S0-CNI-707

Financial Accounting Concepts

PICPA
715 Grant Bldg
Pgh, PA

Commonwealth of PA
Dept of State
State BD of Examiners of Pub Accounts
P.O. Box 2649
Harrisburg PA
17120

Financial Accounting Concepts

Second edition

JAMES H. ROSSELL

WILLIAM W. FRASURE

University of Pittsburgh

CHARLES E. MERRILL PUBLISHING COMPANY

A Bell & Howell Company

Columbus, Ohio

Published by
CHARLES E. MERRILL PUBLISHING COMPANY
A Bell & Howell Company
Columbus, Ohio 43216

Library of Congress Catalog Card Number: 73-88133
International Standard Book Number: 0-675-08860-7

2 3 4 5 6 7 8—78 77

Printed in the United States of America

Preface

Financial Accounting Concepts is, in business parlance, a spin-off from our book *Managerial Accounting* which was first published in 1964 (second edition, 1972). That book emphasizes how to use accounting rather than how to "do" it. It is designed primarily for those who need to understand accounting from a management point of view but who do not necessarily intend to become accountants.

Several instructors who adopted *Managerial Accounting* for its intended use subsequently decided to use the first part of the book along with some supplementary procedural materials for their regular basic accounting courses. *Financial Accounting Concepts* was written in response to that innovation, which corresponds with the increasing trend toward a basic course combining a managerial approach to financial accounting with a highly condensed presentation of the salient principles and procedures ordinarily found in a traditional introductory or basic text.

Financial Accounting Concepts, Second edition, combines the managerial aspects of financial accounting with a concise, but thorough, coverage of the accounting cycle, essential accounting principles, and pertinent fundamental accounting procedures. Chapters 1 through 12 discuss financial statements and critically analyze financial data from an interpretative and management-use point of view. Appendix A contains complete financial statements from annual reports which illustrate specific practices regarding certain issues raised in the first twelve chapters. Chapter 13 examines cost considerations which underlie various financial accounting concepts that are pertinent to the managerial control and decision-making process. As a result, this book emphasizes the managerial aspects of how to use financial accounting, while in Chapters 14 and 15 and Appendix B, it meets the basic needs of those who are interested in knowing how to "do" it.

The book proceeds at a rapid pace with a highly conceptual and managerial approach. Time-consuming involvement in details, mechanics, and techniques is avoided through concentrating on pertinent concepts and procedures. The learning process is fortified by the presentation of examples taken from corporate annual reports to stockholders, references to current accounting and related literature, illustrations of actual applications, and information on relevant historical as well as current research. The questions, problems, and short cases at the end of each chapter have been selected because of their effectiveness in aiding the student to gain and retain mastery of the more important financial concepts.

The second edition of this book combines a comprehensive revision and updating of original content with a substantial amount of new material. Additions or significant changes are provided for several important and timely issues, including:

Earnings per share
Reporting by lines of business
Statement of changes in financial position
Opinions of the Accounting Principles Board
Reporting of leases
Consolidated financial statements
Inventory management

The material in this book is the result of the experiences of the authors in teaching courses in managerial accounting at the undergraduate and graduate levels and in executive development programs at several universities and various in-company management training programs.

As a college text, this book is designed for a one-term course in accounting. It is organized so that each chapter may be used in or out of numerical sequence. Certain chapters or portions of chapters may be omitted. For example, Chapters 14 and 15 and Appendix B may be used following Chapter 3, or inserted at any point after Chapter 1. The sequence of the material selected and the depth to which various topics are probed will depend upon the individual using the book.

The authors gratefully acknowledge the helpful suggestions received from faculty at various colleges who used the first edition of this book. Grateful acknowledgment also is extended to the American Accounting Association, Financial Executives Institute, National Association of Accountants, and numerous publishers for permission to cite their various publications. Particular recognition is due to the many corporate officials who permitted us to use excerpts from their corporate financial statements and annual reports as examples to illustrate different concepts and practices.

Further acknowledgment is made to the American Institute of Certified Public Accountants, Inc., for the numerous citations from or references to *Accounting Trends and Techniques, Accounting Research Bulletins, Opinions of the Accounting Principles Board,* other Institute publications, and various Uniform CPA Examination problems.

James H. Rossell
November, 1973 *William W. Frasure*

Contents

1

The Nature of Accounting and Its Uses

Accounting has been called the "language of business." Business dealings of a financial or quasi-financial nature are expressed in accounting terms or in words substituted for accounting terminology. For example, an individual who purchases a residence for $30,000, paying $5,000 down and signing a mortgage for $25,000, does the following: he makes a "capital expenditure" for land and house of $30,000; he decreases his cash by a $5,000 "disbursement"; and he incurs a "long-term liability" of $25,000. Just as a law student must understand how to use legal terminology and a medical student must learn how to employ medical terminology, so a student of business must know how to use the terminology of accounting.

DEFINITION OF ACCOUNTING

There is a considerable degree of misunderstanding about the nature of accounting. Fundamentally, accounting is an information system by which financial data are recorded, accumulated, and communicated for decision-making purposes. Through financial reporting, information is provided concerning profitability, a vital element in our private enterprise economy. Accounting also provides data for the guidance and control of certain business operations.

The Committee on Terminology of the American Institute of Certified Public Accountants defined accounting as follows:

> Accounting is the art of recording, classifying, and summarizing in a significant manner and in terms of money, transactions and events which are, in part at least, of a financial character, and interpreting the results thereof.[1]

Recording is the mechanical process by which financial transactions and events are systematically placed in accounting records. Such transactions and events are analyzed so that they can be *classified* according to a predetermined system of accounting. Periodically, the information so recorded and classified is *summarized* by the preparation of financial statements and reports to the managers of an enterprise and to other interested parties. *Interpreting* basically refers to that utilization of the recorded, classified, and summarized data which reveals and emphasizes significant changes, trends, and potential developments in the affairs of an enterprise. In 1970, the Accounting Principles Board of the American Institute of Certified Public Accountants issued a statement in which accounting was defined or explained as follows:

> Accounting is a service activity. Its function is to provide quantitative information, primarily financial in nature, about economic entities that is intended to be useful in making economic decisions—in making reasoned choices among alternative courses of action.[2]

Accounting is the process of collecting and measuring economic data and communicating that information to those who need it as a basis for decision making.

---

[1] Accounting Terminology Bulletin Number 1, "Review and Résumé," *Accounting Research and Terminology Bulletins, Final Edition,* p. 9. Copyright 1961 by the American Institute of Certified Public Accountants, Inc.

[2] American Institute of Certified Public Accountants, Inc., Statement of the Accounting Principles Board No. 4, *Basic Concepts and Accounting Principles Underlying Financial Statements of Business Enterprises* (New York, 1970).

APPROACH OF THE BOOK

The first definition above delineates four facets of accounting. In general (as portrayed below), the first three facets refer to the "how to do" part of accounting; the fourth, to the "how to use" aspect of accounting. It is

recording classifying summarizing	interpreting
"how to do"	"how to use"

to this fourth facet of the definition of accounting that this book is directed; principal emphasis will be placed upon the managerial significance of accounting facts, not on the facts themselves. Thus, the goal of this book is not to train accountants as such, but to enable those in or studying for a career in business to understand how accounting is used to formulate certain business decisions and to control certain business operations.

ACCOUNTING: TECHNICAL VIEWPOINT VERSUS MANAGERIAL VIEWPOINT

The reader may have heard accounting related to the sacred art of matching pennies, implying that accounting is merely a routine mechanical process of unvarying precision and petty detail. Or it may be that the reader has heard accountants called tinkerers of the records, indicating it is possible for accountants to obtain different answers in a given situation for each different user of financial information. Rarely are such innuendoes justified. Much of the misunderstanding behind such comments may be traced to the repeated attempts made by accountants to adapt accounting to the diverse needs and objectives with which it is confronted. As an information system, accounting must be adapted to the environment it serves, but it cannot act as a substitute for sound judgment.

From the technical viewpoint alone, accounting must be flexible if it is to satisfy various kinds of needs. First, accounting must follow "generally accepted accounting principles" in the preparation of the financial statements for the annual report to stockholders and other interested parties, or the statements will not be given an unqualified opinion by an independent auditing firm of certified public accountants. (The reader is referred to the second paragraph of the accountants' reports or opinions attached to the financial statements in Appendix A, pages 533 and 540, in which reference is made to generally accepted accounting principles.) In addition, a company with stock listed on any of the stock exchanges must file with the Securities and Exchange Commission periodic financial statements which follow these accounting principles.

The term "generally accepted accounting principles" (GAAP) does not connote a rigid set of accounting rules and procedures by which minutely exact results may always be derived. On the other hand, these principles are far more than vague generalities. They have been (at least until recently), in effect, generalizations from particular business practices. Like most principles, generally accepted accounting principles have been the result of an evolutionary process; they changed in response to changing business practices in a changing society, but usually changed rather slowly.

In 1939, the Committee on Accounting Procedure of the American Institute of Certified Public Accountants began issuing Accounting Research Bulletins. By 1959, 51 bulletins had been issued. Then, in 1959 the Council of the American Institute of CPAs created the Accounting Principles Board (APB), which consisted solely of part-time members. The objective of the APB was to narrow the range of possible different accounting treatments on a given item within the framework of generally accepted accounting principles. During its existence (1959 to mid-1973), the APB issued 31 Opinions which became progressively more complex and detailed. Compliance with these Opinions is insisted on by the SEC in filings with that regulatory agency, and the American Institute of CPAs requires disclosure of any departure from these Opinions in published statements.

The APB received criticism from various sources and on various grounds, one of which was the appearance of questionable independence arising from its members' part-time status. The APB has been replaced by the Financial Accounting Standards Board (FASB), which began operations on March 1, 1973, and which consists of a panel of seven full-time members appointed by the Financial Accounting Foundation. In an attempt to remove the independence related criticism of the APB, during their term on the FASB members must sever all relationships with their former employers. This could be the last chance to have accounting principles set by the private sector. If the FASB should falter, the federal government may well step in to do the rule-setting.

Second, accounting must provide information which is vital and necessary for the proper preparation of various local, state, and federal tax returns. Accounting which follows generally accepted accounting principles for purposes of external reporting to stockholders and the SEC is inadequate for many tax purposes. For example, an item which is income for conventional accounting purposes—such as interest earned on bonds issued by states, municipalities, and other political subdivisions—is not taxable income for federal income tax. There are additional items of income and expense which may be treated in one manner for accounting purposes, but in an entirely different manner for tax purposes. Similarly, another item—such as depreciation expense or the depletion allowance—may be shown at a certain amount for accounting purposes, but at an entirely different amount for tax purposes. Thus, while accountants must record, classify, summarize, and present financial information in a manner which conforms with generally accepted accounting, they must treat some of the same information in an entirely different manner to satisfy tax requirements.

A third variation in accounting data is associated with certain industries. For example, the Interstate Commerce Commission requires railroad and pipe line companies to file periodic financial reports and statements prepared in a manner specified by that commission. Similarly, governmental utility commissions control the financial reporting of utilities, and various governmental agencies exercise control over the financial reporting of insurance companies.

Thus, accounting must furnish financial reports and statements prepared in many different manners according to many different "rules." Yet, while satisfying these diverse obligations, accounting cannot ignore the chief reason for its existence.

The principal reason for the existence of accounting is the aid it provides to management. Accounting should aid management by furnishing information in reports and financial statements. Simply put, financial statements are a means for communicating financial information. Accounting should provide a basis for financial interpretations which assist management in the formulation of certain policy decisions and in the control of current operations. Such internal reporting to management may—and often does—require the collection and presentation of financial information in a manner completely unlike that followed for external reporting. What is needed for reporting to the stockholders, what is legal for tax purposes, or what is required for various governmental agencies may be accounting information which is entirely unsatisfactory for the primary purpose of aiding management to direct the operations of a business. For example, management may wish the internal financial statements to reflect price-level changes to measure performance better over a period of time. Or direct costing may be desired to promote a clearer analysis of costs for pricing policies and future planning. Price-level adjustments to financial statements (to be discussed in Chapter 7) and the use of direct costing (to be discussed in Chapter 13) are considered unorthodox by many because they have not, as yet, been recognized as generally accepted accounting principles. Yet management may be convinced that such innovations are necessary if accounting is to maximize its value for decision-making purposes.

ORGANIZATIONAL RELATIONSHIP OF ACCOUNTING TO MANAGEMENT

The organizational structure necessary to guide the operations of a business differs with the type of business involved, the size and complexity of the company, and the varying philosophies and abilities of the individuals comprising the top management of the company. What may be an excellent organizational arrangement for one company could be almost unworkable for another. Thus, the location, duties, and responsibilities of the accounting function in the overall organizational structure will vary somewhat from company to company. Usually this function is under the direction of an individual whose title is controller.[3]

Shown in the accompanying organization chart is the major segment of the top management organization of a hypothetical large industrial corporation. It must be re-emphasized that the format of any such chart varies from company to company. The specific location of the controllership function is a variable. The chart indicates that both the controller and treasurer are on an equal plane, and that both report to the vice president in charge of finance. Probably the principal variant to this plan is that whereby both the treasurer and the controller are at the company staff level and report directly to the president of the company. Sometimes one individual has the title of Vice President and Controller; in such cases, the treasurer may report to this individual. Similarly, the reverse situation may occur when one person bears the title of Vice President and Treasurer. Again, the same individual may be both secretary and treasurer of a company. It is not uncommon to find, over a period of time, different combinations of these functions in the same company. This lack of uniformity in the location of the controllership function is not peculiar to that function alone. In practically all companies, the organization chart is molded to some degree by the abilities and personalities of the individuals comprising the management.

Assuming an organization chart like the one in Exhibit 1–1, with the controller and the treasurer both reporting to the vice president of finance,

---

[3] Occasionally spelled comptroller, especially when related to governmental operations rather than business enterprises.

EXHIBIT 1–1

A Typical Organization Chart

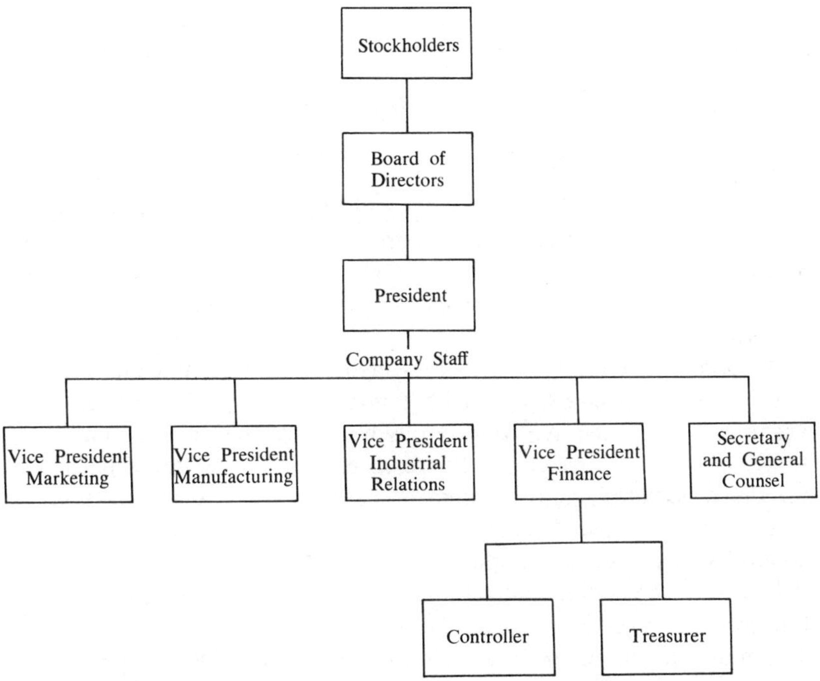

the controller is responsible for the overall accounting function and the treasurer is responsible for the fiscal function.

In a broad sense, the functions allocated to the controller consist of:

> The collection, analysis, and interpretation of the financial information necessary for management use in the operation of the business.
>
> The maintenance of proper accounting records to provide proper reporting to various external groups (e.g., tax authorities, the Securities and Exchange Commission, and other governmental regulatory bodies).

Thus, the controller typically is responsible for the overall system of accounting employed by the company; namely, the maintenance of internal control through the internal audit function, the preparation and explanation of financial analyses and reports, the budgetary control system, the various types of economic and profitability forecasts, and local, state, and federal tax returns.

The functions allocated to the treasurer in a broad sense ordinarily consist of:

> The planning of, and control over, the flow of cash as to sources and applications in conformance with the fiscal policies of the company.
>
> The protection and custody of funds and securities owned by the company.

Thus, the treasurer of the company typically is responsible for maintenance of a proper cash balance, preparation of forecasted cash flows, relationships with banks, investments of excess cash, credit and collection policies, procurement of capital and corporate financing, and the handling of corporate bank accounts.

An analysis of the responsibilities of the controller and the treasurer indicates that no fine line can be drawn between their functions. For example, the specific area of payrolls was mentioned neither under the functions of the controller nor the treasurer. In practice, the responsibility for the preparation and handling of payrolls may be included in the jurisdiction of either function. Whether it be under the duties of the controller or the treasurer, the controllership function must provide for the proper accounting and control of the payroll, and the treasury function must plan for the periodic out-flow of cash to meet the payroll. This illustrates the close liaison that must be maintained between these two separate functions.

THE FIELD OF ACCOUNTING

The field of accounting may be divided into four main categories: private, public, governmental, and institutional accounting.

Private accounting encompasses those persons employed by private business organizations. The preceding section of this chapter which concerned the controller's department provides the reader with an insight into the various facets comprising the area of private accounting. Though, basically, the materials in this book are presented from the point of view of private accounting as an aid to management, the principles discussed are generally applicable to the other three major divisions of accounting.

Public accounting, through independent practitioners, offers professional accounting services on a fee basis to business enterprises of all types, to governmental units, to non-profit institutions, and to the general public. Among the varied services offered to clients by public accountants are audits, design and installation of accounting systems, income tax services, special investigations and reports, and management advisory services. To qualify as a certified public accountant, an individual must pass a uniform comprehensive written examination prepared by the American Institute of Certified Public Accountants and given by the individual states. In addition to the successful completion of the examination, many states require that the individual be registered or licensed to practice public accounting.

Governmental accounting consists of accounting activities performed at national, state, and local governmental levels. Examples of this area at the national level are the General Accounting Office of the United States and the Internal Revenue Service. Due to the wide scope of governmental activities, this division of accounting contains elements of both private and public accounting.

The area of *institutional accounting* refers to the accounting activities of non-profit organizations. Included in this category are charitable organizations, educational institutions, and churches.

Accounting serves many purposes. It often fulfills different needs with somewhat different answers obtained from the same information by following nonuniform but equally acceptable accounting methodologies. Because of its divided obligations, accounting at times appears to possess something akin to a split personality.

QUESTIONS AND PROBLEMS

1–1. Read the article "Horizons for a Profession: The Common Body of Knowledge for CPAs" in the September 1966 issue of *The Journal of Accountancy,* and then choose the proper answer to each of the following six statements.

a. The application of new methods in mathematics, statistics, and probability to problems in the management of formal organizations makes added mathematical capacity for tomorrow's CPAs:

1. optional
2. desirable
3. mandatory
4. too specialized to be worth the time

b. A subject considered to be of highest importance in the common body of knowledge (for tomorrow's beginning CPA) is:
   1. written and oral English
   2. marketing
   3. personnel relations
   4. foreign languages

c. Accounting, while in truth a {a. deterministic / b. probabilistic} process, historically and to the present day is characterized by an appearance of {a. determinism / b. probabilism}.

d. With respect to computers, it is recommended that tomorrow's beginning CPA have:
   1. a generalized acquaintanceship with what computers can do
   2. a knowledge of at least one computer language, ability to diagram an information system, and ability to prepare a program including debugging
   3. the knowledge to double as a computer expert

e. A knowledge of the fundamentals of behavioral science is:
   1. recommended
   2. considered desirable, though not specifically recommended
   3. not recommended

f. The oldest and best established of the quantitative techniques to aid in managerial decisions is:
   1. mathematics
   2. accounting
   3. statistics
   4. probability

1–2. Read the article "The New Financial Executive" in the February 1965 issue of *The Journal of Accountancy,* and then choose the proper answer to each of the following four statements.

a. The effect of electronic data processing (EDP) on the work of the financial executive has been to:
   1. make his job easier
   2. widen his horizon and responsibilities
   3. give him less time for planning because of his preoccupation with the mechanics of EDP

b. The controller, comptroller, or treasurer, depending on what name each company calls its chief financial executive, performs basically the same task today as he did in 1945, only with a different title.
   1. True
   2. False

c. The future financial executive will probably deal with such problems as working for better accounting principles, federal government relations, and labor relations.
   1. True
   2. False

d. The area in the following list that is *not* the concern of the financial executive is:
   1. profit planning
   2. mergers and acquisitions
   3. insurance
   4. research and development costs
   5. cannot choose one: all four areas are his concern

1–3. For both of the following statements, choose the proper answer to each.

a. The members of the board of directors of most corporations are:
   1. appointed by the president of the corporation
   2. selected by management
   3. elected by the stockholders
   4. chosen by holders of preferred stock only

b. The selection of a president for a corporation is made by:
   1. common stockholders
   2. preferred stockholders
   3. common and preferred stockholders
   4. the board of directors

1–4. If management believes that price-level adjustments to financial statements are necessary to make the statements more broadly meaningful, should generally accepted accounting principles be altered to permit the publication of such revised financial statements? Should Congress amend the Internal Revenue Code so that price-level adjustments on financial statements would be allowed?

1–5. What is your concept of the difference between bookkeeping and accounting?

1–6. Is accounting an exact science by which it is possible to measure business and economic data precisely?

1–7. Differentiate between the duties and responsibilities of the controller of a company and those of the treasurer.

1–8. The following news item (names of individual and company have been altered) appeared recently in the financial pages of a local newspaper:

> John Doe, plant accountant for X Co.'s Cleveland plant for six years, has been promoted to the newly created position of division controller, Special Products Division, with headquarters in Pittsburgh.

> Mr. Doe's duties will include internal functional control over plant accountants at special products plants located in four cities, and the establishment of selling prices and pricing policies for all special product items, parts, and accessories.

Do you believe that "the establishment of selling prices and pricing policies" is encompassed in the responsibilities of a typical controller?

1–9. The Woltemar Company has operated profitably since its organization in 1935. Condensed financial statements of the Woltemar Company are reproduced below. Though twenty years apart and covering only two years out of two decades, 1954 and 1974 represent typical years for the company.

Between 1954 and 1974, the Woltemar Company mechanized and modernized its plant. The principal reason for the improvement of the profit margin was the increased labor productivity attributable to the mechanization and modernization. As shown below, an increase in the dollar amount of all items has occurred over the years, and the company has improved its profit margin 20 percent. Moreover, it has always paid an annual $4 dividend to its stockholders. Would you consider the Woltemar Company a "growth" company?

Balance Sheet
as of December 31

	1954	1974
Cash, Receivables, Inventories	$1,000,000	$2,000,000
Property, Plant and Equipment	2,000,000	4,000,000
Total Assets	$3,000,000	$6,000,000
Debts Owed	$ 500,000	$1,000,000
Stockholders' Equity	2,500,000	5,000,000
Total Equities	$3,000,000	$6,000,000

Statement of Income
for the Year

	1954	1974
Sales	$6,000,000	$9,000,000
Costs and Expenses	5,700,000	8,460,000
Net Income	$ 300,000	$ 540,000
Margin of Profit on Sales	5%	6%

1–10. The Runser Company manufactures and sells two products. The results of its operations for the year 1974 are shown below:

THE RUNSER COMPANY
Condensed Statement of Income
for the Year 1974

	TOTAL	PRODUCT ABC	PRODUCT XYZ
Sales	$20,000,000	$10,000,000	$10,000,000
Costs and Expenses	14,000,000	6,000,000	8,000,000
Net Income	$ 6,000,000	$ 4,000,000	$ 2,000,000
Margin of Profit on Sales	$\frac{\$6}{\$20} = 30\%$	$\frac{\$4}{\$10} = 40\%$	$\frac{\$2}{\$10} = 20\%$

The year 1974 was a typical year in the operation of the Runser Company. There is a large unfilled demand for both of the company's products. Each product is independent of the other; neither is part of a product line. Total assets of the company amount to $20,000,000. $15,000,000 of this total is equitably allocated to Product ABC, and $5,000,000 to Product XYZ, as the capital necessary to manufacture and sell each product. Which product do you believe should have priority in a capital expansion program? State clearly any assumptions on your part and any additional information that you would desire.

1–11. Do you believe that generally accepted accounting principles should be revised by a slow evolutionary process and thus appear somewhat antiquated at times, or do you prefer that accounting principles be revised continually by pronouncements of some accounting group, or would it be preferable to have some governmental agency do the rule-making?

1–12. In a few countries a standardized set of accounting rules has been promulgated by an official body. All businesses, regardless of the industry or any peculiar circumstances within a given company, must follow a prescribed, uniform, stereotyped system of accounting. Discuss the advantages and disadvantages of such a procedure.

1–13. To become acquainted with certain available journals in the field of accounting, you are requested to read and submit a brief written summary of one article from a current issue of each of the following four publications:

a. *Journal of Accountancy* (monthly publication)
American Institute of Certified Public Accountants, Inc.

b. *Accounting Review* (quarterly publication)
American Accounting Association

c. *Management Accounting* (monthly publication) (formerly *N.A.A. Bulletin*)
National Association of Accountants

d. *The Financial Executive* (monthly publication) (formerly *The Controller*)
Financial Executives Institute (formerly Controllers Institute of America)

e. *Journal of Accounting Research* (semi-annual publication)
The Institute of Professional Accounting, Graduate School of Business, University of Chicago; and London School of Economic and Political Science, University of London.

f. *Management Adviser* (bimonthly publication) (formerly *Management Services*)
American Institute of Certified Public Accountants, Inc.

1–14. The following segment of a conversation was overheard recently:

> I'm the accountant for XYZ Company. I have complete charge of the books. Once a month, the auditors come in and adjust the books for me and prepare the monthly financial statements for our company.

a. Do you believe the speaker is an accountant?

b. Do you believe that the monthly work of the auditors represents auditing?

1–15. The Interstate Commerce Commission has a prescribed uniform accounting system containing uniform accounting rules for all regulated railroads.

In addition to possible governmental inertia in periodic revision of such a system, do you see any additional dangers in the establishment of uniform accounting rules for American business by governmental decree?

2

The Balance Sheet

The balance sheet provides information which describes the financial standing of a company at a given instant. The time factor is especially significant because the statement conveys a financial message which is valid as of a given date only; yesterday's message would have been slightly different and tomorrow's message will be different. The statement might be visualized as a snapshot of the financial status of a company. Just as such a picture portrays an individual whose current image reflects the cumulative effect of physical change since birth, so a balance sheet presents a current image which reflects the cumulative effect of financial change throughout the lifetime of a company.

During the past 25 years there has been a change from the term "balance sheet" to "statement of financial position" and, in the past few years, a change back to the term "balance sheet." The table on page 16 shows selections taken from a yearly survey of annual reports issued by 600 industrial companies, which clearly indicate this change in terminology:[1]

---

[1] American Institute of Certified Public Accountants, Inc., *Accounting Trends and Techniques in Published Corporate Annual Reports,* 26th ed., p. 67. Copyright 1972 by the American Institute of Certified Public Accountants, Inc.

Title of Statement

	1971	1965	1955	1946
Terminology Applied:				
Balance Sheet	530	470	466	578
Financial Position	49	94	92	12
Financial Condition	21	31	35	6
Other	0	5	7	4
Total	600	600	600	600

ASSETS, LIABILITIES, AND STOCKHOLDERS' EQUITY

Basically, the balance sheet is divided into three sections: assets, liabilities, and equity of the owners. Assets are the resources owned by the company. Liabilities are the debts owed by the company; i.e., claims of creditors. Equity of the owners, usually referred to as stockholders' equity or net worth, is the excess of assets over liabilities. The relationship of the three components of the balance sheet may be expressed as:

Assets − Liabilities = Stockholders' Equity

or as:

Assets = Liabilities + Stockholders' Equity

To illustrate, assume that the assets of a company total \$30,000,000 and that the liabilities amount to \$10,000,000. The stockholders' equity is \$20,000,000. The formal balance sheet is usually presented in one of three or four manners. The most common form of presentation is shown below.

THE FLEMING COMPANY
Balance Sheet
December 31, 1974

ASSETS		LIABILITIES	
		(Details)	
		Total Liabilities . . .	\$10,000,000
		STOCKHOLDERS' EQUITY	
(Details)		(Details)	
		Total Stockholders' Equity	20,000,000
		Total Liabilities and Stockholders' Equity	\$30,000,000
Total Assets	\$30,000,000		

Unlike the accompanying illustration, a published balance sheet shows details of the various items comprising total assets, total liabilities, and total stockholders' equity.

CONDENSED BALANCE SHEET

In presenting a balance sheet, the items constituting assets, liabilities, and stockholders' equity are classified under various headings. The number and type of such headings will vary, depending upon the situation of the company and the type of business. The following condensed balance sheet illustrates those primary classifications which are commonly encountered.

THE FLEMING COMPANY

Balance Sheet

December 31, 1974

ASSETS		LIABILITIES		
Current Assets	$12,000,000	Current Liabilities		$ 4,000,000
Investments	2,600,000	Long-term Debt		6,000,000
Property, Plant and Equipment	14,500,000	Total Liabilities		$10,000,000
Intangibles	400,000			
Deferred Charges	500,000			
		STOCKHOLDERS' EQUITY		
		Capital Stock ..	$ 2,500,000	
		Additional Capital	4,500,000	
		Retained Earnings	13,000,000	
		Total Stockholders' Equity		20,000,000
Total Assets	$30,000,000	Total Liabilities and Stockholders' Equity		$30,000,000

Under each of the five classes of asset headings are listed the specific asset items which comprise that asset group. Likewise, each of the two categories of liabilities are subdivided according to the specific debts owed. The stockholders' equity section furnishes additional information concerning the capital stock, additional capital contributions, and the retained earnings. Before discussing the detailed items appearing on a statement of financial position, however, the principal classifications shown above must be clarified.

Classification of Assets

Current Assets are cash and other assets which are expected to be converted into cash or consumed in business operations within a relatively short period of time, usually one year or less. In addition to unrestricted cash, this category of assets includes such items as temporary investments in readily marketable securities or commercial paper, amounts due from customers for goods sold to them on credit, inventories on hand, and prepaid expenses. Prepaid expenses, shown last in the current asset section, usually represent services or benefits to be received and consumable supplies which will be used in the normal operation of a business instead of being converted into cash. As an illustration, consider a company which two years ago paid in advance a three-year premium on the fire insurance policy covering its building. At the end of two years, the one-year unexpired premium represents an asset of the company. The company will realize this asset as a service or benefit (protection by insurance coverage) rather than in cash.

Reference to the detailed balance sheet on pages 22 and 23 will show that the current assets mentioned above are listed according to the order in which they are expected to be converted into cash.

The classification of Investments is provided for holdings owned of a relatively permanent nature. Included herein are securities of other corporations, advances to affiliated companies, and other long-term investments and equities. Temporary or short-term investments are not included in this classification; such investments are current assets.

Property, Plant and Equipment represents relatively long-lived assets of a tangible nature which are not intended for resale and are used in the operation of the business. These assets include land and depreciable assets such as buildings, machinery, and equipment. This class of assets is often called Fixed Assets.

Intangibles, as a class of assets, possess characteristics similar to those of property, plant and equipment items (fixed assets). Their value, however, does not derive from their physical nature but from the rights conferred by their ownership. Such intangible assets are patents, copyrights, and goodwill; sometimes they are shown under the classification Property, Plant and Equipment, rather than separately.

Deferred Charges represent expenditures made in one fiscal period which are not to be considered a cost of operations in that period, but which are carried forward to become an expense in subsequent periods. An example is an unusually large expenditure for moving and relocating factory machinery which is written off rateably over a period of years. As of any given date, that portion of the initial expenditure which had not yet been considered an expense would be a deferred charge.

Occasionally, additional classifications of assets are encountered, such as "Other Assets." This category might include long-term receivables, special funds, or other assets not readily classified in one of the five preceding groups.

Classification of Liabilities

Current Liabilities are debts to be paid within a relatively short period of time, usually one year or less. Typical examples of current liabilities are amounts owed to trade creditors for materials, supplies, and services purchased on credit; amounts owed on promissory notes for funds borrowed from a bank; accrued or accumulated amounts owed but not yet due (as of the date of the balance sheet) for items such as salaries, taxes, and interest. Occasionally a different type of current liability is encountered when a company has collected or received income in advance of actually earning the amount; i.e., a magazine publishing company receiving a subscription accompanied by a check. Although the cash of the company is increased immediately, the company has not earned the income. It owes a debt to be paid by delivering magazines throughout the life of the subscription rather than by payment of cash.

Long-term Debt refers to liabilities which will not become due within the coming year. In fact, debts like mortgages and bonds may not come due for many years; the balance sheet usually indicates the maturity date of such long-term debts. Any portion of a mortgage or a bond issue that will come due within the coming year is shown as a current liability.

Classification of Stockholders' Equity

Stockholders' Equity, occasionally called net worth of the company, represents the excess of the company's assets over its liabilities. This "excess" is basically derived from two sources: capital contributions by the stockholders and accumulated net earnings which have not been distributed as dividends to the stockholders since the company was established.

The manner in which the capital contributed by the stockholders is presented in the balance sheet depends upon several factors: the type of capital stock, the value assigned to each share of stock, and the dollar amount for which each share of stock is issued. For example, the corporation, by its articles of incorporation, may have only one class of capital stock, or it may have both preferred stock and common stock. In addition, the capital stock may be par value stock or no par value stock. When shares of stock are issued, any consideration received above the par value of par shares or the stated value of no par shares is usually stated separately as Additional Capital, Paid-in Surplus, Capital Surplus, or Capital in Excess of Par Value or Stated Value. A complete discussion of these factors has been reserved until Chapter 12.

Retained Earnings represents the earnings of the company for all years to date which have not been distributed to the owners (stockholders), but reinvested and plowed back into the business. For example, The Fleming Company, since its organization in 1904, has had total net earnings over the years of $40,000,000. Of this, $27,000,000 has been used for dividend declarations and distributed to the stockholders; the remaining $13,000,000, which has been retained in the business, constitutes "Retained Earnings."

DETAILED BALANCE SHEET

The balance sheet illustrated on pages 22–23 is complete for most of the details shown on the typical published statement. Following is a brief explanation of each item appearing on the statement and the basis for the valuation of certain items.

Cash includes actual coin and currency on hand, such negotiable papers as money orders and checks for deposit, and unrestricted balances on deposit with banks.

Marketable Securities are readily marketable government obligations, commercial paper, and stocks or bonds of other corporations which are being held as short-term investments. The securities are listed at cost on the illustrative balance sheet, with a parenthetical note indicating that market prices of the securities exceed cost by a substantial amount. This "paper profit" is unrealized and is not considered profit until the securities are sold and a profit is actually obtained. On the other hand, if the securities had declined considerably below their cost, conservatism would usually require that the securities be written down to their present market value and the cost figure be shown parenthetically.

Accounts Receivable represents amounts due from customers for goods or services sold to them on open account (charge account).

Notes Receivable represents amounts due from customers evidenced by formal written promises to pay and amounts due from others on loans evidenced by signed promissory notes.

Reference to the illustrative balance sheet shows that $3,130,000 is due the business on both accounts and notes receivable, but, based on past experience, the company expects to realize $30,000 less than this amount. The $30,000 represents those receivables which will become bad debts if the company has estimated correctly. A majority of companies in business for some period of time have compiled an experience factor by which they are able to estimate accurately the anticipated amount of bad debts.

Inventories represents the goods and supplies on hand. The type or types of inventory which a company possesses depends upon the business in which the company is engaged. For example, if the company is a merchandising or trading concern, it purchases and sells essentially the same product. Examples of this type of company are F. W. Woolworth Co. and Federated Department Stores, Inc. In the current asset section on the balance sheet of each company is the item:

Merchandise Inventories	$ xxxxxxx

On the other hand, if the company is a manufacturing concern, it produces the finished product it sells. Raw materials are acquired and converted into a finished product by various manufacturing processes. Examples of this type of company are PPG Industries and United States Steel Corporation. The current asset item of "Inventories" on the balance sheet of PPG Industries is detailed in a note to the statements as follows:

Inventories:	
Finished Products	$ xxxxxxx
Work in Process	xxxxxxx
Raw Materials	xxxxxxx
Supplies	xxxxxxx

The following is a brief explanation of each of the four types of inventory encountered in a typical manufacturing business.

Inventory of Finished Goods represents the stock of goods completely manufactured and on hand available for sale.

Inventory of Work in Process represents goods which are partially completed and still in the production process.

Inventory of Raw Materials represents the various materials acquired and on hand which have not yet undergone any manufacturing processes.

Inventory of Supplies consists of those supplies used in the manufacturing processes, which either physically or economically are not considered a part of the finished product, such as abrasives, lubricants, and similar items. In addition to manufacturing supplies, a company normally has an inventory of repair parts for machinery and equipment.

A comprehensive discussion of the determination of the cost assigned to the preceding inventories has been deferred to Chapters 9 and 10. It will suffice at this time to state that some of the more widely used methods employed for inventory valuation are various averaging methods, the first-in, first-out (FIFO) method, and the last-in, first-out (LIFO) method. The illustrative balance sheet above states that The Fleming Company is using the LIFO method.

THE FLEMING
Balance
December

ASSETS

Current Assets:		
Cash		$ 1,075,000
U.S. Government and Other Marketable Securities at cost (quoted market prices aggregate $1,800,000)		1,500,000
Accounts and Notes Receivable, less allowance for doubtful accounts of $30,000		3,100,000
Inventories, on last-in, first-out basis		6,300,000
Prepaid Expenses		25,000
Total Current Assets		$12,000,000
Investments:		
Fund for Property Additions (U.S. Government Securities)	$ 1,800,000	
Investment in and Advances to Affiliated Companies	800,000	
Total Investments		2,600,000
Property, Plant and Equipment—*at cost:*		
Land	$ 2,250,000	
Buildings	6,350,000	
Equipment	12,900,000	
	$21,500,000	
Less: Accumulated Depreciation to Date	7,000,000	
Net Property, Plant and Equipment		14,500,000
Intangibles:		
Trademarks and other intangible assets, less amortization		400,000
Deferred Charges		500,000
Total Assets		$30,000,000

Under the LIFO method the goods "last-in" (most recently acquired) are, for costing and valuation purposes, assumed to be the "first-out": the first sold or used in production. Thus, the inventories physically on hand at a given date are valued at somewhat "ancient" or first-in costs, depending upon how long the company has been on LIFO and whether

COMPANY

Sheet

31, 1974

LIABILITIES

Current Liabilities:

Note Payable to Bank	$ 850,000
Accounts Payable	2,400,000
Accrued Salaries, Wages, Taxes and Interest	250,000
Income Taxes Payable	500,000
Total Current Liabilities	$ 4,000,000

Long-term Debt:

Debentures due 1982	6,000,000
Total Liabilities	$10,000,000

STOCKHOLDERS' EQUITY

Preferred Stock—4% cumulative non-participating, non-convertible, par value $50.00 per share, authorized 50,000 shares; issued and outstanding 20,000 shares	$ 1,000,000	
Common Stock—par value $5 per share, authorized 500,000 shares; issued and outstanding 300,000 shares	1,500,000	
Capital in Excess of Par Value	4,500,000	
Retained Earnings	13,000,000	
Total Stockholders' Equity		20,000,000
Total Liabilities and Stockholders' Equity		$30,000,000

or not the quantity of inventory has changed materially over the years. It is not uncommon for companies which have been on LIFO for a number of years to show inventory amounts on the balance sheet which are considerably below current replacement costs because of rising price levels.

Prepaid Expenses represents those expenditures made for items like insurance premiums, certain taxes, and supply items which are chargeable against future revenues as operating expenses. As they are consumed, they become expenses of operations; until they are consumed, they represent current assets. Although a company may expect to convert all other current assets into cash, it anticipates only services or use from prepaid expenses.

Fund for Property Additions represents assets set aside to facilitate future property acquisitions. Although the illustrated financial statement shows a fund of U.S. Government securities, many funds contain securities of a non-governmental nature. The limiting feature of such a fund is the purpose for which the assets are set aside rather than the nature of the assets contained in it.

Investment in and Advances to Affiliated Companies indicates the amount of ownership that The Fleming Company has in the capital stock and/or bonds of affiliated companies plus loans made to such companies as advances. Through such investments, control may be exercised over other companies which may supply certain inventory items, provide important distributive outlets, or offer various benefits which are vital to the success of The Fleming Company.

Land is building sites and other ground owned and used in operating a business. The original cost of all such land, in our illustration, totals $2,250,000. In accordance with generally accepted accounting principles, the valuation of an asset in the United States is based upon historical cost. This means that the total price paid to acquire an asset represents the cost of that asset throughout its accounting existence. For example, a plot of ground which is owned and used in the operation of the business and which was purchased in 1934 at a cost of $200,000 is valued at $200,000 in the $2,250,000 amount shown for Land on the balance sheet as of December 31, 1974, even though the $200,000 plot of ground may today be worth $500,000.

Buildings of $6,350,000 shows the price paid for all factory buildings, office buildings, and warehouses which the company has acquired over the years, provided that they are still owned and used by the business as of December 31, 1974.

Equipment of $12,900,000 represents the amount paid for all machines, autos, and trucks, and other equipment which the company has acquired (regardless of the year of acquisition), provided that these items are still owned and in use as of December 31, 1974. Some companies prefer to segregate desks, chairs, showcases, cabinets, and similar items in a separate category titled Furniture and Fixtures on the balance sheet.

Accumulated Depreciation to date of $7,000,000 equals that portion of the $19,250,000 original cost of the tangible, long-life property now owned—except land—which has been written off rateably as an expense of operations through the year 1974. Estimated depreciation expense for each year is shown as one of the operating expenses in the statement of income (Chapter 3).

Net Property, Plant and Equipment of $14,500,000 represents the net *book* value or "undepreciated" cost of fixed assets. This dollar amount is not the current value or intrinsic worth of such assets. Instead, it represents that portion of the original price paid for such assets which has not yet been considered a cost of operating the business. For example, if an item of equipment purchased in early 1963 at a cost of $48,000 is still owned and used, the $48,000 is included in the $12,900,000 figure shown for Equipment. Assume that the item under consideration is depreciated over an eighteen-year life, two-thirds (12 years) of which has expired. The $7,000,000 amount shown for Less Accumulated Depreciation to date includes $32,000 for our hypothetical piece of equipment. Therefore, the Net Property, Plant and Equipment amount includes the remaining $16,000, which represents the undepreciated cost of the equipment. This is so, even though our item with a net *book* value of $16,000 may have a current market value of more or less than $16,000, and in spite of the fact that the item purchased 12 years ago for $48,000 may, today, have a replacement cost of $90,000. Historical cost figures shown on financial statements are usually at great variance with current values; this is attributable largely to the changing level of prices and the decreasing value of the dollar. This problem concerns not only the accounting profession but also those in management who use accounting information as an aid in formulating certain business decisions; the problem, and possible remedies for it, is discussed in Chapter 7.

The amount shown for *Trademarks and other intangibles, less amortization,* represents the net carrying value of the intangibles of the company. Intangible fixed assets are those which have no physical substance, such as patents, copyrights, trademarks, franchises, and goodwill. However, ownership of any of these confers certain long-term rights upon the possessor. A patent granted to an inventor has a legal life of 17 years. Copyrights have a legal life of 28 years, with an additional 28-year renewal privilege. Theoretically, a trademark has an unlimited life. Privileges granted by a franchise may or may not have a determinable life. Goodwill, when it appears on financial statements, usually represents a "premium" amount paid to acquire another company or business. The amount of the goodwill purchased is that portion of the consideration paid for the acquired business in excess of the cost of the net tangible assets (assets purchased minus liabilities assumed). Many companies record intangibles as fixed assets at cost and then amortize (write-off) the cost of certain of these assets over a period of years. Other companies, recognizing the debatable value of such assets, either immediately charge off the costs of developing or acquiring intangibles like patents and trademarks as an expense of operations, or show their value at a nominal amount on the balance sheet.

Deferred Charges represent certain expenditures benefiting future years which are written off against income during such future periods. Typical deferred charges are costs of rearranging factory machinery and certain development and experimental costs. Deferred charges, like prepaid expenses, represent certain future benefits to be received, but, unlike prepaid expenses, the actual services have been received or performed.

Note Payable to Bank is a written promise by the business to repay a bank loan of a certain sum at some fixed or determinable future date. Because the note is shown under current liabilities, it will mature within one year. Other notes payable may arise from credit purchases of goods or services from trade creditors when such debts are evidenced by formal written promises to pay.

Accounts Payable are debts owed to trade creditors for unpaid purchases of goods or services. Such debts are on "open account" to distinguish them from debts evidenced by promissory notes.

Accrued Expenses Payable are items such as salaries, wages, certain taxes, and interest—items which represent accumulating debts which have been incurred but not paid, usually because they are not yet due. For example, between pay dates, salaries and wages owed to employees accumulate day by day as a debt of the company. Another example, in some instances, is property taxes which accumulate or accrue on a *pro rata* basis until their due date. Yet another example might be the bonds shown under long-term debt on the illustrative balance sheet: unless the bond indenture called for an interest payment on December 31, 1974, interest has accrued on the bonds since the last interest payment date in 1974.

Income Taxes Payable is the estimated debt owed the government as of December 31, 1974, for payments not yet due on the corporate income tax liability.

Bonds Payable represent long-term borrowing by the corporation incurred by the issuance of bonds. The principal amount of a corporate bond issue, $6,000,000 in the case of The Fleming Company, is payable at the maturity date of the bonds. Interest, however, is usually payable semi-annually. There are many different types of bonds, two of the more common being mortgage bonds and debentures. A mortgage bond issue is secured by a lien on certain property owned by the corporation. A debenture bond issue is not secured by any type of collateral; its security resides in the faith and credit of the corporation.

Preferred Stock is that portion of the ownership equity of the corporation which has certain designated rights which rank ahead of those belonging to common stock. The two preferences most frequently associated with preferred stock are the right to receive dividends before common stockholders and prior claim on assets upon liquidation of the corporation. The illustrative balance sheet shown earlier reveals that The Fleming Company has 4% cumulative preferred stock. This means that the annual $2 dividend (4% × par $50) payable on each share of preferred stock, if unpaid in any year, accumulates and must be paid with the current year's preferred dividend before any dividend can be declared on the common stock. The $2 per share is the maximum dividend on this preferred stock because it is non-participating; it cannot share with the common stock in any additional dividends. Also, it is not convertible into common shares.

Common Stock represents the residual portion of the ownership equity of the corporation. Although it ranks after the preferred stock in receiving designated privileges, it usually has the sole right to vote for the directors of a corporation.

Capital in Excess of Par Value, often called Paid-in Surplus or Capital Surplus, usually represents the amount received in excess of the par value of the shares of stock which have been issued by a corporation. For example, if some of the authorized—but as yet unissued—$5 par value common shares are issued at $25 per share, the $5 par value of each share is shown opposite Common Stock, and the remaining $20 received for each share is shown opposite Capital in Excess of Par Value. A typical additional source of Capital in Excess of Par Value is the capitalization of prior years' earnings by stock dividends; this point is discussed in Chapter 12.

Retained Earnings represents that amount of net earnings or profits which have not been distributed to stockholders out of the total net income earned by a company throughout its existence. It is often called Earned Surplus, Reinvested Income, or Earnings Retained for Use in the Business. Retained earnings are not in the form of cash or any other specific asset.

Bonds and other forms of long-term debt as well as the various items comprising stockholders' equity are illustrated and discussed in much more detail in Chapter 11.

OTHER FORMS FOR THE BALANCE SHEET

The balance sheet illustrated previously shows the assets on the left-hand side of the statement, and the liabilities and stockholders' equity on the right-hand side. While this represents the method most widely employed to present a balance sheet, two additional arrangements are often encountered. One of these lists the assets in detail and total, followed by the liabilities in detail and total, and shows the difference between the two totals as the amount of the stockholders' equity. Illustrated in condensed form by main categories only, it appears as shown below.

The second procedure follows the working capital approach, whereby the statement begins with the subtraction of the current liabilities from

THE FLEMING COMPANY
Balance Sheet
December 31, 1974

ASSETS		
Current Assets		$12,000,000
Investments		2,600,000
Property, Plant and Equipment		14,500,000
Intangibles		400,000
Deferred Charges		500,000
Total Assets		$30,000,000
LIABILITIES		
Current Liabilities	$ 4,000,000	
Long-term Debt	6,000,000	
Total Liabilities		10,000,000
STOCKHOLDERS' EQUITY		
Preferred 4% Cumulative Stock	$ 1,000,000	
Common Stock	1,500,000	
Capital in Excess of Par Value	4,500,000	
Retained Earnings	13,000,000	
Total Stockholders' Equity		$20,000,000

the current assets to arrive at the working capital of the company. To the working capital, assets other than current assets are added and long-term liabilities are deducted to obtain net assets. Finally, the stockholders' equity is itemized and totaled. Obviously, the total of the stockholders' equity must agree with the amount of the net assets. Such a balance sheet, again in condensed form, is illustrated below.

THE FLEMING COMPANY
Balance Sheet
December 31, 1974

Current Assets	$12,000,000
Less: Current Liabilities	4,000,000
Working Capital	$ 8,000,000
Investments	2,600,000
Property, Plant and Equipment	14,500,000
Intangibles	400,000
Deferred Charges	500,000
Total Assets less Current Liabilities	$26,000,000
Less: Long-term Debt	6,000,000
Net Assets	$20,000,000
Stockholders' Equity:	
Preferred 4% Cumulative Stock	$ 1,000,000
Common Stock	1,500,000
Capital in Excess of Par Value	4,500,000
Retained Earnings	13,000,000
Total	$20,000,000

(For a specific illustration of this format, see the balance sheet in the 1972 annual report of The United States Steel Corporation.)

Although three different forms of the balance sheet have been illustrated, additional variations are employed for such specialized endeavors as insurance companies, banks, governmental units, railroads and utilities.

FORMS OF BUSINESS ORGANIZATION

With rare exceptions, businesses in the United States are organized as corporations, partnerships, or sole proprietorships.

A corporation may be defined as "a legal entity operating under a grant of authority from a state or other political autonomy in the form of articles of incorporation or a charter."[2] A partnership, as defined by the Uniform Partnership Act, is "an association of two or more persons to carry on, as co-owners, a business for profit." If a business is owned by one person, it is referred to as a sole proprietorship.

Though the number of businesses organized as sole proprietorships and partnerships greatly exceeds those organized as corporations, corporate business receipts constitute the major portion of the aggregate business receipts that are reported by all three forms of business organizations in this country. The importance of the corporate form of business organization is emphasized by the following figures.[3]

TYPE OF BUSINESS ORGANIZATION	NUMBER OF BUSINESSES	BUSINESS RECEIPTS
Sole Proprietorship	9,429,822	$ 234,334,588,000
Partnership	920,831	84,161,394,000
Corporation	1,658,744	1,560,830,321,000

The significant role of the corporation underlies the use of the corporate approach throughout this text. However, the reader is reminded that the same principles discussed for a corporation are, in the main, equally applicable to the other two forms of business organization.

USES OF THE BALANCE SHEET

The balance sheet of a company indicates to management the financial status of the company as of a given moment. Management uses subsequent statements to disclose, through comparison, changes in the various items which summarize the company's financial condition. An analysis of this and other statements enables management to obtain such vital information as changes in inventory levels, rapidity of accounts receivable collections, and rate of profit earned on the assets employed in the business.

Besides aiding management, other uses of the statement would include those made by creditors interested in the balance sheet as an aid for determining the security of their claims upon the company; stockholders who analyze the balance sheet (and the other financial statements) to

[2] Eric L. Kohler, *A Dictionary for Accountants,* 4th ed. (Englewood Cliffs, N.J.: Prentice–Hall, Inc., 1970), p. 121.

[3] U.S. Dept. of the Treasury, *Statistics of Income, 1969, U.S. Business Tax Returns,* U.S. Treasury Department Publication No. 438 (10–72), p. 3.

determine the soundness of their investment; potential investors who use the statement to guide their future activity; and labor union officials who analyze the financial statement to determine, among other things, the company's "ability to pay."

A governmental use of the statement exists whenever a corporation's stock is listed on one of the stock exchanges which require listed companies to file their financial statements periodically with the Securities and Exchange Commission. Another governmental use arises from one of the schedules on the annual federal corporate income tax return which requires the balance sheet of the company as of the last day of its fiscal year.

Although several important uses of financial statements, with emphasis on the balance sheet, have been summarized, many have not been described. Among others, a company's customers and the public in general are interested in the information disclosed by the financial statements. It is no wonder that today some are prone to criticize accounting statements like the balance sheet; too many different categories of people are attempting to use the identical balance sheet for many different purposes. For example, financial analysts, creditors, and stockholders may want to know what the corporation is currently "worth"; such information may require adjustments to a balance sheet based on the historical cost principle considered preferable or necessary for Securities and Exchange Commission requirements, federal income tax requirements, and generally accepted accounting principles. Therefore, to serve management best or for other special uses, certain items on the balance sheet are often changed or rearranged to facilitate current and meaningful interpretations.

Illustrative Balance Sheet

For illustrations of actual published financial statements, the reader is referred to Appendix A, the Consolidated Balance Sheet of Armstrong Cork Company and the Consolidated Balance Sheet of PPG Industries.

QUESTIONS AND PROBLEMS

2–1. For each of the following four statements, choose the best answer to each and indicate your choice on an answer sheet with the number 1 or 2 or 3.

a. An inventory of store and office supplies on hand should appear on the balance sheet as a:
   1. prepaid expense
   2. portion of inventory of merchandise
   3. property, plant and equipment item

b. On the balance sheet of a magazine publishing company, the amount for subscriptions collected in advance, but as yet unearned, will appear as:
   1. a prepaid expense
   2. a reserve fund
   3. the last current liability

c. Goodwill appears on a company's balance as the result of:
   1. its excellent established business reputation
   2. the excess paid for the net assets of other companies purchased
   3. the action of the board of directors to give recognition to the value of this item so that total assets represent the true value of all assets

d. Retained earnings is another term for:
   1. cash
   2. paid-in surplus
   3. earned surplus

2–2. The Property, Plant and Equipment section of the Balance Sheet of The Fleming Company shows a subtraction of $7,000,000 for Accumulated Depreciation to Date.

Does this $7,000,000 represent cash set aside to acquire new plant and equipment when the old is worn out? If your answer is yes, then explain why Cash, on the same statement, amounts to only $1,075,000. If your answer is no, then explain where the $7,000,000 is.

2–3. The illustrative Balance Sheet of The Fleming Company on page 23 shows Retained Earnings of $13,000,000.

If Retained Earnings are not in the form of cash or any other specific asset, *where* is the $13,000,000?

2–4. Many economists, accountants and businessmen criticize financial statements prepared in accordance with "generally accepted accounting principles." They claim such statements are misleading because they ignore the effect of the past two decades of inflation. To illustrate this point, they take the asset side of the Balance Sheet shown on page 22 and say, "What was done amounts to adding apples, oranges, peaches, pears, etc., and labeling the grand total Total Assets . . . Total Fruit would be more appropriate."

Refer to the Balance Sheet of The Fleming Company, and point out those items which underlie the above quotation. Justify or oppose the position of the critics.

2–5. The following statement appears on page 26 of the text: "Income Taxes Payable is the estimated debt owed the government. . . ."

Give at least three reasons why this liability may be an estimated, rather than an exact, amount.

2–6. Book value (or stockholders' equity) per share of stock is that portion of the total stockholders' equity allocable to a particular class of stock, divided by the number of *outstanding* shares of stock in the same class. The 1972 annual report of Aluminum Company of America discloses the following as of December 31, 1972:

Total stockholders' equity	$1,339,391,979
Portion of above equity applicable to preferred stock:	
Preferred Stock, Par $100	65,990,900
Stockholders' equity applicable to common stock	$1,273,401,079
Common shares issued at December 31	21,871,220
Less issued shares reacquired (treasury stock)	-0-
Common shares outstanding	21,871,220

Therefore, book value (or stockholders' equity) per share of common stock on December 31, 1972, was

$$\frac{\$1,273,401,079}{21,871,220} = \$58.22$$

On this same date, the closing price on the New York Stock Exchange for common stock of Aluminum Company of America was $53⅛.

Discuss the relationship, if any, between the book value (or stockholders' equity) and the market value of a share of stock.

2–7. The 1972 annual report of Armstrong Cork Company shows that the book value (or stockholders' equity) per share, of the common stock on December 31, 1972, was $15.45.

a. Explain what this figure represents.

b. On December 31, 1972, the closing price on the New York Stock Exchange for the common stock on Armstrong Cork Company was $33 per share. Explain why book value (or stockholders' equity per share) and market value are not the same amount.

2–8. The following excerpt (Shareowners' Equity) is taken from the 1972 Balance Sheet of Ingersoll-Rand Company:

Capital Stock:	DEC. 31, 1972	DEC. 31, 1971
Preferred Stock, Authorized and issued 25,255 shares, 6% cumulative $100 par value	$ 2,525,000	$ 2,525,000

	Dec. 31, 1972	Dec. 31, 1971
Preference Stock, authorized—10,000,000 shares, without par value, issued—$2.35 Convertible Series, 3,292,657 shares in 1972 and 3,292,745 shares in 1971....	6,503,000	6,503,000
Common Stock, authorized—30,000,000 shares, $2 par value, issued—15,364,208 shares in 1972 and 15,206,756 shares in 1971...	30,728,000	30,414,000
Capital in excess of par value......	34,559,000	28,051,000
Earnings retained for use in the business	431,076,000	410,275,000
Total Shareowners' Equity	$505,391,000	$477,768,000

Note 6 to the statements reveals that the capital in excess of par increase of $6,508,000 was derived from the company's issuance of shares under incentive stock option plans for key executives.

a. How many shares of common stock were issued during 1972?

b. What was the average amount of consideration received for each share of common stock issued in 1972?

2–9. In the 1972 annual report of Walt Disney Productions, the current liabilities section of the consolidated balance sheet appeared as follows:

	Sept. 30, 1972	Oct. 2, 1971
Notes payable to banks	$ 9,000,000	$ -0-
Accounts payable	16,873,000	31,432,000
Payroll and employee benefits	6,841,000	6,228,000
Property, payroll and other taxes.....	4,217,000	5,320,000
Taxes on income (payable)	14,454,000	3,009,000
Total current liabilities	$51,385,000	$45,989,000

a. Why do the fiscal years of the company end on the dates of September 30, 1972 and October 2, 1971?

b. Why is the estimated liability for income taxes as of each date less than the expense for income taxes for each year ($34,100,000 and $21,800,000 respectively)?

2–10. The Balance Sheets and Notes to the Financial Statements for selected companies for the 1972 fiscal year show the following:

Kellogg Company

Patents, Trade-marks and Goodwill	$ 1

Philip Morris Incorporated

Brands, Trademarks, Patents and Goodwill	202,288,000

Polaroid Corporation	
Patents and Trademarks (at nominal value of $1)	—
Westinghouse Electric Corporation	
Goodwill	85,000,000
American Standard Inc.	
Excess of Cost over Net Assets of	
Businesses Purchased	90,212,000

Required:

a. Why do some companies, such as Kellogg, "carry" goodwill at a nominal figure, while other companies, such as Westinghouse and American Standard, show goodwill at a sizeable amount?

b. Would you consider the goodwill of Westinghouse Electric Corporation to be "worth" more or less than American Standard or Philip Morris?

c. On December 31, 1971, Philip Morris Incorporated showed "Brands, Trademarks, Patents, and Goodwill" at $168,930,000. Explain, or illustrate, the increase in these intangibles during 1972.

d. The Notes to the Financial Statements of Westinghouse Electric Corporation reveal the following:

> Other Assets include goodwill of $85 million in 1972 and $77 million in 1971. Goodwill acquired prior to November 1, 1970, is not being amortized. Goodwill of $8.8 million at December 31, 1972, and $1.6 million at December 31, 1971, resulting from the business combinations subsequent to November 1, 1970, remained to be amortized over the estimated period to be benefited, not to exceed 40 years.

If Westinghouse is amortizing a part of the balance of Goodwill, explain why the amount shown at December 31, 1972, is $8 million higher than the preceding year?

Note: The subject of intangible assets, especially goodwill, is more fully discussed in Chapter 8. Accounting Principles Board Opinion Number 17 pronounced that all intangibles acquired after October 31, 1970, must be written off against earnings over a period not to exceed 40 years or the estimated life of the asset, whichever is shorter. Intangibles acquired prior to November 1, 1970, which do not have a determinable economic life, are not subject to this mandatory amortization.

2–11. The Current Assets section of the Consolidated Statement of Financial Position of RCA Corporation (in the annual report for 1972) included the following:

Receivables (less reserve of $23,158,000) $666,839,000

a. Interpret the meaning of the word "reserve" as it is used in connection with the above Receivables.

b. All dollar amounts in the 1972 financial statements of RCA were rounded off to the nearest one thousand dollars. For a company of this size, do you have any objection to such a procedure?

2–12 In the 1972 annual report of Studebaker-Worthington, Inc., the Property, Plant and Equipment section of the Consolidated Balance Sheet appeared as follows:

	Dec. 31, 1972	Dec. 31, 1971
Property, Plant and Equipment—		
at cost:		
Land	$ 12,606,000	$ 12,537,000
Buildings	103,418,000	90,255,000
Machinery and equipment	172,916,000	159,682,000
	$288,940,000	$262,474,000
Less: Reserve for depreciation . . .	113,731,000	104,440,000
	$175,209,000	$158,034,000

a. What is your understanding of the term "Reserve for depreciation"?

b. To which of the items included in this section is the "reserve" applicable?

2–13. In a "twilight" area between the debt and the shareholders' equity sections of the consolidated balance sheet of The Procter & Gamble Company for the year ended June 30, 1972, appeared the following:

	June 30, 1972	June 30, 1971
Reserves:		
Self-insured risks	$ 5,205,000	$4,181,000
Foreign operations	5,000,000	4,000,000
	$10,205,000	$8,181,000

a. Interpret the two "reserves."

b. Can you justify such a "twilight" section? Are the two "reserves" a debt, *or* a portion of stockholders' equity?

2–14. The Consolidated Balance Sheet of the Carrier Corporation contained the following:

	October 31, 1972
Investment and Other Assets:	
Funds Segregated for Expansion	27,012,000
	48,875,000

What is your interpretation of the word "Funds" under the caption "Investments and Other Assets"?

2–15. A partial condensed summary of the actual Consolidated Balance Sheet as of December 31, 1972 contained in the 1972 annual report of Bristol-Myers Company, is as follows:

ASSETS		LIABILITIES	
Current Assets ..	$554,901,000	Current Liabilities.	$?
Property, Plant and Equipment	?	Other Liabilities ..	?
Other Assets....	?	Long-Term Debt..	?
Excess of cost over net tangible (etc.)	?	Total Liabilities ..	$372,770,000
		STOCKHOLDERS' EQUITY	
		5 items in proper order	
		Total Stockholders' Equity	$481,444,000
Total Assets ...	$854,214,000	Total Liab. and St. Equity	$854,214,000

The following list contains the various asset, liability, and stockholders' equity items which actually appeared on the Consolidated Balance Sheet of Bristol-Myers Company, as of December 31, 1972:

Cash		$ 34,545,000
Land (at cost)		13,299,000
Accounts payable		70,838,000
Short-term borrowings		38,918,000
Buildings (at cost)		135,956,000
Machinery, equipment, fixtures, etc., (at cost)		191,384,000
Construction in progress (of plant, at cost)		8,523,000
Marketable securities (at amortized cost which approximates market)		87,193,000
Capital in Excess of Par Value of Stock		58,008,000
U.S. and foreign taxes on income (payable)		42,320,000
Inventories:		
Finished stock	$86,940,000	
Work in process	33,893,000	
Raw material	33,885,000	
Packaging material	30,315,000	
Total		185,033,000
Accrued expenses (payable)		69,462,000
Prepaid expenses		15,358,000
Prepaid taxes		21,798,000
Accumulated depreciation		130,120,000

Item	Amount
Accounts receivable—customers (less reserves of $10,150,000)	193,844,000
Other receivables (current)	17,130,000
Long-term debt	131,535,000
Other liabilities	19,697,000
Other assets	19,229,000
Excess of cost over net tangible assets received in business acquisitions	61,042,000
Preferred stock—par value $1 per share, authorized 10,000,000 shares; issued $2 convertible series, 1,286,644 shares	1,287,000
Common stock—par value $1 per share, authorized 40,000,000 shares; issued 31,354,522 shares	31,355,000
Retained earnings	391,877,000
Cost of treasury stock:	
Common stock: 24,251 shares	1,083,000

(Notes to the financial statements have been omitted.)

Required

Prepare the complete balance sheet as of this date in proper form.

2–16. The following items have been taken from the books and other records of Brown Corporation on December 31, 1974.

Delivery Equipment	$3,000	Building	$30,000
Land	4,000	Cash	6,000
Furniture and Fixtures	2,000	Mortgage Payable	6,900

Item	Amount
Claims of creditors for amounts due them for merchandise	9,000
Rent collected in advance from tenant who is renting the third floor of the building	100
Claims on customers for merchandise sold on account	20,000
Long-term investment in XYZ Corporation common stock which cost $3,000 and has a current market value of	4,000
Promissory notes received by business from customers	5,000
Accrued interest due to business on notes	50
Interest paid in advance by business on notes	100
Accrued interest owed by the business on the mortgage	100
Inventory of merchandise which costs $20,000 and is marked to sell for	35,000
Promissory notes owed by the business	10,000
Trademarks	1,000
Prepaid insurance	200
Unused stamps, stationery, and other office supply items	650
Estimated corporate federal income taxes payable	3,000
Accrued salaries owed to employees	400

Sales tax collected from customers but not yet remitted to state	200
Amounts withheld from employees' salaries but not yet remitted to federal government for:	
Income taxes	160
F.I.C.A. taxes	40
Employer's unpaid payroll taxes consist of:	
F.I.C.A. taxes	40
State and federal unemployment taxes	60
Capital stock	40,000
Retained earnings	?

Note: The liabilities for the various social security taxes may be listed individually or combined into one item under Current Liabilities on the balance sheet.

Amounts for depreciable assets are net of accumulated depreciation to date.

Required

Prepare a classified balance sheet, *using proper accounting titles.*

2–17. The December 31, 1974, balance sheet of the business of E. G. Burbank (sole proprietor) showed:

Assets	= Liabilities	+ Owner's Equity
\$100,000 =	\$40,000 +	\$60,000

An office desk was then purchased costing \$400; payment was made with \$200 cash and the issuance of a \$200 note. The balance sheet would now show:

Assets	= Liabilities	+ Owner's Equity
\$ ______	= \$ ______	+ \$ ______

2–18. For each of the following statements, choose the best answer and indicate your choice on an answer sheet by the number 1 or 2 or 3.

a. If a company segregates and sets aside cash for a specific future use, the cash so segregated is referred to as a:
   1. fund (an asset)
   2. restriction on retained earnings
   3. retained earnings

b. When a company prices its inventory on a LIFO basis, the dollar amount reported for inventory on the Balance Sheet represents:
   1. current replacement cost
   2. estimated selling price
   3. some amount below current replacement cost if costs have increased since the adoption of LIFO

c. Book value (equity) per share of common stock of Armstrong Cork Company on December 31, 1972, was $15.45. This amount represents:
   1. market value per share on the New York Stock Exchange
   2. the net assets (A-L) per share of common stock per the books of Armstrong Cork
   3. the dollar amount each share would receive if the company were liquidated

d. In general, it may be said that Retained Earnings represents the:
   1. net accumulation of annual net profits and losses over and above amounts declared as dividends to stockholders
   2. amount of cash and any marketable securities accumulated over the years
   3. excess of assets over liabilities

e. Suppose the items listed below were either omitted or treated improperly (as stated) in the preparation of a balance sheet. Indicate in each case the effect of the errors on the equity of the owner (net worth).

   1. An asset was omitted.
      (a) Overstated
      (b) Understated
      (c) No effect
   2. The inventory of merchandise was overvalued.
      (a) Overstated
      (b) Understated
      (c) No effect
   3. A mortgage payable on the real estate was subtracted from (netted against) the total cost of the land and buildings.
      (a) Overstated
      (b) Understated
      (c) No effect
   4. Accrued wages at December 31 were ignored.
      (a) Overstated
      (b) Understated
      (c) No effect
   5. A long-term permanent investment was shown as a current asset.
      (a) Overstated
      (b) Understated
      (c) No effect

2–19. The following items have been taken from the books and other records of T. Rhodes Corporation on December 31, 1974.

Promissory notes owed by the business to trade creditors	$ 10,000
Interest accrued on above notes	120

Bank loan payable in 90 days	12,000
Interest paid in advance to bank on above note payable	180
Cash	16,000
Delivery trucks	10,000
Land	15,000
Buildings	60,000
Merchandise inventory at cost	50,000
Unexpired insurance premiums	1,500
Due to creditors on open account for merchandise purchased	30,000
Due from customers on open account for merchandise sold	40,000
Unused store supplies (bags, cartons, boxes, etc.)	900
Furniture and fixtures	6,000
Goodwill	4,000
Patents	6,000
Accrued salaries owed to employees	600
Salaries paid in advance to employees	100
Dunkirk City bonds owned as temporary investment (market value $25,000), at cost	20,000
Interest accrued on above bonds	200
Mortgage payable on land and buildings	40,000
Interest accrued on above mortgage	400
Promissory notes received by the business from customers	15,000
Interest accrued on certain of the notes from customers	50
Interest collected in advance (unearned) on certain of the notes from customers	80
Unremitted income taxes withheld from employees' salaries	250
Unremitted F.I.C.A. taxes withheld from employees' salaries	50
Unremitted city wage tax withheld from employees' salaries	25
Employer's liability for unpaid F.I.C.A. taxes	50
Employer's unpaid state unemployment tax	25
Employer's unpaid federal unemployment tax	20
Estimated federal income tax payable	2,000
Capital stock	100,000
Retained earnings	?

Required

Prepare a classified balance sheet, *using proper accounting titles.*

3

The Statement of Income

The statement of income presents a financial review of the results of operations of a company over a specific period of time. It summarizes revenues and expenses in a manner which discloses whether a company's activities in a particular fiscal period have resulted in a profit or a loss.

The balance sheet shows the financial status of a company *as of* a given instant; the statement of income shows the profit earned or the loss sustained by a company *over a period* of time. The balance sheet is like a snapshot of a business; the statement of income resembles a moving picture. Just as a balance sheet may be prepared as of any given date, so a statement of income may cover any given period of time—a year, month, week, or even a day.

THE ACCOUNTING PERIOD

The time span between the preparation dates of financial statements is called the accounting or fiscal period. Such periods are normally uniform in length to facilitate management's use of comparative data, the calculation of federal and state income taxes, and conformance with the reporting requirements of various governmental agencies. To aid management, a majority of businesses prepare a statement of income for each month and a balance sheet as of the last day of each month. Consequently, the most common accounting period is one month.

In a broader sense and for most external reporting, the typical accounting period is one year in length. Annual statements are issued to stockholders; income taxes are determined annually; other reporting requirements are tied to a twelve-month period. In addition to comprehensive annual reports, a constantly increasing number of companies are furnishing stockholders with brief quarterly financial statements.

It is not necessary that a fiscal year coincide with the calendar year. Although a majority of businesses have a fiscal year which coincides with the calendar year ending on December 31, there has been a movement, in recent years, to adopt a natural business year in preference to a calendar year. A natural business year is a fiscal year which ends on a date when business activity and inventory levels have reached their lowest point. Thus, many department stores have adopted a fiscal year of February 1 to January 31. The Internal Revenue Service discloses that, based upon corporate income tax returns filed during a recent year, approximately one-half of U.S. corporations have a fiscal year which agrees with the calendar year.

TITLE OF STATEMENT

The statement of income has several alternate titles, as shown by the yearly survey of annual reports issued by 600 industrial companies.[1]

Title of Statement

Terminology Applied:	1971	1965	1960	1955	1946
Income	375	393	382	361	317
Earnings	180	174	152	135	10
Operations	41	24	35	30	10
All Others	4	9	31	74	263
Total	600	600	600	600	600

[1] American Institute of Certified Public Accountants, Inc., *Accounting Trends and Techniques in Published Corporate Annual Reports,* 26th ed., p. 181. Copyright 1972 by the American Institute of Certified Public Accountants, Inc.

REVENUES AND EXPENSES

Basically, the statement of income compares the revenues with the expenses of a specific period. In a given period, revenue ordinarily represents the amount of goods sold and/or services rendered to customers; expenses represent expired costs incurred to produce those revenues. The relationship of the components of the statement of income may be expressed as follows:

Revenue − Expenses = Net Income for Period

Thus, a company with total revenues of $40,100,000 and total expenses of $37,100,000 during a period has a net income of $3,000,000.

CONDENSED STATEMENT OF INCOME

In a statement of income, the revenue items are segregated by source of income, and expense items are categorized by type of expense. The sources of revenue and types of expense will vary depending upon the situation of the company and the nature of its business. The accompanying condensed statement of income illustrates revenue and expense classifications commonly encountered.

THE FLEMING COMPANY
Statement of Income
For the Year Ended December 31, 1974

Revenues:		
Sales (net)	$40,000,000	
Other Revenue	100,000	
Total Revenue		$40,100,000
Expenses:		
Cost of Goods Sold	$24,000,000	
Selling Expenses	7,800,000	
Administrative Expenses	2,200,000	
Other Expenses	200,000	
Income Taxes	2,900,000	
Total Expenses		37,100,000
Net Income for the Year		$ 3,000,000

This statement of income is presented in single-step form. One total amount is shown for revenue, and another total amount for expenses. The difference between the two is the net income (or loss) for the year.

CLASSIFICATION OF REVENUES

Sales represents those products, services, or merchandise which a company sells to its customers during a fiscal period. On financial statements and reports, the amount of sales is usually shown "net" after the subtraction of items such as:

Sales returns, which represents the goods physically returned by customers;

Sales allowances, which summarizes the deductions from original sales price permitted to customers for damaged goods, imperfect goods, or similar causes;

Sales discounts, which is the deductions granted customers for payment of invoices within a stipulated period of time.

This relationship may be summarized as follows:

Gross Sales – Sales returns, allowances, and discounts = Net Sales

Other Revenue is that income derived from sources other than the main source. Examples of such "other" sources for a manufacturing or merchandising company are dividends received on common or preferred stock held as an investment; interest earned on notes receivable, bonds, or savings accounts; rental income from property; and gains from the sale of fixed assets (such as a gain on the sale of a piece of machinery).

CLASSIFICATION OF EXPENSES

Cost of Goods Sold summarizes the cost of the goods which a company has sold to its customers during a period. The determination of the cost of goods sold is discussed in detail later in the chapter.

The difference between net sales (the quantity of goods sold at selling price) and cost of goods sold (the same quantity of goods at cost) is often referred to as the gross margin. This point is also illustrated later in the chapter.

Selling Expenses, often referred to as marketing or distribution expenses, include such items as salesmen's salaries and commissions; payroll taxes on salesmen's salaries and commissions (typical payroll taxes are old-age benefits tax, state and federal unemployment taxes); advertising; depreciation, insurance, and property taxes on the assets of the company which are used in the marketing division of the business; delivery and shipping expenses; and traveling expenses of salesmen.

Administrative Expenses include such items as salaries of office force and company officers; payroll taxes on the above salaries; depreciation, insurance, and property taxes on the assets of the company which are used in the administrative or general office division of the business; directors' fees; expense of telephone and other utilities used in this division of the business; and printing and supplies, if used in the administrative division of the business.

The total of the selling and the administrative expenses is referred to as the *operating expenses.*

Other Expenses consist of those expenses not identified with the cost of the goods sold, nor with the marketing or administrative divisions of the business. Occasionally, these "other expenses" are called financial management expenses and losses. Examples of these expenses include interest expense on bonds payable; interest expense on notes payable; loss from the sale of assets owned (as a loss on the sale of investments held in other companies, or investments in government obligations); and fire or flood loss not covered by insurance.

Income Taxes, on the statement of income of a corporation, represent the company's income tax expense on the net income for the period.

Single-Step Form vs. Multiple-Step Form

The single-step form of the statement of income was illustrated by the statement presented on page 45. Although an increasing number of companies are using this simplified form in their annual reports, the slightly more complex multiple-step form is still widely used. While the single-step form has the distinct advantage of simplicity, the multiple-step form illustrated on page 48 more clearly indicates such important factors as the gross margin (often referred to as "gross profit on sales"), which denotes the spread between net selling prices and the cost of the goods; the average rate of gross margin for the year ($16,000,000 ÷ $40,000,-000, or 40 percent); the ratio of $10,000,000 operating expenses to $40,000,000 net sales (25 percent); and the approximate 50 percent impact of the corporate net income tax rates upon the net income of the company. To show these analyses, many companies prefer the multiple-step statement. In most companies where weekly or monthly statements and operating reports are furnished to management for internal use, the multiple-step form is employed. However, to provide management with vital information which can aid the control of certain current operations and the formulation of certain business policy decisions, greater detail is required than that included on the statement illustrated.

THE FLEMING COMPANY
Statement of Income
For the Year Ended December 31, 1974

Net Sales		$40,000,000
Less: Cost of Goods Sold		24,000,000
Gross Margin on Sales		$16,000,000
Less: Operating Expenses:		
Selling Expenses	$7,800,000	
Administrative Expenses	2,200,000	10,000,000
Net Operating Income		$ 6,000,000
Other Expenses	$ 200,000	
Other Revenue	100,000	100,000
Net Income Prior to Income Taxes		$ 5,900,000
Income Taxes		2,900,000
Net Income for the Year		$ 3,000,000
Net Income (Earnings) per Common Share (see page 55)		$10.03

Detailed Statement of Income

The typical details underlying each major item on the statement of income will be considered next without definition, since they are either self-explanatory or have already been identified. If reference is made to either the single-step or the multiple-step statement of The Fleming Company when the details of each summary item are introduced, their relationship to the statement of income should be readily apparent. It should be understood that these details rarely appear in published statements; to the extent possible, they are retained within the company and used for management guidance.

Net Sales of $40,000,000 is determined in the following manner:

Gross Sales			$40,600,000
Less:	Sales Returns	$ 80,000	
	Sales Allowances	25,000	
	Cash Discounts	50,000	
	State Sales Tax	250,000	
	Federal Excise Tax	170,000	
	Freight Out	25,000	600,000
Net Sales			$40,000,000

To ascertain the Cost of Goods Sold ($24,000,000), a more involved analysis is required. This can be determined under two different assumptions.

Under the first assumption, The Fleming Company is a merchandising concern, which means that it sells substantially the same product that it purchases. To determine the cost of the goods *sold* during the period, it is first necessary to derive the cost of goods *available for sale* in that same period: that is, the sum of the inventory of merchandise on hand at the start of the period and the net cost of the merchandise purchased throughout the period. The next step is to subtract the cost of the goods not sold. Obviously, the cost of unsold goods is the inventory of merchandise on hand as of the end of the period. The difference between the cost of the goods available for sale and the cost of the unsold merchandise is the cost of goods sold. For a merchandising company, this information would be shown as follows:

Inventory of Merchandise, January 1, 1974			$ 5,500,000
Add: Net Purchases:			
Purchases		$24,775,000	
Freight In		225,000	
Less:		$25,000,000	
Purchase Returns	$ 50,000		
Purchase Allowances	25,000		
Purchase Discounts	125,000	200,000	
Net Purchases			24,800,000
Cost of Goods Available for Sale			$30,300,000
Less: Inventory of Merchandise, December 31, 1974			6,300,000
Cost of Goods Sold			$24,000,000

If, under the second assumption, The Fleming Company is a manufacturing company, the composition of the cost of goods sold section is slightly different. In lieu of beginning and ending inventories of purchased merchandise, the company has inventories of finished goods manufactured to be sold. And in place of "net purchases" of merchandise is the cost of goods manufactured. Considering these conditions, the cost of goods sold section of the statement of income appears as follows:

Inventory of Finished Goods, January 1, 1974	$ 5,500,000
Add: Cost of Goods Manufactured	24,800,000
Cost of Goods Available for Sale	$30,300,000
Less: Inventory of Finished Goods, December 31, 1974	6,300,000
Cost of Goods Sold	$24,000,000

The cost of the finished goods manufactured during the period consists of the costs of the raw materials used and the costs of the labor and manufacturing operations incurred at the factory to convert those raw materials into finished goods. A more comprehensive treatment of the determination of the cost of goods manufactured is presented in Chapter 13.

Selling Expenses ($7,800,000 for The Fleming Company) consist of the marketing, advertising, and distribution expenses which are listed below:

Salesmen's Salaries	$4,100,000
Salesmen's Commissions	700,000
Supervision Salaries	200,000
Vacation and Holiday Pay	450,000
Pension Expense	300,000
Compensation and Group Insurance	262,000
Social Security Taxes	300,000
Stationery	18,000
Telephone and Telegraph	83,000
Postage	69,000
Traveling Expenses	294,000
Branch Office Expenses	215,000
Convention Expenses	14,000
Sales Samples	80,000
Trade Publications	6,000
Catalogs and Price Lists	63,000
Displays and Exhibits	17,000
Radio and Television Advertising	225,000
Insurance on Property	98,000

Property Taxes	102,000
Depreciation	200,000
Miscellaneous	4,000
	$7,800,000

Administrative Expenses ($2,200,000 in our illustration) consist of office expenses, headquarters expenses, and certain general expenses as itemized below:

Officers' Salaries	$ 419,000
Office Salaries	635,000
Supervision Salaries	92,000
Vacation and Holiday Pay	100,000
Pension Expense	211,000
Compensation and Group Insurance	127,000
Social Security Taxes	60,000
Employee Publications	11,000
Stationery	3,000
Telephone and Telegraph	7,000
Postage	2,000
Traveling Expenses	75,000
Dues and Subscriptions	8,000
Donations	130,000
Bad Debts	62,000
Credit and Collection Expense	18,000
Legal and Other Professional Services	26,000
Light, Heat, and Water	16,000
Insurance on Property	42,000
Taxes on Property	55,000
Depreciation	100,000
Miscellaneous	1,000
	$2,200,000

Attention is directed to the several detailed expenses appearing under both Selling Expenses and Administrative Expenses; this condition exists because certain operational expenses apply to both divisions. To effect proper control of operations, certain items of expense should be prorated according to the extent to which each division is responsible for their incurrence. The $62,000 bad debts expense attributable to uncollectible accounts incurred by credit sales of merchandise is shown as an administrative expense because it is the administrative division, not the selling or marketing division, which passes on all credit applications.

Other Expenses ($200,000 for The Fleming Company) consist of the following:

Interest Expense on Bonds	$180,000
Interest Expense on Note	6,000
Fire Loss on Equipment	14,000
	$200,000

The preceding expenses are related neither to the cost of the goods sold nor to the selling or administrative activities of the business. Interest expense is not created through business operations, but arises from the financing of the business by outside sources. The loss item is non-recurring and not directly related to the company operations. Thus, on page 48, the category of other expenses is shown immediately after the determination of net operating income.

Other Revenue is derived from other than the main source of income for the company and does not enter into the determination of net operating income. For the year 1974, other revenue of The Fleming Company consists of:

Interest Earned on Investments	$ 85,000
Dividends Received on Investments	5,000
Gain on Sale of Land	10,000
	$100,000

Consideration of the various types of revenue and expenses thus far discussed indicates (as shown by the statement of income on page 48) a net income of $5,900,000 for The Fleming Company. However, this figure is the net income for the year *prior* to the expense for income taxes. As this is written, the United States federal corporate income tax rates are as follows:

Normal tax rate	22% of taxable net income
Surtax rate	26% of taxable net income in excess of $25,000

The overall federal corporate tax rate is 48 percent of taxable net income minus $6,500 (26% surtax on the first $25,000 of income). Application of these tax rates to the $5,900,000 net income of The Fleming Company would produce an amount slightly different from the $2,900,000 expense shown on the statement of income. This is because net income (according to generally accepted accounting principles) and taxable net income (according to the Internal Revenue Code) are not necessarily the same. Certain items of income or expense may be treated in one manner for accounting determination of net income, but in another manner for the determination of taxable net income. We can use two examples to illustrate. Interest earned on bonds issued by a state, municipality, or other political subdivision, though income from an accounting point of view, is excluded in the determination of taxable net income. Depreciation expense may be computed by the straight-line method for accounting purposes, but by an accelerated method for tax purposes. Additional variations between the determination of accounting net income and taxable net income, when significant, are mentioned in the appropriate sections of the text.

The foregoing discussion has made no mention of the proper reporting of major unusual non-recurring type events. In 1966, Accounting Principles Board Opinion No. 9 was issued, which stated:

> . . . that *extraordinary items* should be segregated from the results of ordinary operations and shown separately in the income statement, with disclosure of the nature and amounts thereof.[2]

To aid in clarifying what constitutes an extraordinary item, and how it should be reported, in early 1973 an exposure draft of a proposed APB Opinion was released, which stated:

> Extraordinary items are derived from events and transactions that are distinguished by their *unusual nature* and by the *infrequency of their occurrence*. Thus, to be classified as an extraordinary item, *both* of the following conditions must be met:
>
> (a) *Unusual nature*—the underlying event or transaction must be clearly unrelated to, or only incidentally related to, the ordinary and typical activities of the entity taking into account the environment in which the entity operates. (See discussion in paragraph 13.)
>
> (b) *Infrequency of occurrence*—the underlying event or transaction must be nonrecurring; that is, the event or transaction must be of a type that would not reasonably be expected to recur in the foreseeable future. (See discussion in paragraph 14.)[3]

---

[2] American Institute of Certified Public Accountants, *Accounting Principles Board Opinion No. 9,* "Reporting the Results of Operations" (New York, 1966).

[3] American Institute of Certified Public Accountants, *Proposed Accounting Principles Board Opinion,* "Reporting the Effects of Extraordinary Events and Transactions" (New York, 1973). Also see APB Opinion No. 30.

This proposed opinion reaffirms APB Opinion No. 9 on the presentation of an extraordinary item on the Statement of Income, such as the following:

Net Income before Extraordinary Item(s)	$ xxx
Extraordinary Item(s), less applicable income taxes	xx
Net Income for the Period	$ xx

As an illustration of such reporting, the reader is referred to the recent reports of The Anaconda Company and RCA Corporation. In 1971, The Anaconda Company reported an extraordinary charge (loss) of $302,600,000 due to the expropriation of their Chilean copper properties; in 1972, they reported an extraordinary gain of $80,136,000 on the sale of the assets of the forest products division. And, in 1971, RCA Corporation reported an extraordinary charge of $250,000,000 (net of $240,000,000 estimated tax recovery), when they announced their withdrawal from the general-purpose computer business.

EARNINGS PER SHARE

The Accounting Principles Board in its Opinion No. 15 (May 1969) stated that the earnings per share (or net loss per share) data should be "shown on the face" of the statement of income because of the "significance attached" to it by many people and as an aid in "evaluating the data in conjunction with the financial statements."

The amount of the earnings per share of stock, if a company has only one class of stock (and no securities convertible into stock or stock options or other rights which in the future could dilute earnings per share), is computed by dividing the net income for the period by the weighted average number of shares outstanding during the period. However, reference to the balance sheet of The Fleming Company on page 23 discloses that it has two classes of outstanding stock, non-convertible preferred and common. To calculate earnings per share of *common* stock, the first step is to find the amount of net income for the year allocable to the *common* stock. This would be the net income for the year of $3,000,000 minus the *preferred* stock dividends (shown on page 58) of $40,000 ($2 per share times 20,000 outstanding shares). Therefore there is $2,960,000 allocable to the common stock. The second step is to compute the weighted average number of *common* shares outstanding during the year. Reference to page 23 shows that The Fleming Company had 300,000 shares outstanding at the end of the year. Reference to the balance sheet on page 60 discloses that only 290,000 shares were outstanding at the beginning of the year. Assume that the 10,000 additional shares were sold in the middle of the year. Thus, the weighted average number of common shares outstanding during the year is 295,000. The earnings per common share is derived as follows:

$$\frac{\text{Net income for the year \$3,000,000 — Preferred dividends \$40,000}}{\text{Weighted average number of common shares outstanding of 295,000}} = \$10.03$$

As in many corporations, the capital structure of The Fleming Company is a simple capital structure. However, if the corporation has a complex capital structure due, for example, to possible contingent issuances of common stock due to the future exercise of warrants or stock options, then two earnings per share amounts must be shown on the face of the statement of income. These two earnings per share amounts are referred to as the "primary earnings per share" and "fully diluted earnings per share." The primary earnings per common share amount is based on the average number of shares outstanding during the period, after preferred dividend requirements. The fully diluted earnings per common share amount assumes full conversion of such items as convertible debentures, exercise of outstanding stock options and issuance of shares under an incentive compensation plan. Presented below are two illustrations of such reporting on the statement of income.

BURLINGTON INDUSTRIES, INC.

For the Fiscal Year Ended September 30, 1972

Net earnings per share:	
Primary	$1.86
Fully diluted	1.83

RALSTON PURINA COMPANY

For the Fiscal Year Ended September 30, 1972

Primary earnings per common share—	
Earnings before extraordinary charge	$1.87
Earnings for the year	$1.73
Fully diluted earnings per common share—	
Earnings before extraordinary charge	$1.79
Earnings for the year	$1.66

The detailed and complicated calculations behind these two earnings per share amounts are beyond the scope of this book; the interested reader is referred to Accounting Principles Board Opinion 15 on "Earnings per Share" and APB Opinion 9 on "Reporting the Results of Operations."

Earnings per share data has had increasing widespread usage in recent years. It is vital information for evaluating the trend in operating results over past years and for aid in forecasting the future. In addition, it is definitely necessary information to the financial analyst, the prospective investor, and present stockholders.

THE ACCRUAL BASIS OF ACCOUNTING

The balance sheet contained in the preceding chapter and the statement of income presented in this chapter were prepared in accordance with the accrual basis of accounting. Not all accounting records are maintained on an accrual basis. Instead, some records follow a methodology known as the cash basis of accounting. Although these two accounting bases have much in common, they possess some outstanding differences which should be understood.

Many small businesses and most professional men keep their records on the cash basis of accounting. By this basis, revenue is not recognized until cash is received, regardless of when the service was rendered or the income was earned. Similarly, an item of expense is ignored until cash is paid, regardless of when the actual expense was incurred. To illustrate, let us consider the determination of net income for an attorney in a given period. Determined on the cash basis, income from fees is not viewed as revenue when his services are rendered or when the bill is submitted to the client. Instead, the fee is recognized as revenue in the period when the cash is received, even though he may have rendered the service and "earned" the fee in a prior period. Likewise, his expenses are recognized in the period in which they are paid, regardless of when they were incurred.

Most businesses, due to the nature of their operations, cannot accurately determine their net income for a period by the cash basis of accounting. Take, for example, a company which purchases materials or merchandise with cash and on credit, maintains an inventory of goods on hand, and sells goods to customers for cash and on credit. Determining this company's profit on a basis of when cash is paid to creditors and when it is collected from customers would produce seriously distorted financial statements. Therefore, the company should use the accrual basis of accounting, which permits revenue to be recognized when earned and expenses to be established when incurred.

The illustrated statement of income of The Fleming Company shows gross sales for the year of $40,600,000. Under the accrual basis, the company recognizes revenue when the sale is made and title passes to the customer either upon delivery of goods to the customer or to a common carrier, depending upon the terms of the sale. Therefore, this method recognizes the revenue from a sale as being earned, whether or not cash has been received in payment by the end of the fiscal period. In fact, the balance sheet on page 22 indicates that The Fleming Company has over $3,000,000 of charge sales due from customers as of December 31. Similarly, expenses are recognized as incurred: the amounts shown on the statement of income for salaries and wages represent the actual expense throughout the entire year. Although a small portion of the total amount was not yet paid in cash by the company on December 31 (because the fifty-second weekly payroll period covered the last days of December and the first days of January of the next year), the portion for the last few days of December is not excluded from the total amount of expenses shown for the year. Expenses are recognized as incurred; not as paid. Of course, this situation creates a liability at the end of a fiscal period, shown in the current liabilities section of the illustrated balance sheet.

THE MATCHING CONCEPT

Since an accounting or fiscal period is a small segment of time in relation to the total life expectancy of a typical business, it is highly important that a statement of income properly match expenses and revenue in a given period. An erroneous matching of expenses incurred to create the revenue which belongs to a given period will result in distorted financial statements. For example, if a fiscal period were fifty years long, the acquisition costs of buildings, machinery, and equipment would normally be expenses of producing the revenue of this period. Since fiscal periods are not of such length, the cost of such assets must be allocated equitably (by depreciation expense) throughout their useful life.

The matching concept is one of the justifications for the last-in, first-out method of pricing inventories. If the last goods acquired—regardless of physical flow—are considered the first goods used or sold, they will be expensed at the latest acquisition prices. Such costs would more closely match the related sales revenue of the period: recently incurred costs would be related to sales revenue on nearly the same cost-price level. This point is more fully discussed in the chapters on Inventories.

Today, one of the chief criticisms of accounting is that, because of inflation, the depreciation expense for many fixed assets is insufficient to match the real cost of capital consumed with the revenue produced by its use. For example, a building constructed in 1940 at a cost of $100,000 and with an expected life of 50 years might well have a $300,000 replacement cost today. Yet, since $100,000 was the *cost* of the building, $\frac{1}{50}$ of that cost ($2,000) is expensed each year on the statement of operations. Though the *cost* of the building is matched with revenue each year, it is debatable whether current costs and revenues are matched in an equitable manner. This point is more fully discussed in Chapter 7.

STATEMENT OF RETAINED EARNINGS

The third financial statement, the statement of retained earnings, may be viewed as the connecting link between the balance sheet and the statement of income. The statement of retained earnings discloses the changes during the year in the retained earnings portion of the stockholders' equity. These changes are attributable primarily to two things: the annual net income (or loss) of the company, and the amount of dividends declared to the stockholders throughout the year.

THE FLEMING COMPANY
Statement of Retained Earnings
For the Year Ended December 31, 1974

Balance, Retained Earnings, January 1, 1974...		$11,540,000
Add: Net Income for the Year		3,000,000
		$14,540,000
Less: Dividends Declared		
On Preferred Stock	$ 40,000	
On Common Stock	1,500,000	1,540,000
Balance, Retained Earnings, December 31, 1974		$13,000,000

In this statement, the amount shown for retained earnings on January 1, 1974, agrees with that contained in the balance sheet as of December 31,

1973. The net income for the year 1974 ($3,000,000) is the amount shown by the statement of income (see page 48). The $13,000,000 amount of retained earnings as of December 31, 1974, agrees with that shown on the balance sheet (see page 23). This "tie-together" of the three financial statements may be seen more clearly in the statements on page 60.

During the past fifteen years, there has been a decided trend toward a combined statement of income and retained earnings. Instead of appearing as two separate statements, as discussed and illustrated so far in this chapter, they are often combined into one statement as below. Down to the point of net income for the year, this statement may be in either single-step or multiple-step form. Appendix A discloses that PPG Industries and Armstrong Cork Company employ somewhat separate statements.

THE FLEMING COMPANY
Statement of Income and Retained Earnings
For the Year Ended December 31, 1974

Net Sales	$40,000,000
Cost of Goods Sold	24,000,000
Gross Margin on Sales	$16,000,000
Operating Expenses	10,000,000
Net Operating Income	$ 6,000,000
Excess of Other Expenses over Other Revenue	100,000
Net Income Prior to Income Taxes	$ 5,900,000
Income Taxes	2,900,000
Net Income for the Year	$ 3,000,000
Retained Earnings, January 1	11,540,000
Total	$14,540,000
Dividend Declared	1,540,000
Retained Earnings, December 31	$13,000,000

THE FLEMING COMPANY
Balance Sheet
As of December 31, 1974 and 1973

ASSETS	December 31 1974	December 31 1973
Current Assets	$12,000,000	$11,800,000
Investments	2,600,000	2,400,000
Property, Plant and Equipment	14,500,000	14,165,000
Intangibles	400,000	425,000
Deferred Charges	500,000	550,000
Total	$30,000,000	$29,340,000

LIABILITIES	December 31 1974	December 31 1973
Current Liabilities	$ 4,000,000	$ 5,000,000
Long-term Debt	6,000,000	6,500,000
Total	$10,000,000	$11,500,000
STOCKHOLDERS' EQUITY		
Preferred Stock	$ 1,000,000	$ 1,000,000
Common Stock	1,500,000	1,450,000
Capital in Excess of Par Value	4,500,000	3,850,000
Retained Earnings	13,000,000	11,540,000
Total	$20,000,000	$17,840,000
Total	$30,000,000	$29,340,000

Statement of Income
For the Year Ended December 31, 1974

Net Sales	$40,000,000
Cost of Goods Sold	24,000,000
Gross Margin on Sales	$16,000,000
Operating Expenses	10,000,000
Net Operating Income	$ 6,000,000
Excess of Other Expenses over Other Revenue	100,000
Net Income Prior to Income Taxes	$ 5,900,000
Income Taxes	2,900,000
Net Income for the Year	$ 3,000,000

Statement of Retained Earnings
For the Year Ended December 31, 1974

Balance, Retained Earnings, January 1, 1974	$11,540,000
Net Income for the Year	3,000,000
	$14,540,000
Dividends Declared	1,540,000
Balance, Retained Earnings, December 31, 1974	$13,000,000

REPORTING BY LINES OF BUSINESS

During recent years, there has been a pronounced trend by diversified companies toward voluntary disclosure of sales and profits by divisions or product lines or lines of business. Then, in October 1970, the Securities and Exchange Commission revised Form 10-K. This form is the general form for annual reports to the SEC by companies having securities registered pursuant to the Securities Exchange Act of 1933. One of the revisions, effective for reports filed for fiscal years ending on or after December 31, 1970, is that the financial statements filed with Form 10-K *must* contain, by "lines of business," (i) sales and revenues and (ii) income before tax and extraordinary items, provided the "line of business" accounts for 10 percent or more of the total of each of the two amounts (15 percent, instead of 10 percent, if sales and revenues do not exceed $50,000,000 for the year). Since 10-K is a public document, the same information is being presented in annual reports to stockholders by an increasing number of companies. The SEC, as of the date this is written, has not attempted to define "line of business." It is their position that management of the company is in the most informed position to separate the company into "lines of business" for reporting purposes.

The breakdown shown in the 1972 annual report of Westinghouse Electric Corporation is presented on page 62 as an illustration. This company for years has reported to the stockholders more than just the necessary required financial data. This type of external reporting is similar to that which has been done internally for many years by companies appraising managerial performance by product lines or divisions, as discussed in Chapter 5.

CONSOLIDATED FINANCIAL STATEMENTS

The processes by which organizations grow or expand vary. And the methods by which business organizations do so must take into account various income tax, legal, regulatory, administrative, and financial considerations. One of the most common methods, the subject of this section of the chapter, is the acquisition by one company of the voting stock of another company. Assuming that enough stock is acquired to control the other company, the acquiring company is referred to as the parent company and the company whose stock was acquired as the subsidiary company. Even though both companies retain their separate legal entities,

WESTINGHOUSE COMPANIES

Sales and Income After Taxes

(amounts in thousands of dollars)

	Year Ended December 31, 1972				Year Ended December 31, 1971			
	Sales		Income After Taxes		Sales		Income After Taxes	
	Amount	Percent Contributed	Amount	Percent Contributed	Amount	Percent Contributed	Amount	Percent Contributed
Power Systems	$1,642,697	32%	$ 86,107	43%	$1,504,097	33%	$ 76,292	44%
Consumer Products	875,220	17	6,466	3	759,131	16	(7,731)*	(4)
Industry and Defense:								
Industry	1,743,183	34	52,833	27	1,612,900	35	49,430	28
Defense	428,208	9	11,251	6	406,333	9	11,661	7
Broadcasting, Learning and Leisure Time	351,362	7	23,218	12	304,080	6	25,564	14
Other	45,951	1	18,792	9	43,989	1	20,040	11
Total	$5,086,621	100%	$198,667	100%	$4,630,530	100%	$175,256	100%

* Amounts enclosed in parentheses denote deduction.

consolidated statements combining the net assets and operating activities of both companies are necessary to show the financial condition and operating results of the consolidated organization as a whole.

Consolidated Balance Sheet at Date of Acquisition

To illustrate this discussion, the balance sheets of P Company and S Company as of December 31, 1974, are presented next. Up until this moment both have been completely independent companies. P Company, in Phoenix, manufactures and sells generometers and has been in business twenty years. S Company, in St. Louis, manufactures and sells noskids and is a new (and quite profitable) company, having been founded only two years ago. At this point, please read carefully each company's balance sheet shown on page 64—P Company, the first column *only* (labeled "Before") and S Company in the third column.

Now, on January 1, 1975, P Company acquires an 80 percent interest in S Company by acquiring 80 percent of S's outstanding capital stock in exchange for $440,000 of P's previously authorized but unissued preferred stock. The balance sheet of S Company is unchanged; the only factor that has changed is *who* owns its outstanding capital stock. Now note the two changes in the balance sheet of P Company as shown in the second column (labeled "After") on page 64. The additional asset, Investment in Company S (consisting of 80 percent of the outstanding capital stock of that company), has been financed by issuance of shares of preferred stock (instead of by cash) because of P Company's low cash position.

It is obvious that P Company (now known as the *parent* company) is in control of S Company (now known as the *subsidiary* company) due to its ownership of 80 percent of the voting stock of the latter company. Each company is and may well remain a separate legal entity. Such is the case, for example, with Westinghouse Electric Corporation's 77 percent ownership of Westinghouse Canada, Limited. And it is obvious that each company must continue to gather its own accounting and financial data in order to prepare its separate financial statements. However, because of the significant percentage ownership of P Company in S Company and the intent of long-term control, as well as their similarity in type of business, a set of *consolidated* financial statements should be prepared. A consolidated balance sheet, for example, would reflect the financial position of the overall business enterprise at January 1, 1975. Such a consolidated balance sheet will now be shown (pages 66–67).

At this point, it should be mentioned that the acquisition of S Company was by the "purchase" method. The reader is referred to Chapter 8,

Balance Sheet

	P COMPANY		S COMPANY
	BEFORE (DEC. 31, 1974)	AFTER (JAN. 1, 1975)	BEFORE AND AFTER
ASSETS			
Current Assets:			
Cash	$ 100,000	$ 100,000	$ 40,000
Accounts Receivable (net)	300,000	300,000	100,000
Inventories	400,000	400,000	100,000
Prepaid Expenses	20,000	20,000	10,000
Total Current Assets	$ 820,000	$ 820,000	$250,000
Investments:			
Investment in Company S (80%)		$ 440,000	
Property, Plant and Equipment:			
Cost less Accumulated Depreciation	$2,180,000	2,180,000	$350,000
Total Assets	$3,000,000	$3,440,000	$600,000
LIABILITIES			
Current Liabilities:			
Accounts Payable	$ 200,000	$ 200,000	$ 60,000
Accrued Expenses Payable	100,000	100,000	10,000
Income Taxes Payable	100,000	100,000	30,000
Total Current Liabilities	$ 400,000	$ 400,000	$100,000
Long-term Debt:			
Bonds Payable	$ 600,000	$ 600,000	-0-
Total Liabilities	$1,000,000	$1,000,000	$100,000
STOCKHOLDERS' EQUITY			
Preferred Stock of P Company:			
Issued and Outstanding	$ -0-	$ 440,000	
Common Stock of P Company:			
Issued and Outstanding	500,000	500,000	
Capital Stock of S Company:			
Issued and Outstanding			$200,000
Retained Earnings	1,500,000	1,500,000	300,000
Total Stockholders' Equity	$2,000,000	$2,440,000	$500,000
Total Equities	$3,000,000	$3,440,000	$600,000

page 258, for the distinction between the "purchase" and "pooling of interests" methods of accounting for business combinations. Likewise, it should be noted that since S Company has been in business only two years, it is believed that their recorded asset amounts also reflect the fair value of each of them. Thus, any premium amount in the $440,000 amount paid by P Company for the acquisition of its 80 percent interest in S Company is *goodwill*. Again the reader is referred to Chapter 7, pages 257–62, for a discussion of goodwill, and for the requirement that it be amortized (effective November 1, 1970) over a life not to exceed 40 years.

In arriving at the consolidated balance sheet shown in column four on pages 66–67, little more is involved than cross-adding the items shown by the balance sheet of P Company in column one and the balance sheet of S Company in column two. Note that no formal accounting system exists which contains the combined amounts; the amounts on two separate sets of records simply are being cross-added to prepare the consolidated balance sheet. However, there are two complicating factors. First, there is a premium amount in the $440,000 amount paid by P Company for the 80 percent interest in the net assets of S Company. This excess amount paid over and above that paid for the 80 percent interest in the net assets acquired must be identified and shown as *goodwill* on the consolidated balance sheet. Second, P Company acquired only 80 percent of S Company. Thus, there is a *minority interest* of 20 percent by other owners in the *net* assets (assets minus liabilities) of S Company. This minority interest ownership must be indicated on the consolidated balance sheet. To handle these two factors, note the two sets of offsetting eliminations, labeled (a) and (b), in the third column on pages 66–67.

By issuing $440,000 worth of preferred stock, P Company purchased 80 percent of the *net* assets (assets-liabilities) or stockholders' equity in S Company. But 80 percent of the net assets ($600,000 assets – $100,000 liabilities) or stockholders' equity ($500,000), is only $400,000—$40,000 less than the $440,000 purchase price. And since it was previously noted that S Company's assets were on the statement at their fair value (especially since they were purchased only two years ago when the company was formed), the excess $40,000 represents the purchase of goodwill. Also, in cross-adding the separate balance sheets, there will be some double-counting that must be eliminated. Elimination (a) in the third column on pages 66–67 is designed to both set up the purchased goodwill *and* to eliminate this double-counting, by:

Against P Co. investment cost		$440,000
Offset S Co. equity purchased:		
80 percent of Capital Stock of S Co.....	$160,000	
80 percent of Retained Earnings of S Co.	240,000	400,000
Goodwill purchased		$ 40,000

Balance Sheet
January 1, 1975

	SEPARATE P COMPANY	SEPARATE S COMPANY	ELIMINATIONS	CONSOLIDATED BALANCE SHEET
ASSETS				
Current Assets:				
Cash	$ 100,000	$ 40,000		$ 140,000
Accounts Receivable (net)	300,000	100,000		400,000
Inventories	400,000	100,000		500,000
Prepaid Expenses	20,000	10,000		30,000
Total Current Assets	$ 820,000	$250,000		$1,070,000
Investments:				
Investment in S Company (80%)	$ 440,000		−440,000 (a)	
Property, Plant and Equipment: Cost less Accumulated Depreciation	2,180,000	$350,000		$2,530,000
Goodwill			+ 40,000(a)	40,000
Total Assets	$3,440,000	$600,000		$3,640,000
LIABILITIES				
Current Liabilities:				
Accounts Payable	$ 200,000	$ 60,000		$ 260,000
Accrued Expenses Payable	100,000	10,000		110,000
Income Taxes Payable	100,000	30,000		130,000
Total Current Liabilities	$ 400,000	$100,000		$ 500,000

Long-term Debt:				
Bonds Payable	$ 600,000	-0-		$ 600,000
Total Liabilities	$1,000,000	$100,000		$1,100,000
Minority Interest in S Company			+100,000 (b)	$ 100,000
STOCKHOLDERS' EQUITY				
Preferred Stock of P Company:				
Issued and Outstanding	$ 440,000			$ 440,000
Common Stock of P Company:				
Issued and Outstanding	500,000			500,000
Capital Stock of S Company:				
Issued and Outstanding		$200,000	−160,000 (a) − 40,000 (b)	
Retained Earnings	1,500,000	300,000	−240,000 (a) − 60,000 (b)	1,500,000
Total Stockholders' Equity	$2,440,000	$500,000		$2,440,000
Total Equities	$3,440,000	$600,000		$3,640,000

The consolidated balance sheet is designed to show the financial position of the consolidated business entity. In so doing, it must give recognition to equities of outsiders. The consolidated balance sheet on pages 66–67, obtained by cross-adding, contains *all* the assets and liabilities of S Company. But outsiders, the minority stockholders of S Company, have a 20 percent interest in the net assets of S Company. Elimination (b) in the third column above segregates this minority interest by:

Equity (net assets) retained by S Co. shareholders:	
20 percent of Capital Stock of S Co.	$ 40,000
20 percent of Retained Earnings of S Co.	60,000
Equals Minority Interest	$100,000

In practice, this minority interest of others in a subsidiary usually is shown on the consolidated balance sheet as a separate item *between* the liabilities and stockholders' equity sections. Occasionally it will be shown as a liability and occasionally as a segment of stockholders' equity.

At this point, it would be possible to quickly terminate this brief overview of consolidated financial statements because the basic point has been made; namely, consolidated statements are designed to present the financial picture of the total combined business organization. In so doing, the effect of intra-organization transactions must be eliminated and the equities of any minority interests in any part of the overall combined organization clearly indicated. However, it is worthwhile to discuss additional factors affecting consolidated financial statements that occur subsequent to the date of acquisition by one company of another. Therefore, next presented, on pages 69–71, are the Statements of Income and Retained Earnings for the next year, 1975, of P Company and S Company, and the Balance Sheet of each at the end of the next year, December 31, 1975.

Consolidated Financial Statements One Year After Acquisition

To prepare the Consolidated Statement of Income, note that the separate statements of income of each company have simply been cross-added down through the line for income taxes. This is possible because there have *not* been any financial transactions between the two companies during 1975 that affect the statement of income. (If there had been any such transactions, such as the sale of merchandise from one to the other, the reader can appreciate that the sale by one and the purchase by the other are offsetting items to be eliminated with a further possible adjustment for any resulting intercompany profit on the sale-purchase. On such complicating factors, the reader is referred to a standard book in the area of advanced accounting principles.) Note that the *consolidated* statement of income, down through the line for income taxes, contains 100 percent of the revenue items (net sales) of S Company and 100 percent of the

Statement of Income
For the Year Ended December 31, 1975

	SEPARATE P COMPANY	SEPARATE S COMPANY	CONSOLIDATED STATEMENT OF INCOME
Net Sales	$1,622,000	$510,000	$2,132,000
Cost of Goods Sold	900,000	300,000	1,200,000
Gross Margin on Sales	$ 722,000	$210,000	932,000
Marketing and Administrative Expenses	200,000	100,000	300,000
Net Operating Income	$ 522,000	$110,000	$ 632,000
Other Expenses: Interest Expense on Bonds	30,000	-0-	30,000
Net Income before Income Taxes	$ 492,000	$110,000	$ 602,000
Income Taxes	250,000	50,000	300,000
			$ 302,000
Net Income of Subsidiary Applicable to Minority Interests			12,000
Net Income for the Year	$ 242,000	$ 60,000	$ 290,000

Changes in Retained Earnings
For the Year 1975

	P COMPANY	S COMPANY	CONSOLIDATED
Retained Earnings, January 1, as shown by January 1, 1975, balance sheet	$1,500,000	$300,000	$1,500,000
Net Income, 1975, as shown by above Statement of Income	242,000	60,000	290,000
80 percent of S Company net income to P Company*	48,000		
	$1,790,000	$360,000	$1,790,000
Dividends Declared	100,000	10,000	100,000
Retained Earnings, December 31, as shown by December 31, 1975, balance sheet	$1,690,000	$350,000	$1,690,000

* Could have been shown above on Separate P Company Statement of Income

Balance Sheet

December 31, 1975

	SEPARATE P COMPANY	SEPARATE S COMPANY	ELIMINATIONS	CONSOLIDATED BALANCE SHEET
ASSETS				
Current Assets:				
Cash	$ 150,000	$ 60,000		$ 210,000
Accounts Receivable (net)	350,000	140,000		490,000
Inventories	550,000	145,000		695,000
Prepaid Expenses	50,000	5,000		55,000
Total Current Assets	$1,100,000	$350,000		$1,450,000
Investments:				
Investment in S Company (80%)	$ 480,000		—480,000 (a)	
Property, Plant and Equipment:				
Cost less Accumulated Depreciation	2,080,000	$320,000		$2,400,000
Goodwill			+ 40,000 (a)	40,000
Total Assets	$3,660,000	$670,000		$3,890,000
LIABILITIES				
Current Liabilities:				
Accounts Payable	$ 250,000	$ 80,000		$ 330,000
Accrued Expenses Payable	150,000	20,000		170,000
Income Taxes Payable	30,000	20,000		50,000
Total Current Liabilities	$ 430,000	$120,000		$ 550,000

Long-term Debt:				
Bonds Payable	$ 600,000	-0-		$ 600,000
Total Liabilities	$1,030,000	$120,000		$1,150,000
Minority Interest in S Company			+110,000 (b)	$ 110,000
STOCKHOLDERS' EQUITY				
Preferred Stock of P Company:				
Issued and Outstanding	$ 440,000			$ 440,000
Common Stock of P Company:				
Issued and Outstanding	500,000			500,000
Capital Stock of S Company:				
Issued and Outstanding		$200,000	−160,000 (a) − 40,000 (b)	
Retained Earnings	1,690,000	350,000	−280,000 (a) − 70,000 (b)	1,690,000
Total Stockholders' Equity	$2,630,000	$550,000		$2,630,000
Total Equities	$3,660,000	$670,000		$3,890,000

cost and expense items (cost of goods sold, marketing and administrative expenses, and income taxes) of S Company. Thus, the consolidated statement includes all $60,000 of the net income of S Company. But 20 percent of the $60,000 net income does not belong to the consolidated organization, but to "outsiders"—the minority interest in S Company. Therefore, to arrive at the net income for the year of the consolidated organization, the $12,000 amount (20 percent of $60,000) must be removed. The $290,000 consolidated net income is the sum of the entire $242,000 net income of P Company and $48,000 (80 percent of $60,000) of the net income of S Company.

The analysis showing the changes in retained earnings during 1975 contains the only intercompany transaction, namely, the dividend declared and paid by S Company. The $10,000 dividend has been distributed 20 percent ($2,000) to the outside minority interest and 80 percent ($8,000) to P Company. Where is this receipt of $8,000 in cash reflected on P Company's statements? In the current asset, cash, of course, but also in retained earnings. Note that retained earnings includes *all* 80 percent of the $60,000, or $48,000, of the net income of S Company. To understand exactly what has taken place, an explanation is necessary of what is technically known as the equity method of accounting for intercompany investments. By the use of the equity method, the amount shown on the parent company's balance sheet as "Investment in Subsidiary" includes not only the initial purchase price, but also the parent company's pro rata share of the *retained* net income (or loss) of the subsidiary since the time of its acquisition by the parent company. In effect, the parent company each year takes up its full share of the subsidiary's net income as an increase in its "Investment" and then reduces it by the amount it (the parent) actually receives in the form of dividends declared by the subsidiary. Thus, of the $48,000 net income allocable to the parent company, to date $8,000 has been "received" (in the form of dividends) while $40,000 technically has not as yet been received and is included in the asset "Investment in S Company" on the balance sheet of the parent company, as next explained.

On the two balance sheets for separate P Company, its Investment in S Company (80 percent) is shown at:

December 31, 1975	$480,000
January 1, 1975	440,000
Increase during 1975	$ 40,000

This $40,000 increase in the investment is P Company's $48,000 share of S Company's net income for 1975 less the $8,000 of it actually received as a dividend distribution from S Company. It should also be noted that exactly the same two eliminations are necessary to arrive at the December 31, 1975, consolidated balance sheet as were necessary a year earlier; only the dollar amounts are different because of the 1975 profit and dividend of S Company. Elimination (a) in the third column on pages 70–71 is designed to both set up the same original $40,000 of purchased goodwill and offset the investment of P against 80 percent of the stockholders' equity of S, by:

Against P Co. investment		$480,000
Offset S Co. equity:		
80 percent of Capital Stock of S Co.	$160,000	
80 percent of Retained Earnings of S Co.	280,000	440,000
Goodwill originally purchased		$ 40,000

And, again, elimination (b) sets up the 20 percent minority interest of the "outsiders" in the net assets of S Company, by:

S Co. equity (net assets) of outsiders:	
20 percent of Capital Stock of S Co.	$ 40,000
20 percent of Retained Earnings of S Co.	70,000
Equals Minority Interest	$110,000

Note the $10,000 increase in the minority interest since January 1. This is their share of the net income of S Company for 1973 (20 percent of $60,000) of $12,000 less the $2,000 of it received as their share of the dividend (20 percent of $10,000) declared by S Company.

Obviously, this abbreviated discussion of consolidated statements has avoided many complicating factors that arise in actual business dealings. However, it has met the goal of presenting the general principles by which consolidated statements are derived and the reasoning for so doing. The reader interested in an in-depth study of the subject is referred to the several chapters on the subject that will be found in the usual advanced accounting principles book.

QUESTIONS AND PROBLEMS

3–1. Answer the following three statements true or false:

a. The exact earnings of a business entity cannot be definitely determined before the end of the life of the business.

b. The Statement of Income is a more useful statement to those in management than the Balance Sheet.

c. For the full year of 1974, Marshall Company shows the following data for Heat and Light Expense:

Total for services rendered by the utility companies.	$1,000
Cash payments to the utility companies	900
Accrued utility expenses payable	100

If Marshall Company is on the accrual basis, Heat and Light Expense on the Statement of Income will be $1,000.

3–2. For each of the following six statements, choose the best answer to each and indicate your choice on an answer sheet with the number 1, 2, or 3.

a. Cost of goods sold represents the volume of goods sold during the year at:
   1. selling price
   2. cost
   3. value

b. One of the "key" dollar amounts readily shown by a multiple-step statement of income that is not separately set out on a single-step statement is:
   1. cost of goods sold
   2. net operating income
   3. depreciation expense

c. An uninsured tornado loss on a factory building should appear on the statement of income as:
   1. a part of cost of goods sold
   2. an operating expense
   3. an "other expense" item

d. Dividends on common stock declared during the year reduce:
   1. the net income for the year Never reduce income
   2. retained earnings at the date declared
   3. federal income tax expense of the corporation

e. When a company costs its inventory on a LIFO basis, the dollar amount reported for cost of goods sold on the Statement of Income represents:
   1. most recent costs
   2. the oldest costs
   3. some amount below current replacement cost if costs have increased since the adoption of LIFO

f. Cash dividends to stockholders are:
   1. an expense on Statement of Income
   2. a distribution of corporate profits of stockholders
   3. a return of the capital investment

3–3. The 1972 annual report of Arvin Industries, Inc. presented the Consolidated Statement of Operations and Retained Earnings for the 52 weeks ended December 31, 1972, in the single-step form, similar to that illustrated on page 45. The following list contains the various items of "Revenues" and "Costs and Expenses" which actually appeared on the statement:

Cost of goods sold	$170,348,460
Interest expense	3,120,050
Net sales	205,483,128
Selling, general and administrative expenses	19,344,009
Income taxes	5,902,732
Other income—net	716,026
Earnings per common share	?

Net income per share of common stock is based on an average of 5,557,787 shares outstanding during the year. None of the authorized preferred shares have been issued.

Required

Prepare the consolidated statement of operations (statement of income) in single-step form and compute earnings per common share. The "Net Earnings" for the year was $7,483,903. (Notes to the financial statements have been omitted.)

3–4. The 1972 annual report of The Coca-Cola Company presented the Consolidated Statements of Profit and Loss and Earned Surplus (separate statements) for the year ended December 31, 1972, in the multiple-step form for the statement of profit and loss, similar to that illustrated on page 48. The following list contains the various items which actually appeared on the statements:

Selling, general, and administrative expenses	$ 522,614,889
Net sales	1,876,192,397
Other deductions	10,921,861
Earned surplus, beginning of year	622,374,362
Cash dividends paid	97,912,992
Cost of goods sold	995,340,910
Income taxes	172,644,000
Other income	15,486,690

Earnings per share amounted to $3.19.

Required

Prepare the Consolidated Statements of Profit and Loss and Earned Surplus. The balance of earned surplus (retained earnings) on December 31, 1972, was $714,618,797. (Notes to the financial statements have been omitted.)

3–5. The financial statements contained in the 1972 annual report of the Westinghouse Electric Corporation show the following assets, liabilities, and stockholders' equity items as of December 31, 1972, and the income and expenses for the year 1972.

Cash and marketable securities	$ 139,227,000
Investments	183,706,000
Accounts payable—trade	351,045,000
Income taxes currently payable	29,091,000
Deferred current income taxes	116,441,000
Accumulated depreciation	1,005,690,000
Inventories	866,901,000
Equity in income from non-consolidated subsidiaries and affiliated companies	25,702,000
Interest expense	56,699,000
Accrued payrolls and payroll deductions	157,113,000
Sales (net)	5,086,621,000
Cost of sales	3,877,876,000
Prepaid and other current assets	150,169,000
Income taxes (expense)	147,167,000
Land and buildings	702,671,000
Construction in progress	92,005,000
Customer receivables	1,016,191,000
Non-current liabilities	81,101,000
Common stock—par value $3.125, authorized 120,000,000 shares; issued 88,464,492 shares	276,452,000
Retained earnings, December 31	1,145,711,000
Distribution, administrative and general expenses	783,116,000
Cumulative preferred stock—par value $100, authorized 374,846 shares; 304,820 shares issued and outstanding	30,482,000
Depreciation	103,240,000
Minority interest in net income of consolidated subsidiaries	3,329,000
Capital in excess of par value	486,312,000
Cost of treasury stock (common; 364,778 shares)	8,838,000
Short-term loans and current portion of long-term debt	208,346,000
Retained earnings, January 1	1,028,892,000
Dividends declared for the year:	
Preferred stock	1,158,000
Common stock	81,966,000
Poolings of interests adjustments directly to retained earnings (plus)	1,276,000

Long-term debt (principally debentures)	629,109,000
Minority interest	65,302,000
Other income	57,771,000
Deferred income taxes—non-current	42,187,000
Other assets	273,707,000
Machinery and equipment	1,424,404,000
Other current liabilities	233,437,000
Net income per common share	$2.24

Required

Prepare in proper form:

a. Consolidated Balance Sheet.
b. Consolidated Statement of Income (multiple-step form).
c. Consolidated Statement of Retained Earnings.
(Notes to the financial statements have been omitted.)

3–6. The MBA Corporation was organized three years ago by three energetic young college graduates. You are employed as "business manager." Since the chief accountant of the company resigned two weeks ago and has not been replaced yet, your most pressing need is for financial statements for the year just ended. You decide to prepare the statements yourself.

The following amounts are disclosed by the records:

Cash	$ 8,000
Accrued Expenses Payable	500
Land, Buildings, and Equipment	76,000
Accounts Receivable	9,300
Net Sales	159,000
Paid-in Surplus	7,500
Common Stock (Par $10)	30,000
Gain on Sale of Marketable Securities	2,800
Accounts Payable	3,000
Accumulated Depreciation to date	12,000
Mortgage Payable (includes installments totaling $4,000 due in 1975)	40,000
Prepaid Expenses	300
Inventory, January 1, 1974	30,000
Estimated Doubtful Accounts	100
Purchases (net of returns and discounts)	90,000
Retained Earnings, December 31, 1974	19,500
Permanent Investments (present market value $4,500)—at cost	3,000
Retained Earnings, January 1, 1974	11,300
Dividend Income	400
Inventory, December 31, 1974	23,500

Estimated Income Taxes Payable	7,500
Selling, General, and Administrative Expenses	37,500
Income Tax Expense	7,500
Dividends Paid	10,500
Interest Expense on Mortgage	2,000

Required

Based upon your few weeks of instruction to date, prepare in proper form:

a. Balance Sheet, as of December 31, 1974.

b. Statement of Income and Retained Earnings, for the year ended December 31, 1974. (Use multiple-step form for portion pertaining to statement of income.)

3–7. For each of the following statements, choose the best answer to each and indicate your choice on an answer sheet with the number 1, 2, or 3.

a. As of December 31, 1972, the Aluminum Company of America had 21,871,220 shares of $1 par value common stock outstanding. Mr. Jones owns 100 of these shares. Through his broker, he sells the 100 shares at $53 per share (on the New York Stock Exchange) and the shares are purchased by Mr. Smith at $54 through his broker. The effect of this transfer of ownership of 100 shares upon the financial statements of ALCOA is:
   1. none
   2. changes Balance Sheet but not the Statement of Income
   3. varied effect on the financial statements

b. When a corporation originally issues stock at a price in excess of par (if par value stock) or in excess of stated value (if no par value stock), this excess amount, per the corporate records, results in:
   1. "Other Income" on the Statement of Income
   2. an increase in Capital or Paid-in Surplus on the Balance Sheet
   3. Earnings Retained in the business

c. The primary responsibility for presenting fairly the financial statements (indicating the financial position and the results of operations) contained in the company's annual report is that of:
   1. the C.P.A. firm which does the audit and attaches its opinion to the statements in the annual report
   2. the company itself
   3. the SEC (Securities and Exchange Commission)

d. Assume a mercantile business employs the accrual basis of accounting. The cost of goods sold figure is the same as:
   1. the total cash paid for merchandise purchased

2. the total cash paid for merchandise purchased plus amounts still owed for merchandise purchased
3. the total cost of merchandise purchased, increased, or decreased by the net change in the inventory of merchandise from the beginning to the end of the fiscal period

e. On the balance sheet, the amount representing the difference between the cost of the property, plant and equipment and the accumulated depreciation to date is:
   1. estimated current value
   2. estimated liquidation value
   3. estimated unexpired or unrecovered cost

3–8. The accounting records of Texas Products Corporation show the following assets and liabilities *as of* December 31, 1973, and the income and expenses *for the year* 1973.

Cash	$ 10,000	Rent Collected in Advance	100
Accounts Receivable	12,000	Mortgage Payable	10,000
Notes Receivable	6,000	Capital Stock	40,000
Accrued Interest Receivable	30	Retained Earnings, January 1, 1973	11,098
RCA Common Stock (market value $11,000)	10,000	Dividends Paid	5,000
Land	4,000	Sales	199,000
Building	30,000	Sales Returns and Allowances	1,000
Accumulated Depreciation	6,000	Sales Discounts	2,000
Furniture and Fixtures	5,000	Inventory of Merchandise, December 31, 1973	19,000
Accumulated Depreciation	1,000	Prepaid Insurance	470
Goodwill	5,000	Inventory of Office Supplies	300
Accounts Payable	14,290	Inventory of Merchandise, January 1, 1973	14,500
Notes Payable	4,000	Purchases	140,000
Accrued Property Taxes Payable	700	Freight In	1,500
Estimated Federal Income Taxes Payable	5,000	Purchase Returns and Allowances	1,000
Federal Income Taxes Withheld	200	Purchase Discounts	1,000
F.I.C.A. Taxes Withheld	60	Sales Salaries	16,000
F.I.C.A. Taxes Payable	60	Advertising	2,400
Federal Unemployment Tax Payable	240	Transportation Out	2,000
State Unemployment Tax Payable	150	Store Expenses	408
		Social Security Taxes—Sales Salaries	1,448
		Office Salaries	14,000
		Office Expenses	350
		Insurance	600
		Depreciation of Building	750

Depreciation of Furniture and Fixtures...	400	Cash Dividends Received	400
Property Taxes	1,200	Rent Earned	800
Utilities Expense	825	Interest Expense (on Notes)	200
Bad Debts	200	Interest on Mortgage..	400
Social Security Taxes—Office Salaries	1,267	Loss on Sale of Plant and Equipment	1,000
Interest Earned (on Notes)	150	Estimated Federal Income Taxes	5,000

Note: Social security taxes (showing rates as this is written) consist of the following:

Federal Old Age and Survivors Insurance Tax (F.I.C.A.), including Medicare	5.85%
Federal Unemployment Tax	0.4%
State Unemployment Tax (maximum rate is dependent on state law; actual rate may be lower due to merit rating based on company's employment experience)	2.8%

Thus 9.05% of salaries equals the company's social security taxes (no employee earned in excess of the amount subject to the various payroll taxes).

Required

Prepare the three financial statements in proper form.

Notes: The operating expenses of the business may be presented in one category as "Operating Expenses" or segregated between "Selling Expenses" and "General and Administrative Expenses." The final amount arrived at on the Statement of Retained Earnings must agree with the amount shown for Retained Earnings on the Balance Sheet as of December 31, 1973.

3–9. Prepare in proper form for the T. Cobb Corporation:

a. Balance Sheet, as of December 31, 1974.

b. Statement of Income and Retained Earnings, for the year ended December 31, 1974. (Use multiple-step form for portion pertaining to statement of income and also show the earnings per share of common stock.)

The following amounts (in thousands of dollars) are disclosed by the records:

Cash	$ 3,000
Land, Buildings, and Equipment, at original cost	60,000
Net Sales	100,000
Accounts Payable	4,000
Inventory, January 1, 1974 (on FIFO basis) at cost	15,000

Purchases (net of returns and discounts)	57,500
Estimated Income Taxes Payable	5,000
Income Tax Expense	10,000
Marketing Expenses	11,000
Inventory, December 31, 1974 (on FIFO basis) at cost	12,500
Retained Earnings, January 1, 1974	30,000
Retained Earnings, December 31, 1974	?
Estimated Doubtful Accounts	100
Prepaid Expenses	100
Accumulated Depreciation to date	20,000
Accounts Receivable	8,000
Accrued Expenses Payable	800
Interest Expense	240
Investment (10%) in Foreign Company, at cost	4,000
Intangible Assets (principally goodwill)	500
6% Preferred Stock, Par $100; 10,000 shares issued and outstanding	?
Capital in Excess of Par and Stated Value	8,000
Dividends from Foreign Company	700
Notes Payable to Bank (short-term)	1,000
3% Debentures, due 1980	7,000
Common Stock, No Par—stated value of $5; 800,000 shares issued and outstanding	?
Administrative Expenses	9,000

Dividends Paid:

On Preferred .... 6% ($6.00 per share)

On Common ....$4.00 per share

(No additional shares were issued in 1974.)

Note: Neither the preferred stock nor the bonds are convertible into common stock.

3–10. Prepare in proper form (including headings) for the Wrangall Corporation:

a. Balance Sheet, as of December 31, 1974.

b. Statement of Income and Retained Earnings (combined), for the year ended December 31, 1974. (Use multiple-step form for portion of the combined statement pertaining to statement of income.) Compute the earings per share of common stock.

Cash	$ 3,000
Land, Buildings and Equipment, at original cost	60,000
Net Sales	100,000
Freight In	500
Accounts Payable	4,000
Inventory, January 1, 1974 (on FIFO basis) at cost	15,000

Purchases (net of returns and discounts)	57,000
Estimated Income Taxes Payable	5,000
Income Tax Expense	10,000
Marketing Expenses	11,000
Inventory, December 31, 1974 (on FIFO basis) at cost. . .	12,500
Retained Earnings, January 1, 1974	30,000
Retained Earnings, December 31, 1974	37,240
Estimated Doubtful Accounts	100
Prepaid Expenses	100
Accumulated Depreciation to date	20,000
Accounts Receivable	8,000
Accrued Expenses Payable	760
Interest Expense	450
Permanent Investment (10%) in Affiliated Company, at cost	4,000
Intangible Assets (principally goodwill)	500
6.5% Preferred Stock—Par $20; 200 shares issued and outstanding	4,000
Capital in Excess of Par and Stated Value	3,000
Dividends from Affiliated Company	950
Notes Payable to Bank (short-term)	1,000
7% Debentures, due 1990	4,000
Common Stock, No Par—stated value of $5; 1,200 shares issued and outstanding	6,000
Administrative Expenses (including bad debts)	9,000
Dividends Paid:	
On Preferred . . . . 6.5% ($1.30 per share). .	260
On Common . . . . $2.50 per share	3,000
(No additional shares were issued in 1974)	
Mortgage Payable (including installments of principal totalling $500 due in 1975)	3,000

Note: Neither the preferred stock nor the bonds are convertible into common stock.

3–11. Select three assets on the balance sheet of the company in problem 3–9 or 3–10 (whichever was assigned) and state some other cost or "valuation" basis which might have been used to determine the dollar amount (gross or net) of the assets.

3–12. Read the two articles mentioned below and answer the four questions. Questions a and b are based upon the article, "How's the Annual Report Coming?" from *Fortune,* January 1964.
Questions c and d are based upon the article, "The Development of Accounting Principles" from *The Journal of Accountancy,* September 1964.

Choose the number 1, 2, or 3 of each of the four questions to indicate the selection of the proper answer to each, according to the articles.

a. From a *logical* point of view, the annual report to the stockholders of a company *should* be a report from:
   1. the members of the board of directors
   2. the president of the corporation
   3. the controller and treasurer of the corporation

b. Honest financial reporting, in large part, by major American corporations:
   1. has become a way of life
   2. lags behind such financial reporting found in European countries
   3. is the exception rather than the rule

c. The development of accounting principles should be by:
   1. a cooperative effort of industry, the Institute, various other professions, trade associations, and government
   2. edicts of the Accounting Principles Board ratified by the Institute
   3. legislation

d. Complete uniformity in accounting practices is:
   1. the ultimate goal of the Accounting Principles Board
   2. possible within the next five years
   3. not attainable

3–13. As sole owner, R. E. Lee started a merchandising business on July 1, 1973, called the Virginia Merchandise Mart. The following facts were taken from the books and records as of June 30, 1974, the end of his first year in business. The fiscal year of the business is July 1 to June 30.

Cash	$ 9,675	Bad Debts	280
Sales	110,700	Fire Loss on Office Equipment	1,500
Rent Collected in Advance	100	Gain on Sale of Investments	2,800
Transportation In	2,170	Purchase Returns and Allowances	1,180
Transportation Out	1,109	Sales Salaries	10,000
Prepaid Insurance	400	Social Security Taxes—Sales Salaries	600
Insurance on Merchandise	420	Building	30,000
Insurance on Office Equipment	80	Accrued Salaries Payable	485
Cash Dividends Received	350	State Income Tax Withheld	27
U.S. Grant Corporation Capital Stock (permanent investment)	7,150	Prepaid Advertising	75
Store Equipment	8,000	Inventory of Store Supplies	125
Depreciation of Store Equipment	600	Store Supplies Expense	422

Heat, Light and Water Expense	972
Sample Expense	487
Notes Payable	1,500
Federal Unemployment Tax Payable	50
Notes Receivable	4,000
Purchase Discounts ...	512
Interest Expense	82
Insurance on Delivery Equipment	290
Federal Income Tax Withheld	200
Interest on Mortgage ..	700
Insurance on Building .	396
Land	5,000
Accrued Interest Payable	15
Office Equipment	4,000
Office Supplies Expense	514
Interest Earned	190
Miscellaneous Selling Expenses	321
Repair Expenses	401
Purchases	72,310
Inventory of Merchandise, July 1, 1973 ...	28,000
Inventory of Merchandise, June 30, 1974 ..	32,500
Property Taxes	1,200
Accrued Property Taxes Payable	600
Miscellaneous General Expenses	123
Delivery Truck Expenses	1,780
Federal F.I.C.A. Taxes Withheld	100
Federal F.I.C.A. Taxes Payable	100
Depreciation of Office Equipment	400
Advertising	697
Sales Returns and Allowances	1,200
State Unemployment Tax Payable	140
Mortgage Notes Payable	17,500
Accrued Commissions Receivable	200
Commissions Earned ..	200
Sales Discounts	1,027
Delivery Equipment ...	6,500
Accounts Receivable ..	16,525
Depreciation of Delivery Equipment	1,000
Office Salaries	5,000
Social Security Taxes—Office Salaries	300
Rent Earned	350
Accrued Interest Receivable	40
Accounts Payable	6,883
Telephone and Telegraph Expense	196
Trademarks	100
Depreciation of Building	600
Insurance on Store Equipment	70
R. E. Lee, Capital	?

On July 1, 1973, R. E. Lee made an initial capital investment in the business of $79,500. During the fiscal year ended June 30, 1974, he made added investments of $10,000 and withdrawals of $6,445.

Required

a. Prepare the following three financial statements in proper form:
   1. Balance Sheet as of June 30, 1974. The amounts listed above for depreciable plant and equipment items are net amounts after depreciation to June 30, 1974, was deducted.
   2. Statement of Income for the year ended June 30, 1974.
   3. Statement of Owner's Equity (or Capital) for the year ended June 30, 1974.

b. Prepare the following financial analysis:
   1. Current ratio as of June 30, 1974.
   2. Working capital as of June 30, 1974.
   3. Rate (%) of gross profit for the year ended June 30, 1974.
   4. Rate (%) of net operating income for the year ended June 30, 1974.

c. What amount (in dollars) has been *paid* for each of the following expenses during the year? (Assume no other facts.)
   1. Total Salaries of $15,000.
   2. Property Taxes of $1,200.
   3. Total Interest Expense of $782.

d. What amount (in dollars) has been *collected* for each of the following income items during the year? (Assume no other facts.)
   1. Interest Earned of $190.
   2. Commissions Earned of $200.
   3. Rent Earned of $350.

3–14. The "natural business year" of a company coincides with the company's annual cycle of activity. The natural business year ends when inventories on hand, receivables from customers, and loans owed to banks are at their lowest point in the annual activity cycle.

Required

a. What are the advantages of using a natural business year rather than the calendar year for a company's fiscal year? Name some possible disadvantages.

b. Suggest logical fiscal closing dates if the concern is a:
   1. manufacturer of automobiles
   2. brewery
   3. refiner of gasoline
   4. manufacturer of wallpaper
   5. publisher of school and college books
   6. department store
   7. college

3–15. Company P acquired 90 percent of the capital stock of Company S on January 1, 1975, at a cost of $110,000. The following data are submitted at December 31, 1975:

	Company P	Company S
Capital Stock (Par $100)	$500,000	$75,000
Retained Earnings, January 1, 1975	180,000	45,000
Net Income for Year 1975, from *own* separate operations	45,000	5,000
Dividends Paid during 1975	30,000	4,500

Required

What amounts should appear on the Consolidated Balance Sheet as of December 31, 1975 (assuming the equity method which was the method used in the chapter) for:

1. Minority Interest
2. Goodwill
3. Consolidated Retained Earnings

3–16. Parent Company acquired an 80 percent interest in Subsidiary Company on January 1, 1975. Their *separate* financial statements reveal the following:

Parent Company retained earnings, January 1, 1975	$40,000
Parent Company net income for the year 1975	60,000
Subsidiary Company net income for the year 1975......	70,000
Subsidiary Company dividends during year 1975	25,000
Parent Company dividends during year 1975	-0-

Required

On the December 31, 1975, Consolidated Balance Sheet, what will be the amount for Consolidated Retained Earnings?

3–17. If Parent Company in Problem 3–16 paid $114,000 for the stock of Subsidiary Company on January 1, 1975, what would be the amount shown for "Investment in Subsidiary" on Parent Company's separate balance sheet at December 31, 1975?

3–18. Old Beulah Corporation was incorporated in 1948. The balance sheet disclosed the following stockholders' equity section at December 31, 1974.

6 percent Cumulative, Non-Participating, Non-Convertible, Preferred Stock—Par $100, authorized 400,000 shares; issued and outstanding 100,000 shares	$ 10,000,000
Common Stock—Par $50, authorized 1,000,000 shares; issued 600,000 shares, of which 100,000 are in the treasury	30,000,000
Capital in Excess of Par	15,000,000
Retained Earnings (total)	55,000,000
	$110,000,000
Less: Treasury Stock, Common (100,000 shares @ $70 cost)	7,000,000
Total Stockholders' Equity	$103,000,000

During 1974 no shares of either class of stock were sold or purchased. The treasury stock was purchased in 1969. There are no dividends in arrears on the preferred stock.

The Statement of Retained Earnings for 1974 disclosed the following:

Retained Earnings, January 1, 1974			$52,600,000
Net Income for the Year 1974		$5,000,000	
Dividends during 1974:			
On Preferred Stock			
($6 per share)	$ 600,000		
On Common Stock			
($4 per share)	2,000,000	2,600,000	2,400,000
Retained Earnings, December 31, 1974			$55,000,000

Required

Compute the 1974 earnings per common share.

3–19. Prepare in proper form (including headings) for the Fairchance Corporation:

a. Balance Sheet, as of December 31, 1974

b. Statement of Income and Retained Earnings (combined), for the year ended December 31, 1974. (Use *multiple-step form* for portion of the combined statement pertaining to statement of income.) Include the earnings per share of common stock.

The following dollar amounts (in thousands of dollars) are disclosed by the records:

Cash	$ 4,500
Net Sales	85,000
Accounts Payable	3,600
Estimated Income Taxes Payable	2,500
Income Tax Expense	5,500
Prepaid Expenses	300
Accrued Expenses Payable	600
Administrative Expenses (including bad debts)	7,000
Interest Expense	300
Intangible Assets (principally goodwill)	1,200
Capital in Excess of Par	16,500
U.S. Treasury and Other Readily Marketable Securities (at cost)	350
Treasury Stock, Common (100,000 shares at cost)	1,000

Inventory, January 1, 1974, at cost (on FIFO basis) or market, the lower	14,500
Inventory, December 31, 1974, at cost (on FIFO basis) or market, the lower	12,500
Retained Earnings, January 1, 1974	27,625
Retained Earnings, December 31, 1974	?
6% Debentures (including installments of $500 payable annually commencing July 1, 1975 for 10 years)	5,000
Common Stock, Par $5; 2,100,000 shares issued (of which 100,000 shares are in the Treasury)	10,500
5% Preferred Stock—Par $50; issued and outstanding 50,000 shares	?
Accumulated Depreciation to date	10,000
Marketing Expenses	9,000
Purchases (net of returns, allowances and discounts)	46,000
Land, Buildings, and Equipment, at original cost	55,000
Accounts Receivable	10,000
Transportation In	200
Dividends from Japanese Distributorship	500
Investment of 10% in Japanese Distributorship (at cost)	7,500
Estimated Doubtful Accounts	350
Notes Payable (to bank; short-term)	800

Dividends Paid:

On Preferred ... 5% ($2.50 per share)

On Common ... $1.50 per share on 2,000,000 shares outstanding.

Note: Neither the preferred stock nor the bonds are convertible into common stock. During the year of 1974 no shares of stock were issued, sold, or reacquired as treasury shares.

3–20. a. If a retail company this year purchases a building at a cost of $100,000 and settles the acquisition by a check for $40,000 and a mortgage payable of $60,000 due in 1985, what is the effect of this single transaction on their balance sheet? (Give name of item and amount of change. Indicate if there is no change.)

	Name of item	$ Amount
Assets:		
Increase	____________	________
Decrease	____________	________
Liabilities:		
Increase	____________	________
Decrease	____________	________
Stockholders' Equity:		
Increase	____________	________
Decrease	____________	________

b. If a company on the accrual basis has goods in inventory at a cost of \$3,000 (previously purchased but as yet not paid for) and *now* sells these goods for \$5,000 (on charge), the effect of *this* single transaction on their statement of income only is:

Net Sales	\$________
Cost of Goods Sold	\$________
Gross Margin	\$________
Net Income for Year	\$________

c. The sale of the goods from inventory immediately above changes which of the following items on the balance sheet (of the company selling the goods)? By how much?

	Name of item	\$ Amount
Assets:		
Increase	________________	__________
Decrease	________________	__________
Liabilities:		
Increase	________________	__________
Decrease	________________	__________
Stockholders' Equity:		
Increase	________________	__________
Decrease	________________	__________

d. Land used by the company for twenty years as an employee parking lot is no longer needed. It had originally cost \$50,000 and is now sold for \$150,000 cash. What is the effect of this sale of land on the company's statement of income?

4

Statement of Changes in Financial Position

The balance sheet, the statement of income, and the statement of retained earnings are the principal financial statements which *historically* have been presented. Within a company, they guide the decision-making process of management; externally, they provide information to creditors, stockholders, potential investors, and other interested parties. In addition to these statements, most companies make extensive use of various types of reports, budgets, supplementary schedules, and additional statements as aids in planning and controlling operations. Of these, the most frequently encountered is the statement of source and application of funds (which just recently had its name changed to *statement of changes in financial position* to reflect a broader concept of the term funds). Although not a new statement, it has not appeared with any frequency in the annual reports of corporations until recently; it has been widely used by various companies over many years as a pertinent tool of internal analysis. In October 1970, the Securities and Exchange Commission revised Form 10-K. This form is the general form for annual reports by companies having securities registered pursuant to the Securities Exchange Act of 1934 and the Securities Act of 1933. One of the revisions, effective for fiscal years ending on or after December 31, 1970, is that the financial statements filed with Form 10-K *must* contain the statement of source and application of funds (statement of changes in financial position). Then, in December 1970, an exposure draft of the proposed Accounting Principles Board Opinion titled "Reporting the Sources and Uses of Funds" said in its opinion "such a statement (funds statement) should be included as one of the *basic* financial statements in financial reports of a business entity." Thus, this financial statement now should be considered one of the principal financial statements along with the balance sheet and statement of income and retained earnings. Accounting Principles Board Opinion No. 19, dated March 1971, and titled "Reporting Changes in Financial Position," requires (for fiscal years ending after September 30, 1971) such a statement to accompany both the balance sheet and statement of income and retained earnings. This opinion also recommends that the title of the statement be Statement of Changes in Financial Position (rather than Sources and Uses of Funds as contained in the exposure draft of opinion) because of the broad concept used in determining "funds."

The word *funds* has several different connotations. To illustrate the various connotations of the term, using some simple examples, assume that it is 11:00 A.M. on a Wednesday morning, and someone says to you: (1) "Do you have enough funds for lunch today?" In this case you will think only in terms of the very very short run, an hour, and you will probably base your reply on the amount of your most liquid current asset. In this case *funds* means cash to you.

However, if the person should say: (2) "Do you have enough funds for an evening out tonight?" the time period has been slightly lengthened. In this case you will think in terms of the very short run, eight hours or so, and could base your reply on your present cash position *plus* any amount you might expect to receive this afternoon from liquidating (selling) readily marketable securities owned (as cashing in your Series E Bonds). In this case *funds* means the *sum* of your first two *current assets*.

But, if the person should say: (3) "Do you have enough funds for skiing this weekend?" the time period has again been lengthened. Though still thinking in terms of a relatively short run, now you will probably base your reply on the sum of your first three current assets; cash, readily marketable securities, and any accounts receivable you expect to collect from some of your friends within a few days.

On the other hand, if the person should say: (4) "Will you have enough funds for the big dance in a few weeks?" you will think in terms of a slightly longer time period. Considering this intermediate length time period, you will probably base your reply on the sum of the three current assets (cash, readily marketable securities, and accounts receivable) *minus* accounts payable for your charge account purchases which will come due within the next few weeks.

Then, if the person should say: (5) "Will you have enough funds to purchase an automobile within the next six months to a year?" you will now base your reply on a somewhat "long run" time period perspective. In this case you will probably consider the effect of the change that will occur in the intervening time period in your net working capital, the total of your current assets (cash, readily marketable securities, receivables, *and* inventory) *minus* your total current liabilities (accounts and notes payable, taxes payable, etc.). This meaning of funds, namely working capital, has been widely used in the past, especially prior to 1971.

Finally, if the person should say: (6) "I've just made a real deal; bought a $25,000 house, no down payment, completely financed by a 25-year mortgage, and no payments due for two years. Thus, there is no effect on my funds—is there?" Your answer is, "Yes, there is an effect on 'funds,' despite the fact your acquisition of the house causes no immediate change in any current asset item or any current liability item." Now you have based your answer on the "all financial resources" concept of funds as required by Accounting Principles Board Opinion No. 19, dated March 1971. In this expanded concept of funds, the $25,000 mortgage payable incurred is viewed as a source of funds even though no current liability has been affected and the $25,000 house acquired is viewed as a use of funds even though no current asset has been affected. On this point Accounting Principles Board Opinion No. 19 is very specific:

> However, a funds statement based on either the cash or the working capital concept of funds sometimes excludes certain financing and investing activities because they do not directly affect cash or working capital during the period. For example, issuing equity securities to acquire a building is both a financing and investing transaction but does not affect either cash or working capital. To meet all of its objectives, a funds statement should disclose separately the financing and investing aspects of all significant transactions that affect financial position during a period. These transactions include acquisition or disposal of property in exchange for debt or equity securities and conversion of long-term debt or preferred stock to common stock.[1]

The material which follows in this chapter is limited to the sixth meaning above for *funds,* namely, the broad concept embracing all changes in financial position and including all aspects of the company's financing and investing activities even if no item of working capital is directly affected.

---

[1] American Institute of Certified Public Accountants, Inc., Accounting Principles Board Opinion No. 19, *Reporting Changes in Financial Position,* paragraph 6 (New York, 1971).

For example, on March 31, 1972, Ralston Purina Company called for redemption its outstanding 4⅞% convertible subordinated debentures. Substantially all of the debentures were converted into common stock. The Statement of Changes in Financial Position for the Year Ended September 30, 1972 of Ralston Purina Company included the following items:

Under sources of funds:	
Issuance of common stock for conversion of debentures—contra below	$39,052,000
Under uses of funds:	
Reduction of long-term debt:	
Conversion of debentures—contra above	39,052,000
Current maturities and retirements	41,488,000

It is obvious that additional meanings for the word *funds* are possible. And it is apparent that all the usages of *funds* are important when considered in their particular context. However, the material which follows in this chapter is limited to the sixth meaning above for *funds*.

The statement of changes in financial position reports the sources and the disposition of funds which have flowed through a business during a particular period of time. Some have referred to it as a "where-got" (sources), "where-gone" (uses) statement. The term *funds* is used here in a relative, rather than a general, sense. These funds consist of more than cash alone or even cash plus readily marketable securities. A business *is* concerned with its cash position and cash flow; it is *also* vitally concerned with the broader picture presented by the flow of all financial resources.

To illustrate the importance of a statement of changes in financial position, let us assume that a stockholder, a creditor, or some executive of a company is furnished the following financial statements (reproduced on pages 97–99):

Comparative Balance Sheet, as of December 31, 1973 and 1974
Statement of Income, for the year 1974
Statement of Retained Earnings, for the Year 1974

After studying the above statements, our hypothetical reviewer might muse as follows:

> I think that I understand these financial statements, but I'm still puzzled. I see that the company had a net income during 1974 of

> $3,000,000. In addition, $700,000 was received from issuing common stock. This is a total of $3,700,000. Of this, $1,540,000 went for dividends. This leaves $2,160,000. Then, by comparing the amounts on the balance sheet at the end of each year, I can see that working capital was increased by $1,200,000. This still leaves $960,000 unaccounted for. Where is it?

In answering such questions, the statement of changes in financial position is invaluable for it shows the specific sources from which funds were derived and the various applications or uses to which the funds were placed during the year.

ILLUSTRATION OF THE STATEMENT OF CHANGES IN FINANCIAL POSITION

While there is no stereotyped form for the statement of changes in financial position, the statement shown below is arranged in a typical manner. This statement, covering the year 1974, has been prepared for The Fleming Company from the following: comparative balance sheets as of December 31, 1973 and 1974; specific items from the statement of income and statement of retained earnings for the year 1974; and an analysis of certain supplementary data.

THE FLEMING COMPANY

Statement of Changes in Financial Position

For the Year Ended December 31, 1974

Working Capital, January 1, 1974			$6,800,000
Source of Funds:			
Operations:			
Net Income for the Year, per Statement of Income		$3,000,000	
Plus expenses which did not require use of funds in current year:			
Depreciation of plant and equipment	$1,640,000		
Amortization of intangible assets and deferred charges	75,000		
Fire loss on equipment	14,000		
	$1,729,000		

Less profit on sale of land included below in proceeds from sale	10,000	1,719,000	
Funds provided by operations		$4,719,000	
Proceeds from sale of land.		275,000	
Proceeds from insurance on equipment destroyed by fire		46,000	
Issuance of common stock:			
Common stock sold	$ 350,000		
Common stock issued for acquisition of land— see contra below	350,000	700,000	
Total Sources		$5,740,000	
Uses of Funds:			
Purchase of building		$1,350,000	
Purchase of equipment		600,000	
Land acquired by issuance of common stock— see contra above		350,000	
Addition to fund for property additions		200,000	
Retirement of bonds		500,000	
Declaration of dividends:			
On preferred stock	$ 40,000		
On common stock	1,500,000	1,540,000	
Total Uses		$4,540,000	
Increase in Working Capital (see tabulation below)			1,200,000
Working Capital, December 31, 1974			$8,000,000

Changes in Working Capital:

	DECEMBER 31, 1974	DECEMBER 31, 1973	INCREASE OR (DECREASE)
Current Assets:			
Cash	$ 1,075,000	$ 1,280,000	$ (205,000)
Marketable Securities	1,500,000	1,500,000	—
Receivables	3,100,000	3,500,000	(400,000)
Inventories	6,300,000	5,500,000	800,000
Prepaid Expenses	25,000	20,000	5,000
Total	$12,000,000	$11,800,000	$ 200,000

Current Liabilities:			
Note Payable	$ 850,000	$ 1,300,000	$ (450,000)
Accounts Payable	2,400,000	2,900,000	(500,000)
Accruals Payable	250,000	200,000	50,000
Income Tax Payable	500,000	600,000	(100,000)
Total	$ 4,000,000	$ 5,000,000	$(1,000,000)
Working Capital	$ 8,000,000	$ 6,800,000	$ 1,200,000

DATA FOR PREPARATION OF THE STATEMENT OF CHANGES IN FINANCIAL POSITION

The following condensed financial statements and an analysis of certain supplementary data were used to determine the *sources* and the *uses* of funds, as illustrated in the preceding Statement of Changes in Financial Position for The Fleming Company.

THE FLEMING COMPANY

Comparative Balance Sheet

As of December 31, 1974 and 1973

	December 31, 1974	December 31, 1973	Increase or (Decrease)
	ASSETS		
Current Assets:			
Cash	$ 1,075,000	$ 1,280,000	$ (205,000)
Marketable Securities...	1,500,000	1,500,000	—
Receivables	3,100,000	3,500,000	(400,000)
Inventories	6,300,000	5,500,000	800,000
Prepaid Expenses	25,000	20,000	5,000
Total	$12,000,000	$11,800,000	$ 200,000
Investments:			
Fund for Property Additions	$ 1,800,000	$ 1,600,000	$ 200,000
Affiliated Companies ...	800,000	800,000	—
	$ 2,600,000	$ 2,400,000	$ 200,000
Property, Plant and Equipment:			
Land	$ 2,250,000	$ 2,165,000	$ 85,000
Buildings	6,350,000	5,000,000	1,350,000
Equipment	12,900,000	12,400,000	500,000
	$21,500,000	$19,565,000	$ 1,935,000

Accumulated Depreciation	(7,000,000)	(5,400,000)	1,600,000
Net	$14,500,000	$14,165,000	$ 335,000
Intangibles, less amortization	$ 400,000	$ 425,000	$ (25,000)
Deferred Charges	$ 500,000	$ 550,000	$ (50,000)
Total Assets	$30,000,000	$29,340,000	$ 660,000

LIABILITIES

Current Liabilities:			
Note Payable	$ 850,000	$ 1,300,000	$ (450,000)
Accounts Payable	2,400,000	2,900,000	(500,000)
Accruals Payable	250,000	200,000	50,000
Income Tax Payable ...	500,000	600,000	(100,000)
Total	$ 4,000,000	$ 5,000,000	$(1,000,000)
Long-term Debt:			
Debentures	$ 6,000,000	$ 6,500,000	$ (500,000)
Total Liabilities	$10,000,000	$11,500,000	$(1,500,000)

STOCKHOLDERS' EQUITY

Preferred Stock (Par $50)	$ 1,000,000	$ 1,000,000	—
Common Stock (Par $5) ..	1,500,000	1,450,000	50,000
Capital in Excess of Par Value	4,500,000	3,850,000	650,000
Retained Earnings	13,000,000	11,540,000	1,460,000
Total Stockholders' Equity	$20,000,000	$17,840,000	$ 2,160,000
Total Liabilities and Stockholders' Equity	$30,000,000	$29,340,000	$ 660,000

THE FLEMING COMPANY

Statement of Income

For the Year Ended December 31, 1974

Revenues:		
Sales (net)	$40,000,000	
Other Revenue	100,000	
Total Revenue		$40,100,000

Expenses:		
Cost of Goods Sold	$24,000,000	
Selling Expenses	7,800,000	
Administrative Expenses	2,200,000	
Other Expenses	200,000	
Income Taxes	2,900,000	
Total Expenses		37,100,000
Net Income for the Year		$ 3,000,000

Note: $1,640,000 of depreciation of buildings and equipment, $25,000 amortization of intangible assets, and $50,000 amortization of deferred charges are included in the expenses shown above.

THE FLEMING COMPANY

Statement of Retained Earnings

For the Year Ended December 31, 1974

Balance, Retained Earnings, January 1, 1974		$11,540,000
Add: Net Income for the Year		3,000,000
		$14,540,000
Less: Dividends Declared		
On Preferred Stock	$ 40,000	
On Common Stock	1,500,000	1,540,000
Balance, Retained Earnings, December 31, 1974		$13,000,000

The way in which the principal financial statements of The Fleming Company and supplementary data were used to prepare the Statement of Changes in Financial Position on pages 95–97 will be explained by a description of the composition of the statement's two major divisions.

SOURCES OF FUNDS

The typical sources of funds in a business are:

Funds generated by operations,
Disposal of non-current assets,
Increase in long-term debt, and
Issuance or sale of additional capital stock.

Reference to the financial statements of The Fleming Company (pages 97–99) will reveal whether funds were provided by each of the above sources, although the exact amount provided cannot be determined until each source is examined and modified for any changes required by an analysis of supplementary data. The actual amount of funds provided by each source was determined as follows.

Funds generated by operations was the result of the current year's operating activities. The statement of income indicates a net income of $3,000,000 for the year, but the company's operations generated funds which exceeded this figure. This difference is because the net income was computed by subtracting expenses from revenues, and certain expenses did not require the use of funds. For example, the footnote to the statement of income states that $1,640,000 of depreciation expense on buildings and equipment is included in expenses. This amount does not represent an outward flow of funds this year. The actual outflow of funds occurred in prior years when the fixed assets now being depreciated were acquired. The $1,640,000 of depreciation expense represents the current year's allocation of a portion of the total original cost of those fixed assets. Thus, to determine funds provided by operations, this type of expense must be added back to the previously determined net income for the year. Similarly, the $25,000 current year's amortization or write-off of intangible assets and the $50,000 amortization of deferred charges must also be added back to net income for the year.

During the year 1974, a fire destroyed some of the company's equipment which had been acquired several years ago at a cost of $100,000. To the date of the fire, the equipment had been depreciated a total of $40,000, leaving $60,000 as the undepreciated balance or unrecovered cost of the equipment. Since the company does not completely insure its equipment against fire hazards, only $46,000 was collected from the insurance company. Therefore, a $14,000 fire loss was incurred by the company. In summary:

Cost of equipment destroyed by fire	$100,000
Accumulated depreciation to date	40,000
Undepreciated balance	$ 60,000
Proceeds received from insurance company	46,000
Amount of fire loss	$ 14,000

The fire loss of $14,000 is one of the items contained in "Other Expenses" on the statement of income. Although this amount is definitely a loss to the company, no funds were expended (actually $46,000 of funds were received). Consequently, this $14,000 represents another expense which must be added back to the previously determined net income to ascertain the funds provided by operations during the year.

The comparative balance sheets show that the land amount was increased by $85,000 during 1974. An analysis of this item shows that the $85,000 is a net of two separate transactions. Land of $350,000 was acquired during the year and land that had originally cost $265,000 was sold during the year. In summary:

Land, at cost:	
Amount, December 31, 1973	$2,165,000
Acquired	350,000
	$2,515,000
Sold	265,000
Amount, December 31, 1974	$2,250,000

Supplementary data reveals that the land, originally acquired at a cost of $265,000, was sold for $275,000. Since the entire proceeds of $275,000 is shown as a source of funds on the statement of changes in financial position, the $10,000 profit on sale of land, which had been included in the net income for the year, must now be subtracted from net income to determine the funds provided by operations. This adjustment provides a more accurate figure for funds provided by operations, for the sale of land is not directly related to the usual operations of the company.

An alternative method for determining the *funds generated by operations* is possible; perhaps it may be more logical. Actually, the previously calculated $4,719,000 source of funds from operations is a "net" source. Reference to the statement of income shows that:

Funds came in from business operations as follows:	
Sales revenues	$40,000,000
Other revenues (excluding $10,000 profit on sale of land)	90,000
Funds in from operations	$40,090,000
Funds went out due to business operations as follows:	
Cost of goods sold	$24,000,000
Selling *and* Administrative *and* Other Expenses totaled $10,200,000, but included $1,729,000 of expenses which didn't use funds (depreciation of $1,640,000, amortization of $75,000 and the loss of $14,000)	8,471,000
Income Taxes	2,900,000
Funds out due to operations	$35,371,000
Net Funds from operations	$ 4,719,000

Either this method or that previously discussed of adjusting the net income for the year are acceptable for determining the funds provided by operations. Obviously, both methods should give the same result.

Disposal of non-current assets by The Fleming Company occurred twice during the year. Both of these entered into the adjustments which were previously made to the funds provided by operations. The exact amount of funds provided by each of these disposals must be shown on the statement of changes in financial position. The sale of land provided $275,000 of funds. And the fire, which inadvertently "disposed" of some of the company's equipment, provided $46,000 of funds from the insurance company. Additional analysis of the comparative balance sheet does not indicate any other disposals of non-current assets, any decrease in investments, or any sale of buildings or equipment. Moreover, the decreases in intangibles and deferred charges have already been reconciled to the amounts written off during the current year as amortization expense.

Increase in long-term debt provides funds for a company. No such source of funds occurred during the current year for The Fleming Company.

Issuance of additional capital stock provided funds when 5,000 shares of the $5 par value common stock were sold for $70 per share or $350,000, and 5,000 additional shares also were issued to acquire a tract of land fairly appraised at $350,000. The $700,000 of funds provided is reflected in the stockholders' equity section of the balance sheet by increases in the following two items:

Common Stock (10,000 shares @ $5)	$ 50,000
Capital in Excess of Par Value (10,000 shares @ $65)	650,000
Funds provided by issuance of common stock.	$700,000

Consequently, the statement of changes in financial position must show $700,000 of *funds provided* by the issuance of common stock, preferably segregated as follows on the statement:

Issuance of common stock:	
Common stock sold	$350,000
Common stock issued for acquisition of land—see contra below	350,000

And, because the common stock issued to acquire the land did not affect working capital (current assets minus current liabilities), an offset item on the statement of changes in financial position under *funds used* would show:

Land acquired by issuance of common stock—
see contra above $350,000

In summary, the statement of changes in financial position must reflect the above financing and investing activities of the company in the same manner *as if* the entire $700,000 of stock had been *sold* for cash and then $350,000 of the cash had been used to *purchase* the land.

USES OF FUNDS

The typical applications or uses of funds in a business are as follows:

Acquisition of non-current assets,
Reduction of long-term debt,
Purchase of outstanding capital stock, and
Declaration of cash dividends.

Reference to the financial statements of The Fleming Company (pages 97–99) will reveal whether funds were utilized for each of the preceding applications. Although the financial statements may not readily disclose the exact amount of funds that have been applied, an examination of each indicated application can determine the exact amount of each use of funds. The actual amount of funds employed by each use was determined as follows.

Acquisition of non-current assets did occur, as an analysis of the supplementary data underlying changes in these assets (shown by the comparative balance sheet) discloses that funds were used during the year to increase investments, buy a plant building, purchase new equipment, and acquire land (by the issuance of common stock).

The fund for property and plant additions (to be used to acquire additional facilities in approximately five years) was increased $200,000 by the purchase of U.S. Government bonds. An additional plant building was purchased for $1,350,000, and new equipment was also purchased for $600,000. However, the comparative balance sheet shows a net increase of only $500,000 for equipment, since $100,000 of equipment was destroyed by fire. Also, land was acquired for $350,000 by the issuance of common stock.

To prepare a statement of changes in financial position it may be necessary to analyze the amount of net change in the accumulated depreciation to date. In the present case, the net increase of $1,600,000 shown on the comparative balance sheet is readily accounted for as follows:

	ACCUMULATED DEPRECIATION TO DATE ON		
	BUILDINGS	EQUIPMENT	TOTAL
Balance, December 31, 1973	$1,500,000	$3,900,000	$5,400,000
Depreciation expense for 1974 per statement of income	200,000	1,440,000	1,640,000
Total	$1,700,000	$5,340,000	$7,040,000
Removal of portion allocated to assets disposed of during year...	—	40,000	40,000
Balance, December 31, 1974	$1,700,000	$5,300,000	$7,000,000

Reduction of long-term debt in the amount of $500,000 is shown by the comparative balance sheet. An examination reveals that, although the debenture bonds were not scheduled to mature for several years, funds were used during the year to retire prematurely a portion of the bonds by purchasing them at face on the open market.

Purchase of outstanding capital stock did not occur, as reference to the comparative statement of financial position indicates that neither preferred stock nor common stock was reacquired during the year. Instead, additional common stock was issued.

Declaration of cash dividends are disclosed by the statement of retained earnings; $1,540,000 of funds were used during the year for dividends to stockholders.

The reader is referred to pages 535 and 541 of Appendix A for the illustrative statements of changes in financial position of Armstrong Cork Company and PPG Industries.

SUMMARY

An important use of the statement of changes in financial position is that made by management to indicate the sources and uses of the company's financial resources, to show financial changes not readily apparent by the traditional analysis of the balance sheet and statement of income, and to aid those responsible for financial decisions and future planning within the firm. Another important use of this statement is that made by investors and various other parties external to the firm in evaluating the company's financial position.

Although a large majority of companies historically prepared this statement for internal use only, recent pronouncements by the Accounting Principles Board and the Securities and Exchange Commission have made the inclusion of this statement in published annual reports and on Form 10-K mandatory, since it furnishes considerable additional financial information to stockholders, financial analysts, and other interested parties.

QUESTIONS AND PROBLEMS

4–1. The following information was prepared by the G. Edwards Corporation. There were no disposals of fixed assets during 1974.

G. EDWARDS CORPORATION
Balance Sheet

	December 31	
	1974	1973
Current Assets	$20,000,000	$18,000,000
Current Liabilities	9,000,000	8,500,000
Working Capital	11,000,000	9,500,000
Property, Plant and Equipment	50,000,000	45,000,000
Accumulated Depreciation to date	22,000,000	20,000,000
Net Property, Plant and Equipment	28,000,000	25,000,000
Stockholders' Equity	$39,000,000	$34,500,000
Stockholders' Equity Evidenced By:		
Capital Stock, Par $50	$15,000,000	$15,000,000
Capital in Excess of Par	4,000,000	4,000,000
Retained Earnings, January 1	15,500,000	13,500,000
Net Income for the Year	6,000,000	3,000,000
	21,500,000	16,500,000
Dividends during the Year	1,500,000	1,000,000
Retained Earnings, December 31	20,000,000	15,500,000
Stockholders' Equity	$39,000,000	$34,500,000

Required

Prepare a statement of changes in financial position for 1974.

4–2. The balance sheets of the Mart Merchandising Corporation at December 31, 1974 and 1973, were as follows:

	December 31, 1974		December 31, 1973	
	(Amounts represent thousands of dollars)			
ASSETS				
Current Assets:				
Cash		$ 1,000		$ 1,650
Accounts Receivable	$5,400		$3,800	
Less: Allowance for Doubtful Accounts	100	5,300	90	3,710
Notes Receivable		500		250
Inventory of Merchandise		8,100		7,800
Prepaid Expenses		225		250
Total Current Assets		$15,125		$13,660
Land, Building and Equipment:				
Land		$ 2,100		$ 2,100
Building	$9,150		$8,000	
Less: Accumulated Depreciation	1,250	7,900	800	7,200
Furniture and Fixtures	$ 850		$ 620	
Less: Accumulated Depreciation	90	760	60	560
Net Land, Building and Equipment		$10,760		$ 9,860
Intangible Assets (at cost less amortization:				
Patents, Goodwill, Trademarks, etc.		$ 435		$ 750
Total Assets		$26,320		$24,270
LIABILITIES				
Current Liabilities:				
Accounts and Accruals Payable		$ 9,500		$ 8,300
Long-term Debt:				
Bonds Payable		2,000		1,000
Total Liabilities		$11,500		$ 9,300

STOCKHOLDERS' EQUITY

Contributed Capital:		
Capital Stock (Par $100) . . .	$10,000	$12,000
Premium on Capital Stock . .	600	1,000
Total	$10,600	$13,000
Retained Earnings	4,220	1,970
Total Stockholders' Equity	$14,820	$14,970
Total Creditors' and Stockholders' Equity	$26,320	$24,270

During 1974:

A new roof which cost $150,000 and a $1,000,000 addition to the building were added to the Building amount.

Some of the old fixtures and furniture having a total cost of $170,000 and accumulated depreciation to date of $20,000 were sold for $125,000. New modernistic furniture was purchased for $400,000.

The Depreciation Expense on furniture and fixtures for 1974 was $50,000.

Bonds in the amount of $1,000,000 were issued at par.

20,000 shares of capital stock were retired during the year at a cost of $2,400,000. The $400,000 excess of redemption price over par value was charged against the Premium on Capital Stock.

The only two items directly affecting the Retained Earnings during the year were net profit or loss for the year and dividend declarations of $250,000.

Required

Prepare a statement of changes in financial position for 1974.

4–3. The following column appeared on page one of the Wall Street Journal on August 4, 1969.[2]

The Outlook

Appraisal of Current Trends in Business and Finance

Trying to assess the behavior of the stock market is a bit like trying to assess the behavior of the fairer sex. In each instance, the endeavor can be highly hazardous.

---

[2] Reprinted with permission of the Wall Street Journal

Women, we of course know, are intrinsically fascinating, exasperatingly complicated and wildly unpredictable. But they also are magnificently simple, at least according to an older and wiser colleague here. The simplicity, he says, is not readily apparent to the dazzled male eye—until one recognizes that women are composed of fat, muscle and bone, precisely the same ingredients (though the arrangement differs slightly) that go into the far less mystifying male form. This fact of science, our colleague claims, tends to be overlooked by men who are bewildered by female behavior.

The parallel, to be sure, is less than perfect. But it is a fact that the stock market is intrinsically fascinating, exasperatingly complicated and wildly unpredictable. Is it also magnificently simple? Few stock market observers would say so. But most would at least agree that there are some fat-muscle-and-bone fundamentals in the composition of the market that tend to be overlooked in times such as this—when the Dow-Jones industrial stock average has fallen 14.6% in the last 2½ months.

When a person buys a share of stock, this normally enables him to gain a share in the profits of the particular company, through dividend payments. If the company's profits picture happens to be bright, a share of its stock would normally be expected to sell at a relatively high price, in terms of earnings. Conversely, the stock of another company whose profits picture happens to be bleak would normally be expected to sell at a relatively low price, in terms of earnings.

In short—and there is nothing very mysterious about it—the price of a stock normally reflects the health of the particular company's earnings.

The relationship between the price of a share of stock and the earnings that underlie the share is usually expressed as a "price-earnings ratio." If a particular stock sells at $15 per share, and the company earns $1 per share annually, the stock carries a price-earnings ratio of 15-to-one, or simply 15 in the jargon of Wall Street.

The relationship of price to earnings provides a simple means of gaining perspective not only on the price of a single stock but on many stocks taken as a whole. For example, it is possible to compute a price-earnings ratio for the 30 stocks that make up the Dow-Jones industrial average. At the end of last week, the Dow-Jones industrial average, at 826.59, was 13.9 times the $59.38 combined per-share earnings of the 30 Dow-Jones stocks for the 12 months ended March 28.

The table below attempts to place the latest price-earnings ratio for the Dow-Jones industrial stocks into post-World War II perspective. Figures for past years are based on the Dow-Jones average at each year's end and on full-year earnings.

Year	*Ratio*	*Year*	*Ratio*
1948	7.7	1960	19.1
1950	7.7	1962	17.9
1952	11.8	1964	13.6
1954	14.4	1966	13.6
1956	15.0	1968	16.3
1958	20.9	1969	13.9

The table shows that the Dow-Jones stocks are selling at prices that are relatively low in terms of earnings. The price-earnings ratio generally was higher than at present through most of the current decade, as well as through a considerable part of the 1950s. Indeed, the only period in the postwar years in which the ratio was consistently lower than now was the pre-1954 era. The current ratio seems positively depressed when compared with the levels that prevailed in the 1958–64 period. In the third quarter of 1961, the ratio reached nearly 25-to-one, almost twice last week's level.

Another way of gaining perspective on the current price-earnings level is to see how it compares with ratios that prevailed near the finish of past periods of expanding business, shortly before a recession.

There have been four major recessions in the postwar era, and in each corporate profits declined substantially. Just before the first of these recessions, in 1948–49, the price-earnings ratio of the Dow-Jones stocks stood at 8.5, far less than at present. Before the second, in 1953–54, the ratio was at 10.0, also below the present level. But before the 1957–58 recession, in which profits fell especially steeply, the ratio was 14.4, higher than now. And before the 1960–61 setback, it stood at 18.2, far higher than now.

Still another way of assessing the current price-earnings level is to observe the "quality" of the earnings that go into the ratio. Besides actual profits, companies also gain funds through depreciation. These depreciation funds represent sums deducted each year by corporations from pre-tax profits for the depreciation of such fixed assets as machine tools.

While they don't show up as profits in company earnings reports, these depreciation funds are nearly as good as profits, in the view of many analysts. Cash from depreciation can be plowed into new facilities, and the more a company can finance such spending out of depreciation, the more its current earnings can be freed for dividend payments.

Currently, for each dollar of after-tax profits, U.S. corporations produce more than 90 cents in depreciation money. Through all the 1960s and nearly all the 1950s, depreciation funds have amounted to well over 50 cents per dollar of earnings. But in earlier postwar years, there was relatively little depreciation money backing up each dollar of earnings. In 1948, when the price-earnings ratio stood at 7.7, depreciation amounted to only 30 cents per dollar of earnings.

The unpredictability of today's stock market is plainly apparent. Will the economy soon enter a recession? If so, will profits shrivel? Can companies continue to produce depreciation funds at a high rate? But it is also a very simple fact that in terms of earnings stocks generally are selling at prices higher than in early postwar years but lower than in most recent years. In this inflationary time, that's quite a distinction.

—Alfred L. Malabre Jr.

Required

After rereading paragraphs 12, 13, and 14 in the above 15-paragraph column, discuss what you believe is meant by:

a. actual profits

b. depreciation funds

c. depreciation funds are nearly as good as profits

d. cash from depreciation can be plowed into new facilities

4–4. The Management Planning Committee of Fineview Corporation has finalized plans for next year. Included in their planning are the following items:

a. Funds are to be obtained by issuing debenture bonds at the beginning of the year due in ten years in the amount of $2,500,000 with interest payable semi-annually at the rate of 8 percent a year.

b. Securities held as "permanent" investments in a fund for plant expansion (a non-current asset) and having a cost of $500,000 are to be sold for $800,000.

c. Within current assets is a short-term investment in U.S. Government Securities, at a cost of $100,000. This will be sold at cost.

d. Capital expenditure projects costing $3,000,000 are to be undertaken.

e. Working capital should be increased by $600,000 because of the contemplated capital expenditure program.

f. Continue making quarterly dividend payments of $.37½ a share on the 1,000,000 shares outstanding.

g. The controller has prepared the following projected statement of income for next year:

FINEVIEW CORPORATION
Estimated Statement of Income
For Next Year

Net Sales		$16,000,000
Cost of Goods Sold		9,000,000
Gross Margin on Sales		$ 7,000,000
Marketing and Administrative Expenses	$3,000,000	
Depreciation Expense	1,000,000	4,000,000
Net Operating Income		$ 3,000,000
Interest Expense on Bonds (debentures)		200,000
		$2,800,000
Gain on Sale of Permanent Investments		300,000
Net Income Before Income Taxes		$ 3,100,000
Income Tax Expense		1,600,000
Net Income After Income Taxes		$ 1,500,000

Required

Prepare an estimated statement of changes in financial position for next year. Because the amounts are estimates based on plans rather than actual results of what has already happened, the statement will not "balance." Therefore, "balance" the statement by an item indicating the dollar amount by which the objectives of the Management Planning Committee will fall short or be more than fulfilled if all the estimates turn out to be fact.

4–5. A major stockholder of Nunnery Hill Company, when he received the company's annual report on March 20, 1974, stated that something definitely had to be wrong with the financial statements. The Statement of Income for 1973 reported a net loss for the year of $40,000; yet, a comparison of the December 31, 1972 and December 31, 1973 Balance Sheets showed that working capital increased by $25,000.

During the year 1973, the company paid $15,000 for new equipment. Depreciation expense of $50,000 was deducted on the Statement of Income. In 1973, $30,000 was borrowed (new long-term debt) from the Prudential Insurance Company for 10 years.

Required

Prepare a statement of changes in financial position to show whether the stockholder is right or wrong.

4–6. Consecutive balance sheets of Allegheny Equipment Company contained the following:

	December 31, 1974	December 31, 1973
Property, Plant and Equipment (at cost):		
Machinery and Equipment . . .	$350,000	$300,000
Accumulated Depreciation to date	165,000	170,000
Unrecovered Cost	$185,000	$130,000

During the year 1974, machinery and equipment was sold at a gain of $2,000 (shown as "other income" on the Statement of Income). New machinery and equipment was purchased at a cost of $80,000. Depreciation expense on machinery and equipment in 1974 (per the Statement of Income) amounted to $20,000.

Required

Calculate the proceeds received from the sale of the machinery and equipment.

4–7. The Marin Manufacturing Corporation commenced business on December 31, 1971. On that date, its initial balance sheet appeared as follows:

Balance Sheet
December 31, 1971

Working Capital (Current Assets less Current Liabilities)	$ 2,000,000
Property, Plant and Equipment (at cost)	8,000,000
Net Assets	$10,000,000
Capital Stock (Par $50)	$10,000,000
Capital in Excess of Par Value	-0-
Retained Earnings	-0-
Stockholders' Equity	$10,000,000

During the first four years of business, the Marin Manufacturing Corporation operated at exactly the break-even point each year. The statements of income for the four years appeared as follows:

Comparative Statements of Income
For the Years Ended December 31

	1975	1974	1973	1972
Net Sales	$8,000,000	$6,000,000	$7,000,000	$5,000,000
Costs and Expenses	8,000,000	6,000,000	7,000,000	5,000,000
Net Income for Year	-0-	-0-	-0-	-0-

During this time, there were no acquisitions of additional fixed assets nor disposals of any of the original items owned on December 31, 1971. Each year's depreciation expense amounted to $500,000 ($8,000,000 cost of plant ÷ average composite life of 16 years); this expense was included in the costs and expenses amounts shown by the above statements of income. No dividends were declared during the four years.

Required

a. Prepare a balance sheet as of December 31, 1975.

b. Prepare a single statement of changes in financial position covering the four-year period of January 1, 1972, to December 31, 1975.
Note: Assume that all "funds provided (net)" were used to increase working capital.

c. Why was not a portion of the funds provided by operations used for dividends to the stockholders?

d. Assume that annual depreciation expense was $1,000,000 (average composite life of plant only 8 years) instead of $500,000 (thus each year indicates a $500,000 net loss), and:
   1. redo requirements a and b.
   2. explain why increased depreciation expense did not "provide" additional funds.

e. Assume that annual depreciation expense was $250,000 (average composite life of plant is 32 years) instead of $500,000 (thus each year indicates a $250,000 net income before tax), and:
   1. redo requirements a and b. Assume a corporate income tax rate of 50 percent.
   2. explain why operations which resulted in an annual "net income after tax" of $125,000 provided less funds than operations at break-even point or at a net loss.

4–8. The following is the final portion of a conversation which took place in the office of A. C. Van Dusen, Vice-President—Finance, in late January of 1975:

M. A. ROBINSON, DIVISION MANAGER OF PRODUCT CHAMP: "Look, don't give me such a hard time. I'm working *for* the Company. Either I get $10,000,000 for our capital expansion program to increase our output and competitive position for Champ, or Champ perishes. It's our biggest profit maker at present, but Octopus, Inc., and Noodles, Ltd., are not only increasing capacity but making rapid technological advances. Although we are presently on top, we can't stand still. Remember what happened to Tippetts Company with its generometers when they stood pat with a winning hand several years ago."

A. C. VAN DUSEN: "But, we just don't have the funds. Available funds are already committed."

H. E. DAER, TREASURER: "And look at our overall cash position. It is $1,000,000 less than one year ago."

J. HUDSON, C.P.A., CONTROLLER: "Money is limited, you know. We just don't grind the printing press to make more."

M. A. ROBINSON: "Look, you fellows are only concerned with the sacred art of matching pennies. I've thoroughly analyzed our proposed $10,000,000 capital expansion program. It's a low risk program. It betters all your benchmarks by any of your fancy schemes: payback, MAPI formula, or rate of return computed by the discounted cash flow method."

J. HUDSON: "Your program may be a worthy one, but it will have to wait at least one year before we can embark on it. If you want to see where our cash came from and where it went in the past year, Mr. Daer can draw up a cash flow statement for you."

M. A. ROBINSON: "No, that isn't necessary. Thirty years ago, as an engineering student in college, I learned the basics of accounting. They still haven't changed: debits are still on the left. I know that 'cash' flows constantly among the various items constituting working capital and other items. I even understand the difference between the cash and the accrual basis of accounting. I've completely analyzed our 1974 statements (attached). We made a profit of $10,000,000 and only paid out $2,000,000 in dividends. Furthermore, we issued additional capital stock during the year. Yet cash goes down and working capital remains almost the same. You number jugglers haven't convinced me that funds are tight."

J. HUDSON: "I can see what is causing the confusion. Now look at our 1974 financial statements while I take ten minutes and prepare a 'where got' and 'where gone' analysis for you. Technically this is known as a statement of changes in financial position."

THE VAN DUSEN MANUFACTURING COMPANY

Comparative Balance Sheet

	December 31	
	1974	1973
Current Assets:		
Cash	$ 3,000,000	$ 4,000,000
United States Government Bonds (at cost)	3,100,000	3,000,000
Accounts Receivable (less estimated doubtful accounts)	22,900,000	19,000,000
Inventories	50,000,000	51,000,000
Prepaid Expenses	1,000,000	1,000,000
Total Current Assets	80,000,000	78,000,000
Less: Current Liabilities:		
Accounts Payable	29,000,000	27,000,000
Accrued Expenses Payable	3,000,000	2,000,000
Estimated Income Taxes Payable	7,000,000	9,000,000
Total Current Liabilities	39,000,000	38,000,000
Net Working Capital	41,000,000	40,000,000
Investment (10%) in Foreign Distributorship (at cost)	5,000,000	3,000,000
Property, Plant and Equipment:		
Land	12,000,000	10,000,000
Buildings	40,000,000	35,000,000
Accumulated Depreciation to date	18,000,000	17,000,000
	22,000,000	18,000,000
Machinery and Equipment	79,000,000	70,000,000
Accumulated Depreciation to date	29,340,000	25,000,000
	49,660,000	45,000,000
Net	83,660,000	73,000,000

Goodwill; and Patents less Amortization to date	900,000	3,000,000
Total Assets, less Current Liabilities	130,560,000	119,000,000
Bonds Payable	17,560,000	21,000,000
Stockholders' Equity	$113,000,000	$ 98,000,000
Stockholders' Equity represented by:		
Capital Stock (Par $100)	$ 40,000,000	$ 35,000,000
Paid-in Surplus	22,000,000	20,000,000
Reinvested Earnings	51,000,000	43,000,000
	$113,000,000	$ 98,000,000

THE VAN DUSEN MANUFACTURING COMPANY

Statement of Income and Retained Earnings

For the Year Ended December 31, 1974

Net Sales		$200,000,000
Cost of Goods Sold		140,000,000
Gross Margin on Sales		60,000,000
Marketing and Administrative Expenses	$31,900,000	
Depreciation of Plant, Machinery and Equipment and Amortization of Patents	7,100,000	39,000,000
Net Operating Income		21,000,000
Other Income:		
Dividends from Foreign Distributorship		2,000,000
		23,000,000
Other Expenses:		
Loss on Disposal of Machinery and Equipment	$ 938,000	
Interest on Bonds Payable	800,000	1,738,000
		21,262,000
Income Taxes		9,262,000
Net Income prior Extraordinary Charges		12,000,000
Write-off of Goodwill		2,000,000
Net Income for the Year		10,000,000
Retained Earnings, January 1, 1974		43,000,000
		53,000,000
Dividends, 1974		2,000,000
Retained Earnings, December 31, 1974		$ 51,000,000

Additional analysis discloses:

a. A portion of the long-term debt was retired at par (face) in 1974.

b. The 1974 capital expansion program resulted in acquisitions of land and buildings. No land or buildings were disposed of during 1974. A considerable amount of new machinery and equipment was acquired during 1974; part was for expansion purposes and part was to replace technically obsolete equipment.

c. No patents were acquired or sold during 1974. The patents had a remaining life of 10 years on January 1, 1974, and are being amortized over this life.

d. Goodwill, which had appeared on the balance sheet at a fixed constant amount for several years, was written off in its entirety in 1974, as an extraordinary charge against earnings.

e. Technologically obsolete machinery and equipment was disposed of as follows during 1974:
   1. Machinery and equipment with an unrecovered cost (book "value") of $1,100,000 was sold for $200,000.
   2. Machinery and equipment with an unrecovered cost (book "value") of $40,000 was scrapped; the scrap was sold for $2,000.

f. On January 1, 1971, the company changed its inventory pricing method from FIFO to LIFO. In 1974 alone, it is estimated that this saved the company $1,000,000 in income taxes.

Required

Assume that you are Mr. J. Hudson, Controller. Using the above financial statements and additional supplementary data, prepare a statement of changes in financial position for 1974. As a check on the amount of one of the sources of funds, namely the amount provided by operations, determine that amount by both the regular method and the alternative method. Support clearly, by supplementary schedules or calculations, the amount of new machinery and equipment purchased in 1974.

4–9. The letter—with editor's comment thereon—reproduced below is from the November 15, 1962, issue of *FORBES*.[3]

Depreciation

Sir: You mention U.S. corporations dipping into their "depreciation accruals" (*FORBES*, Oct. 1, p. 7) to raise money for plant and equipment.

---

[3] *FORBES* Magazine, November 15, 1962, copyright Forbes Inc., 1962. Used by permission.

Your magazine and many other business periodicals consistently make this error. No funds are *provided* by depreciation; the funds had already been expended when the capital asset was acquired.

A greater disservice is being done by statements about funds being provided through depreciation. Some businessmen actually have the impression that the more equipment they purchase, the more funds they will generate as their depreciation climbs.

The fact remains that internal funds—some of it profits, some of it depreciation money—are providing the capital dollars.

—Ed.

Required

In not more than 100 words, reconcile the views of the author of the letter and the editor of *FORBES* with respect to "depreciation provides funds or money."

5

Measuring Management Performance, Return on Capital, Other Measurements

The primary objective of a private enterprise concern is profit. Management is charged with the responsibility to plan and direct the affairs of a company toward the attainment of this goal.

In Chapter 1, one of the principal reasons expressed for the existence of accounting was the aid it provides to management. Thus, attention should be focused upon the managerial significance of the data provided by the accounting information system which reveals changes and indicates significant developments in the affairs of an enterprise.

One of the functions of the interpretive area of accounting should be the proper appraisal of the results of past business activities for measurement of performance: financial statements and supplementary data should be analyzed for significant relationships to measure performance in relation to the profitability of the enterprise. The aim of any such analytical review is to provide a guide for future actions.

When judging the degree of success or failure of a business, the paramount question is how to measure performance. Traditionally there has been reliance, in varying degrees, on certain time-honored and generally useful financial analyses and ratios like working capital, current ratio, net earnings per share on outstanding stock, rate of profit on stockholders' equity, percent of profit to sales, turnover of inventories, ratio of stockholders' equity to liabilities, and many others. The selection of the measurements to be used often depends upon the category of the individual making the analysis; e.g., stockholder, creditor, financial analyst, plant manager of the company, or director of the corporation. And, all too often, numerical ratios or rates are themselves used as answers for measurement of performance rather than as initiators of further analysis and future planning.

PERCENT OF NET INCOME TO NET SALES

Historically, the percentage margin of profit on sales, expressed as the relationship of the net income to the net sales for the period, has been the ratio most widely employed to measure past performance and to plan future actions. This ratio is computed as follows:

$$\text{Margin Percentage} = \frac{\text{Net Income for the Period}}{\text{Net Sales for the Period}}$$

With rare exceptions, internal reports to management and external reports to stockholders and the public always indicate the percentage margin of profit. For example, the 1972 Annual Report of Caterpillar Tractor Co. contains "Significant Trends Since Incorporation" (April 15, 1925), which include the following (dollar amounts expressed in millions):

		PROFIT				PROFIT	
YEAR	SALES	AMOUNT	% OF SALES	YEAR	SALES	AMOUNT	% OF SALES
1925	$ 13.8	$ 3.3	23.7%	1943	$171.4	$ 7.6	4.4%
1926	20.7	4.3	20.9	1944	242.2	7.3	3.0
1927	26.9	5.7	21.3	1945	230.6	6.5	2.8
1928	35.1	8.7	24.9	1946	128.4	6.1	4.8
1929	51.8	12.4	24.0	1947	189.1	13.5	7.1
1930	45.4	9.1	20.1	1948	218.0	17.5	8.0
1931	24.1	1.6	6.5	1949	254.9	17.2	6.7
1932	13.3	(1.6)	(12.2)	1950	337.3	29.2	8.7
1933	14.4	.4	2.5	1951	394.3	15.8	4.0
1934	23.8	3.8	16.0	1952	480.8	22.7	4.7
1935	36.4	6.2	17.2	1953	437.8	20.6	4.7
1936	54.1	10.2	18.9	1954	406.7	25.9	6.4
1937	63.2	10.6	16.7	1955	533.0	36.0	6.8
1938	48.2	3.2	6.7	1956	685.9	55.5	8.1
1939	58.4	6.0	10.3	1957	649.9	40.0	6.2
1940	73.1	7.8	10.7	1958	585.2	32.2	5.5
1941	102.0	7.7	7.6	1959	742.3	46.5	6.3
1942	142.2	7.0	4.9	1960	716.0	42.6	6.0

		PROFIT				PROFIT	
YEAR	SALES	AMOUNT	% OF SALES	YEAR	SALES	AMOUNT	% OF SALES
1961	734.3	55.8	7.6	1967	1,472.5	106.4	7.2
1962	827.0	61.9	7.5	1968	1,707.1	121.6	7.1
1963	966.1	77.3	8.0	1969	2,001.6	142.5	7.1
1964	1,216.6	129.1	10.6	1970	2,127.8	143.8	6.8
1965	1,405.3	158.5	11.3	1971	2,175.2	128.3	5.9
1966	1,524.0	150.1	9.9	1972	2,602.2	206.4	7.9

Many regard the margin percentage as the key measurement of management's performance. This measurement is important to indicate the spread between revenue and expenses of the period, and it is conceded that without a margin of profit a company "has nothing." But the percent of net income to net sales is not *the* principal measurement of performance. Consider these percentages of profit, based on figures taken from the 1972 annual reports of:

	PERCENTAGE OF PROFIT (AFTER INCOME TAX) ON SALES
Weyerhaeuser Company (Year Ended December 31, 1972)	8.8%
Procter & Gamble Company (Year Ended June 30, 1972)	7.8%
United States Steel Corporation (Year Ended December 31, 1972)	2.9%
The Kroger Co.[1] (Year Ended December 30, 1972)	0.6%

It is incorrect to conclude from these figures that Weyerhaeuser Company is the most profitable company or that it is about one and one-eighth times as profitable as Procter & Gamble Company. And it is erroneous to assume that United States Steel Corporation is almost five times as profitable as The Kroger Co. These margins of profit disregard the amount of capital employed by each company to produce the volume of sales on which the margin of profit has been earned.

RETURN ON CAPITAL

Used alone, the possible inadequacy of the percentage margin of profit on sales as a measurement of performance may be illustrated by assuming

[1] The margin of profit on sales for The Kroger Company excludes an extraordinary loss on discontinued operations, which materially affects profits.

a company with sales of $1,000,000 and a net income of $100,000. On the surface, its 10% margin of profit indicates a highly profitable business. But, if the capital employed in this same company is $2,600,000, the profit on capital employed is only 3.8%, about equal to that earned on a savings account at a bank.

In the determination of return on capital for a business, the term "capital" may not be employed in the usual accounting or financial usage of the word; namely, to indicate the excess of assets over liabilities. From an economic point of view, the use of total assets as the "capital" of a business is more broadly meaningful for measuring the performance of management. It is the *total* assets of a company, not some smaller amount, which are available to management in the operation of a business. Thus, for measuring the performance and effectiveness of management, the total of all assets entrusted to its use appears to be a valid base and return on capital may be computed as follows:

$$\text{Return on Capital} = \frac{\text{Net Income for the Period}}{\text{Total Assets}}$$

Reference to the preceding four companies whose 1972 percentages of profit on sales were cited reveals the following returns on total assets (based on their annual report figures):

	PERCENTAGE RETURN (AFTER INCOME TAX) ON CAPITAL (TOTAL ASSETS)
Weyerhaeuser Company	6.47%
Procter & Gamble Company	11.62%
United States Steel Corporation	2.39%
The Kroger Co.	2.80%

Though Weyerhaeuser Company had a margin of profit on sales of about one and one-eighth times that of Procter & Gamble Company, the latter has a return on capital about 80 percent *larger*. And United States Steel Corporation, which had a margin of profit on sales almost five times that of The Kroger Co., has a rate of return on capital which is about 20 percent *smaller*.

The rate of return on capital depends upon two factors. The first of these, the margin percentage of profit on sales, has been illustrated. The second factor is turnover of capital employed. Using total assets as the capital employed, the turnover of capital employed is determined as follows:

$$\text{Turnover of Capital} = \frac{\text{Net Sales for the Period}}{\text{Total Assets}}$$

The turnover of capital is an indication of management's effectiveness in using the total capital of the business to generate sales volume. In a sense, it indicates how diligently management is working the assets to generate the sales volume. Obviously, as shown by our four illustrative companies, the turnover depends in part upon the type of business.

	TURNOVER OF CAPITAL
Weyerhaeuser Company	.73
Procter & Gamble Company	1.49
United States Steel Corporation	.83
The Kroger Co.	4.67

Both Weyerhaeuser Company and United States Steel Corporation have a capital turnover of less than once a year. But Kroger Co. has a turnover of almost five times a year.

Before proceeding into the controversial areas embodied in the concept of return on capital, a summary of the pertinent points already discussed is in order. Return on capital, though not a new concept, has been widely accepted by management as a tool for measuring performance. Today, the top managements of many companies feel that performance should be measured by the profit earned on capital employed.

This performance depends upon:				This performance is measured as follows:
Percentage of profit on sales	×	Turnover of capital	=	Return on Capital
$\frac{\text{Net Income}}{\text{Sales}}$	×	$\frac{\text{Sales}}{\text{Total Assets}}$	=	$\frac{\text{Net Income}}{\text{Total Assets}}$

The rate of return on capital employed may be determined directly, without resort to the two dependent factors, by dividing the profit earned by the capital employed. However, to prevent overlooking the two dependent factors which produce the return on capital, it is advisable to compute separately the percentage of profit on sales and the turnover of capital. Then, the multiplication of these two factors will give the rate of return on capital. The procedure, applied to the four companies, is:

	Percentage of profit on sales	×	Turnover of capital	=	Percentage return on capital
Weyerhaeuser Co.	8.8%	×	.73	=	6.47%
Procter & Gamble Co.	7.8%	×	1.49	=	11.62%
U.S. Steel Corp.	2.9%	×	.83	=	2.39%
The Kroger Co.	0.6%	×	4.67	=	2.80%

It must be remembered that different types of businesses cannot be validly compared on a single basis, like percentage of profit on sales or turnover of capital. Return on capital, the result of both factors, is the common denominator necessary for comparative purposes, since it equitably compares a company which has a high profit margin on sales and low turnover, with another which has a low margin on sales but a high turnover. The concept of return on capital employed uses sales, capital, and profit to provide an index to a company's performance.

Today, many single companies are diversified to the extent that their range of items sold is almost as varied as if our four illustrative companies were in reality only one company with four separate divisions selling timber, soap, steel, and food. For example, in 1972, RCA had the following distribution of its net sales: home products and other commercial products and services, 52 percent; broadcasting, communications, publishing, and education, 21 percent; vehicle renting and related services, 17 percent; space, defense, and other government business, 10 percent. As a result, return on capital has become a prime tool or common denominator for measuring and comparing performance by product lines, divisions, and plants within a company. Where decentralization of management and operations allows each division, plant, or product line to be treated as if it were a separate business, it is not uncommon to find year-end bonuses based on the performance of individual segments of the business, with performance measured by the return on capital employed.

Return on Capital—Illustrative Case

Using the financial statements for Holliday Corporation, an assumed company, the complexities involved in the determination of a rate of return on capital employed may be clearly illustrated.

Determination of the Capital Base (Denominator)

Total Assets vs. Other Bases. The amount of capital, the base on which the rate of return is calculated, is usually the total assets of a company. On December 31, 1974, the balance sheets of both Holliday

HOLLIDAY CORPORATION

Balance Sheet

December 31, 1974 and 1973

ASSETS	1974	1973
Current Assets:		
Cash	$ 350,000	$ 400,000
U.S. Government and Other Marketable Securities (at cost)	500,000	550,000
Accounts Receivable	2,400,000	2,200,000
Inventories (LIFO basis)	2,500,000	2,400,000
Prepaid Expenses	50,000	50,000
Total Current Assets	$ 5,800,000	$ 5,600,000
Property, Plant and Equipment:		
Buildings and Equipment (cost)	$12,200,000	$11,300,000
Less: Accumulated Depreciation to Date	4,700,000	4,200,000
	$ 7,500,000	$ 7,100,000
Land (cost)	1,100,000	1,000,000
Construction in Progress	600,000	300,000
Total Property, Plant and Equipment	$ 9,200,000	$ 8,400,000
Total Assets	$15,000,000	$14,000,000

LIABILITIES	1974	1973
Current Liabilities:		
Accounts Payable	$ 1,100,000	$ 1,200,000
Accrued Wages and Salaries	200,000	150,000
Income Taxes Payable	1,100,000	850,000
Miscellaneous Payables	600,000	300,000
Total Current Liabilities	$ 3,000,000	$ 2,500,000
Long-term Debt:		
Debentures, Due May 1, 1987	3,000,000	3,000,000
Total Liabilities	$ 6,000,000	$ 5,500,000
STOCKHOLDERS' EQUITY		
Capital Stock, $10 par value Authorized 500,000 shares Outstanding 300,000 shares	$ 3,000,000	$ 3,000,000
Capital Contribution in Excess of Par	1,000,000	1,000,000
Retained Earnings	5,000,000	4,500,000
Total Stockholders' Equity	$ 9,000,000	$ 8,500,000
Total Equities	$15,000,000	$14,000,000

Note: The last-in, first-out basis of stating inventories was adopted by the company on January 1, 1957. Accordingly, the carrying value of these inventories was approximately $1,500,000 below current replacement cost at December 31, 1974, and $1,400,000 below current replacement at December 31, 1973.

HOLLIDAY CORPORATION

Statement of Income

For the Years Ended December 31, 1974 and 1973

	1974	1973
Net Sales	$29,000,000	$25,000,000
Cost of Goods Sold	19,000,000	16,000,000
Gross Margin on Sales	$10,000,000	$ 9,000,000
Selling, General, Administrative Expenses	7,000,000	6,400,000
Net Operating Income	$ 3,000,000	$ 2,600,000
Other Income:		
Interest Income	17,000	16,000
Other Charges:		
Interest on Long-term Debt	(90,000)	(90,000)
Net Income prior Income Taxes	$ 2,927,000	$ 2,526,000
Income Taxes	1,427,000	1,226,000
Net Income for the Year	$ 1,500,000	$ 1,300,000

Note: Depreciation included in costs and expenses amounted to $600,000 in 1974 and $550,000 in 1973.

Corporation and Competitor Corporation show that the management of each company has $15,000,000 of total capital or assets for use in business operations. Though the balance sheets show that the financial policies of the two companies differ on the utilization of sources of funds to raise capital, the fact remains that the management of each company has the same amount of total capital to use in the operation of the business.

Holliday Corporation—Summary Balance Sheet

Various Assets	$15,000,000	Current Liabilities	$ 3,000,000
		Long-term Debt	3,000,000
		Stockholders' Equity	9,000,000
	$15,000,000		$15,000,000

Competitor Corporation—Summary Balance Sheet

Various Assets	$15,000,000	Current Liabilities	$ 3,000,000
		Long-term Debt	-0-
		Stockholders' Equity	12,000,000
	$15,000,000		$15,000,000

While these financial policies are vital factors in the long-run stability of the company and the return accruing to the stockholders, return on capital employed measures performance of management in everything entrusted to its control, namely total assets, regardless of the source of the assets. Thus, though the stockholders of both companies may be interested in the earnings based on the respective $9,000,000 and $12,000,000 investments, and though creditors, bankers, and financial analysts may be interested in the respective 1:1:3 and 1:0:4 ratios of current debt to long-term debt to stockholders' equity, the performance of each company's management should be judged according to the profit earned on the $15,000,000 of capital available to each. The business manager should be measured in terms of the yield earned on that total capital irrespective of the source of the resources, be it from equity of owners, by long-term debt, or through current liabilities.

Average Total Assets. Because a balance sheet indicates total assets as of a given instant, many companies use some method of averaging total assets to obtain the capital base. An averaging procedure lessens the effect caused by an unusual event which might temporarily distort total assets. Likewise, the period-end total asset amount includes the effect of the current period's profit not distributed as dividends; averaging will reduce the factor of attempting to earn profit this period on a portion of this period's profit. Also, whenever return on assets is used internally to measure management performance at the plant or divisional level, the use of other than a year or month-end amount will lessen the temptation of the local manager to improve temporarily his rate of return by some unsound method of decreasing the asset base as of a given moment.

The limited financial information given for Holliday Corporation permits a simple average of assets as of the beginning and end of 1974. Such an average, $14,500,000 in this case, theoretically appears more valid for a capital base than does the midnight December 31, 1974, amount of $15,000,000. For internal reporting, management would have month-end and quarter-end total asset amounts available for determining an average total asset base. As the base against which to measure earnings at each division and plant monthly, one company, for example, uses a progressing two-month to thirteen-month average of the assets at each location for the months of January through December each year.

Omission of Specific Assets from Capital Base. In certain instances, management may deem it appropriate to remove specific assets from the total asset amount to arrive at a more realistic capital base against which to measure the profit earned for the period. Thus, if the management of Holliday Corporation believes that performance should be measured by the profit earned on the assets *used,* the temporarily idle capital tied up in construction in progress could be removed in the determination of average total assets. In this case, the average capital base would be \$14,050,000, as follows:

$$\text{Average Assets Used} = \frac{(\$15{,}000{,}000 - 600{,}000) + (14{,}000{,}000 - 300{,}000)}{2}$$

This procedure recognizes that nothing can be earned on this asset until the plant is completed and in operation.

Many companies use stockholders' equity plus long-term debt for the capital base. In effect, capital employed in such cases is total assets minus current liabilities. On this point, an N.A.A. study states:

> . . . companies using equity plus long-term debt as their investment base reason that, since current liabilities are temporary in nature, management should not be expected to earn a return on assets supplied by short-term creditors.[2]

Valid as such reasoning may be, the theory which holds management responsible for earning a return only on total assets in excess of current liabilities is somewhat at odds with the concept that management's performance should be judged on *all* capital entrusted to its control. However, any business using such a base for capital employed will find itself in accord with the method of General Motors Corporation, Armco Steel Corporation, and Westinghouse Electric Corporation. Some companies use more than one base for computing rate of return; General Motors, for example, in addition to calculating the rate of return on total assets minus current liabilities, calculates the rate of return on total assets.

Addition of Specific "Assets" to Capital Base. In certain instances, it may be necessary to add "missing assets" to the total asset amount already shown to arrive at an equitable base for capital employed in the business. A distorted and unrealistic rate of return may occur in the case of a company which does not own, but instead leases, a portion of its tangible fixed assets. At present, under generally accepted accounting, usually only assets *owned* appear on the balance sheet; usually disclosure of *rented* property is shown by a note to the financial statements.[3] Thus, when a company leases a considerable amount of its fixed assets, either

---

[2] National Association of Accountants Research Report No. 35, *Return on Capital as a Guide to Managerial Decisions* (New York, 1959), p. 9.

[3] Under certain circumstances a rented asset is included among the fixed assets of a company. This can occur when the lease agreement is in reality an installment purchase contract. See Chapter 8, pages 253 and 256.

the total asset amount used as capital employed must be increased to show a realistic rate of return on a company-wide basis, or some discount factor must be applied to a rate predicated upon an abnormally low asset base. The problem is far more critical when comparative performance of management is attempted on a plant-by-plant basis. For example, divisional statements may show that Plant A owns $10,000,000 of tangible fixed assets, whereas Plant B, of comparable capacity and producing the same product, owns only $2,000,000 of tangible fixed assets and rents the remainder under long-term leases. Direct comparison of the profits earned on the capital employed for both plants is impossible unless an adjustment is made to the divisional balance sheet of Plant B for the assets it uses but does not own; no method of adjustment satisfactory to all has yet been developed. One method used, as reported in the N.A.A. study, is:

> Where, as is often the case, lease arrangements are merely forms of borrowing, some companies capitalize the interest factor imputed in rental payments to develop a capital value for inclusion in rate of return calculations.[4]

If, in fact, a lease agreement is an installment purchase contract, accounting principles dictate that the substance rather than the legal form of the agreement must be reflected in the financial statements. Such a lease is called a financing lease. The payments required under the lease are discounted at the interest rate the lessee pays for its long-term debt. This amount is shown as an asset on the balance sheet. The liability is included among the long-term liabilities. For more on this point, the reader is referred to the section of chapter eight on leaseholds. In any case, those in management should be cognizant of the possible distortion in rates of return when attempting to evaluate performance of a plant which leases a portion of its assets. Some companies, for example, include all purchased *and* leased assets in the base to arrive at total assets used in the business by various divisions.

Adjustment of Specific Assets in the Capital Base. It is possible that the effect on a particular company's capital employed base of the factors mentioned in the preceding sections may be minor in comparison to the effect caused by inequities in the valuations used for the property, plant and equipment owned. Consider the amount shown by the balance sheet of Holliday Corporation on page 125 in this chapter. Should the base

---

[4] N.A.A. Research Report No. 35, *Return on Capital as a Guide to Managerial Decisions,* p. 11.

amount of capital employed in the business reflect the buildings and equipment at their depreciated cost of $7,500,000 as of December 31, 1974, or at some other amount? These amounts include fixed assets and

Buildings and Equipment (cost)	$12,200,000
Less: Accumulated Depreciation to date	4,700,000
	$ 7,500,000

their accumulated depreciation to date in all types of dollars, dependent upon when the assets were acquired. In addition, the amount shown for accumulated depreciation to date may reflect the effect of accelerated depreciation.[5] Therefore, it may be extremely difficult to determine an equitable dollar amount for the property, plant and equipment in the total assets of $15,000,000 shown by the balance sheet in the determination of a capital employed base.

The non-comparability of similar items is extremely critical when the rate of return for one plant or division of the company is compared against another. For example, the figures above may include a building constructed for Division A of Holliday Corporation in early 1950 at a cost of $1,000,000 and a building of identical type and size constructed in early 1970 for Division B at an inflated cost of $3,000,000. Assume that each building, when constructed, had an estimated useful life of 50 years and that straight-line depreciation is used. The balance sheet prepared as of December 31, 1974, will reflect, among Division A's

DIVISION A—HOLLIDAY CORPORATION

Balance Sheet

December 31, 1974

ASSETS

Cash		$ xxxxxxxx
Accounts Receivable		xxxxxxxx
Inventories (LIFO basis)		xxxxxxxx
Property, Plant and Equipment:		
Building, at cost	$1,000,000	
Less: Accumulated Depreciation to date ($20,000 × 25 years)	500,000	500,000
Other plant & equipment items, net of accumulated depreciation		xxxxxxxx
Total Assets		$x + 500,000

[5] A detailed analysis of the various methods of depreciation is presented in Chapter 6, and the effect of a changing price level is discussed in Chapter 7.

various assets, a building which has been depreciated \$20,000 annually (\$1,000,000 cost ÷ 50 years) for the past 25 years. Total assets of Division A will include a "\$500,000 building." On the other hand, the balance sheet as of this same date for Division B will reflect, among that division's total assets, a building which has been depreciated \$60,000 annually (\$3,000,000 ÷ 50 years) for the past five years. Total assets of Division B will include a "\$2,700,000 building," a figure 5⅖ times larger than that for Division A. Not only will the denominator—capital employed—be disproportionately higher for Division B, but the numerator —profit earned—will reflect a charge for three times as much depreciation expense. If divisional managerial performance is measured by the profit earned on the capital employed and no adjustment is made for the above distortions, obviously Division A is the place to work.

DIVISION B—HOLLIDAY CORPORATION

Balance Sheet

December 31, 1974

ASSETS		
Cash		\$ xxxxxxxx
Accounts Receivable		xxxxxxxx
Inventories (LIFO basis)		xxxxxxxx
Property, Plant and Equipment:		
Building, at cost	\$3,000,000	
Less: Accumulated Depreciation to date (\$60,000 × 5 years)	300,000	2,700,000
Other plant & equipment items, net of accumulated depreciation		xxxxxxxx
Total Assets		\$x + 2,700,000

To compensate for such inequities, three possible courses of action will be suggested. The first of these is to do nothing with the dollar amounts based upon original cost: use the figures exactly as shown by the divisional balance sheets, then compensate for inequities by recognizing that divisions like A and B, though producing the same product by the same process, cannot possibly earn the same rate of return. One method of such compensation establishes different target rates of return for Divisions A and B. This first course of action, using fixed assets in the capital base on an "as is" basis of original cost less accumulated depreciation thereon, is the method presently employed by Armstrong Cork Company and Westinghouse Electric Corporation. A strong argument for such a procedure, though directed at company rather than divisional level as previously shown, is the following statement by I. Wayne Keller, former Vice President of Armstrong Cork Company:

> Personal experience has demonstrated that, where assets reflected in the published financial statements are used as the capital employed at the company level, there is a ready acceptance of the figure. When other values are used, confusion is created which detracts from the true purpose of effective use of the ratios.[6]

Keller continues:

> The prime danger in departing from the published financial statements is that management time, which should be devoted to holding and improving the ratios, will be diverted to attacks upon the validity of the amount of capital used in determining the ratios.[7]

Note that these statements argue against *any* modification of the actual conventional accounting figures. Admitting the validity of Keller's point, it is difficult to believe that, if it were applied at the divisional or plant level, the plant managers would not be as confused about why they need not obtain identical rates of return.

A second possible remedy for distortion is to include all fixed asset amounts in the capital base at replacement value. For example, one company using this method developed a series of index numbers with the period 1947–1949 equal to 100. Then the fixed assets at each division were listed by year of acquisition and converted to common like-type dollars by index numbers. The N.A.A. study indicates that two of the 42 companies in its report make adjustments for changing price levels.

> One of these companies revalues its fixed assets by use of currently published indexes of construction prices in an attempt to approximate replacement cost. The other company uses such indexes in addition to insurance figures.[8]

While this method of adjusting fixed assets provides for equalization of dollar values, it makes no provision for older facilities and equipment that may be less efficient and require greater maintenance expense. And, though most index numbers move in a somewhat common direction, there

---

[6] I. Wayne Keller, "The Return on Capital Concept," *N.A.A. Bulletin* (March, 1958), p. 15.

[7] *Ibid.*, p. 17.

[8] N.A.A. Research Report No. 35, *Return on Capital as a Guide to Managerial Decisions,* p. 11.

is always an argument over the validity of the particular index number(s) used for any such adjustment. Because of rapidly changing prices during the past 20 years, it may be more equitable to adjust fixed assets by index numbers, imperfect as the method may be, than to do nothing. See Chapter 8 for a more complete discussion on this issue.

A third method of modifying the fixed asset amounts is to add back the accumulated depreciation to date; i.e., include the fixed assets in the capital base at original cost, rather than cost less accumulated depreciation to date. Thus, the capital employed base for Division A of Holliday Corporation would include the building at $1,000,000 (rather than $500,000), and the capital base for Division B would include the building at $3,000,000 (rather than $2,700,000). The buildings would then be in the respective divisional capital bases in a 1 to 3 ratio, rather than the former 1 to $5\frac{2}{5}$ ratio. There are three predominant arguments advanced for such a procedure. First, it is a rough adjustment for the changing value of the dollar, and it provides some equalization between older plants constructed at relatively low cost and newer plants built at high cost. While the newer plants still appear to be penalized to some degree (e.g., the 1 to 3 ratio in Divisions A and B for identical buildings), the newer plant should be more efficient and require less maintenance expense. The second argument for including fixed assets in the base at gross (original cost) is that the conventional accounting procedure of writing down such assets by periodic depreciation is intended to amortize the cost of the fixed assets systematically and has little to do with any change in the efficiency of such assets. Regardless of the portion of original cost amortized, a 25-year-old building is nearly as efficient for production as one five years old. A seven-year-old turret lathe is relatively efficient compared to one a year old; otherwise, action should be taken to replace the seven-year-old lathe. And a new truck will not deliver the goods any better or faster than a three-year-old truck kept in a proper state of repair and maintenance. The third argument is more subtle in its implications. Because floor space is one of the most costly operating factors in business today, the inclusion of the fixed assets in the capital base at cost attempts to force the divisional manager to get rid of "junk." For example, consider the equipment and machinery portion of the fixed assets per the balance sheet of Division A:

Equipment and Machinery at cost	$2,100,000	
Less: Accumulated Depreciation to date.......	1,100,000	$1,000,000

Included is a fully depreciated 15-year-old drill press which had originally cost $100,000. Thus, the above amounts include:

Drill press, at cost	$ 100,000	
Less: Accumulated Depreciation to date	100,000	$ -0-

Though it was replaced two years ago by a new, modern, more efficient piece of equipment, the old drill press still stands idly in one corner of the plant "just in case" or because "you never know." After all, it is fully depreciated. Thus, it is not costing anything—only valuable floor space! The add-back of accumulated depreciation to date means that the division manager must measure his profit earned against a capital base which includes the original $100,000 cost of the old drill press, or dispose of it. Among companies which, for various reasons, include fixed assets at original cost in the capital employed base is E. I. duPont de Nemours & Company.

An additional asset, inventories, may merit consideration in the determination of an equitable capital base. This is especially the case if the company has been on LIFO for some time. For example, the balance sheet on page 125 in this chapter indicates that if Holliday Corporation had not adopted LIFO, the December 31, 1974, amount for inventories would be $4,000,000 instead of $2,500,000. When measuring performance, management should be charged with earning on the $4,000,000 current cost of the inventories, rather than on a lower figure resulting from a change in an accounting method 20 years ago.

In summary, the points made in the preceding five sections indicate that judgment must be used to decide whether to include, exclude, or modify certain assets or their stated amounts in the determination of an equitable capital base. In part, the materiality of amount is a factor. The particular uses to be made of the measure of performance must be considered. And consistency should be maintained to minimize any charge of "number juggling."

Determination of the Profit Earned (Numerator)

The determination of the amount of profit earned, the numerator with which the rate of return is calculated, is subject to many judgmental factors. Reference is again made to the financial statements of Holliday Corporation; specifically, the statement of income on page 126. Consider whether the "profit earned" should be viewed as:

Net income for the year ($1,500,000 per the statement of income),
Net income prior to income taxes ($2,927,000),
Net operating income ($3,000,000), or
Some other measure of profit earned.

Conventional accounting fairly presents the fact that Holliday Corporation has a net profit of $1,500,000 for 1974. This is the resultant amount based on overall performance of the company. And, if the rate of return of Holliday Corporation is to be measured against that of Competitor Corporation or that of the industry as a whole, a numerator of $1,500,000 as the profit earned appears equitable. From this point of view, profit after all income and expense factors (including income taxes) is a fair measure of profit earned. Basically, all companies are subject to the same tax rates in a given period.

However, if Holliday Corporation intends to compare its overall performance in 1974 with that of preceding years, it may be more equitable to use a profit earned amount which is not influenced by changing tax laws and tax rates. The effect of changing tax laws and rates, over which management has no control, may be illustrated from the following information selected from the annual reports of Armstrong Cork Company:

REPRESENTATIVE YEARS	FROM ANNUAL REPORTS[9] EARNINGS BEFORE INCOME TAXES	INCOME TAXES	NET EARNINGS	INCOME TAXES AS % OF EARNINGS BEFORE TAX
1972	$78,261,000	$36,500,000	$41,761,000	46.6%
1970	31,563,000	13,750,000	17,813,000	43.6%
1968	69,241,000	34,350,000	34,891,000	49.6%
1965	63,693,000	30,000,000	33,693,000	47.1%
1963	55,162,000	28,100,000	27,062,000	50.9%
1961	37,331,012	18,825,000	18,506,012	50.4%
1956	27,020,380	13,700,000	13,320,380	50.7%
1951	18,648,831	10,119,231	8,529,600	54.3%
1947	15,803,429	6,154,837	9,648,592	38.9%
1944	11,763,658	7,544,660	4,218,998	64.1%
1939	5,470,006	1,029,812	4,440,194	18.8%

These figures reflect fairly constant federal income tax *rates* (approximately 48 percent to 52 percent) since the excess profits tax was repealed on January 1, 1954. However, these *dollar* amounts for income taxes have been affected by changing federal provisions for such items as depreciation, the investment credit, and tax surcharges for several of the years from 1954 to date, as well as by changes in foreign income tax laws

[9] As mentioned in Chapter 3, in any specific year, net income for tax purposes usually differs from net income for accounting purposes. And over the years, both accounting principles and tax laws have changed. But the above figures are sufficiently representative to illustrate the effect of increasing and decreasing tax rates.

and rates. Also, the amounts for any one year could be distorted due to various other factors, such as the extensive production interruptions which occurred in 1970. Note the effect of the excess profits tax during World War II (e.g., 1944) and again during the Korean War (e.g., 1951). In between these two wars—"the good old days"—the prevailing tax rate was approximately 38 percent. And, prior to 1940, income taxes were a comparatively small cost of doing business. Thus, it is evident why some companies, in measuring the performance of management on a comparative basis, prefer to use a profit earned amount which is prior to income taxes. If this is the preference of the management of Holliday Corporation, a profit earned amount of $2,927,000 may better measure those factors which are under the control of management.

Theoretically, if rate of return is based upon total assets, interest expense should not be deducted when determining the profit earned numerator. In this respect, interest expense is a payment to creditors who have supplied short-term and/or long-term capital, just as dividends are distributions to the owners who have supplied capital. Should this concept be utilized by Holliday Corporation, a profit earned of $3,017,000 before income taxes and interest on debt should be measured against total assets employed.

When return on capital is used for measuring the performance of management in the *operation* of the business, the best measure of profit earned may be the net operating income. For 1974, Holliday Corporation had a $3,000,000 net income from operations; i.e., from the production and sale of its products. For Holliday Corporation, this procedure would exclude the other income item of interest earned during the year. Consideration also should be given to the exclusion of the asset, the securities on which the interest was earned, from the asset base. Consistency should be maintained in the determinations of "capital" and "income."

In the determination of the profit earned numerator, there is much to recommend the exclusion of non-recurring items which may occasionally appear as Other Income or Other Charges or as Extraordinary Gains or Losses. For example, a gain on the disposal of plant and equipment items is unrelated to the basic purpose for which a business is operated. And a casualty loss attributable to a flood or fire is outside the normal operations of the usual company. Such non-operating income and expense items should not be permitted to distort a measure of operating performance.

SUMMARY—RETURN ON CAPITAL

Normally, profits do not just happen, but are the result of operations properly planned. Management needs proper criteria for appraising past operations and planning future operations; in recent years, management has come to rely rather heavily upon return on capital for the common denominator to measure effectiveness of past operations so that intelligent decisions can be made with respect to future operations.

The calculation of a numerical rate of return on capital does not provide an "answer." Investigation and analysis of the causes of the calculated numerical rate is vital if the tool is to be useful. In the final analysis, return on capital can be improved only by management action to increase sales volume, decrease costs, reduce or minimize assets employed, or some combination of these three factors.

In recent years, the increased size and the widely diversified operations of many companies have resulted in a trend toward a decentralized form of business organization. Thus, performance of management in terms of profit responsibility has also been localized, and return on capital has assumed increasing importance as a method of measuring performance at the divisional, plant, or product-line level. Therefore, in addition to the basic problems concerning which assets to include in the base, how to value these assets, and how to determine net income, there is the added problem of equitably allocating certain assets to the divisions, plants, or product lines. For example, should the capital invested in a headquarters office building be allocated to the divisions, and if so, how?[10] In principle, the problem of equitable allocation of common assets to divisions is the same as the equitable allocation of common costs and expenses to divisions, plants, and the departments within a plant.[11]

In this chapter, the discussion of return on capital has concerned only the appraisal of past operating performance. This performance may be measured at the company level, division or plant level, and by product lines. Evaluations of such performance may be made by comparisons with competitor companies, industry-wide statistics, with all businesses as a whole, and with the company's own predetermined goals. All of this should aid the planning of future actions. Return on capital is also used as a tool for capital planning by evaluating proposed acquisitions of capital assets, a subject beyond the scope of this book.

Conflict: Overall Company vs. Divisional Objectives

It is possible that a conflict may arise between the objectives of the top management of the company and the actions of a particular division of that company when return on capital is used as a measurement of per-

---

[10] For a discussion of methods used in practice, the following two reports published by the National Association of Accountants are recommended: N.A.A. Research Report No. 35, *Return on Capital as a Guide to Managerial Decisions,* Chapter 4; N.A.A. Accounting Practice Report No. 14, *Experience with Return on Capital to Appraise Management Performance,* pp. 11–14.

[11] See Chapter 13 for the allocation of common manufacturing costs.

formance. Assume that a company *as a whole* has an *objective overall* return on capital of 15%, but at present is obtaining only a 10% return. However, Division A of this company has consistently been the best divisional performer of the company. Currently its own return on capital is at 30%. Division A has an investment opportunity which will significantly increase its current volume of business. This additional volume, though profitable, will only yield a 25% rate of return on its required investment and thereby would reduce the division's overall rate of return on its assets. The management of Division A would be inclined to reject this new business. Yet, for the company as a whole, the added business would provide an increase in the company's overall rate of return. Obviously, to optimize *total company* profit *in dollars,* the new business should be accepted if it will produce any rate of return in excess of 10%. However, such action should not permit the management of Division A to be "penalized" for the consequent reduction in its rate of return.

OTHER MEASUREMENTS

Many specific ratios and measurements may be determined from an analysis of financial statements. Most accounting principles texts contain a chapter on statement analysis, and there are several books devoted entirely to this area; such sources are replete with the determination and significance of various ratios and measurement devices. However, the majority of these measurements deal with specific segments of the basic return on capital formula. The common segmented ratios and measurements are listed below under the appropriate portion of the return on capital formula. Each of these measurements will be illustrated using the financial statements of Holliday Corporation on pages 125 and 126. Though the overall rate of return on total assets contains the detailed measurements and ratios discussed below, the analysis of component factors aids the determination of why the overall rate is a given amount.

RETURN ON CAPITAL

Percentage of net profit on sales	×	Turnover of capital	=	Return on capital
		Related segmented measurements		
(1) Percentage of gross margin on sales		(1) Turnover of receivables		(1) Return on stockholders' equity and the leverage factor
(2) Percentage of operating profit on sales		(2) Turnover of inventory		

Percentage of Profit

The percentage of net profit for the year on sales (5.17%) measures the rate of return on net sales after all costs and expenses. In effect, each \$1.00 of net sales produced approximately \$.05 profit. All other profit percentages are segments of this overall profitability ratio.

$$\frac{\text{Net Income for the Year}}{\text{Net Sales}} = \frac{\$\ 1{,}500{,}000}{\$29{,}000{,}000} = 5.17\%$$

The percentage of gross margin on sales (34.48%) measure the relationship of gross margin to net sales. In effect, each \$1.00 of net sales represents a recovery of the cost of the goods sold of approximately \$.65½ and produces a gross margin of \$.34½ to cover operating expenses and provide net income.

$$\frac{\text{Gross Margin on Sales}}{\text{Net Sales}} = \frac{\$10{,}000{,}000}{\$29{,}000{,}000} = 34.48\%$$

The percentage of operating profit on sales (10.34%) measures the basic profitability of sales, Holliday Corporation's primary purpose in business.

$$\frac{\text{Net Operating Profit}}{\text{Net Sales}} = \frac{\$\ 3{,}000{,}000}{\$29{,}000{,}000} = 10.34\%$$

This ratio excludes the effect of the somewhat unrelated items of other income and other charges.

Turnover

Turnover of capital, with capital defined as total assets, was discussed and illustrated beginning on page 121 in this chapter. The turnover of average total assets, unadjusted for any of the reasons previously discussed, was twice for Holliday Corporation during the year 1974.

$$\frac{\text{Net Sales}}{\text{Average Total Assets per books}} = \frac{\$29{,}000{,}000}{\$14{,}500{,}000} = 2 \text{ times}$$

Usually, all other turnover figures in general use by companies for analysis are segments of this overall turnover figure.

The turnover of accounts receivable, nine times in 1974, is determined by dividing the net credit sales (total net sales of \$29,000,000 minus cash sales of \$8,300,000) by the average accounts receivable. In this illustration only the amount of accounts receivable at the beginning and end of the year were available; a more representative average could be computed

$$\frac{\text{Net Sales on credit}}{\text{Average Accounts Receivable}} = \frac{\$20{,}700{,}000}{\$\ 2{,}300{,}000} = 9 \text{ times}$$

by using month-end balances. The turnover figure is a measure of the liquidity of receivables. A turnover of nine times means that the accounts receivable as of a given date will be collected in approximately one and one-third months. The usual expression of the average collection period is in days, in this case approximately 41 days, computed as follows:

$$\frac{\text{Average Accounts Receivable}}{\text{Net Sales on credit}} \times \text{Number of Days in period} = \frac{\$\ 2{,}300{,}000}{\$20{,}700{,}000} \times 365 = 41 \text{ days}$$

The turnover of inventories, assuming that Holliday Corporation is a merchandising concern and not a manufacturer, would be computed by dividing the cost of the merchandise sold by the average inventory at cost. However, the "cost" of these two items is not comparable for Holliday Corporation. Because the inventories are on a LIFO basis, their amounts are stated in somewhat ancient costs; the cost of goods sold amount basically represents current costs. To secure a realistic inventory turnover figure for Holliday Corporation, one should use similar "costs," which is possible in this case because of the footnote to the balance sheet (see page 125). The inventory turnover of almost five times a year, computed below, means that the company has sold and replaced its overall average inventory almost five times a year.

$$\frac{\text{Cost of Goods Sold}}{\text{Average Inventories at replacement cost}} = \frac{\$19{,}000{,}000}{\frac{1}{2}\ (\$4{,}000{,}000 + \$3{,}800{,}000)} = 4.87 \text{ times}$$

Return

Return on capital was discussed and illustrated beginning with page 121 of this chapter. Recognizing all the limitations subsequently mentioned concerning the data to be used in such a calculation, it is assumed that Holliday Corporation computed its rate of return on capital as follows:

$$\frac{\text{Net Income for the Year}}{\text{Average Total Assets}} = \frac{\$\ 1{,}500{,}000}{\$14{,}500{,}000} = 10.345\%$$

The return of 10.345% for 1974 represents rate of profit earned on all of the capital available for use by management.

From the view of the stockholders of the company, the rate of return on only the stockholders' equity is of primary interest. Based upon the financial statements on pages 125 and 126, the rate of return on stockholders' equity (17.14% for 1974) is determined by dividing the net income for the year by the average stockholders' equity.

$$\frac{\text{Net Income for the Year}}{\text{Average Stockholders' Equity}} = \frac{\$1{,}500{,}000}{\$8{,}750{,}000} = 17.14\%$$

From the overall viewpoint of measuring the management's performance, this particular measurement is limited, because it measures profit against only a portion of the total capital used. The rate of return on stockholders' investment, while of prime concern to groups like investors, is of limited overall use, because it is only a segment of the total; it is more akin to a measurement of financial management than to a measurement of the management based on operations of the company. This may be seen more clearly when it is realized that Holliday Corporation is trading on the equity. Trading on the equity occurs whenever a business finances a portion of the total assets owned with sources of funds other than those provided by the equity of common stockholders. These additional sources of funds are principally of three types:

1. Preferred stock with a fixed dividend rate (Holliday Corporation has not issued preferred stock).
2. Long-term debt with a limited return (Holliday Corporation issued $3,000,000 of debentures due in 1987).
3. Short-term debt with a limited or no return (Holliday Corporation had $2,500,000 of current liabilities as of December 31, 1973, and $3,000,000 of such short-term debt as of December 31, 1974. Since none of this debt includes interest bearing notes payable, the assets provided by such funds are employed without cost to Holliday Corporation).

If the cost for use of such funds is less than the return their use earns for the common stockholders, the leverage factor is favorable; a reverse situation would indicate unfavorable leverage. In the case of Holliday Corporation, the leverage factor is favorable: the return on the average stockholders' equity is 17.14%, while the return on average total assets is 10.345%. This is attributable to the leverage factor, the ratio of assets to stockholders' equity (1.6571), computed as follows:

$$\frac{\text{Assets (average)}}{\text{Stockholders' Equity (average)}} = \frac{\$14{,}500{,}000}{\$\ 8{,}750{,}000} = 1.6571$$

The leverage factor of 1.6571 times the return on assets of 10.345% equals the return on stockholders' equity of 17.14%.

SIGNIFICANCE OF MEASUREMENTS AND RATIOS

Any measurement or ratio is meaningless unless it is analyzed for cause and related to other relevant data.

Much data is available for comparison; for example, Dun & Bradstreet, Inc., annually publishes 14 ratios for many lines of business. If Holliday Corporation were a paper box and container manufacturer, it could compare its yearly and five-year averages with those published by this source. A rate of net profit on net sales for 1971 in excess of 2.60% would indicate that the company was above the median point on margin for this year. And since the median collection period by paper box manufacturers for receivables was 34 days during this period, Holliday Corporation could compare its collection experience against this median.[12] If Holliday Corporation were in the petroleum industry, the *Annual Financial Analysis of a Group of Petroleum Companies* published by The Chase Manhattan Bank, N.A., would indicate that in 1971 it should have earned in excess of 10.7 percent on stockholders' equity and in excess of 10.1 percent on borrowed and invested capital to be above the probable average of the overall industry. And, if Holliday Corporation were a manufacturer of primary nonferrous metals, *The Quarterly Financial Report for Manufacturing Corporations* for the third quarter of 1972, compiled by the Federal Trade Commission, would enable the company to compare its figures for the third quarter of 1972 to the following for that industry:

Profit per dollar of sales, before federal income taxes	4.6%
Profit per dollar of sales, after taxes	3.2%
Profit on stockholders' equity after taxes	4.9%
Current assets to current liabilities	2.28

and to such as the following for *all* manufacturing corporations.

Profit per dollar of sales, before federal income taxes	7.2%
Profit per dollar of sales, after taxes	4.2%
Profit on stockholders' equity, after taxes	10.1%
Current assets to current liabilities	2.05

These are but a few of the examples of the comparative data available for comparison and analysis.

Any resultant numerical ratio must be viewed in its proper context. A given numerical answer may be good in one situation and poor in another, or it may be both from different points of view. For example, a high inventory turnover may be excellent because it indicates a mini-

---

[12] Reprinted by special permission from DUN'S, 1972, copyright 1972, Dun & Bradstreet Publications Corporation.

mum investment of funds in this asset, but a high turnover could also indicate the possibility of lost sales attributable to an insufficient quantity of goods on hand.

CONCLUSION

Management judgment should pre-empt any ratio or measurement. No group of ratios answers a problem any more than a computer can think: ratios can only indicate areas for investigation. Intelligent managerial use of such ratios is required to unearth cause and effect.

In addition, all ratios and financial measurements must be viewed in their proper perspective. First, no two companies, even those in the same business, are exactly alike in their operations or in products produced and sold. Second, generally accepted accounting principles permit alternative methods of treating items. Third, though the dollar sign is a common denominator, it is subject to changing value. Fourth, though history does repeat itself, it is always difficult to compare past results with future plans. In effect, only general, not specific, conclusions should be drawn from comparative financial data.

QUESTIONS AND PROBLEMS

5–1 Following are the condensed financial statements of Fala Corporation:

Balance Sheet
as of December 31, 1974

Cash	$ 10,000	Accounts Payable		$ 10,000
Marketable Securities	5,000	Accrued Expenses Payable		20,000
Accounts Receivable (net)	20,000	Total Current Liabilities		$ 30,000
Inventories	25,000	Long-term Debt (mortgage)		20,000
Total Current Assets	$ 60,000	Total Liabilities		$ 50,000
Investments	30,000	Capital Stock	$50,000	
Plant & Equipment (net)	60,000	Retained Earnings	50,000	100,000
Total Assets	$150,000	Total Equities		$150,000

Statement of Income and Retained Earnings for the Year 1974

Net Sales		$300,000
Cost of Goods Sold		160,000
Gross Margin on Sales		$140,000
Operating Expenses		90,000
Net Operating Income		$ 50,000
Other Income (from securities and investments)	$2,800	
Other Expenses (interest on debt)	1,800	1,000
Net Income before Tax		$ 51,000
Income Taxes		21,000
Net Income for Year		$ 30,000
Retained Earnings, January 1, 1974		40,000
		$70,000
Dividends on Capital Stock		20,000
Retained Earnings, December 31, 1974		$ 50,000

Required

a. Margin of profit on sales (net income for year as a percentage of sales)
b. Turnover of "capital" (capital defined as total assets as of December 31)
c. Return on "capital"
d. Leverage factor
e. Return on stockholders' equity (use Stockholders' Equity at December 31)

5–2. The following conversation took place in the office of A. Schreib, President of Harvey Corporation:

A. SCHREIB, PRESIDENT OF HARVEY CORPORATION: "Summarizing our two meetings of last month, I think that the possible acquisition of Young Corporation by us would be no bargin. True, our management consultant, Mr. Malloy, says that we can probably acquire Young Corporation at a reasonable price. But, as I recall the tenor of our previous meetings, we thought we might well be acquiring a mediocre company."

E. WOODS, TAX MANAGER OF HARVEY CORPORATION: "I'm still confused. What's being considered? Are we thinking of the purchase of Young's total assets or the acquisition of their outstanding capital stock? The tax consequences are different."

E. B. MALLOY, MANAGEMENT CONSULTANT: "I say first things first. Are you or aren't you interested in acquiring Young Corporation? It isn't often that such a solid company is available; it was only through an unusual contact that I unearthed the possibility. To my way of thinking, tax possibilities should be considered only after a decision to acquire has been made."

M. K. EVANS, EXECUTIVE VICE-PRESIDENT: "Don't fail to consider one vital point: while their basic product is similar to ours, it really isn't competitive. In fact, it would be an excellent item to supplement our own line."

J. HOWARD, CONTROLLER: "Frankly, I'm not impressed by the whole idea. Look at their profit margin. It's only 5% on sales; ours is 8%. They started business at approximately the same time we did, yet their sales volume is 80% of ours. Their assets and their annual net profit each are one-half of ours. They certainly are not a growth company like us. To my way of thinking, acquiring Young Corporation would be acquiring long-term trouble."

A. SCHREIB: "Basically, I must agree. And I know that your comparative figures are not distorted; for example, they use accelerated depreciation as we do, and they also adopted LIFO at the same time we did. Frankly, I think their problem is management. I've never been impressed by their deadpan attitude and lack of sparkle. They don't give their company a good image. Now, what do you think of this—let's buy them out, fire their management, and rattle-shake-and-roll their operation so it produces a decent margin of profit?"

E. B. MALLOY: "Now wait a minute; let's unscramble three points. First, larger numbers don't prove growth. There is a difference between true growth and mere expansion. Second, I think that their management are sound people. To lose them could be disastrous: what do you know about manufacturing their basic product? Third, and most important, I believe their company is at least as profitable as yours; thus, it would be a wonderful acquisition. Throughout your discussion, you have been looking at only one thing, percentage margin of profit on sales. True, yours is better. But you are comparing unlike things. Their product is different from yours. For example, a service station couldn't expect the same percentage margin on a gallon of gasoline and a quart of oil. You are ignoring the turnover of capital investment which is needed for an overall appraisal. Now look at these compartive figures I've worked out which consider both margin and turnover. Together they give the whole picture, the return on capital concept, which I think is a fairer manner to appraise the performance of the company and its management. First, let me show you the 1973 comparisons and explain what they imply."

Required

Assume that you are E. B. Malloy, Management Consultant. Using the financial statements of both companies, shown on pages 146–47, prepare the comparative figures which you believe he presented to the management in accordance with the comments above concerning margin, turnover, and return on capital. Indicate clearly your basis and determination of each item.

HARVEY CORPORATION

Balance Sheet

	AS OF DECEMBER 31	
	1975	1974
ASSETS		
Current Assets	$ 5,500,000	$ 5,000,000
Property, Plant and Equipment:		
Cost	15,500,000	14,000,000
Accumulated Depreciation to Date	8,500,000	7,500,000
Net	7,000,000	6,500,000
Total Assets	$12,500,000	$11,500,000
LIABILITIES AND STOCKHOLDERS' EQUITY		
Current Liabilities	$ 3,000,000	$ 2,500,000
Long-term Debt—4% Bonds	1,000,000	1,000,000
Stockholders' Equity	8,500,000	8,000,000
Total Equities	$12,500,000	$11,500,000

HARVEY CORPORATION

Statement of Income and Retained Earnings

	FOR YEAR ENDED DECEMBER 31	
	1975	1974
Net Sales	$10,000,000	$ 9,600,000
Less Costs and Expenses	8,400,000	8,064,000
Net Income before Income Taxes	1,600,000	1,536,000
Less Income Taxes (50%)	800,000	768,000
Net Income for the Year (8%)	800,000	768,000
Retained Earnings, January 1	3,184,000	2,816,000
	3,984,000	3,584,000
Dividends	400,000	400,000
Retained Earnings, December 31	$ 3,584,000	$ 3,184,000

YOUNG CORPORATION

Balance Sheet

	As of December 31	
	1975	1974
ASSETS		
Current Assets	$ 2,100,000	$ 2,100,000
Property, Plant and Equipment:		
Cost	8,300,000	7,500,000
Accumulated Depreciation to Date	4,200,000	3,800,000
Net	4,100,000	3,700,000
Total Assets	$ 6,200,000	$ 5,800,000
LIABILITIES AND STOCKHOLDERS' EQUITY		
Current Liabilities	$ 1,000,000	$ 800,000
Long-term Debt—4% Bonds	2,500,000	2,500,000
Stockholders' Equity	2,700,000	2,500,000
Total Equities	$ 6,200,000	$ 5,800,000

YOUNG CORPORATION

Statement of Income and Retained Earnings

	For Year Ended December 31	
	1975	1974
Net Sales	$ 8,000,000	$ 7,500,000
Less Costs and Expenses	7,200,000	6,750,000
Net Income before Income Taxes	800,000	750,000
Less Income Taxes	400,000	375,000
Net Income for the Year	400,000	375,000
Retained Earnings, January 1	1,175,000	1,000,000
	1,575,000	1,375,000
Dividends	200,000	200,000
Retained Earnings, December 31	$ 1,375,000	$ 1,175,000

5–3. The Regular Department Store typically sells 95% of its volume on regular 30-day charge account and 5% for cash; installment time-payment sales are insignificant. In the most recent year, $75,000,000 of sales were on regular charge account.

The store has always earned a profit, but sales volume has been declining each year for the past several years. The Board of Directors and top management of the company are under pressure from disgruntled stockholders.

Attached are the most recent financial statements of the Regular Department Store.

Required

a. Compute, for the most recent year, the following ratios for Regular Department Store:
   1. Current ratio

REGULAR DEPARTMENT STORE

Balance Sheet

	AS OF JANUARY 31	
	1975	1974
ASSETS		
Current Assets:		
Cash	$ 2,000,000	$ 2,000,000
United States Government Securities (short term)	27,000,000	19,000,000
Accounts Receivable (net of estimated doubtful accounts)	15,000,000	17,000,000
Merchandise Inventories (priced at the lower of cost or market)	24,000,000	31,000,000
Supply Inventories and Prepaid Expenses	2,000,000	2,000,000
Total Current Assets	70,000,000	71,000,000
Properties and Equipment (at cost):		
Land	600,000	670,000
Buildings, Fixtures and Equipment	6,750,000	7,000,000
Less: Accumulated Depreciation	4,450,000	4,400,000
Net	2,300,000	2,600,000
Leasehold Improvements (less amortization)	200,000	230,000
Net Properties and Equipment	3,100,000	3,500,000
Total Assets	$73,100,000	$74,500,000

LIABILITIES AND STOCKHOLDERS' EQUITY

Current Liabilities:		
Accounts Payable	$ 6,400,000	$ 8,200,000
Accrued Expenses and Miscellaneous	1,400,000	1,660,000
Income Taxes Payable	1,600,000	2,000,000
Total Current Liabilities	9,400,000	11,860,000
Stockholders Equity:		
Preferred Stock		
Authorized, issued, and outstanding: 20,000 shares of no par value, non-callable, $7.00 per share, cumulative dividends; stated at liquidating value	2,000,000	2,000,000
Common Stock		
Authorized 1,000,000 shares of no par value; issued and outstanding: 650,000 shares, at stated value	21,000,000	21,000,000
Earned Surplus—representing earnings reinvested in the business....	40,700,000	39,640,000
Total Stockholders' Equity	63,700,000	62,640,000
Total Liabilities and Stockholders' Equity	$73,100,000	$74,500,000

REGULAR DEPARTMENT STORE

Statements of Income and Retained Earnings

	FOR THE YEARS ENDED JANUARY 31	
	1975	1974
Net Sales	$80,000,000	$95,000,000
Deductions:		
Cost of Merchandise Sold	55,000,000	65,400,000
Wages and Salaries	14,600,000	16,500,000
Other Expenses—net	3,000,000	4,000,000
Rents	1,000,000	1,100,000
Depreciation on Buildings and Equipment	300,000	300,000
Property, Social Security, and State Taxes	1,100,000	1,200,000
Total Costs and Expenses	75,000,000	88,500,000

Net Income before Income Taxes	5,000,000	6,500,000
Income Taxes	2,500,000	3,300,000
Net Income for the Year	2,500,000	3,200,000
Retained Earnings, February 1	39,640,000	37,880,000
Total	42,140,000	41,080,000
Cash Dividends:		
Preferred Stock—\$7.00 per share ...	140,000	140,000
Common Stock—\$2.00 per share....	1,300,000	1,300,000
Total Dividends	1,440,000	1,440,000
Retained Earnings, January 31	\$40,700,000	\$39,640,000

2. Average collection period for accounts receivable
3. Inventory turnover
4. Margin of profit (net income for the year as percentage of sales)
5. Return on investment (net income for year as percentage of average stockholders' investment)

b. Based upon your evaluation of results obtained from the above five ratios, you, as a management trainee in the company, are requested to give your impression of the performance of the present management of the Regular Department Store. In your answer, comment upon the result of each of your five computations.

5–4. Compare the result of each of your five computations in problem 5–3 with those of other department stores *and* give your evaluation of Regular Department Store versus other department stores. Financial data is available from many sources for department stores, one of which is published in *Dun's Review* under the caption "The Ratios of Retailing."

5–5. The following are the most recent financial statements of Springfield Corporation:

SPRINGFIELD CORPORATION
Condensed Balance Sheet
December 31, 1974

ASSETS		
Current Assets (Schedule A)		\$ 800,000
Investments		50,000
Property, Plant and Equipment (net)......		650,000
Total Assets		\$1,500,000
LIABILITIES		
Current Liabilities	\$300,000	
Long-term Debt	100,000	
Total Liabilities		400,000

STOCKHOLDERS' EQUITY

Capital Stock (par $100)	$800,000	
Retained Earnings	300,000	
Total Stockholders' Equity		$1,100,000

SPRINGFIELD CORPORATION
Condensed Statement of Income
For the Year Ended December 31, 1974

Net Sales		$2,500,000
Less: Cost of Goods Sold (Schedule B)		1,700,000
Gross Margin on Sales		$ 800,000
Less: Operating Expenses		500,000
Net Operating Income		$ 300,000
Other Expenses	$6,000	
Other Revenue	3,000	3,000
Net Income before Income Taxes		$ 297,000
Estimated Income Taxes		147,000
Net Income for the Year		$ 150,000

SPRINGFIELD CORPORATION
Statement of Retained Earnings
For the Year Ended December 31, 1974

Retained Earnings, January 1, 1974	$ 210,000
Add: Net Income for the Year	150,000
Total	$ 360,000
Less: Dividends	60,000
Retained Earnings, December 31, 1974	$ 300,000

Schedule A

CURRENT ASSETS

Cash	$ 190,000
Accounts Receivable	175,000
Notes Receivable	5,000
Marketable Securities	47,000
Inventory of Merchandise	380,000
Prepaid Expenses	3,000
Total Current Assets	$ 800,000

Schedule B

COST OF GOODS SOLD

Inventory of Merchandise, January 1			$ 420,000
Purchases		$1,710,000	
Transportation In		20,000	
Gross Cost of Merchandise Purchased		$1,730,000	
Less:			
Purchase Returns and Allowances	$30,000		
Purchase Discounts	40,000	70,000	
Net Cost of Merchandise Purchased			1,660,000
Cost of Merchandise Available for Sale.			$2,080,000
Less: Inventory of Merchandise, December 31			380,000
Cost of Goods Sold			$1,700,000

Required

From the foregoing data for the Springfield Corporation, you are asked to determine and explain the significance of:

a. The working capital as of December 31, 1974.

b. The current ratio (working capital ratio) as of December 31, 1974.

c. The acid test ratio as of December 31, 1974.
Note: Acid test ratio = Cash, Receivables and Marketable Securities to Current Liabilities.

d. The merchandise turnover during the year 1974 in number of days.

e. The average number of days' sales uncollected as of December 31, 1974. (The amount of cash sales during the year was insignificant.)

f. The profit earned in 1974 per share of capital stock. (No change in outstanding capital stock took place during the year.)

g. The rate of gross margin for 1974.

h. In recent years, there has been a marked increase among companies using rate of return on capital employed to measure performance. A company's performance, for example, may be measured by the profit earned (net income) on the capital (total assets) employed. This performance is measured as follows:

$$\text{Return on Capital Employed} = \frac{\text{Net Income}}{\text{Total Assets}}$$

This performance is dependent upon:

$$\text{Margin of Profit} = \frac{\text{Net Income}}{\text{Net Sales}}$$

and

$$\text{Turnover of Capital} = \frac{\text{Net Sales}}{\text{Total Assets}}$$

The interrelationship of the components may be expressed as follows:

$$\frac{\text{Return on Capital Employed}}{\dfrac{\text{Net Income}}{\text{Total Assets}}} = \frac{\text{Margin of Profit}}{\dfrac{\text{Net Income}}{\text{Net Sales}}} \times \frac{\text{Turnover of Capital}}{\dfrac{\text{Net Sales}}{\text{Total Assets}}}$$

Compute the 1974 rate of return on the capital employed for the Springfield Corporation supported by its two components.

5–6. The following is a comparative statement of income for Walter Good Company:

	For the Year Ended		
	Dec. 31, 1974	Dec. 31, 1973	Percentage Change
Net Sales	$1,070,000	$1,000,000	+ 7%
Cost of Goods Sold	693,000	700,000	– 1%
Gross Margin	$ 377,000	$ 300,000	+26%
Operating Expenses	57,000	60,000	– 5%
Net Income before Income Taxes	$ 320,000	$ 240,000	+ 33%

Sales revenues have increased 7%, while cost of goods and operating expenses have decreased 1% and 5%. As a result, net income (prior income taxes) has increased 33%; 1974 has been a banner year! However, further investigation reveals that in 1974 selling prices were 10% higher than in 1973.

Required

a. What was the sales *volume* percentage change from 1973 to 1974?

b. Indicate what change took place in *unit* cost of goods sold in 1974 as compared to 1973.

c. Comment on the trend of operating expenses.

5–7. Using the financial statements of Harvey Corporation given in problem 5–2:

a. Determine the following as of the last day of the fiscal year:
   1. Working capital
   2. Current ratio (also known as working capital ratio)
   3. Book value per share (stockholders' equity per share) of common (or capital) stock. The average number of shares outstanding during 1975 was $450,000.

b. Determine the following for the fiscal year:
   1. Margin of profit (net income as a percentage of sales)
   2. Turnover of capital, with capital defined as total assets (sales divided by total assets)
   3. Return on capital (net income divided by total assets, i.e., your answer to b.1 multiplied by your answer to b.2)
   4. Leverage factor (assets divided by stockholders' equity)
   5. Return on stockholders' equity (net income divided by stockholders' equity, i.e., your answer to b.3 multiplied by your answer to b.4)

5–8. Harvey Corporation (see problem 5–7) is a manufacturer of paper and allied products. Compare the results of six of your eight calculations (ignore a.1 and a.3) for Harvey Corporation with those for the industry. Industry data is available from many sources, one of which is the *Quarterly Financial Report for Manufacturing Corporations,* compiled since 1947 by the Federal Trade Commission.

Required

How, in your opinion, does Harvey Corporation as an individual company compare with companies in its industry?

5–9. Using the annual report of a company furnished to you by your instructor:

a. Determine the following as of the last day of the fiscal year:
   1. Working capital
   2. Current ratio (also known as working capital ratio)
   3. Book value per share (stockholders' equity per share) of common (or capital) stock

b. Determine the following for the fiscal year:
   1. Margin of profit (net income as a percentage of sales)
   2. Turnover of capital, with capital defined as total assets (sales divided by total assets)
   3. Return on capital (net income divided by total assets, i.e., your answer to b.1 multiplied by your answer to b.2)
   4. Leverage factor (assets divided by stockholders' equity)
   5. Return on stockholders' equity (net income divided by stockholders' equity, i.e., your answer to b.3 multiplied by your answer to b.4)

5–10. For the past several years, *Fortune* has published an annual "Fortune Directory" of the 500 largest U.S. industrial corporations (ranked by sales). Using the most recent issue, compute profit as a percentage of assets for the first five companies in the list. Then, compare this ratio with two given percentages, profit to sales and profit to "invested capital." Does the comparison suggest any relationships? As an added assignment, you may wish to extend your calculations and comparisons beyond the first five companies and employ appropriate statistical techniques to reveal any possible correlation of size of company, return on assets, margin of profit, and return on invested capital.

5–11. The chief postulate of our private enterprise system is that the individual's quest for gain maximizes the public welfare. As regards capital, for example, prospective returns are presumably highest from those uses currently most favored by consumers and, of these, from those in which additional capital repesents the least cost means of production. Capital allocation in response to profit expectations occurs at two levels: first, by investor selection among enterprises; and, second, by management selection among projects. The motivations and competitive conditions essential to smooth functioning of this allocation system are not always fully realized. Nevertheless, by the criteria of material output and public acceptance, it works quite well.

Does accounting contribute to effective operation of the allocation system? Discuss.

5–12.

EARLE WRIGHT CORPORATION

(Case in abbreviated form)

Earle Wright Corporation of Arkansas City, Kansas, has manufactured a complete line of widgets for many years. During these years, both sales volume and capital invested in the business have *steadily* increased. For example:

YEAR	NET SALES	NET EARNINGS (PER STATEMENT OF INCOME)	TOTAL ASSETS (PER BALANCE SHEET)
1947	$150,000,000	$10,000,000	$ 95,000,000
1952	200,000,000	9,000,000	135,000,000
1957	250,000,000	11,000,000	170,000,000
1961	302,800,000	18,500,000	213,000,000
1965	374,700,000	33,700,000	277,700,000
1969	552,300,000	58,100,000	487,700,000
1972	684,470,000	41,761,000	588,241,000

One director of the company recently raised the question, "Is ours *really* a *growth* company?" His concern arose from his recent reading (see attached references on page 161) and his application of the "rate of return on capital employed" concept to the financial data of

Earle Wright Corporation. This particular director feels (along with an increasing number of those in the managements of many companies) that a company's performance should be measured by the *profit earned* on the *capital employed.*

This performance is measured as follows:		This performance is dependent upon:		
. . . .		. . . .		. . . .
Return on Capital Employed	=	Margin of Profit	×	Turnover of Capital
. . . .		. . . .		. . . .

$$\frac{\text{Profit Earned}}{\text{Total Assets}} = \frac{\text{Earned Profit}}{\text{Sales}} \times \frac{\text{Sales}}{\text{Total Assets}}$$

When the director applied this "formula" to the financial data of the Earle Wright Corporation for the past 22 years, he obtained the following results:

	Return	=	Margin	×	Turnover
1951	11.59%		9.10%		1.27
1952	11.66%		9.54%		1.22
1953	12.01%		9.61%		1.25
1954	12.67%		10.78%		1.18
1955	14.88%		11.91%		1.25
1956	12.46%		10.56%		1.18
1957	10.16%		8.93%		1.14
1958	12.03%		11.04%		1.09
1959	15.53%		13.29%		1.17
1960	12.13%		11.00%		1.10
1961	13.03%		12.00%		1.09
1962	13.68%		12.67%		1.08
1963	16.44%		15.51%		1.06
1964	17.00%		16.50%		1.03
1965	16.05%		16.16%		.993
1966	14.05%		14.33%		.985
1967	10.01%		10.57%		.947
1968	11.80%		11.95%		.988
1969	9.80%		10.93%		.896
1970	5.09%		6.82%		.746
1971	9.13%		11.35%		.804
1972	10.40%		11.48%		.905

Note: Amounts may not exactly cross-multiply due to rounding of numbers.

Note: Over the years, the amounts are not exactly comparable, due to:

Change in the method of accounting for wholly owned foreign subsidiaries.

Change in the method of accounting for the investment credit.

Acquisition of other companies (1968).
Sale of certain businesses (1969).
Lengthy strikes (1970).

"See," he said, "our rate of return in 1972, though satisfactory, is less than it was 22 years ago. Though our margin is excellent, our turnover of capital keeps deteriorating."

When questioned by the other directors about discrepancies between his numbers and those based upon the company's financial statements, he replied, "Oh, I adjusted the raw financial data. For example, I used profit before income taxes and exclusive of miscellaneous income and other expenses. And I used 'gross' total assets by adding back accumulated depreciation to date, plus a few other minor adjustments." When accused of juggling the numbers, the director's defense was, "This is what some other companies do, companies that are larger and more profitable than ours."

This director then went on to get a few other things off his chest: "The typical corporate annual report—ours included—is likely to convey the impression that the reporting corporation is a growth company. Normally, the president's letter to the stockholders speaks of the year's financial results in glowing terms. It indicates that sales have increased over the preceding year or why they will be improved in the immediate future; that earnings per share are improved or should be in the coming years; that specific costs have been controlled effectively; and that dividends have been maintained or slightly increased. Along with the president's letter, the typical annual report contains narrative, pictures, and graphs concerning new products introduced, other companies purchased or acquired, increased emphasis on research and development, additional outlays for capital expenditures, improved employee benefits, and other favorable indicators. Finally, the financial statements are presented. Often a quick glance or cursory examination is all that the typical reader of an annual report affords to the financial statements. He is convinced that the company is in fine shape; the financial statements are certified, and, in the main, this year's dollar amounts for items like total assets, net income, sales, etc., are greater than the amounts of the preceding year. Obviously, this is another growth company.

"But is it a growth company? Perhaps it is only an expanding company; is there a difference? Those who provide information to aid management in formulating certain policy decisions and in controlling current operations are—or should be—aware of the distinction. A growth company is to be desired; an expanding company to be challenged. Measuring the performance of management to determine whether or not a company is a growth company may conceivably differ from measurements employed by analysts, bankers, investors, or lenders.

"When judging the degree of success or failure of a business firm, the first question is: how do you *measure* a business? Traditionally, there has been general reliance, in varying degrees to be sure, on certain standard and generally accepted financial analyses and ratios like working capital, current ratio, acid test, net earnings per share, rate of profit on stockholders' equity, net profit on sales, gross profit on sales, turnover of inventories, ratio of stockholders' equity to total liabilities, and others.

"At this point it is pertinent to ask, 'Why not *measure* a business firm in the same manner that many companies today are measuring themselves?' " The concept of Return on Capital Employed is a measuring tool that uses sales, invested capital, and profit as an index to a company's performance. Today, management is conscious of how effectively it is using its available capital. Until recently, most businesses emphasized the rate of profit on sales. The possible inadequacy of this measurement, when used alone, may be illustrated by assuming a company with sales of $1,000,000 and a net profit of $100,000. On the surface, a 10% margin of profit indicates a profitable business; but if the capital employed by this same company is $3,300,000, the profit on capital employed is only 3%, less than that earned on Series E Bonds. Return on Capital Employed, though not a new concept, has been widely accepted by management in recent years as a tool for measuring performance. Today, the top managements of many companies feel that a company's performance should be measured by the *profit earned* on the *capital employed* in the business.

"Rate of return appears to be a relatively stable measurement device when measuring the performance of a company over a period of years. It should be an aid in determining whether a company is a growth company or merely an expansion company. Over a period of time, an increase in the dollar amounts shown on the financial statement of a company may indicate expansion in the sense that the company is larger. However, the company may not be a growth company; it may be simply 'fatter.' This point was emphasized by T. G. Mackensen when he was a special studies analyst for the H. J. Heinz Company: 'True growth comes from the ability of management to employ successfully additional capital at a satisfactory rate of return. The company that is merely expanding at declining rates of return on investment will eventually be brought to a stop by lack of expansion capital.'[13]

"Based on an application of the return on investment concept to various industries and several companies within these industries, Harvey O. Edson summarized his study as follows:[14]

---

[13] "Modern Techniques of Financial Analysis for Management Planning: An AMA Symposium," *Journal of Accountancy* (February, 1954), p. 175. (Copyright © 1954, by the American Institute of Certified Public Accountants, Inc.)

[14] Harvey O. Edson, "Setting a Standard for Your Company's Return on Investment," *The Controller* (now *Financial Executive*) (September, 1958).

1. For the total company return, a range of 20 percent–35 percent before taxes would be considered quite satisfactory.
2. Within protected product lines, a 30 percent–40 percent experience would be quite adequate over an extended period of time.
3. Your ROI should be better, certainly, than that of the related industry experience indicated on our table. Remember, these are over-all averages, and the ratios are depressed by the poor, below-average performers. Possibly your industry average might be the low point in your desirable range.
4. Develop individual ROI ratios for the best companies within your industry. Conceivably that factor would become the high point of your ROI range.
5. The more competitive the general conditions within your specific industry are, the narrower and lower the probable range of ROI will be.
6. Well-protected product lines, i.e., (a) special arts and methods not known to the general trade, or (b) patent protected, should show higher rates of return than more competitive lines."

Case Considerations

a. As an illustrative experiment, use the summary annual report figures of Earle Wright Corporation to determine how the director calculated the 1972 return, margin, and turnover.

b. Do you believe that Earle Wright Corporation is a growth company?

c. Should the "profit earned" be the:
   1. Net Income for the Year
   2. Net Income prior Income Taxes
   3. Operating Profit before Income Taxes
   4. Some other measure of "profit earned"

d. Should the "capital employed" be the:
   1. Total assets, per the balance sheet
   2. Average total assets
   3. Gross total (or average) assets—add back depreciation to date
   4. Net Worth (Stockholders' Equity)
   5. Net Worth plus Long-term Debt (Assets minus Current Liabilities)
   6. Some other measure of "capital employed"

e. Should the rate of return be determined for:
   1. The company as a whole
   2. The product lines (or divisions or plants) within the company

f. Should the rate of return be compared with:
   1. Past experience within the company
   2. A predetermined goal of the company
   3. Current budget forecast of the company
   4. Other companies in the same industry

EARLE WRIGHT CORPORATION

Balance Sheet

As of December 31

	1972	1971
ASSETS		
Current Assets (cash, receivables, inventories, etc.)	$ 239,100,000	$ 232,200,000
Long-term Receivables	37,500,000	33,500,000
Property, Plant and Equipment (at cost)	491,100,000	463,100,000
Less: Accumulated depreciation to date	(191,000,000)	(172,600,000)
Miscellaneous Assets	11,500,000	4,200,000
Total Assets	$ 588,200,000	$ 560,400,000
LIABILITIES		
Current Liabilities (Payables due within one year)	$ 73,500,000	$ 79,700,000
Miscellaneous Liabilities	25,400,000	21,000,000
Long-Term Debt	75,200,000	70,900,000
Total Liabilities	$ 174,100,000	$ 171,600,000
STOCKHOLDERS' EQUITY		
Capital Stock Outstanding	$ 42,700,000	$ 39,600,000
Contributed Capital in Excess of Par	42,100,000	40,400,000
Earnings Retained in Business	329,300,000	308,800,000
Total Stockholders' Equity	$ 414,100,000	$ 388,800,000

EARLE WRIGHT CORPORATION

Statement of Income

For the Year

	1972	1971
Net Sales	$684,470,000	$564,000,000
Miscellaneous Income (net)	6,200,000	6,400,000
	690,670,000	570,400,000
Costs and Expenses	612,409,000	506,100,000
Net Earnings before Income Tax	78,261,000	64,300,000
Income Tax Expense	36,500,000	28,800,000
Net Earnings for Year	$ 41,761,000	35,500,000
Net Earnings per Share	$1.60	$1.36

References

1. "Annual Report on American Industry," *Forbes.* The January 1, 1971 issue rates 659 major companies.
2. National Association of Accountants, Research Report No. 42, *Long Range Profit Planning,* December 1, 1964.
3. Robert Morris Associates, *Annual Statement Studies.*
4. "Watch That Waistline!", *Forbes,* May 15, 1970.
5. Keith Powlison, "Obstacles to Business Growth," *Harvard Business Review,* Vol. 31, No. 2 (March–April 1953), 48–56.
6. F. J. Muth, "Return on Capital Employed—A Measure of Management," N.A.C.A. *Bulletin,* Vol. XXXV, No. 6 (February, 1954).
7. R. B. Read, "Return on Investment—Guide to Decisions," N.A.C.A. *Bulletin,* Vol. XXXV, No. 10 (June, 1954).
8. "Return on Investment: Gist of a Technical Service Survey," N.A.C.A. *Bulletin,* Vol. XXXV, No. 6 (February, 1954).
9. "How H. J. Heinz Manages Its Financial Planning and Controls," *Financial Management Series 106,* American Management Association.
10. National Association of Accountants, Research Report No. 35, *Return on Capital as a Guide to Managerial Decisions,* December 1, 1959. This 107-page booklet contains much excellent source material. Part I, Rate of Return for Measuring Periodic Profit Performance, discusses how various companies calculate rate of return, how it is analyzed and used, and the use of return on capital as a guide in pricing. Part II, Using Rate of Return in Capital Planning, analyzes many methods including the discounted cash flow method.
11. National Association of Accountants, Accounting Practice Report No. 14, *Experience with Return on Capital to Appraise Management Performance,* February 1962.
12. John F. Beckman, "Managing ROI on Business Contracts—Through Simulation," *Management Adviser,* Vol. 10, No. 1 (January–February 1973), 28–38.

6

Property, Plant and Equipment: Acquisition and Depreciation

Property, plant and equipment, often called fixed assets, comprise a significant portion of the total assets of most companies; on the next page the survey of the 1972 annual reports of some typical large industrial companies illustrates this fact. Because of the relative importance of fixed assets, this chapter and the following two contain an examination of the accounting principles and practices which apply to this category of assets.

Property, plant and equipment represent relatively long-lived tangible assets which are used in the operation of the business and not held for sale. Examples of these assets are building site land; depreciable assets like buildings, machinery, and equipment; and depletable natural resources like oil, timber, and mineral deposits. Occasionally, the scope of the term *property, plant and equipment* (or *fixed assets*) is broadened to include intangibles. Intangible fixed assets, as a class, possess characteristics similar to those of tangible property, plant and equipment items. Their value, however, does not originate in their physical substance, but is attributable to the rights conferred by their ownership. Examples of such intangible assets are patents, copyrights, trademarks, and goodwill.

Each accounting period should be systematically charged with its share of the cost of fixed assets (tangible and intangible) possessing a determinable or estimated life.[1] The terms regularly employed to identify the allocation of such costs to the applicable accounting periods are:

Depreciation . . . the periodic charge for tangible assets other than natural resources.
Depletion . . . . . . the periodic charge for natural resources.
Amortization . . . the periodic charge for intangible assets.

COMPANY	PROPERTY, PLANT AND EQUIPMENT[2]				NET P. P. & E. AS % OF TOTAL ASSETS
	COST	ACCUMUL. DEPREC.	NET	TOTAL ASSETS	
	(AMOUNTS IN MILLIONS OF DOLLARS)				
General Motors Corporation	14,748	9,270	5,478	18,273	30%
General Electric Company	4,449	2,312	2,137	7,402	29%
U.S. Steel Corporation	10,084	5,928	4,156	6,570	63%
DuPont (E. I.) de Nemours	5,689	3,575	2,114	4,284	49%
Gulf Oil Corporation	10,862	5,444	5,418	9,324	58%
Swift and Company	486	233	253	936	27%
General Dynamics Corporation	820	482	338	1,015	33%
Kraftco Corporation	892	433	459	1,245	37%
RCA Corporation	1,435	664	771	3,137	25%
Union Carbide Corporation	4,729	2,775	1,954	3,718	53%
United Aircraft Corporation	917	658	259	1,223	21%

This chapter and chapter seven discuss property, plant and equipment and the related facets of depreciation. Chapter eight discusses natural resources and their depletion and intangible assets and their amortization.

An understanding of the distinguishing characteristics of two types of expenditures is necessary for a discussion of fixed assets and their periodic write-off. Presented next are the fundamental concepts necessary for such understanding.

CAPITAL EXPENDITURES AND REVENUE EXPENDITURES

An expenditure is the contracting of a liability for the acquisition of an asset or the incurring of an expense. An understanding of the basic differences between *capital* and *revenue* expenditures is a prerequisite to the determination of the cost of fixed assets, which costs may be ultimately depreciated, depleted, or amortized.

[1] Building site land does not have a determinable life.

[2] Exclusive of intangibles where separately stated.

A capital expenditure benefits future fiscal periods as well as the current one; it results in an increase in the carrying value of an asset, usually a fixed asset, on the balance sheet. A revenue expenditure benefits only the current fiscal period; it results in the increase in an item of expense on the statement of income.[3] These are concise explanations of the two terms; neither term can be defined to coincide perfectly with the various treatments given expenditures under practical implementations in business. The differentiation between capital and revenue expenditures will be illustrated by examples.

First, ABC Company purchases a second-hand delivery truck and incurs the following four expenditures in connection with this acquisition:

Invoice from X Company for second-hand truck	$2,000
Invoice from Z Company to have the truck completely overhauled prior to placing the truck into service	300
Cost of gasoline and oil for the first week's operation of the truck	50
Driver's salary for the week	150

Which of these four expenditures should be capitalized? One of the guiding principles underlying the classification of expenditures is that expenditures made to place a fixed asset in condition, in position, and ready for use should be capitalized. Accordingly, the capitalized cost of the above truck is $2,300. This amount represents the cost of the newly acquired fixed asset as an addition to existing property, plant and equipment. The other two expenditures, totaling $200, are revenue expenditures; they represent expenses concerned with the operation of the acquired asset and should be deducted from revenue on the statement of income.

A second example is used to illustrate an extension of the guiding principle already established. DEF Company, located in Buffalo, N.Y., purchases a piece of machinery and incurs the following expenditures:

Cost of machine, f.o.b. Cleveland, Ohio	$6,000
State sales tax	200
Freight charges to Buffalo	150
Insurance on machine while in transit	25
Cost to install machine in plant	200
Cost to break-in machine	125
Total	$6,700

Theoretically, the total cost of $6,700 may be capitalized as an addition to property, plant and equipment. All six of the expenditures are in-

[3] Revenue expenditures are often referred to as operating expenditures.

curred in acquiring the machine and placing it in condition, in position, and ready for use: no usable asset is acquired until $6,700 has been expended. Also, if the terms of purchase with the vendor in Cleveland were f.o.b. Buffalo, installed and ready to operate, the vendor's invoice for the machine would be approximately $6,700. To some degree, however, actual company practice may differ from the concepts embodied in accounting theory. Many companies have established a policy of charging to revenue all expenditures which are less than a stated amount—for example, $100. If this were the situation with the company in the second example, the $25 for insurance included in the above total could be expensed rather than capitalized. Also, in practice, many companies capitalize installation costs but expense breaking-in costs. This practice is followed when it is considered impractical to segregate breaking-in costs when the break-in operations are performed by the company's own employees. The pertinent point involved here is that the company follows a *consistent* policy for all expenditures which concern similar property acquisitions.

When considering what treatment a given expenditure should receive, it is entirely possible to arrive at one answer which is in accord with accounting theory, a second that conforms with company policy, and a third which complies with federal income tax regulations and related court decisions. For example, the state sales tax on the purchase of the above machine could be viewed in theory as a capital expenditure, but it may be treated as a revenue expenditure if it is deductible for purposes of federal income tax.[4] Due to the borderline nature of certain expenditures, such as major repairing and overhauling of equipment, the area of capital versus revenue expenditures results in much tax litigation.

One of the most concise and clear summaries of the differences between capital and revenue expenditures was that made years ago by the Board of Tax Appeals in the Illinois Merchants Trust Company case, in which the Board said:

> In determining whether an expenditure is a capital one or is chargeable against operating income, it is necessary to bear in mind the purpose for which the expenditure was made. To repair is to restore to a sound state or to mend, while a replacement connotes a substitution. A repair is an expenditure for the purpose of keeping the property in an ordinarily efficient operating condition. It does

[4] There is a general state sales tax in all but a few of the 50 states. In the majority of such states, owing to the wording of the state statute, the tax may be deducted in the year incurred for federal income tax puroses; but in a few states the tax must be capitalized as a portion of the cost of the capital asset and recovered through depreciation.

> not add to the value of the property, nor does it appreciably prolong its life. It merely keeps the property in an operating condition over its probable useful life for the uses for which it was acquired. Expenditures for that purpose are distinguishable from those for replacements, alterations, improvements or additions which prolong the life of the property, increase its value, or make it adaptable to a different use. The one is a maintenance charge, while the others are additions to capital investment which should not be applied against current earnings.[5]

Management should adhere to sound policies in distinguishing between capital and revenue expenditures; mishandling of these items will distort certain amounts in the balance sheet and prevent the matching of applicable costs with related revenue on the statement of income. In addition, management should be aware in its planning that many borderline cases, for tax purposes, are subject to a degree of control. For example, a deferred maintenance policy which causes the replacement of a worn-out motor on a large piece of machinery with a new motor costing $1,000 probably is a capital expenditure; but, a continuing maintenance policy which results only in periodic *repairs* and minor replacements of the parts to the original motor probably constitutes revenue expenditures. Incidentally, an expenditure such as the one immediately above, *if* deemed a capital expenditure, usually increases property, plant and equipment in a manner other than by adding the amount directly to the "cost" figure already on the records. Usually it is charged against accumulated depreciation to date rather than shown as an addition to cost. This is a procedure often used when a major replacement of a component part or an improvement in effect "makes good" prior years' depreciation or extends life; e.g., a new roof installed on a ten-year-old brick kiln.

DEPRECIATION

Concept of Depreciation

The term *depreciation* is employed in the periodic write-off of the cost of all items of property, plant and equipment except such tangible assets as land and natural resources and certain long-lived intangible assets. The term *depreciation* denotes the periodic cost allocation against revenue of such tangible assets as buildings, machinery, and equipment. These

[5] *Illinois Merchants Trust Company, Executor, Estate of William B. Manierre,* CCH December 1952, BTA 103 (acq.), reproduced by permission of Commerce Clearing House, Inc.

fixed assets have a limited useful life; physically, they deteriorate from use and from the action of the elements. An adequate repair and maintenance policy may slow, but cannot halt, this deterioration. In addition, such tangible fixed assets gradually become obsolete as a result of improved models, new inventions, and changes in consumer demand. The term depreciation includes both concepts: loss of serviceability from physical deterioration and loss of utility from gradual obsolescence.

Equitable methods must be used to write off the cost of fixed assets like buildings, machinery, and equipment items as their useful lives decrease. If the length of an accounting period exceeded or at least equalled the life of the fixed assets owned by a company, the depreciation problem would not exist. Thus, if a fiscal period were 50 years, practically all fixed assets would be an expense of the 50-year period. However, the one-year fiscal period is customary in business. Therefore, each fiscal period should be systematically charged with its proportionate share of the cost of fixed assets so that such cost will be fairly allocated as expense to each fiscal period throughout the estimated useful lives of the assets. In effect, the cost of each fixed asset is a long-term prepaid expense which, by some equitable method, must be prorated over its useful life as an expense to be matched against revenue during each period.

Definition of Depreciation

An explanation of the term depreciation is contained in a release by the Committee on Terminology of the American Institute of Certified Public Accountants:

> Depreciation accounting is a system of accounting which aims to distribute the cost or other basic value of tangible capital assets, less salvage (if any), over the estimated useful life of the unit (which may be a group of assets) in a systematic and rational manner. It is a process of allocation, not of valuation.[6]

Depreciation accounting must be recognized as a process of allocation of cost, not as a process of constantly valuing or revaluing fixed assets according to what they are currently "worth." In accounting usage, depreciation does not attempt to measure the decline in value of a fixed asset. Instead, depreciation is a process by which the cost of a fixed asset is equitably distributed over the years of its estimated useful life.

---

[6] Accounting Terminology Bulletin Number 1, "Review and Résumé, *Accounting Research and Terminology Bulletins, Final Edition,* p. 25. Copyright 1961 by the American Institute of Certified Public Accountants, Inc.

The Three Unknowns

The determination of that portion of the cost of a tangible fixed asset which is to be allocated to each fiscal period as depreciation expense requires decisions with respect to three factors: the cost (or other basic value) of the fixed asset, its salvage value (if any), and the estimated useful life of the asset. In varying degrees, the determination of these three factors is a matter of judgment, experience, fact, and educated guess. Rarely are all three of the unknowns capable of exact determination at the time a fixed asset is acquired. In fact, it may not be until years later, when the fixed asset is disposed of, that all three factors are finally capable of precise calculation. The necessity of resolving these unknowns at the time a fixed asset is acquired—coupled with perfect vision when using hindsight—has produced much litigation in the tax courts. Therefore, a résumé of the pertinent points that should be considered in making decisions concerning each of these three factors is presented next.

Cost (or Other Basic Value)

Basically, cost is the sum of the actual expenditures involved in acquiring and placing a fixed asset in operating condition. As discussed earlier in this chapter, such cost is often in excess of that paid to the vendor. A piece of machinery purchased f.o.b. shipping point has an acquisition cost in excess of that paid to the seller of the machine. The total cost of the asset, the amount to be depreciated, frequently includes items like freight charges, installation costs, and break-in expenditures. These points were discussed earlier, but there are additional factors which must also be resolved in certain instances.

Consider the case of a company which purchases land and a second-hand factory building for a lump sum price of $500,000. What is the cost of the building, which is subject to depreciation; what is the cost of the land, which is not subject to depreciation? If the purchase agreement does not explicitly specify the portion of the $500,000 purchase price allocable to each, an equitable allocation must be made. One possible method of allocation is to use the values at which each is assessed for property taxes, as follows:

	ASSESSED VALUE	PERCENT OF TOTAL	APPORTIONMENT OF PURCHASE PRICE
Land	$100,000	¼	$125,000
Building	300,000	¾	375,000
Total	$400,000		$500,000

Another method of apportioning the total purchase price is by an independent appraisal of the land and the building. In addition to the $375,000 cost apportioned to the building, additional capital expenditures may be incurred in getting this second-hand fixed asset into condition and ready for use.

Another situation in which the cost of a fixed asset is not readily determinable is in the case of a company constructing a fixed asset itself for its own use. Without getting involved in the details, the reader can easily appreciate that, while the material costs could be identified without too much difficulty and the labor costs might be readily segregated equitably, the proration of many of the appropriate general overhead expenses like heat, light, telephone, and administrative salaries would require careful analysis and would not be capable of precise apportionment. If all applicable costs are not equitably allocated between the fixed asset under construction and the goods being produced for sale, distorted financial information will result which could seriously mislead management if the dollar amount involved is material.

Occasionally a basis other than cost is used for establishing the dollar amount assigned as the value of the asset acquired. This situation occurs when land and buildings are donated to a company to induce it to establish a plant in a specific locality. In such an instance, the fixed assets may be shown on the financial statements at market value at the time of acquisition. Another situation is presented when fixed assets are acquired through the issuance of the company's own capital stock. Should such assets be shown at their own market value or at the value of the shares issued to acquire the assets?[7]

Cost (or other basic value) is not always readily determinable, nor is it always subject to precise measurement. Nevertheless, the determination must be made in as equitable a manner as possible.

Salvage (If Any)

The amount to be depreciated over the estimated useful life of a fixed asset is the difference between the cost and the salvage value of the asset. Salvage value, as used in the determination of depreciation, is the estimated amount which will be realized from a tangible fixed asset at the time it is sold or otherwise disposed of at the end of its estimated useful life. To ascertain the total amount to be depreciated, salvage value must be determined at the time the asset is acquired; yet it may be many years before the exact salvage amount is actually ascertainable. In the case of

[7] This point is discussed in Chapter 12.

some assets, salvage value might represent a substantial portion of the original cost, as new automobiles purchased by automobile rental agencies which dispose of them after only a very limited period of use. However, in the case of other assets, salvage value may be negligible or non-existent; for example, the cost of scrapping an asset may approximate its junk value. Often this is the case with a building; a similar situation occurs with certain machinery in industries where technological or style changes are very frequent. Past experience is usually the most valid basis for estimating salvage value. If there is no past experience available for new types of fixed assets like an atomic power plant or Disneyland, judgment appears to be the best basis for estimating salvage value. Rather than salvage value, a company may wish to use *net* salvage value (salvage value reduced by the estimated cost of removing, dismantling, or junking the asset). A company should be consistent in its use of either salvage value or net salvage in determining its depreciation allowances.

Estimated Useful Life

The third factor to be predetermined to allocate depreciation expense equitably is the estimated useful life of the asset. Estimated useful life is not necessarily the useful life inherent in the asset; rather, it is the period over which the asset is expected to be useful in the business of the particular company. Identical depreciable assets may conceivably have different estimated useful lives for different companies.

If someone were to ask, "What is the estimated useful life of an automobile?" his question could not be answered properly until answers had first been furnished for several other questions, among which would be these:

> What is the repair and maintenance policy for the automobile? Is it a scheduled program of adequate maintenance, or is it of the bare minimum necessity type?
>
> Is the automobile kept in a garage, or does it stand out in all kinds of weather?
>
> How many miles is the automobile driven per year?
>
> Assuming that the usual operator is a skilled and experienced driver, are there occasions when young, inexperienced operators drive the car? If so, how frequently do such occasions occur?
>
> Is the automobile viewed as simply a means of transportation or in some other manner? In other words, do model changes and innovations which cause gradual obsolescence mean that it will be more quickly disposed of than would otherwise be the case?

From the foregoing, it is apparent that estimated useful life is dependent upon many factors, chief among which are the company's policy on repairs and maintenance; wear and tear from operations, climatic and other local conditions; human behavior; economic changes; inventions; and normal obsolescence. Estimated useful life is a matter of judgment and should be forecasted according to past experience and all other pertinent data. An estimated life for a depreciable asset, once determined, should be changed if at some time in the future conditions clearly warrant such a change. Many companies review such estimates periodically.

From 1934 through July 11, 1962, the only guide to useful lives for depreciable assets justifiable for income tax purposes was Bulletin "F," issued by the Treasury Department. Last completely revised in January, 1942, Bulletin "F" listed estimated useful lives for approximately 5,000 types of assets. Illustrative items included in the list were:

ITEM DESCRIPTION	LIFE (YEARS)
Factory buildings	50
Office buildings	67
Warehouses	75
Apartment buildings	50
Brick kilns	25
Hotel carpets and rugs	6
Blast furnaces (iron and steel industry)	25
Passenger automobiles	5
Salesmen's automobiles	3
Office desks	20
Generators, large units above 3,000 kv.-a	28
Aircraft engines	6,000 flying hours

For two reasons, the estimated lives listed in Bulletin "F" were not to be accepted as final answers. First, the average useful life figure was intended only as a rough guide or starting point from which a company should estimate life based upon the period over which the depreciable asset was expected to be useful in the business of that particular company. Second, the accelerated pace of technological innovation and increasingly rapid changes in economic conditions rendered the list somewhat antiquated since it was released in January of 1942. Bulletin "F" was intended only as a guide; in reality, however, it acted as a "par" against which the Internal Revenue Service compared the depreciable lives used by companies. And, in addition, the burden of proof for deviations from Bulletin "F" lives was placed on the taxpayer.

On July 11, 1962, the Treasury Department issued *Depreciation Guidelines and Rules,* officially known as "Revenue Procedure 62–21." Instead of establishing lives on individual items of depreciable property, as did Bulletin "F," the guideline lives contained in Revenue Procedure 62–21 apply to only about 75 broad classes of assets. Each class is assigned a guideline life for tax purposes. These 75 broad classes are enumerated as subdivisions of the following four groups of depreciable assets used in business:

Group One:	Assets used by business in general
Group Two:	Non-manufacturing activities (excluding transportation, communications, and public utilities)
Group Three:	Manufacturing
Group Four:	Transportation, communications, and public utilities

Group One contains assets in common use by all businesses, like office furniture, automobiles, trucks, and office machines. The other three groups contain all the equipment and productive machinery used by a specific industry. The following examples are selected at random from the four groups and 75 classes of depreciable assets enumerated in Revenue Procedure 62–21.

GROUP	CLASS	CLASS DESCRIPTION	LIFE (YEARS)
One	1	Office Furniture, Fixtures, Machines, and Equipment	10
	2	Transportation Equipment:	
		(b) Automobiles, including taxis	3
		(d) General-purpose trucks:	
		Light (actual unloaded weight less than 13,000 pounds)	4
		Heavy (13,000 pounds or more)	6
	4	Buildings (other than special purpose structures)	
		Type of Building (four of thirteen):	
		Apartments	40
		Factories	45
		Office Buildings	45
		Warehouses	60
Two	1	Agriculture:	
		(a) Machinery and Equipment (including fences)	10
		(d) Farm Buildings	25
	6	Recreation and Amusement (other than land improvements or structures)	10
	7	Services (Personal and Professional)	10

Three	4	Chemicals and Allied Products	11
	5	Electrical Equipment:	
		(a) Electrical Equipment	12
		(b) Electronic Equipment	8
	8	Glass and Glass Products	14
	17	Petroleum and Natural Gas:	
		(c) Petroleum Refining	16
	19	Primary Metals:	
		(a) Ferrous Metals	18
		(b) Nonferrous Metals	14
	28	Tobacco and Tobacco Products	15
Four	3	Electric Utilities	
		(a) Hydraulic production plant	50
		(b) Nuclear production plant	20
		(c) Steam production plant	28
		(d) Transmission and distribution facilities	30
		Each guideline class includes the related land improvements.	
	7	Pipeline Transportation	22

Note that the guideline life for the entire class of office furniture, fixtures, machines, and equipment is ten years. Under Bulletin "F" each individual item in this category had a separate life, ranging from five years for a typewriter to fifty years for an office safe. The new and shorter lives contained in the "guideline lives" are intended to give recognition to factors like more rapid obsolescence caused by changing technology, new inventions, and foreign competition. While the shorter lives have been referred to as "equivalent to a tax cut" and a "stimulus to continued economic growth," ultimately such lives had to be justified by the business utilizing them. The guideline lives, or possibly even shorter lives being used by a business at present, had to be consistent with the actual practice of the business in retiring and replacing its depreciable assets. The reasonableness of the lives used was gauged by a technique known as the "reserve ratio" test; i.e., the comparison of the ratio of accumulated depreciation to date to the cost of the assets in the particular guidelines class, with a predetermined range within which the ratio should fall.

On January 11, 1971, President Nixon announced, effective January 1, 1971, two important changes with respect to depreciation allowances on business *equipment* (e.g., machinery and equipment; but *not* buildings and real estate improvements). They are:

a. the introduction of the Asset Depreciation Range (ADR) System, which permits business equipment to be depreciated over lives that are not more than 20 percent shorter nor 20 percent longer than the "guideline lives" established by the Treasury Department on July 11, 1962; years are rounded to the nearest half year.

b. the termination of the complex "reserve ratio test" effective December 31, 1970, so that the life over which business equipment is written off need no longer be consistent with actual practice in retiring and replacing such depreciable assets (see above).

In describing these changes, the literature abounds with such terms as "promote economic growth," "increase the competitiveness of U.S. goods in world markets," "create new jobs," "offset the toll inflation has taken in the value of depreciation deductions," "stimulate the economy in 1971," and "adjust the imbalance in tax distribution attributable to the Tax Reform Act of 1969."

Then, the Revenue Act of 1971 was passed by Congress and signed by President Nixon on December 10, 1971. One of the provisions contained in this Act is the establishment of the Class Life Asset Depreciation Range system with respect to depreciation. This provision codified the Asset Depreciation Range (ADR) system; it is now part of the "tax law" whereas previously it was only a Treasury Department "regulation." Also, this same provision of the Act absorbed the guideline lives. Thus, the Class Life Asset Depreciation Range system has combined the ADR system established by the Treasury Department in 1971 and the guideline lives system established by the Treasury Department in 1962.

When the triumvirate of unknowns, cost (or other basic value), salvage value (if any), and estimated useful life has been resolved, an answer must, in turn, be supplied to an involved question: what method of depreciation should be used?

DEPRECIATION METHODS

The objective of any depreciation method should be to allocate the cost less salvage value of a depreciable fixed asset over the estimated useful life of that asset in a manner which is both systematic and rational. The depreciation methods used today by a majority of the firms located in the United States may be divided into the following two categories:

(1) Those methods characterized by the cost minus salvage divided by life procedure:
   (a) Straight-line method
   (b) Units-of-production method

(2) Those methods characterized by the accelerated depreciation procedure:
   (a) Declining balance method
   (b) Sum-of-the-years' digits method

To illustrate and explain the various methods of depreciation, assume the following facts for a new machine purchased on January 1, 1973:

Cost (invoice price plus other applicable capital expenditures)	$8,000
Estimated salvage value	250
Estimated useful life:	
In years	5
In units of production	25,000

Straight-Line Method

The method of depreciation most commonly used for many years has been the straight-line method. The theory underlying this method of apportionment is that depreciation is a function of time. The straight-line method produces a uniform annual depreciation expense for each year of the asset's life. The annual depreciation charge is obtained by dividing the amount to be depreciated, cost minus salvage value, by the number of years of estimated useful life. Applying this method to the facts provided above, the annual depreciation expense amounts to $1,550, computed as follows:

$$\text{Annual depreciation} = \frac{\text{Cost} - \text{estimated salvage value}}{\text{Estimated life (in years)}}$$

$$\text{Annual depreciation} = \frac{\$8{,}000 - \$250}{5 \text{ years}}$$

$$\text{Annual depreciation} = \$1{,}550$$

Assuming no changes or revisions during the four years in cost, estimated salvage value, or estimated useful life for the above piece of machinery, the table below summarizes the effect on the financial statements of the resulting straight-line depreciation.

	Statement of Income For the Year	Balance Sheet as of December 31				
Year	Depreciation Expense	Cost	–	Accumulated Depreciation to date	=	Cost Less Accumulated Depreciation
1973	$1,550	$8,000	–	$1,550	=	$6,450
1974	1,550	8,000	–	3,100	=	4,900
1975	1,550	8,000	–	4,650	=	3,350
1976	1,550	8,000	–	6,200	=	1,800
1977	1,550	8,000	–	7,750	=	250*
	$7,750					

* Estimated salvage value

An alternative manner of expressing estimated life when straight-line depreciation is used is by a percentage rather than actual years. In the above illustration, the amount to be depreciated (cost minus salvage value) may be multiplied by 20 percent rather than divided by five to obtain the annual depreciation allocation. Similarly, a depreciable fixed asset with a four-year life would have a depreciation rate of 25 percent, and an asset with a 12-year life would have a depreciation rate of 8⅓ percent. The multiplier is obtained by dividing 100 percent by the number of years in the estimated useful life of an asset.

The principal advantages of straight-line depreciation are the relative simplicity of computation and the ease with which the concept is understood. The disadvantage advanced by most critics is that this method of depreciation does not give recognition to fluctuations in the actual use made of the asset. If the asset is a building, the effect of such fluctuations probably would be minor. But, if the asset is a machine whose usage might be expected to fluctuate widely from period to period, straight-line depreciation may not be realistic. Also, in the later years of life, when efficiency of operation of the asset may be somewhat lower and repair and maintenance expenses may tend to increase rather sharply, a constant straight-line depreciation charge plus an increasing repair and maintenance expense may produce an unreasonably high total for the two operating expenses.

Units-of-Production Method

The units-of-production method allocates the depreciable basis of a fixed asset according to the use made of that asset during each period. It recognizes that assets which receive irregular use, like certain machinery or trucks, should be depreciated according to their usage rather than by the passage of time. Units of production or output may be expressed in an estimated number of working hours or the number of units of goods to be produced by a machine. In the case of an automobile or truck, units of production or output may be expressed in an estimated number of miles that may be expected from the vehicle. The unit depreciation charge is calculated by dividing the fixed asset's life (expressed in the estimated total number of measurement units) into the acquisition cost less anticipated salvage value of the asset. Applying this method to the assumed facts stated on page 176, the unit depreciation expense for the machine amounts to 31¢ per unit produced; it is computed as follows:

$$\text{Depreciation expense per unit} = \frac{\text{Cost} - \text{estimated salvage value}}{\text{Estimated life (in units)}}$$

$$\text{Depreciation expense per unit} = \frac{\$8{,}000 - \$250}{25{,}000 \text{ units}}$$

$$\text{Depreciation expense per unit} = 31¢$$

Assume that there are no changes in the basic facts employed in the original unit depreciation charge, and that the machine's output during the ensuing years is as follows:

1973	6,000 units
1974	4,000 units
1975	7,000 units
1976	5,000 units
1977	3,000 units
	25,000 units

From the above information, the depreciation expense for each period, in this case each year, can be readily obtained by multiplying the previously computed unit rate of 31¢ by the number of units produced during each period. For example, the depreciation expense for 1973 would be 31¢ × 6,000 units or $1,860. The following table summarizes the effect on the financial statements of depreciation determined by the units-of-production method.

	Statement of Income For the Year	Balance Sheet As of December 31				
Year	Depreciation Expense	Cost	−	Accumulated Depreciation to date	=	Cost Less Accumulated Depreciation
1973	$1,860	$8,000	−	$1,860	=	$6,140
1974	1,240	8,000	−	3,100	=	4,900
1975	2,170	8,000	−	5,270	=	2,730
1976	1,550	8,000	−	6,820	=	1,180
1977	930	8,000	−	7,750	=	250*
	$7,750					

* Estimated salvage value

The chief advantage of the units-of-production method of depreciation is that the cost of the asset is allocated as expense in proportion to the use made of the asset in securing its related revenue. To some extent in the case of certain depreciable assets, this method makes possible a more accurate matching of expenses with revenue than does the straight-line method of depreciation. Though the arithmetic calculation of depreciation is elementary when the units-of-production method is used, the method does require that a record be maintained of the unit output or the hours worked by a particular asset or group of assets.

To compensate for unusual situations which might occur when highly abnormal operating conditions prevail, certain companies which use a units-of-production method establish both minimum and maximum amounts for the depreciation expense in any one year. For example, if an asset is idle throughout the entire year, it does depreciate to some extent. If, on the other hand, a machine is required to produce 10,000 units instead of the 2,000 units normally produced in a year, the machine has not necessarily depreciated five times as much.

Background of Accelerated Depreciation

Prior to 1954, the straight-line method of depreciation was used almost to the complete exclusion of all other methods in the determination of periodic depreciation expense. In 1953, one source, in comparing the use of various methods of depreciation, stated with respect to the straight-line method:

> This is by far the most common method, and is used by more than 90% of all taxpayers entitled to the deduction.[8]

Then, as today, some companies used the units-of-production method for selected assets. In a few instances, a limited version of the declining balance method of depreciation was used for rental housing. But the straight-line method of depreciation was by far the preferred method.

The foregoing is not intended to imply that the straight-line method was the only method of depreciation thought to be justifiable at the time; but, with few exceptions, it was the only method used. Nevertheless, for many years preceding 1954, literature in accounting and related areas devoted considerable attention to a discussion of other methods of depreciation. Among the other methods proposed were the accelerated methods of depreciation known as the declining balance method and the sum-of-the-years' digits method.

Accelerated methods of depreciation provide greater charges in the early years of the asset's life and progressively smaller charges in later years. Theoretically, the continually decreasing periodic depreciation expense will be counter-balanced by an increasing expense for repairs and maintenance as the asset ages. Thus, the total of these two operating expenses, depreciation plus repair and maintenance expense, would approximate an equal amount for each year of the life of the asset. In

---

[8] *Prentice-Hall 1954 Federal Tax Course, Students Edition* (Englewood Cliffs, N.J.: Prentice-Hall, Inc., 1953), p. 2009.

theory, the situation might be illustrated as follows (amounts not related to previous examples):

YEAR OF LIFE	DEPRECIATION EXPENSE	REPAIR AND MAINTENANCE EXPENSE	TOTAL OF THE TWO OPERATING EXPENSES
1st year	$1,000	$ 0	$1,000
2nd year	800	200	1,000
3rd year	600	400	1,000
4th year	400	600	1,000
5th year	200	800	1,000

In theory, it is not difficult to justify this method for many assets. For example, the trends illustrated above for depreciation expense and repair and maintenance expense typically represent the operation of a privately owned automobile. Similar conditions prevail with certain depreciable assets used in business.[9] In fact, an additional argument favoring a depreciation method which produces decreasing annual charges can be advanced. Assets having revenue-producing possibilities which are considerable at the time of their acquisition and shortly thereafter could conceivably lose this advantage long before the end of their estimated useful life because of the inability to forecast accurately the long-range market demand for the products produced by such assets. Thus, heavy depreciation in the early years of the life of an asset might produce a more rational allocation of its cost.

Despite long-standing arguments favorable to accelerated depreciation, prior to 1954 business almost completely rejected the use of any method of accelerated depreciation. Why did this condition exist? Probably because such methods were not acceptable for income tax purposes. But, on August 16, 1954, the President signed into law a new income tax code containing provisions pertaining to accelerated depreciation retroactive to January 1, 1954. Reaction by accountants and the business community was immediate. In fact, what had been largely interesting theory suddenly became common practice. Even the Committee on Accounting Procedure of the AICPA reacted quickly when in October, 1954, it stated:

> The declining-balance method is one of those which meets the requirements of being "systematic and rational" (*Accounting Terminology Bulletin No. 1,* paragraph 56). In those cases where the expected productivity or revenue-earning power of the asset is relatively greater during the earlier years of its life, where maintenance

---

[9] There have been a few studies which tend to discredit this idea. They indicate that maintenance costs have varied little with the age of the asset.

charges tend to increase during the later years, the declining-balance method may well provide the most satisfactory allocation of cost. The conclusions of this bulletin also apply to other methods, including the "sum-of-the-years' digits" method, which produce substantially similar results.[10]

Declining Balance Method

The declining balance method of depreciation is one of two commonly used methods which provide larger depreciation charges during the first years of the asset's life and steadily decreasing charges over the estimated useful life of the asset. By this method, a fixed rate is applied to the *cost* (*not* to the cost minus salvage value) of the asset in the first period to determine that period's depreciation expense. In each subsequent period, the depreciation expense is computed through application of the same fixed rate to the remaining balance (cost minus accumulated depreciation to date) of the asset.

In theory, the fixed rate is determined by extracting the root, equivalent to the estimated life, of a quotient which is obtained by dividing the salvage value by the cost of the asset. Using the same assumed facts as those shown on page 176, the fixed rate is calculated as follows:

$$\text{Fixed rate of depreciation} = 1 - \sqrt[n]{\frac{\text{Salvage value}}{\text{cost}}}$$

$$\text{Fixed rate of depreciation} = 1 - \sqrt[5]{\frac{250}{8{,}000}}$$

$$\text{Fixed rate of depreciation} = 50\%$$ [11]

The first table on page 182 summarizes the effect that the theoretical fixed rate used to calculate declining balance depreciation would have on the resulting financial statements.

There are at least two reasons which explain why the theoretical fixed rate is seldom encountered in practice. First, this rate involves rather complex calculations. Second, the Internal Revenue Code of 1954 states that the maximum rate that may be used is twice the straight-line rate. Thus, for the machine in our example, the effective fixed rate that would

---

[10] Accounting Research Bulletin No. 44, "Declining-Balance Depreciation," paragraph two, *Accounting Research and Terminology Bulletins, Final Edition.* Copyright 1961 by the American Institute of Certified Public Accountants, Inc.

[11] Figures were purposely chosen which would simplify arithmetic and add to clarity of presentation. Rarely would the rate equal an even percentage. For example, if cost is $1,000, salvage is estimated at $100, and life is 10 years, application of the formula would give a fixed rate of 20.5672%.

actually be used for tax purposes is twice the straight-line rate of 20 percent, or 40 percent[12]; thus, it is commonly referred to as the double declining balance method of depreciation. Use of this rate can lead to a few complications. For example, if the permissible tax rate of 40 percent

					Statement of Income For the Year	Balance Sheet As of December 31				
Year	Cost less Accumulated Depreciation on Machine on January 1	×	Fixed Rate	=	Depreciation Expense	Cost	–	Accumulated Depreciation to date	=	Cost less Accumulated Depreciation
1973	$8,000	×	50%	=	$4,000	$8,000	–	$4,000	=	$4,000
1974	4,000	×	50%	=	2,000	8,000	–	6,000	=	2,000
1975	2,000	×	50%	=	1,000	8,000	–	7,000	=	1,000
1976	1,000	×	50%	=	500	8,000	–	7,500	=	500
1977	500	×	50%	=	250	8,000	–	7,750	=	250*
					$7,750					

* Estimated salvage value

(twice the straight-line rate) is used, the results shown in the preceding table would be changed to the following (rounded to the nearest dollar):

					Statement of Income For the Year	Balance Sheet As of December 31				
Year	Cost less Accumulated Depreciation on Machine on January 1	×	Fixed Rate	=	Depreciation Expense	Cost	–	Accumulated Depreciation to date	=	Cost less Accumulated Depreciation
1973	$8,000	×	40%	=	$3,200	$8,000	–	$3,200	=	$4,800
1974	4,800	×	40%	=	1,920	8,000	–	5,120	=	2,880
1975	2,880	×	40%	=	1,152	8,000	–	6,272	=	1,728
1976	1,728	×	40%	=	691	8,000	–	6,963	=	1,037
1977	1,037	×	40%	=	415	8,000	–	7,378	=	622*
					$7,378					

* More than estimated salvage value of $250.

Note that, at the end of the estimated useful life, the remaining carrying value or undepreciated cost of $622 exceeds the estimated salvage value of $250. Similarly, total depreciation is $7,378, not $7,750. For these

[12] Similarly, if an asset had a six-year life which would produce a straight-line rate of 16⅔ percent, the permissible effective fixed percentage rate for declining balance depreciation would be 33⅓ percent.

reasons, the income tax law permits a change during the life of the asset from the double declining balance method to the straight-line method so that unrecovered cost less salvage value may be depreciated over the remaining estimated useful life. Presumably, if no such switch to straight-line is made and the asset is continued in use beyond the fifth year, depreciation at the permissible fixed rate on the unrecovered cost of the asset can be continued until it has been depreciated down to the salvage value. Conversely, sometimes the application of twice the straight-line rate will depreciate an asset down to salvage value before the end of its originally estimated useful life. Then, depreciation charges should cease before the termination of estimated useful life, for in no case should an asset be depreciated below its estimated salvage value.

Sum-of-the-Years' Digits Method

The sum-of-the-years' digits method of depreciation, like the declining balance method, produces gradually decreasing depreciation charges over the estimated useful life of the asset. This method, unlike the declining balance method, is somewhat easier to compute and avoids the problem of a possible remaining excess of unrecovered cost at the end of estimated useful life. Under the sum-of-the-years' digits method, the depreciation expense for any given year is computed by multiplying the total cost less salvage value by a changing fraction. In any year, the fraction used requires a numerator which corresponds to the remaining years of estimated life of the asset and a denominator which equals the sum of the numerical sequence formed by the years in the asset's total life. Using the original example of a machine with a five-year life, the numerator of the applicable fraction for the first year would be 5, for the second year 4, and so on until it reached 1 for the last year of life. The denominator of the

					Statement of Income For the Year	Balance Sheet As of December 31				
Year	Cost less Salvage Value	×	Fraction	=	Depreciation Expense	Cost	−	Accumulated Depreciation to date	=	Cost less Accumulated Depreciation
1973	$7,750	×	5/15	=	$2,583	$8,000	−	$2,583	=	$5,417
1974	7,750	×	4/15	=	2,067	8,000	−	4,650	=	3,350
1975	7,750	×	3/15	=	1,550	8,000	−	6,200	=	1,800
1976	7,750	×	2/15	=	1,033	8,000	−	7,233	=	767
1977	7,750	×	1/15	=	517	8,000	−	7,750	=	250*
					$7,750					

* Estimated salvage value

fraction each year would be 15, the sum of the numbers designating the years in the total life; that is, 1 + 2 + 3 + 4 + 5. Thus, the depreciation expense for the first year would be $5/15$ of the cost minus salvage value of the machine, for the second year, $4/15$ of the cost minus salvage value. Using the assumed facts on page 176, the table above summarizes the effect of the sum-of-the-years' digits method of depreciation on the information provided by the financial statements.

Any company intending to use either of the two accelerated methods of depreciation for federal income tax purposes should be aware of the provisions of Section 167(c) of the 1954 Internal Revenue Code (and the changes made by the Tax Reform Act of 1969 and the Revenue Act of 1971) which states, generally, that the tangible fixed asset, to be eligible for such depreciation, must have a useful life of three years or more, be acquired after December 31, 1953, and be an unused new asset (second-hand assets are not eligible).

In recent years, some of the accelerated depreciation provisions have been suspended, reinstated, altered, repealed, or modified for income tax purposes. An awareness of these changes is necessary when planning for new capital expenditures.

The Investment Credit and Accelerated Depreciation Suspension Act, P.L. 89–800, signed by the President on November 8, 1966, contained the following two principal provisions:

1. The 7 percent investment credit, to be discussed in Chapter 7, was suspended on property acquired or constructed during the period of October 10, 1966, through December 31, 1967.
2. Accelerated depreciation (both double declining balance and sum-of-the-years' digits methods), discussed in this chapter, was prohibited on *buildings* (but *not* on machinery, equipment, etc.) if ordered or if construction was started during the period of October 10, 1966, through December 31, 1967.

The aim of these two provisions was to discourage capital expenditures and thus decrease or restrain one of the inflationary pressures on the economy. There were certain minor exceptions to the above two provisions, designed chiefly to benefit the small businessman, which are beyond the scope of this book. These two provisions were not "repealed"; rather they were to have been "suspended" for approximately 15 months. When the economy suddenly turned down, due to many factors, the suspension was quickly terminated, ahead of schedule, effective principally with property acquired after March 9, 1967.

The Tax Reform Act of 1969, P.L. 91–172, signed by the President on December 30, 1969, contained the following principal provisions:

1. Repealed the 7 percent investment credit, to be discussed in Chapter 7, effective April 18, 1969.
2. Reinstituted the concept of rapid amortization, to be discussed in Chapter 7.
3. The only accelerated depreciation method permitted for new real business property (office buildings; not machinery, equipment, etc.) purchased or constructed after July 24, 1969, is the 150 percent declining balance method. In effect, for new buildings, the maximum rate is 1½ times the straight-line rate. If a new building with an estimated life of 50 years is acquired, the 150 percent declining balance method would result in annual depreciation rate of 3 percent (1½ times the 2 percent straight-line rate) on the diminishing balance. Note that the double declining balance and the sum-of-the-years' digits method are *still available* for new personalty business (machinery, equipment, etc.) property.
4. The above deceleration of accelerated depreciation does *not* apply to *new* real property which is principally new residential rental property, e.g., a new apartment building. Both the double declining balance method and the sum-of-the-years' digits method may still be used on new residential rental property.
5. A 125 percent declining balance method may be employed to depreciate *used* residential rental property with a life of 20 years or more at acquisition.

The aim of the repeal of the investment credit and the deceleration of accelerated depreciation was to aid in curbing the inflationary aspects of the economy. The chief aim of the other provisions is to better environmental conditions and housing.

The Revenue Act of 1971, signed by the President on December 10, 1971, contained the following provisions, which are still in effect as of the date of this writing:

1. Restored the 7 percent investment credit, to be discussed in Chapter 7, effective, basically, August 16, 1971.
2. Codified and combined the guideline lives and ADR into the Class Life Asset Depreciation Range system.

The object, once again, of such provisions was to stimulate the economy by measures such as the above encouragement given to capital expenditures.

COMPARISON OF PRINCIPAL DEPRECIATION METHODS

The summary presented below of the preceding detailed tables clearly indicates the effect of the various methods on the information provided by the financial statements. When the units-of-production method is used, the depreciation expense for the period varies directly with the use made of the asset. When the straight-line and the accelerated methods of depreciation are used, passage of time, rather than usage, usually determines the depreciation expense for the period; the amount of expense is the resultant of the specific method selected. A comparison of results for

ANNUAL DEPRECIATION EXPENSE ON THE STATEMENT OF INCOME

YEAR	STRAIGHT-LINE	UNITS-OF-PRODUCTION	DECLINING BALANCE[13]	SUM-OF-YEARS' DIGITS
1973	$1,550	$1,860	$3,200	$2,583
1974	1,550	1,240	1,920	2,067
1975	1,550	2,170	1,152	1,550
1976	1,550	1,550	691	1,033
1977	1,550	930	415	517
	$7,750	$7,750	$7,378	$7,750

the first two years, based upon our assumed facts, reveals that, of the $7,750 amount (cost less salvage value) to be allocated over the five-year life of the asset in a "systematic and rational manner," 40 percent is distributed as expense in the first two years by the straight-line method;

	METHOD OF DEPRECIATION		
YEAR	STRAIGHT-LINE	DECLINING BALANCE	SUM OF-YEARS' DIGITS
1973.............	$1,550	$3,200	$2,583
1974.............	1,550	1,920	2,067
	$3,100	$5,120	$4,650
% of $7,750.............	40%	66%	60%

[13] Using the tax method of double the straight-line rate.

the declining balance and the sum-of-the-years' digits methods distribute 66 percent and 60 percent of it in the same time period. A reverse situation prevails in the later years of life. What, then, should determine the method of depreciation selected?

Selection of a Depreciation Method

The selection of a depreciation method should be based, theoretically, on the premise that one method will most fairly provide the proper information for management guidance. A depreciation method should allocate the cost of an asset equitably over its useful life so that the closest possible matching occurs each period between expired costs and related revenue. Thus, each company must base its selection of the method or methods of depreciation to be employed upon the kind of information it needs for management guidance, the nature of its business, and the types of depreciable plant and equipment items which are involved. It is not uncommon for a given company to use different depreciation methods for the various classifications of depreciable property it owns.

An additional factor must also be considered in selecting proper depreciation methods. While the above approach may be fine theory from the point of view of financial reporting, the effect of a federal corporate income tax rate of approximately 50 percent should not be ignored. If the accelerated methods of depreciation, rather than straight-line, are used, the impact of income taxes may be reduced. Both accelerated methods provide greater depreciation expense in the earlier years of an asset's life; this reduces, in these years, the net income subject to tax. The amount of the decrease in taxes payable during such years is approximately 50 percent of the amount by which accelerated depreciation exceeds straight-line depreciation on the assets involved. For a company of any size, the dollar amount involved may be material. In fiscal year 1972, for example, it resulted in an increase in the deferred tax liability of Campbell Soup Company by $5,743,000. This current tax deferral conserves additional funds which can be alternatively employed in the business; but what of the future—those later years when accelerated depreciation is less in amount than straight-line depreciation? Discussion of this point is reserved for the next chapter.

As with so many decisions required of management, a policy concerning depreciation methods must be resolved with an awareness of tax consequences. Each company must make its decision based on past experiences, present status, and expected future results. Any decision based solely on a gamble that tax rates will move one way or another could be disastrous. Many companies have resolved the dilemma concerning depreciation methods by adopting one or more methods to present fairly the financial results and a different method or methods for income taxes. For example, Reynolds Metals Company uses straight-line depreciation for financial accounting and the declining balance method for income taxes. But, while this procedure solves one problem, it creates another. The financial statements will be distorted if the statement of income shows a smaller depreciation expense and a larger net income than does the tax return; because of the excess depreciation deducted on the tax return, the actual federal income taxes for the year will be less than the amount that would be allocable to the net income shown by the financial statement of income. To prevent such distortion, a provision for deferred income taxes should be provided for in the financial statements; this point is discussed at the beginning of the next chapter. As an example of such a situation, the 1972 Annual Report of Armstrong Cork Company states:

> The company generally uses straight-line depreciation for financial reporting purposes and accelerated depreciation as permitted for tax purposes, at rates calculated to provide for the retirement of assets at the end of their useful lives. . . . Taxes deferred to future years ($4,415,000 in 1972 and $2,212,000 in 1971) represent timing differences resulting from the use of accelerated depreciation for tax purposes and straight-line depreciation for financial reporting, and other items that are handled differently for tax and financial reporting purposes.

Group and Composite Rate Depreciation

For clarity, the theory underlying the depreciation methods explained and the facts employed to illustrate such theory in examples have been limited to the depreciation of a single asset. Many companies, regardless of the depreciation method or methods selected, apply these methods to homogenous groups of fixed assets rather than to specific units. For example, a delivery service might depreciate, upon acquisition, a fleet of trucks as a group rather than individually. Similarly, a department store might depreciate its showcases as a group; another business might use group depreciation for its office typewriters.

When the group method of depreciation is used, useful life is estimated for the group as a whole to establish a depreciation rate. This rate of depreciation is then applied to the total cost of the group for the previously determined life or until the group of assets is fully depreciated. Use of the group method assumes that early retirement of a specific item will be offset by late retirement of another in the same group. Any unduly large variation in this predicted pattern of retirements would necessitate an adjustment in the group rate of depreciation.

The composite method of depreciation differs from the group method in that the composite category contains depreciable assets unlike each other in form, but like each other in that they are all used in a specific segment of the business. For example, the composite may be an open hearth unit, the overall life of which is 25 years; the composite may contain everything in it from the building with a 50 year life, charging machines with a 20 year life, and ingot molds with a 5 year life. A composite life of 15 years may be used for office equipment; but whenever the office equipment is segregated into groups, group lives could be:

Furniture, fixtures, and filing cases	20 years
Mechanical equipment	8 years
Safes	50 years

The averaging technique used by a composite rate will be a time saver if the rate does not require frequent revisions. Accuracy of a composite rate is always subject to greater debate than the more commonly employed group method.

REVISION OF ESTIMATED USEFUL LIFE

The periodic depreciation expense for a fixed asset may be changed because of a revision in the asset's originally estimated useful life. Usually, such revisions are not made unless the amount involved is material.

As an illustration of the problems created by the revision of estimated useful life, assume that a machine costing $30,000 was originally estimated to have a useful life of ten years and no salvage value. At the end of five years, it is ascertained that the machine still has ten years of useful life remaining: the machine has an overall useful life of fifteen years instead of ten. The company uses the straight-line method of depreciation. What action, if any, should be taken to adjust the financial statements for the excess depreciation taken during the first five years? What should the revised annual depreciation charge be for the next ten years?

Theoretically, $2,000 instead of $3,000 depreciation should have been expensed in each of the past five years. The past overstatement of this expense has understated net income each year by $1,000 and has produced a cumulative effect of a $5,000 understatement in retained earnings reinvested in the business. Similarly, assets are also understated by $5,000. As shown below, the property, plant and equipment section of the balance sheet at the end of the fifth year indicates that $15,000 of unrecovered cost remains to be depreciated, while the amount would be $20,000 if useful life had been correctly anticipated. In principle, the correction of this situation would require that retained earnings reinvested in the business be increased $5,000 by means of a special credit (or charge, if life should be shortened) on the current statement of income to adjust for the $1,000 understatement of net income each year for five years, and that the assets of the company be increased $5,000 by changing

	BASED UPON AN ESTIMATE OF	
	10-YEAR LIFE	15-YEAR LIFE
Machinery (at cost)	$30,000	$30,000
Less: Accumulated depreciation to date	15,000	10,000
Unrecovered cost	$15,000	$20,000

the amount shown for "Less: Accumulated depreciation to date" from $15,000 to $10,000. In this manner, unrecovered cost of $20,000 would be equitably allocated over the remaining ten years of life as an annual $2,000 charge against revenue.

In practice, a more realistic method is usually followed. By this method, the remaining unrecovered cost of $15,000 is divided by the revised estimated remaining life of ten years to derive a $1,500 annual depreciation charge against revenue. This procedure has the effect of ultimately having all costs and expenses reflected in operations on the statement of income. By either method, the full $30,000 of original cost will be allocated over fifteen years.

Accounting theorists are not in agreement about the proper procedure to be employed when a revision of estimated useful life is necessary. Many of their arguments center around sophisticated distinctions, as whether the error in establishing useful life was routine and mechanical or an error in judgment, and whether the events leading to a revision of life were of an unusual nature. Those in management should be aware of the effect of any revisions in estimated life upon the financial data which they employ in the guidance of the business.

Management should also be aware of the necessity of revising the estimated useful life of depreciable assets whenever conditions warrant such adjustments. Such periodic reviews may either increase or decrease estimated remaining life. For example, in 1959 Walt Disney Productions increased the remaining life of Disneyland from its life of seven years originally established in 1955 to ten years; in 1967 it was extended to twelve years. On the other hand, many companies have found it necessary to revise downward the estimated remaining life of many assets. A period of rapid technological changes produces more rapid obsolescence of certain depreciable assets than originally anticipated. In addition, certain depreciable assets like machinery may have their remaining useful life shortened by extraordinarily heavy usage (i.e., daily plant operations may increase from one to three eight-hour shifts). Management should consider possible complications with the Treasury Department when contemplating any redetermination of estimated remaining useful life of depreciable assets. Such contemplated revisions should be made only when the change in useful life is significant and there is a clear and convincing basis for the redetermination.

QUESTIONS AND PROBLEMS

6–1. Letter an answer sheet from a through f and then for each of the following expenditures, place a "C" if the item is a capital expenditure or if it can be capitalized; place an "R" only if the item is definitely a revenue (operating) expenditure.

a. The cost of a new battery and battery cables for the company's second-hand delivery truck purchased *two days ago.* The other cables were worn through in one spot and the battery (apparently original equipment) was worn out.

b. The cost of a new battery for a company auto used by salesmen. The company purchased the auto *two years ago* and depreciates it over four years; the original battery, now being replaced, wore out.

c. The cost to the University of Bellevue for putting in stone and concrete sidewalks where students had worn paths over the years across the *grass* lawn.

d. The cost to the University of Bellevue for *reseeding* portions of the lawn worn by student traffic, student recreational activities, and ROTC drills. The original cost of the lawn had been capitalized in "Land."

e. The cost of a set of basic medical *encyclopedias* needed in the office library of a doctor.

f. The cost of the *annual* one-year subscription to the American Medical Journal needed in the office library of a doctor.

6–2. Van Sickle Merchandising Company purchased a used delivery truck for $2,500. Prior to placing the truck in use, it sent the truck to the Butler Garage for overhauling and reconditioning. The itemized bill received from the Butler Garage disclosed:

Overhauling motor	$150
Reconditioning chassis	100
New delivery truck body	500
Two new tires to replace "bald" ones	70
Spotlight	30
Gasoline and oil	15
Anti-freeze (non-permanent)	10
State inspection sticker (semi-annual)	5
Total	$880

What portion of the $880 should be capitalized and what portion should be expensed? Prepare your answer in accord with accounting theory rather than company policy or tax considerations.

6–3. At December 31, 1974, the balance sheet of the Beulah Corporation disclosed:

Property, Plant and Equipment, at cost:		
Land	$ 500,000	
Buildings	2,000,000	
Machinery	700,000	
Automobiles (10 @ $4,000)	40,000	
Total	$3,240,000	
Accumulated Depreciation to date	1,000,000	
Unrecovered Cost		$2,240,000

During 1975, the following events affecting the various property, plant and equipment items occurred:

a. To increase its employee parking area, the corporation purchased adjacent land for $100,000 and a building on it for $50,000. It cost $3,000 to raze the building and $2,000 to level the land.

b. An air-conditioning unit was purchased and installed in each of the ten company automobiles, cost $500 each. The autos had never been air-conditioned.

c. Each automobile received its usual 10,000 mile tune-up and had new spark plugs and points installed at a cost of $15 each.

d. A piece of machinery (original cost $100,000) with an estimated life of 10 years was completely rebuilt at a cost of $40,000 during the eighth year (1975) of its life, extending its estimated useful life for seven more years from January 1, 1975. For this item, see the explanation of "CA" at the beginning and end of problem 6–4 and on page 167.

e. The buildings were painted at a cost of $25,000. The corporation's maintenance policy includes painting its buildings every fifth year. The corporation last painted them in 1970.

f. Depreciation expense (total) for the year as shown by the statement of income was $350,000.

Required

At December 31, 1975, the balance sheet of the Beulah Corporation would show:

Property, Plant and Equipment, at cost:		
Land	$	
Buildings		
Machinery		
Automobiles (10 autos)		
Total	$	
Accumulated Depreciation to date		
Unrecovered Cost		$

6–4. For each of the items below, you are to indicate the preferred accounting treatment. Letter your answer sheet from a through j, and opposite these letters place:

- "C" if the item is a capital expenditure and increases an asset.
- "CA" if the item is a capital expenditure but is chargeable against accumulated depreciation to date.
- "R" if the item is a revenue expenditure and increases an expense item on the statement of income.

a. The Talbot Co. spent $8,600 during the year for experimental purposes in connection with the development of its product. This is approximately the same amount that the company has been spending for this purpose annually for many years.

b. In April, the West Co. paid cash of $2,800 because a suit was lost in defense of a patent infringement case.

c. The Miller Co., plaintiff, paid $5,000 for legal fees in December, in connection with a successful infringement suit on its patent. No damages were awarded. (See page 252.)

d. The Placey Company recently purchased land and two buildings for a total cost of $35,000 and entered the purchase on the books. Razing costs of $1,200 were incurred in removing the smaller building, which had an appraised value at acquisition of $6,200, to make room for new construction.

e. On June 1, the Geneva Hotel installed a sprinkler system throughout the building at a cost of $13,000. As a result, the insurance rate was decreased by 40 percent.

f. A motor in one of Company B's trucks was overhauled at a cost of $600. It is expected that this will extend the life of the truck for two years.

g. An improvement, which extended the life but not the usefulness of the assets, cost $6,000.

h. Joe Donald and Frank Rice, maintenance repair men, spent five days in unloading and setting up a new $6,000 precision machine in the plant. The wages earned in this five-day period totaled $240.

i. The Edison Electric Utility Company recorded the first six months' interest on 6 percent, $100,000 ten-year bonds sold six months ago. The bonds were sold to finance the construction of a hydroelectric plant. Six months after the sale, the construction of the hydroelectric plant was completed and operations were begun.

j. The Hiway Supermarket Co. paid a special "tax" assessment. The special assessment provided funds for the construction of public streets in the area in which the market was located.

Note: This problem has been adapted from a problem on the Uniform CPA Examination.

"CA" represents a capital expenditure, but one that is chargeable against accumulated depreciation to date rather than shown as an addition to cost. This is a procedure often used when a major replacement of a component part or an improvement in effect "makes good" prior years' depreciation or extends life; e.g., a new roof installed on a ten-year-old brick kiln.

6–5. The Finance Committee of Unocheck Corporation is debating the proper treatment of a contemplated $300,000 renovation cost of its $1,000,000 25-year-old office building (new roof, new elevators, new front on first three floors, complete new plumbing and wiring, etc.). While the expenditure may lengthen the life of the building, it might also be viewed as either making good prior years' depreciation, or a property addition, or merely bringing the building back to its original condition. If the renovation is undertaken, paid for, and completed in December of the current year, show how the current year's estimated statements would be changed if the expenditure is:

STATEMENT OF INCOME		(1) AN ADDITION TO BUILDINGS	(2) A RESTORATION OF PRIOR DEPRECIATION	(3) A REVENUE EXPENDITURE
Net Sales	$10,000,000	$10,000,000	$10,000,000	$10,000,000
Costs and Expenses	7,000,000			
	$ 3,000,000	$	$	$

Income Tax (50%)	1,500,000			
Net Income	$ 1,500,000	$	$	$
Balance Sheet ...				
Current Assets ..	$ 8,000,000	$ 7,700,000	$ 7,700,000	$ 7,700,000
Building	$ 1,000,000	$	$	$
Accumul. Depreciation	—500,000			
	$ 500,000	$	$	$
Other Assets	3,000,000	3,000,000	3,000,000	3,000,000
	$11,500,000	$	$	$
Current Liabilities	$ 4,500,000	$	$	$
Stockholders' Equity	7,000,000			
	$11,500,000	$	$	$

Note: Ignore any possible depreciation on the $300,000.

Note: For the second alternative, see the explanation of "CA" at the beginning and end of problem 6–4 and on page 167.

6–6. The Roddy Manufacturing Corporation decided to construct a new plant on the outskirts of Erehwon, Ohio, and incurred the following expenditures:

Purchase price of land including an old farmhouse (Approximate apportionment of expenditure is $235,000 to land and $15,000 to house)		$ 250,000
Net cost of clearing land:		
Razing house	$1,000	
Less sale of scrap	200	
	$ 800	
Removing trees, stumps, brush	3,200	4,000
Leveling land (cut down small hill and filled ravine)		32,000
Cost of building (paid to contractor)		2,000,000
Cement driveways and walks		6,000
Fence around property		3,500
Landscaping (grass, trees, shrubbery, etc.) ...		4,500
Total		$2,300,000

Required

a. What portion of the $2,300,000 should be capitalized as the cost of the:

Land?
Land Improvements (attachments)?
Building?

b. Should any portion of the $2,300,000 be treated as an operating expenditure?

6–7. Letter an answer sheet from a through t and then for each of the following expenditures, place a "C" if the item is a capital expenditure or if it can be capitalized; place an "R" only if the item is definitely a revenue (operating) expenditure.

a. The cost of moving old machinery from several old plants to another much larger building and cost of reinstalling the machinery; object was to consolidate the company's operating activities.

b. Purchase and installation of an excellent quality vinyl-asbestos floor in the reception office of a steel company. The flooring covered a hardwood floor so badly worn that it couldn't be refinished.

c. Landscaping expenditures incurred in the construction of a shopping center.

d. Cost of installing a police signaling system by a jewelry store.

e. Repairs on the main office building of a steel company to the gutters which were damaged by a heavy snow storm.

f. Interest, during construction, on funds borrowed to finance new capital projects by Sacramento Municipal Utility District.

g. The cost of a new engine (motor) in the company's delivery truck.

h. Interest paid to MNBT Bank by ABC Department Store on funds borrowed to carry excess inventory needed during the fall-Christmas season.

BNP Bank purchased a membership in the Wildwood Country Club, to be used by officers of the bank in the bank's business:

i. The initiation fee of $300 and the required purchase of stock, $800, in the country club.

j. The monthly dues in the club.

k. Cost of a new battery for the salesman's auto; the old battery was ruined by neglect during a sub-zero cold wave.

l. Architect's fee for plans for a new office building just constructed.

m. Special tax assessment for prorata share of the cost of a sewer line, replacing septic tanks.

n. Painting the office building of the company; it had not been painted for seven years.

o. Annual termite inspection fee of $100 paid for inspection of the company's various buildings in Florida.

p. Firman Company purchased an ancient three-story building in the old French quarter of New Orleans. Though the architects retained by Firman Company recommended that the company demolish the building, permission could not be obtained from local authorities because of the historical and architectural value of the building. Therefore, the company expended $50,000 to place the building in condition so that it could again be used for revenue producing purposes.

q. Dental fees paid by an actor for necessary new bridgework to replace bridgework broken when he made a series of TV prize fight pictures.

r. Expenditure of $100, to State Department of Revenue, for license plates for delivery truck.

s. Title search on a tract of ground purchased as a building site.

t. Cost of tuition for a college program of study (for the typically successful, full time, day school candidate for a degree).

6–8. The depreciation policy and procedures of Willetts Manufacturing Company for its various types of depreciable assets (for both book and income tax purposes) are as follows:

a. For depreciable assets acquired prior to January 1, 1954:
   1. Straight-line depreciation for all buildings, machinery, equipment, and furniture and fixtures.

b. For depreciable assets acquired since January 1, 1954:
   1. Accelerated depreciation on new depreciable assets acquired with an estimated life of three years or more, as follows:
      (a) Declining balance (tax method) on all buildings.
      (b) Sum-of-the-years' digits method on all machinery, equipment (including trucks), and furniture and fixtures.
   2. Straight-line depreciation on used depreciable assets acquired; also on new depreciable assets which have an estimated life of less than three years.

c. For depreciable assets acquired since January 1, 1958:
   Same policy as for those acquired since January 1, 1954. The 20 percent initial depreciation allowance is *not* used. (See Chapter 7 for discussion of 20 percent initial depreciation allowance.)

d. In all cases, the company computes depreciation to the nearest full month. All amounts are rounded to the nearest dollar.

Required

Complete a depreciation schedule for selected depreciable assets of the Willetts Manufacturing Company by stating the following for each asset shown below:

a. Method of depreciation used.

b. Amount of accumulated depreciation to date, as of January 1, 1973.

c. Amount of depreciation expense for the year 1973.

ITEM	DATE ACQUIRED	COST	SALVAGE	LIFE (YEARS)
Brick factory building	Jan. 3, 1952	$305,000	$5,000	50
Machinery (lathe)	July 1, 1953	18,500	500	20
Machinery (drill press) ...	Jan. 2, 1967	36,800	800	8
Furniture and Fixtures	Jan. 2, 1968	20,000	500	10
Machinery—used	July 2, 1968	16,000	1,000	5
Office building	Jan. 2, 1969	500,000	-0-	50
Fixtures—used	Oct. 1, 1971	14,000	-0-	10
Plant building	Jan. 2, 1973	500,000	-0-	50
Machinery (lathe)	Jan. 2, 1973	74,000	2,000	8

Note: Problem 6–8 does not consider the Class Life Asset Depreciation Range system (effective in 1971).

6–9. ROC Corporation purchased a piece of new machinery on January 2, 1973. ROC Corporation is the original user of the machinery: cost $60,000; estimated salvage value $5,000; estimated useful life 10 years. (The corporation did *not* elect to use the 20 percent additional one-shot first-year depreciation allowance as discussed in Chapter 7 on this acquisition.) Compute the *1973 and 1974* expense for depreciation if ROC Corporation uses the:

a. Straight-line method

b. Declining balance method (tax method—twice straight-line rate)

c. Sum-of-the-year's digits method

6–10. Assume the information given in problem 6–9, except that the machinery purchased was second hand machinery.

Required

Compute the *maximum* allowed depreciation expense for both 1973 and 1974.

6–11. For each of the following statements, choose the best answer to each and indicate your choice on an answer sheet with the number 1, 2, or 3.

a. Depreciation accounting is the process of:
   1. revaluing the asset on the balance sheet as it wears out
   2. expensing the cost of the asset in a systematic manner as a charge against revenues so as to determine an accurate profit for the period
   3. providing for replacement of the asset when its useful life is ended

b. Accelerated depreciation, approved by the Revenue Act of 1954, was an attempt by Congress to:
   1. update generally accepted accounting principles
   2. "stimulate" the economy
   3. give recognition to a long established business practice with respect to depreciation methods used in business

c. The "guideline lives" are the result of:
   1. an Act of Congress
   2. a Treasury Department release
   3. a study by the American Institute of CPAs

d. Accelerated depreciation:
   1. usually expenses the total cost (less any salvage) of the asset in a shorter number of years than straight-line depreciation
   2. is available on all fixed assets, except land, acquired since January 1, 1954
   3. is not mandatory; straight-line depreciation may still be elected

6–12. Assume the following facts with respect to a new machine purchased by Fairbanks Manufacturing Company on January 2, 1973:

Cost:		
Invoice price	$110,000	
Transportation charges	2,000	
Installation charges	4,000	
Total cost of machine		$116,000
Estimated salvage value		$ 4,000
Estimated life:		
In years		Ten
In units-of-production		100,000

The company did not use the 20 percent depreciation allowance discussed in Chapter 7.

Required

Determine for each of the two years, 1973 and 1974, the depreciation expense per year by each of four methods. Units produced are: 10,000 in 1973; 20,000 in 1974. Present your answers in the form of the following chart (round to nearest dollar if necessary).

YEAR	STRAIGHT-LINE	UNITS-OF-PRODUCTION	SUM-OF-YEARS' DIGITS	DECLINING BALANCE (TAX METHOD)
1973				
1974				

6–13. Assume the following facts for a new machine purchased by Richmond Products, Incorporated, on January 2, 1973:

Cost:		
Invoice price	$22,500	
Transportation charges	500	
Installation charges	1,000	
Total cost of machine		$24,000
Estimated salvage value		$ 600
Estimated Life:		
In years		Three
In units-of-production		93,600

Required

Determine the depreciation expense per year for each of the three years and the accumulated depreciation at the end of the third year by each of the following methods:

a. Straight-line

b. Units-of-production

c. Sum-of-years' digits

d. Declining balance (tax method)

Notes: Units produced are: 30,000 in 1973, 32,000 in 1974, 31,600 in 1975. The company did not use the initial 20 percent depreciation allowance discussed in Chapter 7.

6–14. A new type of machinery, a generometer, was purchased by Whittier Company on January 1, 1970, at a cost of $31,000. It was estimated that the generometer would have an estimated useful life to the company of approximately ten years and salvage value of approximately $1,000. Because of the invention of a new high-speed and extremely efficient type of generometer which was recently developed and sold to Whittier's competitors, it became reasonably certain early in 1974 that, by the end of 1975, the old style generometer would have to be junked and replaced by the new style generometer and that salvage value would be negligible rather than $1,000. Such rapid obsolescence was not anticipated in estimating the useful life of Whittier's present generometer. Compute the depreciation expense for the year 1974, assuming that the company uses straight-line depreciation (and did not use the initial 20 percent depreciation allowance discussed in Chapter 7).

6–15. If not previously assigned, problem 4–3 may be used at this point.

7

Property, Plant and Equipment: Depreciation (continued)

DEPRECIATION AND DEFERRED INCOME TAXES

In the discussion in Chapter 6 concerning the selection of a depreciation method, it was stated that many companies use the straight-line method for financial reporting and adopt an accelerated method of depreciation for income tax purposes. This practice raises two problems: first, the alleviation of any possible distortion in financial reporting; and second, the extent to which the resulting deferred tax liability actually will become payable in future years. These two points will now be given necessary additional explanation.

The first problem concerns the distortion that might occur in financial reporting when the statement of income shows a smaller amount for depreciation expense than the tax return does, and when the statement also indicates a reduced expense for the year's federal income tax payments because of the excess depreciation deducted on the tax return. To alleviate such possible distortion, the AICPA's Committee on Accounting Procedure recommended that:

> There may be situations in which the declining-balance method is adopted for income-tax purposes but other appropriate methods are used for financial accounting purposes. In such cases, account-

> ing recognition should be given to deferred income taxes if the amounts thereof are material, except in those rare cases, such as are mentioned in paragraph 8, where there are special circumstances which may make such procedure inappropriate. The foregoing provision as to accounting recognition of deferred income taxes applies to a single asset, or to a group of assets which are expected to be retired from service at about the same time; in this case an excess of depreciation taken for income-tax purposes during the earlier years would be followed by the opposite condition in later years, and there would be a tax deferment for a definite period. It applies also to a group of assets consisting of numerous units which may be of differing lengths of life and which are expected to be continually replaced; in this case an excess of depreciation taken for income-tax purposes during the earlier years would be followed in later years by substantial equality between the annual depreciation for income-tax purposes and that for accounting purposes, and a tax deferment would be built up during the earlier years which would tend to remain relatively constant thereafter. It applies further to a gradually expanding plant; in this case an excess of depreciation taken for income-tax purposes may exist each year during the period of expansion in which event there would be a tax deferment which might increase as long as the period of expansion continued.[1]

This pronouncement gave formal recognition to interperiod tax allocation. However, alternative procedures for so doing were then used by different companies. As a result, in 1967 the Accounting Principles Board issued Opinion No. 11, "Accounting for Income Taxes." This opinion extended the principle of income tax allocation and prescribed that what is now known as the deferred method be used. This is the method used in the illustration which follows.

To illustrate the application and effect of the principle of interperiod tax allocation, assume the following facts covering the four-year period of 1973 through 1976 for the Static Corporation:

Sales, each year	$1,000,000
All expenses prior income taxes except depreciation on special lathes, each year	800,000

For ease of illustration, a federal corporate income tax rate of 50%.

---

[1] Accounting Research Bulletin No. 44, "Declining-Balance Depreciation," paragraph four, *Accounting Research and Terminology Bulletins, Final Edition*. Copyright 1961 by the American Institute of Certified Public Accountants, Inc.

Purchase in January 1973 of special lathes at a cost of $225,000, scrap value of $25,000, and life of four years. For depreciation of these lathes, the company has decided to use straight-line depreciation for financial reporting purposes and sum-of-years' digits depreciation for tax purposes. Thus depreciation charges will be:

	STRAIGHT-LINE DEPRECIATION ON FINANCIAL STATEMENTS	SUM-OF-YEARS' DIGITS DEPRECIATION ON TAX RETURN
1973	$ 50,000	$ 80,000
1974	50,000	60,000
1975	50,000	40,000
1976	50,000	20,000
	$200,000	$200,000

Except for depreciation on the special lathes, all items of income and expense are identical for financial reporting and tax purposes.

The accompanying illustrative segments of the condensed financial statements reflect the effect of these assumed facts over the four-year period.

Reference to the statements on p. 204 reveals that the actual income tax liability for 1973 is $60,000. However, if the straight-line depreciation used on the statement of income for financial reporting had also been used on the tax return, the tax would have been $75,000. Therefore, tax of $15,000 has been postponed or deferred until later years. This deferred income tax is shown on the balance sheet, often as a liability, following the current liabilities and any long-term debt, but prior to the stockholders' equity section.[2] To alleviate possible distortion in the reported profits shown by the statement of income, the provision for federal income tax expense is shown at an amount representing the tax that would have been incurred if the straight-line amount of depreciation shown by the statement of income had been deducted on the tax return. On most published statements of income, only the total $75,000 income tax provision or expense is shown, not the segregation into expense currently payable and expense payable at some indefinite future date.

In 1974, the deferred tax liability increases in a similar manner but by a smaller amount; namely, $5,000, which is equal to 50 percent (the

[2] Reference to pages 537 and 541 of Appendix A will reveal like treatment on the Consolidated Balance Sheets of Armstrong Cork Company and PPG Industries.

STATIC CORPORATION

(amounts in thousands of dollars)

Statement of Income

		1973		1974		1975		1976
Sales		$1,000		$1,000		$1,000		$1,000
Less all expenses except depreciation on special lathes		800		800		800		800
		$ 200		$ 200		$ 200		$ 200
Straight-line depreciation on special lathes		50		50		50		50
Net income prior tax		$ 150		$ 150		$ 150		$ 150
Provision for federal income tax	$60		$70		$80		$90	
Provision for deferred federal income tax	15	75	5	75	(5)	75	(15)	75
Net income for the year		$ 75		$ 75		$ 75		$ 75

Corporate Tax Return Calculation

	1973	1974	1975	1976
Sales less expenses (per above)	$200	$200	$200	$200
Sum-of-years' digits depreciation on special lathes	80	60	40	20
Taxable income	$120	$140	$160	$180
Corporate income tax, assuming 50% rate	$ 60	$ 70	$ 80	$ 90

Balance Sheet

	Dec. 31, 1973	Dec. 31, 1974	Dec. 31, 1975	Dec. 31, 1976
Liability section:				
Deferred federal income tax	$15	$20	$15	$ 0

assumed tax rate) of the excess of accelerated depreciation of $60,000 over straight-line depreciation of $50,000.

In 1975, the situation is reversed. Straight-line depreciation shown on the statement of income exceeds the amount for accelerated depreciation deducted on the tax return. Thus, a portion of the previously expensed but deferred tax liability becomes payable. The tax expense on the income statement is $75,000, but $80,000 is payable, $5,000 of which represents previously deferred income tax. By the end of 1976, the end of estimated useful life of the special lathes, the deferred tax liability has been eliminated.

The Static Corporation, over the four-year period, has paid the same amount of federal income taxes that it would if it had never used accelerated depreciation for taxes. Despite this apparent "breakeven" answer in overall tax payments, the company has received one definite benefit: by deferral of tax payments, it has had extra monies for three years to use in the business on which it should expect to earn a return. Unless there are extenuating circumstances, a company is practically forced to use accelerated depreciation, at least for taxes, to take advantage of this free use of money.

Furthermore, the situation illustrated has been for an absolutely static type of company. All other things have been held equal to simplify the illustration; no new equipment, for example, has been purchased for four years. This is unrealistic, since practically all businesses are constantly acquiring new depreciable assets. These new assets, as acquired, are similarly available for accelerated depreciation. This is the gist of the other problem raised in the preceding chapter, the long-run effect of accelerated depreciation. It is a matter of conjecture whether, in future years, the deferred tax liability actually will become payable. Barring a change in the tax code, it is possible that the majority of businesses will continue to acquire new depreciable assets in a quantity more than sufficient to offset the effect of decreasing accelerated depreciation deductions on older assets. For many companies, the deferred income tax payable amount, under long-term liabilities, has increased over the years to what now has become a very sizeable figure.

Rapid Amortization

Closely akin to the problems raised by accelerated depreciation are those arising from rapid amortization. During World War II, the Korean conflict, and for a period thereafter, certificates of necessity were issued by the government to permit those fixed assets certified as necessary for the war effort or national defense to be written off for tax purposes in 60 months. This special amortization privilege meant that these assets could be "depreciated" over a period much shorter than their probable useful life. Any portion of a facility not so certified would be eligible for only normal depreciation. For example, assume a plant building completed in early January, 1951, at cost of $10,000,000, on which a 75 percent certificate of necessity is obtained. Also assume that it has no salvage value and a normal estimated useful life of 40 years. Three-fourths of the building ($7,500,000) would be "amortized" over five years, and one-fourth would be "depreciated" over forty years. Thus, the total allocation to expense, at least for income taxes for the years 1951 through 1955, would amount to $1,562,500. But, for the next 35 years, 1956 through 1990, it would amount to only $62,500. Some companies have reflected rapid amortization on the financial statements in the same amount as that deducted for income taxes. Other companies have shown the equivalent of normal depreciation, $10,000,000 divided by 40 years ($250,000), on the financial statements while deducting on the tax return the amounts

YEAR	AMORTIZATION OF 75% OF BUILDING $7,500,000 ÷ 5 YEARS	DEPRECIATION OF 25% OF BUILDING $2,500,000 ÷ 40 YEARS	SUM OF YEARLY AMORTIZATION AND DEPRECIATION
1951	$1,500,000	$ 62,500	$ 1,562,500
1952	1,500,000	62,500	1,562,500
1953	1,500,000	62,500	1,562,500
1954	1,500,000	62,500	1,562,500
1955	1,500,000	62,500	1,562,500
1956	0	62,500	62,500
⋮	⋮	⋮	⋮
1990	0	62,500	62,500
	$7,500,000	$2,500,000	$10,000,000

shown in the last column of the above table. The American Institute of Certified Public Accountants, through its Committee on Accounting Procedure, attempted to bring some standardization into practice.[3]

[3] For details, see *Accounting Research Bulletin No. 27; Accounting Research Bulletin No. 43,* p. 76.

It is interesting to note that the term amortization, rather than depreciation, has been employed to denote the write-off of such tangible fixed assets as buildings, machinery, and equipment when these are covered by certificates of necessity.[4] Such practice conflicts with the usual usage of the term amortization which is ordinarily reserved to indicate the write-off of intangible fixed assets.

Though no new certificates of necessity have been issued since 1959, this discussion is pertinent for several reasons. First, the financial statements of many companies still show the effect of such rapid amortization. The 1960 annual report of Union Carbide Corporation contained the following note to the financial statements:

> The cost of facilities constructed by the Corporation under Certificates of Necessity issued by the United States Government is amortized for tax purposes over a period of 60 months from the date of completion and is charged against income over the same period. During the year 1960, such amortization amounted to $11,640,000, including normal depreciation of approximately $5,424,000. After the year 1960, the remaining amount to be amortized is approximately $8,109,000.

Reference to the 1960 annual report of PPG Industries would disclose that the company was still amortizing emergency facilities but that, unlike Union Carbide Corporation, charged to income only normal depreciation and established a deferred tax liability in a manner identical to that previously discussed in connection with accelerated depreciation. A second reason for a review of what at present may appear to be past history is to alert the reader to the possibility that a portion of the net fixed assets, cost less depreciation to date, of some companies may be somewhat understated owing to their rapid write-off for financial reporting purposes as well as for tax purposes. A third reason for a review of rapid amortization is to point out the weakness in any management policy decision which overemphasizes present tax consequences at the sacrifice of possible long-run effects. Consider the case of a company which received a certificate of necessity on a new facility near the close of World War II. For a short period, while income tax rates were exceedingly high because of the excess profits tax, the company benefited substantially from a tax standpoint owing to rapid amortization. But shortly after the close of the war, the repeal of the excess profits tax reduced the effective tax rate to only 38 percent. Continued rapid amortization at this tax rate pro-

---

[4] Even building site land is subject to rapid amortization if covered by a certificate of necessity.

duced a much smaller tax savings.[5] Then, just as the facility was fully amortized, the Korean conflict began in June of 1950. Regular tax rates quickly rose to 52 percent, and an excess profits tax was reimposed. The company now found itself at a distinct disadvantage, because little, if any, of the depreciable base of the World War II facility remained for write-off at a much greater tax savings. Moreover, the substantially reduced asset base provided an additional handicap when the company used this base to determine its excess profits. While managers must consider tax consequences in their planning, they should not attempt to outguess future tax changes at the sacrifice of sound planning. A fourth reason for the review is that the concept of rapid amortization recently has been resurrected and made applicable to four widely diverse types of property.

The Tax Reform Act, signed into law by President Nixon on December 30, 1969, contains three provisions for rapid amortization and one for rapid depreciation. First, rapid amortization over 60 months, instead of the regular depreciation allowance, may be elected for certified pollution control facilities placed in service between January 1, 1969, and December 31, 1974, on plants in operation before January 1, 1969. Second, rapid amortization over 60 months, instead of regular depreciation over the usual 14 year life, may be elected for new rolling stock of railroads placed in service between January 1, 1970, and December 31, 1974. Third, rapid amortization over 60 months, instead of regular depreciation allowance, may be elected for certified coal mine safety equipment placed in service between January 1, 1970, and December 31, 1974. And, fourth, within specified dollar limits, capital expenditures between July 25, 1969, and December 31, 1974, for the rehabilitation of slum and substandard housing rented to low or moderate income persons may be written off by rapid depreciation over five years using the straight-line method.

Initial Depreciation Allowance

A new concept of depreciation was introduced to United States businessmen by the Small Business Tax Revision Act of 1958. Though a discussion of the technical income tax provisions concerning depreciation is beyond the scope of this book, an appreciation of the basic factors is necessary to a proper evaluation of alternative courses of action and a correct interpretation of resulting financial facts. For these reasons and for a possible indication of the future course which income tax provisions

---

[5] Some companies availed themselves of the provision to abandon special amortization and to write off any unamortized balance by regular depreciation over remaining normal useful life.

concerning depreciation may take, an understanding of the additional first-year depreciation allowance is important. Though a part of the Small Business Act, the new provision applies to all businesses, large or small.

In addition to regular depreciation, straight-line or accelerated, this provision in the tax Code permits an initial 20 percent one-shot depreciation allowance in the year during which qualifying property is acquired. To be eligible for this allowance, the depreciable asset must be tangible personal property (i.e., machinery and equipment, not buildings) with a remaining useful life of at least six years at the date of acquisition. The tangible personal property may be either new or used. However, the application of the initial 20% allowance is limited to a maximum of $10,000 of such property acquired by a corporation in any one year. (It is possible for sole proprietorships and partnerships to receive slightly greater benefits than corporations.) The initial allowance is applied to $10,000 maximum of the cost of such assets, not cost less salvage value. The regular first-year depreciation is then computed on cost minus the 20 percent initial allowance (and minus salvage value unless the double declining balance depreciation method is used). Regular depreciation may be straight-line or accelerated depreciation if the property qualifies as new property; only straight-line depreciation may be employed if it is used property.

To illustrate this concept, assume that a corporation purchases a piece of new machinery in January for $45,000. The machine has an estimated useful life of ten years and a salvage value of $3,000. The company elects to use its maximum $10,000 annual amount available for the 20 percent initial allowance on this asset. Sum-of-the-years' digits depreciation is regularly employed by this company for this type of fixed asset. The depreciation expense for the first year would be $9,273, computed as follows:

Initial allowance, 20% of $10,000	$2,000
Sum-of-the-years' digits depreciation:	
$\frac{10}{55}$ of $40,000[6]	7,273
Depreciation expense for the year	$9,273

The obvious question at this point is why one should be so concerned with one tax provision which can at best increase the total depreciation expense of a corporation by $2,000 in any one year. The most important reason is the implication of things to come. The concept of an initial

[6] Cost of $45,000 minus $2,000 initial depreciation allowance minus $3,000 salvage value.

depreciation allowance, while new to United States businessmen, is established practice in certain other countries. For example, Great Britain and Canada permit a similar type of initial depreciation allowance with rates that are far more liberal in order to enable business to amortize a larger portion of the cost of the property more quickly; their varying rates are applicable to the *total* cost of the assets, not to a limited \$10,000 of total cost for all fixed assets acquired in any one year. The Congress of the United States has considered (but not passed) bills to liberalize the present initial depreciation allowance. Tax laws, once envisioned solely as a means of raising revenue, now appear to be taking on additional "duties." It is interesting to note that the last four federal income tax changes which liberalized depreciation allowances occurred during the "recession" years of 1954, 1958, 1962, and the "recovery" year of 1971. In 1954, an attempt was made to increase industrial activity through greater expenditures for *new* plant, equipment, and machinery. In 1958, an attempt was made to aid small businesses. In 1962, the new guideline lives were hailed by Secretary of the Treasury Dillon as "a major stimulus to our continued economic growth." Then, in January of 1971, these guideline lives were modified by the ADR System as discussed in Chapter 6. There is the possibility that, if such additional depreciation provisions like initial depreciation allowances of varying rates on different types of plant, machinery, and equipment should be adopted in the United States, such periodic revisions in the tax structure could greatly influence the flow of capital into or out of specific industries.

Credit for Investment in Certain Depreciable Property

The Revenue Act of 1962 introduced a new and far-reaching concept known as the 7 percent investment credit. The announced aim of the investment credit is to encourage modernization and expansion of productive facilities and thereby increase productivity and profitability. The amount of the credit is based upon new capital investment and in the form of a reduction in the income taxes otherwise payable.

During the past twelve years, the investment credit has been an on-again off-again provision and altered several times by Act of Congress. An awareness of these changes is believed desirable so that one may be knowledgeable about one of the methods that has been used in an attempt to fine-tune the economy and the possible impact that such changes have had over the years. These various changes will be presented later; the following discussion is based on the present status of the investment credit.

The application of this tax concept has had widespread effect on many management decisions, including the decisions to consider leasing buildings, but buying machinery and equipment; to determine when to buy and when to sell certain depreciable assets; to consider the acquisition of new assets instead of used ones; to contemplate, if reasonable, the assigning to newly acquired property a useful life of at least seven years; to study the advantages and disadvantages of capitalizing borderline items as a portion of the cost of certain newly acquired depreciable assets; and to weigh the different accounting methods for the investment credit because of the possible impact on net earnings for the year. The underlying reasons for the effect of the investment credit upon these decisions will be apparent from a short presentation of the salient points comprising this tax "benefit."

The investment credit is based upon the amount of certain new and used tangible depreciable property acquired during the year. Normally, all personal tangible property qualifies for the credit; e.g., machinery, equipment, trucks, and office furniture. Non-personal tangible property such as buildings does not qualify.

The credit is equal to 7 percent of the "qualified investment" made during the year. An investment is not fully qualified for the 7 percent credit unless it has a useful life of at least seven years. Thus, the effective percentage is less for assets with a shorter life, as follows:

IF USEFUL LIFE IS	THE APPLICABLE PERCENTAGE OF THE INVESTMENT WHICH QUALIFIED IS	WITH A RESULTANT EFFECTIVE INVESTMENT CREDIT OF
Less than 3 years	None	None
3 or 4 years	33⅓%	⅓ of 7% = 2⅓%
5 or 6 years	66⅔%	⅔ of 7% = 4⅔%
7 years or more	100 %	7%

These percentages apply to the *total* cost of all *new* eligible property acquired. But the maximum qualified investment in *used* eligible property acquired in any one year which is eligible for the credit is $50,000 (for most corporations; the limitation may be different for some other types of business entities).

To illustrate these considerations in determining the investment credit, assume that a cement manufacturing corporation acquired and placed into service the following six assets in 1973.

ASSET	YEARS OF LIFE	COST	APPLICABLE PERCENTAGE	QUALIFIED INVESTMENT
Special tools (new) . .	2	$ 25,000	(1) None	$ -0-
Tractor units, over-the-road (new)	4	60,000	33⅓%	20,000
Company airplane (new)	6	150,000	66⅔%	100,000
Machinery (new)	20	80,000	100 %	80,000
Machinery (used) . . .	10	80,000	(2) 100 %	50,000
Office building (new) .	45	500,000	(3) None	-0-
Total qualified investment				$250,000
				.07
Investment credit				$ 17,500

(1) Life less than 3 years
(2) Applicable only to $50,000 maximum on used assets
(3) Buildings not eligible for the credit

Several technical points must be mentioned about the investment credit of $17,500 for the sake of accuracy. First, the credit reduces the corporate tax liability that would otherwise be payable. Second, in general, the maximum credit allowed against the tax liability is the lesser of the amount of the actual tax liability itself, or $25,000 plus one-half of the tax liability in excess of $25,000. Third, any excess credit not used in a given year may be carried back or forward against tax liabilities of other years under certain conditions. Fourth, if any properties are prematurely disposed of (e.g., a ten-year life asset is sold after four years), a portion of the tax credit may have to be repaid. Fifth, the investment credit is not 7 percent but 4 percent on property acquired for use in a public utility business.

Among the various possibilities of accounting for the investment credit, the two methods which are predominant will be presented. One method regards the investment credit as simply a tax reduction in the current period when the assets are acquired (the "flow-through" method). The other method regards the credit as a benefit to be recognized prorata over the productive life of the assets acquired (the "deferral" method) rather than all in the year of acquisition. It should be remembered that the overall long-run effect will be identical regardless of which of the two procedures is used. However, the year to year effects will differ. To illustrate the two methods of financial reporting for the investment credit, assume the following for a given company:

1. New machinery with a class life of ten years is purchased in January, 1973, at a cost of $100,000. Salvage value is negligible.
2. Company uses straight-line depreciation method for both external financial reporting and income tax purposes. The company does not use the 20 percent initial depreciation allowance or ADR.
3. State corporate income taxes are not a factor.
4. Maximum amount of investment credit can be utilized as a reduction of the federal income tax liability. The company does not exceed the various limitations on the use of the investment credit.
5. The investment credit is $7,000 (7 percent × $100,000).
6. Annual depreciation expense is $10,000 ($100,000 ÷ 10) on the full cost of the new machinery.
7. Total 1973 depreciation expense is $300,000 ($290,000 on old assets + $10,000 on the new machinery).
8. $450,000 of the 1973 tax liability of $500,000 has been paid by December 31, 1973.
9. The company keeps this particular piece of machinery at least seven years and thus does not lose any portion of the maximum credit of 7 percent. In other words, none of the original $7,000 credit is "recaptured" by the government because of early disposition of the machinery.

The flow-through method, which views the investment credit as a tax reduction in the current period, results in the acquired machinery being reflected on the statement of financial position at its original full cost, $100,000, and annual depreciation expense, $10,000, based on this full cost as a charge against revenues on the statement of income. The $7,000 investment credit is reflected as a reduction in the current liability for federal income taxes payable as a result of the reduction of federal income tax expense of the year. This procedure results in the following statement presentation.

Balance Sheet

As of December 31, 1973

Property, Plant and Equipment:		Current Liabilities:	
(partial only)		Federal Income Taxes	
Machinery, at cost	$100,000	Payable ($50,000	
Less: Accumulated		less $7,000 credit)	$43,000
depreciation	10,000		
	$90,000		

Statement of Income

For Year Ended December 31, 1973

Net Sales	$10,000,000
Cost of Goods Sold	6,000,000
Gross Margin on Sales	$ 4,000,000
Operating Expenses (except Depreciation)	2,700,000
	$ 1,300,000
Depreciation ($290,000 + 10,000)	300,000
Net Income before Federal Income Taxes	$ 1,000,000
Federal Income Taxes of $500,000, less $7,000 credit	493,000
Net Income for the Year	$ 507,000

The deferral method, which views the investment credit as a benefit to be recognized prorata over the productive life of the acquired machinery, results in the asset being reflected in the statement of financial position at only $93,000 ($100,000 full cost less the $7,000 "discount" or government subsidy on purchase), and annual depreciation expense, $9,300 ($93,000 ÷ 10), based on this *net* cost as a charge against revenues on the statement of income.[7] The $7,000 investment credit is reflected as a reduction in the current liability for federal income taxes payable. However, federal income tax expense for the year is not reduced by the credit of $7,000; the expense remains at its original $500,000.[8] Thus, the net income for the year is $700 higher annually for ten years than it otherwise would be because of a charge of only $9,300 for depreciation expense instead of $10,000. This procedure results in the statement presentation on page 215.

Regardless of which of the two methods is used, the long-run effect, over ten years in this case, will be identical. The first method, which views the investment credit as a tax reduction in the year in which the asset is acquired, recognizes the full benefit in the first fiscal period. The second method, which views the investment credit as a reduction in the cost of the asset, recognizes the benefit prorata over the life of the acquired asset.

[7] Another method is to show machinery at $100,000 and a Deferred Investment Credit of $7,000; then write off depreciation at $10,000 annually while amortizing the investment credit as a reduction of income tax expense in the amount of $700 annually.

[8] Depreciation for tax purposes is still based on the full cost amount of $100,000.

Balance Sheet

As of December 31, 1973

Property, Plant and Equipment:		Current Liabilities:	
(partial only)		Federal Income Taxes	
Machinery, at cost	$100,000	Payable ($50,000	
Less: Credit	7,000	less $7,000 credit)	$43,000
	$ 93,000		
Less: Accumulated			
depreciation ...	9,300		
	$ 83,700		

Statement of Income

For Year Ended December 31, 1973

Net Sales	$10,000,000
Cost of Goods Sold	6,000,000
Gross Margin on Sales	$ 4,000,000
Operating Expenses (except Depreciation) ..	2,700,000
	$ 1,300,000
Depreciation ($290,000 + 9,300)	299,300
Net Income before Federal Income Taxes	$ 1,000,700
Federal Income Taxes	500,000
Net Income for the Year	$ 500,700

The difference in the timing of the tax benefit is illustrated by the following summary:

INVESTMENT CREDIT RECOGNIZED AS A BENEFIT:	1973	NEXT NINE YEARS	TEN-YEAR TOTAL
In year asset is acquired	$7,000	$ -0-	$7,000
Prorata over years of asset's life	700	6,300	7,000

Thus the investment credit has caused further diversification in the manner in which a given financial situation may be handled for reporting purposes. For example, Washington Steel Corporation uses the flow-through method as disclosed by the Notes to Financial Statements. Following is the explanatory excerpt from their 1972 Annual Report:

> The investment credit is accounted for by use of the flow-through method. Investment credit of $146,000 in 1972 was used to reduce the provision for federal income tax.

On the other hand, Briggs & Stratton Corporation uses the deferral method as disclosed by the Notes to Financial Statements. Following is the explanatory excerpt from their 1972 Annual Report:

> The Company has followed the deferral method of accounting for the Federal investment tax credit and the remaining unamortized credit of $953,368 at year end is being amortized over the life of the related assets. Amortization of $130,711 in 1972 and $138,446 in 1971 is reflected in the statement of income.

Evidence indicates that the majority of companies use the flow-through method.

As was stated earlier, the investment credit has been altered several times by Act of Congress. Initially, the provision for the investment credit (in the Revenue Act of 1962) required that the basis of the property be reduced by the amount of the credit. For example, *if* the $100,000 of new machinery in the previous illustration had been acquired in 1962 or 1963 (instead of 1973), the basis for depreciation would have been only $93,000; i.e., $100,000 minus 7 percent of $100,000. This meant that $7,000 less of depreciation could be expensed over the 10-year life of the machinery. Therefore, at an assumed 50 percent tax rate, subsequent income taxes would have been increased by $3,500 (50 percent × $7,000) during the 10 years. The long-run benefit was not a tax savings of $7,000, but only 50 percent of that amount, or $3,500. This is illustrated by the following summary:

	1962	NEXT NINE YEARS	TEN-YEAR TOTAL
Tax *reduction* because of credit	$7,000	$ -0-	$7,000
Tax *increase* because of reduced depreciation expense (50% × $700 smaller annual depreciation)	350	3,150	3,500
Tax savings	$6,650	($3,150)	$3,500

The provision for the investment credit in the Revenue Act of 1964 eliminated the requirement that the basis of the property must be reduced by the amount of the credit before depreciation is calculated. Thus, the long-run benefit starting with 1964 was the full amount of the credit and not one-half of it as just illustrated, *if* the asset was purchased on or after January 1, 1964. For example, the $100,000 of new machinery in the previous illustration, since it was acquired in 1973, has a basis for depreciation of the full $100,000. Therefore, the entire $7,000 credit is a tax savings.[9]

Then, the Investment Credit and Accelerated Depreciation Suspension Act, P. L. 89–800, signed by the President on November 8, 1966, suspended the 7 percent investment credit on property acquired or constructed during the period of October 10, 1966, through December 31, 1967. One of the aims of this provision was to discourage capital expenditures and thus decrease or restrain one of the inflationary pressures on the economy. There were certain minor exceptions to this provision, designed chiefly to benefit the small businessman. The investment credit was not "repealed"; rather it was to have been "suspended" for approximately 15 months. When the economy suddenly turned down, due to many factors, the suspension was quickly terminated, ahead of schedule, effective principally with property acquired after March 9, 1967.

Next, the 7 percent investment credit was repealed effective April 18, 1969, by the Tax Reform Act of 1969 signed into law on December 30, 1969. This move was one of several measures taken in an attempt to curb the inflationary aspects of the economy.

The Revenue Act of 1971, signed by the President on December 10, 1971, restored the 7 percent investment credit for equipment acquired, basically, after August 15, 1971. Also in determining the amount of the "qualified investment," the useful life brackets were shortened by one year. It is interesting to note that the Revenue Act of 1971 specifically states that, ". . . no taxpayer shall be required to use . . . any particular method of accounting for the credit. . . ." Thus the Act sanctions both the "flow-through" and "deferral" methods previously discussed, and, the Act goes on to state, ". . . taxpayer shall disclose, in any such report, the method of accounting for such credit used by him for purposes of such report. . . ." With the restoration of the investment credit, several minor changes were made (e.g., extension of the carryover period for unused credits under certain conditions; only a 4% credit instead of the previous 3% credit for eligible public utility property) which are beyond the scope of this book.

---

[9] The Revenue Act of 1964 also contained a provision for adding back to basis, for subsequent depreciation charges over remaining life, the tax credit reductions made to property acquired in 1962 and 1963.

POSSIBLE TRANSITION TO PRICE-LEVEL ADJUSTMENTS

All of the discussion to this point, both in the preceding chapter and in this chapter, has been based upon the concept of allocating the *cost* of fixed assets to operations as an expense of doing business. At times, it has been necessary to discuss certain facets of the problem which appear to deviate somewhat from this idea. In fact, there exists in the United States today a strong minority opinion favoring change in one of the basic conventions of accounting; namely, that the basis for depreciation, original cost, should be replaced by a basis which makes allowances for changes in the price level.

The concept of depreciation based on current costs rather than on actual original cost, though at present not generally accepted, might well become "generally accepted" in the future. In this connection, it is interesting to note the pattern of changes which have occurred in depreciation practices. Accelerated depreciation methods such as declining balance and sum-of-the-years' digits were commonplace in many European countries long before their general acceptance in the United States in 1954. Japan, Sweden, Britain, and a few other countries have long made considerable use of variations of initial depreciation allowances, the first limited application of which did not occur in the United States until 1958. And now, in countries where inflation has been somewhat severe, various methods of price-level depreciation have become effective.[10]

After approximately two decades of inflation, and notwithstanding a few recessions, there is need to question whether long-term assets should be depreciated on the basis of historical cost or whether depreciation amounts and the related assets should be adjusted to reflect changes in price levels. The discrepancy between replacement and historical cost exists because monetary units cease to be a reliable measure when prices are changing rapidly.

Effect of Changing Price Level on Property, Plant and Equipment

Approaching the problem first from the point of view of the balance sheet, how significant is the following information shown by the 1972 annual report of Bethlehem Steel Corporation?

Property, plant and equipment, at cost	$5,146,395,000
Less: Accumulated depreciation	3,015,881,000
Net	$2,130,514,000

[10] Some such countries are Italy, Formosa, Brazil, Argentina, and The Netherlands.

These amounts include assets and their accumulated depreciation to date in terms of all types of dollars. These figures might well include non-depreciable land acquired at the inception of the corporation in 1905; a building still in use which was acquired in 1935 when a dollar was worth $2.42; another building purchased in 1946 when the dollar was worth $1.60; machinery purchased in 1960 when a dollar was equal to $1.05; and equipment purchased in 1969 when the dollar was worth $0.94.[11] Bethlehem Steel Corporation has followed the generally accepted accounting principle of stating the property, plant and equipment items at historical cost less accumulated depreciation and amortization to date based upon those costs. Thus, the total figures are a conglomeration of all different types of past dollars.

The non-comparability of similar items is clearly illustrated by analyzing the following situation. A company constructed a brick building at a cost of $1,000,000 and put it into use on January 1, 1953; a second brick building, basically identical to the first was constructed at a cost of $2,000,000 and put into use on January 1, 1968. Each building, when constructed, had an estimated useful life of 40 years. Annual straight-line depreciation on the first building was $25,000, but was $50,000 on the identical second building. Thus, the property, plant and equipment section of the balance sheet as of December 31, 1972, would contain the following:

Building	$1,000,000	
Less: Accumulated depreciation		
to date ($25,000 × 20 years)	500,000	$ 500,000
Building	$2,000,000	
Less: Accumulated depreciation		
to date ($50,000 × 5 years)	250,000	1,750,000

This information is presented fairly in terms of historical cost. But because the statement contains dollars unadjusted for price-level changes, such information may be meaningless to the user of financial statements; or it may be misleading if he assumes that the second building is "worth" three and one-half times the first building. The confusion stemming from the non-comparability of reported financial data has been partially responsible for a decreasing usefulness of the traditional balance sheet to the point where it may be that the assets shown thereon represent only unabsorbed dissimilar costs not yet charged to operations.

---

[11] Based upon purchasing power of the dollar expressed in terms of reciprocals of the wholesale price index compiled by the Department of Labor, Bureau of Labor Statistics. Base year of 1967 equals 100.

One suggested method of alleviating the situation is to adjust the figures by an index number.[12] Of the various index numbers available, one possibility would be the Building Cost Index published weekly by *Engineering News-Record,* a McGraw-Hill, Inc. publication. Calculations based on these records, which use a base year of 1913, would indicate that setting January 1953 = 100, the index rose to 161 in January 1968 and 253 in December 1972. Expressed in current dollars, the amounts stated for the two buildings could be restated as follows on December 31, 1972:

Building	$2,530,000	
Less: Accumulated depreciation to date ($63,250 × 20 years)	1,265,000	1,265,000
Building	$3,142,857	
Less: Accumulated depreciation to date ($78,571 × 5 years)	392,855	2,750,002

The significance of these amounts is readily apparent because of the deliberate simplification in the original facts selected to illustrate the principle. The actual conversion of an item to current prices may be achieved by multiplying its original cost at date of acquisition by a fraction whose numerator is the current index number and whose denominator is the index number at the time of the asset's purchase. Accumulated depreciation to date is similarly converted by applying the fraction to accumulated depreciation based on the original cost.

The chief criticisms advanced against price-level adjustments to balance sheet amounts are definitely worthy of comment. One criticism is that if the basis of historical cost dollars is abandoned, no completely objective data remain as the basis for accounting, because any revaluations made or index numbers employed are estimates based upon judgment. Furthermore, such adjustments may be more misinterpreted by those using financial statements than are the present statements based

[12] No index number exists with which some weakness cannot be found. The two used in this portion of the chapter are used solely for illustrative purposes and not because *their* specific use is recommended. However, most similar type indexes move in like fashion. For example:

YEAR	CONSUMER PRICE INDEX 1957–59 = 100	GNP IMPLICIT PRICE DEFLATOR 1958 = 100
1941	51.3	47.2
1951	90.5	85.6
1961	104.2	104.6
1971	141.1	141.6

upon original cost. Another argument advanced against price-level adjustments is that the degree of inflation in this country is not sufficient to warrant such adjustments. One should not ignore the reverse situation which occurred during the depression of the 1930s when many assets purchased in the 1920s had to be written down, not up! In addition, how can management appraise past performance if accounting does not furnish financial information based upon past costs? Though portions of these opinions may be valid, they do not resolve the problem or provide much aid in the solution of a greater problem not yet discussed: the effect of price-level changes upon the statement of income.

Effect of Changing Price Level on the Statement of Income

As an introductory illustration of the effect of the changing value of the dollar upon reported profit, assume the following facts:

> In 1955, land is purchased at a cost of $10,000. The general price index is 100.
> In 1975, the land is sold for $20,000. The general price index is 200.

Using the historical cost convention for profit measurement results in an apparent profit of $10,000; however, there is no real profit, because the general price index has doubled. An additional complication could be added by assuming the existence of an index of land values of 100 in 1955 and 250 in 1975. If the land was sold for only $20,000, orthodox accounting would show a book profit of $10,000, whereas there is a $5,000 real loss in current dollars based on an index of land values; rather than a $10,000 profit, management may be responsible for a $5,000 loss.

Many accountants, economists, and businessmen argue persuasively that reported profits reflecting historical cost depreciation are grossly overstated and that, as a result, the consumption of productive capital is being taxed. This occurs, it is contended, because the failure to measure depreciation in present cost prevents matching current costs against current revenue in determining reported profits. Orthodox depreciation computed on original cost of assets acquired at prices substantially lower than those currently prevailing involves matching depreciation allowances computed in one monetary unit against current income expressed in another or less valuable unit. This leads to overstatement of profit and overpayment of income taxes; it may result in impairment of capital, inability to replace existing plant facilities, and the distribution of dividends from an income that is partially fictitious. These points are developed in the following illustration.

Illustrative Case

In the first column of the following statement of income, prepared in an orthodox manner in accordance with generally accepted accounting principles, the reported net income for the year is $100,000. Of this amount, 60 percent is distributed to stockholders by dividends, and 40 percent is plowed back into the business.

Statement of Income
For the Year 1974
(in thousands of dollars)

	Column One: Per Generally Accepted Accounting	Column Two: Per Price-level Depreciation
Net Sales	$1,000	$1,000
Less: Cost of Goods Sold	600	600
Gross Margin	$ 400	$ 400
Less: Selling and Administrative Expenses	150	150
	$ 250	$ 250
Less: Depreciation Expense	50	100
Net Income prior Income Taxes	$ 200	$ 150
Less: Income Taxes (50% rate)	100	100
Net Income for the Year	$ 100	$ 50
Disposition of Net Income for the Year:		
To stockholders (dividends)	$ 60	$ 60
To retained earnings	40	−10
	$ 100	$ 50

Depreciation expense is segregated from cost of goods sold and from selling and administrative expenses so that total depreciation expense of the year may be isolated for analysis. Inventories are priced on a LIFO basis, which results in an amount which closely approximates current costs for the cost of goods sold during the year. Thus, in both Column One and Column Two of the statement of income down to the item of depreciation expense, current or recent costs are fairly matched with current revenue: to this point, net income is measured in units of approximately equal purchasing power.

Reference to the contrasting statements of income presented in parallel columns above indicates different amounts for depreciation expense. Column One shows $50,000 of depreciation expense based on the historical acquisition cost of depreciable property, regardless of changing price levels, and is in accordance with generally accepted accounting principles. Column Two sets forth the depreciation expense at $100,000 to give effect to the changing value of the dollar; it is not in accordance with generally accepted accounting principles.[13] Many would argue that the $200,000 amount shown in Column One as the net income for the year prior to income taxes is not accurate as the statement no longer matches current costs with current revenue; the $50,000 of depreciation expense is based on past historical costs rather than current costs. On the other hand, the $150,000 amount shown in Column Two as net income for the year prior to income taxes does fairly present the results of operations, because current costs have been matched with current revenue; income determination is in units of approximately equal purchasing power. Basically, this is the same argument that is advanced to justify LIFO.[14] From a theoretical point of view, it is difficult not to embrace price-level depreciation for depreciable fixed assets when the LIFO concept is accepted for the pricing of goods.

On these statements of income, income taxes will approximate $100,000 in both cases, because price-level depreciation is not an allowable deduction for tax purposes. Therefore, Column One shows net income for the year of $100,000 and follows generally accepted accounting, while Column Two indicates net income of only $50,000. Since dividends of $60,000 have been distributed to shareholders during the year, the $40,000 of remaining "profits" is retained and reinvested in the business, as reflected by Column One. On the other hand, Column Two indicates that such dividend payments, out of a "real" profit of only $50,000, have impaired capital to the extent of $10,000. Thus, proponents of price-level depreciation maintain that depreciation on a basis of historical cost overstates profit and results in an effective tax rate in excess of 50 percent. In turn, this may cause an impairment of capital, an inability to replace existing plant facilities, and the payment of dividends from a dollar income that is partially fictitious.

The effect of recalculating depreciation on a current basis varies among industries. The percentage reduction in net income, when depreciation is adjusted to reflect changes in price levels, will be less in a company with a

---

[13] The arbitrary selection of a multiple of two for depreciation expense will be supported by comments in the next paragraphs.

[14] See Chapters 9 and 10; also brief references in Chapters 2 and 3.

preponderance of such short-lived depreciable fixed assets as the tools, dies, and patterns used by an automobile manufacturer than in a company owning a substantial amount of long-lived assets, such as a steel producer and a public utility. *Engineering News Record* shows that the Construction Cost Index rose from 100 in 1940 to 273 in 1955. Based upon this trend, it has been stated that

> Over the 15-year period the rate (of cost increase) was approximately 7 percent per annum compounded. . . . By using this 7 percent per annum figure, we can get an indication of the over-all inadequacy of depreciation on facilities which have a life of 25-years, and which have been bought in equal physical amounts each year. . . . In short, to recover purchasing power under these assumptions, our regular depreciation allowance needs to be multiplied by 2.15. . . . If the average life of facilities were ten years, instead of 25, the multiple of 2.15 would drop to 1.42. . . . If the life averaged only five years . . . the multiple would drop to 1.22. . . .[15]

It should be remembered that acceptance of depreciation computed on a current basis for income tax purposes would increase expenses and reduce reported profits, thus decreasing the income tax paid. This might necessitate increasing the general tax rates. Such a combination of factors, dependent upon amount of and variation in the average life of long-term assets, would affect various companies and industries differently. In turn, this could lead to a redistribution of the overall tax burden among such companies and industries.

Price-Level Depreciation (and other price level adjustments)

As of yet, there is no "official" sanction in the United States of price-level depreciation (or any other accounting price-level adjustments). The American Institute of Certified Public Accountants, through its Committee on Accounting Procedure, stated, back in 1953:

> It has been suggested in some quarters that the problem be met by increasing depreciation charges against current income. The committee does not believe that this is a satisfactory solution at this time. It believes that accounting and financial reporting for general use will best serve their purposes by adhering to the generally accepted concept of depreciation on cost, at least until the dollar is

---

[15] Benjamin F. Fairless, "Steel's Depreciation Problem," 64th general meeting of the American Iron and Steel Institute, May 24, 1956.

> stabilized at some level. An attempt to recognize current prices in providing depreciation, to be consistent, would require the serious step of formally recording appraised current values for all properties, and continuous and consistent depreciation charges based on the new values. Without such formal steps, there would be no objective standard by which to judge the propriety of the amounts of depreciation charges against current income, and the significance of recorded amounts of profit might be seriously impaired.[16]

The Securities and Exchange Commission, which has authority to police the financial reporting of a large segment of our economy attributable to business corporations, in 1948 and again in 1954 denied requests of registrants to reflect depreciation on replacement cost in financial statements filed with the Commission.[17]

The American Accounting Association, through its Committee on Concepts and Standards Underlying Corporate Financial Statements, has stated, with respect to the question of modification of financial statements:

> In periodic reports to stockholders, the primary financial statements, prepared by management and verified by an independent accountant, should, at the present stage of accounting development, continue to reflect historical dollar costs.
>
> There is reason for believing that knowledge of the effects of the changing value of the dollar upon financial position and operating results may be useful information, if a practical and substantially uniform method of measurement and disclosure can be developed.[18]

And, then with respect to methods of disclosure, stated:

> Management may properly include in periodic reports to stockholders comprehensive supplementary statements which present the effects of the fluctuation in the value of the dollar upon net income and upon financial position.
>
> Such supplementary statements should be internally consistent; the income statement and the balance sheet should both be ad-

---

[16] Accounting Research Bulletin No. 43, "Restatement and Revision of Accounting Research Bulletins," p. 68, *Accounting Research and Terminology Bulletins, Final Edition*. Copyright 1961 by the American Institute of Certified Public Accountants, Inc.

[17] Securities and Exchange Commission, 14th Annual Report, p. 111, and 20th Annual Report, p. 107.

[18] *Accounting Concepts and Standards Underlying Corporate Financial Statements, Supplementary Statement No. 2,* August 1951, American Accounting Association; reaffirmed in 1957 by the Committee.

> justed by the same procedures, so that the figures in such complementary statements are coordinate and have the same relative significance.[19]

The decade of the 1960s saw several significant moves in the direction of price-level adjustments on published financial statements. In addition to many excellent articles in the various professional journals, several significant studies were made on the subject of price-level adjustments, among which are those cited in the following four paragraphs.

In 1961, the Accounting Principles Board of the American Institute of CPAs authorized a research study concerning the potential effect of price-level adjustments on financial statements. The study was published in 1963 and recommended that supplementary financial statements should be presented by companies giving effect to changes in the general price level.[20] As shown later in this chapter by the illustrative statements of Indiana Telephone Corporation, historical dollar amounts are converted to general purchasing power dollars. Thus, for example, assets are stated at cost (in terms of general purchasing power) and *not* at "current value."

As a result of Accounting Research Study No. 6, *Reporting the Financial Effects of Price-Level Changes,* the Accounting Principles Board prepared a research draft of a proposed pronouncement which included an illustrative set of supplementary price-level statements. On the basis of this research draft, a field test was conducted on 18 companies which restated their financial statements by making general price-level adjustments. This field test, sponsored by the Accounting Principles Board, seems to confirm the viewpoint of Accounting Research Study No. 6. Following is the opening paragraph of the article by Paul Rosenfield (who is a project manager in the accounting research division of the American Institute of CPAs) describing the field test on the financial statements of the 18 companies:

> Eighteen companies recently participated in a field test of general price-level accounting and many of the participants were surprised with the results. In spite of the modest rate of inflation in the United States in recent years, differences between financial statement amounts before and after restatement for general price-level changes were significant for many of the companies. The differ-

---

[19] *Ibid.*

[20] American Institute of Certified Public Accountants, Inc., Accounting Research Study No. 6, *Reporting the Financial Effects of Price-Level Changes* (New York, 1963).

ences varied widely from company to company and even between years for the same company. Net income was a larger amount after restatement than before restatement for some companies and a smaller amount for others.[21]

In 1969, the Accounting Principles Board issued Statement No. 3, "Financial Statements Restated for General Price-Level Changes." In commenting on Statement No. 3, George C. Watt stated ". . . (Statement No. 3) . . . is commendable, for it represents standby capacity ready for either, at some subsequent date, mandatory supplemental disclosure or, in the event of runaway inflation, mandatory application in the preparation of the primary financial statements."[22] Statement No. 3, (an APB Statement, not an APB Opinion), 71 pages in length, suggests supplementary information (statements) restated for general price-level changes using the Gross National Product Implicit Price Deflator and "provides recommendations on how to prepare and present" such supplementary information.

It should be noted that *A Statement of Basic Accounting Theory,* published by the American Accounting Association in July, 1966 (prepared by a Committee to Prepare a Statement of Basic Accounting Theory), recommends that current cost financial statements be shown along with historical cost statements. Though not an "official" statement of the American Accounting Association, the publication of the *Statement* was approved by its Executive Committee.

None of the foregoing precludes any company from including in its reports paragraph explanations, graphs or tables, and supplementary schedules or statements to enhance the explanation of the effect of price-level changes. Many companies have done so.

Thus, depreciation based upon the historical cost of depreciable property, regardless of changing price levels, remains a generally accepted accounting principle in the United States. Such principles are resistant to change, and changes occasionally require a lengthy process of establishing substantial recognition of the need. Although the three organizations cited above exercise considerable leadership in striving for better methods of financial reporting, they do not have sole responsibility. Corporate financial statements are representations of the reporting corporation, and corporate management has the primary responsibility for its own statements.

---

[21] Paul Rosenfield, "Accounting for Inflation—A Field Test," *The Journal of Accountancy,* Volume 127, Number 6 (June, 1969), 45.

[22] George C. Watt, "Price-Level Accounting Americanized," *The Price Waterhouse Review,* Volume 14, Number 3 (Autumn, 1969), 50.

Most of the foregoing discussion has centered on price-level adjustments with respect to property, plant, equipment and the depreciation of it; that is the subject of this chapter and, for most companies, the dollar amounts involved are material. It should be emphasized that all relevant items on all financial statements should be similarly treated, not just property, plant, equipment and the depreciation of it; for example, on the Statement of Income of Indiana Telephone Corporation every item on that statement has been restated by the Gross National Product Implicit Price Deflator (see page 231 and Appendix A).

Possible Progression Toward Price-Level Depreciation

Next presented is a summary of references to, and present applications of, price-level depreciation in the financial statements and supplementary data used for external reporting. They indicate a possible movement, as yet of untested strength, toward price-level depreciation.

Shortly after the close of World War II, many companies were concerned with the inadequacy of depreciation allowances attributable to the rapid increase in costs then being experienced. United States Steel Corporation, in its annual report for 1947, attempted to give partial effect to increasing replacement costs by showing on the statement of income, in addition to regular depreciation expense, an amount of $26,300,000 titled "Added to Cover Replacement Cost." The next year, 1948, page 5 of the annual report of United States Steel Corporation contained the following statement:

> However, in view of the disagreement existing among accountants, both public and private, and the stated position of the American Institute of Accountants, which is supported by the Securities and Exchange Commission, that the only accepted accounting principle for determining depreciation is that which is related to the actual number of dollars spent for facilities, regardless of when or of what buying power, U.S. Steel has adopted a method of accelerated depreciation on cost instead of one based on purchasing power recovery.

Because of the unacceptability of a depreciation basis other than original cost, most companies have limited themselves to devices such as comments, graphs, and charts in their annual reports to reflect the effect of a changing price level. Typical is the following from the Financial Review portion of the 1952 annual report of Westinghouse Electric Corporation:

> Operating costs for 1952 included $21,836,000 for depreciation and amortization of facilities. This computation, conforming with generally accepted accounting practice and federal income tax regulations, is based on the original cost of facilities. However, because of the reduced purchasing power of the dollar, this amount of depreciation does not provide adequate funds for replacement of obsolete or worn-out facilities which were bought over a period of several decades. The annual amount of depreciation computed on the basis of current replacement costs of existing facilities and using present depreciation rates is estimated to be $29,580,000. This compares with depreciation actually allowed on such facilities of $21,836,000.

In the Financial Summary section of its 1960 annual report, United States Steel Corporation made the following statement:

> Under the tax code the depreciation allowable in the calculation of taxable income must be based on the prices often paid years ago —25 years or more in the case of United States Steel—for the items subject to depreciation. But amounts so determined cannot at today's inflated prices possibly have buying power equivalent to that originally expended and thus be sufficient to meet current needs if the enterprise is just to "stay even." The deficiency amount which should realistically be regarded as depreciation is thus treated as income and on that pretense over half of it taxed away. This is more than inimical to growth; it puts a tax on just keeping even.
>
> Illustrative of the seriousness of these matters are the facts of United States Steel. For the post-war years, 1946–1960, United States Steel's recorded wear and exhaustion—sometimes called depreciation—aggregated $2,872,000,000. Of this amount, $2,671,000,000 was deductible in determining taxable income. If, each year, depreciation had been sufficient to recover the appropriate *buying* power—not just the number—of dollars originally expended, the total would have been $4,276,000,000. The deficiency from this amount needed to stay even was $1,605,000,000, on which taxes were levied as though it were income.

In its 1972 report, immediately following the financial statements, Gulf States Utilities Company presented the following information:

> Value of Original Plant Dollars Declines
>
> The Company's utility facilities were constructed over a period of many years and consequently "Net Plant" as stated on the books

> represents the investment of dollars of widely different value. Because of this fact, the "Total plant less accumulated provision for depreciation" shown on the Balance Sheet on pages 14 and 15 of this report which is stated as "Original Cost" does not reflect the effect that the declining purchasing power of the dollar has had on the current valuation of the Company's property.
>
> The effect of such dollar depreciation on the Company can be illustrated by applying the Consumer Price Index, as published by the Bureau of Labor Statistics, to the original cost dollars shown as "Total plant less accumulated provision for depreciation." By doing this, the figure would become $1,420,180,000 which is $402,828,000 or 39.6 percent greater than the amount as shown on the Balance Sheet.
>
> The management will continue to strive for regulatory recognition of such decreases in the value of the dollar and the need for consideration of this factor in rate making.

Until recently, the only formal recognition given price-level problems in published financial statements was the very limited adoption of a method which involves earmarking a portion of retained earnings as an allocation for higher plant replacement costs. It is an attempt to place the reader of the financial statements on guard against the fact that a portion of retained earnings may be partially phantom in nature. Replacement of plant facilities is contemplated at higher price levels. Depreciation expense on the statement of income and fixed assets on the balance sheet are still shown at amounts based on historical cost.

In 1952, after four years of work on the problem of determining business income, a "Study Group on Business Income," composed of business executives, economists, labor leaders, government officials, lawyers, and accountants, released its deliberations. Approximately 70 percent of the 44 members recommended eventual determination of income in units of approximately equal purchasing power. One of the conclusions of the study group was:

> For the present it may well be that the primary statements of income should continue to be made on bases now commonly accepted. But corporations whose ownership is widely distributed should be encouraged to furnish information that will facilitate the determination of income measured in units of approximately equal purchasing power, and to provide such information wherever it is practicable to do so as part of the material upon which the independent accountant expresses his opinion.[23]

---

[23] American Institute of Certified Public Accountants, Inc., *Changing Concepts of Business Income* (New York: The Macmillan Company, 1952), p. 105. Copyright (1952) American Institute of Certified Public Accountants, Inc.

A step in this direction was taken by the Indiana Telephone Corporation beginning with its 1954 annual report, in which contrasting financial statements were presented in parallel columns. A minor portion of the financial statements is shown below to illustrate the publication of dual statements.

Statement of Income

Year 1972

	Column A Historical Cost	Column B Historical Cost Restated for Changes in Purchasing Power of Dollar
	⋮	⋮
Depreciation provision, Note 1(b)	$2,053,700	$2,620,440
	⋮	⋮
Net Income, Note 1(a)	$2,126,274	$1,798,597

Statement of Assets and Capital

December 31, 1972

	Column A Historical Cost	Column B Historical Cost Restated for Changes in Purchasing Power of Dollar
Telephone Plant, at original cost, Note 1(a):		
In service	$37,084,382	$47,050,796
Less: Accumulated depreciation	11,842,883	16,041,306
	25,241,499	31,009,490
Plant under construction	968,792	977,559
	26,210,291	31,987,049
	⋮	⋮
Total Investment in Telephone Business	$28,169,146	$33,759,371

Common Shareholders' Interest:		
Common stock, no par value, authorized 500,000 shares, issued 492,086 shares	4,251,785	6,678,779
Retained earnings (Note 4)	7,937,320	4,675,412
	12,189,105	11,354,191
Less: Treasury stock, 4,336 shares, at cost	(5,192)	(8,130)
Stock discount and expense	(76,267)	(123,194)
Total common shareholders' interest	12,107,646	11,222,867
Unrealized effects of price level changes, Note 1(a)	—	6,475,004
Total Investment in Telephone Business	$28,169,146	$33,759,371

Column A amounts are based upon generally accepted accounting principles. Column B figures are restated for changes in the purchasing power of the dollar. The conversion of the fixed assets (and a minor dollar amount of certain other assets) into current dollars, as shown by Column B of the balance sheet, causes an adjustment of stockholders' equity. While a presentation of this type is an obvious aid to a utility seeking a fair return on the fair value of its property, the statements also are a pioneering attempt to show the effect of the changing value of the dollar upon financial statements.[24] Because of the current interest in price-level adjustments, the complete financial statements of Indiana Telephone Corporation, the notes thereto, and the opinion of the independent public accountants are reproduced in full in Appendix A-3.

> Notes to Financial Statements (below is portion of Notes 1(a) and 1(b))
>
> (a) *Explanation of financial statements.* In the accompanying financial statements, costs measured by the dollars disbursed at the time of the expenditure are shown in "Column A—Historical Cost." In "Column B—Historical Cost Restated for Changes in Purchasing Power of Dollar" (where the amounts in A and B differ), these dollars of cost have been restated in terms of the price level at December 31, 1972, as measured by the Gross National Product Implicit Price Deflator. Since 1954, the Corporation has presented supplemental financial information recognizing the effect of the change in the purchasing power of the dollar relating to telephone plant and depreciation expense in the annual report to shareholders.

[24] The first comprehensive writing in this area is a book by Henry W. Sweeney, *Stabilized Accounting* (New York: Harper & Brothers, 1936).

In computing the amounts set forth in Column B of the accompanying financial statements, the Corporation has followed the methods set forth in Statement No. 3 released in June, 1969, by the Accounting Principles Board of the American Institute of Certified Public Accountants, except that, contrary to Statement No. 3, the effects of price level changes on long-term debt and preferred stock have been reflected as income in the year in which the debt and preferred stock are retired (as required by the specific instruments under which they were issued) and not refinanced. The Accounting Principles Board has tentatively taken the position that all such amounts should be taken into income in the year of price level change. In the opinion of the Corporation's management and of its independent public accountants, such tentative viewpoint of the Accounting Principles Board does not result in a proper determination of income for the period. "Unrealized Effects of Price Level Changes" recognizes the excess of adjustments on the Statement of Assets over the adjustments of Common Shareholders' Interest. (b) *Recovery of capital and return on capital.* Under the law of Indiana, the Corporation is entitled to recover the fair value of its property used and useful in public service by accruing depreciation based on the "fair value" thereof and is entitled to earn a fair return on such "fair value." The amount shown in Column B for telephone plant approximates the fair value of the property as determined based on the principles followed by the Public Service Commission of Indiana in an order dated September 1, 1967, authorizing the Corporation to increase its subscriber rates.

In the accompanying financial statements, Column A includes depreciation expense based on historical cost and Column B includes depreciation expense, as well as other expenses, on the basis of historical cost repriced in current dollars to reflect the changes in the purchasing power of the dollar. Also, the annual reports to the Indiana Commission are in the same basic form shown herein.

Few other U.S. companies in their published financial statements have taken a similar approach to reveal the effect of price-level depreciation (and other price-level adjustments) upon the results of their operations; several have made such adjustments on their statements used only for internal purposes.

The most significant proposal for the recognition of price-level adjustments (as of this writing, May 1973) in financial statements, is that for the United Kingdom and Ireland. Following is a summary of the proposal as presented in the "Executive News Briefs" by Arthur Andersen & Co.

The Accounting Standards Steering Committee (ASSC), which is responsible for the development of accounting standards in the

United Kingdom and Ireland, has released a proposed statement of standard accounting practice, *Accounting for Changes in the Purchasing Power of Money.*

The draft proposes that companies having shares quoted on a recognized stock exchange be required to present supplementary price-level adjusted financial statements to their shareholders in addition to basic unadjusted historical cost statements. It recommends that other companies also present such supplementary statements to their shareholders. The supplementary statements are to present the company's financial position at the end of its latest fiscal year, its results for that year and the comparative amounts for the preceding year. The draft specifies the use of a consumer price index.

The procedures recommended for effecting the adjustments to the data presented in the historical cost financial statements are similar in most respects to procedures recommended in Accounting Principles Board Statement No. 3 (1969), *Financial Statements Restated for General Price-Level Changes.* While APB Statement No. 3 has had little, if any, practical effect on practice in the United States, because its conclusions were recommendations that did not require adoption by any company, the boldness of the ASSC proposal in *requiring* supplemental price-level statements for listed companies is likely to affect financial reporting, not only in the United Kingdom and Ireland, but in other parts of the world as well. As the chairman of the ASSC notes in his foreword to the draft, "It is vital that managements and users of financial statements should appreciate the effect of inflation on for example, profits, price structures, dividend policy and cover, borrowing powers, demands for additional working capital, and the return on invested capital." The increasing rate of inflation in many countries in recent years brings a greater urgency to the need for data that indicate the effects of inflation.

Should this recommendation be adopted, the United Kingdom and Ireland will have taken a significant forward step in recognizing the effect of inflation. Adoption of this requirement in the United Kingdom and Ireland could lead in time to similar requirements in other countries, including the United States.[25]

Summary: Price-Level Depreciation

The argument concerning price-level depreciation is not settled; much information developed through research studies and various publications

[25] Arthur Andersen & Co., "Executive News Briefs," Vol. 1, No. 4, April 1973.

concerning the pros and cons of the situation is available for the person who wishes to pursue the subject further.[26]

It should be remembered that the objective price-level depreciation, like that of historical cost depreciation, is not founded upon the concept of replacement of tangible capital, but the recovery and maintenance of tangible capital; the amount recovered may be reinvested in anything or in nothing. Inflation cannot be cured by any form of accounting. The objective of price-level depreciation is to prevent the loss of capital through inflation by permitting the recovery of capital in an amount equal to the dollars of purchasing power originally invested in the facilities.

If management believes that the effect of price-level changes warrants the recasting of the financial information which it needs to control operations and to formulate certain business policies, such adjustments should be made. There is no requirement that internal financial reporting must follow generally accepted accounting principles. Financial reports using a constant (rather than a fluctuating) dollar may well aid management in comparing operating results of one plant with another and in comparing the operating results of a specific division today with its performance of some years ago. In some instances, such adjusted information may prove invaluable as an aid in the formulation of pricing policies and in decisions regarding capital expansion programs. Realistic dividend policies may be more equitably established, and the information could prove useful in labor-management discussions. Thus, although price-level depreciation is not valid for tax purposes or external financial reporting, it may be the method which best fulfills the chief purpose for which accounting exists, namely, as an aid to management.

QUESTIONS AND PROBLEMS

7–1. For each of the following statements, choose the best answer and indicate your choice on an answer sheet.

---

[26] Especially recommended are the following studies published by the American Accounting Association:

"Price Level Changes and Financial Statements, Case Studies of Four Companies," by Ralph C. Jones.

"Price Level Changes and Financial Statements, Basic Concepts and Methods," by Perry Mason.

"Effects of Price Level Changes on Business Income, Capital and Taxes," by Ralph C. Jones.

"A Statement of Basic Accounting Theory," by the American Accounting Association (1966).

Many current articles concerning price-level depreciation are available in the various business, financial, and accounting journals.

a. Price-level depreciation is:
   1. shown on 20 percent of United States published financial statements
   2. a tax gimmick
   3. an attempt to match current costs against current revenues and thus maintain capital investment intact

b. Increased depreciation expense to reflect current costs was first shown on the operating statement of:
   1. Indiana Telephone Company in 1955
   2. U.S. Steel Corporation in 1947

c. Any permission, by a change in the Revenue Act, to use price-level depreciation for income tax purposes would be least advantageous to:
   1. public utilities
   2. steel companies
   3. auto manufacturers

d. Wiggle Manufacturing Corporation's new lathe (problem 7–3) cost $31,000 more than the old one because of:
   1. price-level changes
   2. its being a better piece of machinery
   3. both 1 and 2

e. A majority of accountants believe that any company using price-level depreciation for external reporting:
   1. should write up fixed assets
   2. should show that long-term debt will be paid off in cheaper dollars
   3. is not following generally accepted accounting principles

f. Price-level depreciation is somewhat similar to LIFO in its effect on the:
   1. Statement of Income
   2. Balance Sheet
   3. income taxes

g. The suspension of the investment credit from October, 1966, to March, 1967, was accompanied by the suspension of accelerated depreciation on buildings.
   1. True
   2. False

h. Coats Manufacturing Company in 1973 purchased a brand new office building to expand its operations. Which of the following provisions apply to the $700,000 cost of the building:
   1. 20 percent initial one-shot depreciation
   2. 7 percent investment credit (on all or part)
   3. accelerated depreciation (DB at 150 percent of S-L rate)
   4. accelerated depreciation (SYD)

5. all of the above
6. 1 and 2
7. 1 and 3
8. 2 and 3
9. 1, 2, and 3
10. 1, 2, and 3 or 4
11. 3 or 4
12. none of the above

7–2. If the company in problem 6–12 uses straight-line depreciation for its financial statements and double declining balance depreciation for tax purposes, what will be the approximate dollar amount of its deferred income tax liability on the Balance Sheet prepared at *December 31, 1974?* Assume a 50 percent tax rate and no other facts.

7–3. The Harrison City plant of Wiggle Manufacturing Corporation is preparing the next issue of its local house organ (company newspaper for employees). Among the usual news items, the company plans a very short educational story for its employees to be titled, "Why 'Depreciation Dollars' Don't Go Far Enough." The article will be supplemented by pictures of two turret lathes. The planned textual draft of the article, submitted to company headquarters for approval, is as follows:

> In 1957, the Harrison City plant bought a turret lathe (picture above) for $8,000. Last year, 1973, when it came time to replace this lathe, the plant had $8,000 (set aside in depreciation allowances) and $200 from the sale of the old lathe. But the cost of the new lathe (picture below), same model, was $21,000. With attachments needed to do more advanced work, total cost was $39,000. The added $31,000 had to come from only one place—our profits. At Wiggle's rate of profit last year, it would take nearly a million dollars in sales to make enough profit to replace one lathe that keeps one employee per shift on the job. "Depreciation" just isn't enough.

Required

Criticize the script.

7–4. H. C. Carlson Corporation purchased a piece of machinery on January 2, 1973, at a cost of $15,000. Estimated useful life is eight years and estimated salvage value is $400. The machinery purchased was new, not used. The corporation *did* elect to use the total annual $10,000 amount allowed for 20 percent initial one-shot depreciation on this particular acquisition.

Required

Compute the *maximum* allowable depreciation expense for 1973. The company wishes to "recover" the investment in this new machine as quickly as possible.

7–5. Assume the information given in problem 6–9 except that:

a. The machinery purchased was second-hand used machinery.

b. The corporation *did* elect to use the total annual $10,000 amount allowed for 20 percent initial one-shot depreciation on this particular acquisition.

Required

Compute the *maximum* allowable depreciation expense for both 1973 and 1974.

7–6. Based upon your study of the annual report of Indiana Telephone Corporation (reproduced in Appendix), which shows price-level adjustments in the financial statements, answer each of the following by inserting check marks at *all* the proper places:

Fixed Assets are shown at:
- Cost less accumulated depreciation .... ________
- Cost of property repriced in current dollars less accumulated depreciation to date on current dollar basis .... ________

Long-term Debt is shown:
- In the traditional manner .... ________
- At an adjusted amount to reflect the fact that "good" dollars were borrowed and the debt will be repaid in "cheap" dollars .... ________

Net Income for the year, as shown by the Statements of Income, reflects depreciation expense:
- Based upon original historical cost .... ________
- Based upon current price levels .... ________

7–7. Assume that Flamingo Corporation, a manufacturer of electrical household appliances, acquired the following fixed assets on January 3, 1973:

	COST	ESTIMATED SALVAGE
New items:		
Automobiles	$ 20,000	$ 3,000
Light general purpose trucks	30,000	5,000
Heavy general purpose trucks	60,000	7,000
Office furniture, fixtures, equipment, and office machines	50,000	2,000
Machinery, equipment, dies, jigs..	400,000	15,000
Office building	1,000,000	-0-

Used items:		
Office machines; estimated useful life remaining is five years	60,000	-0-
	$1,620,000	

Required

a. Prepare and complete a columnar schedule containing the following column headings:

   1. Item (list the seven acquired fixed assets)
   2. Cost
   3. Guideline Group and Class
   4. Life (years) (per Revenue Procedure 62–21)
   5. Eligibility for 20 percent Initial Depreciation
   6. Estimated Salvage
   7. First Year Depreciation Choices:
      7a. Straight-line
      7b. Sum-of-Years' Digits
      7c. Declining Balance (Tax Method)

   Column 5 should be filled in with the word "Yes" or "No" for each of the seven fixed assets acquired. *Select* the machinery and equipment for the 20 percent initial allowance.

   In columns 7a, 7b, and 7c, compute the 1973 depreciation expense for each of the seven fixed assets by every method allowable for the particular asset. For any item where the arithmetic becomes involved, show only the arithmetic equation by which the amount would be computed.

b. If the Asset Depreciation Range (ADR) system (effective January 1, 1971; see discussion in Chapter 6, page 174) had been elected to modify the guideline lives listed in column 4 for requirement a, what are the *shortest* lives over which each of the seven assets could have been depreciated? (Note: Years should be rounded to the nearest half year.) Would the adoption of ADR have changed the depreciation *method* used on any of the seven depreciable assets?

7–8. Go back to problem 7–7 and add to your columnar schedule the following three additional column headings:

   8. Determination of Investment Credit:
      8a. Amount eligible
      8b. Applicable percentage
      8c. Qualified investment

   Only the data in columns 1, 2, and 4 is necessary to complete these additional columns.

Total column 8c and multiply by 7 percent to determine the investment credit.

7–9. The comments below are from a footnote supplementing Justice Jackson's separate opinion in a Supreme Court case, Power Comm'n vs. Hope Gas Co. (1944), 320 U.S. 591.

> "To make a fetish of mere accounting is to shield from examination the deeper causes, forces, movements, and conditions which should govern rates. Even as a recording of current transactions, bookkeeping is hardly an exact science. As a representation of the condition and trend of a business, it uses symbols of certainty to express values that actually are in constant flux. It may be said that in commercial or investment banking or any business extending credit, success depends on knowing what not to believe in accounting. Few concerns go into bankruptcy or reorganization whose books do not show them solvent and often even profitable. If one cannot rely on accountancy accurately to disclose past or current conditions of a business, the fallacy of using it as a sole guide to future price policy ought to be apparent. However, our quest for certitude is so ardent that we pay an irrational reverence to a technique which uses symbols of certainty, even though experience again and again warns us that they are delusive. Few writers have ventured to challenge this American idolatry, but see Hamilton, Cost as a Standard for Price, 4 Law and Contemporary Problems 321, 323–25.***"

Required

Give your recommendations to alleviate the causes which create situations of the type portrayed in the above comments of Justice Jackson.

7–10. The Wabash Corporation purchased a brand new piece of machinery on January 2, 1973; cost $87,500; estimated salvage value $4,500; estimated useful life 9 years. The 20 percent one-shot initial depreciation allowance for the year is used on this acquisition. Compute, for 1973, the *total* depreciation expense (*include* one-shot amount), by:

a. straight-line

b. sum-of-years' digits

c. declining balance (tax method)

7–11. The Canyon Corporation purchased a brand new piece of machinery on January 2, 1973; cost $100,000; estimated salvage value $3,000; estimated useful life 10 years. The 20 percent one-shot initial depreciation allowance for the year is used on this acquisition. Compute, for 1973, the *total* depreciation expense, by:

a. straight-line

b. sum-of-years' digits

c. declining balance (tax method)

7–12. If the machinery in problem 7–11 had been *used* machinery, what would have been the *maximum* depreciation permitted in 1973 for "generally accepted accounting" and "income tax" purposes (same amount for both).

7–13. Assume that the Whittier Construction Corporation acquired the following fixed assets on January 3, 1973.

	COST	ESTIMATED SALVAGE	LIFE (YEARS)
New, Unused:			
Office furniture and fixtures	$ 50,000	$ 2,000	10
Machinery—all purpose	100,000	5,000	10
Office building	400,000	-0-	45
Equipment and Machinery .	200,000	20,000	15
Used, Second-Hand:			
Equipment and tools	100,000	-0-	10

Required

Compute the amount of the investment credit. (The Company had an income tax expense for the year of $1,000,000.)

7–14. Skadden, Inc., a retailer, was organized during 1966. Skadden's management has decided to supplement its December 31, 1969, historical dollar financial statements with general price-level financial statements. The following general ledger trial balance (historical dollar) and additional information have been furnished.

1. Monetary assets (cash and receivables) exceeded monetary liabilities (accounts payable and bonds payable) by $445,000 at December 31, 1968. The amounts of monetary items are fixed in terms of numbers of dollars regardless of changes in specific prices or in the general price-level.
2. Purchases ($1,840,000 in 1969) and sales are made uniformly throughout the year.
3. Depreciation is computed on a straight-line basis, with a full year's depreciation being taken in the year of acquisition and none in the year of retirement. The depreciation rate is 10 percent and no salvage value is anticipated. Acquisitions and retirements have been made fairly evenly over each year and the retirements in 1969 consisted of assets purchased during 1967 which were scrapped. An analysis of the equipment account reveals the following:

YEAR	BEGINNING BALANCE	ADDITIONS	RETIREMENTS	ENDING BALANCE
1967	—	$550,000	—	$550,000
1968	$550,000	10,000	—	560,000
1969	560,000	150,000	$60,000	650,000

4. The bonds were issued in 1967 and the marketable securities were purchased fairly evenly over 1969. Other operating expenses and interest are assumed to be incurred evenly throughout the year.
5. Assume that Gross National Product Implicit Price Deflators (1958 = 100) were as follows:

ANNUAL AVERAGES		INDEX	CONVERSION FACTORS (1969 4TH QTR. = 1.000)
1966		113.9	1.128
1967		116.8	1.100
1968		121.8	1.055
1969		126.7	1.014
QUARTERLY AVERAGES			
1968	4th	123.5	1.040
1969	1st	124.9	1.029
	2nd	126.1	1.019
	3rd	127.3	1.009
	4th	128.5	1.000

SKADDEN, INC.
Trial Balance
December 31, 1969

	Debit	Credit
Cash and receivables (net)	$ 540,000	$
Marketable securities (common stock)	400,000	
Inventory	440,000	
Equipment	650,000	
Equipment—Accumulated depreciation		164,000
Accounts payable		300,000
6% First mortgage bonds, due 1987		500,000
Common stock, $10 par		1,000,000
Retained earnings, December 31, 1968	46,000	
Sales		1,900,000
Cost of sales	1,508,000	
Depreciation	65,000	
Other operating expenses and interest	215,000	
	$3,864,000	$3,864,000

Required

a. Prepare a schedule to convert the Equipment account balance at December 31, 1969, from historical cost to general price-level adjusted dollars.

b. Prepare a schedule to analyze in historical dollars the Equipment—Accumulated Depreciation account for the year 1969.

c. Prepare a schedule to analyze in general price-level dollars the Equipment—Accumulated Depreciation account for the year 1969.

d. Prepare a schedule to compute Skadden, Inc.'s general price-level gain or loss on its net holdings of monetary assets for 1969 (ignore income tax implications). The schedule should give consideration to appropriate items on or related to the balance sheet and the income statement.
(Uniform CPA Examination problem)

7–15. There has been a good deal of criticism of the traditional "historical" cost records and the data which they reflect, especially during times of inflation or deflation. In order to assist in the interpretation of accounting reports as normally prepared, many accountants have suggested that the recorded cost data be first utilized in the preparation of the conventional financial statements, and then, as a supplementary technique, these statements be converted into dollars having a uniform purchasing power through the application of price indexes to the recorded dollar amounts. There has been some considerable difference of opinion among these accountants as to whether to use a "general" price index, such as the wholesale commodity price index, or the cost of living index, or, on the other hand, to use a more "specific" price index that is more applicable to the industry involved, or to the particular items being converted (for instance, using a construction index for the conversion of plant and equipment items, or using a special price index constructed for a specific industry).

Required

Give arguments for and against each of these two types of indexes. (Uniform C.P.A. Examination problem.)

8

Property, Plant and Equipment: Depletion, Amortization, Disposal of Fixed Assets

DEPLETION

Depletion is the term employed to describe the write-off or amortization of fixed assets characterized as natural resources. As timber or coal, oil, ore, and other mineral deposits are removed or extracted from their natural position, the costs applicable to the removed portion of these natural resources, often called wasting assets, are expensed against revenue of the period. Depletion and depreciation are similar in that both refer to the systematic process of allocating the cost, less salvage value, of tangible fixed assets over their estimated useful life as charges against revenues of the periods benefited by such assets. Depletion and depreciation differ in that depletion is primarily related to the physical removal or diminution of a fixed asset, while depreciation is not ordinarily related to an actual reduction of the physical properties of a fixed asset.

Depletion expense is customarily determined in the same manner that depreciation expense is calculated under the unit of production method. For illustrative purposes, assume that in January, 1973, the Berkeley Oil

Corporation purchases oil lands in a single tract at a cost of $15,300,000.[1] It is estimated that the residual value, or surface rights, of the land is $300,000. Recoverable oil reserves are estimated to be 50,000,000 barrels. Therefore, the "unit" (per barrel) depletion charge is determined as follows:

$$\text{Unit depletion charge} = \frac{\text{Cost of natural resource} - \text{residual value}}{\text{Recoverable reserves}}$$

$$\text{Unit depletion charge} = \frac{\$15{,}300{,}000 - \$300{,}000}{50{,}000{,}000 \text{ barrels}}$$

$$\text{Unit depletion charge} = 30¢ \text{ per barrel of oil}$$

If 2,000,000 barrels of oil are extracted and sold in 1973, the depletion expense for the year will be determined as follows:

$$\text{Depletion expense} = \text{Unit depletion charge} \times \text{number of barrels recovered}$$
$$\text{Depletion expense} = 30¢ \times 2{,}000{,}000 \text{ barrels}$$
$$\text{Depletion expense} = \$600{,}000$$

In future years the unit depletion charge must be revised if a material change occurs in any of the factors employed in the original determination. For example, a material change in the estimated quantity of recoverable reserves would require an adjustment in the unit depletion charge.

As of December 31, 1973, the fixed assets section of the balance sheet should contain the following explanation:

Property, Plant and Equipment (on the basis of cost):		
Oil Properties	$15,300,000	
Less: Accumulated depletion to date	600,000	$14,700,000
Plant and Equipment	$........	
Less: Accumulated depreciation to date	......	....
Net Property, Plant and Equipment		$........

A complete statement of income for the year is presented next. The $600,000 depletion expense shown is the allowance previously computed and is based upon *cost* factors. However, the $425,500 amount for federal income taxes is not based upon the $1,200,000 net income figure shown on the operating statement. This is attributable to the special provision in the federal income tax code which provides for a percentage depletion allowance to the owner of an economic interest in a natural resource.

---

[1] For simplification of the illustration which follows, it has been assumed that the company purchases the oil lands. More frequently, natural resources like oil deposits are acquired for development through leasing.

BERKELEY OIL CORPORATION
Statement of Income
For the Year Ended December 31, 1973

Net Sales		$5,000,000
Less:		
Cost of Goods Sold, Selling, Administrative and General Expenses	$2,850,000	
Intangible Drilling Costs	200,000	
Exploration and Development Expenses	50,000	
Depreciation Expense	100,000	
Depletion Expense	600,000	3,800,000
Net Income before Federal Income Taxes		$1,200,000
Less: Federal Income Taxes		425,500
Net Income for the Year		$ 774,500

While a detailed discussion of the income tax factors applicable to depletion is definitely beyond the scope of this book, recognition of the highlights of this tax provision will provide a better understanding of the related accounting practices.

A brief historical review of federal income tax provisions affecting depletion discloses a constant liberalization in the amount of depletion allowed as a tax deduction. The Revenue Act of 1913 limited depletion, based upon the cost of the natural resource, to 5 percent of gross income. World War I caused depletion to become a congressional favorite. Congress fostered the discovery and development of underground natural resources by the introduction of the discovery value method of depletion for mines, oil, and gas. Then, the Revenue Act of 1926 introduced percentage depletion on oil and gas by providing for a depletion deduction of 27½ percent of gross income (changed to 22 percent in late 1969), with a maximum limitation of not more than 50 percent of taxable income of the taxpayer computed without the allowance for depletion, but in no case less than if computed on cost. In 1932, Congress introduced percentage depletion on mines at varying rates for different minerals and eliminated the discovery value method for those mines permitted to use the percentage method. Between 1932 and 1954, periodic revenue acts passed by Congress extended percentage depletion to additional natural resources and further reduced the application of the discovery value method as a basis of depletion. In addition, the percentage rates were increased for many minerals. The Code of 1954 extended percentage depletion to practically all natural resources and completely eliminated the discovery value method of depletion from the tax code. The Tax Reform Act of 1969 reduced some of the percentage depletion rates. Today, the depletion allowance or deduction for federal income taxes is the greater of the:

1. Cost method
2. Percentage method (percentage of the gross income from the producing property). However, the percentage depletion allowance must be limited to 50 percent of the taxable income computed with the depletion allowance excluded.

At present, percentage depletion rates are applicable to over one hundred natural resources and minerals. Some illustrative rates are:

22%	......	oil and gas, sulphur, uranium.
22%	......	if from deposits in the U.S.: asbestos, bauxite, mica, cobalt, lead, manganese, nickel, zinc, etc.
15%	......	if from deposits in the U.S.: gold, silver, copper, iron ore.
14%	......	ball, china, and sagger clay; refractory clay, borax, potash, granite, limestone, etc.
10%	......	coal, sodium chloride, lignite, etc.
7½%	......	clay and shale, if used or sold for use in manufacture of sewer pipe or brick.
5%	......	gravel, peat, sand, etc.

Since 1926, when the principle of percentage depletion was first established, volumes have been written on the pros and cons of the subject; often the factual economic considerations are confused by political considerations. The usual justification for different depletion percentages is the varying degrees of risk involved in locating and extracting the different types of natural resources and the relative importance of the different resources to the national defense and welfare.

By continuing with the Berkeley Oil Corporation illustration used previously in this discussion, the federal income tax allowance for depletion expense can be determined. To stress the principles involved in the tax calculations, assume that the item of income and all of the expenses—except depletion—shown on the preceding statement of income are identical for company accounting and for taxes. Similarly, assume that the net sales amount ($5,000,000) agrees with the defintion of gross income as prescribed by the tax regulations; namely, the amount for which the company sells the oil in the immediate vicinity of the well.

Cost depletion, as previously determined, amounted to $600,000. The unit depletion charge of 30¢ was multiplied by the number of barrels of oil extracted and sold. The percentage depletion allowance is .22 times the gross income of $5,000,000 derived from the property, or $1,100,000. For tax purposes, the greater of cost depletion or percentage depletion must be used in any given year. However, in the case of Berkeley Oil Corporation, the deduction cannot be $1,100,000, because this amount exceeds the limitation placed upon percentage depletion: 50 percent of taxable net income determined prior to the deduction for depletion. Reference to the statement of income discloses that the limiting net income figure is $1,800,000 ($5,000,000 of gross income less $3,200,000 of expenses except depletion). Fifty percent of this net income is $900,000, the maximum allowance for percentage depletion.

In summary, the periodic depletion allowance for income taxes, which is not necessarily the same amount for general accounting, is the larger of (1) or (2) below unless (3) is smaller than (2), in which case the allowance is the larger of (1) or (3).

(1) Cost depletion method:

Unit depletion charge	× barrels sold	
30¢	× 2,000,000	= $600,000

(2) Percentage depletion method:

%	× gross income	
22%	× $5,000,000	= $1,100,000

(3) Limitation on percentage method:

50%	× taxable net income prior depletion deduction	
50%	× $1,800,000	= $900,000

Cost depletion, like depreciation, ceases when the cost of the property has been recovered. However, percentage depletion continues as long as gross income is obtained from the property and the results of operations yield a net income for the period. By percentage depletion, it is not unusual for a taxpayer to recover an amount greater than the cost of the property.

Those charged with management responsibilities of a financial nature in an extractive industry should be aware of the interrelationship of percentage depletion and accelerated depreciation. A considerable number of companies purposely have not availed themselves of the opportunity to employ accelerated depreciation, since percentage depletion is limited to 50 percent of taxable income before the depletion deduction and accelerated depreciation might reduce this base to such an extent as to reduce also the percentage depletion allowance.

AMORTIZATION

Intangible fixed assets possess characteristics which are similar to those of tangible property, plant and equipment items. However, intangibles have no bodily substance: their value is attributable to the rights conferred by their ownership.

Similar to the process by which tangible fixed assets are depreciated, the cost of intangible fixed assets possessing a determinable life should be systematically charged against revenue during each fiscal period by a process referred to as amortization. Unlike tangible fixed assets, where the accumulated depreciation to date is shown as a contra item subtracted from the original cost of the assets, intangible fixed assets are usually directly reduced by each period's amortization. The Consolidated Balance Sheet of Textron, Inc. as of December 30, 1972, illustrates this procedure.

Property, plant and equipment, at cost:	
Land and buildings	$131,827,000
Machinery and equipment	437,040,000
	$568,867,000
Less accumulated depreciation	325,905,000
Net property, plant and equipment	$242,962,000
Amount paid over value assigned to net assets of companies acquired, less amortization	$ 51,335,000
Patents, at cost less amortization	$ 12,516,000

Usually intangible fixed assets like leasehold improvements, leases, and leaseholds are shown at cost less amortization to date. However, in the past, it has been somewhat common practice to show intangibles like patents, goodwill, trademarks, and brand names at a nominal value, usually one dollar.[2]

The Committee on Accounting Procedures of the American Institute of Certified Public Accountants stated that intangibles may be classified into the following two types:

1. Those having a term of existence limited by law, regulation, or agreement, or by their nature (such as patents, copyrights, leases, licenses, franchises for a fixed term, and goodwill as to which there is evidence of limited duration);
2. Those having no such limited term of existence and as to which there is, at the time of acquisition, no indication of limited life

---

[2] For illustration, see December 31, 1972, balance sheet of Kellogg Company.

> (such as goodwill generally, going value, trade names, secret processes, subscription lists, perpetual franchises, and organization costs).[3]

This same reference also indicated the preferred procedures to be followed for the amortization of these two broad classes of intangible assets.

> *Type (a)* The cost of type (a) intangibles should be amortized by systematic charges in the income statement over the period benefited, as in the case of other assets having a limited period of usefulness. If it becomes evident that the period benefited will be longer or shorter than originally estimated, recognition thereof may take the form of an appropriate decrease or increase in the rate of amortization or, if such increased charges would result in distortion of income, a partial write-down may be made by a charge to earned surplus.
>
> *Type (b)* When it becomes reasonably evident that the term of existence of a type (b) intangible has become limited and that it has therefore become a type (a) intangible, its cost should be amortized by systematic charges in the income statement over the estimated remaining period of usefulness. If, however, the period of amortization is relatively short so that misleading inferences might be drawn as a result of inclusion of substantial charges in the income statement, a partial write-down may be made by a charge to earned surplus, and the rest of the cost may be amortized over the remaining period of usefulness.[4]

The above two references from APB No. 43 were superseded on November 1, 1970, by APB Opinion No. 17. The conclusions contained in APB Opinion No. 17 are:

> The Board concludes that a company should record as assets the costs of intangible assets acquired from others, including goodwill acquired in a business combination. A company should record as expenses the costs to develop intangible assets which are not specifically identifiable. The Board also concludes that the cost of each type of intangible asset should be amortized by systematic charges

[3] Accounting Research Bulletin No. 43, "Restatement and Revision of Accounting Research Bulletins," p. 37, *Accounting Research and Terminology Bulletins, Final Edition*. Copyright 1961 by the American Institute of Certified Public Accountants, Inc.

[4] *Ibid.*, pp. 38–39.

> to income over the period estimated to be benefited. The period of amortization should not, however, exceed 40 years.[5]

With this background of long-term intangibles, the methods of their presentation, and the methods for their amortization, a brief description of each of the more commonly encountered intangibles is presented next.

A *patent* is an exclusive right granted by the United States Patent Office to an inventor, permitting him to use, sell, manufacture, or permits the use by others through royalty agreements of his invention. The legal life of a patent is 17 years and is not renewable. Thus, the cost of a patent is amortized over its legal life or its estimated economic useful life, whichever is shorter.

The amortization basis of a patent depends upon several factors. If a patent is purchased from another party, the basis is the amount paid for it. However, if a patent is developed, its cost would include items such as legal and filing fees, the cost of drawings and working models, and the research and development expenditures which have led to the patent. The major portion of these costs of developing a patent are normally the costs for the research, experimental, and development work. Many companies operate large research laboratories which continually work on a variety of projects, including ideas which may lead to the procurement of patents. Some companies capitalize such expenditures as a portion of the cost of patents obtained, and then periodically amortize such costs against revenue. More often, due to the fact that it is a continually recurring cost, companies charge such research and development expenditures to operations as they are incurred. This latter procedure also eliminates the problem of deciding how much overall research and development cost should be allocated to each specific patent obtained as a capitalized cost.

Often it is said that a patent has no proven worth until it has stood the test of an infringement suit. Thus, the costs involved in successfully defending the first infringement suits may properly be capitalized as a part of the cost of the patent; the cost of unsuccessful suits plus the cost of the then valueless patent would be expensed.

A *copyright* is an exclusive right granted by the federal government to an author or artist permitting him to use, sell, or reproduce his literary or artistic creation. The legal life of a copyright is 28 years, with a renewal privilege of an additional 28 years. Because of the short revenue-producing life of most copyrighted items, their cost is usually amortized over a relatively few years rather than over their legal life.

---

[5] American Institute of Certified Public Accountants, Inc., *Opinion of the Accounting Principles Board, Number 17,* "Intangible Assets," p. 334. Copyright (1970) by the American Institute of Certified Public Accountants, Inc.

The costs of developing a copyrighted item and the copyright fee are usually nominal and thus are expensed in the period incurred. However, a copyright may be purchased at a considerable cost; then the purchase price is capitalized and systematically amortized as a periodic charge against revenue.

A *franchise* is an exclusive privilege granted by the federal, state, or other governmental unit to a company permitting the use of certain public property. Such franchises are usually associated with public utility companies and grant exclusive privileges like the use of rights-of-way for transportation purposes and the use of public property for the laying of gas mains.

The life of a franchise may be a definite number of years, an indefinite number of years, or perpetual. If life is a definite number of years, the cost (if any) should be amortized over the shorter of its contract life or estimated economic useful life. If life is for an indefinite number of years, any cost involved in obtaining the franchise should be amortized fairly rapidly, since the franchise could be revoked at any time. Theoretically, the cost of a perpetual franchise (e.g., franchises by the federal government granting rights-of-way to the land-grant railroads west of the Mississippi River and franchises by certain local governmental agencies to cable TV companies) need not be amortized as long as the franchise possesses income-producing value.

Normally, the acquisition cost of a franchise is nominal unless an existing franchise has been purchased from another company. Those using financial statements should be aware that any dollar amount appearing on a balance sheet for franchises may be completely unrelated to its worth.

Franchises may require periodic payments like yearly license or rental fees to a governmental unit; any such expenditures should be expensed as incurred.

Occasionally, dealer franchises are encountered whereby a manufacturer of a product grants a dealer the privilege of marketing a product within a given territory. Such business agreements require analysis and treatment as those granted by governmental agencies.

A *leasehold,* acquired by a contract called an operating lease, is an agreement giving the lessee the right to use the property of the lessor, or owner, for a prescribed period. In return he must make a series of regular payments on dates specified in the contract. Unless the lessee makes a lump sum deposit at the outset of the contract, nothing appears in the balance sheet of the lessee to indicate the existence of the lease. The periodic rental payments made by the lessee are included in his operating costs. Thus it is possible for a company to lease (rather than purchase) a considerable amount of fixed assets and thereby indicate on the balance sheet no dollar amount for fixed assets, leasehold, or obligation for future rentals. However, if the amount is material, Accounting Principles Board Opinion Number 5 requires that adequate disclosure be made.[6] This would be done through footnotes to the financial statements.

Typical of the disclosure required is the following footnote from the 1972 annual report of the Cook Paint and Varnish Company:

> Note E—*Long-Term Lease Commitments*
>
> At November 30, 1972, the Company had 97 long-term leases expiring on various dates to 1983, with present minimum annual rentals of $532,230.

Also note the following from the 1972 annual report of F. W. Woolworth Company:

> Note 8—*Long-Term Leases*
>
> Minimum annual rentals in effect at December 31, 1972, under more than 4,300 store property leases are summarized as follows:

Leases expiring during:	
Next five years	$ 20,800,000
Six to ten years	29,450,000
Eleven to twenty years	73,004,000
Twenty-one to thirty years	18,945,000
Subsequently	1,313,000
	$143,512,000

> Total rent charged to expense for the year, including rentals based on a percentage of sales but excluding payments of real estate taxes, insurance and other expenses required under some leases, amounted to $146,231,000 in 1972.

---

[6] American Institute of Certified Public Accountants, Inc., *Accounting Principles Board Opinion No. 5,* "Reporting of Leases in Financial Statements of Lessee" (New York, 1964). For additional information on leases, the reader is also referred to:

American Institute of Certified Public Accountants, *Accounting Principles Board Opinion No. 7,* "Accounting for Leases in Financial Statements of Lessors" (New York, 1966).

American Institute of Certified Public Accountants, *Accounting Principles Board Opinion No. 27,* "Accounting for Lease Transactions by Manufacturer or Dealer Lessors" (New York, 1972).

American Institute of Certified Public Accountants, *Accounting Principles Board Opinion No. 31,* "Disclosure of Lease Commitments by Lessees" (New York, 1973).

In some instances the lease agreement is, in fact, an installment purchase contract. These leases are called financing leases. The various payments under the agreement are in reality debt payments rather than rental payments. In such instances accounting principles dictate that the substance rather than the legal form of the agreement must be reflected in the financial statements; it should be recorded as a purchase agreement. While it can be difficult in practice to ascertain if a lease is an operating lease or a financing lease, the characteristics of each can be described. Under an operating lease the agreement is for only a portion of the asset's life. The lessor pays all the costs usually associated with ownership, such as property taxes. The agreement does not provide for the transfer of title from the lessor to the lessee. The lease may or may not be cancellable. In contrast, a financing lease is noncancellable by either party except under the most unusual circumstances. Should the term of the lease be less than the life of the asset, then the agreement gives the lessee an option to purchase the leased asset on or before the termination of the lease for a nominal amount relative to the property's expected value at time of purchase. Under a financial lease the lessee rather than the lessor pays those costs usually borne by the owner, e.g., taxes, insurance and maintenance.[7] The payments required under the lease are discounted at the interest rate the lessee pays for its long term debt. This amount is shown as an asset on the balance sheet, indicating that the property right is acquired by a lease agreement. The liability is included among the long-term liabilities. (See Chapter 11, pages 336–37.)

Typical of the format for disclosure of the property rights in a balance sheet is that found in the 1972 annual report of Armco Steel Corporation:

Property, Plant and Equipment—At Cost	
Land, land improvements, and leaseholds	$ 68,425,000
Buildings	249,978,000
Machinery and equipment	1,647,692,000
Other	83,889,000
Construction in progress	31,653,000
Total	$2,081,637,000
Less accumulated depreciation	1,010,985,000
Property, Plant and Equipment—Net	$1,070,652,000
Unamortized Lease Rights	148,579,000
⋮	⋮
Long-Term Debt	381,882,000
Long-Term Lease Obligations	171,760,000

[7] The financing lease is discussed in Accounting Principles Board Opinion Number 5. See sections number 9, 10, 11, 12.

From "Financial Summary"
Long-Term Leases
Armco has entered into lease agreements for the use of facilities that have been constructed with funds provided from the proceeds of Industrial Revenue Bonds. The lease agreements provide for the payment in annual amounts ($16,000,000 in 1973, and in generally decreasing annual amounts to approximately $14,000,000 in 1980 through 1991 and approximately $7,000,000 in 1992 and 1993) sufficient to service principal and interest (combined effective rate of approximately 4.8%) on the bonds. Amounts, which comprehend lease rights, equivalent to the aggregate lease payments generally are being amortized and charged to income on a straight-line basis over the estimated productive lives of the facilities, which for the most part are shorter than the terms of the leases. Armco has options to purchase the facilities at any time during the term of the leases at the scheduled redemption prices of the bonds or for nominal amounts at the end of the lease periods.

The cost of the property right is amortized over its useful life as any other comparable asset would be. Thus, under certain financial leases where a purchase option exists, the cost of the property right will be amortized over a period longer than the term of the lease.

A company enters into financing lease agreements so as to minimize the portion of its capital tied up in fixed assets. In the typical case it minimizes capital investment by avoiding the need to raise additional capital through borrowing (e.g., bonds, mortgages) or equity capital (e.g., a new stock issue). In some cases it minimizes its investment in fixed assets by selling off properties currently owned and then immediately leasing them for a substantial period. Such a transaction is called a sale and leaseback. By entering into a sale and leaseback agreement the managers of the company are able to free capital previously invested in fixed assets for other activities. It is important to note that the accounting procedures specified in A.P.B. 5 do *not* alter the financial liquidity advantages of the financial lease. However, it does require the balance sheet to reflect the effects of the event as if the company had borrowed the necessary funds. Thus, it does alter the desirability of leasing assets relative to purchasing them in those instances where the disclosure of the asset and the debt on the balance sheet would significantly alter the picture presented of the firm's financial position, e.g., the calculation of the rate of return or the ratio of total debt to total equity.

Leasehold Improvements consist of any improvements or alterations made by the lessee to leased property. Since such additions revert to the lessor at the termination of the lease, leasehold improvements usually are amortized over the life of the improvement or the period of the lease, whichever is shorter. Consider the properties section of the December 31, 1972 Balance Sheet of F. W. Woolworth Co.

Properties, at Cost (Note 1):	
Land and buildings	$238,032,000
Furniture, fixtures and equipment	414,161,000
	$652,193,000
Accumulated depreciation	215,883,000
	$436,310,000
Buildings on leased ground, less amortization	32,273,000
Alterations to leased and owned buildings, less amortization	123,070,000
	$591,653,000

Observe that the last two items, excluding the portion constituting alterations to owned buildings, represent leasehold improvements subject to amortization.

Goodwill is a term which conveys different meanings to different people. To the layman, the term may imply a successful company which has fine facilities, markets excellent products, and has outstanding customer relations. To the accountant, the term usually means the capitalized value of any expected future excess profits to be earned by the company, possibly, but not necessarily, as a result of the intangibles considered by the layman. In any case, goodwill, as an intangible fixed asset appearing on a balance sheet, normally represents the amount actually paid, in the acquisition of a going business, in excess of the value of the net tangible assets acquired. But, to the businessman who has paid this excess amount to acquire another company, the use of the term goodwill as a caption representing the excess payment could be completely misleading. While the motivating factor for the premium payment by the businessman might be expected future excess earnings, the acquisition of another company could be undertaken to assure a source of supply of raw materials, as part of a diversification program, to secure a tax advantage, or for some other reason. Practically, regardless of the "goodwill" of a company, this intangible asset should never appear as a recorded asset unless it has been purchased.

There are two methods of accounting for business combinations. They are known as the "purchase" method and the "pooling of interests" method. A detailed analysis of the criteria for each method is beyond the scope of this book. APB Opinion No. 16, effective November 1, 1970 spells out the rules for each and the interested reader is referred to this

47-page source for any in-depth study desired. The conclusions of APB Opinion No. 16, in full, are:

> The Board concludes that the purchase method and the pooling of interests method are both acceptable in accounting for business combinations, although not as alternatives in accounting for the same business combination. A business combination which meets specified conditions requires accounting by the pooling of interests method. A new basis of accounting is not permitted for a combination that meets the specified conditions and the assets and liabilities of the combining companies are combined at their recorded amounts. All other business combinations should be accounted for as an acquisition of one or more companies by a corporation. The cost to an acquiring corporation of an entire acquired company should be determined by the principles of accounting for the acquisition of an asset. That cost should then be allocated to the identifiable individual assets acquired and liabilities assumed based on their fair values; the unallocated cost should be recorded as goodwill.[8]

As an illustration, assume the following condensed balance sheet of Kenneweg Corporation immediately prior to its acquisition of Wilson Company:

Various Assets	$22,000,000
Various Liabilities	$12,000,000
Stockholders' Equity:	
Outstanding Preferred Stock, Par $100	-0-
Outstanding Common Stock, Par $100	4,000,000
Additional Capital Contributions by Stockholders in Excess of Par	1,500,000
Reinvested Earnings	4,500,000
	$22,000,000

Kenneweg Corporation, bent upon a program of expansion and diversification, is interested in acquiring the Wilson Company. The Wilson Company has been in business for many years, has a fine established business reputation, and manufactures an excellent staple product which appears to have outstanding future prospects. It is anticipated that the pattern of above-average profits generated by Wilson Company will continue if the

[8] American Institute of Certified Public Accountants, Inc., *Opinions of the Accounting Principles Board, Number 16,* "Business Combinations," p. 283. Copyright (1970) American Institute of Certified Public Accountants, Inc.

company is acquired by Kenneweg Corporation. Continued negotiations end with the acquisition of Wilson Company by Kenneweg Corporation. Kenneweg Corporation acquires the net tangible assets of Wilson Company for $2,000,000. These net tangible assets consist of:

Various assets acquired and fairly valued at	$1,900,000
Liabilities assumed of	200,000
Net tangible assets	$1,700,000

The excess payment of $300,000 is for goodwill purchased. This business combination should be accounted for by the "purchase" method.

Settlement of the $2,000,000 purchase price might be by a cash payment of that amount. However, in this illustration assume that Kenneweg Corporation issues preferred stock in exchange for the business of Wilson Company. In the exchange, 20,000 shares of the $100 par stock are issued. The resultant condensed balance sheet of Kenneweg Corporation would now reflect the following factors:

Various Assets:		
Original amount		$22,000,000
Tangible assets acquired from Wilson Company		1,900,000
Goodwill purchased		300,000
		$24,200,000
Various Liabilities:		
Original amount	$12,000,000	
Liabilities of Wilson Company assumed	200,000	$12,200,000
Stockholders' Equity:		
Outstanding Preferred Stock, Par $100		2,000,000
Outstanding Common Stock, Par $100		4,000,000
Additional Capital Contributions by Stockholders in Excess of Par		1,500,000
Reinvested Earnings		4,500,000
		$24,200,000

Assets have been increased $2,200,000; $1,900,000 of tangible assets have been acquired, and $300,000 of goodwill has been purchased. Liabilities have increased by $200,000 of debts assumed. The $2,000,000 settlement made by the issuance of 20,000 shares of preferred stock has increased stockholders' equity that same amount.

Since the term *goodwill* conveys various meanings to those using financial statements, many companies have avoided it by employing more descriptive alternatives. One such term is that shown by the Consolidated

Balance Sheet of R. J. Reynolds Industries, Inc. At December 31, 1972, it showed:

Cost in excess of net assets of businesses acquired	$163,465,000

Purchased goodwill may appear to have an unlimited life. By theory, then, it might be maintained that, once paid for, goodwill should remain intact on the balance sheet at its purchase price. This was the recommended procedure previously quoted for such a "type b" intangible asset. However, this same reference provided for the amortization of such "type b" intangibles when subsequent events justify their write-off. Because the unlimited life of goodwill is debatable and its subsequent value is highly questionable, many companies do systematically amortize the asset. A review of published financial statements indicates that many companies carry this intangible asset at a nominal value, like one dollar. However, per APB No. 17, goodwill acquired on or after November 1, 1970, *must* be amortized over a life not to exceed 40 years. Generally speaking, under the present federal income tax code, no amortization of goodwill is deductible for tax purposes; only at the date of sale or liquidation of a company may such an item be considered for income tax purposes.

The examples which follow are intended to illustrate the varying terminology and procedures used in accounting for goodwill acquired *prior to* and *after* APB No. 17 which became effective on November 1, 1970. From the 1972 annual report of The Magnavox Company:

	December 31	
	1972	1971
Excess of cost over net assets of acquired companies	$8,289,000	$6,825,000

Excess of Cost Over Net Assets of Acquired Companies: The excess of cost over net assets of acquired companies resulting from transactions initiated after October 31, 1970, is being amortized over forty years. Excess of cost over net assets acquired of $5,756,000 relating to acquisitions prior to October 31, 1970 is considered by management to have an indefinite life and accordingly is not being amortized.

Similarly, from the 1972 annual report of Dow Chemical Company:

	December 31	
	1972	1971
Goodwill	$79,890,532	$77,323,480

Goodwill: The excess of the cost of investments in consolidated subsidiaries over carrying value of assets acquired is shown as goodwill. Goodwill arising after October 1970 is amortized over 40 years. In the opinion of management, goodwill arising prior to that date requires no amortization.

The General Foods Corporation, in their 1972 annual report, treats the problem in a slightly different manner:

	April 1	
	1972	1971
Goodwill, less amortization of $960,000 in 1972 (Note 3)	$92,284,000	$95,046,000

Goodwill ($11,738,000) acquired after October 31, 1970, the effective date of Opinion Number 17 of the Accounting Principles Board, is being amortized by the straight-line method over a period of 40 years. Also, based upon the continuing evaluation of goodwill by management, amortization was commenced in fiscal 1972 for $30,370,000 of goodwill acquired prior to November 1, 1970. This goodwill is also being amortized by the straight-line method over a period of 40 years. The balance of the goodwill ($51,136,000) acquired prior to November 1, 1970, continues to be carried at cost.

And, from the 1972 annual report of National Can Corporation:

	December 31	
	1972	1971
Intangibles, excess of cost over net assets of acquired companies	$11,280,068	$11,295,268

Portion of Note A:

The Corporation believes that the excess of cost over the fair value of the net assets of acquired companies is of such a nature that no diminution in value is expected in the foreseeable future and, accordingly, such excess attributable to acquisitions initiated prior to November 1, 1970, are not being amortized. However, in accordance with Opinion No. 17 of the Accounting Principles Board of the American Institute of Certified Public Accountants, the excess of cost over the fair value of the net assets of companies acquired after October 31, 1970, is being amortized over a forty (40) year period with annual amortization of $15,200 was charged to earnings.

Note 6 to the financial statements in the 1972 annual report of American Home Products Corporation reads as follows:

> Intangible assets at December 31, 1972 consist of $81,443,000 of goodwill, trademarks, formulae, etc., acquired since January 1, 1954, which is not being amortized since the Company believes there has been no diminution in value of these assets, and $2,596,000 for patents and patent rights acquired since January 1, 1950, which are being amortized over the term of each patent.

In August 1970, Opinion No. 17 of the Accounting Principles Board was issued, making amortization of goodwill mandatory effective November 1, 1970. Such goodwill acquired in a merger accounted for as a purchase must be recorded and written off against earnings over a period of up to 40 years. This Opinion is applicable only to acquisitions on and after November 1, 1970. Thus, alternative methods of accounting for goodwill acquired prior to that date may persist for several years.

Organization Costs consist of those expenditures incurred at the formation of a corporation for items such as incorporation and charter fees, legal and accounting fees, printing of stock certificates, underwriting fees, and expenses incident to the sale of the stock. In theory, this "type b" intangible has an unlimited life because such organization costs benefit all future years of corporate life. In practice, because the total dollar amount involved is not usually a considerable sum and the asset is of uncertain worth, organization costs are customarily written off in the first year, or the first few years, of business. Prior to 1954, organization costs were deductible for federal income taxes only in the year of dissolution. The Internal Revenue Code of 1954 allows corporations an election to deduct certain organization costs ratably over a period of 60 months or more, beginning with the month the corporation commences business. This election applies only to the expenditures incurred before the end of the corporation's first taxable year and does not apply to organization costs as expenditures involved in the issuing of securities.

A trademark is a distinctive symbol (a drawing or an emblem) which is used to distinguish a company's product or products from those of other companies. The trademarks of many companies are most valuable assets. Yet, trademarks seldom appear on a balance sheet at other than a nominal figure. The costs involved in developing a trademark are often expensed as incurred, because the useful life of a trademark is so indefinite. Trademarks may be registered with the federal government for an indefinite life.

The preceding sections have presented the salient points with respect to those intangible fixed assets most often encountered. Other intangibles occasionally shown by financial statements are brand names, formulas, designs, research and development costs, subscription lists, scripts, film rights, mining or timber rights, and licenses.

DISPOSAL OF FIXED ASSETS

Disposals of depreciable fixed assets create problems which must be resolved correctly to insure the proper effect upon periodic financial statements; inaccurate solutions may unwittingly mislead both internal management and outside reviewers of the company's financial reports. To illustrate the typical problems which arise through such disposals, the following facts are assumed to apply to a piece of machinery which was purchased by a company on January 5, 1972:

Cost:	
Invoice price	$ 9,800
Freight (capitalized)	300
Installation (capitalized)	100
Total cost of machine	$10,200
Estimated salvage value	$ 200
Estimated useful life	Five years
Depreciation method:	
Regular straight-line	
Computed to nearest full month	
Neither group nor composite methods used	
Fiscal year of company coincides with calendar year	

The December 31, 1974, balance sheet of the company showed for this particular asset:

Machinery	$10,200	
Accumulated depreciation to date[9]	6,000	
Cost less accumulated depreciation		$ 4,200

Three different types of situations are created by making the following three assumptions about the manner by which the machine is disposed of on March 31, 1975:

(1) Sold the machine for $5,000 cash.

(2) Sold the machine for $3,500 cash.

(3) Traded in the piece of machinery for another machine priced at $12,000. Received a trade-in allowance of $3,500 (the amount for which it could have been sold for cash) and paid the balance of $8,500 in cash.

---

[9]Annual depreciation of ($10,200 – $200)/5 years or $2,000 times three full years to date.

Under all three assumptions, recognition first must be provided for the additional depreciation which accumulated between December 31, 1974, and the date of the disposal in 1975. Since the company computes depreciation to the nearest full month, depreciation for three months, one-fourth of a year, of 1975 will amount to $500.[10] Thus, total accumulated depreciation to the date of disposal is $6,500.

Under the first assumption, there is a $1,300 gain on the sale of the piece of machinery, computed as follows:

Cost (total) of machine	$10,200
Less accumulated depreciation (6,000 + 500)	6,500
Cost less accumulated depreciation	$ 3,700
Cash received from sale	5,000
Gain on disposal	$ 1,300

Under the three assumptions provided, the summary tables which follow indicate the effect of the sale on the financial statements. Using the first assumption, the balance sheet as of March 31, 1975, reflects the increase in the cash balance attributable to the $5,000 cash receipt. The property, plant and equipment section of the statement reflects a $3,700 net decrease attributable to the removal of the $10,200 machine and its contra item of accumulated depreciation to date of $6,500 (actually $6,000 as of January 1 plus $500 additional for the first three months of 1975). The statement of income for the first three months of the year, of course, includes the $500 of depreciation expense allocated to this period of time. In addition, the non-operating section of the statement of income discloses the $1,300 gain on disposal of the machinery. The resulting overall net income for the period which is not distributed as dividends increases the retained earnings of the company.

Under the second assumption (if the machine is sold for $3,500 cash), there is a loss of $200, since the cash received is $200 less than the $3,700 amount which represents the cost of the machine less accumulated depreciation. Reference to the following tables indicates that the effect of this sale upon the pertinent items contained in the financial statements would be similar to that explained under the first assumption.

The third assumption (if the old machine is traded in for a new machine) also results in a $200 loss on disposal of the old machine, as indicated below:

---

[10] To simplify depreciation computations, many companies charge one-half a year's depreciation in the year of acquisition and one-half a year's depreciation in the year of disposal, regardless of the actual specific dates.

Cost (total) of old machine	$10,200
Less accumulated depreciation (6,000 + 500)	6,500
Cost less accumulated depreciation	$ 3,700
Trade-in allowance received	3,500
Loss on disposal	$ 200

As in the second assumption, $3,500 is "received." However, under the second assumption, the machine was disposed of by an outright sale and the receipt was in cash; under the third assumption, the receipt is a trade-

Balance Sheet
As of March 31, 1975

	First Assumption	Second Assumption	Third Assumption
Current Assets:			
Cash	+ 5,000	+ 3,500	− 8,500
Property, Plant and Equipment:			
Machinery	−10,200	−10,200	{ +12,000 −10,200
Less: Accumulated depreciation	− 6,500	− 6,500	− 6,500
Net	− 3,700	− 3,700	{ +12,000 − 3,700
Stockholders' Equity:			
Retained Earnings	The gain or loss on disposal becomes a portion of the net income for the period retained and reinvested in the business		

Statement of Income
For the Three Months Ended March 31, 1975

	First Assumption	Second Assumption	Third Assumption
Operating Expenses:			
Depreciation of Machinery	+ 500	+500	+500
Other Income:			
Gain on Disposal of Fixed Assets	+1,300		
Other Expenses and Losses:			
Loss on Disposal of Fixed Assets		+200	+200

in allowance. Thus, the new machine, priced at $12,000, requires a cash outlay of only $8,500 as follows:

Cost of new machine	$12,000
Less trade-in allowance received	3,500
Cash disbursed to acquire new machine	$ 8,500

Reference to the preceding tables indicates the effect of the trade-in of the old machine for a new machine upon the financial statements. The balance sheet reflects the decrease in the cash balance attributable to the $8,500 disbursement for the new machine. The property, plant and equipment section of the statement reflects a net increase of $8,300 produced by the $12,000 increase for the acquisition of the new machine and a $3,700 net decrease attributable to the disposal of the $10,200 old machine and its accumulated depreciation to date of $6,500. The statement of income for the period, as for the second assumption, includes the $500 of current depreciation expense on the old machine and the $200 loss on the disposal of this machine.

While the theory followed above regarding the trade-in of one asset for a similar type of new asset is sound as theory, it does not agree with the income tax provisions regarding trade-ins. Federal income tax provisions require that, for the typical trade-in situation just illustrated, no gain or loss be recognized when property used in business is exchanged for property of a like kind.[11] Because the tax provisions prevent such gains or losses on trade-in from being recognized as income or expense, the cost of the new asset acquired must be adjusted in the following manner for tax purposes:

$$\text{Basis of new asset} = \text{Cost of new asset} \begin{cases} + \text{ Non-recognized loss} \\ - \text{ Non-recognized gain} \end{cases}$$

Thus, the $12,000 new machine acquired by trade in our third assumption would have a tax basis of $12,200 because of the addition of the $200 non-recognized loss on the disposal of the old machine. And for taxes, depreciation of the new machine would be based upon $12,200 rather than $12,000. Rather than use one method for general accounting and another for taxes in such situations, many companies simply follow the tax method for general accounting purposes when the dollar amount involved is not significant. In such a case, the balance sheet under the third assumption would indicate an increase in Machinery of $12,200 instead of $12,000, and the Loss on Disposal of Fixed Assets of $200 on the statement of income would be eliminated.

[11] Internal Revenue Code, Section 1031.

Those in management who are responsible for decisions regarding acquisitions and disposals of items of property, plant, and equipment should be aware of the foregoing principles. The disposal of a fixed asset by *sale,* accompanied by the purchase of a similar fixed asset, normally will produce a gain or loss situation for both general accounting and tax purposes. On the other hand, the acquisition of a similar new fixed asset resulting from disposal of the old asset by *trade-in* normally will not produce a taxable gain or deductible loss. Proper planning will provide the method to be employed to maximize company interests.

The businessman should also be aware of the fact that normally, when the group or composite method of depreciation is used, no gain or loss is recognized for either general accounting or taxes when an asset is sold, scrapped, or traded in. Under normal circumstances, when specific assets which are a part of a group are retired, it is assumed that any individual gains and losses on such disposals will offset each other.

QUESTIONS AND PROBLEMS

8–1. The Ft. Yukon Oil Company purchased oil lands in January, 1974, at a cost of $100,000,000 containing approximately 1,000,000,000 barrels of recoverable oil. 40,000,000 barrels of oil were produced and sold in 1974. Gross income (Sales) from the property amounted to $30,000,000 in 1974 and total deductions (Expenses) except for depletion amounted to $18,000,000.

Required

a. What amount normally would be shown for Depletion Expense (on cost) on the company's Statement of Income?

b. On the company's tax return:
   1. What is the maximum depletion deduction for federal income tax purposes?
   2. If the deductions were $24,000,000 instead of $18,000,000, what is the maximum depletion deduction?
   3. If the deductions were $10,000,000 instead of $18,000,000, what is the maximum depletion deduction?

8–2. Scranton Coal Company purchased a coal mine which contained approximately 20,000,000 tons of recoverable coal in January, 1974, at a cost of $5,000,000. 1,000,000 tons of coal were mined and sold in

1974. Gross income from the property amounted to $8,000,000 in 1974, and total deductions (expenses) except for depletion amounted to $6,000,000.

Required

a. What amount would be shown for Depletion Expense on the company's Statement of Income?

b. On the company's tax return:
   1. What is the maximum depletion deduction for federal income taxes?
   2. If the deductions were $6,800,000 instead of $6,000,000, what would be the maximum depletion deduction?
   3. If the deductions were $7,600,000 instead of $6,000,000, what would be the maximum depletion deduction?

8–3. If not previously assigned, problem 2–10 may be used at this point. This problem is concerned with intangible assets.

8–4. For each of the following statements, choose the best answer and indicate your choice on an answer sheet.

a. If a company's balance sheet shows an amount for goodwill, such an amount represents:
   1. the purchase price of going businesses acquired in excess of their net tangible assets (less amortization to date)
   2. the arbitrary value the company has assigned to its own established business reputation generated through excellent customer relations and by marketing profitably well accepted products
   3. the excess of the appraised value of the company over and above the amount actually shown by stockholders' equity

b. Petroleum companies usually don't use accelerated depreciation because:
   1. percentage depletion gives them enough of a tax advantage
   2. of the limitation on percentage depletion
   3. it isn't generally accepted accounting

c. Many companies show goodwill at $1 because of:
   1. income tax advantages
   2. conservatism and the debatable dollar amount to the reader of financial statements
   3. its negligible development cost

d. Percentage depletion:
   1. gives oil and gas companies abnormally high profits
   2. is based upon equity, risk, necessity to national defense, and welfare of the nation
   3. resulted from the Oklahoma-Texas oil lobby in 1926

e. A patent:
   1. has a life of 28 years
   2. is an intangible fixed asset
   3. is a guarantee of an invention

8–5. On July 1, 1974, M. L. Thompson Corporation traded in an old piece of machinery for a new but similar machine. The old machine had cost $7,900 when purchased January 2, 1964. Estimated life of 15 years and salvage value of $400, both established at the date of acquisition, had never been changed for old machine. The December 31, 1973, balance sheet showed for this particular old asset:

Machinery	$7,900	
Accumulated depreciation to date	5,000	$2,900

The company uses straight-line depreciation but does not use either the group or composite methods. When the trade-in occurred on July 1, 1974, the corporation received a trade-in allowance of $950 for the old machine (the amount for which it could have been sold for cash) and paid the balance of $8,100 in cash for the new machine, which was priced at $9,050.

Required

a. Compute the gain or loss on the disposal of the old machine.

b. For tax purposes, such a gain or loss is not recognized. Therefore, compute the depreciation basis of the new machine for tax purposes.

8–6. A used building purchased on July 1, 1962, for $800,000 with no salvage and a life of 20 years, was sold on December 31, 1974, for $430,000 cash. Compute the gain or loss on sale of the building.

8–7. A used building purchased in January 1961 for $600,000 with no salvage and a life of 30 years was sold on July 1, 1974, for $300,000 cash. Compute the gain or loss on sale of the building.

9

Inventories and Cost Determination

Inventory represents the cost of goods owned as of a specific date. The type of inventory which a company owns depends upon the company's business: if the company is a merchandising concern, it purchases and sells the same product. For example, in the Balance Sheet of F. W. Woolworth Co. as of December 31, 1972, the inventory appeared as follows:

Merchandise inventories (Note 1) $653,058,000

On the other hand, a manufacturing concern produces the finished product which it sells. Its inventories consist of raw materials not yet placed into production, work in process (partially completed goods in production), and finished goods available for sale. In addition, a manufacturing company usually has inventories of manufacturing supplies, repair parts, containers, and packaging supplies; usually it also maintains an inventory of finished parts which it has produced or purchased. A typical presentation of inventories by a manufacturing-type company is contained in Note 4 to the Balance Sheet of Ingersoll-Rand Company as of December 31, 1972:

Note 4: Inventories: The composition of inventories at December 31, 1972 is as follows:

Raw materials and supplies	$ 31,609,000
Work in process	96,753,000
Finished goods	215,298,000
	$343,660,000

Variations from the two examples presented above will be encountered in businesses differing from typical merchandising or manufacturing endeavors. For example, in the current asset section of the Balance Sheet of The Detroit Edison Company as of December 31, 1972, the inventories appeared as follows:

Inventories	
Fuel	$46,342,000
Construction and maintenance materials	33,739,000
Merchandise for resale	756,000

Various analyses of published financial reports indicate that inventories comprise a major segment of total current assets as well as a considerable portion of total assets. Examine the accompanying survey of the 1972 annual reports of eleven large industrial companies.[1] For comparison, one utility company and one retail merchandising company are also shown. Because of the sizeable investment which inventories represent in the typical company, this chapter discusses the major principles and practices which apply to cost determination, valuation, and management of inventories.

Cost Determination

The determination of the cost of a company's inventory as of a specific date, except in unusual and isolated situations, is *not* a simple matter. Many valid and logical methods are available to a business enterprise. To illustrate, assume the following set of elementary facts for a company that

[1] These are the same eleven companies that were used in Chapter 6 for a comparison of fixed assets to total assets. Reference to both of these tables discloses that the total of inventories *and* net property, plant, and equipment comprise from 38 percent to 75 percent of total assets for the typical company. Similarly, the total inventories and net property, plant, and equipment comprise 95 percent and 72 percent of total assets for Detroit Edison and F. W. Woolworth. The above percentages are intended only to convey a general panorama of the relative components of total assets. Unusual situations in any one company may skew comparative figures. In utility companies, fixed assets normally predominate (i.e., 92 percent of total assets in Detroit Edison).

COMPANY	AMOUNTS IN MILLIONS OF DOLLARS INVENTORIES	CURRENT ASSETS	TOTAL ASSETS	INVENTORIES AS PERCENTAGE OF CURRENT ASSETS	TOTAL ASSETS
General Motors Corporation .	$4,200	$10,539	$18,273	40%	23%
General Electric Company ...	1,759	3,979	7,402	44	24
U.S. Steel Corporation	790	1,753	6,570	45	12
Du Pont (E. I.) de Nemours	793	1,823	4,284	43	19
Gulf Oil Corporation	667	2,936	9,324	23	7
Swift and Company	254	494	936	51	27
General Dynamics Corporation	102	637	1,015	16	10
Kraftco Corporation	433	740	1,245	58	34
RCA Corporation	436	1,807	3,137	24	14
Union Carbide Corporation ..	743	1,628	3,718	46	20
United Aircraft Corporation .	347	843	1,223	41	28
Utility:					
Detroit Edison Company ..	81	183	2,752	44	3
Merchandise:					
F. W. Woolworth Co.	653	909	1,720	71	37

commences business to buy and sell a single product on July 1 and has the following flow of goods during July:

July 1—Purchase of one item	$100 cost
July 20—Purchase of one item	110 cost
July 30—Sale of one item	180 selling price

What is the cost of the one item of inventory on hand at July 31? If it is assumed that the one sold was the first one purchased, the first-in, first-out (FIFO) concept, then the inventory cost of the one on hand is $110. But, if it is assumed that the one sold was the last or most recent one purchased, the last-in, first-out (LIFO) concept, then the inventory cost of the one on hand is $100. A third answer is possible by computing an average cost for both items purchased. In this simplified example, the average cost of each of the two items purchased is $105 (total cost of $210 divided by the quantity of two items); thus, the inventory cost of the one on hand is $105.

At this point, recall that one of the objectives of accounting is to present fairly the operating results of the period. The method used to determine the cost of an inventory at the end of a fiscal period should not be viewed principally as a means of determining a dollar amount to be presented as a current asset on the balance sheet. To present fairly the operating results of the period, attention must be directed to the cost determination of the goods sold during the period. The diagrams presented next reflect the effect resulting from the three methods of cost determination on the operating statements.

If the first-in, first-out (FIFO) method is used, then, *theoretically,* the oldest unit of inventory has been sold. As shown below, matching the

Assumption: FIFO costing		Balance Sheet, July 31	
		Current Assets:	
July 1—Purchase one ..	$100	Inventory (FIFO basis)	$110
July 20—Purchase one ..	$110	Statement of Income for July	
July 30—Sale of one of the two above units of inventory at		Sales	$180
		Cost of Goods Sold	100
	$180	Gross Margin	$ 80

$100 cost against the $180 revenue results in a gross margin of $80 when a FIFO flow of costs is assumed. If the last-in, first-out (LIFO) method is used, then, theoretically, the most recently acquired unit has been sold. As shown, matching the $110 cost against the $180 revenue results in a gross margin of $70 when a LIFO flow of costs is assumed. When an average cost method is used, theoretically no particular unit is assumed to have been sold or retained in inventory. As shown below, matching the $105 of cost against the $180 of revenue results in a gross margin of $75 when the total cost of the two units is averaged. An analysis of these

Assumption: LIFO costing		Balance Sheet, July 31	
		Current Assets:	
July 1—Purchase one ..	$100	Inventory (LIFO basis)	$100
July 20—Purchase one ..	$110	Statement of Income for July	
July 30—Sale of one of the two above units of inventory at		Sales	$180
		Cost of Goods Sold	110
	$180	Gross Margin	$ 70

three diagrams indicates the effect of an assumed flow of costs on both the portion of acquisition costs identified with goods in inventory and the portion of acquisition costs assigned to the goods sold during the period. It should be emphasized that the selection of any method of cost deter-

Assumption: AVERAGE costing		Balance Sheet, July 31	
		Current Assets:	
July 1—Purchase one ..	$100	→ Inventory (avg. cost basis)	$105
July 20—Purchase one ..	$110		
		Statement of Income for July	
At this point, on hand are: At $105, two units		→ Sales	$180
		→ Cost of Goods Sold	105
July 30—Sale of one of the two above units of inventory at	$180	Gross Margin	$ 75

mination of inventory is *not* predicated upon the actual manner by which the goods physically move into and out of an inventory. For example, a company may use the LIFO method of cost determination even though, as a matter of policy, it attempts to physically dispose of its goods on the FIFO basis. A more comprehensive treatment of the methods of the cost determination of inventory and cost of goods sold is presented in succeeding pages.

To determine the cost of an inventory item, additional factors must be considered. For example, if a retail concern purchases an item for its inventory from a vendor at an invoice price of $50, this amount usually will not represent the full or total cost of the item. In addition to the invoice cost, consideration should be given to related direct costs (e.g., transportation and insurance during transit) and related indirect costs (e.g., storage and handling). Whether such costs are allocated to items of inventory as a portion of cost or immediately expensed against revenue of the period depends upon the policy of the particular company. For a manufacturing company, the determination of the total cost of inventory items is complicated further by various alternative cost accounting methods employed to allocate manufacturing costs to specific products.[2] Those who use financial information for comparative analyses (e.g., between companies) should be aware that, in addition to possible non-comparability of figures determined by FIFO, LIFO, or average cost, the cost determination policy, under any of these methods, will vary from company to company even within the same industry. Failure to consider

[2] See Chapter 13.

related direct and indirect costs in addition to the actual invoice cost may lead to erroneous managerial decisions.[3]

Cash discounts on purchased goods should be considered in the cost determination of inventory items. Assume that the $50 inventory item mentioned in the preceding paragraph is purchased by the company with terms of 2 percent discount if paid for within thirty days. While a majority of companies appear to view the $1 discount as a savings with a resulting inventory cost of only $49, other companies view the $1 discount as an item of miscellaneous income earned by the company and cost the inventory item at $50. From a theory point of view, the latter method is debatable, because nothing is earned by simply paying invoices in time to take advantage of cash discounts; income is recognized only when items are *sold* at a profit, not when purchased at a reduced cost.

Perpetual and Non-Perpetual Inventory Systems

Inventories may be accounted for by a perpetual inventory system which requires continuously maintained records indicating the amount of each individual item of inventory on hand at any given time. Or inventories may be accounted for by a non-perpetual inventory system which necessitates a physical count of the items to determine the amount of the inventory at a specific date. The non-perpetual system is often referred to as a periodic inventory system. A perpetual inventory system may be maintained only in terms of physical quantities of items or in terms of both physical quantities and dollars of cost.

Even though a business maintains its inventory record on a perpetual basis, it is necessary to verify the accuracy of these records by actual physical counts of the various inventory items. Such physical counts may be made at periodic intervals for selected inventory items during the year, or by a systematic continuous method which verifies each item of inventory at least once a year, or by complete annual physical count as of a given date. Regardless of the safeguards imposed by internal control systems to prevent inaccuracies and despite the advances in inventory control made possible by electronic computers, discrepancies do occur

[3] For example, a review by the Comptroller General of the United States of selected activities in the management of food supply by the Military Subsistence Supply Agency disclosed that transportation costs of approximately $600,000 annually which were applicable to perishable foods furnished to commissary stores were not being added to the prices charged such stores but, in effect, were being absorbed by the Government; see Report to the Congress of the United States by the Comptroller General of the United States, *Review of Selected Activities in the Management of Food Supply by the Military Subsistence Supply Agency, Department of Defense,* November 1961.

between an inventory quantity kept by perpetual records and the quantity obtained by a periodic physical count. The causes of such discrepancies, due to the "people" element in any system, range from clerical error to theft. The auditing standards of the public accounting profession require verification of inventories. To implement this standard, certain auditing procedures are followed, including the physical count or measurement of a sample of the company's inventory to test how well the company itself has performed the periodic physical count function.

Illustrative Facts

To present more fully the underlying theories involved in

(1) the determination of the cost to be deferred in inventory as of a specific date, and

(2) the determination of the cost applicable to the goods sold or used during a specific period of time,

the accompanying facts are assumed to present and compare the results under various cost determination methods for a single item (#156) of inventory.

	Item #156	
July 1	Inventory of 300 units, each at a cost of $50	
	PURCHASES AT VARYING COSTS AS INDICATED	SALES; ALL AT THE PRICE OF $80 PER UNIT
July 5	200 @ $52	
10		100
20	200 @ $55	
25		400
30	200 @ $57	
Totals	600 purchased	500 sold
July 31	Inventory of 400 units	

For clarity of comparison, the beginning inventory of 300 units is costed at $50 per unit for each inventory method illustrated. Though many methods of cost determination for the pricing of inventories are in use, only three methods are used extensively.[4] They are: first-in, first-out; average cost; and last-in, first-out.

[4] For a comprehensive survey relative to the frequency with which the various methods of cost determination are used in practice, see the latest annual edition of *Accounting Trends and Techniques in Published Corporate Annual Reports,* by the American Institute of Certified Public Accountants, Inc.

FIRST-IN, FIRST-OUT COST DETERMINATION METHOD							ITEM #156		
	RECEIVED (OR PURCHASED)			ISSUED (OR SOLD)			BALANCE ON HAND		
DATE	QUANTITY	UNIT COST	AMOUNT	QUANTITY	UNIT COST	AMOUNT	QUANTITY	UNIT COST	AMOUNT
July 1							300	$50	$15,000
5	200	$52	$10,400				300 200	50 52	25,400
10				100	$50	$ 5,000	200 200	50 52	20,400
20	200	55	11,000				200 200 200	50 52 55	31,400
25				200 200	50 52	20,400	200	55	11,000
30	200	57	11,400				200 200	55 57	22,400
Totals	600	—	$32,800	500	—	$25,400			

First-In, First-Out (FIFO) Method

The FIFO method of cost determination is based upon a flow of costs in which the first or earliest costs incurred are the first costed out of inventory. The method only assumes that the first items purchased or received are those items which are first sold or issued. The FIFO method of cost determination may be used regardless of the manner or order in which the actual goods are physically removed from inventory. Reference to the perpetual inventory record on page 278 clearly illustrates the issuance of 100 units on July 10 and 400 units on July 25 from the oldest priced units on hand at the time of each issuance. Thus, the net income for July, as shown by the statement of income, matches the earliest incurred costs with current revenue. And, since the goods are theoretically removed and costed from inventory in the same sequence as acquired, the ending inventory, shown as a current asset on the balance sheet at July 31, reflects the cost of the last 400 units acquired.

The FIFO method has been subject to much criticism because of its apparent failure to match current costs with current revenue. For example, the above inventory record indicates a cost of goods sold amount of $25,400 for the 500 units issued during July. The earliest costs of $50 and $52 are matched against revenue of the period. But the latest incurred and most current cost is $57 per unit. Because management is inclined to compare the most recent or current costs with the current selling price for decision-making purposes, the FIFO concept (as used for income determination) may be at variance with management's thinking when costs are not relatively stable.

The first statement of income (FIFO-perpetual) on page 289 shows a gross margin of $14,600. In a period of rising cost prices, as in our illustration, the FIFO method may somewhat overstate the income of the period, because it does not match current costs with revenue. Though the most current cost incurred is $57 per unit, the period's income has been determined by matching the oldest costs of $50 and $52 against current revenue of $80 per unit. And, in a period of falling cost prices, the reverse situation would occur: FIFO would tend to understate income of the period by matching the older higher costs against revenue.

The use of FIFO for the cost determination of inventory presented in balance sheets is not subject to the same degree of criticism. Because the first goods "in" are assumed to be the first goods "out," the last goods "in" are presumed to be those on hand at the balance sheet date. Reference to the preceding inventory record reveals that the ending inventory of 400 units consists of the most recent acquisitions totaling 400 units.

Thus, the inventory amount of $22,400 reflects the most recent costs of $55 and $57 per unit. Similarly, in a period of declining cost prices, the inventory amount would reflect the most recently incurred acquisition costs; as will be discussed shortly, there is a procedure whereby such declining costs may be written down to current replacement cost in case this amount is less than the most recently incurred acquisition costs. As shown by the diagram below, the FIFO method of cost determination allocates the total $47,800 cost of available goods (opening inventory of $15,000 plus purchases of $32,800) by charging the earliest acquisition costs against revenue of the period and deferring the most recent acquisition costs in inventory.

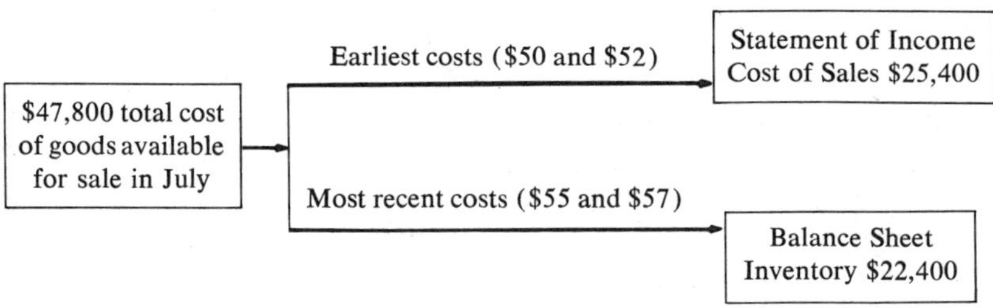

The analysis of the perpetual inventory record and the first statement of income on page 289 reveal the effect of FIFO on the financial statements.

The preceding discussion assumed that a perpetual inventory record of both quantity and dollars was maintained for inventory item #156. Now, consider the FIFO method under a non-perpetual or periodic inventory system. The company's records still indicate the following minimum information about the opening inventory and acquisitions during the period:

July 1	Inventory of 300 units	@ $50	$15,000
5	Purchase of 200 units	@ 52	10,400
20	Purchase of 200 units	@ 55	11,000
30	Purchase of 200 units	@ 57	11,400
	900		$47,800

A physical inventory count at July 31 reveals that there are 400 units on hand. The FIFO method of inventory assumes that the ending inventory consists of the latest 400 units acquired. Thus, the ending inventory is costed at the latest unit costs incurred to acquire the number of units presently on hand, as follows:

200 units × $57 =	$11,400	(last acquisition)
200 units × $55 =	11,000	(next to last acquisition)
400	$22,400	

When the ending inventory is stated at the latest incurred costs, the remaining (and earliest) portion of incurred costs is allocated to the units disposed of during the period, as follows:

July 1	Cost deferred in inventory of 300 units ...	$15,000
During July ..	Cost incurred for purchase of 600 units ...	32,800
	900 units ...	$47,800
July 31	Cost deferred in inventory of 400 units ...	22,400
For July	Cost charged against sales of 500 units ...	$25,400

It should be noted from this presentation and the second statement of income (FIFO-periodic) shown on page 289 that the FIFO method of cost determination gives identical results regardless of whether a perpetual or periodic inventory system is in use.

Last-In, First-Out (LIFO) Method

The LIFO method for the cost determination of inventory as of a specific date and for the cost of the goods sold or used during a specific period is somewhat the reverse of the FIFO method. The LIFO method is based upon a flow of costs whereby the last costs incurred are the first costed out of inventory as stock items are issued. The method assumes that the last items purchased (or received) are the first to be sold (or issued), regardless of the actual order in which the goods are physically issued from inventory. Reference to the perpetual inventory record below reveals that 100 units were issued on July 10 and 400 units were issued on July 25 from the latest priced units on hand at the time of each issuance. On a statement of income for July, current revenue would be matched with costs which are more current than those resulting from the FIFO method.

The LIFO method has been the subject of much discussion and wide adoption since World War II. It should be remembered that these years have been characterized by increasing costs and rising selling prices. From a theoretical point of view, LIFO is advocated for this type of situation, because it results in a more realistic net income by matching more current costs (usually higher) against revenue. For example, the following inventory record indicates a cost of goods sold of $26,400 for the 500 units issued during July. Except when the inventory level (on July 25) temporarily fell under the opening July 1 quantity on hand, the recent

LAST-IN, FIRST-OUT COST DETERMINATION METHOD							ITEM #156		
	RECEIVED (OR PURCHASED)			ISSUED (OR SOLD)			BALANCE ON HAND		
DATE	QUANTITY	UNIT COST	AMOUNT	QUANTITY	UNIT COST	AMOUNT	QUANTITY	UNIT COST	AMOUNT
July 1							300	$50	$15,000
5	200	$52	$10,400				300 200	50 52	25,400
10				100	$52	$ 5,200	300 100	50 52	20,200
20	200	55	11,000				300 100 200	50 52 55	31,200
25				200 100 100	55 52 50	21,200	200	50	10,000
30	200	57	11,400				200 200	50 57	21,400
Totals	600	—	$32,800	500	—	$26,400			

costs of $55 and $52 are matched against revenue of the period. The revenue from the first 200 units to be issued in August will be matched with the most recent acquisition cost of $57 per unit on July 30. It is contended that this is how management actually makes plans; i.e., by matching the current or most recent costs with current revenue. Past costs, while important as a guide in planning, are secondary to current costs in decision-making.[5]

The third statement of income (LIFO-perpetual) on page 289 shows a gross margin of $13,600. In a period of increasing costs, as in our illustration, the LIFO method will result in a smaller net income than will the FIFO method. This is because the higher, more recent costs are matched against current revenue of $80 per unit. By theory, the reduced margin of $1,000, which results from the use of LIFO, may be defended on the basis that the lower margin is more realistic: it matches more current costs with current revenue in income determination.

From a practical standpoint, tax considerations exert an even greater influence than the theoretical aspects mentioned so far. For example, when R. J. Reynolds Tobacco Company adopted LIFO in 1957, it reduced its earnings before taxes for that year by $26,897,049 and, accordingly, its income taxes by appoximately $14,555,000. Because LIFO assumes that materials and other cost elements used in production or sold are the most recent acquisitions, LIFO boosts production costs and the subsequent cost of the goods sold in periods of rising costs. So long as costs continue to increase, the tax advantage continues. Presumably, R. J. Reynolds did not expect their cost prices to drop below their January 1, 1957, level.

While LIFO is logical from the standpoint of stating the results of current operations by charging against revenue the more recent and current costs, it may seriously distort the dollar inventory amount shown by the balance sheet. Because the last goods "in" are assumed to be the first goods "out," the old first goods "in" are presumed to be those on hand at the balance sheet date. Reference to the preceding inventory record discloses that, though 500 units are sold during July, 200 of the 300 old $50 units on hand at the start of the period are assumed to be still on hand. In fact, all 300 of the old units would be presumed to be still on hand if the inventory level had not dropped below 300 units on July 25 (a point which the LIFO-periodic system ignores, as will be shown). Thus, the inventory amount of $21,400 reflects the somewhat ancient cost

[5] A logical extension of this reasoning would lead to a NIFO (next-in, first-out) concept. A sale of a unit normally leads to the purchase of another unit for inventory. Thus, it is the cost of the next unit "in" which should be compared with the revenue from the present unit sold to more perfectly match costs with revenue.

of $50 for half of the units. That $50 cost will remain as long as at least 200 units are on hand, regardless of the time that may elapse or the amount of the increase in current replacement cost. This resulting understatement of the current asset is sometimes called the "LIFO cushion" or "LIFO reserve."

The preceding discussion assumed that a perpetual inventory record showing both quantity and dollars was maintained for inventory item #156. Now, consider the use of the LIFO method under a non-perpetual or periodic inventory system. The company's records would still indicate the following minimum information concerning the opening inventory and acquisitions during the period:

July 1	Inventory of	300 units	@ $50	$15,000
5	Purchase of	200 units	@ 52	10,400
20	Purchase of	200 units	@ 55	11,000
30	Purchase of	200 units	@ 57	11,400
		900		$47,800

A physical inventory count at July 31 reveals that there are 400 units on hand. The LIFO method assumes that the ending inventory consists of the earliest 400 units acquired; the ending inventory is costed at the earliest unit costs incurred to acquire the number of units presently on hand, as follows:

300 units × $50 =	$15,000	(earliest acquisition)
100 units × 52 =	5,200	(next to earliest acquisition)
400	$20,200	

When the ending inventory is stated at the earliest or oldest costs, it is the remaining and most recent portion of incurred costs ($27,600) which is allocated to the units disposed of during the period. It should be noted from this presentation and the fourth statement of income (LIFO-

July 1	Cost deferred in inventory of 300 units ...	$15,000
During July ..	Cost incurred for purchase of 600 units ...	32,800
	900 units ...	$47,800
July 31	Cost deferred in inventory of 400 units ...	20,200
For July	Cost charged against sales of 500 units ...	$27,600

periodic) shown on page 289 that the LIFO method of cost determination will not give identical results for the perpetual and the periodic system whenever the inventory quantity level decreases, *during* the period, so that some of the older cost layers are assumed to have been issued prior to the acquisition of additional goods. The application of

LIFO by the periodic system more aptly parallels the underlying theory of LIFO, because it ignores fluctuating inventory levels *during* the period. Thus, the LIFO base of 300 units at $50 each will never be reduced until the inventory quantity drops below 300 units as of the close of the fiscal period.

As shown by the diagram below, the LIFO method of cost determination allocates the total $47,800 cost of available goods (opening inventory of $15,000 plus purchases of $32,800) by charging the most recent costs against revenue of the period and deferring the earliest or oldest costs in inventory.[6] This analysis is based upon the periodic system of LIFO discussed immediately above and shown by the fourth statement of income (LIFO-periodic) on page 289.

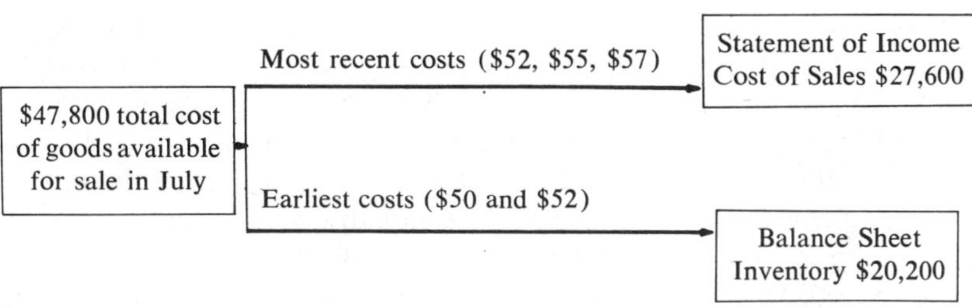

Average Cost Methods

Though there are several variations in the method by which an average cost may be determined, the most common procedure determines the average unit cost by weighting the calculation in relation to the differing

[6] These comments regarding LIFO have been presented for an uncomplicated situation: no trouble is encountered in applying the theory and following the cost flow for one stock item. However, consider a company with many different items of inventory, or a diversified company that manufactures everything from light bulbs to appliances, motors, and generators. Similarly, think of the complications when a company changes models of an existing product or drops a product line but adds a new line in its place. And, in a manufacturing concern, the difficulty of tracing the various factors of cost through succeeding stages of production to finished goods inventory may be quite complex. An analysis of such complicating factors is beyond the scope of this book and is not necessary for an understanding of the LIFO concept. It is sufficient to say that such complicating factors have been overcome without an impossible amount of clerical work. Illustrations later in this chapter reveal actual companies with such complications which are on LIFO. Among the procedures in use to minimize LIFO difficulties is the grouping of many inventory items into a few "pools" and the use of the "dollar value" method by the application of index numbers to year-end inventories.

quantities of goods acquired at varying costs. The weighted average unit cost is determined by dividing the total dollar cost of units available for sale or issue by the total number of such units.

Moving Average Method

If a perpetual inventory record is maintained showing both quantity and cost price, a new weighted average unit cost must be determined at the time of each acquisition if the unit purchase price differs from the unit cost of those items already on hand. When the weighted average method is used in conjunction with such a perpetual inventory system, it is called the moving average method. Reference to the assumed facts on page 277 and to the perpetual inventory record and accompanying unit cost calculations on the next page reveals the determination of cost by the moving average method. On July 5, when the month's first purchase of stock item #156 is made, the 200 units purchased increase the balance on hand to 500. Dividing the $25,400 total cost by the 500 available units results in a weighted average unit cost of $50.80. This unit cost is used for the cost determination of all units on hand *and* all units issued or sold until additional units are acquired at a cost other than the present $50.80; in this case, on July 20.

The moving average method is affected by both past costs and most recent costs in the determination of both the July 31 inventory amount and the cost of the goods sold during July. To a degree, the averaging procedure levels out a fluctuating unit cost; the amount of cost deferred in inventory as of a given date and the amount of cost allocated to the units sold during the period usually fall between the amounts as determined by FIFO and LIFO. Comparison of the fifth statement of income (moving average-perpetual) with the preceding four statements on page 289 illustrates this point. In a period of rising costs indicated by our assumed facts, the moving average unit cost will lag and be less than most recent costs. In a period of falling costs, this same lag will result in a moving average unit cost which exceeds most recent costs.

Weighted Average Method

The weighted average method involves the same basic concepts and results in the same general effects as the moving average method. The weighted average method is used when an averaging effect on costs is desired by the company which uses the periodic inventory system or employs the perpetual inventory system only for quantities. At certain intervals, as at the end of each month when financial statements are prepared, a weighted average unit cost is computed. This unit cost is then used to

MOVING AVERAGE COST DETERMINATION METHOD							ITEM #156		
	RECEIVED (OR PURCHASED)			ISSUED (OR SOLD)			BALANCE ON HAND		
DATE	QUANTITY	UNIT COST	AMOUNT	QUANTITY	UNIT COST	AMOUNT	QUANTITY	UNIT COST	AMOUNT
July 1							300	$50.00	$15,000
5	200	$52	$10,400				500	50.80	25,400
10				100	$50.80	$ 5,080	400	50.80	20,320
20	200	55	11,000				600	52.20	31,320
25				400	52.20	20,880	200	52.20	10,440
30	200	57	11,400				400	54.60	21,840
Totals	600	—	$32,800	500	—	$25,960			

Computation of weighted average unit cost:

July 5 — July 20 — July 30

$$\frac{\text{Total cost}}{\text{Total units}} = \frac{\$25{,}400}{500} = \$50.80 \qquad \frac{\$31{,}320}{600} = \$52.20 \qquad \frac{\$21{,}840}{400} = \$54.60$$

determine both the cost of all units on hand in inventory at that date and the cost of all units sold or issued during the period. Using the assumed data on page 277, the weighted average unit cost of $53.11 may be determined as follows:

July 1	.....	Opening inventory	300 units @ $50 =	$15,000
5	.....	Purchased	200 units @ 52 =	10,400
20	.....	Purchased	200 units @ 55 =	11,000
30	.....	Purchased	200 units @ 57 =	11,400
			900	$47,800

$$\text{Weighted average unit cost} = \frac{\text{Cost of units available for sale}}{\text{Number of units available for sale}}$$

$$\text{Weighted average unit cost} = \frac{\$47{,}800}{900} = \$53.11$$

The 400 units on hand at July 31, as determined by a physical count or by a perpetual inventory record maintained for quantities only, multiplied by the weighted average unit cost of $53.11, defers $21,244 of cost in inventory as a current asset. The 500 units sold during July, multiplied by the same $53.11 unit cost, results in a cost of goods sold of $26,556 to be charged against the July revenue. A comparison of the diagram below with the two preceding diagrams for FIFO and LIFO shows the effects of the different methods upon the determination of costs deferred in inventory and costs charged against revenue of the period.

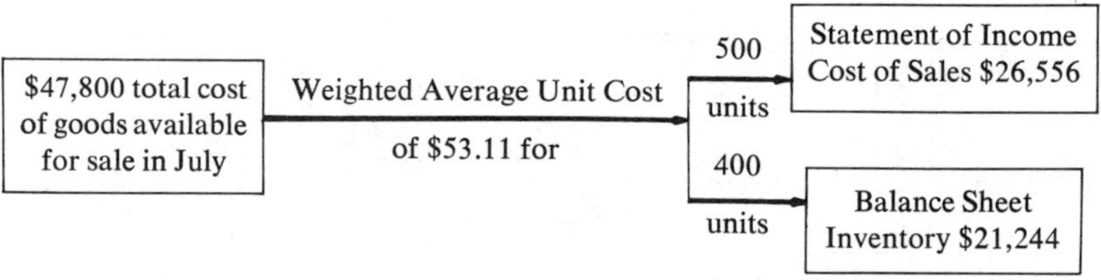

An analysis of the sixth statement of income (weighted average-periodic) below reveals the same general effect upon gross margin, when compared to FIFO and LIFO, as that caused by the moving average method.

Illustrative Comparison of Cost Methods

The six illustrative statements of income shown below have been referenced repeatedly regarding the comparative effects of the three principal methods of cost determination. A study of these statements, the summary presented below, and a review of the underlying principles of each inventory method are suggested at this point.

Statement of Income (through Gross Margin)
Month of July

	Units	First-In, First-Out (Perpetual)		First-In, First-Out (Periodic)	
Sales	500		$40,000		$40,000
Cost of Goods Sold:					
Inventory, July 1	300	$15,000		$15,000	
Purchases	600	32,800		32,800	
Available for Sale	900	$47,800		$47,800	
Inventory, July 31	400	22,400		22,400	
Cost of Goods Sold	500		25,400		25,400
Gross Margin on Sales			$14,600		$14,600

	Units	Last-In, First-Out (Perpetual)		Last-In, First-Out (Periodic)	
Sales	500		$40,000		$40,000
Cost of Goods Sold:					
Inventory, July 1	300	$15,000		$15,000	
Purchases	600	32,800		32,800	
Available for Sale	900	$47,800		$47,800	
Inventory, July 31	400	21,400		20,200	
Cost of Goods Sold	500		26,400		27,600
Gross Margin on Sales			$13,600		$12,400

	Units	Moving Average (Perpetual)		Weighted Average (Periodic)	
Sales	500		$40,000		$40,000
Cost of Goods Sold:					
Inventory, July 1	300	$15,000		$15,000	
Purchases	600	32,800		32,800	
Available for Sale	900	$47,800		$47,800	
Inventory, July 31	400	21,840		21,244	
Cost of Goods Sold	500		25,960		26,556
Gross Margin on Sales			$14,040		$13,444

Cost Determination Method	Inventory System	Balance Sheet July 31 Current Asset Inventory	Statement of Income for July		
			Sales	Cost of Goods Sold	Gross Margin on Sales
First-in, first-out	Perpetual	$22,400	$40,000	$25,400	$14,600
First-in, first-out	Periodic	22,400	40,000	25,400	14,600
Last-in, first-out	Perpetual	21,400	40,000	26,400	13,600
Last-in, first-out	Periodic	20,200	40,000	27,600	12,400
Moving average	Perpetual	21,840	40,000	25,960	14,040
Weighted average	Periodic	21,244	40,000	26,556	13,444

Before proceeding further, a few points basic to all of the preceding discussion should be reiterated to prevent possible misinterpretations. First, to clearly isolate the varying effects of the different cost determination methods, an opening inventory of $15,000 (300 units at $50 each) was assumed for each of the six illustrations. Normally, this would not occur unless this is the first month of business and the beginning inventory constitutes a portion of the initial capital investment or the business is a going concern now changing its inventory method from a plan whereby in the past each item of inventory always has been specifically identified with its own individual acquisition cost. In fact, if a zero opening inventory is assumed, the varying effects of the three principal cost determination methods would be as discussed. Whatever the inventory method selected, the July 31 current asset amount listed in the table immediately above will become the August 1 amount of opening inventory and thus continue the effect of the method used in July. Second, a period of rising costs was selected for the illustrative examples and the rate of the cost increase condensed into the one-month illustration might better be viewed as a panorama of a longer period of time. Even a one-year period can result in a significant change. It has already been mentioned that the use of LIFO reduced the net income of R. J. Reynolds Tobacco Company by $26,897,049 before tax and by $12,342,049 after tax. Similar results were experienced by Westinghouse Electric Corporation during 1956, its first year on LIFO; increasing costs were charged against revenue rather than deferred to year-end inventory, and net income was reduced $25,000,000 before tax and $12,000,000 after tax. Third, the effects of the various cost determination methods of inventory should be considered for increasing, decreasing, and stable cost levels. In general, an increasing cost level has been characteristic of the past twenty years. The long-run effect of LIFO upon income determination, in a period of increasing cost levels, is indicated by the excerpts taken from the annual reports of companies shown on pages 310–11. Decreasing cost levels would give opposite effects. Such an experience occurred in the late 1950's when copper prices decreased sharply. Companies with copper inventories on LIFO were forced to match lower, not higher, current costs against revenue. For an illustration of the effects of such a situation, see page 308. If cost levels were stable over a considerable period of time, any of the three inventory cost determination methods theoretically would produce identical results. Fourth, even if it were assumed that over a long period of time what goes up comes down, the aggregate income of the business entity for this lengthy period would not necessarily be identical regardless of its inventory method. Federal and state income tax rates change. And even if tax rates were stable over a long period of time, the company that pays a lower tax in year one which is offset by a higher tax in year ten has benefited by the "time-value" of the additional funds it has had for use in the business during the intervening years.

QUESTIONS AND PROBLEMS

9–1 The Mason-Dixon Company purchases and sells a single commodity. Records of the company disclose the following activity with respect to this one item of inventory during January:

Inventory balance, January 1	1000 units at $15 unit cost ..	$15,000
Weekly purchases, in order of acquisition	500 units at $16 unit cost ..	$ 8,000
	500 units at $17 unit cost ..	$ 8,500
	500 units at $18 unit cost ..	$ 9,000
	1000 units at $21 unit cost ..	$21,000
Total January purchases	2500	$46,500
Daily January sales totaled	2000 units at $30 unit price ..	$60,000
Inventory balance, January 31	1500 units	

Required

Complete the statement of income, as far as gross margin on sales, assuming that the company is on:

a. FIFO

b. LIFO

c. Weighted Average

	FIFO	LIFO	Weighted Average
Net Sales	$60,000	$60,000	$60,000
Cost of Goods Sold:			
Inventory, January 1 . .	$15,000	$15,000	$15,000
Purchases			
Cost of Goods Available for Sale	$	$	$
Inventory, January 31 . .			
Cost of Goods Sold	$	$	$
Gross Margin on Sales . . .	$	$	$

9–2. The Jeb Stuart Company purchases and sells a single commodity. Records of the company disclose the following activity with respect to this one item of inventory during January:

Inventory balance, January 1	1000 units at $25 unit cost . .	$25,000
Weekly purchases, in order of acquisition	500 units at $25 unit cost . .	$12,500
	500 units at $27 unit cost . .	$13,500
	500 units at $28 unit cost . .	$14,000
	500 units at $32 unit cost . .	$16,000
Total January purchases	2000	$56,000
Total January sales . .	2000 units at $35 unit price . .	$70,000
Inventory balance, January 31	1000 units	

For each of the following statements, choose the best answer to each and indicate your choice on an answer sheet with the number 1, 2, 3, or 4.

a. If inventory costs are accounted for on a FIFO basis, the cost of the January 31 inventory is:

1. $27,500

2. $30,000
3. $26,000
4. None of the above

b. If on FIFO, the January cost of goods is:
1. $56,000
2. $43,500
3. $51,000
4. None of the above

c. If on FIFO, the gross margin on the statement of income would be:
1. $19,000
2. $14,000
3. $16,500
4. None of the above

d. If inventory costs are accounted for on a LIFO basis (non-perpetual), the cost of the January 31 inventory is:
1. $25,000
2. $30,000
3. $26,000
4. None of the above

e. If on LIFO, the January cost of goods sold is:
1. $40,000
2. $65,000
3. $56,000
4. None of the above

f. If on LIFO, the gross margin on the statement of income would be:
1. $ 5,000
2. $14,000
3. $20,000
4. None of the above

g. If inventory costs are accounted for on a weighted average basis, the cost of the January 31 inventory is:
1. $25,000
2. $29,000
3. $27,000
4. None of the above

h. And, if on weighted average, the January cost of goods sold is:
1. $58,000
2. $54,000
3. $50,000
4. None of the above

i. And, if on weighted average, the gross margin on the statement of income would be:
1. $16,000

2. $20,000
3. $12,000
4. None of the above

9–3. Manson Company sells over 100 different products; the facts presented pertain to only one of these products. The January 1, 1974, inventory contained 400 units, each of which had been purchased at a cost of $6. During 1974, cost prices rose steadily, but competitive conditions forced the company to keep its selling price at $15 per unit throughout the year. During 1974, Manson Company made the following purchases and sales of this product:

January 27	Purchased	300 units @	$ 7
April 15	Sold	400 units @	15
August 13	Purchased	500 units @	8
November 28	Sold	400 units @	15

A physical inventory count on December 31, 1974, revealed 400 units on hand.

Required

a. Compute the cost of the December 31, 1974, inventory balance.

b. Prepare a statement of income for the year 1974 through the point of gross margin on sales. Indicate clearly the determination of the cost of goods sold amount.

For comparison, requirements a and b are to be prepared under each of the following six assumptions:

Perpetual inventory system maintained for both quantities and amounts	Periodic inventory system
1. First-in, first-out basis	2. First-in, first-out basis
3. Last-in, first-out basis	4. Last-in, first-out basis
5. Moving average basis	6. Weighted average basis

Carry unit cost calculations to the nearest cent.

9–4. Manson Company, which had been subject to rising cost levels in 1974 (see problem 9–3), experienced stable costs for goods acquired in 1975. And, throughout 1975, the company maintained a selling price of $15 per unit. During 1975, Manson Company made the following purchases and sales:

February 16	Purchased	300 units @	$ 8
June 18	Sold	500 units @	15
October 23	Purchased	500 units @	8
December 11	Sold	200 units @	15

A physical inventory count on December 31, 1975, revealed 500 units on hand.

Required

For 1975, solve requirements a and b as stated for problem 9–3, except, for comparison, assume only the periodic inventory system throughout. This will limit the comparison to assumptions 2, 4, and 6 as listed in the preceding problem. Remember that the ending inventory under each of the three assumptions in the preceding problem will be the opening inventory for this problem.

9–5. Manson Company, which had, at first, been subject to rising cost levels and then, to stable costs (see problems 9–3 and 9–4), experienced declining costs for goods acquired in 1976. Despite falling costs, the company was able to maintain a selling price of $15 per unit throughout the year. During 1976, Manson Company made the following purchases and sales:

March 18	Purchased	500 units @	$ 6
May 5	Sold	400 units @	15
July 31	Purchased	300 units @	5
November 16	Sold	500 units @	15

A physical inventory count on December 31, 1976, revealed 400 units on hand.

Required

For 1976, solve requirements stated for 1975 in the preceding problem.

9–6. Manson Company, which had experienced rising, stable, and declining acquisition costs (see problems 9–3, 9–4, and 9–5) on the product in question, believed that this product would soon become obsolete because of a recent technological break-through which would revolutionize the product. Therefore, in January of 1977, they quickly sold the 400 units in their opening inventory for $10 each and discontinued the product.

Required

a. Compute the gross margin on the 1977 sale of the 400 units by matching the revenue received ($4,000) with the January 1 inventory carrying cost. (See the three December 31 inventory amounts arrived at in problem 9–5.)

b. Summarize the results of Manson Company's experience over the period 1974–1977 by preparing and completing the following table:

YEAR	FIRST-IN, FIRST-OUT			LAST-IN, FIRST-OUT			WEIGHTED AVERAGE		
	SALES	COST OF SALES	GROSS MARGIN	SALES	COST OF SALES	GROSS MARGIN	SALES	COST OF SALES	GROSS MARGIN
1974									
1975									
1976									
1977									
Totals									

c. The management of Manson Company is considering a change in its inventory pricing method for all of its products. For years, the weighted average method has been used, but the management believes that this method is a compromise between FIFO and LIFO, which makes both the balance sheet and the statement of income somewhat unrealistic. Furthermore, it believes that it is at a tax disadvantage, because it does not use LIFO. The short-lived experience and resultant profit pattern encountered with the product in question over the years 1974–1977 is true for about 50 percent of the company's volume. The other 50 percent of volume is characterized by rising costs and rising selling prices. On the whole, you believe management favors a 100 percent switch to LIFO. Prepare a statement giving your recommendations and the reasons behind your recommendations.

9–7. The timing of certain events over which management *does* have control can have an impact on certain short-run financial results. Consider the following case concerning the timing of the company's year-end purchase of 10,000 units of Product A.

BOULDER CORPORATION

Balance Sheet

December 31, 1973

ASSETS		LIABILITIES	
Current Assets:		Current Liabilities:	
Various	$200,000	Various	$150,000
Inventory of Merchandise	100,000		
Total Current Assets	$300,000		

The January 1, 1974, inventory of merchandise of $100,000 consisted of 20,000 units of Product A at $5 each. During 1974, Boulder Corporation sold 80,000 units at $12 each and purchased 70,000 units at $7 each. Because the year-end inventory quantity is only one-half its level of a year ago, the company plans to purchase 10,000 units in early January of 1975; current replacement cost is still $7 per unit. Following are the resultant 1974 financial statements; they assume; first, that the company is on FIFO; second, that the company is on LIFO.

Statement of Income

For the Year Ended December 31, 1974

	FIFO Basis	LIFO Basis
Net Sales	$960,000	$960,000
Cost of Goods Sold	520,000	540,000
Gross Margin	$440,000	$420,000
Operating Expenses	220,000	220,000
Net Income before Income Tax	$220,000	$200,000
Federal and State Income Taxes @ 50%	110,000	100,000
Net Income for Year	$110,000	$100,000

Balance Sheet

December 31, 1974

	FIFO Basis	LIFO Basis
Current Assets:		
Various	$330,000	$330,000
Inventory of Merchandise	70,000	50,000
Total Current Assets	$400,000	$380,000
Current Liabilities:		
Various	160,000	150,000
Working Capital	$240,000	$230,000
Current Ratio	2.50 to 1	2.53 to 1

Required

Assume that, instead of replacing inventory in early January of 1975, Boulder Corporation replaces the liquidated inventory in late December of 1974 by purchasing (and paying for) 10,000 units at $7 each to restore the inventory quantity to its January 1, 1974, level. Assuming first FIFO, then LIFO, prepare:

a. Revised statements of income for 1974.

b. Revised partial balance sheets as of December 31, 1974.

c. Revised calculations of working capital and current ratio.

d. Short statement concerning the differing effect upon the flow of funds.

e. Short statement giving your recommendations to Boulder Corporation about the timing of year-end purchases of merchandise.

9–8. Stonewall Jackson Company purchases and sells a single commodity, "Champ." Records of the company disclose the following activity for "Champ" during January of 1974:

	Units	Unit Cost
Inventory balance, January 1	500	$10
Purchases during month:		
January 10	1,000	$11
January 20	2,000	12
Total purchases	3,000	
Sales during month:		
January 5	200	
January 15	800	
January 25	2,100	
Total sales	3,100	
Inventory balance, January 31	400	

Indicate the inventory cost at January 31 and the cost of goods sold for the month of January under six different possible methods by choosing from among the following possible answers:

1.	$ 4,200	8.	4,400	15.	35,800
2.	4,000	9.	4,100	16.	4,701
3.	4,571	10.	35,200	17.	35,429
4.	4,800	11.	35,900	18.	36,167
5.	4,667	12.	34,100	19.	35,299
6.	35,600	13.	31,000		
7.	36,000	14.	37,200		

a. Method: FIFO. Perpetual inventory is maintained and units sold are costed out of inventory currently.
   Inventory, January 31: Answer .... ( )
   Cost of goods sold: Answer .... ( )

b. Method: FIFO. No perpetual inventory record is operated.
   Inventory, January 31: Answer .... ( )
   Cost of goods sold: Answer .... ( )

c. Method: LIFO. Perpetual inventory is maintained and units sold are costed out of inventory currently.

Inventory, January 31: Answer .... ( )
Cost of goods sold: Answer .... ( )

d. Method: LIFO. No perpetual inventory record is operated.
Inventory, January 31: Answer .... ( )
Cost of goods sold: Answer .... ( )

e. Method: Moving average. Perpetual inventory is maintained and units are costed out of inventory currently.
Inventory, January 31: Answer .... ( )
Cost of goods sold: Answer .... ( )

f. Method: Weighted average.
Inventory, January 31: Answer .... ( )
Cost of goods sold: Answer .... ( )

9–9. This problem contains several statements designed to test your knowledge of the effects upon financial statements caused by differing methods of pricing inventories and costing goods issued or sold. Indicate your answer to each statement by choosing from among the following three possibilities:

1. FIFO
2. LIFO
3. Moving average

a. During a period of constantly rising prices for goods purchased:
Ending inventory will be highest using .... ( )
Cost of goods sold will be lowest using .... ( )
Net profit for the period will be lowest using .... ( )

b. During a period of constantly falling prices for goods purchased:
Ending inventory will be lowest using .... ( )
Cost of goods sold will be lowest using .... ( )
Net profit for the period will be highest using .... ( )

c. The pricing method that most nearly matches current costs with current revenue is .... ( )

d. In a period of rising prices, the inventory on the balance sheet is valued nearest to current cost when the inventory method used is .... ( )

e. An inventory method which, normally, may be used for federal income taxes only if it is used for general accounting is .... ( )

f. In situations where there is a rapid inventory turnover, an inventory method which produces almost the same results as FIFO is .... ( )

9–10. Assume the following facts for the first month of business of Elterich Company. (The March 1 inventory of 400 units constitutes a portion of the original investment in the business.)

			Units	Unit Cost
March	1	Inventory of Merchandise balance . .	400	$6.00
	5	Units purchased	200	7.00
	12	Units sold	300	
	20	Units purchased	500	8.00
	31	Units sold	600	

There were 200 units in the inventory of merchandise at March 31. The company does not use a perpetual inventory method.

a. *Weighted Average Method of Cost Determination:*

Cost is determined by multiplying the number of units on hand at the end of the period by the weighted average unit cost. The weighted average unit cost is determined by dividing the total cost of units available for sale by the total number of units available for sale during a particular period. Compute the cost of merchandise inventory as of March 31.

b. *First-in, First-out Method of Cost Determination:*

1. Cost is determined by assuming for pricing purposes that the first units purchased will be the first units sold. Thus, the final inventory will be priced at the latest unit costs incurred to acquire the number of units on hand. Compute the cost of merchandise inventory as of March 31.
2. If the final inventory of merchandise had consisted of 600 units instead of 200 units, what would have been the cost of the inventory?

c. *Last-in, First-out Method of Cost Determination:*

1. Cost is determined by assuming for pricing purposes that the last units purchased will be the first units sold. Thus, the final inventory will be priced at the earliest unit costs incurred to acquire the number of units on hand. Compute the cost of merchandise inventory as of March 31.
2. If the final inventory of merchandise had consisted of 600 units instead of 200 units, what would have been the cost of the inventory?

d. *Comparative Results of Various Methods of Inventory Pricing:*

In addition to the facts assumed initially, use net sales of $9,000 (900 units @ $10 selling price) to complete the comparative table provided on page 301.

The table shows that, due to price fluctuations, inventory values at the end of the accounting period—and reported profits for the period—will differ under various methods of inventory pricing. Observe that changes in the amount of the gross margin on sales during the first month of business correspond exactly with the increase or decrease in the ending inventory. This occurs because the cost of goods sold is affected inversely by variations in the cost of the ending inventory. It should be recognized that the inventory method used initially must be consistently followed in subsequent months.

1. During a period of rising cost prices, what method of inventory pricing tends to reduce the amount of reported profit?
2. During a period of falling cost prices, what method of inventory pricing tends to maximize the inventory shown on the balance sheet?

COMPARATIVE TABLE SHOWING EFFECT OF VARIOUS METHODS OF INVENTORY PRICING

	WEIGHTED AVERAGE	FIRST-IN, FIRST-OUT	LAST-IN, FIRST-OUT
Net Sales	$9,000	$9,000	$9,000
Cost of Goods Sold:			
Inventory of Merchandise, March 1	$2,400	$2,400	$2,400
Purchases			
Cost of Merchandise Available for Sale	$	$	$
Less: Inventory of Merchandise, March 31			
Cost of Goods Sold	$	$	$
Gross Margin on Sales	$	$	$

10

Inventories (concluded)

THE LOWER OF COST OR MARKET

To this point, all of the discussion has centered on the principal methods employed to determine the *cost* of inventory for the balance sheet and the *cost* of goods sold for the period's operating statement. Market conditions may occur so that the *cost* of the items contained in an inventory exceeds that at which the goods currently can be replaced. Competitive conditions often force selling prices down when replacement costs decrease. Therefore, it may be unrealistic to defer in inventory a cost amount in excess of current replacement cost. Such a decline might logically be charged against revenue in the period when the decline occurred rather than in a succeeding period when the goods are sold. The use of cost or market, the lower, recognizes this concept in the valuation of inventories.

The recommendation of the AICPA concerning the application of the lower of cost or market with respect to inventory pricing is as follows:

> A departure from the cost basis of pricing the inventory is required when the utility of the goods is no longer as great as its cost. Where there is evidence that the utility of goods, in their disposal in

> the ordinary course of business, will be less than cost, whether due to physical deterioration, obsolescence, changes in price levels, or other causes, the difference should be recognized as a loss of the current period. This is generally accomplished by stating such goods at a lower level commonly designated as *market*.[1]

For the meaning of the term market, the AICPA states:

> As used in the phrase *lower of cost or market,* the term *market* means current replacement cost (by purchase or by reproduction, as the case may be) except that:
>
> (1) Market should not exceed the net realizable value (i.e., estimated selling price in the ordinary course of business less reasonably predictable costs of completion and disposal); and
>
> (2) Market should not be less than net realizable value reduced by an allowance for an approximately normal profit margin.[2]

Not all accountants completely agree with certain of the details stated immediately above by the AICPA with respect to the upper and lower limits used to determine market figures. Because these theoretical details are unnecessary for a basic understanding of the lower of cost or market, the issue will be avoided in the forthcoming example by assuming that market falls within these limits.

The concept of the lower of cost or market should not be viewed as another method of cost determination of inventory. First, cost must be determined by one of the three principal methods which have been discussed. Then, cost should be compared to market. For federal income tax purposes, a business may value its inventories either at cost or at the lower of cost or market. Once the valuation method has been selected, it may not be changed without the permission of the Internal Revenue Service. However, a business may not value its inventory at the lower of cost or market for tax purposes if it determines the cost of the inventory by the use of the LIFO method.

When a company values its inventory by the lower of cost or market, its application may be on an item by item basis or on the inventory total as a whole or on a basis of separate groups of the inventory. The table below illustrates the determination of inventory at the lower of cost or market by the first procedure. If the company values its ending inventory

---

[1] Accounting Research Bulletin No. 43, "Restatement and Revision of Accounting Research Bulletins," p. 30, *Accounting Research and Terminology Bulletins, Final Edition*. Copyright 1961 by the American Institute of Certified Public Accountants, Inc.

[2] *Ibid.*, p. 31.

at cost, on a FIFO basis, its valuation is $6,500. But, if the company has selected the lower of cost or market as its valuation basis, the inventory will be shown at $6,300 if market is applied to the inventory as a whole, since that amount is $200 less than cost. And if the application of the lower of cost or market is made to the inventory on an item by item basis, the inventory will be shown at $6,210, because that amount is $290 less than cost. Again, the company must be consistent from year to year in the procedure by which the lower of cost or market is determined.

INVENTORY AT DECEMBER 31, 1974

ITEM	QUANTITY	UNIT PRICE		INVENTORY AT		C OR M,
		COST (1)	MARKET (2)	COST	MARKET	LOWER
AB	100	$ 9.00	$8.50	$ 900	$ 850	$ 850
CD	400	10.00	9.40	4,000	3,760	3,760
EF	300	2.00	2.10	600	630	600
GH	200	5.00	5.30	1,000	1,060	1,000
				$6,500	$6,300	$6,210

(1) As determined, for example, by FIFO.
(2) Meaning current replacement cost.

The use of the lower of cost or market, which allows inventory to be shown at an amount below cost, is consistent with the principle of conservatism. As noted in other chapters, many accounting procedures are based on this principle, which never anticipates profits but always anticipates and provides for losses. If the company with the assumed facts of the preceding paragraph values its December 31, 1974 inventory at the lower of cost or market amount of $6,210, the write-down of the inventory by $290 will constitute a charge against revenue for the year 1974. Thus the reduction of net income is made in the year of the decline, not in 1975 when the goods are sold. Regardless of the direction in which selling prices of the goods actually may move in 1975, the charge against the revenue realized from such sales will be the $6,210 of "cost" deferred in inventory, not the actual cost of $6,500.

As previously stated, an analysis of methods used by companies for determining cost of inventories showed that the great majority used FIFO, LIFO, or average cost. However, this same analysis reveals that, as a basis of pricing, the use of the lower of cost or market very greatly exceeds the use of cost as a basis.[3]

[3] See latest edition of *Accounting Trends and Techniques*.

Examples of the use of the lower of cost or market illustrate the concepts just presented. The Balance Sheet of Fruehauf Corporation at December 31, 1972 showed:

Current Assets:	
Inventories (Note B)	$105,805,368

The "Summary of Accounting Principles" section contained the following disclosure as to determination of both "cost" and "market."

> *Inventories*—Inventory amounts are based upon physical determinations during the year and have been stated at the lower of cost or market prices. Cost prices are determined by the first-in, first-out method, and market prices represent the lower of replacement cost or estimated net realizable amount.

The 1972 annual report of Ingersoll-Rand Company discloses the fact that cost has been reduced by an allowance for obsolete inventory. It is

Current Assets
Inventories

Note 1—*Summary of Significant Accounting Policies*

Inventories: Inventories are valued at the lower of cost less allowances for obsolescence, principally on the first-in, first-out basis, or market.

Note 4—*Inventories:* The composition of inventories at December 31, 1972 is as follows:

Raw materials and supplies	$ 31,609,000
Work in process	96,753,000
Finished goods	215,298,000
	$343,660,000

not unusual to use different cost determination methods for different segments of inventory as shown by the Statement of Financial Position of American Metal Climax, Inc., at December 31, 1971.

Current Assets:	
Inventories (Note 7)	$159,190,000

Note 7:

Metals refined and in-process at the lower of cost (primarily last-in, first out) or market (at December 31 market quotations: 1971, $130,000,000)	$ 66,280,000

Metal fabricated products, etc., at the lower of cost (primarily first-in, first-out) or market ..	47,340,000
Ores, concentrates, and chemicals, at the lower of average cost (primarily) or market	25,840,000
Operating supplies, at average cost, less reserves	19,730,000
	$159,190,000

The valuation basis is somewhat different for each of the four classes of inventory, and three different cost determination methods are employed.

As shown by the Balance Sheet of Exxon Corporation, formerly Standard Oil Company (New Jersey), at December 31, 1972, both FIFO and LIFO are used as cost determination methods and both are valued at lower of cost or market.

Current Assets:

Inventories

Crude oil, products, and merchandise	$1,546,213,000
Materials and supplies	199,228,000

Summary of Accounting Principles

Inventories—Crude oil, products, and merchandise inventories are carried at the lower of current market value or cost (approximately 60 percent determined under the first-in, first-out method and the remainder under the last-in, first-out method). Inventories of materials and supplies are valued at cost or less.

While the use of LIFO coupled with the lower of cost or market is mandatory for external reporting, federal income tax regulations specifically prohibit the use of the lower of cost or market when cost is determined by LIFO. The paramount reason for this restriction on the use of LIFO can be shown by a simplified illustration. Assume a time period of rising cost levels followed by a time period of falling cost levels. Ignoring factors such as a changed tax rate, the total profit earned over the sum of *all* time periods should be identical whether FIFO or LIFO is used.

Time period one:

First purchase	1 unit @ $4 cost price
Second purchase	1 unit @ $6 cost price
Then, first sale	1 unit @ $10 selling price

Time period two:

On hand	1 unit @ $6 FIFO; $4 LIFO
First purchase	1 unit @ $3 cost price
Then, first sale	1 unit @ $10 selling price

As shown by the summary results for two time periods, LIFO has resulted in a higher total margin of $1. And the ending inventory at LIFO is overstated because current replacement cost of $3 per unit is below the old LIFO base of $4 per unit. The regulations of the Treasury Department prohibit the write-down of the LIFO inventory from $4 to $3, with the resultant $1 market decline loss charged against income of the second period. The net effect of such a lower of cost or market concept coupled with LIFO would constitute a return to FIFO: the ending inventory would be reduced to $3 and the margin of the second time period would be reduced to $6. If it is assumed that over the life of the business entity, all other things remain equal (they never do), total

Time period one:

Statement of Income

	FIFO	LIFO
Sale of 1 unit	$10	$10
Cost of 1 unit	4	6
Margin	$ 6	$ 4

Balance Sheet

	FIFO	LIFO
Ending Inventory of 1 unit at a cost of	$6	$4

Time period two:

Statement of Income

	FIFO	LIFO
Sale of 1 unit	$10	$10
Cost of 1 unit	6	3
Margin	$ 4	$ 7

Balance Sheet

	FIFO	LIFO
Ending Inventory of 1 unit at a cost of	$3	$4

Sum of periods one and two:

Statement of Income

	FIFO	LIFO
Margin	$10	$11

Time period three:

On hand .... 1 unit @ $3 FIFO; $4 LIFO

Final sale .... 1 unit @ $10 selling price

No ending inventory

Statement of Income

	FIFO	LIFO
Sale of 1 unit	$10	$10
Cost of 1 unit	3	4
Margin	$ 7	$ 6

Sum of periods one, two, and three:

Statement of Income

	FIFO	LIFO
Margin	$17	$17

margin will be identical. If the business entity is liquidated in an assumed third time period, the counteracting effects in the three periods will result in identical total margins, because total costs of $13 have been matched against the sale of three units for $30. While the long-run concept may be theoretically sound, it is no satisfaction to a company on LIFO which encounters the situation shown at the end of the second time period. The penalty for matching current costs against current revenue in the second time period is an overstated ending inventory—and an overstated profit for the period for income tax purposes according to those who have actually encountered such a periodic down-swing of cost levels.

ILLUSTRATIVE RESULTS OF FIFO VS. LIFO

Those who use financial information as a guide to planning and as a basis for certain business decisions must be alert to the varying effects of the different inventory methods and to consequent possible distortions in the financial information produced from these methods.

Partial non-comparability of financial data, even between companies in the same industry, is possible for many reasons already discussed in preceding chapters. In addition to the varying methods of accounting for items such as depreciation, intangible assets, and research and development costs, the user of financial information should be cognizant of the varying methods of cost determination of inventories. As an example, consider the following from the December 31, 1973, consolidated balance sheets of:

Able Corporation

Current Assets:
Inventories, at the lower of cost (first-in, first-out) or market $250,000,000

Baker Corporation

Current Assets:
Inventories, at the lower of cost (last-in, first-out) or market $500,000,000

Because of their different methods of cost determination of inventories, it is inaccurate to state that Baker's inventory is double that of Able's. Baker's inventories, for the most part, have been on a LIFO basis for many years. If Baker had costed their inventories on a FIFO basis, the total dollar amount shown above on the balance sheet would be much higher; this would be disclosed in their financial summary, somewhat as follows:

> The LIFO basis values inventories conservatively during periods of rising cost levels. On a FIFO basis the year-end 1973 inventories would have been $100.0 million in excess of the $500.0 million shown under current assets. This excess increased $10.0 million during 1973.

Similarly, the companies' net incomes are not directly comparable in any one year. In 1973, Baker's net income was approximately $5,000,000 less than if they had been on FIFO. And, Baker's cash flow was improved by approximately $5,000,000 in 1973 by that amount of reduction in its income taxes for the year. Only the future can decide whether such a tax savings is temporary or permanent. At least companies on LIFO will have had the interest-free use of such funds in the intervening years.

A person using financial statements contained in an annual report should always remember that the accompanying information in "notes to the statements," in the "accounting principles and policies" section, and/or in the "financial review," are an integral part of the statements. For example, the 1972 annual report of Caterpillar Tractor Co. shows the following on the balance sheet:

Current Assets:
Stated on basis of cost using principally "last-in, first-out" method:
Inventories (note 1C) $706,900,000

Then "note 1C" clearly presents the following additional information:

> A major portion of the inventories is stated on the basis of the "last-in, first-out" method of inventory accounting adopted in 1950. This is a generally accepted accounting method designed to allocate incurred costs in such a manner as to relate them to revenues more nearly on the same cost-price level than would the "first-in, first-out" method used prior to 1950. The general effect is to include in "costs allocated to year" (and not in inventories) a major portion of the increases in costs which result from rising price levels.
>
> If the "first-in, first-out" method had been in use, inventories would have been $244.4 million and $241.8 million higher than reported at December 31, 1972 and December 31, 1971, respectively.

If material in amount, it is required in SEC filings that companies disclose the amount by which LIFO inventories are below current cost levels. Similarly, such a disclosure was shown on the December 31, 1972 balance sheet of Bethlehem Steel Corporation when that company presented its inventories as follows:

Current Assets:	
Inventories (Note B)	$481,705,000

Bethlehem Steel Corporation, which adopted LIFO in 1947 for a major segment of its inventories, presents the following information in Note B:

Ore, fluxes, fuel and coal chemicals	$121,231,000
Pig iron, alloys, scrap and manufacturing supplies	75,238,000
Finished and semi-finished products	218,709,000
Contract work in progress	66,527,000
	$481,705,000

> The amounts included above for inventories valued by the LIFO method are less than replacement or current cost by $220,000,000 at December 31, 1972.

Many companies which adopted LIFO many years ago, still have a considerable portion of their inventory stated at cost levels as of the date of their adoption of LIFO. Generally speaking, only quantity increases in year-end inventories since the adoption date of LIFO enter into inventory at a current cost level. One of the few times when the old LIFO base costs can be liquidated occurs when a company has a lower year-end inventory quantity this year than it had last year. Fluctuating inventory levels *during* a particular year may be ignored by using LIFO only at year-end to cost quantities.

The foregoing discussion definitely is not intended to belittle certain accounting methods. The past 30 years have produced a tremendous improvement in accounting methods and procedures. The tolerance range of variations in acceptable procedures has been greatly narrowed, and future years will see additional improvement. External forces such as inflation and high tax rates coupled with changing tax laws have also plagued accounting methodology. From an income determination point of view, LIFO does more accurately match current costs with current revenue for many companies. Constant revisions in the tax code since 1939, when LIFO was first introduced, today permit any taxpayer who has an inventory to use the LIFO method upon the approval of the Internal Revenue Service. Because of rising costs and high tax rates,

LIFO has become increasingly advantageous to companies. Thus, the "cost" of the inventory shown by the balance sheet is often only an indication of outdated past costs deferred for a given quantity of goods. In the future, as accounting becomes less a tool of management and more a measurement of management's performance (as discussed in Chapter 5), it is believed that the balance sheet will reassert its importance on a level equal to that of the statement of income; that it will be less a *balance* sheet and more an indicator of financial position.

Effect of Differing Inventory Methods

The managerial significance and use of accounting data in the area of inventories is of prime importance with respect to many decisions which must be made in the management of any business. No repetition of the differing effects of the inventory cost determination methods, under alternative conditions, will be restated at this point. It is sufficient to say that the selection of a particular method has ramifications far beyond the determination of what portion of the total cost of goods is to be deferred in inventory as an asset and what portion is to be allocated as a charge against revenue of the period.

While an understanding of the differing cost flows possible under the various cost determination methods is important, those in management should be fully cognizant of all the resultant effects produced by the method selected. If a company uses LIFO, total assets may need restating prior to their use as an amount of capital employed for the determination of profit earned on capital employed as a measure of performance. Working capital amounts and ratios may be distorted; comparisons in the same company from period to period or between like companies in the same industry at a given moment may be misleading. Inventory turnover ratios are affected by the choice of the cost determination method. The impact of income taxes on the net income for the year will affect the flow of funds of the company. The cost of an item of inventory, per the records of the company, may be completely useless as a possible aid in management's deliberations concerning the establishment of an equitable selling price. To the extent that such ramifications mentioned are not understood, they may lead to improper decisions by those in management who use financial data for planning.

One partially redeeming factor to these comments is that, whatever the method of inventory costing and inventory valuation selected, it must be used consistently from year to year. Otherwise, any set of comparative financial data would be practically worthless. Consistency in method is required for both income tax purposes and for external reporting. In this respect, it should be remembered that the certificate of the independent public accountant concludes with an opinion on the company's published statements that they "were prepared in conformity with generally accepted accounting principles applied on a basis *consistent* with that of the preceding year." While this does not preclude a change in a company's inventory method, as from FIFO to LIFO, the effect of such change must be disclosed for that year. When Westinghouse Electric Corporation changed its inventory method in 1956, the accountants' report or "certificate" by the independent certified public accountants concluded with:

> . . . in conformity with generally accepted accounting principles applied on a basis consistent with that of the preceding year, apart from the change to the LIFO (last-in, first-out) method of inventory valuation, which we approve. As a result, approximately $25,000,000, representing rising inventory cost levels during 1956, was excluded from valuation of year-end inventories, which had the effect of reducing net income after taxes by about $12,000,000.

In addition to the factors which have been discussed, the selection of an inventory cost determination method should be partially influenced by the company's type of business. For example, LIFO is more advantageous to a company in an industry characterized by the large inventories in relation to total assets. Companies in certain of the metal industries fall into this category and thus find LIFO advantageous, during rising cost levels, because of their relatively slow inventory turnover. On the other hand, many retail stores, drug companies, and beverage companies are on FIFO or average cost methods because of a relatively low quantity of inventory in relation to total assets or because of a high turnover rate.

INVENTORY MANAGEMENT

Management of inventory encompasses a wide range of varying activities within a business. In scope, these activities range from the actual planning for purchases of materials and goods, through scheduling and control in all stages of production for a manufacturing business, to the ultimate delivery of the product to the customer. Excess inventory results in idle capital and often increased expenses. Lack of sufficient inventory results in lost sales and often increased expenses. Increasingly today, more scientific approaches are being employed in the management of inventory as businesses strive toward the utopian goal of having just the right amount of goods on hand in exactly the right places at precisely the time they are needed.

Carrying Costs of Inventory

Reference to the table on page 273 indicates the considerable capital investment which most companies must tie up in inventories. The cost which must be incurred to carry such inventories is not so obvious. Without attempting to make an all inclusive list, carrying costs include expenses such as:

Handling costs—upon receipt and issuance of goods plus any intervening handling due to sorting, inventory counting, and relocation.

Storing costs—for depreciation, maintenance, property taxes, utilities (or lease or rent expense) and other operating expenses of storage areas and warehouses.

Financial costs—for paper work relating to all phases of inventory maintenance from purchase orders for raw materials to accounting costs for perpetual record of finished goods; local taxes on inventory balances; and insurance covering inventory.

Risk costs—as obsolescence on certain items, possible physical deterioration, breakage, theft, and price declines.

Capital costs—for interest on loans needed to carry inventory; imputed cost of interest at prevailing rate of funds tied up in inventory.

While such carrying costs will vary from company to company, reliable estimates indicate that these costs usually range from 15 percent to 25 percent annually on the original inventory cost. One manufacturing company with a fairly short production cycle has stated that its carrying costs amount to 20 percent. Another company involved in domestic production for foreign shipment and sale estimates its carrying costs at 34 percent. Regardless of the percentage, the multiplication of even a minimum percentage by the inventory amounts shown for selected companies earlier in this chapter results in a staggering total dollar cost for maintenance of inventories. Instances are encountered in which such costs approach the annual net income after taxes for a company. Thus, the concern of companies with respect to the maintenance of proper inventory levels is understandable.

Basic Objectives of Inventory Management

Present business practices validate the premise that some irreducible minimum amount of inventory is mandatory. Theoretically that amount would be predicated, in a manufacturing company, upon a perfect blend of timing in the receipt of previously ordered raw materials based on the length of the production cycle so that the finished goods are completed on exactly the date necessary to ship them to the customer for arrival on his required delivery date—all at the most efficient level of activity in order to minimize costs. As long as people are involved, such perfection will not be possible. Yet, the theoretical concept contains the basic objectives of inventory management: it emphasizes the attempt to maintain an inventory amount where its carrying cost is properly equated with the gain to be derived from having the inventory available.

One of the basic objectives, then, is customer satisfaction. Availability of finished goods for proper delivery date must not be forfeited by maintaining too small a finished goods inventory. Profits result only from the *sale* of goods at an amount in excess of cost. Yet, to maximize this profit, additional costs to carry an excessive quantity of inventory must not be incurred. In addition to matching customer requirements to inventory size, management must maintain proper product quality during the various stages of production. Consideration of customer satisfaction, then, results in at least a four-way interaction affecting inventory management: the sales group desires an overabundance of inventory to prevent the loss of a single sale due to stock-outs; the financial group wishes to minimize inventory levels; the production group is interested in an economical level of factory operations and cost reduction of the product; and the customers often want unrealistic delivery dates, product quality, and service.

Another basic objective of inventory management is reduction or control of costs of operations throughout the company. The ramifications of this objective are multitudinous; a few examples will illustrate the point. First, what is the most economical quantity of a specific raw material to order? Larger, but less frequent, purchase orders will decrease cost per unit for the paper work involved in ordering the materials, inspecting it upon arival, and subsequent bookeeping for recording the purchase and payment of the bill. In addition, larger purchase orders may reduce raw material costs due to decreased transportation costs resulting from carload lot rates and quantity discounts on larger orders from vendors. Against such decreased costs must be matched the increased carrying costs. Second, and more complicated, what is the most economical quantity of a product to process through the various stages of manufacturing in one run? In addition to the differing effects caused by those production costs which vary somewhat directly with the volume of production (e.g., power and direct labor) and those production costs which are relatively fixed in total amount (e.g., depreciation and property taxes on the plant building), many additional factors must be considered. Production planning must evaluate the availability of the facilities at the given time for the given volume of this product against other demands for the use of the same facilities. A steady, prolonged, production period—as opposed to seasonal demands—for products must be evaluated; temporary excess inventory may increase carrying costs. Similarly, indirect personnel costs, as unemployment compensation resulting from a fluctuating size of work force, hiring and training expenses, severance pay, overtime premium pay, and the image of the company as seen by its employees and community, must not be overlooked. These and other tangible and intangible factors must be weighed in the determination of the most economical lot-size of a product to manufacture. Third, and likewise complicated for a large organization, is the determination in which warehouses, in what quantities, and for how many products shall inventories of finished goods be maintained. Factors like location and size of customers, differentials in warehousing costs, and differing transportation costs must be considered. These examples illustrate the scope of inventory management in the area of effective cost control.

In summary, effective inventory management requires that the functions of purchasing, production (for a manufacturing business), and marketing be executed as efficiently as possible in relation to the costs of carrying the inventories of raw materials, work in process, and finished goods.

Inventory Management—How?

Effective inventory management has been studied by almost all medium- to large-sized businesses, and the object of many books and articles. Only a few of the considerations involved and the approaches taken will be mentioned here; detailed studies are available for the person desiring information in depth.

One of the primary factors in effective management is a proper evaluation of the composition of the inventory. Different portions of the total inventory may require different control procedures; for example, one study of inventories maintained by manufacturing companies revealed:

An analysis of an inventory generally will show:

A. 70% of the dollar inventory value in 10% of the quantity of items
B. 25% of the dollar inventory value in 25% of the quantity of items
C. 5% of the dollar inventory value in 65% of the quantity of items[4]

---

[4] John E. Martin, "Production Control," *The Arthur Andersen Chronicle,* Vol. 13 (July, 1953), 149.

Other studies based on this "ABC" plan show very close correlation to the above relationships. Class "A" items should be scheduled for very frequent receipt—daily, if feasible—to minimize investment in inventory. At the other extreme, Class "C" items should be scheduled for receipt perhaps only a few times a year to minimize all of the paper work costs which any acquisition entails. Similar principles are, of course, applicable to a retail business. The "how" for effective inventory management and control must be different for $500 diamond rings and $2 charm bracelets.

The business trend to cut inventories will continue; care must be taken regarding how and where to cut. Recently, top management of a medium-sized steel company ordered a total inventory cut of 10 percent during the year. After the anguished screams had subsided, a thorough analysis of the inventory composition was made; it was found that 30 percent of the total inventory had not moved in four years. A planned inventory control program caused a reduction of total inventory considerably in excess of 10 percent when the "how" factor of inventory management was applied to specific items or groups rather than to total inventory.

In recent years, the "how" of effective inventory management has become increasingly scientific in approach. Practical applications of statistical techniques and advanced mathematical formulae by operations-research procedures, coupled with the use of electronic data processing equipment, have contributed greatly to inventory management.

Analytical methods using mathematical formulae are employed increasingly to aid the solution of the three problems mentioned in the section on "Basic Objectives of Inventory Management." To balance the carrying cost of inventory against cost savings resulting from less frequent but larger purchases of goods, the most economical order quantity (called the E. O. Q.) may be determined by a formula, as discussed and illustrated in the appendix to the narrative of this chapter. As a management aid in production planning, the most economical lot-size or quantity to manufacture (called the E. M. Q.) may be computed by mathematical techniques. And, by linear programming, the warehousing question of what quantities of which goods to store for minimum transportation costs (called the transportation-line theory) may be tackled.

A terse summary of one large company's present management of finished goods inventory is indicative of the trend. This particular well-diversified manufacturing company has plants and warehouses at many locations throughout the United States as well as some foreign operations. All domestic operations are linked by a private leased electronic communication system to the company's computer center, located near corporate headquarters. All sales orders, regardless of their point of origin, are transmitted to the computer center. Within thirty minutes, it is possible to determine which warehouses have the particular inventory item and from which warehouse it will be shipped to the customer, notify the salesman's office of the origin point of shipment, get the shipment started, adjust the perpetual inventory records, and process the paper to bill the customer.

Inventory Management—By Whom?

Historically, management of inventory appears to have been the responsibility of the purchasing function of a company; this is probably its focal point yet today. One large manufacturing company presently has its inventory management distributed by delegating responsibility for control of raw material inventories to a central purchasing office, work in process inventories to each plant manager, and finished goods inventories to the marketing manager of each product line. For all companies except the smallest, such management methods appear doomed.

The need for more science in business management will require a new approach to management control systems, and inventory management is a portion of any management control system. The use and application of financial, accounting, and economic data by analytical methods employing statistical techniques and mathematical formulae and models, aided by high-speed computers, will require a new approach to inventory control and management. It appears that the purchasing department approach to inventory management will soon be replaced by a new concept that will require a control group which is versed in financial-accounting-behavioral-economic concepts, which possesses a thorough knowledge of mathematics, and which is able to speak the language of the computer.

Inventory Management—By What?

Many companies have extensive inventory control systems, yet these systems do not always work. Why? Usually a deficiency in the system is blamed; the problem is often misunderstanding of "what" controls inventories.

A company's inventory control system may contain all the paper work, formulae, and electronic data processing equipment necessary to its needs ranging from the perpetual inventory stock cards illustrated in chapter 9 to the newest in computers. Yet, do these *control* inventory? Consider two illustrative cases which are quite typical.

The first case concerns a large oil company with extensive overseas operations. Commissary stocks for their Near East location usually required a lead time of six months from the date requisitioned to the date of delivery by refrigerated ship. Basic control was by the typical perpetual inventory cards, accompanied by minimum-maximum quantity points, for each food item. The cards were maintained by a bright young accounting graduate a few months out of school. When quantities reached the designated minimum level, he reordered. Orders were approved after review by his immediate supervisor; at first, the orders were carefully examined; later, in only a perfunctory manner, because the young man had "caught on." Unknown to the young man, during his third month on the job, his immediate supervisor and the mess chef embarked on a campaign to serve brussels sprouts twice a day before the excess inventory spoiled. The young man watching the perpetual inventory cards reordered brussels sprouts when they hit the minimum level. Then he remembered the six months lead time for refrigerated items and doubled the order. Suddenly he remembered a point he had learned in college—watch the monthly consumption pattern. "My gosh, how these fellows like brussels sprouts," he said as he again doubled the order! The company ended up with double the quantity that had been on hand prior to the commencement of the "eating campaign." Was the inventory control system inadequate?

The second case concerns a large manufacturing company which employed a computer to control inventories. One division had a large inventory of a certain type of small motor which it had manufactured that had become obsolete. In a desperate effort to unload the small motors, selling price was reduced to a point considerably below cost. The motors were sold, and this fact dutifully recorded by the computer. But, being a marvellous machine, the computer then proceeded to reorder more such motors. Someone had failed to push a button. At the originating division, the production line was set up for the manufacture of more obsolete small motors. Only very persistent questioning by one of the workmen on the production line halted the operation before it had gone very far. Was the inventory control system inadequate?

The obvious point of both cases is that paper and machines do not control; they only aid control. In the final analysis, real control must be by human beings. And, due to the increasing complexities in business, the humans must acquire much additional knowledge if inventory management, in the broadest sense, is to be effective. While giant mathematical computers cannot grind out orders to businessmen because human judgments are necessary for the consideration of many factors affecting our complex society, the expanding scientific method of inventory management should be used to aid, not to replace, human judgment.[5]

---

[5] The following excerpt is from page seven of *Observations on Financial Inventory Accounting—What It Is and What It Could Be, Department of Defense,* by the Comptroller General of the United States, May 17, 1972:

> Over the years, the Department of Defense's inventory quantity records have been inaccurate and unreliable. We have issued several

APPENDIX
ECONOMIC ORDER QUANTITY DETERMINATION

The accounting function has been one of the most important sources of information to management. This information has been used in the exercise of the basic management function: decision making with regard to the acquisition and allocation of scarce resources (the economist's *factors of production*) among competing activities or ends. The size, complexity, diversity, and geographical dispersion of the modern business enterprise have greatly increased management's needs for a variety of informational inputs to its decision-making process. Where formerly accounting information, both direct and derived, had been adequate for management's needs, it is now becoming apparent that information generated by, and peculiar to, other organizational functions is also required by today's decision makers. The recent development of workable models of some of the other primary and subsidiary systems of the organization to complement the existing financial, or accounting, models has contributed to this expansion of informational needs. These newer models, such as facilities location models, quality control models, production scheduling models, inventory control models, etc., have been developed by many investigators in many disciplines. Significant contributions have been made by statisticians and mathematicians and by those trained in the fields of operations research or management science. Many of these newer models specify certain kinds of accounting information as inputs. In addition, improved accounting models have been developed, and the accounting profession has adopted and adapted many of the non-accounting models for its own use. Thus, the requirements for accounting information have increased apace with the requirements for nonaccounting information. Satisfaction of these expanded requirements will require that accountants become knowledgeable of these newer mathematical and statistical models. This does not imply that accountants should be mathematical or statistical sophisticates.[6] It does imply an awareness and

---

reports showing the extent of inaccuracies and the resulting effects on management decisions. Our latest report, "Army Inventories—Inaccuracies, Effects, and Ways to Improve," issued in February 1971 emphasizes this perennial problem.

> . . . the Army thought it had $439 million of inventory in 1969 that did not exist; the Army also found $391 million of inventory in 1969 it did not know it had.

[6] Mathematics and accounting are not incompatible. In fact, Paciolo, a celebrated Italian mathematician, is generally credited with being the pioneer of double-entry bookkeeping in 1494. For an interesting account of this man's life and work in accounting see R. G. Brown and K. S. Johnston, *Paciolo on Accounting* (New York: McGraw-Hill Book Company, 1963).

a modicum of understanding of these symbolic models to the end that their utilization by accounting practitioners may be enhanced, whenever justified. As mentioned on page 317, one of the mathematical and statistical techniques commonly employed is that for the determination of economic order quantity. The use of this technique is now presented.

The importance of inventories as an asset has been referred to previously. The role of the accountant in achieving effective control of this major asset item has also been noted. Inventories, whether they are merchandise, raw materials, work in process, finished goods, or supplies, would thus appear to be of basic concern to management at all levels of the enterprise. Although many analytical techniques (models) have been developed to assist management in its planning and control of inventories, there are fundamentally only two questions to which these techniques address themselves. These are the questions of when to order and how many to order. In this section we will briefly set forth the essential features of one decision model—the classical deterministic model—for answering these two questions. It is classical since it represents the first significant inventory model, and deterministic since it does not take uncertainty into account.

The essence of the classical deterministic model is contained in two diagrams. The following diagram, which depicts the behavior of inventory over time for some specific item which is stocked in anticipation of a demand for it, is shown below:

EXHIBIT 10–1

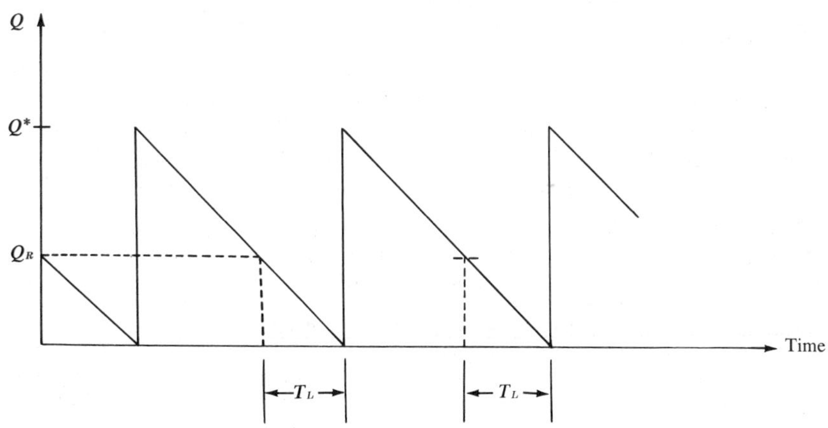

This diagram represents the following: the item is withdrawn from the storeroom at a constant, or nearly constant, rate until the inventory level, Q, reaches Q_R, the reorder point. At this moment in time a replenishment order is initiated for a quantity, Q^*. The time interval from the initiation of this replenishment order until the physical items ordered are received and available for disbursement from the storeroom is called the Lead Time, T_L. The Lead Time is assumed to be constant, or nearly so. Items are withdrawn from the storeroom at the same constant rate during the Lead Time. At the instant that the inventory reaches zero the replenishment order is received at the storeroom and the inventory level immediately increases to Q^*, the predetermined order quantity. This saw-tooth pattern is repeated. The adjective *deterministic* which is used to describe the model results from the assumed constancy of both the withdrawal rate and the Lead Time.

The order quantity, Q^*, is a specific value of the decision variable "how many to order" and is subject to management determination. It is assumed that in making this quantity determination, management is interested in minimizing over a specified time-period the sum of the variable costs associated with the resulting inventory. The specified time period is generally taken to be one year. The relevant variable costs can be included in one or the other of two variable cost categories: ordering costs or carrying costs.[7] The relationship of each of these variable cost categories to order quantity, Q, is depicted in the second diagram.

The ordering costs over some specified time period are a function of the demand or requirement in units for the item in question over the time period, S; the cost in dollars associated with placing an order, C_R, and the number of units of the item specified on the order, Q. The time period demand, S, divided by the number of units ordered each time an order is placed, Q, will give the number of orders placed during the time period. For example, if annual demand is 1000 units and the order quantity is specified to be 100 units then $1000 \div 100 = 10$ orders per year. Multiplication of the number of orders placed per time period by the cost of placing each order, C_R, will yield the time period ordering costs. Thus, to continue with the preceding example, if ordering costs are $5.00 per

---

[7] The choice of variable costs as the relevant costs eliminates the necessity for considering the purchase price or the manufacturing cost of the item in question. Over any specified time period, say one year, the assumed constant withdrawal rate, say X pieces per day, uniquely determines a time period quantity, say $Y = 260X$ pieces per year, whose dollar value is constant regardless of how many pieces of the item are ordered at any one time. A constant, in this case one of dollar value, is not subject to management determination and need not enter into its decision-making model. The problem of "price breaks" is not considered in this elementary exposition.

order, then the annual ordering costs will be 10 orders per year times \$5.00 per order or \$50.00. It will be seen from this very rudimentary analysis and from the second diagram that the time period ordering costs, $SC_R \div Q$, decrease as the quantity ordered, Q, is increased. The ordering cost component of total variable costs operates to make Q as large as possible.

The carrying costs over some time period are a function of the number of units Q of the item specified on the order and the cost I in dollars associated with carrying one unit in inventory per time period. This cost, I, is the sum of a number of relevant cost sub-components: investment costs (interest or opportunity costs), warehousing costs, obsolescence costs, spoilage or shrinkage costs, pilferage costs, and taxes. These costs are generally determined on a percentage basis and then applied to the cost of the item per unit to give a dollar cost per unit per time period. Thus, if the total of the relevant cost sub-components is determined to be 25 percent per year, then for an item costing \$4.00 per unit, the carrying cost per unit per year would be calculated as 0.25 times \$4.00, or \$1.00. Assuming that the carrying cost per unit per time period has been determined, there remains only the problem of determining the number of units of the item to which this unit carrying cost is applicable in order to calculate the total time period carrying costs. The first diagram, the behavior of inventory over time, shows that the number of units in inventory is constantly changing. Sometimes there will be Q^* units in inventory, the next instant there will only be $(Q^* - 1)$ units, and so forth until we reach the point at which there will be zero units in inventory and then the whole process repeats itself. How many units are in inventory, on the average, over the time period? It can be shown for the model depicted that if the order quantity is for Q^* units then this is equivalent to having $(Q^* \div 2)$ units in inventory over the entire time period. Thus, if the order quantity is for 100 units and the withdrawal rate is constant, as shown in the exhibit, then this is no different from a carrying cost viewpoint than having $100 \div 2 = 50$ units in inventory at all times. Based upon this reasoning the carrying costs are determined from the expression $(Q \div 2)I$, or $(QI \div 2)$. The second diagram shows that carrying costs per time period increase as the quantity ordered, Q, increases. The carrying cost component of total variable costs operates to make Q as small as possible.

The characteristics of the two opposing cost components are summarized in the Total Variable Cost (TVC) curve which is defined as

$$TVC = \frac{SC_R}{Q} + \frac{QI}{2}$$

EXHIBIT 10–2

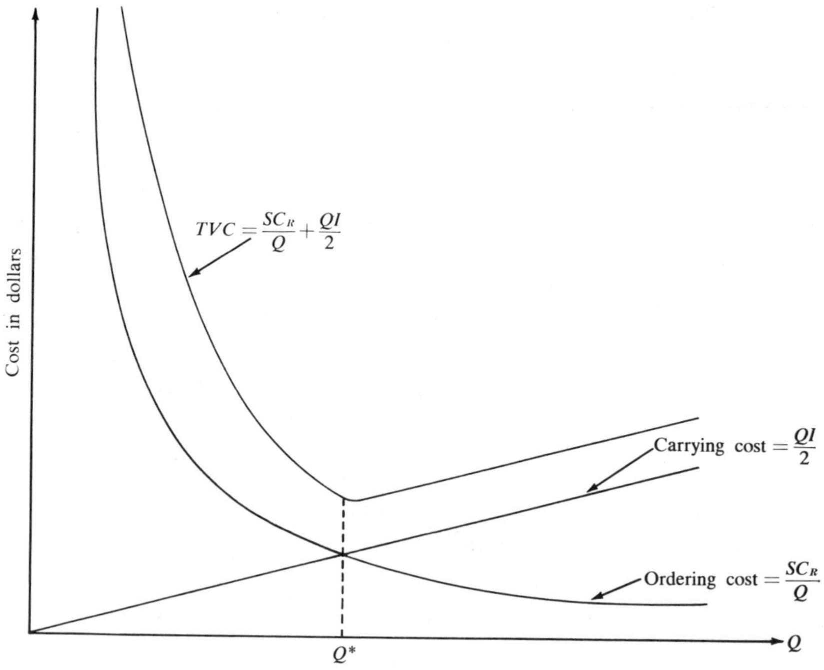

It is this total variable cost that management would like to minimize. The curve of TVC is seen to be high for small order quantities Q; to decrease as Q is increased until some minimum point is reached, Q^*; and thereafter to increase as Q continues to increase. Referring to the diagram it will be seen that the minimum point on the TVC curve appears to be where the two cost component curves intersect (have the same value). This is indeed the case and leads to a method for determining Q^*, that order quantity which minimizes TVC. Equating the expression for the two cost components, $\frac{SC_R}{Q}$ and $\frac{QI}{2}$, and solving the resulting equation for Q will yield

$$Q^* = \sqrt{\frac{2SC_R}{I}}$$

The value of Q that minimizes Total Variable Cost, a specific value of Q, is generally designated Q^* or *E.O.Q.*, The Economic Order Quantity. Assuming that values for S, C_R, and I are available, the formula provides a fairly simple mechanism for calculating Q^* and answers the question of how many to order.

The question of "when to order" may be approached in the following manner. If Q^* units are ordered each time an order is placed and S units are required per time period, then

$$\frac{S}{Q^*} = \text{number of orders that will be placed per time period.}$$

$$1 \div \frac{S}{Q^*} = \frac{Q^*}{S} = \text{time interval between orders expressed as a fraction of the time period.}$$

Example: Suppose that the following data are available for an item for which Q^* and the time interval between orders are required:

$$S = 400 \text{ units per year}$$
$$C_R = \$7.50 \text{ per order}$$
$$I = \$0.60 \text{ per unit per year}$$

Then,

$$Q^* = \sqrt{\frac{2SC_R}{I}} = \sqrt{\frac{2(400)\ (\$7.50)}{\$0.60}}$$

$$Q^* = \sqrt{\frac{6000}{0.60}} = \sqrt{10000}$$

$$Q^* = 100 \text{ units}$$

$$\text{Number of orders per year} = \frac{S}{Q^*} = \frac{400}{100} = 4$$

$$\text{Time interval between orders} = \frac{Q^*}{S} = \frac{100}{400} = \frac{1}{4} \text{ year, or order every 3 months}$$

The basic inventory model presented here has many variations. Models which incorporate uncertainty, probabilistic models, have also been constructed.

One note of caution: A mathematical or statistical model is not a substitute for mature and considered judgment. It is an adjunct to such judgment. If an answer given by a model does not accord with your judgment, you are well-advised to check the model.

QUESTIONS AND PROBLEMS

10–1. A few years ago, at one of a company's divisions, an EDP system was installed (by a management consulting firm). The system worked well, so the management consulting firm departed. Sometime thereafter it was discovered that the inventory on the company's records exceeded the actual physical inventory by $300,000. This was due to the failure to record some of the issuances of goods from inventory. Therefore, the shortage, item by item, was tabulated for the $300,000 of missing goods and fed into the computer to reduce the records for inventory by $300,000 and bring it into agreement with the actual physical inventory on hand. What do you think happened then? (Remember the case of the small motors mentioned near the end of this chapter.)

10–2. The same oil company that had the trouble with the brussels sprouts mentioned near the end of this chapter also had trouble with inaccurate typists at their Near East location. The order went out to write, not type, all future orders. An order was handwritten very distinctly for "8 tuns of cheese" and sent to headquarters in New York. Note: a *tun* of cheese is a round wheel of cheese. What do you think happened?

10–3. Select the one best answer to each of the following statements.

a. If a company values its inventory at the lower of cost or market, and cost (determined by one of the acceptable cost determination methods) is $10, replacement cost $9, and selling price $23, the inventory will be shown on the published balance sheet at (assuming no other factors):
   1. $9.00
   2. $9.50
   3. $10.00
   4. $23.00

b. The industry (according to Accounting Trends and Techniques) which shows most companies on LIFO is:
   1. bakery
   2. nonferrous metals (metals other than iron)

c. For a heavy manufacturing company, annual carrying cost for inventory, as a percentage of the dollar amount of the inventory, approximates:
   1. 5 percent
   2. 20 percent
   3. 40 percent

d. The "LIFO reserve" for Westinghouse Electric Corporation (principally on LIFO since January 1, 1956) and for Caterpillar Tractor Company (principally on LIFO since January 1, 1950) is:
   1. negligible in amount
   2. significant in amount

e. From a theory point of view (and also practice by many companies), an inventory item purchased at $50 (invoice amount) plus $2 for shipping charges less $1 cash discount for paying the invoice promptly, should result in the inventory being shown at a cost of:

1. $49
2. $50
3. $51
4. $52

f. The purchase price of a certain inventory item changes frequently. The cost of the inventory of this item at year end will be the same if perpetual records are kept as it would be under a periodic inventory method only if the cost is computed under the:

1. weighted average method
2. first-in, first-out method
3. last-in, first-out method

(Adapted from Uniform CPA Examination)

10–4. Henderson Company is wholly dependent upon ABC Company for its source of supply of a raw material which it uses in large quantities. Any interruption in the operation of ABC Company would force Henderson Company to suspend its own operations. The status of current union negotiations between ABC Company and its employees indicates that the company is faced with either a prolonged strike six weeks hence or a substantial wage increase. In the event of a prolonged strike, Henderson Company will lose its source of supply, as none other will be available domestically and transportation costs from foreign sources are prohibitive. In the event of a wage increase, cost prices to Henderson Company probably will be increased substantially for this raw material. As the person in the management of Henderson Company charged with the responsibility for inventory management of raw materials, what analyses would you prepare to aid the determination of what quantity, if any, of this raw material should be stockpiled within the next six weeks?

10–5. Big Steel Company, like many large steel companies, has carried its inventories on a LIFO basis for many years. As a result, the inventory dollar amount is considerably below current replacement cost. Also, like most steel companies, Big Steel Company has a fiscal year that coincides with the calendar year. In mid-July, after prolonged labor negotiations, an industry-wide strike closes Big Steel Company. In late October, not knowing when the strike will end (it actually ended in mid-November after 116 days), you, as a consultant to the company, are presented with the following problem:

> Our inventories are severely depleted below our January 1 level. Considerable inroads will be made into our LIFO basis, assuming that we

> cannot build inventory quantities back up to their past January 1 level by this December 31. Assuming no inventory build-up will be possible by December 31, we lose two ways. First, any build-up after December 31 must go into inventory at the then current prices. Second, the partial liquidation of our LIFO base this year will have an abnormal effect on income because of the sale of that equivalent quantity of goods at current selling prices contrasted with the exceedingly low cost basis. What can we do?

Assuming that no inventory build-up is possible by December 31, what possible courses of action would you present to Big Steel Company?

10–6. Select the one best answer to each of the following statements.

a. When inventories are values at the lower of cost or market, "market" refers to:
   1. the price that the market will bear
   2. present selling price
   3. current replacement cost

b. Due to automation, high-speed computers, and electronic data processing, inventory quantities can now be controlled by:
   1. machines
   2. people pushing buttons on machines
   3. machines as an aid to intelligent people

c. The industry (according to *Accounting Trends and Techniques*) which shows most companies on LIFO is:
   1. bakery
   2. non-ferrous metal
   3. chemicals

d. LIFO, coupled with C or M, the lower, is:
   1. a reversion to FIFO, when costs decline, and therefore not legal for tax purposes
   2. never used for external reporting purposes

e. Utility companies are not greatly concerned with the problems of whether or not to shift to LIFO.
   1. True.
   2. False.

f. NIFO, rather than LIFO, could present a more realistic picture of economic income.
   1. True.
   2. False.

g. The LIFO "cushion" is:
   1. the amount inventories are below current replacement cost
   2. shown by most balance sheets, because of its materiality
   3. a provision for a possible decline in prices

h. A company can switch *to* LIFO any year it wishes (assuming Internal Revenue Service approval of the technical mechanics of the Company's LIFO system).
   1. True
   2. False

10–7. Montebello Company sells three products. Inventories at December 31 for two successive years are as follows:

	DECEMBER 31, 1973			DECEMBER 31, 1974		
PRODUCT	COST (FIFO)	MARKET	C OR M, THE LOWER	COST (FIFO)	MARKET	C OR M, THE LOWER
A	$10,000	$10,000	$?	$10,000	$12,000	$?
B	9,000	9,200	?	16,000	17,000	?
C	11,000	8,000	?	7,000	7,000	?
Total	$30,000	$27,200	$?	$33,000	$36,000	$?

Condensed statements of income for the two successive years are as follows:

	1973		1974	
Net Sales		$220,000		$300,000
Cost of Goods Sold:				
Inventory, January 1 .	$ 25,000		$?	
Purchases	122,000		$162,000	
	$147,000		$?	
Inventory, December 31	?		?	
Cost of Goods Sold		?		?
Gross Margin on Sales ..		$?		$?
Selling & Administrative Expenses		50,000		60,000
Net Income before Income Taxes		$?		$?

Required

a. Complete the above comparative statements of income assuming that Montebello Company values inventories on the basis of cost (FIFO).

b. Complete the above comparative statements of income assuming that Montebello Company values inventories on the basis of the lower of cost (FIFO) or market, with the cost or market determination based on each individual product in inventory. Inventory is reflected in the cost of goods sold section at the lower of cost or market, not necessarily cost.

c. Prepare a report analyzing the effect of the two valuation bases upon reported profits. Include in the report your recommendations to Montebello Company concerning the choice of a valuation basis for inventories.

10–8. The statements of income for Stonewall Company for the past four years reveal the following facts:

	1970	1971	1972	1973
Net Sales	$100,000	$100,000	$100,000	$120,000
Cost of Goods Sold .	70,000	72,000	68,000	84,000
Gross Margin	$ 30,000	$ 28,000	$ 32,000	$ 36,000
Operating Expenses .	24,000	29,000	23,000	23,000
Net Income or (Loss)	$ 6,000	$ (1,000)	$ 9,000	$ 13,000

On September 6, 1974, a fire completely destroyed the store and merchandise. The inventory of merchandise on hand at the start of the year was $15,000; purchases to the date of the fire totaled $35,000; sales up to September 6, 1974, amounted to $60,000. What was the approximate cost of the inventory destroyed in the fire? No perpetual inventory records have been maintained by Stonewall Company. Thus, Stonewall Company is having difficulty with the fire insurance company concerning the amount of loss sustained. Support your answer with all necessary computations.

Note: The rate of gross margin (gross margin divided by net sales) has been fairly constant for the past several years.

10–9. Proprietor Kent purchased 5,000 units of Product X for $32,000. He expects to sell all of them this year while incurring operating expenses of $3,600. He desires a net profit for the year equal to 20 percent (before tax) of net sales. What unit selling price will be necessary to accomplish this objective?

10–10.* Gay Manufacturing Company uses steel in the production of its finished product. At any given time, its three inventories (raw materials, work in process, finished goods) all contain steel: raw steel, steel in goods in process, steel in finished goods. While the levels of the inventories may fluctuate during the year, assume an overall total

* This problem has been adapted from "Should LIFO Be Adopted in 1956?" by R. A. Hoffman, *The Price Waterhouse Review*, September, 1956; with permission of Price Waterhouse & Co.

inventory of steel (in all categories) of 18,000 tons at the end of each year, 1956 through 1960, the same quantity as there was at the end of 1955. Steel wage increases per hour over the five years are: 1956—17¢; 1957—12¢; 1958—12¢; 1959—12¢ and 1960—12¢. Assume a price increase in steel (thus, an increase in cost of steel, a raw material, to Gay Manufacturing Company) of 60¢ per ton for each 1¢ per hour wage increase granted to steelworkers.

a. If Gay Manufacturing Company adopts LIFO for the steel portion of its inventory, what will be the estimated tax reductions for the years 1956 through 1960? Use a tax rate of 54% (federal plus state).

b. How could further tax reductions be attained by expanding the scope of the LIFO election in these years? Federal Income Tax Regulations of the Treasury Department state, "a manufacturer or processor who has adopted LIFO can elect to have such methods confined to raw materials only (including those included in goods in process and in finished goods)."

c. Do you believe that the LIFO method of costing inventories and goods sold is a sound accounting procedure or merely a tax savings device? Explain.

10–11. Compute the Economic Order Quantity *EOQ* for an article which has a yearly demand S of 7500 units, a cost per order C_R of \$7.20, and a carrying cost per unit per year I of \$1.20. What is the Total Variable Cost *TVC* for this *EOQ*?

11

Long-Term Debt

The typical business entity has two principal sources of capital: creditors' equity (debt) and owners' equity (investment). The illustrative summary balance sheet shown below indicates that the sources of the $50,000,000 capital (total assets) of ABC Company are $15,000,000 of debt equity and $35,000,000 of ownership equity. The typical business will always have some amount of current liabilities representing debts like accounts payable, taxes payable, and accrued salaries and wages. In addition to exercising proper administration of current or short-term debt,

ABC COMPANY
Balance Sheet
December 31, 1974

ASSETS		EQUITIES	
Current Assets ...	$12,000,000	Current Liabilities .	$ 5,000,000
Property, Plant and Equipment (net)	38,000,000	Long-term Debt ..	10,000,000
		Total Liabilities ..	$15,000,000
		Owners' Equity ...	35,000,000
Total Assets	$50,000,000	Total Equities	$50,000,000

the management of the company (particularly the treasurer and the finance committee) must be aware of the effects of decisions concerning ways of raising and managing the more permanent capital of the company; namely, the long-term debt and the investment of the owners. This chapter and the next one will be concerned with the salient factors of these long-term equities of a business entity.

Long-term debt refers to liabilities which will not become due within a short period of time, usually a year. Such debt may be evidenced by long-term promissory notes, bonds, mortgages, or some other form of instrument. The balance sheet usually indicates the maturity date of such long-term debts; any portion of the debt that will become due within the coming year should be shown as a current liability.

FORMS OF LONG-TERM DEBT

Principal forms of long-term debt are promissory notes, bonds, and mortgages. Illustrations from the balance sheets of Litton Industries, Inc., Century Electric Company, Procter & Gamble Company, and Season-All

LITTON INDUSTRIES, INC.
July 31, 1972

Note B—Long-term liabilities: Long-term liabilities at July 31, 1972 consisted of the following:

Notes payable to insurance companies:	
Due to 1984 with interest from 3½% to 4⅞%	$ 60,895,000
Due to 1993 with interest from 5.35% to 7.0%	11,778,000
Notes payable to banks:	
Due to 1977 with interest at ¼% to ¾% above published bank borrowing rates	125,000,000
Due 1977 to 1980 with interest at 6⅛% to 6⅝%	67,188,000
Due 1975 to 1982 with interest at 7⅞% to 8%	14,792,000
Bonds payable to 1984 with interest at 6¼%	15,625,000
Notes due December 1, 1976 with interest at 8¾%	60,000,000
Miscellaneous debt due to 1994 with average interest at 5%	63,058,000
	$418,336,000

Industries, Inc. are presented as examples of these forms of long-term debt.

The Notes to Financial Statements of Litton Industries, Inc. show long-term indebtedness in the form of notes owed to insurance companies and banks, and other such debt. Reference to Note D of the Balance Sheet of Century Electric Company discloses the installment payment dates of the debt, the covenant regarding the maintenance of working capital, and the restriction on dividends until the debt is liquidated.

CENTURY ELECTRIC COMPANY

December 31, 1971

Long-Term Debt—less portion classified as current liability—Note D	$6,207,000

Note D—*Long-Term Debt*

The long-term notes payable to banks are payable on April 30th and October 30th of $250,000 each with final installment of $1,350,000 due April 30, 1973, with interest at ½ of 1% above prime rate. The loan agreement provides, among other things, that the Company shall maintain working capital of at least $10,500,000, shall not make expenditures for property, plant, and equipment in any year in excess of its total depreciation without approval of the banks and shall not pay dividends on its capital stock in excess of the cash dividends paid in 1967 plus 4% thereof compounded for each year after 1967.

The balance sheet of Procter & Gamble Company discloses that a portion of its long-term debt is in the form of bonds. Debentures are a form of bonded indebtedness secured only by the general credit of the company.

THE PROCTER & GAMBLE COMPANY AND SUBSIDIARY COMPANIES

June 30, 1972

Long-term Debt	
Debentures, 7%, less unamortized discount of $994,000	$ 99,006,000
Debentures, 3⅞%	31,867,000
Other, principally debt of subsidiaries	102,191,000
	$233,064,000

The majority of the long-term debt of Season-All Industries is in the form of a mortgage on real estate owned by the company.

SEASON-ALL INDUSTRIES, INC.

December 31, 1972

Long-Term Debt—less portion due within one year	
Mortgages payable	$1,067,251
Note payable—bank	350,000
	$1,417,251

In addition to the three principal forms of long-term debt illustrated above, there are other forms of such indebtedness like long-term loans payable, accounts payable, and contracts payable. Long-term leases, as discussed on pages 253–56 in Chapter 8, also may give rise to long-term debt for the property involved. As was explained in Chapter 8, leases are classified into two types, operating and financing. The operating lease gives rise to a commitment by the lessee to make a series of periodic payments during the term of the lease to the owner of the property in return for its use during the period of the lease. The obligation under such a lease is shown in the footnotes to the balance sheet. Typical of the form in which operating leases are disclosed is the following excerpt from the 1972 annual report of the F. W. Woolworth Co.:

Notes to Financial Statements

Note 8—*Long-Term Leases*

Minimum annual rentals in effect at December 31, 1972 under more than 4,300 store property leases are summarized as follows:

Leases expiring during:	
Next five years	$ 20,800,000
Six to ten years	29,450,000
Eleven to twenty years	73,004,000
Twenty-one to thirty years	18,945,000
Subsequently	1,313,000
	$143,512,000

The financing lease is essentially an installment purchase despite the leasing form in which the agreement is cast. A.P.B. No. 5 (see Chapter 7) requires that in the case of financing leases the substance of the transaction rather than the legal form be disclosed. Thus, in the case of a financing lease the payments required by the lease are discounted to the date the lease begins at the interest rate the Company pays on its long-term debt. This amount is shown as a non-current liability on the balance sheet. The Century Electric Company disclosed its obligation under various financing leases in its 1971 annual report in the following manner:

> Note D—*Long-term debt.* Long-term debt at December 31, 1971, consisted of the following:

Notes payable to banks	$1,850,000
Capitalized lease obligations	5,092,500
	$6,942,500
Portion included in current liabilities	735,500
	$6,207,000

> The capitalized lease obligations relate to land, buildings, machinery and equipment leased from two municipalities, which were financed by sale of industrial revenue bonds and bear interest at various rates from 4.1% to 7.75%. Lease obligations with the City of Lexington, Tennessee, at December 31, 1971, was $2,302,500. Lease obligations with the County of Alcorn, Corinth, Mississippi, at December 31, 1971, was $2,790,000.

The annual payments made under a financing lease are treated as if they were payments on a debt, e.g., a mortgage or installment purchase. One part is considered a payment of interest on the obligation disclosed on the balance sheet. The balance of the payment is applied to payment on the principal of the debt.

Types of Bonds

Bonds are usually classified by the type of lien, if any, which they have upon the assets of the issuing company and by any special privileges which the bonds confer upon their holder. An exhaustive treatment of the various types of bonds is beyond the scope of this book, yet an understanding of the more common types of bonds is necessary for a person involved with financial matters.

Debenture bonds are backed only by the general credit of the issuer. No specific assets are pledged as security for the debt represented by such borrowing. In the preceding section, it was shown that The Procter and Gamble Company incurred long-term debt by issuing this type of bonds.

Subordinated debentures represent long-term debt which ranks below debt owed to certain other creditors. For example, the 1972 annual report of International Harvester Company showed slightly over \$100,000,000 of such debt.

Long-Term Debt:	
Promissory note	
3½% due 1982	\$45,000,000
Subordinated debentures	
4⅝% due 1988	50,520,000
4.80% due 1991	52,037,000
Sinking fund debentures	
8⅝% due 1995 (Face value \$100,000)	99,856,000
6¼% due 1998	50,000,000
Eurodollar revolving credit agreements	
7% due 1977	20,000,000
6⅞% due 1977	5,000,000
Other (Face value \$142,713; weighted average 6.2%)	142,634,000
Total	\$465,047,000

With respect to payment of principal and interest, the 4⅝ percent and 4.80 percent debentures, backed by the general credit of the company, are subordinated to certain other debts of International Harvester Company such as the 8⅝ and the 6¼ percent debentures and any current notes payable to banks.

Mortgage bonds are secured by a lien on property of the issuing corporation. For example, at December 31, 1972, Iowa-Illinois Gas and Electric Company had \$138,742,000 of its debt in First Mortgage Bonds. Such bonds are a lien on substantially all of the properties of the company.

Sinking fund bonds require the issuer of the bonds periodically to set aside or remit a specific sum of money or some of the bonds themselves if such bonds have been reacquired, usually to a trustee under the bond indenture, toward the retirement of the bonds. For example, as of December 31, 1972, approximately one-half of the long-term debt of Arvin Industries, Inc., consisted of:

5.1% Sinking Fund Debentures, due 1990 .... \$16,500,000

Frequently, contributions to a sinking fund are used by the fund's trustee to purchase outstanding bonds in the open market or call the appropriate amount by lot, whichever course requires the least funds. In such a case, the sinking fund is in reality a "purchase fund."

Serial bonds are issued on a single date, but mature at different dates. The Schuylkill County (Pennsylvania) Municipal Authority, for example, had an issue of serial bonds dated July 1, 1962, to mature in installments on July 1 of the years indicated in the following schedule:

PAR AMOUNT	COUPON INTEREST RATE	YEAR OF MATURITY	PAR AMOUNT	COUPON INTEREST RATE	YEAR OF MATURITY
$100,000	2.75%	1965	$ 130,000	3.70%	1974
100,000	2.90%	1966	140,000	3.75%	1975
105,000	3.00%	1967	145,000	3.80%	1976
110,000	3.10%	1968	150,000	3.85%	1977
110,000	3.20%	1969	160,000	3.85%	1978
115,000	3.30%	1970	165,000	3.90%	1979
120,000	3.40%	1971	175,000	3.90%	1980
125,000	3.50%	1972	1,453,000	4.00%	1987
130,000	3.60%	1973	4,767,000	4.25%	2002

Convertible bonds may be exchanged at the option of the bondholder for a stipulated amount of stock of the same corporation. The exchange usually must be made within a certain time period and may require an additional cash payment by the bondholder. In effect, the bondholder—a creditor—becomes a stockholder—an "owner"—upon such a conversion. An example of convertible bonds is contained in the 1972 annual report of Virginia Electric and Power Company as follows:

Convertible Debentures
20 Year 3⅝% due May 1, 1986
Authorized and outstanding $50,000,000
Convertible: Into Common Stock at $33.00 per share

Income bonds represent debt on which the interest is paid in a given year only if the net earnings of the issuing corporation are sufficient to cover the amount of the interest. Whether any unpaid interest accumulates depends upon the bond indenture. Often, these bonds arise from a reorganization of the company. For example, the October 31, 1972 Balance Sheet of the Pittsburgh Brewing Company showed:

Long-term Debt—5% Sinking Fund Income
Subordinated Debentures due Oct. 31, 1992
(Net of debentures reacquired) (Note 4) $2,458,100

Note 4 to the balance sheet disclosed that the income bonds were issued pursuant to a plan of reorganization adopted by the board of directors on November 27, 1957. Frequently, the trust indenture of income bonds requires that the board of directors decide whether the periodic interest will be paid. Thus, these interest payments are formalized in a manner very similar to that of dividend declarations on preferred stock. If interest is in arrears on income bonds, this does not mean that the bonds themselves are in default.

Refunding bonds are issued by a corporation in exchange for, or to raise funds to redeem, a currently outstanding bond issue.

Callable bonds are those which the issuing corporation may, if it wishes, redeem prior to the maturity date by giving proper notice to the bondholders. An example of a mortgage bond issue that is both refunding and callable is shown in the 1972 annual report of Virginia Electric and Power Company, as follows:

First and Refunding Mortgage Bonds

			OUTSTANDING
Series E	2¾%,	due March 1, 1975 ...	$ 61,200,000
Series F	3%,	due March 1, 1978 ...	10,000,000
Series G	2⅞%,	due June 1, 1979 ...	20,000,000
Series H	2¾%,	due Sept. 1, 1980 ...	20,000,000
Series I	3⅜%,	due Dec. 1, 1981 ...	20,000,000
Series J	3¼%,	due Oct. 1, 1982 ...	20,000,000
Series K	3⅛%,	due May 1, 1984 ...	25,000,000
Series L	3¼%,	due June 1, 1985 ...	25,000,000
Series M	4⅛%,	due Oct. 1, 1986 ...	20,000,000
Series N	4½%,	due Dec. 1, 1987 ...	20,000,000
Series O	3⅞%,	due June 1, 1988 ...	25,000,000
Series P	4⅝%,	due Sept. 1, 1990 ...	25,000,000
Series Q	4⅞%,	due June 1, 1991 ...	30,000,000
Series R	4⅜%,	due May 1, 1993 ...	30,000,000
Series S	4½%,	due Dec. 1, 1993 ...	30,000,000
Series T	4½%,	due May 1, 1995 ...	60,000,000
Series U	5⅛%,	due Feb. 1, 1997 ...	50,000,000
Series V	6⅞%,	due Dec. 1, 1997 ...	50,000,000
Series W	7⅛%,	due Jan. 1, 1999 ...	85,000,000
Series X	7¾%,	due June 1, 1999 ...	75,000,000
Series Y	9%,	due Apr. 1, 2000 ...	85,000,000
Series Z	8⅞%,	due Sept. 1, 2000 ...	85,000,000
Series AA	7⅜%,	due March 1, 2001 ...	90,000,000
Series BB	7½%,	due Sept. 1, 2001 ...	50,000,000
Series CC	7⅜%,	due June 1, 2002 ...	100,000,000(1)
		Total Outstanding	$1,111,200,000

(1) Issued June 1972.
INTEREST: Semiannually.

Often callable bonds, if called before maturity, require the issuing corporation to pay the bondholder a specific premium above the par of the bond.

Although additional types of bonds could be enumerated and described, these types and combinations of these provide an adequate insight into the bonds which are commonly encountered.

INTEREST COST OF A BOND ISSUE

The usual bond issue requires the issuing corporation to make periodic interest payments at a fixed rate on the face (or par) amount of the bonds. Typically, such interest payments are made semi-annually; for example, a $10,000,000 face (par amount), ten-year bond issue, bearing an interest rate of 6 percent payable semi-annually on June 30 and December 31, would require interest payments of $300,000 on each of these two dates.

The individual bonds constituting a given issue bear a face (or par) value of a designated amount, such as $1,000, $500, or $100. Thus, if the $10,000,000 bond issue consisted of $1,000 par value bonds, 10,000 bonds would be issued; if the face of each bond was only $500, then 20,000 such bonds would be sold.[1]

If the $10,000,000 bond issue is sold at par (or face), the annual interest cost is 6 percent of that amount, or $600,000. However, it is rarely possible to predetermine the exact interest rate required to sell a bond issue at precisely the par amount. Typically, bonds are issued at a price above or below par. This premium or discount at issuance is a modification of the contractual interest rate of the bond issue to determine an adjusted interest rate based upon factors such as the current conditions of the money market, the credit rating of the company, and present interest rates.

Assume that the previously mentioned $10,000,000, ten-year, 6 percent bond issue is sold at a premium; namely, at 110, i.e., 110 percent of par. Basically, the bonds are sold at a premium because the contractual interest rate of 6 percent is greater than necessary under the circumstances prevailing at the time the bond issue is sold. The premium received of $1,000,000, 10 percent of the par of the issue, is not income to the corporation. In effect, it is an amount collected at the issuance of the

[1] Care should be exercised in reading stock and bond quotations. For example, a stock quoted at 105 on the New York Stock Exchange indicates a price of $105 per share. But a bond quoted at 105 on the same exchange indicates a price of 105 percent of the par or face value of the bond; the actual dollar price of a bond cannot be determined without a knowledge of its par value.

bonds that will result in an adjustment to the interest expense of the corporation as interest is paid during the ten-year life of the debt. Therefore, the adjusted interest rate to the corporation is not 6 percent, but only 5 percent, determined as follows:

Cash received by corporation:	
Face (par) plus premium upon issuance of bonds	$11,000,000
Cash to be distributed by corporation:	
Annual interest payments of (6% of $10,000,000) $600,000 for 10 years	$ 6,000,000
Face (par) of bonds to be paid at maturity	10,000,000
	$16,000,000
Excess of total disbursements over receipts	$ 5,000,000
Average net cost per year for 10 years	$ 500,000
Adjusted annual interest rate $\left(\frac{\$500{,}000}{\$10{,}000{,}000}\right)$	5%

Though the contractual interest of 6 percent on $10,000,000 ($600,000) is paid to the bondholders each year, this amount represents a net interest cost of only $500,000. The $1,000,000 premium received at issuance is amortized over the ten-year life of the bonds as a reduction of the interest expense actually paid. On a straight-line basis, this amortization is $100,000 per year. In effect, each year's interest payments totaling $600,000 represent $500,000 of expense and $100,000 of return to the bondholders of the premium received by the company at issuance of the bonds.

When bonds bear a contractual interest rate which is less than the rate required by prevailing market conditions for the risk involved, they are sold at a discount. Such discount is similar to interest paid in advance to the purchasers of bonds. Assume that a $10,000,000, ten-year, 6 percent bond issue is sold at a discount; namely, at 90, or 90 percent of par. In effect, the discount of $1,000,000 is interest paid in advance and will result in an adjustment to the interest expense of the corporation as interest is paid during the ten-year life of the debt. Therefore, the adjusted interest rate to the corporation is not 6 percent, but 7 percent, determined as follows:

Cash received by corporation:	
Face (par) less discount upon issuance of bonds	$ 9,000,000
Cash to be disbursed by corporation:	
Annual interest payments of (6% of $10,000,000) $600,000 for 10 years	$ 6,000,000
Face (par) of bonds to be paid at maturity	10,000,000
	$16,000,000

Excess of total disbursements over receipts	\$ 7,000,000
Average net cost per year for 10 years	\$ 700,000
Adjusted annual interest rate $\left(\frac{\$700,000}{\$10,000,000}\right)$	7%

The \$1,000,000 discount incurred at issuance of the bonds is amortized over the ten-year life of the bonds as an addition to the interest actually paid. On a straight-line basis, this amortization of \$100,000 per year increases the annual interest cost from the \$600,000 of interest actually paid to an adjusted cost (disregarding the time differential) to the company of \$700,000.

Statement Presentation of Bonded Indebtedness Factors

Bonds payable, at face or par, represent long-term debt. Any portion of this debt that will come due within the coming year should be shown as a current liability with a corresponding reduction in long-term indebtedness.

The balance of the unamortized bond premium or discount as of a given date is shown as an adjustment to the face amount of the long-term debt. The amount of premium not yet written off is added to the face amount of the long-term debt and the unamortized discount is subtracted from this face amount. As the premium or discount is amortized, the net balance of the debt will be decreased or increased so that it will equal the face amount at maturity. Illustrative of this method of presentation is the following from the 1972 annual report of the Procter & Gamble Company:

Long-Term Debt (partial only):		
Debentures, 7%	\$100,000,000	
less Unamortized Discount	994,000	\$99,006,000

The costs involved in the issuance of bonds for items such as printing, legal and accounting fees, and underwriting commissions are added to the discount upon issuance or subtracted from the premium, and then amortized as a component of the discount or premium.

On the statement of income for the period, the item Interest Expense on Long-term Debt, shown as a non-operating expense, is usually an amount adjusted for the period's amortization of any applicable premium or discount. Occasionally, the details are separately stated, as in the 1972 Statement of Net Revenue of the Sacramento Municipal Utility District, which shows:

Interest on long-term debt	\$18,520,428
Amortization of bond premium, bond redemption premium, discount and expense, net	137,595
Total income deductions	\$18,658,023

Often, the terms of a bond issue, as contained in the bond indenture, require the issuing corporation to accumulate a sinking fund by installment contributions so that the assets necessary to retire the debt will definitely be available in liquid form at the maturity date. The segregated asset, Sinking Fund, should not be shown as a current asset, because the amount is not available as working capital for business operations; instead, this fund should be shown in a non-current classification of assets. Reference to the December 31, 1972, Balance Sheet of Sacramento Municipal Utility District discloses the following special asset section:

SEGREGATED FUNDS, consisting of cash and securities, at cost:	
For construction purposes	$40,316,528
For nuclear fuel	1,228,198
In reserve funds for Revenue Bonds	20,295,529
	$61,840,255

Often the annual sinking fund requirements for a bond issue may be fulfilled by purchasing or calling certain of the outstanding bonds and delivering them to the trustee of the fund in satisfaction of the current installment due to the fund.

A bond indenture or other long-term debt agreements may require a restriction on the retained earnings of a corporation until the debt is retired. Any such restriction on retained earnings may be in conjunction with, or independent of, any sinking fund requirements. The usual purpose of such a restriction on retained earnings is to limit dividend declarations, thus keeping an equivalent amount of assets in the business until the debt is liquidated. Presented below are two illustrations of such restrictions.

JONES & LAUGHLIN STEEL CORPORATION

Consolidated Statement of Financial Position

December 31, 1970

Liabilities (partial only):	
Long-term debt (Note F)	$317,137,000
Shareholders' Equity (partial only):	
Income retained in the business	$409,044,000

Portion of Note G:

At December 31, 1970, all income retained in the business was restricted under the provision of the bank credit agreements dated September 1, 1970, and accordingly, no amount was available for payment of cash dividends on common stock.

UNITED AIRCRAFT CORPORATION
Consolidated Balance Sheet
December 31, 1970

Liabilities (partial only):	
Long-term debt	$233,770,300
Stockholders' Equity (partial only):	
Earnings retained in the business	$343,951,072

Financial Comments (partial only):

Dividends

The terms of the loan agreements relating to the Corporation's 5% sinking fund notes and of the indentures relating to the three issues of subordinated debentures include certain provisions restricting the availability of retained earnings for payments of cash dividends on the common stock. Under these provisions, $231,335,884 of the retained earnings of $343,951,072 at December 31, 1970, was free of such restrictions.

The first illustration shows a situation in which the restriction on retained earnings was so complete that no dividends could be declared by Jones & Laughlin Steel Corporation at December 31, 1970. The second illustration presents a situation where the restriction on the retained earnings of United Aircraft Corporation was relatively unimportant. Cash dividends of United Aircraft, each year for the preceding five years, amounted to approximately $1.80 per share (about $21,770,000 each year). With net earnings exceeding $45,000,000 each year for the preceding five years and *unrestricted* retained earnings of $231,335,884 at December 31, 1970, the restriction on retained earnings was of considerably less significance than it was for Jones & Laughlin.

A corporation may purchase its own bonds on the market and hold them as treasury bonds. These treasury bonds may then be cancelled, resold, or used to meet a sinking fund requirement. Treasury bonds are not an asset but are shown as a reduction of the long-term indebtedness of the corporation, as shown in the following illustration taken from the 1972 Annual Report of Cities Service Company.

3% Sinking Fund Debentures due 1977; excludes debentures in treasury of $8,700,000	$39,300,000

A discussion of the factors influencing decisions on whether to raise needed additional capital by the incurrence of long-term debt or by the issuance of capital stock will be presented after the basic factors constituting stockholders' equity have been discussed in the next chapter.

QUESTIONS AND PROBLEMS

11–1. On January 1, 1974, the Severna Park Manufacturing Company sells 1,000 ten-year, 6 percent, sinking fund bonds. Face (par) value for each bond is $1,000. Interest is to be paid semi-annually on June 30 and December 31. Annually, according to the provisions of the bond indenture, $100,000 (less the earnings in the fund each year) is to be deposited with a trustee to provide the amount needed to retire the bonds at maturity. Also, the company is required to restrict retained earnings in an amount equal to the balance of the fund.

Required

a. Complete the form below under the three assumptions for the original issue price of the bonds.

	BONDS SOLD AT		
DESCRIPTION OF FACTS	FACE (100%)	95 (95%)	105 (105%)
January 1, 1974			
(1) Face of total issue ..	$	$	$
(2) Upon issuance, total amount of:			
Bond discount ..		$	
Bond premium ..			$
June 30, 1974			
(1) Semi-annual interest payment ...	$	$	$
December 31, 1974			
(1) Semi-annual interest payment ...	$	$	$
(2) Amount of annual straight-line amortization of:			
Bond discount ...		$	
Bond premium ..			$
(3) Interest Expense on Bonds (net) shown by annual statement of income	$	$	$

b. Complete the form below for the sinking fund and restriction on retained earnings requirements.

DESCRIPTION OF FACTS	AMOUNT
December 31, 1974	
(1) First annual contribution to sinking fund	$
(2) Restriction on retained earnings	$
December 31, 1975	
(1) Second annual contribution to sinking fund (during 1975 the fund increased $5,000 because of income earned on the first contribution	$
(2) Additional restriction on retained earnings, equal to total increase in fund during 1975	$
December 31, 1983	
(1) Tenth annual contribution to sinking fund (during 1983 the fund increased $45,000 because of income earned on the $900,000 balance in the fund as of December 31, 1982)	$
(2) Additional restriction on retained earnings, equal to total increase in fund during 1983	$
January 1, 1984	
(1) Retirement of bond issue (no bonds had been redeemed during ten years) will require the use of the sinking fund to the extent of	$
(2) This retirement of the bonds will permit the removal of the restriction on retained earnings in the amount of	$

11–2. Approximately eight years from December 31, 1974, management plans to add to plant capacity by an estimated expenditure of $160,000. It is decided that, annually, beginning with December 31, 1974, $20,000 shall be set aside in a Plant Extension Fund. The amount of the annual contribution to the fund will be reduced by whatever amount the fund increases during the current year due to its earnings. It is also decided that a portion of retained earnings will be restricted (formally titled Retained Earnings Restricted for Plant Extension), the amount of which restriction is to be kept equal to the related fund. Each December 31, a restriction of retained earnings will be made for the total increase in the amount of the fund that year.

At December 31, 1981, the balance of the Plant Extension Fund is $144,200, including $4,200 of interest earned by the fund during 1981 and already recorded, but excluding the last annual contribution to be made on December 31, 1981. No additional provision has been made to restrict retained earnings since December 31, 1980.

The following table shows the actual accumulation of the fund:

YEAR ENDED	INCOME EARNED BY FUND	ANNUAL CONTRIBUTION DECEMBER 31	TOTAL FUND
December 31, 1974	$ —	$20,000	$ 20,000
December 31, 1975	800	19,200	40,000
December 31, 1976	1,600	18,400	60,000
December 31, 1977	3,000	17,000	80,000
December 31, 1978	3,400	16,600	100,000
December 31, 1979	5,000	15,000	120,000
December 31, 1980	3,600	16,400	140,000
December 31, 1981	4,200	?	160,000

Required

a. Determine the amount of the contribution to the Plant Extension Fund on December 31, 1981.

b. Determine the amount of the additional restriction made to retained earnings on December 31, 1981.

c. If an additional plant building is purchased on January 8, 1982, for $157,000, what will happen to:
1. the balance remaining in the Plant Extension Fund?
2. the restriction on retained earnings?

Note: Assume no further plant extension is contemplated.

11–3. **Required**

a. Where would a fund (e.g., Sinking Fund for Bond Redemption, Plant Extension Fund) be shown in the balance sheet?

b. How would a restriction on retained earnings (e.g., Retained Earnings Restricted for Bond Redemption, Retained Earnings Restricted for Plant Extension) appear in the balance sheet?

c. Where would the income earned by a fund (e.g., Income Earned by Sinking Fund, Income Earned by Plant Extension Fund) during a given year be reflected on the annual statement of income?

d. What is the purpose of a fund?

e. What is the purpose of a restriction on retained earnings?

f. Why have *both* a fund and a restriction on retained earnings?

g. Discuss this statement: "Once the bonds have been retired (or the plant expansion program completed) and the restriction on retained earnings removed (causing a sudden increase in unrestricted retained earnings), the corporation is in an excellent position to pay a large dividend."

Note: This problem may be used independently or as an additional requirement to either of problems 11–1 or 11–2.

11–4. a. Compute the selling price of a face (par) $1,000 bond if the market quotation is:

93	94½	95¼
111	100½	102⅜

b. Compute the selling price of a face $500 bond if the market quotation is 97⅞.

c. On May 1, 1974, West Lafayette Manufacturing Company issued $100,000 of 6 percent first mortagage bonds at 98½. Face of each bond is $1,000. The bonds are payable in ten years, with interest payable semiannually on May 1 and November 1.

One of the bonds was purchased by Brown, an individual investor, on May 1, 1974. On August 13, 1974, Brown sold the bond to Smith at 99 plus accrued interest. Smith held the bond until December 13, 1974, when he sold it to Green at 98 plus accrued interest.

Determine the following:

1. Cost of bond to Brown
2. Gain or loss on sale of bond by Brown
3. Interest earned on the bond by Brown
4. Cost of bond to Smith (exclusive of accrued interest)
5. Gain or loss on sale of bond by Smith
6. Interest earned on the bond by Smith

11–5. R & F Corporation has issued $1,000,000 of 5 percent debenture bonds at par to mature in 20 years. The bond indenture requires the corporation to accumulate a sinking fund and to restrict retained earnings for dividend declarations.

Required

Select the best answer to the following three statements:

a. On the balance sheet, the Sinking Fund would be shown as:

1. an investment asset
2. a current asset
3. a restriction on retained earnings
4. a fixed asset

b. On the same balance sheet, the amount of the restriction on retained earnings would be shown as:
   1. an investment asset
   2. a current asset
   3. a portion of the stockholders' equity section
   4. a reduction of bonds payable

c. On the statement of income for the year, the annual $50,000 of interest expense on the bonds would be shown as:
   1. an administrative expense
   2. a financial management expense (Other Expenses and Losses section) to be deducted after the determination of net operating income.
   3. a portion of cost of goods sold, because the proceeds from the bond were used to build a new manufacturing plant
   4. not shown at all, but treated as are dividends on capital stock (i.e., as a distribution of the net income for the year and, thus, a direct charge against retained earnings)

11–6. For each of the following statements, choose the one best answer to each and indicate your choice on an answer sheet with a number.

a. The establishment of a fund (e.g., sinking fund for bond redemption) out of cash:
   1. decreases the amount of current assets
   2. decreases the amount of total assets
   3. increases the amount of current assets
   4. increases the amount of total assets
   5. changes the amount of total retained earnings
   6. none of the above

b. The incurrence of long-term debt as a method of securing funds for a capital expansion program is indicative of:
   1. a venturesome "gambling" management
   2. the manner in which a majority of new capital has been raised from *external* sources by companies since World War II (see end of next chapter)
   3. ultra-conservatism in management
   4. none of the above

c. A company sells $1,000,000 face (par) of 8 percent bonds at a premium, viz., 105 (105 percent of par). They mature in 20 years. The annual interest expense (after amortization of premium on a straight-line basis) shown on the income statement for any of the twenty years is:
   1. $77,500
   2. $80,000
   3. $82,500
   4. none of the above

d. A company sells 200 5 percent bonds at a discount, viz., 90 (90 percent of par). The face amount of each bond is $500, and they mature in ten years. The annual interest expense (after amortization of discount on a straight-line basis) shown on the income statement for any of the ten years is:
   1. $5,000
   2. $6,000
   3. $7,000
   4. none of the above

e. Assume you purchase a $1,000 face (par) bond from a corporation the day it is issued (April 1) for 105. The bond bears an annual interest rate of 8 percent, payable April 1 and October 1. Then you sell the bond on July 1 for 104½ plus accrued interest. You will have:
   1. $5 capital loss and $20 of interest income
   2. $15 capital gain and no interest income
   3. $5 capital loss and $40 of interest income

f. Income bonds pay interest:
   1. only once every year
   2. when the company receives revenues
   3. when the company earns enough to have first met its preferred dividend requirements
   4. when net earnings of the year cover interest requirements
   5. if company wishes to pay interest

12

Stockholders' Equity

Stockholders' equity, often referred to as shareholders' equity, capital, or net worth, represents the excess of the company's assets over its liabilities. Basically, stockholders' equity is derived from two sources—capital contributions by the stockholders (and possibly others) and net earnings reinvested in the business.

CAPITAL STOCK AND ITS TERMINOLOGY

One of the two sources of stockholders' equity is capital contributions. On the typical balance sheet, the amount of capital contributions is subdivided into two categories. The first of these two categories is "capital contributed for, or assigned to, shares, to the extent of the par or stated value of each class of shares presently outstanding."[1] The second category is "capital in excess of par or stated value." The first category of contributed capital is discussed in this section, and the second, in the following section.

[1] Accounting Terminology Bulletin Number 1, "Review and Résumé," p. 30, *Accounting Research and Terminology Bulletins, Final Edition.* Copyright 1961 by the American Institute of Certified Public Accountants, Inc.

Various terms commonly encountered in relation to shares of capital stock will be discussed and illustrated prior to any detailed analysis of an entire stockholders' equity section.

One such category of terms concerns the present status of the total number of shares of capital stock authorized in the charter granted to the corporation by the state in which the company is incorporated. For example, Hershey Foods Corporation, as of December 31, 1972, had 20,000,000 shares of common stock authorized, 12,528,710 shares issued, and 704,905 shares of treasury stock. Using these amounts, it is possible to illustrate certain capital stock terminology as follows:

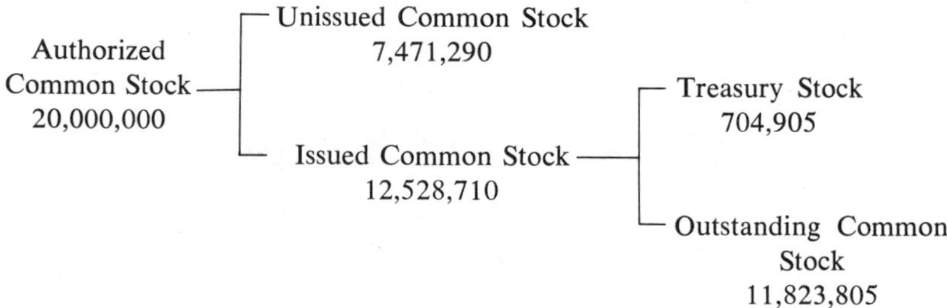

Of the 20,000,000 authorized shares, 7,471,290 shares are *unissued,* since they have never been sold, whereas 12,528,710 have been *issued.* But, of the 12,528,710 shares which have been issued and for which the corporation has received consideration, 704,905 have been reacquired by the company and not cancelled but held in *treasury;* the remaining 11,823,805 shares of the issued shares remain *outstanding* in the hands of the public.

A second category of terms relates to the predetermined dollar amount, if any, assigned to each share and printed on the face of the stock certificates. If a predetermined fixed dollar amount is assigned to each share of capital stock, the stock is known as *par value* stock. It is unfortunate that the word *value* is coupled with the word *par* because the dollar amount designated as par is an arbitrary amount and rarely reflects the value of the stock. For example, few would know offhand, or be interested in knowing, the present par value of the shares of common stock of the following corporations:

	PAR
United States Steel Corporation	$30
Bethlehem Steel Corporation	8
General Motors Corporation	1⅔
Aluminum Company of America	1
Sterling Precision Corporation	.10
Carrier Corporation	2.50

Starting with New York in 1912, state corporation codes have been amended so that today all states permit the issuance of *no-par value* stock. No-par value stock has no specific or predetermined fixed dollar amount assigned to each share. However, some state corporation codes require the assignment of a *stated value* per share to no-par stock, and certain states permit the board of directors to assign a stated value. Any stated value assigned to no-par shares removes them from the category of "true" no-par stock and makes them very similar to par stock. Typical examples of no-par stock issues are the following:

Caterpillar Tractor Co., common stock, no-par value
Minnesota Mining and Manufacturing Company, common stock, without par value
Beatrice Foods Co., common stock, without par value, stated value per share of $3.65
Standard Brands Incorporated, common stock, without par value, stated value per share—$2.00

A third category of terms describing capital stock relates to the different classes of stock. If a corporation has only one class of stock, like Exxon Corporation and Gulf Oil Corporation, the stock may be referred to only as *capital* stock. But, if a corporation has more than one class of stock, one class may be called *preferred* stock, and the other, *common* stock.[2] Preferred stock has certain designated rights which supersede those belonging to common stock. The two preferences most frequently associated with preferred stock are the right to dividends before common stock and a prior claim on assets in event the company is liquidated. In exchange for such preferences, all other rights are usually reserved to the common stock, whose principal reserved right is often the right to vote for the directors of the corporation. To explain the different rights attached to different classes of stock, two illustrations are presented. First, Scott Paper Company has stock outstanding of the following classes:

Cumulative preferred shares without par value:
$3.40 series
$4.00 series
Common shares without par value

Both series of preferred stock have equal preference for assets and dividends and are entitled to $100 per share if the company is involuntarily liquidated. Since both series of preferred are *cumulative,* any dividends not declared when due accumulate and should any such dividend arrearages ever occur, they must be paid before any dividends can be declared

[2] It is not unusual to find a company with just one class of stock designating it as common, rather than capital, stock.

on the common stock. Neither series of preferred stock has any voting rights except on default of dividends for one year. Other than this possible restriction, the common stock has the sole voting power. Second, United States Steel Corporation had, until 1966, the following two classes of outstanding stock:

Preferred stock, 7% cumulative, par value $100
Common stock, par value $16⅔ per share

In any liquidation, the preferred stock was entitled to preference over the common to the par amount of $100 per share. The preferred also had preference over the common to cumulative dividends of 7 percent per annum. During the depression of the 1930's, the dividends on the preferred fell in arrears. Since the stock was cumulative, such arrearages had to be paid (and were in 1936 and 1937) before any dividends could be paid on the common stock. Should preferred stock of a company be *non-cumulative* in nature, any dividends not declared will lapse. Note that when the preferred stock is par stock, as in the case of United States Steel Corporation, the annual dividend rate is expressed as a percent of par, in this instance 7 percent of $100 or $7 annually (actually $1.75 per quarter) per share. But, when the preferred stock is no-par stock, as in the case of Scott Paper Company, the annual dividend rate is expressed as so many dollars per share. Unlike the owners of preferred stock of Scott Paper Company, the preferred stockholders of United States Steel Corporation were entitled to vote; in fact, each share of preferred had six votes. (Note: On January 1, 1966, United States Steel Corporation exchanged this preferred stock for debentures). Occasionally preferred stock is *participating* preferred stock. Then, the preferred stock is entitled to participate with the common stock and receive additional dividends over and above the stipulated preferred dividend rate once the common stockholders have received a certain dividend. However, most preferred stock is *non-participating;* preferred stockholders normally are entitled to only the fixed dividend rate regardless of the amount of dividends declared to the common stockholders.

CAPITAL IN EXCESS OF PAR OR STATED VALUE

The term Capital in Excess of Par or Stated Value refers to the second category of the contributed capital portion of the stockholders' equity.

There are several terms widely used as alternates for Capital in Excess of Par or Stated Value. Capital Surplus, which has been objected to by accounting authorities for many years because of possible misinterpretation, is still widely used to denote this portion of the stockholders' equity.[3] A survey of 600 annual reports issued in 1971 discloses the following frequencies of use for the various terms which describe this portion of contributed capital.[4]

Capital surplus	122	
Paid-in surplus	29	
Total retaining term "surplus"		151
Capital in excess of par or stated values	142	
Additional paid-in capital	132	
Paid-in capital, or other paid-in capital	25	
Additional capital, or other capital	45	
Other captions using the term "capital"	25	
Captions avoiding use of term "capital"	6	
Total replacing term "surplus"		375
		526
No such items presented on balance sheets		74
		600

Some of the usual sources of contributed capital in excess of the amount assigned to the par or stated value of outstanding shares are as follows:

1. Capital contributed for shares as a result of the original issuance of par-value shares at amounts exceeding their par value. Usually this excess is referred to as "premium on capital (or common or preferred) stock."
2. Capital contributed for shares as a result of the original issuance of no-par value shares at amounts exceeding their stated value.
3. From treasury stock transactions.
4. From the issuance of additional shares of the corporation's own stock as the result of a stock dividend.
5. Capital contributed other than for shares of stock. Occasionally such a source of contributed capital results from assets donated to a corporation.

[3] For a comprehensive analysis of the objections to the term "capital surplus," see Accounting Terminology Bulletin Number 1, "Review and Résumé," pp. 28–32, *Accounting Research and Terminology Bulletins, Final Edition.* Copyright 1961 American Institute of Certified Public Accountants, Inc.

[4] Condensed from American Institute of Certified Public Accountants, *Accounting Trends and Techniques in Published Corporate Annual Reports,* 26th ed., p. 163. Copyright (1972) American Institute of Certified Public Accountants, Inc. This reference also clearly indicates the trend in past years away from either capital surplus or paid-in surplus and toward alternate titles.

Four illustrations are presented to clarify the first four sources of contributed capital. The December 31, 1972, Balance Sheet of Gulf States Utilities Company illustrates the first source; namely, premium on par value capital stock (on their preferred stock, $100 par value).

Capital Stock (details not reproduced) and Retained Earnings:	
Preferred stock, cumulative, $100 par value ..	$117,500,000
Common stock, without par value	187,579,725
Premium on preferred stocks	655,236
Retained earnings	139,354,411
Total capital stock and retained earnings ..	$445,089,372

The Balance Sheet amount of Additional Capital at October 31, 1972, shown by The Firestone Tire & Rubber Company is clarified by an attached Statement of Additional Capital indicating the source of the increase in Additional Capital during the year. In this case, the increase comes from source two enumerated above; namely, the issuance of no-par value shares at an amount exceeding the stated value.

Balance at Beginning of Year	$188,725,000
Excess of Proceeds over Stated Value from Sales of Common Stock (without Par Value) Under the Incentive Stock Option Plan	409,000
Balance at End of Year	$189,134,000

The notes to the financial statements contained in the annual report of the Coca-Cola Company include the following schedule to support the December 31, 1972 amount of $59,087,550 shown by the Balance Sheet as Capital Surplus:

	CAPITAL SURPLUS
Balance January 1, 1971	$46,510,457
Sale of stock (191,028 shares of previously unissued and 17,220 shares of treasury) to employees exercising stock options	7,668,031
Balance December 31, 1971	54,178,488
Sale of stock to employees exercising stock options	4,908,986
Other	76
Balance December 31, 1972	$59,087,550

This contains two illustrations of the third source enumerated; namely, additional capital resulting from the disposal of treasury stock at an amount exceeding its acquisition cost.

The 1972 annual report of Litton Industries, Inc., discloses, on the Statement of Additional Paid-in Capital, the item of:

Excess of market value over par value of common stock issued for stock dividend	$20,956,000

This is illustrative of the fourth source enumerated above; namely, a stock dividend when market value exceeds par or stated value. The theory underlying a stock dividend is discussed later in this chapter.

Summary—total contributed capital. Contributed capital represents the *total* amount contributed to the corporation by the stockholders (and possibly by others if there are donated assets) in the form of assets and services. This total amount typically is subdivided into two categories: *capital stock*—that portion of the contributed capital assigned to shares in the amount of the par or stated value of the various classes of shares of outstanding stock, and *capital in excess of par or stated value*—that portion of the contributed capital in excess of the amount assigned to the par or stated value of the various classes of stock.[5]

RETAINED EARNINGS

The second principal source of stockholders' equity is retained earnings. Retained earnings, often still called "earned surplus," represents that portion of the company's total net earnings over the years of its existence which has *not* been distributed to the stockholders as dividends, but reinvested in the business. The term "undivided profits" could be used to explain the meaning of retained earnings if there were no possibility that the word "undivided" might imply that such an amount was actually to be divided among the stockholders at some stated time in the future. Of course, the amount of retained earnings or undivided profits, though legally available for dividend declaration, normally could not be paid out as dividends, because it merely represents the amount already plowed back into the business in various forms as additional working capital, plant and equipment, investments in subsidiaries; i.e., an overall increase in the net assets of the company.

---

[5] Rarely is stock issued at a discount (i.e., for less than par value) because of the possible individual stockholder liability to creditors of the corporation to the extent of the discount in the event of the corporation's failure. Basically, there is no reason to issue shares at a discount when the opportunity exists to authorize no-par shares or when par may be predetermined at almost any given amount at the time the application is filed for a corporate charter.

Despite the previously mentioned opposition to the term *surplus,* its usage, though declining, is still encountered. The survey of 600 annual reports discloses the following.[6]

Number of Companies	
Replacing the term "earned surplus"	573
Retaining the term "earned surplus"	27
	600

The phrase most frequently used in lieu of *earned surplus* is *retained earnings.* Such usage follows the recommendation of the Committee on Terminology of the American Institute of Certified Public Accountants, that:[7]

> The term earned surplus be replaced by terms which will indicate source, such as retained income, retained earnings, accumulated earnings, or earnings retained for use in the business. In the case of a deficit, the amount should be shown as a deduction from contributed capital with appropriate description.

The term deficit should be used as the opposite to retained earnings, as illustrated by the 1972 Statements of LTV, Inc.

Retained Earnings (deficit) .... (101,915,000)

Possible restrictions upon retained earnings, as mentioned earlier in connection with long-term debt, will be more fully discussed in a subsequent section of this chapter.

ILLUSTRATIVE PRESENTATION OF STOCKHOLDERS' EQUITY

To summarize the pertinent factors presented to this point regarding stockholders' equity, it is worthwhile to explain an illustrative set of facts for a fictitious company, the McCandless Corporation.

> FACTS: On January 2, 1974, the McCandless Corporation received its charter with an authorized capital of 3,000 shares of preferred stock, 7 percent non-cumulative, non-participating, par value $100; and 6,000 shares of no-par common stock. The following transactions affecting stockholders' equity occurred during 1974:

---

[6] Condensed from American Institute of Certified Public Accountants, *Accounting Trends and Techniques in Published Corporate Annual Reports,* 26th ed., p. 165. Copyright (1972) American Institute of Certified Public Accountants, Inc.

[7] Accounting Terminology Bulletin Number 1, "Review and Résumé," p. 31, *Accounting Research and Terminology Bulletins, Final Edition.* Copyright 1961 by the American Institute of Certified Public Accountants, Inc.

January	3	Issued 1,000 shares of preferred stock for cash at par.
January	4	Issued 2,000 shares of common stock for cash at $55 per share. The McCandless Corporation is incorporated in a state which permits the company to allocate a portion of the proceeds from the issuance of no-par stock to a capital in excess of stated value category. The directors of the McCandless Corporation established a stated value of $50 per share on all common no-par stock.
January	15	Issued 100 shares of common no-par stock in payment of attorney's costs of $5,500 incurred in the organization of the corporation.
February	9	In consideration for the corporation's locating a large plant in its vicinity, the City of Erewhon unconditionally donated land with a fair market value of $20,000. The donation was legal under the state law.
February	12	Issued 100 shares of preferred stock to Mr. Doe in payment for an adjacent plot of land which the directors valued at $10,000.
March	12	Issued 500 shares of preferred stock for cash at $103 per share.
April	14	Issued 1,000 shares of common no-par stock at $56 per share.
December	31	The net income for the year was $40,000.
December	31	The directors declared a 7 percent dividend on the preferred stock and a $2 per share dividend on the common stock.

Each of the foregoing transactions is analyzed for its effect upon stockholders' equity in the following summary:

SUMMARY ANALYSIS

DATE	PREFERRED STOCK ISSUED		COMMON STOCK ISSUED		CAPITAL IN EXCESS OF PAR OR STATED VALUE	RETAINED EARNINGS
	NUMBER OF SHARES	AMOUNT @ $100 SHARE	NUMBER OF SHARES	AMOUNT @ $50 SHARE		
Jan. 3	1,000	$100,000			$ -0-	
4			2,000	$100,000	10,000 (1)	
15			100	5,000	500 (1)	

SUMMARY ANALYSIS (cont.)

DATE	PREFERRED STOCK ISSUED: NUMBER OF SHARES	PREFERRED STOCK ISSUED: AMOUNT @ $100 SHARE	COMMON STOCK ISSUED: NUMBER OF SHARES	COMMON STOCK ISSUED: AMOUNT @ $50 SHARE	CAPITAL IN EXCESS OF PAR OR STATED VALUE	RETAINED EARNINGS
Feb. 9	—	—	—	—	20,000 (2)	
12	100	10,000			-0-	
Mar. 12	500	50,000			1,500 (3)	
Apr. 14			1,000	50,000	6,000 (1)	
Totals	1,600	$160,000	3,100	$155,000		
	(1) Capital in Excess of Stated Value of No-Par Stock				$16,500	
	(2) Capital from Donated Land				20,000	
	(3) Premium on Preferred Stock				1,500	
	Total Capital in Excess of Par or Stated Value				$38,000	
Dec. 31	Net income for the year increases retained earnings					$ 40,000
31	Dividend declarations reduce retained earnings:					
	On preferred: 7 percent of $160,000 or $7 times 1,600 shares					(11,200)
	On common: $2 times 3,100 shares					(6,200)
Retained earnings reinvested in the business at December 31						$ 22,600

The summary analysis of the facts may be presented in the following format as a portion of the balance sheet:

SOLUTION

STOCKHOLDERS' EQUITY

Contributed Capital:

7 percent, Non-cumulative, Non-participating

Preferred Stock, Par $100

Authorized	3,000 shares	
Less: Unissued	1,400 shares	
Issued and Outstanding ..	1,600 shares ..	$160,000

Common Stock, No-Par Value,

$50 Stated Value

Authorized	6,000 shares	
Less: Unissued	2,900 shares	
Issued and Outstanding ..	3,100 shares ..	155,000

Capital in Excess of Par or Stated Value:		
Premium on Preferred Stock	$ 1,500	
Capital in Excess of Stated Value	16,500	
Capital from Donated Land	20,000	38,000
Total Contributed Capital		$353,000
Retained Earnings		22,600
Total Stockholders' Equity		$375,600

DIVIDENDS

The usual corporate notice of a dividend declaration will read similarly to the following:

> At a meeting held October 1, your Board of Directors declared a cash dividend of $1 per share to shareholders of record at the close of business on November 1 and payable on December 1.

It is on the first date, the date that the dividend is declared (October 1), that the dividend becomes a liability of the corporation; retained earnings are decreased and current liabilities are increased by the total amount of the dividend declaration. It is on the third date, the date that the dividend is paid (December 1), that the liability for the dividend is liquidated; current liabilities and current assets are decreased by the total amount of the dividend. The intermediate date, the date of record (November 1), is the last day on which anyone who has recently purchased shares can have them transferred to his name to receive the dividend already declared. On the New York Stock Exchange, usually a stock sells "ex-dividend" on the third business day before the record date.

Asset dividends. The typical profit distribution is a cash dividend to the stockholders, as discussed in the preceding paragraph. However, though not too common a practice, a dividend which distributes corporate profits may be paid with assets other than cash. For example, in addition to quarterly cash dividends, Standard Oil Company (Indiana) had a special year-end dividend, during the years 1948–1963, payable in shares it owned of Standard Oil Company (New Jersey).

Stock dividends. A stock dividend is an issuance of additional shares of the corporation's own stock to its shareholders, not a distribution of cash or any other assets. In effect, a stock dividend is a permanent capitalization of earnings; it causes a decrease in retained earnings and an increase in contributed capital but does not change the total amount of stockholders' equity. Technically, a stock dividend is not a distribution of corporate earnings, but a capitalization of such earnings: such a dividend does not change any stockholder's proportionate equity in the company.

The effect of a stock dividend upon the stockholders' equity section of the balance sheet is (1) to decrease retained earnings by the "fair value" of the shares issued, (2) to increase capital stock by the par or stated value amount of the shares, and (3) to increase capital in excess of par or stated value by the amount of the excess of "fair value" over par or stated value. On the date a stock dividend is declared, retained earnings are decreased. But no current liability for "dividends payable" is created, as for an asset dividend. Since a stock dividend is only a shift from retained earnings to contributed capital without any effect upon the total dollar amount of stockholders' equity, the "stock dividend payable" amount remains within the stockholders' equity section between the declaration and payment dates. A typical presentation of this situation is the following from the December 31, 1966, statement of Consolidated Financial Position of RCA Corporation:

Shareholders' Equity	
Capital stock, no par, at stated value	
$3.50 cumulative first preferred stock, shares authorized 920,300, outstanding 183,639 (preference on liquidation $100 per share, $18,363,900)	$ 2,971,000
Common stock, authorized 80,000,000 shares; issued 59,458,337 shares	39,639,000
2 percent stock dividend payable, 1,184,597 shares	790,000
Capital surplus	411,835,000
Reinvested earnings	237,702,000
Total Shareholders' Equity	$692,937,000

The above 2 percent stock dividend was payable on January 30, 1967.

"Fair value" per share, as determined by the directors of a company, typically has a reasonable relationship to market value.[8] For example, to determine the fair value per share for its 1 percent stock dividend declared on November 13, 1956, Sears, Roebuck and Co. used the closing market price per share on the day preceding the stock dividend declaration, adjusted to give effect to the stock dividend. The approximate

[8] An exception to the procedure of capitalizing the fair value per share for a stock dividend could occur when the fair value per share is less than the legal minimum required to be capitalized according to the law of the state of incorporation. In this case, the higher amount—legal minimum per share—would be capitalized. Such a situation might occur if fair value per share is less than par value.

market price per share on the stock dividend record date was used by Ashland Oil, Inc., to determine fair value per share for its 2 percent stock dividend in 1960.

The Committee on Accounting Procedure of the AICPA recommended that an amount equal to the fair value of shares to be issued by a stock dividend should be capitalized by a transfer from Retained Earnings to Common Stock and Capital in Excess of Par when the shares issued as a dividend are less than approximately 20 percent to 25 percent of the shares previously outstanding.[9] For example, the Board of Directors of PPG Industries, on October 10, 1962, declared a stock dividend of 2 percent (that is, at the rate of one share for each 50 shares held), payable on January 21, 1963. The Company's "earnings retained for use in the business" was reduced $46.26 for each share of the common stock issued as a result of this stock dividend. Of that sum, the par value of $10.00 per share was transferred to capital stock, and $36.26 per share was transferred to "capital contributed for stock in excess of par value."

A stock dividend is a formal recognition by the company that such an amount is to be permanently retained in the business. Notices to shareholders concerning stock dividend declarations typically contain statements as: "The stock dividend was declared with the objective of conserving cash for the continuing growth of the Corporation's business" (RCA Corporation, January 30, 1967); and "The purpose of this stock dividend is to effect a capitalization of earnings which will conserve working capital in the interests of the Company's business" (Ashland Oil, Inc., August 1, 1960). Because, theoretically, a stock dividend "gives" a stockholder "nothing" (merely more shares of stock but with each share representing a proportionately smaller equity in the corporation), the typical stock dividend is not taxable income to the recipient for federal income tax purposes.

Illustration of Effect of Dividends upon Stockholders' Equity

The corporate codes of the 50 states differ with respect to possible dividend declarations (both cash and stock dividends) from "capital in excess of par or stated value" (paid-in surplus or capital surplus) and, though rarely encountered because an appraisal write-up of assets is not generally accepted accounting, any "recorded appreciation of assets" (appraisal or revaluation surplus). This is beyond the scope of the present

---

[9] Accounting Research Bulletin No. 43, "Restatement and Revision of Accounting Research Bulletins," Chapter 7, *Accounting Research and Terminology Bulletins, Final Edition.* Copyright 1961 by the American Institute of Certified Public Accountants, Inc.

discussion. Therefore, assume in the two cases below that dividend declarations are from retained earnings (earned surplus).

The following stockholders' equity section was taken from the balance sheet of the Skoner Corporation, a fictitious company, as of December 31, 1974:

Stockholders' Equity

Capital Contributions		
Common Stock—Par $100:		
Authorized	80,000 shares	
Less: Unissued	50,000 shares	
Issued and Outstanding	30,000 shares	$3,000,000
Capital in Excess of Par:		
Premium on Common Stock	$70,000	
Capital from Donated Land	50,000	120,000
Retained Earnings		1,380,000
Total Stockholders' Equity		$4,500,000

Case one. The board of directors met and declared a 5 percent cash dividend ($150,000) on January 2, 1975, payable February 1, to stockholders of record on January 15. Assuming no changes in stockholders' equity other than those caused by the declaration and payment of the dividend:

1. The summary form on the next page presents the revised amounts constituting the stockholders' equity section of the balance sheet;
2. Shows the revised book value per share; and
3. Shows the change in equity of a stockholder owning 20 shares of stock.

Case two. Revert to the original stockholders' equity section as of December 31, 1974, and assume that the directors had declared, on January 2, a stock, instead of a cash, dividend payable on February 1 to stockholders of record on January 15. The dividend was equal to one share for every 20 shares outstanding (5 percent). The board of directors placed a "fair value" of $160 per share on the shares issued as a result of the 5 percent stock dividend. The cash dividend decreases stockholders' equity (specifically, retained earnings) by the total amount of the dividend and the book value per share by the amount of the per share dividend because of the asset distribution. The stock dividend capitalizes the fair value ($160) of the shares issued (1,500) without affecting total stockholders' equity; retained earnings is decreased $240,000 ($160 × 1,500 shares), but contributed capital is increased the same amount—common stock by \$150,000 (\$100 par × 1,500 shares) and capital in excess of par by \$90,000 (\$60 × 1,500 shares). Furthermore, the proportionate equity of the stockholder is unchanged; 21 shares represent the same equity as the 20 previous shares.

SUMMARY

	BEFORE DIVIDEND	AFTER CASH DIVIDEND	AFTER STOCK DIVIDEND
Outstanding Common Stock	\$3,000,000	\$3,000,000	\$3,150,000
Capital in Excess of Par	120,000	120,000	210,000
Retained Earnings	1,380,000	1,230,000	1,140,000
Total Stockholders' Equity	\$4,500,000	\$4,350,000	\$4,500,000
Number of shares outstanding ..	30,000	30,000	31,500
Book value per share	\$150.00	\$145.00	\$142.86
Equity per corporate books of assumed stockholder	\$150.00 × 20	\$145.00 × 20	\$142.86 × 21
	\$3,000	\$2,900	\$ 3,000
Cash received by stockholder ...	—	\$100	\$ -0-

STOCK SPLIT

A stock split involves the issuance of additional shares to present stockholders without changing the total dollar amount of any of the items constituting the stockholders' equity section of the balance sheet. To illustrate this point, analyze case three for Skoner Corporation.

Case three. Revert to the original stockholders' equity section as of December 31, 1974, and assume that the directors had recommended

	BEFORE SPLIT	AFTER SPLIT
Outstanding Common Stock	\$3,000,000	\$3,000,000
Capital in Excess of Par	120,000	120,000
Retained Earnings	1,380,000	1,380,000
Total Stockholders' Equity ..	\$4,500,000	\$4,500,000
Number of shares outstanding	30,000	60,000
Book value per share	\$150	\$75
Equity per corporate books of assumed stockholder	\$150 × 20	\$75 × 40
	\$3,000	\$3,000

(and the stockholders approved) a two for one stock split effective on February 1, with par value of each share to be reduced from $100 to $50. Only the number of shares changed, having doubled because of the two for one split. But par per share has been halved; if the stock had been no-par stock without a stated value, even this formality would not have been necessary. Note that the individual stockholder, who now has twice as many shares, still has identical equity in the company. The only possible gain to an individual stockholder would be if the market value per share on the stock exchange does not drop to exactly one-half of its former price; this is a distinct possibility because stock splits are viewed as "bullish" by the market.

A typical reason for a stock split is "to increase the number of outstanding shares for the purpose of effecting a reduction in their unit market price and thereby, of obtaining wider distribution and increased marketability of the shares."[10] In a similar vein, the Westinghouse Electric Corporation said the following about a proposed two for one stock split in 1971, "It is believed that a stock split will result in a broader base of ownership and enhanced marketability of the Corporation's stock and increased public interest in the Corporation's business." And, in 1972, concerning a two for one stock split, the Minnesota Mining and Manufacturing Company stated, "The Management believes that the stock split . . . will bring the market price of the common stock within a trading range more attractive to the small individual investor and thus will be to the advantage of the Company and its stockholders."

There are two basic differences between a stock dividend and a stock split. The former results in a permanent capitalization of earnings by the transfer of a given dollar amount from retained earnings to contributed capital, while the latter need not involve any transfer. The second basic difference is the number of shares involved. There is no doubt that a 3 percent distribution of shares is a stock *dividend,* while a 300 percent distribution is a stock *split*. But where is the line to be drawn to distinguish between the two? On this point, the following recommendation of the Committee on Accounting Procedure of the AICPAs is as reasonable an answer as any:

> The committee believes that the corporation's representations to its shareholders as to the nature of the issuance is one of the principal considerations in determining whether it should be recorded as a stock dividend or a split-up. Nevertheless, it believes that the issuance of new shares in ratios of less than, say, 20% or

[10] *Ibid.*, p. 49.

> 25% of the previously outstanding shares, or the frequent recurrence of issuances of shares, would destroy the presumption that transactions represented to be split-ups should be recorded as split-ups.[11]

Rarely is a split encountered in which shares are distributed in a ratio of less than an additional one-half share for each full share currently outstanding.

TREASURY STOCK

Treasury stock is the corporation's own stock which was fully paid for when issued and has later been reacquired but not cancelled. Because its acquisition results in a reduction of the number of shares of stock outstanding in the hands of the public, such an acquisition is usually reflected as a reduction in stockholder's equity to the extent of the cost of such shares. An example of the usual presentation of treasury stock is shown by the following, taken from the December 31, 1972, Consolidated Balance Sheet of Continental Can Company:

Stockholders' Equity

Capital Stock	
$4.25 Cumulative Preferred (stated value $100)	$ 5,525,000
Common (par value $1)	29,175,000
Paid in Surplus	222,288,000
Retained Earnings	441,349,000
	$698,337,000
Less—Common Stock in Treasury, at Cost (106,524 shares)	2,954,000
	$695,383,000

Slightly more than two-thirds of the 600 survey companies covered in the analysis of 1971 annual reports by the 1972 edition of *Accounting Trends and Techniques* published by the AICPA referred to treasury stock in their reports.

To illustrate the effect of the acquisition and subsequent disposal of treasury stock, assume the following stockholders' equity section of a balance sheet:

Stockholders' Equity
(before purchase of treasury stock)

Capital Contributions:

---

[11] *Ibid.*, p. 53.

Capital Stock, par $100; 600,000 shares authorized; 400,000 shares issued and outstanding	$40,000,000
Capital in Excess of Par:	
Premium on Capital Stock	2,000,000
Retained Earnings	25,000,000
Total Stockholders' Equity	$67,000,000

If the corporation now purchases 1,000 shares of its own outstanding capital stock at $102 per share, total assets (specifically, cash) is decreased $102,000 and total stockholders' equity is decreased the same amount. Within the stockholders' equity section shown below (which now totals $66,898,000), the wording opposite the capital stock amount is altered to indicate that, though 400,000 shares are still issued, 1,000 of these are no longer outstanding in the hands of the public. The cost of the 1,000 shares of treasury stock is usually subtracted, as shown, to

Stockholders' Equity
(after purchase of treasury stock)

Capital Contributions:	
Capital Stock, par $100; 600,000 shares authorized; 400,000 shares issued (of which 1,000 are in the treasury)	$40,000,000
Capital in Excess of Par:	
Premium on Capital Stock	2,000,000
Retained Earnings	25,000,000
	$67,000,000
Less: Cost of Treasury Stock (1,000 shares)	102,000
Total Stockholders' Equity	$66,898,000

arrive at the decreased total of stockholders' equity. Now, assume that the 1,000 shares of treasury stock are sold for $104 per share at a later date. The "gain" of $2 per share is not income within the usual meaning of the term and thus should not affect retained earnings.[12] Rather, the entire proceeds, including the so-called "gain," constitute contributed capital. As shown by the stockholders' equity below, the $104,000 increases stockholders' equity that same amount by an increase in capital in excess of par by $2,000 (the $2 per share excess of selling price over cost) and by the removal of the $102,000 deduction for the cost of the treasury stock. Because all of the issued stock is again outstanding, the wording opposite the capital stock amount of $40,000,000 is identical to that prior to the purchase of the treasury stock. Retained earnings

[12] Nor is it taxable income by the provisions of the Internal Revenue Code.

has remained unchanged during the treasury stock transactions; normally, it would be affected only by net income for the intervening period and by any dividend declarations.

Stockholders' Equity
(after sale of treasury stock)

Capital Contributions:		
Capital Stock, par $100; 600,000 shares authorized; 400,000 shares issued and outstanding		$40,000,000
Capital in Excess of Par:		
Premium on Capital Stock	$2,000,000	
From Disposition of Treasury Stock	2,000	2,002,000
Retained Earnings		25,000,000
Total Stockholders' Equity		$67,002,000

The reasons for acquiring treasury shares are varied. Sometimes, management desires to remove excess capital no longer needed in the business; then, the treasury shares actually might be retired rather than remain as treasury shares. Often, shares are purchased on the market; then, these treasury shares, rather than some of the unissued shares, are sold to fulfill employee stock purchase and stock option plans for executives and key employees. Preferred shares are often reacquired and temporarily held as treasury stock under a plan calling for the periodic redemption and retirement of a specified amount of preferred stock. In certain instances, common shares are reacquired and held as treasury stock so that they may be used when the company's convertible preferred stock is tendered for conversion into common shares. Occasionally, treasury stock is used to make payments to the company's employees under an incentive compensation plan.

The possibility of a restriction on the retained earnings of the company because of its acquisition of treasury shares is included in the discussion of restrictions on retained earnings in the next section of this chapter.

RESTRICTIONS ON RETAINED EARNINGS

The amount of retained earnings is not represented by any specific asset, nor is there any relationship between the amount of cash and the amount of retained earnings. Retained earnings (earned surplus) represents that portion of the total amount of the company's net earnings over the years of its existence which has not been distributed to the stockholders as dividends, but which has been reinvested in the business. Thus, retained earnings represents a source of assets, but not any specific asset. Theoretically, it represents the amount legally available for dividend declarations. Of course, it would be rare for a board of directors to consider the total amount of retained earnings as actually available for dividend declarations, because retained earnings are usually plowed back into the business as added working capital, for new plant and equipment, and in various other forms.

In addition to the practical limitation of considering total retained earnings as legally available for dividend declarations, there are often formal *restrictions* on retained earnings limiting dividend declarations. These formal restrictions on retained earnings are of two general types: voluntary restrictions based upon management policies and legal or contractual restrictions.

As an illustration of the effect of a voluntary restriction upon retained earnings, refer to the stockholders' equity section of the balance sheet of the McCandless Corporation on page 362. This statement shows $22,600 of retained earnings legally available for dividend declarations. However, assume that it is the desire of management formally to restrict dividend declarations to permit the retention of assets in the business for future plant expansion. In accordance with this plan, three-fourths of retained earnings are to be restricted until the contemplated future expansion has been accomplished. Disclosure of this restriction, at December 31, 1974, may be presented by revising the retained earnings portion of the previously presented stockholders' equity section on page 362 as follows:

Retained Earnings:		
Unrestricted	$ 5,650	
Restricted:		
For Future Plant Expansion	16,950	
Total Retained Earnings		$22,600

The total amount of retained earnings ($22,600) is unchanged; the total amount has merely been subdivided, by vote of the board of directors, to indicate that $16,950 is retained for a specific purpose. No cash or any other assets have been segregated or set aside by the establishment of this restriction; segregation would require the establishment of a special fund as one of the assets of the corporation.

Sometimes, the unrestricted amount of retained earnings ($5,650 in the illustration) is referred to as the "free" retained earnings. Such a caption on this item may be definitely misleading to the user of financial data, since he might believe that this amount is definitely earmarked and available for dividends. Actually, it (as well as the $16,950) has already been reinvested in the business and is distributed among the various assets of the company.

Occasionally, the restricted amount of retained earnings ($16,950 in the illustration) is referred to as either the "appropriated" or "reserved" retained earnings. These capitions may be similarly misleading to those using financial data. Nothing of a tangible nature has been segregated, appropriated, reserved, or set aside to expand the plant; the restriction only indicates the intention of management to use assets in the manner indicated someday.

To avoid these possible misinterpretations, a marked trend toward a revised presentation which indicates restrictions by a footnote to the financial statements has occurred in recent years. Such a presentation would appear as follows:

Retained Earnings (Note 1) $22,600

Notes to Financial Statements:

Note 1: By resolution of the Board of Directors, $16,950 of retained earnings is restricted for plant expansion purposes and thus decreases possible dividend declarations by that amount; only $5,650 of retained earnings is unrestricted.

Additional illustrations of this presentation will be shown in subsequent examples.

Some of the additional voluntary restrictions upon retained earnings occasionally encountered are those:

For Working Capital
For Contingencies
For Sudden Obsolescence of Fixed Assets
For Higher Costs of Replacing Fixed Assets
For Possible Casualty Losses

All restrictions on retained earnings are established by reducing the amount of the unrestricted (free) retained earnings to indicate the intention of the directors to limit dividend declarations and thereby keep an equivalent amount of assets in the business for the use indicated by the title of the restriction established on retained earnings. Any voluntary restriction may be removed in the same manner by which it was established; namely, by vote of the board of directors.

The second basic type of formal restrictions on retained earnings consists of those required for legal purposes and/or contractual arrangements. Typical of this category are those restrictions required:

By Long-term Indebtedness
By Credit and Loan Agreements
For Redemption of Preferred Stock
By Purchases of Treasury Stock

Restrictions such as these are not voluntary; they are mandatory and are required to fulfill stipulated agreements.

Two examples of restrictions occasioned by the incurrence of long-term debt through notes and bond issues have already been presented on pages 344–45. Both Jones & Laughlin Steel Corporation and United Aircraft Corporation disclosed restrictions by notes to the financial statements. In the case of the former company, the restriction completely eliminated the possibility of cash dividends on September 1, 1970; while, for the latter company, the restriction will have little, if any, effect upon dividend declarations.

Similarly, the notes to the financial statements contained in the 1972 annual report of Litton Industries, Inc. show a restriction of greater than seventy-five percent of its retained earnings due to its long-term debt, principally notes payable (reproduced on page 334). A portion of "Note E," to the statements reads as follows:

> Under the terms of the Company's borrowing agreements, consolidated earnings retained in the business of approximately $58,983,000 were available for cash dividends at July 31, 1972.

Similar to the manner by which retained earnings may be restricted because of the raising of additional capital through the incurrence of debt, so restrictions may also be imposed when equity capital is raised through the issuance of preferred stock. Often, a corporation's charter of incorporation will place limitations on dividend declarations as long as any preferred stock is outstanding.

To protect creditors, many state corporate codes require that corporations maintain a stipulated amount of *legal* or *stated* capital. The legal provisions of these state codes are varied and highly technical, and thus beyond the scope of this discussion. However, it should be apparent to the reader that the creditors of a company could be left in an untenable position should the company's management use corporate resources to acquire considerable treasury stock while continuing with a liberal dividend policy on the remaining outstanding shares. To prevent such a possibility, many states require that retained earnings be restricted by the cost of the treasury stock to limit dividend declarations. This restriction on retained earnings limits the *total* of all distributions to stockholders through returns *of* capital investment (corporate acquisitions of treasury stock) and by returns *on* capital investment (corporate dividend declarations) to the amount of retained earnings. Thus, the required legal capital cannot be impaired by any attempt to do two things with the resources provided by retained earnings . . . return capital and pay dividends; dividends can be declared only to the extent that resources provided by retained earnings have not been used for treasury stock acquisitions. Illustrative of this type of restriction is the following from the annual report (financial review section) of Scott Paper Company, with respect to its Reinvested Earnings at December 31, 1971, in the amount of $318,289,000.

> The company holds in the treasury 619,132 of its issued common shares, acquired at a cost of $18,635,000. Under Pennsylvania law, reinvested earnings in that amount are restricted and are not available for dividends.

Unlike voluntary restrictions on retained earnings, legal and/or contractual restrictions cannot be removed until the commitment which required the restriction has been fulfilled.

FACTORS IN PLANNING THE FINANCIAL STRUCTURE

Planning the financial structure of the company is a top management function. In so doing, two basic sources of funds are available to management. These sources are debt and ownership equity—the two segments of the right-hand side of the balance sheet which provide the resources or assets shown by the left-hand side of the statement. Like any plan, that for the financial structure of the company should be reviewed and revised as required by changing conditions. Initially, as the business is formed, and continually, as the business requires additional funds, balance should be maintained in the financial structure. The company must have an adequate ownership equity as the base upon which to incur debt, as an individual buying a home should have an adequate ownership equity (the down payment) upon which to incur debt (the mortgage payable).

General Factors Which Influence the Determination of a Proper Balance

The balance maintained between debt and ownership equity will vary in accordance with many factors, one of which is the philosophy of the top management of the company. At one extreme is the idea that debt, other than the bare minimum of current liabilities, is to be abhorred, that all risk should be avoided whenever possible. At the other extreme is the "thin" corporation whose small ownership equity and heavy debt ratio creates financial leverage so great that, at times, the soundness of the financial structure is questionable. In between is the philosophy that all current factors must be considered in determining a balance which assures financial soundness while providing an equitable return on the investment of the owners.

A second factor to consider in determining the proper distribution between debt and ownership equity is the type of industry. The utility industry, for example, with its basic profit stability, steady growth in most cases, and heavy investment in long-lived plant and equipment, usually has a higher total debt to total assets ratio than that of many other industry groups. In Exhibit 12–1, note that the percentage of total

EXHIBIT 12–1

Percentages of Debt and Stockholders' Equity to Assets

	IN PERCENTAGES	
MAJOR INDUSTRIAL GROUPS	TOTAL DEBT TO TOTAL ASSETS	TOTAL STOCKHOLDERS' EQUITY TO TOTAL ASSETS
Agriculture, Forestry, and Fisheries	59	41
Mining	43	57
Manufacturing	44	56
Transportation, Communication, Electric, Gas, and Sanitary Service	54	46
Wholesale Trade	57	43
Retail Trade	55	45
Finance, Insurance, and Real Estate	85	15
Services	69	31

Source: United States Treasury Department, Internal Revenue Service, *Statistics of Income, 1968, Corporation Income Tax Returns*, March, 1972.

debt to total assets is 54 percent for utilities, while the same ratio is 44 percent for manufacturing corporations. However, these statistics may be misleading, because they consider only industry groups; for example, in Exhibit 12–2, note the wide variation within the manufacturing group.

EXHIBIT 12–2

Sources of Capital (Total Assets), as of December 31, 1972

	PERCENT OF TOTAL ASSETS			
INDUSTRY	CURRENT LIABILITIES	NONCURRENT LIABILITIES[2]	TOTAL LIABILITIES	STOCKHOLDERS' EQUITY
All manufacturing corporations	24.6	22.2	46.8	53.2
Durable goods	27.2	21.5	48.7	51.3
Transportation equipment	34.4	17.7	52.1	47.9
Motor vehicles and equipment[1]	30.1	14.0	44.1	55.9
Aircraft and parts[1] . . .	43.6	21.8	65.4	34.6
Electrical machinery, equipment and supplies	31.3	21.4	52.7	47.3
Other machinery	26.0	19.1	45.1	54.9
Metalworking machinery and equipment[1]	25.4	15.6	41.0	59.0
Other fabricated metal products	29.0	21.0	50.0	50.0
Primary metal industries .	17.9	30.5	48.4	51.6
Primary iron and steel[1]	19.4	28.6	48.0	52.0
Primary nonferrous metals[1]	15.7	33.3	49.0	51.0
Stone, clay, and glass products	18.7	22.7	41.4	58.6
Furniture and fixtures . . .	26.6	16.3	42.9	57.1
Lumber and wood products, except furniture . .	21.4	30.1	51.5	48.5
Instruments and related products	23.9	12.9	36.8	63.2
Miscellaneous manufacturing and ordnance	35.3	18.9	54.2	45.8
Nondurable goods	21.8	22.9	44.7	55.3
Food and kindred products	27.3	22.5	49.8	50.2
Dairy products[1]	28.6	18.1	46.7	53.3
Bakery products[1]	24.3	23.0	47.3	52.7
Alcoholic beverages[1] . .	21.6	21.6	43.2	56.8
Tobacco manufacturers . .	23.6	26.1	49.7	50.3
Textile mill products	25.2	22.0	47.1	52.9

EXHIBIT 12–2

(Continued)

	PERCENT OF TOTAL ASSETS			
INDUSTRY	CURRENT LIABILITIES	NON-CURRENT LIABILITIES[2]	TOTAL LIABILITIES	STOCKHOLDERS' EQUITY
Apparel and other finished products	39.1	17.4	56.5	43.5
Paper and allied products	16.8	29.6	46.4	53.6
Printing and publishing	21.8	23.0	44.8	55.2
Chemicals and allied products	20.1	22.4	42.5	57.5
Basic chemicals[1]	18.3	27.2	45.5	54.5
Drugs[1]	22.1	14.8	36.9	63.1
Petroleum refining and related industries	16.7	22.6	39.3	60.7
Petroleum refining[1]	16.6	22.7	39.3	60.7
Rubber and miscellaneous plastic products	25.7	25.1	50.8	49.2
Leather and leather products	30.5	17.5	48.0	52.0

[1] Included in major industry above
[2] Principally long-term debt
Source: Federal Trade Commission—*Quarterly Financial Report for Manufacturing Corporations.*

Not only is there a wide variation in the total debt to total assets ratio, but also within the composition of total debt itself, i.e., the proportion of both current liabilities and non-current liabilities to total assets.

Regardless of the philosophy of the top management of the company and the industry group or subdivision thereof of which the company is a part, a third factor, the conditions within the given company itself, may greatly negate the influence of the first two. For the individual company, its growth rate of sales, trend of profit margins, competitive position within the industry, vulnerability to cyclical fluctuations, and present ratio of debt to assets, are all considerations which exert considerable influence on the availability of particular sources of funds.

In addition to these variables which influence the balance between debt and ownership equity, management must consider the effect of various specific factors, presented next, in its determination of the best source of funds.

Effect of Specific Factors

Many specific factors, considered in planning the financial structure of the company for their long-run effect, must be weighed when choosing the proper sources of capital to be utilized in any given instance. Several of these factors will be mentioned as guidelines to be employed for shaping this kind of decision.

One prime factor is that of control. Normally, creditors do not vote, while stockholders do. If additional capital is raised by a large stock issue, control is unaffected in most large companies where it is rare to find any single stockholder owning as much as 1 percent of the outstanding voting stock. But, in the small to medium-sized company, such a stock issue, if purchased by other than present stockholders, might lead to a shift in control and management of the company. Thus, other things being equal, management of a smaller company might be inclined to maintain control by raising additional capital through borrowing (debt) or the issuance of some class of non-voting stock (ownership equity).

A second factor is income taxes. Interest paid on debt is a deductible business expense. Dividends declared on stock are not a business expense; dividends are the distribution of a portion of the after-tax net income to the owners of the corporation. If $10,000,000 of additional capital is raised at an annual gross cost of 4 percent when the tax rate is 50 percent, the full cost of $400,000 annually is out-of-pocket to the company if it represents dividends because the capital was procured through a stock issue; but if the capital was obtained by borrowing, the out-of-pocket cost is only $200,000 ($400,000 of interest paid less a $200,000 reduction in taxes to be paid). Any calculation such as this is subject to many refinements; only the basic point of this second factor has been presented.

Third, debt matures at some specific future date and must be repaid. But stockholders are owners of the company, and their investment does not carry a maturity date. Creditors may take legal action against the company and perhaps force its liquidation if the debt is not repaid when due. Ownership equity carries with it no such possibility; the claims of creditors have preference over the claims of owners on the assets of the company. Debt requires payment at specific dates; occasionally, these dates may find the company in a strained financial position.

The rigidity of the claim on the income of the company is a fourth factor to consider. Debt requires paying a predetermined, fixed, interest rate regardless of the profit or loss situation of the company at a particular time. (An exception, of course, is an issue of income bonds when it is not required to accumulate the interest if it is not earned in some year.)

Dividends are not a fixed claim upon earnings of the company; the frequency and the rate of dividends on stock are at the discretion of the board of directors of the company. In poor years, dividends may be omitted; in prosperous years, extra dividends may be declared. Normally, the only recourse of an unhappy stockholder is to vote against the present directors or sell his stock. (An exception, of course, is an issue of preferred stock which is cumulative in regard to dividends.)

A fifth factor in the determination of a proper debt-ownership ratio is financial leverage. As discussed in Chapter 5, trading on the equity is profitable and favorable to the common stockholders when funds procured through debt or preferred stock issues are employed in the business profitably enough to earn a greater return than the fixed cost (of interest or preferred dividends) incurred for the use of the funds.

Closely related to the leverage factor is that of earnings per share of common stock. Regardless of management's feeling concerning the importance of earnings per share, it is a key factor in the appraisal of a company's performance by financial analysts as well as prospective and present stockholders. Thus, this sixth factor must be considered in planning the financial structure of the company; the proceeds from any additional common stock issue should be employed profitably enough in the business to avoid any dilution of earnings per share.

Last, and not very specific, is the factor of gazing into the crystal ball and coming up with the right answers for future economic and environmental conditions. For example, consider those who raised additional capital by a 20-year bond issue in 1916 as opposed to those who did likewise in 1939. Many who borrowed in 1916 found it difficult or impossible to meet the interest charges on the debt during the depression of the 1930s and were forced into bankruptcy. But most of those who borrowed funds for 20 years in 1939 experienced no difficulty in meeting the interest charges in the ensuing years. To the contrary, at maturity in 1959, they found that, owing to the changed value of the dollar, they were paying off debt with cheap dollars although good dollars had been borrowed. Many other facets, like changing tax rates, wars, inventions, and laws, preclude any perfect weighing of all the specific factors involved in planning the financial structure of a company.

Because any company is only a minute segment of a dynamic economic system subject to changing political, legal, economic, and ethical considerations, it is impossible to prepare any static and complete list of specific factors and their effect upon management's decisions in the determination of the most feasible sources of capital to employ. Thus, these considerations should be viewed only in regard to present conditions. What sources of capital are companies currently employing? The statistics in Exhibit 12–3 are indicative of the present situation.

EXHIBIT 12–3

Sources Utilized for Expansion of U.S. Corporations[1]

<table>
<tr><td>YEAR</td><td>1959</td><td>1961</td><td>1963</td><td>1965</td><td>1967</td><td>1969</td><td>1971</td></tr>
<tr><td>Amount of expansion in billions of dollars[2]</td><td>$38.5</td><td>$40.0</td><td>$46.7</td><td>$66.6</td><td>$84.8</td><td>$97.8</td><td>$125.6</td></tr>
<tr><td colspan="5">Sources of financing of above expansion:
Internal sources ....
Retained earnings (net income less dividends) plus depreciation expense
External sources ....
Principally new stock and new long-term borrowing</td><td colspan="3">
In the range of 62% to 81%

In the range of 38% to 19%</td></tr>
<tr><td colspan="5">Composition of external sources:
New stock issues
New bond issues and other long-term borrowing</td><td colspan="3">
Varied widely with an approximate range between 2 to 1 and 6 to 1 in favor of new bond issues and other long-term borrowing</td></tr>
<tr><td colspan="8">[1] All U.S. corporations excluding banks, savings and loan associations, insurance companies, and investment companies.
[2] Expansion consists of: increase in net working capital, investment in additional plant and equipment in the U.S., and investment in other assets including fixed assets of foreign subsidiary companies—principally the second of the three items.
Source: Securities and Exchange Commission, Statistical Bulletin: Working Capital of U.S. Corporations.</td></tr>
</table>

The patterns of these statistics, which have varied little in the past several years, indicate that approximately three-fourths of business expansion is financed from funds provided by current profitable operations (net income for the period less dividends and plus the depreciation expense, since this expense does not require the use of funds). The use of external financing sources accounts for approximately one-fourth of business expansion. And the predominate method of utilizing the external sources is through the incurrence of long-term debt, not by stock issues.

QUESTIONS AND PROBLEMS

12–1. The following stockholders' equity section was taken from the balance sheet of Nanty-Glo Corporation as of December 31, 1974:

Capital Stock, Par $100; 1,000,000 shares authorized; issued and outstanding 200,000 shares	$20,000,000
Additional Paid-in Capital	5,000,000
Retained Earnings	15,000,000
Total Stockholders' Equity	$40,000,000

For the succeeding year, 1975, the corporation had a net income for the year of $4,000,000. Quarterly dividends paid during the year (on March 15, June 15, September 15, and December 15) *totaled* $4 per share for the year. No shares were sold or reacquired during the year. At December 31, 1975, market value per share was $300.

Required

Complete the below stockholders' equity sections at December 31, 1975, assuming:

a. Only the information above.

b. The above information plus a year-end 5 percent stock dividend.

c. The above information, exclusive of the year-end stock dividend (i.e., ignore requirement b), plus a four for one stock split on December 31. Assume a proportionate change in the par of each share.

	REQUIREMENT A	REQUIREMENT B	REQUIREMENT C
Capital Stock; 1,000,000 shares authorized;	Par $100	Par $ ____	Par $ ____
issued and outstanding are ..	200,000 shares	____ shares	____ shares
Capital Stock at par	$20,000,000	$	$
Additional Paid-in Capital ...	$ 5,000,000	$	$
Retained Earnings ...	$	$	$
Total Stockholders' Equity	$	$	$

12–2. For each of the following statements, choose the one best answer to each and indicate your choice on an answer sheet with a number.

a. When United States Steel Corporation, in 1966, exchanged $175 principal amount of 4⅝ percent subordinated debentures for each outstanding $100 par value 7 percent cumulative preferred share, the effect upon earnings per share of common stock (assume no other changes in the capital structure) was:

1. to increase earnings per share

2. none
3. to decrease earnings per share

b. In the average manufacturing company, if assets equal 100 (percent), then, approximately:
1. liabilities will be 40 and stockholders' equity 60
2. liabilities will be 60 and stockholders' equity 40
3. liabilities will be 50 and stockholders' equity 50

c. In the average utility company (transportation, gas, electric, communication, sanitary service), if assets equal 100 (percent), then approximately:
1. liabilities will be 30 and stockholders' equity 70
2. liabilities will be 50 and stockholders' equity 50
3. liabilities will be 70 and stockholders' equity 30

d. Since World War II, most corporate expansion has been financed by:
1. profits not distributed in dividends (plus add-back of depreciation expense)
2. incurring long-term debt
3. new stock issues

e. If a corporation had total assets of 100 (percent), it would be a "thin" incorporation if:
1. liabilities are 50 and stockholders' equity 50
2. liabilities are 10 and stockholders' equity 90
3. liabilities are 90 and stockholders' equity 10

12–3. Old Beulah Corporation was incorporated in 1946. The balance sheet disclosed the following stockholders' equity section as December 31, 1974.

6 percent Cumulative, Non-Participating, Non-Convertible, Preferred Stock, Par $100; 400,000 shares authorized; 100,000 shares issued and outstanding	$ 10,000,000
Common Stock, Par $50; 1,000,000 shares authorized; 600,000 shares issued, of which 100,000 are in the treasury	30,000,000
Capital in Excess of Par	15,000,000
Retained Earnings (total)	55,000,000
	$110,000,000
Less: Treasury Stock, Common (100,000 shares @ $70 cost)	7,000,000
Total Stockholders' Equity	$103,000,000

During 1974 no shares of either class of stock were sold or purchased. The treasury stock was purchased in 1969. There are no dividends in arrears on the preferred stock.

The Statement of Retained Earnings for 1974, disclosed the following:

Retained Earnings, January 1, 1974			$52,600,000
Net Income for the Year 1974		$5,000,000	
Dividends during 1974:			
On Preferred Stock ($6 per share) .	$ 600,000		
On Common Stock ($4 per share) .	2,000,000	2,600,000	2,400,000
Retained Earnings, December 31, 1974			$55,000,000

Required

Compute the 1974 Earnings per common share.

12–4. Refer to the facts in the preceding problem. Then on January 1, 1975, Old Beulah Corporation sold one-half of its treasury stock at $90 per share. Assuming no other facts, prepare below the stockholders' equity section of the balance sheet on January 1, 1975, immediately after the sale of treasury stock.

6 percent Cumulative Preferred Stock (unchanged)	$ 10,000,000
Common Stock, Par 50; 1,000,000 shares authorized;	
______________________________	
(complete the description for common stock)	
Capital in Excess of Par	$
Retained Earnings (total)	$
	$
Less: Treasury Stock, Common ( ) ..	
Total Stockholders' Equity	$

12–5. For each of the following statements, choose the one best answer to each and indicate your choice on an answer sheet with a number.

a. The establishment of a restriction on retained earnings (e.g., restriction for contingencies):
   1. changes the amount of total assets
   2. changes the amount of total liabilities
   3. changes the amount of *total* retained earnings
   4. changes the amount of *total* stockholders' equity
   5. none of the above

b. When an issue of preferred stock is purchased and permanently retired (cancelled) by the issuing corporation for less than its original issue price, proper accounting for the retirement:

1. increases the amount of dividends available to common shareholders
2. increases the contributed capital of the common shareholders
3. increases reported net income for the period
4. increases the treasury stock held by the corporation
(Adapted from Uniform CPA Examination)

c. The sale for $15,000 of 1,000 shares of treasury stock (par $20) which had cost $18,000 results in a *decrease* in stockholders' equity *at the time it is sold of:*
1. $2,000
2. $3,000
3. $5,000
4. $15,000
5. none of the above

d. If you own 100 shares of a stock and subsequently receive a 5 percent stock dividend, followed a year later by a two for one stock split, you then own:
1. 205 shares
2. 210 shares
3. 195 shares
4. none of the above

e. A cash dividend distributes earnings, a stock dividend capitalizes earnings, a stock split normally does not affect retained earnings.
1. True
2. False

12–6. For each of the following statements, choose the best answer to each and indicate your choice on an answer sheet with a number.

a. The incurrence of long-term debt as a method of securing funds for a capital expansion program is indicative of:
1. a venturesome "gambling" management
2. the manner in which a majority of new capital has been raised from *external* sources by companies since World War II
3. ultra-conservatism in management
4. none of the above

b. Treasury stock is *usually* shown on a company's balance sheet as:
1. an investment
2. a reduction in stockholders' equity
3. unissued stock
4. a reduction of liabilities
5. outstanding stock

c. Restrictions on retained earnings *normally:*
1. freeze cash
2. freeze earnings
3. freeze dividends

4. guide management planning
5. reduce corporate taxes
6. reduce profits
7. none of the above

d. The maximum amount of treasury stock which a company can purchase is:
1. unlimited
2. limited only by its cash position
3. limited only by its net income for the year
4. limited by certain provisions in many state corporation codes, for the protection of creditors
5. limited only by the Securities and Exchange Commission

12–7. For each of the following statements, choose the best answer to each and indicate your choice on an answer sheet with a number.

a. The declaration of a cash dividend to be paid at a later date has the following effect on the company's financial statements at the time of *declaration:*
1. reduces cash and retained earnings
2. reduces retained earnings and increases current liabilities
3. no effect
4. reduces net income for the period

b. When a previously declared cash dividend is paid, it has the following effect on the company's financial statements at the time of *payment:*
1. reduces cash and current liabilities
2. reduces cash and retained earnings
3. no effect
4. reduces net income for the period

c. The declaration of a stock dividend to be "paid" at a later date (by the issuance of unissued shares) has no effect on either *total* liabilities or *total* stockholders' equity at the time of *declaration.*
1. True
2. False

d. A stock split has no effect on either *total* assets, *total* liabilities, or *total* stockholders' equity.
1. True
2. False

e. A cash dividend distributes earnings, a stock dividend capitalizes earnings, a stock split does not affect retained earnings.
1. True
2. False

f. Retained earnings are permanently capitalized by:
1. a stock split

2. a stock dividend
3. a cash (asset) dividend
4. cancellation of Treasury stock

g. An "Irish" dividend is a slang term for a:
   1. distribution of inventory instead of cash
   2. reverse stock split
   3. dividend declared on March 17
   4. dividend from excess profits resulting from lucky ventures

Brain

12–8. From the following information selected from the balance sheets of three different corporations as of December 31, 1974, determine the missing facts:

	DE SOTA CORPORATION	HALL CORPORATION	ELLSWORTH CORPORATION
Total Assets	$500,000	$700,000	$?
Total Liabilities .	?	300,000	100,000
Issued and Outstanding Capital Stock	250,000	300,000	600,000
Retained Earnings	?	?	(200,000)*
Total Stockholders' Equity	300,000	?	?

* Indicates Deficit

12–9. For the year ended December 31, 1974, the Statement of Income of Lunga Corporation disclosed a net income for the year of $90,000. The only changes in Retained Earnings during 1974 were attributable to dividends declared and the net income for the year. Comparative balance sheets were as follows:

LUNGA CORPORATION

Comparative (Condensed) Balance Sheets

	DECEMBER 31, 1973		DECEMBER 31, 1974	
Total Assets		$800,000		$810,000
Total Liabilities		$350,000		$290,000
Issued and Outstanding Capital Stock	$300,000		$300,000	
Retained Earnings	150,000		220,000	
Total Stockholders' Equity		450,000		520,000
Total Equities		$800,000		$810,000

Required

a. Calculate the amount of cash dividends declared during 1974.

b. Prepare a Statement of Retained Earnings for the year ended December 31, 1974.

12–10. In answering this problem, insert a plus sign, a minus sign, or a zero in each of the twelve squares to indicate the effect of dividends and stock splits.
Insert a plus if the total dollar amount of the item increases.
Insert a minus if the total dollar amount of the item decreases.
Insert a zero if the total dollar amount of the item is unchanged.

ITEM	CASH DIVIDEND	STOCK DIVIDEND	STOCK SPLIT
Capital Stock Outstanding (Par)			
Capital in Excess of Par			
Retained Earnings			
Total Stockholders' Equity			

Note: Fair Value per share exceeds par value per share.

12–11. Pavuvu Corporation was organized in 1921 and has operated continuously since that date. The authorized capital stock of the corporation is 10,000 shares with a $50 par value per share. The information that follows is taken from the balance sheets on the dates indicated.

	DECEMBER 31, 1973	DECEMBER 31, 1974
Capital Stock Outstanding	$350,000	$400,000
Premium on Capital Stock	50,000	52,000
Retained Earnings	220,000	250,000

On December 1, 1974, one thousand shares of previously unissued stock were sold for cash.

A 4 percent dividend ($2 per share) was declared on September 15, 1974, to stockholders of record on October 10, 1974, payable October 31, 1974.

Required

Determine the following:

a. Total amount of dividend declared and paid in 1974.

b. Per share price of stock issued December 1, 1974.

c. Since a Statement of Income has not been provided, calculate the net income or net loss for the year 1974. Indicate clearly your method in arriving at the amount of the profit or loss.

12–12. As of December 31, 1974, the following amounts are shown on the balance sheet of the Banika Corporation:

Cash	$ 200,000	
Accounts Receivable	300,000	
Estimated Doubtful Accounts		$ 3,100
Inventories	250,000	
Machinery and Equipment	400,000	
Accumulated Depreciation—Machinery and Equipment		120,000
Notes Payable		60,000
Accounts Payable		150,000
Capital Stock Issued		600,000
Premium on Capital Stock		12,000
Retained Earnings		210,000
Treasury Stock (100 shares at cost)	5,100	
	$1,155,100	$1,155,100

The authorized capital stock of the corporation is 30,000 shares of $50 par value stock.

Banika Corporation was organized in July, 1942.

The balance sheet as of December 31, 1973, showed Retained Earnings of $175,000.

Cash dividends of $30,000 were declared (and paid) in 1974.

Required

a. Prepare, in proper form, the stockholders' equity section of the balance sheet as of December 31, 1974.

b. Calculate the book value per share as of December 31, 1974.

c. Inasmuch as a Statement of Income has not been provided, calculate the net income or net loss for the year 1974. Indicate clearly your method in arriving at the amount of the net income or loss.

12–13. The following facts were selected from various sections of the balance sheet of the Keim Corporation as of December 31, 1974:

Capital Stock, $100 par value; 14,000 shares authorized; 8,800 shares issued, of which 800 shares are in the treasury	$880,000
Treasury Stock (800 shares)	80,000
Premium on Capital Stock	27,500
Retained Earnings (unrestricted)	226,000

Retained Earnings Restricted by Treasury Stock Purchases	80,000
Accumulated Depreciation to Date	22,500
Retained Earnings Restricted for Bond Redemption	24,000
Capital in Excess of Par from Donated Assets	6,500
Sinking Fund for Bond Redemption	24,000

Required

a. Using the above information:
   1. prepare the stockholders' equity section of the balance sheet as of December 31, 1974.
   2. compute the book value per share of outstanding stock as of December 31, 1974.

b. A cash dividend of $40,000 was declared and paid during the first week of January, 1975. Compute the book value per share immediately after the payment of the cash dividend. (Assume no other changes in the stockholders' equity section.)

c. In addition to the cash dividend in requirement b. above, the company declared and paid a stock dividend of one share for every forty shares outstanding and valued the dividend shares at $120. The dividend was declared and paid during the second week of January, 1975. Compute the book value per share immediately after the payment of the stock dividend. (Assume no other changes in the stockholders' equity section other than that noted in requirement b. above.)

12–14. The stockholders' equity section of the consolidated balance sheet of United States Steel Corporation at December 31, 1937, appeared as follows:

Capital Stock and Surplus	
United States Steel Corporation	
Preferred 7% Cumulative Stock—Par Value $100 (Authorized 4,000,000 shares; issued 3,602,811 shares)	$ 360,281,100.00
Common Stock—Par Value $100 (Authorized 12,500,000 shares; issued 8,703,252 shares)	870,325,200.00
Capital Surplus	81,250,021.42
Earned Surplus of U.S. Steel Corporation and Subsidiary Companies	280,356,143.55
Total Capital Stock and Surplus	$1,592,212,464.97

On this same balance sheet, the property category was subdivided into tangible and intangible amounts. The intangible assets were shown at $260,368,521.53.

During the 36 years following the formation of U.S. Steel in 1901, a total of $508,302,500 of intangible assets was written off. Following a change in the capital structure of U.S. Steel in April of 1938, the board of directors authorized a further write-off of the intangibles, from $260,368,521.53 to the nominal amount of $1.00.

Amendments to the certificate of incorporation of U.S. Steel, proposed by the board of directors, were adopted by the stockholders at the annual meeting in April of 1938. These amendments effected the following changes in the corporate capital structure:

a. Common stock changed from $100 par value shares to no-par value shares.

b. Authorized common shares were increased from 12,500,000 shares to 15,000,000 shares.

A stated capital amount of $75 per share was set on the 8,703,252 outstanding common no-par shares. The decrease of $25 per share in capital stock resulted in a transfer of this amount to capital surplus. Capital surplus then consisted of:

Premium on par value common stock	$ 81,250,021.42
Transfer from common capital stock	217,581,300.00
Total capital surplus	$298,831,321.42

It was against this total capital surplus that the intangible assets were written down to $1.00.

For the year 1938, the corporation had a net loss of $7,717,453.69. No dividends were declared on the common stock, but regular dividends totaling $7 per share were declared on the preferred stock.

Required

a. Prepare the stockholders' equity section of the consolidated balance sheet of the United States Steel Corporation at December 31, 1938.

b. To what degree was the real value of the intangible assets affected by the book reduction to $1?

c. Why were the intangible assets not written off against earned surplus (retained earnings)?

12–15. The stockholders' equity section of the Consolidated Balance Sheet of Texaco Inc. appeared as follows as of December 31, 1960:

Stockholders' Equity (Note 3):	
Capital stock—par value $25:	
Shares authorized—75,000,000	
Shares issued—62,440,298 including treasury stock	$1,561,007,450
Paid-in capital in excess of par value (Note 4)	118,748,636
Retained earnings used in the business	1,078,033,813
	$2,757,789,899
Less—Capital stock held in treasury—691,024 shares, at cost	21,074,871
Total stockholders' equity	$2,736,715,028

(Notes not reproduced)

At a special stockholders' meeting in July, 1961, the stockholders approved an increase in Texaco's authorized capital stock from 75,000,000 shares with a par value of $25 each, to 150,000,000 shares with a par value of $12.50 each. In August of 1961, Texaco distributed one new share of stock for each share held by the stockholders of record on July 19, 1961 (in effect, a 2 for 1 split). As a result, the number of issued shares was exactly doubled. Other transactions affecting stockholders' equity in 1961 were:

a. Net income for the year was $430,116,577.

b. Cash dividends paid during the year totaled $191,510,329.

c. Treasury shares sold to stock option holders during the year resulted in an increase to paid-in capital in excess of par value in the amount of $1,196,575, and left 1,303,567 treasury shares at a cost of $20,853,893 as of December 31, 1961.

Required

a. Prepare the stockholders' equity section of the consolidated balance sheet as of December 31, 1961.
b. Compute the book value per share of outstanding stock as of December 31, 1961, and compare it to market value (57⅜) on that same date.

12–16. Tenaru River Corporation was incorporated on August 9, 1944, with an authorized capital consisting of 4,000 shares of 5 percent cumulative, nonparticipating preferred stock of $100 par value and 5,000 shares of no-par common stock. The corporation was incorporated in a state whose corporate code (law) permits the crediting of a capital in excess of stated value account with a portion of the proceeds from the sale of no-par shares. The directors of the corporation passed a resolution stipulating that $40 per share should be credited to the Common Stock—No-Par account.

The following information was taken from the stockholders' equity section of the balance sheet of Tenaru River Corporation as of December 31, 1974:

Preferred Stock Outstanding—5 percent Cumulative	$300,000
Common Stock Issued—No Par	188,000
Treasury Stock—Common No Par (200 shares at cost)	8,500
Retained Earnings (free)	120,000
Retained Earnings Restricted for Contingencies ...	20,000
Premium on Preferred Stock	15,000
Retained Earnings Restricted for Plant Expansion .	30,000
*Appreciation of Fixed Assets	10,000
Capital in Excess of Stated Value	7,000
Capital from Donated Assets	12,000
Retained Earnings Restricted by Treasury Stock Purchases	8,500

* Land purchased in 1942 was written up $10,000 during 1974.

Required

In the proper form prepare the detailed stockholders' equity section of the corporation's balance sheet as of December 31, 1974.

12–17. For each of the following statements, choose the one best answer to each and indicate your choice on an answer sheet with a number.

a. When a given company, as a very few have done, increases a given fixed asset, as land, on its balance sheet from historical cost to current cost, it:

1. increases total assets
2. increases total stockholders' equity
3. increases liabilities
4. is not conforming to generally accepted accounting principles
5. 1 and 2
6. 1, 2, and 3
7. 1 and 3
8. 1, 2, 3, and 4
9. 1, 3, and 4
10. 1, 2, and 4
11. none of the above

b. A plant site (land) donated by a township to a company that plans to open a new factory should be shown on the company's statement of financial position at:

1. the nominal cost of taking title to it

2. its market value
3. one dollar (since the land cost nothing but should be included in the balance sheet)
4. the value assigned to it by the company's directors
(Adapted from Uniform CPA Examination)

c. When Indiana Telephone Corporation increased its Telephone Plant (fixed assets) from historical cost to current cost, it also resulted in an increase in:
1. liabilities
2. retained earnings
3. stockholders' equity (total)
4. depreciation expense for the year
5. 2 and 4
6. 3 and 4

12–18. Shaffer Corporation, incorporated in 1923, would be characterized by many as a growth company. The last ten years have been especially profitable, but the past decade has also been marked by a tight financial situation. Rapid expansion has been financed solely from internal sources. It became apparent, in mid-1974, that, if the company is to continue its expansion and growth, additional capital of $40,000,000 must be raised from external sources in early 1975. Following are Shaffer Corporation's financial statements, in condensed form, for 1974:

Balance Sheet

December 31, 1974

Current Assets	$ 80,000,000
Current Liabilities	50,000,000
Working Capital	$ 30,000,000
Property, Plant and Equipment (net)	200,000,000
Stockholders' Equity	$230,000,000
Details of Stockholders' Equity:	
5% Cumulative, Non-Participating, Non-Convertible Preferred Stock, Par $100; 500,000 shares authorized; none issued	$ -0-
Common Stock, Par $100; 2,000,000 shares authorized; 1,000,000 shares issued and outstanding	100,000,000
Capital in Excess of Par	10,000,000
Earnings Reinvested in the Business	120,000,000
	$230,000,000

Statement of Income and Earnings Reinvested in the Business

For the Year 1974

Net Sales	$300,000,000
Cost of Goods Sold	180,000,000
Gross Margin (40 percent)	$120,000,000
Marketing and Administrative Expenses	75,000,000
Net Operating Income (15 percent)	$ 45,000,000
Income Taxes (50 percent rate)	22,500,000
Net Income for the Year	$22,500,000
Earnings Reinvested in the Business, January 1	105,500,000
	$128,000,000
Dividends in 1974; $8 per share	8,000,000
Earnings Reinvested in the Business, December 31	$120,000,000

Assume that:

a. The new financing to raise an additional $40,000,000 is accomplished successfully as of January 1, 1975. The cost of capital is 5 percent regardless of the external source utilized.

b. The funds are immediately employed in the business to produce an increased volume of production and sales at costs and prices the same as those of the preceding year; i.e., no change in rates of gross margin, net operating income, and income taxes.

c. The sales volume for 1975 is $345,000,000.

d. The dividend rate of 8 percent on the $100 par value common stock is to be maintained.

e. Only the common stock is voting stock.

Required

a. Compute earnings per share of common stock for 1974.

b. A statement of income (include calculation of earnings per share of common stock) and earnings reinvested in the business for the year 1975 if the $40,000,000 of capital is raised by:
   1. Issuing 400,000 shares of 5 percent preferred stock at par
   2. Issuing 5 percent bonds at par
   3. Issuing 250,000 shares of common stock at $160 per share (An $8 dividend per share on $160 raised per share equals 5 percent cost of capital.)

c. State your choice of the three methods of raising the additional $40,000,000 of capital and the reasons for your decision.

12–19. On January 1, 1974, four men formed a corporation to manufacture and sell astro-powered cigarette lighters. The certificate of incorporation authorized 40 shares of no-par value capital stock. The only issuance of stock was to the incorporators, as follows:

Mr. A—10 shares @ $100	$1,000
Mr. B—10 shares @ $100	1,000
Mr. C—10 shares @ $100	1,000
Mr. D—10 shares @ $100	1,000
Total contributed capital	$4,000

$300,000 of additional capital was raised by the issuance of "Fifteen-year 2 percent Debenture Bonds" in registered form and one-year 9 percent notes, as follows:

Mr. A—Bonds and notes	$ 50,000
Mr. B—Bonds and notes	50,000
Mr. C—Bonds and notes	50,000
Mr. D—Bonds and notes	50,000
	$200,000
Investors other than stockholders—Bonds	100,000
Total debt	$300,000

This capital structure is known as a "thin incorporation," because the primary initial source of capital is from loans, not stock investment.

Required

a. What is the purpose of such an obviously excessive debt structure?

b. Give all possible arguments to prove that interest expense on debt is, in reality, the payment of dividends.

12–20. The following stockholders' equity section was taken from the balance sheet of Tulagi Corporation as of December 31, 1973:

Stockholders' Equity

Capital Stock, Par $100:		
Authorized	200,000 shares	
Less: Unissued	150,000 shares	
Outstanding	50,000 shares	$ 5,000,000

Capital in Excess of Par	500,000
Retained Earnings	6,000,000
Total Stockholders' Equity	$11,500,000

For the succeeding year, 1974, the corporation had a net income (after taxes) of $1,000,000. Below are six different stockholders' equity sections of the balance sheet as of December 31, 1974. Each indicates that corporate net worth has been affected by some type or types of capital transactions during 1974. If additional shares of stock were issued, assume that fair market value per share at the date of issuance was $200. Indicate the capital transaction(s) which occurred by choosing from among the following six possibilities:

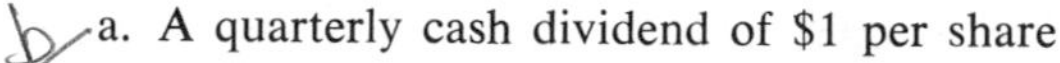

a. A quarterly cash dividend of $1 per share

b. A quarterly cash dividend of $1 per share and the sale (issuance) of 2,000 additional shares for cash early in the third quarter

c. A 10 percent stock dividend

d. A two for one stock split

e. A two for one stock split in January and a 4% stock dividend in December

f. A quarterly cash dividend of $1 per share and a year-end 4% stock dividend

Required

From the above choices, select the one best answer to each of the following six resultant stockholders' equity sections.

a.

Capital Stock, Par $50 (100,000 shares outstanding)	$ 5,000,000
Capital in Excess of Par	500,000
Retained Earnings	7,000,000
Total Stockholders' Equity	$12,500,000

b.

Capital Stock, Par $100 (50,000 shares outstanding)	$ 5,000,000
Capital in Excess of Par	500,000
Retained Earnings	6,800,000
Total Stockholders' Equity	$12,300,000

c.

Capital Stock, Par $100 (52,000 shares outstanding)	$ 5,200,000
Capital in Excess of Par	700,000
Retained Earnings	6,400,000
Total Stockholders' Equity	$12,300,000

d. Capital Stock, Par $100

(52,000 shares outstanding)	$ 5,200,000
Capital in Excess of Par	700,000
Retained Earnings	6,796,000
Total Stockholders' Equity	$12,696,000

e. Capital Stock, Par $100

(55,000 shares outstanding)	$ 5,500,000
Capital in Excess of Par	1,000,000
Retained Earnings	6,000,000
Total Stockholders' Equity	$12,500,000

f. Capital Stock, Par $50

(104,000 shares outstanding)	$ 5,200,000
Capital in Excess of Par	1,100,000
Retained Earnings	6,200,000
Total Stockholders' Equity	$12,500,000

12–21. This problem concerns consolidated financial statements. Select the one best answer to each of the following three statements.

a. Consolidated statements are used to present the result of operations and the financial position of:
   1. a company and its branches
   2. a company and its subcontractors
   3. a company and its subsidiaries
   4. any group of companies with related interests

b. Consolidated statements are intended primarily for the benefit of:
   1. stockholders of the parent company
   2. taxing authorities
   3. creditors of the subsidiary companies
   4. management of the subsidiary companies

c. H is the parent company and would probably treat K as an investment, not a consolidated subsidiary, in the proposed consolidated statement of H, J, and K if:
   1. H and J manufacture electronic equipment; K manufactures ball bearings
   2. H and J manufacture ball-point pens; K is a bank
   3. all three companies manufacture steel products; H owns 100 percent of J but only 98 percent of K

12–22. This problem concerns corporate capital transactions. Select the one best answer to each of the following:

a. The purchase of treasury stock will:
   1. reduce the number of authorized shares
   2. increase total assets

3. reduce total stockholders' equity
4. reduce total liabilities

b. One hundred shares of treasury stock originally purchased and carried at $101 per share (par is $100) are sold for cash at $104 per share. The sale of the treasury stock will:
   1. increase outstanding capital stock by $10,400
   2. increase retained earnings by $300 and capital contributions by $10,100
   3. increase total stockholders' equity by $10,400, of which $300 will increase "capital in excess of par"
   4. have no effect on total stockholders' equity

c. Because of the possibility of litigation against the company, the board of directors voted to create a "surplus reserve" for contingencies in the amount of $100,000. This restriction on retained earnings will:
   1. set aside cash in a fund
   2. increase liabilities
   3. decrease total stockholders' equity
   4. have no effect on total retained earnings.

d. One year later, the board of directors voted to remove the unnecessary restriction on retained earnings (see part "c"); litigation against the company no longer appeared probable. This "closing" of the surplus reserve for contingencies of $100,000 will:
   1. free "frozen" assets, thus permitting larger dividend payments
   2. increase the year's net profit by $100,000
   3. increase total stockholders' equity
   4. have no effect on total retained earnings

e. When the board of directors authorized the write-up of certain fixed assets to values established by a reliable appraisal, it increased fixed assets on the balance sheet and also increased:
   1. appreciation of fixed assets (revaluation or appraisal surplus)
   2. retained earnings
   3. net profit for the year
   4. working capital

f. A calendar year corporation declared a cash dividend on December 15, to stockholders of record on December 29, payable on January 15. The December 31 balance sheet showed the dividend as a current liability. When the dividend is paid on January 15, it will:
   1. decrease retained earnings and current liabilities
   2. decrease cash and current liabilities
   3. have no effect on the balance sheet
   4. reduce net profit by the amount of the dividend

12–23. Savo Island Corporation was incorporated on January 2, 1973. The information below pertains to the first two years of its business, as reflected by the following stockholders' equity section of the statements of financial position at the end of each year.

	DECEMBER 31, 1973	DECEMBER 31, 1974
Capital Contributions:		
Common Stock—par $100; 2,000 shares authorized; 1,500 and 1,600 shares issued respectively at the end of each year, of which 100 shares are in the treasury	$150,000	$160,000
Capital in Excess of Par:		
Premium on Common Stock	5,000	10,000
Retained Earnings	51,500	95,500
Total	206,500	265,500
Deduct Cost of Treasury Stock—Common (100 shares)	10,500	10,500
Total Stockholders' Equity	$196,000	$255,000

Additional information:

The 100 shares of treasury stock were purchased on August 1, 1973.

There were no issuances of capital stock in December of either year. The 100 shares issued in 1974 were sold on February 8, 1974.

As yet, the company has no regular quarterly dividend policy. To date, each December 1 the company has declared a year-end dividend as follows:

December 1, 1973—3 percent ($3 per share)
December 1, 1974—4 percent ($4 per share)

Each dividend was payable on December 29 to stockholders of record on December 15.

Required

Indicate your answer to each of the six statements below by choosing from among the following seventeen possible answers:

1. $ 4,500	7. $56,000	13. $170.00
2. 4,200	8. 6,000	14. 95,500
3. 4,185	9. 6,400	15. 44,000
4. 55,700	10. 3,820	16. 50,000
5. 51,500	11. 140.00	17. Some other amount not given
6. 47,300	12. 150.00	

a. The total amount of the dividend declared and paid in 1973 was . . . . ( )

b. The net income for 1973, the first year of business was . . ( )

c. Book value per share of stock at December 31, 1973, was ( )

d. The per share price received for the stock issued on February 8, 1974, was . . . . ( )

e. The total amount of the dividend declared and paid in 1974 was . . . . ( )

f. The net income for 1974 was . . . . ( )

12–24. "In essence, stock splits and stock dividends may be likened to slicing a pie a little more finely—more slices but the same amount of pie."[13]

Do you agree? Explain.

---

[13] *New York Times,* February 28, 1972, page 47, column 6, "Personal Finance." © 1972 by The New York Times Company. Reprinted by permission.

13

Framework, Behavior, and Flow of Manufacturing Costs

Earlier chapters have explained how the periodic gross margin of a business is obtained by matching the cost of goods sold during a period with the revenues realized from their sale. These chapters have also explained that the cost of saleable goods, which should be associated with revenues of future periods, is retained in the periodic inventory. In trading concerns (e.g., wholesalers and retailers), the costs ordinarily associated with the items in the inventory are the acquisition costs (i.e., the prices paid when they were purchased). Similarly, acquisition costs also represent the costs of the items which a trading concern sells during a period.

In a manufacturing enterprise, the determination of the cost of the items sold and the cost of the items retained is more involved; complication is created by the production process of the manufacturing concern. Unlike a trading company, which ordinarily inventories and sells the same items it originally bought, a manufacturer purchases raw materials and, through a production process, transforms their physical nature into new items which are to be sold. As explained in Chapter 3, the manufacturer arrives at the cost of goods sold by first adding the acquisition costs of the raw materials used and, perhaps, transportation and handling charges to the cost of labor and other conversion costs incurred to determine the cost of producing the finished goods. Then, when finished goods are sold, their calculated cost represents cost of goods sold during a period. The raw materials, plus the labor and other costs incurred in converting these materials into finished goods which are not included in the cost of goods sold during a period, represent costs which should be associated with future revenues. Until this association becomes possible by future sales, these costs should be properly identified and, according to their characteristics, classified under one of the three inventories described below:

(1) Raw Materials Inventory—the acquisition cost of raw materials not yet placed in the manufacturing process.
(2) Work in Process Inventory—the cost of raw materials and related conversion costs of goods still in the production process.
(3) Finished Goods Inventory—the cost of raw materials and related conversion costs of completely processed goods which are on hand and available for sale.

A comparison of the costs of the items sold and the items retained by a trading company with those of a manufacturing concern can be made by studying the abbreviated financial statements presented below:

Statement of Income

Trading Company			Manufacturing Company		
Sales		$90,000	Sales		$90,000
Cost of Goods Sold:			Cost of Goods Sold:		
Inventory of Merchandise 1/1	$ 60,000		Inventory of Finished Goods 1/1 .	$ 60,000	
Net Cost of Purchases ..	45,000		Cost of (Finished) Goods Manufactured ...	45,000	
Available for Sale	$105,000		Available for Sale	$105,000	
Inventory of Merchandise 1/31	55,000		Inventory of Finished Goods 1/31 .	55,000	
Cost of Goods Sold ..		50,000	Cost of Goods Sold ..		50,000
Gross Margin on Sales		$40,000	Gross Margin on Sales		$40,000

Balance Sheet

Trading Company		Manufacturing Company	
Current Assets:		Current Assets:	
Inventory of Merchandise	$55,000	Inventory of Raw Material	$38,000
		Inventory of Work in Process	5,500
		Inventory of Finished Goods	55,000

Notice that the cost of items sold in a trading company is determined by the net cost of purchases adjusted for changes in the inventory of merchandise, while the cost of items sold by a manufacturing concern is determined by the cost of (finished) goods manufactured adjusted by changes in the inventory of finished goods. For the manufacturing concern to know the cost of the finished goods manufactured, it must adjust the cost of raw material purchased by changes in the inventory of raw material, and it must adjust the cost of material used, labor consumed, and other production charges by changes in the inventory of work in process. These adjustments force a manufacturing concern to keep three separate categories of costs for items retained and to reflect these categories on its balance sheet, while a trading company needs only a single inventory.

The initial step taken by a trading concern to ascertain the basic cost of the items in its inventory may also be used to obtain the basic cost of the items in the raw materials inventory of a manufacturing concern. Under either situation, the acquisition cost of an inventory item may be obtained from the invoice of a vendor. While the pricing methods employed—FIFO, LIFO, average, etc.—may complicate the valuation process to a degree, the unit acquisition costs are readily identifiable. But, beyond this point, the manufacturer must employ different cost identification procedures. No longer are unit costs given; they must be determined. In addition to the pricing methods employed, the valuations placed on the work in process inventory, finished goods inventory, and the cost of goods sold in a manufacturing concern depend upon, and are determined by, the calculation of the unit cost of an item at each stage. It is this need for unit cost accumulation, identification, determination, and reporting that requires a kind of accounting known as manufacturing accounting, or, by its all-inclusive term, cost (or industrial) accounting.

In instances where the problem can be satisfactorily solved through using totals, the information needed can be obtained directly by routine financial accounting which records, accumulates, presents, and reports events of a financial character. However, in most instances, totals provide inadequate answers, because they do not give management as much useful information as it should obtain from the accounting records. For example, they do not show the amount of material, labor, and other manufacturing cost which is applicable to each item produced. Cost accounting furnishes this information and arranges the detailed cost figures in ways which aid managerial control and certain policy decisions. But, rather than a different kind of accounting, cost accounting is an extension of financial accounting. Both systems gather and report data in accordance with generally recognized accounting principles. Cost accounting, however, concentrates upon the material, labor, and related costs which are required to make and sell each product.

The costs of making and selling products represent the total costs which are deducted from sales revenue to obtain period profit. Total costs, in a manufacturing activity, include the costs of two distinctly different functions which should be classified as manufacturing cost and commercial expenses. The commercial expenses of a manufacturer, like those of a trading concern, should be divided into three groups: distribution (selling or marketing) expenses, administration expenses, and financial expenses. Distribution expenses consist of the costs of selling and delivering products after they have been produced and are ready for sale. Administration expenses cover the overall costs of directing and controlling the enterprise. Financial expenses include items like interest and other costs relating to borrowed capital. Manufacturing cost, often called production cost or factory cost, is the sum of the material, labor, and manufacturing expenses which enter into the cost of production. It is this latter phase of total cost which constitutes the primary consideration of cost accounting.

The determination of a reliable period gross profit is considered, by many, to be the fundamental objective of manufacturing accounting. Unless the cost of goods produced, the valuation of inventories, and the cost of goods sold can be established accurately, it is impossible to periodically achieve such an objective. Among the three foregoing requisites, the most difficult to obtain is the accurate determination of the cost of the goods produced. Such determination requires proper recognition of the three elements of manufacturing cost: direct material, direct labor, and manufacturing overhead. These elements are discussed in the next section.

THE ELEMENTS OF MANUFACTURING COST

Direct materials (sometimes called raw materials) refers to all materials that become an intrinsic part of, and can be readily and practically associated with, the finished product. That material which is consumed in the productive process or becomes an integral, nonassociative part of the finished product is classified as indirect material; rivets, tacks, glue, thread, and grease are examples of this latter category.

Direct labor (sometimes called productive labor) is the labor effort applied by the worker, either by physical contact or through the medium of a machine, upon materials to transform them into finished products. That labor which cannot feasibly be associated with the finished products or is not performed directly upon the material being converted into finished products is classified as indirect labor. Inspectors, general helpers, foremen, cleaners, and other such labor costs belong in this category.

Manufacturing overhead (sometimes called factory burden, manufacturing expense, indirect cost, or simply "overhead") consists of all factory costs, except direct material and direct labor, which are connected with the production of a product. The distinguishing feature of this heterogeneous mixture of manufacturing costs is their inability to be traced to individual units of product. They are either incurred jointly to benefit a group of products or in such insignificant individual units that the expense of tracing them to finished products is prohibitive. Unlike direct materials and direct labor, which can be readily and directly associated with a finished product, manufacturing overhead costs must be indirectly related to finished products through some equitable assignment. Some of the many types of manufacturing costs which are included in manufacturing overhead are:

Indirect material
Indirect labor
Property taxes—factory
Fire insurance—factory
Light, heat and power—factory
Repairs and maintenance—factory
Depreciation of factory equipment and machinery
Depreciation of factory building

FINANCIAL STATEMENTS OF A MANUFACTURER

It is customary for a manufacturing enterprise to summarize its production activities by preparing a separate statement or schedule showing the components of the cost of goods manufactured, as revealed by the statement on page 408.

Three major components in the preceding statement are the elements of manufacturing cost which provide total charges into production of $42,500 during January. A fourth is the cost of (finished) goods manu-

THE MALLOY MANUFACTURING COMPANY

Statement of Cost of Goods Manufactured
For the Month Ended January 31, 1974

Direct material:			
Raw material inventory, January 1, 1974		$30,000	
Purchases	$31,000		
Less: Purchase returns and allowances	3,000	28,000	
Material available for use		$58,000	
Less: Raw material inventory, January 31, 1974		38,000	
Direct material used			$20,000
Direct labor			15,000
Manufacturing overhead:			
Indirect labor		$ 1,900	
Property taxes—factory		600	
Fire insurance—factory		800	
Light, heat and power—factory		1,100	
Repairs and maintenance—factory		500	
Depreciation of factory equipment and machinery		1,400	
Depreciation of factory building		1,200	
Total manufacturing overhead			7,500
Total manufacturing costs originating this period			$42,500
Add: Work in process inventory, January 1, 1974			7,000
Total manufacturing costs			$49,500
Less: Work in process inventory, January 31, 1974			4,500
Cost of goods manufactured			$45,000

factured, a cost which is obtained by adjusting the total manufacturing costs originating this period for the difference between the beginning and ending work in process inventories. This adjustment is necessary, because a decrease in the work in process inventory means that the cost of finished goods produced exceeds the cost of the charges placed into production during a period, while an increase in the work in process inventory means that the cost of the finished goods completed is less than the charges entered into production. The $45,000 cost of goods manufactured is in turn reflected on the statement of income of a manufacturing company as a replacement for "net purchases" that would appear on the income statement of a trading concern. A statement of cost of goods manufactured, frequently called a statement of production, can be converted into a statement of cost of goods sold simply by adjusting the cost of goods manufactured for the difference between the beginning and ending finished goods inventories. Using the cost of goods manufactured computed in the preceding statement, this determination would be made by the method shown in the following schedule:

Cost of goods manufactured	$ 45,000
Add: Finished goods inventory, January 1, 1974	60,000
Cost of goods available for sale	$105,000
Less: Finished goods inventory, January 31, 1974	55,000
Cost of goods sold	$ 50,000

If the additional lines of the above schedule had been added to the preceding statement, the title of that statement would have changed to statement of cost of goods manufactured and cost of goods sold. With this statement, the amount for cost of goods sold can be shown on the statement of income as a single item. There should be no difference between the statement of income of a manufacturer and that of a trading concern when the cost of goods sold is shown as a single amount. In fact, under this condition, the only significant difference between the financial statements of a manufacturing business and those of a trading concern would appear on the balance sheet under "Current Assets," because three inventory items would replace a single item: the manufacturer's statement would show raw materials inventory, work in process inventory, and finished goods inventory, while the trader's statement would show only merchandise inventory.

The cost of goods sold cannot be ascertained unless the cost of producing finished units is first determined, and knowledge of the cost of manufacturing finished units in turn requires recognition of the costs which should be associated with partly completed units. Approximations of this information can, under certain conditions, be obtained through a deductive process. For example, if the ending inventory of raw materials is subtracted from the sum of the beginning raw material inventory plus period net purchases, the remainder may be presumed to represent the material issued during the period. Then, if the material issued plus the labor and overhead incurred during the period is reduced by the estimated material, labor, and overhead associated with partly completed products, the remainder may be considered the cost of the products completed during the period. Finally, the estimated cost of products completed plus the beginning finished goods inventory less the ending finished goods inventory may be accepted as the cost of goods sold during the period. This procedure is unsatisfactory for three major reasons:

(1) The dollar amount of each inventory should be determined on the basis of a physical or perpetual inventory at the end of each period.
(2) Waste, spoilage, and theft are either overlooked or inadequately recognized.
(3) The problem of assigning realistic values to partly completed products is extremely difficult. This difficulty intensifies as the variety of different products increases.

All three of the above objections can be overcome by the correct use of a proper system of cost accounting. In fact, the third and most perplexing objection involves what many believe to be the basic problem of cost accounting. This problem, restated as a question, is: How can the proper amounts of material, labor, and overhead be determined for completed and partly completed products? If only one product is involved, a reasonable and usable answer could be obtained through following the approximation procedures previously explained. But, if more than one kind of product is manufactured, no simple calculation would provide answers which would make due allowances for one product using more material, labor, or overhead than another. Instead, some means must be used which will give proper consideration to these differences. This requires a recognition of the nature of the productive process and the selection of a method or system which fits the facts of the situation involved. Cost accounting does this by using two basic methods of assigning manufacturing costs to individual products: process costing and job order costing.

PROCESS COSTING

Process costing assigns manufacturing costs to individual units when the productive output is continuous and routine. This method is used by manufacturing concerns which mass-produce standardized products for warehouse stock to be sold to customers whose identity is usually unknown; it is suitable whenever the identity of a single product unit is lost. Process costing is usually found in industries like cement, flour, coal, sugar, paper, rubber, tobacco, dairy, automobile, textile, steel, chemical, electrical appliances, and oil refining. Also, certain public utilities like electric power, gas, water, and steam heat cost their products by process costing. Since many of the industries listed do have some special job production, it should not be presumed that they depend exclusively on process costing.

In continuous process production, a product ordinarily moves from raw material to finished form through a designated sequence of departments or cost centers. A department or cost center is one operation or a cluster of homogeneous operations wherein a specific step is performed in the completion of a product. The department or cost center provides the basis for process costing. Costs are accumulated by the department for a time period, like a month, without any attempt to associate costs with individual units. At the end of the period, the total costs collected for the department are divided by the physical output of the department to obtain an average unit cost. The average unit cost of the completed units times the number of units transferred becomes, in effect, the cost of the material entering succeeding departments, or the cost of the products placed into finished goods, if all productive operations have been completed.

A process costing system requires that a record of manufacturing costs and physical output be maintained by the department for each period of time. Not only will such a record provide the basis for the calculation of average unit costs, but, if the proper organizational structure is present, it will permit the measuring of performance within each area of responsibility. This record, known as a cost of production report, shows the cost of the direct material, direct labor, and manufacturing overhead used to process a unit through each department and the cost of each unit of finished product. To explain the cost flow as it appears on a cost of production report, it is assumed that Baldrige Manufacturing Company produces a single product which is processed through three departments, incurring the following department costs:

	CUTTING	ASSEMBLING	PAINTING
Direct Material	$16,000	$2,000	—
Direct Labor	8,000	4,000	$12,000
Manufacturing Overhead	4,000	2,000	6,000

Assuming that 8,000 units are started and completed in each department and that there are no beginning or ending inventories, the cost of production report is shown on the following page.

This example has been highly simplified to emphasize the essentials of the flow of product costs in process costing. It ignores problems like lost units, multiple products, increase in units, and departmental opening and closing inventories. There is no need here to go into the extensive and detailed study required to cover the numerous and sometimes complex variations which might be encountered. The problem of inventories, however, arises regularly and therefore requires explanation at this point.

In the example provided, 8,000 units were started and completed during the period in each department. More frequently than not, the

BALDRIGE MANUFACTURING COMPANY
Cost of Production Report
For the Month of January, 1974

	Cutting		Assembling		Painting	
Quantity schedule (units):						
Started in process . . .	8,000					
Received in department			8,000		8,000	
Transferred to next department	8,000		8,000			
Transferred to finished goods					8,000	
	Total Cost	Unit Cost	Total Cost	Unit Cost	Total Cost	Unit Cost
Departmental costs:						
Direct material	$16,000	$2.00	$ 2,000	$ .25	-0-	-0-
Direct labor	8,000	1.00	4,000	.50	$12,000	$1.50
Manufacturing overhead	4,000	.50	2,000	.25	6,000	.75
Total departmental costs	$28,000	$3.50	$ 8,000	$1.00	$18,000	$2.25
Cost transferred into department			28,000	3.50	36,000	4.50
Total cost accumulated	$28,000	$3.50	$36,000	$4.50	$54,000	$6.75
Cost transferred to next department . .	$28,000	$3.50	$36,000	$4.50		
Cost transferred to finished goods . . .					$54,000	$6.75

situation is complicated by: first, units that were started by a department in prior periods and completed in the current period; and second, units that were started by a department in the current period but not completed. Since all of the costs of units both started and completed were incurred in the current period and since only a part of the cost of the other two types of units belongs to the current period, the three types of units cannot be added together. Instead, they must be converted to a common denominator, termed *equivalent unit,* which is equal to one unit which is 100 percent completed. Sometimes, the assumption is made that all units in the beginning and ending inventories are 50 percent completed. Consequently, it would take two such units to equal a unit that was both started and completed during the period. In other instances, all units in the work in process inventories are ignored, or the beginning and ending inventory units are assumed to be equal. Although expedient, none of these methods should be used when departmental inventories are significant and substantial differences exist between the beginning and ending inventories. Instead, a more exact procedure should be employed.

A more precise determination of the equivalent units of production can be obtained through a valid estimate of the actual stages of completion. For example, if 10,000 units were completed during the period, 4,000 additional units were 75 percent completed at the end of the period, and 2,000 units were only 50 percent completed at the beginning of the period, the number of equivalent units completed would be 12,000, determined as follows:

Units finished during month	10,000
Plus: 75% × 4,000 units at end of month	3,000
	13,000
Less: 50% × 2,000 units at start of month	1,000
Equivalent units produced during month	12,000

If total costs incurred during the period were $24,000 the cost of an equivalent unit would be $2.00. The 4,000 units in the ending inventory would be costed at $1.50 apiece. The 10,000 units completed would be costed at $2.00 for the 8,000 units both started and completed and at $1.00 plus whatever costs had already been accumulated on each of the 2,000 units which comprised the beginning inventory. Obviously, such a calculation applies only when the three elements of cost have equal stages of completion. Otherwise, equivalent units of production must be computed separately for material, labor, and manufacturing overhead.

This condition frequently exists when material is not added beyond the initial department.

JOB ORDER COSTING

Job order costing assigns manufacturing costs to individual units when the productive output is neither continuous nor stereotyped. This method is used by manufacturing concerns that produce in accordance with special designs or specifications which are supplied by the customer. Repeat orders may be infrequent and rarely is productive output scheduled for warehouse stock. Instead, production ordinarily lags behind the receipts of customers' orders. This method should be used whenever it is possible physically to distinguish each unit or each group of units from all other units throughout the productive process. For example, it is the only method adaptable to the construction industry. It is ideally suited to account for the costs of any single unit like a turbine, locomotive or aircraft. Also, it is applicable to factories and workshops where identical or similar products are covered by a single production order (e.g., printing, foundry or furniture).

In job order production, a product or group of products moves from raw material to finished form through one or more departments. The department, however, is not the primary determinant in calculating product unit cost. Nor is dominant importance attached to the time period. The all-important factor is the job, or order, for which costs are accumulated, regardless of the number of time periods involved, until the job is finished. Upon completion, the total costs accumulated for the job divided by the number of units produced is the product unit cost.

Throughout the productive process, material, labor, and manufacturing overhead costs are collected on a separate form reserved for each job. This form, or summary sheet, is called a job order cost sheet or job cost sheet, and it contains spaces to record the material, labor, and overhead costs that are identified with each job by a job order number. (Individual job order numbers provide correct identification when several jobs are moving through the factory at the same time.) In addition, the job cost sheet usually shows other pertinent information like date ordered, number of items to be produced, date completed, specifications, and a description of the job. An example of a job cost sheet is shown on page 415.

Job order cost sheets should be designated to provide a manufacturing concern with the information it needs. Consequently, their content, arrangement, and form differ among various users. Although the example provided has been highly simplified to show the basic cost requirements,

Job Order Cost Sheet

WILDWOOD MANUFACTURING COMPANY

Customer	Allison Brothers and Company	Job Order Number	9474
Specifications	Attached	Date Ordered	10/18/—
Blueprint	Attached	Date Commenced	12/1/—
Description	Generator No. 226A4	Date Completed	12/13/—
Quantity	10	Date Shipped	12/15/—

Direct Materials

Date	Department	Requisition	Amount
12/1	71	4128	$3,000
12/1	72	4129	2,000
12/1	73	4210	1,000
		Total	$6,000

Direct Labor

Date	Department	Operation	Amount
12/1–6	71	112	$2,400
12/6–10	72	231	1,600
12/10–13	73	317	1,000
		Total	$5,000

Manufacturing Overhead

Date	Department	Basis	Amount
12/6	71	D.L. Hours	$2,880
12/13	72	Machine hours	960
12/13	73	200% of D.L.	2,000
		Total	$5,840

Summary

Direct Material	$ 6,000
Direct Labor	5,000
Manufacturing Overhead	5,840
Total Manufacturing Cost	$16,840
Units Produced	10
Unit Cost	$ 1,684
Selling Price	$28,000
Manufacturing Cost	16,840
Gross Margin	$11,160
Commercial Expenses (30% of Sales)	8,400
Net Profit	$ 2,760

it does contain information concerning the profitability of the job. This knowledge can be used as a guide for future price quotations on similar jobs. In addition to aiding pricing decisions, job cost information helps management to appraise manufacturing efficiency by providing current product costs for comparison with past product costs or estimated product costs.

ACCOUNTING FOR COST ELEMENTS

The two preceding sections have explained how given amounts of direct material, direct labor, and manufacturing overhead are combined to obtain unit product costs under both process costing and job order costing. But neither section explained how the proper amounts of these cost elements are ascertained. The purpose of this section is to describe how such amounts are obtained.

Direct material costs are obtained from material requisitions which show the type, quantity, unit cost, and total cost of materials used in production. If the material is issued to a job, the job order number is shown on the requisition. The total cost of all requisitions bearing a specific job number represents the cost of direct material for a particular job. In process costing, departmental costs are identified by substituting the name or number of the department for the job order number on the material requisitions.

Direct labor costs are computed by using work or time tickets which show, among other things, the time worked, rate of pay, total earnings, description of work, and employee's name. If the work was performed on a job, the job order number is shown so that all time tickets bearing a given job number will, when totaled, provide the direct labor cost on that job. In process costing, the department identification is used, not the job order number. If an employee works in only one department, time tickets are not required under process costing, since the departmental direct labor costs can be obtained from the payroll or clock cards which show the amount of time worked each day.

Manufacturing overhead costs are not as readily traced to product units as the prime costs of direct material and direct labor. Since these costs are not associated directly with the products produced, it is impossible to measure exactly how much manufacturing overhead cost should belong to a given product. Total manufacturing overhead, however, is incurred because of production and is a proper part of the cost of manufacturing products. Consequently, some feasible method must be devised to charge an equitable amount of manufacturing overhead to each product unit.

Although manufacturing overhead costs cannot be traced directly to a unit of product, they can be traced directly to a unit of activity. These units are: first, producing departments in which operations are performed directly upon the product being manufactured; and second, service departments in which particular benefits are provided for producing departments or producing and other service departments. The expenses incurred in operating both types of departments represent the total manufacturing overhead costs which belong to the products manufactured. Individual expenses may be traced directly to producing departments and indirectly to product units; they may be traced directly to service departments, indirectly to producing departments, and then again indirectly to product units. An illustration of this tracing procedure is provided by the Manufacturing Overhead Distribution Sheet shown on page 418.

In the following simplified illustration, each manufacturing overhead expense was assigned directly to the three producing and the two service departments by the most equitable basis obtainable for this company. That is, departmental time tickets were used to ascertain how much of the total indirect labor expense belonged to each department; department material requisitions were used to establish the amount of the indirect material that had been issued to each department; property taxes were prorated according to the cubic space occupied by each department; fire insurance was allocated according to the dollar value of equipment and space associated with each department; departmental square footage was used to prorate other expense; meters measured each department's share of light, heat, and power; and the dollar amount of equipment located in each department was used to prorate the total expense from depreciation of equipment.

After each manufacturing overhead expense was directly assigned to the appropriate department, the total cost for the general service department was distributed to the storeroom and the three producing departments according to the number of man hours associated with each department. Storeroom had 1,000; finishing, 5,000; assembling, 6,000; and cutting, 8,000. The $23,600 cost in the general service department came to $1.18 per man hour for the 20,000 total man hours. The $1.18 hourly rate times the number of man hours in each department was the share of the general service department's cost which was distributed to each department. A similar procedure was used to distribute the $8,880 adjusted total cost of the storeroom to the three producing departments. In this instance, however, costs were distributed according to the dollar value of material requisitions which had been issued to each department. Finishing received $8,000 of material requisitions; assembling, $2,000; and cutting, $30,000.

Manufacturing Overhead Distribution Sheet

Departmental Overhead	Total	Producing Departments			Service Departments	
		Cutting	Assembling	Finishing	Storeroom	General
Indirect labor	$ 32,900	$12,200	$ 8,700	$ -0-	$ -0-	$ 12,000
Indirect material	36,200	14,000	9,000	6,200	2,400	4,600
Property taxes—factory	11,400	4,400	3,000	2,000	1,000	1,000
Fire insurance—factory	8,300	3,200	2,000	1,100	800	1,200
Light and heat—factory	25,100	13,800	4,600	3,700	1,200	1,800
Depreciation of equipment	28,500	13,500	6,000	5,500	1,700	1,800
Other	16,600	7,300	4,100	3,400	600	1,200
Total	$159,000	$68,400	$37,400	$21,900	$ 7,700	$ 23,600
General		9,440	7,080	5,900	1,180	(23,600)
Storeroom		6,660	444	1,776	$(8,880)	
	$159,000	$84,500	$44,924	$29,576		
Machine hours		5,000				
Direct labor hours			10,000			
Direct labor costs				$20,000		
Rate per machine hour		$ 16.90				
Rate per labor hour			$4.4924			
Rate per labor dollar				147.88%		

After all manufacturing overhead costs had been distributed and accumulated in the three producing departments, an equitable basis was selected for apportioning the total department costs to the products that were worked on in each department: that factor which correlated most closely with the generation of overhead in each department was chosen. Analyses revealed that causal relationship existed between manufacturing overhead and machine hours in the cutting department and between manufacturing overhead and direct labor hours in the assembling department. In the finishing department, direct labor hours and direct labor cost were about equally desirable; direct labor cost was selected, because it was more readily obtainable. The unit of production method was considered and rejected, since the variety of the multiple products being produced made that method inequitable; no common unit could be equitably associated with all products. Material cost was considered for the cutting department, but no logical relationship could be established between the material costs of the products and the manufacturing overhead used in their production. For example, one product requiring a small amount of processing but made with high-priced material would have been charged with far more than its fair share of manufacturing overhead.

As shown in the lower part of the preceding Manufacturing Overhead Distribution Sheet, the basis selected to apportion departmental manufacturing overhead costs caused departmental manufacturing overhead rates to be established as follows:

Cutting Department	$16.90 per machine hour
Assembling Department	$4.4924 per labor hour
Finishing Department	147.88% per labor dollar

Using the above departmental cost rates, manufacturing overhead costs may be assigned to a given unit of product by ascertaining and employing relevant product data. For example, if a product required twelve minutes in the cutting department, twenty minutes in the assembling department, and one dollar of labor cost in the finishing department, its manufacturing overhead cost would be $6.3563, computed as follows:

Cutting Department:	Twelve minutes × $16.90 per machine hour =	$3.38
Assembling Department:	Twenty minutes × $4.4924 per labor hour =	1.4975
Finishing Department:	One dollar labor cost × 147.88% =	1.4788
Total manufacturing overhead cost		$6.3563

The use of a manufacturing overhead distribution procedure provides a convenient arrangement for apportioning manufacturing overhead to the various products worked on in each department. Such a distribution sheet, however, cannot be prepared until the end of the period, after the total cost of each manufacturing overhead expense item has been ascertained. This means that the manufacturing overhead applicable to each unit of product manufactured during a period cannot be determined until the end of the period. Under process costing, when production is for warehouse stock, this timing presents little difficulty. Under job order costing, when production is for customer order and a job may be completed and shipped in the early part of a period, it is impractical to wait until the end of the period to find out what the job costs. Proper control of cost is impossible if management has to wait long after a job is completed to learn the cost of a job. Instead, it is advantageous to charge a finished job at the time it is completed with a reasonable share of manufacturing overhead so that the total cost of the job becomes available immediately. How can this be done when the actual amount of these expenses is often not known until the end of the period?

Jobs can be charged with manufacturing overhead at any time by predetermined applicable manufacturing overhead rates for each department. This requires that an estimate of departmental expenses and related activity be made before a period begins. Then, the estimated departmental expenses divided by the estimated activity measure will provide a predetermined overhead rate. A problem arises, however, as to how to make reliable expense estimates. One approach is to determine the individual expense-activity relationship which has existed in the past, and then to project this relationship for the level of activity expected in the future. If events which invalidate the historical relationship have occurred, adjustments should be made to correct those expenses that are involved. After the total amount of each manufacturing overhead expense has been estimated for a period, all manufacturing overhead expenses should be assigned and distributed to service and producing departments and then related to estimated activity measures as they previously were on the manufacturing overhead distribution sheet. Since this action is taken before a period commences, not at the end of a period, a manufacturing overhead budget, rather than a manufacturing overhead distribution sheet, is prepared.

Through predetermined rates, manufacturing overhead can be charged whenever the machine hours, direct labor hours, direct labor cost, or other applicable activity measure is known. Practicality, however, usually demands that such charges be made either weekly or monthly and when the job is completed. In this manner, manufacturing overhead charges can be made in a convenient and orderly fashion and still enable the manufacturing overhead applicable to a job to be known when the job is finished. Before illustrating the effect of predetermined manufacturing overhead rates on financial statements, cost behavior will be examined to provide a better understanding of the influence of manufacturing overhead on total manufacturing cost.

COST BEHAVIOR

Certain costs tend to remain unchanged in amount regardless of the volume of activity or production, while others tend to vary in proportion to changes in activity. Unless this distinction is recognized and given due consideration, cost accumulations and analyses may inadequately inform those in management who use such data. Knowledge of this distinction depends upon an understanding of *activity variations* and the *variability of costs*.

When the volume of production is homogeneous, activity can be measured by quantities of physical output. For instance, the activity or volume of a single product plant can be measured by the number of units produced. But, if production is so heterogeneous that output in units is not a suitable measure, it is necessary to select some common denominator by which all types of physical output can be reduced to comparable measurement. Commonly used measurement bases are direct labor hours, machine hours, and direct labor cost.

A most significant characteristic of cost variability is that *total* manufacturing costs do not tend to vary in direct proportion to changes in aggregate activity. This fact, combined with the knowledge that direct material and direct labor costs tend to vary in proportion to productive output, suggests that changes in all or a part of the remaining element of manufacturing cost (manufacturing overhead costs) correlate more closely with some factor other than production volume. This suggestion implies that additional factors must be used to establish the degree of variability existing among those costs comprising manufacturing overhead.

In a typical manufacturing enterprise, manufacturing overhead costs can be divided into at least the two following principal categories of variability:

(1) Costs which tend to fluctuate in proportion to the total volume of production, but are not ordinarily identified as being generated by any specific unit of output. Such costs tend to be a function of productive activity; they display characteristics of variability similar to those associated with direct material and direct labor costs. Consequently, these costs may be classified as variable manufacturing overhead costs.

(2) Costs which tend to be constant in total amount within a specified range of productive volume. Since this range ordinarily covers a period of time within which management expects production to be handled by existing facilities and organization, these costs may be considered a function of time instead of productive activity. Some such costs are fixed because of their inherent nature; others are fixed by the action of management. Regardless of whether their fixity results from inherent qualities or is a matter of managerial decision, those costs may be classified as fixed or non-variable manufacturing overhead costs.

Some costs do not fall precisely into either category, because they possess both fixed and variable characteristics. Consequently, the fixed component of this type of cost may be included in the fixed category, while the variable component may be combined with other costs comprising the variable category. These costs are described as semi-variable costs.

An understanding of the role played by both variable and fixed manufacturing overhead costs is a vital prerequisite to proper interpretations of cost data. The total amount of a variable cost like indirect materials tends to change with the volume of production, but the cost per unit tends to remain constant. Fixed costs like depreciation, property taxes, and fire insurance react in an opposite manner; though the total amount is constant, the cost per unit tends to vary inversely with the volume of production. Total manufacturing overhead cost is a composite of variable, fixed, and semi-variable components, and, consequently, it possesses an overall semi-variable character.

COST FLOW

Exhibits 13–1, 13–2, and 13–3 emphasize the significance of the cost-volume relationship under each of three different types of cost flows. Through holding all other cost determinants constant during two months of operations, the influence of a change in volume is isolated in each instance. The two months of activity illustrated by each model are based upon the following assumptions:

(1) A single product is manufactured.
(2) 10,000 units of product represent the normal monthly volume of production.
(3) Production is continuous mass production.

(4) Unit selling price is a constant $5.00 amount throughout the two-month period.
(5) No inventory is on hand as of January 1.
(6) During January, 10,000 units are produced, and 8,000 units are sold. Production costs are:

Direct material	$10,000
Direct labor	10,000
Variable manufacturing overhead costs	6,000
Fixed manufacturing overhead costs	4,000

(7) During February, 5,000 units are produced, and 4,000 units are sold. Production costs are:
   (a) All variable costs are "perfect" variables and equal 50% of the amount of total variable costs in January, since production volume has been reduced by one-half.
   (b) Total fixed costs of $4,000 remain unchanged from the amount incurred in January.

Exhibit 13–1 traces the cost flow and shows the effect upon financial statements of manufacturing costs which are generated by the operation of an actual cost system. In January, the $30,000 cost of production divided by the 10,000 units produced provides a $3.00 average unit cost of production. Since there was no beginning inventory, the $3.00 unit cost of production becomes the unit cost of goods sold on the January statement of income. The $16,000 gross margin in January results from selling 8,000 units which cost $3.00 apiece ($24,000) for $5.00 per unit ($40,000). The 2,000 unsold units times their $3.00 unit cost become the $6,000 inventory shown on the balance sheet as of January 31.

In February, the 50 percent reduction in productive activity reduces the cost of production to $17,000. This amount divided by the 5,000 units produced provides an average unit cost of production of $3.40, which is $.40 greater than the unit cost of production in January. This increase occurs because the $4,000 of fixed manufacturing overhead was apportioned to 10,000 units in January, while it is apportioned to only 5,000 units in February. None of this increase is attributable to the variable costs, because the unit cost of direct material, direct labor, and variable manufacturing overhead is identical in both months. When the 5,000 units costing $3.40 apiece are combined with the 2,000 units in the beginning inventory which cost $3.00 apiece, 7,000 units, costing a total of $23,000, are available for sale during February. The company uses a weighted average unit cost of $3.286 to cost both the 3,000 units on hand on February 28 and the 4,000 units which are sold during the month.[1]

---

[1] Weighted average unit cost =

$$\frac{\$23{,}000 \text{ (Cost of goods available for sale)}}{7{,}000 \text{ (No. of units available for sale)}} = \$3.286.$$

EXHIBIT 13–1

Flow of Costs
Actual Cost System

MONTH OF JANUARY

COST OF PRODUCTION		STATEMENT OF INCOME			BALANCE SHEET AS OF JANUARY 31	
Direct Material	$10,000	Sales (8,000 units × $5.00)		$40,000	ASSETS	
Direct Labor	10,000	Cost of Goods Sold:			Current Assets:	
Manufacturing Overhead:		Cost of Production (10,000 × $3.00)	$30,000			
Variable	6,000	Less: Inventory, January 31 (2,000 × 3.00)	6,000		Inventory	$6,000
Fixed	4,000	Cost of Goods Sold (8,000 × 3.00)		24,000		
Cost of Production ..	$30,000	Gross Margin on Sales		$16,000		
		Less: Operating Expenses:				
Unit Cost of Production:		Marketing Expenses	$ 4,000			
$30,000 ÷ 10,000 units = $3.00		Administrative Expenses	1,000	5,000		
		Net Operating Income		$11,000		
		Rate of Gross Margin: $16,000 ÷ $40,000 = 40%				

EXHIBIT 13–1 (*Continued*)

MONTH OF FEBRUARY

COST OF PRODUCTION

Direct Material	$ 5,000
Direct Labor	5,000
Manufacturing Overhead:	
Variable	3,000
Fixed	4,000
	$17,000

Unit Cost of Production:
$17,000 ÷ 5,000 units = $3.40

STATEMENT OF INCOME

Sales (4,000 units × $5.00)			$20,000
Cost of Goods Sold:			
Inventory, Feb. 1	(2,000 × $3.00)	$ 6,000	
Cost of Production	(5,000 × 3.40)	17,000	
Cost of Goods Available for Sale	(7,000 × 3.286)	$23,000	
Inventory, Feb. 28	(3,000 × 3.286)	9,858	
Cost of Goods Sold	(4,000 × 3.286)		13,142
Gross Margin on Sales			$ 6,858
Less: Operating Expenses:			
Marketing Expenses		$ 4,000	
Administrative Expenses		1,000	5,000
Net Operating Income			$ 1,858

Rate of Gross Margin:
$6,858 ÷ $20,000 = 34%

BALANCE SHEET AS OF FEBRUARY 28

ASSETS

Current Assets:	
Inventory	$9,858

A comparison of the two income statements reveals that the rate of gross margin has decreased from 40 percent in January to 34 percent in February. How could this unfavorable development occur when, in both months, exactly 80 percent of the units produced are sold, the selling price remains constant, the variable unit costs are identical, and the total fixed costs remain unchanged? The answer to this question is found in the only factor which does change, and this is volume. Volume is solely responsible for the variance in the gross profit rate.

Furthermore, a comparison of the two balance sheets reveals that the cost assigned to the inventory in February has increased disproportionately to the increased number of units in the inventory. The $6,000 inventory has increased 64 percent to $9,858, while the number of units in the inventory has increased from 2,000 to 3,000, or only 50 percent. How should a plant manager interpret this phenomenon? Should he presume: that the units in inventory are worth more because of the smaller number of units produced by February's decreased activity; that the value assigned to the inventory is unduly inflated; or that idle plant costs have been included in the valuation of an asset on the balance sheet?

Exhibit 13–1 and the foregoing discussion indicate that, while all other factors remain constant, a change in volume of productive activity may cause certain financial statements to hinder, rather than aid, management's appraisal of operating conditions. This confusing situation may be alleviated by using alternative costing methods which will isolate the effect of volume changes. Such alternative methods include:

(1) A historical (actual) cost system which utilizes a normal manufacturing overhead rate.
(2) A historical (actual) cost system which utilizes the theory of direct costing.
(3) A predetermined (standard) cost system which may, or may not, utilize direct costing theory.

Alternative one will be presented by Exhibit 13–2 and the accompanying discussion. Exhibit 13–3, accompanied by a related explanation, will present alternative two. Alternative three is not illustrated because it provides, depending upon whether absorption or direct costing theory is being followed, a manufacturing overhead cost flow comparable to alternative one or two. Alternative three, however, differs radically from the other two alternatives in its treatment of direct material and direct labor costs. Under a standard cost system flow, all three cost elements are ascertained by predetermined costs. Then the cost elements, so calculated, are compared with their related actual costs to disclose monetary variances for measurement and control purposes. This is a brief and incomplete description of standard costs, but a meaningful coverage of the subject is beyond the scope of this book.[2]

To prevent widely fluctuating unit costs due to volume changes from affecting the usefulness of cost data contained on financial statements and other reports, the effect of volume upon unit costs must be isolated. Variable costs, which tend to change in proportion to production volume, present little difficulty. Fixed costs, which tend to be constant in total amount regardless of volume, are the crux of the problem. For example, if fixed manufacturing overhead costs amount to $10,000 and one unit of product is produced, the fixed manufacturing overhead applicable to this unit is $10,000; if 5,000 units are produced, the unit manufacturing overhead cost would be only $2.00. Consequently, when activity fluctuates from period to period, changes in unit costs will occur unless fixed costs are stabilized per unit regardless of the volume of activity. Constant fixed manufacturing overhead costs per unit can be obtained by dividing the estimated annual total amount of such costs by the estimated annual volume of production, and then using the derived unit fixed manufacturing overhead cost to cost each unit produced throughout the year. This calculation provides an estimated or normal fixed manufacturing overhead unit rate and will accomplish two important objectives: first, the elimination of changes in unit cost which are due solely to changes in the volume of production; and second, the provision of a predetermined fixed manufacturing overhead rate which, when combined with a predetermined variable manufacturing overhead rate, may be used for costing at any time during a period. In our illustration, the fixed manufacturing overhead amounts to $4,000 a month ($48,000 a year), while the normal volume of activity is 10,000 units a month (120,000 units per year). A normal fixed manufacturing overhead rate would be calculated as follows:

$$\text{Normal fixed manufacturing overhead rate} = \frac{\$48{,}000}{120{,}000 \text{ units}} = \$.40 \text{ per unit}$$

Exhibit 13–2 traces the flow of manufacturing costs through the pertinent financial statements when a normal fixed manufacturing overhead rate is used in conjunction with an otherwise actual cost system. It discloses, for the month of January, results identical to those shown in Exhibit 13–1, because January is a month of normal productive volume. Thus, in Exhibit 13–2, the fixed manufacturing overhead charged to production by the normal fixed manufacturing overhead rate ($.40 ×

[2] For a more comprehensive coverage of standard costs, see James H. Rossell and William W. Frasure, *Managerial Accounting,* Second Edition (Columbus, Ohio: Charles E. Merrill Publishing Company, 1972), Chapter 13.

EXHIBIT 13–2

Flow of Costs

Actual Cost System with Normal Fixed Manufacturing Overhead Rate

MONTH OF JANUARY						
COST OF PRODUCTION		STATEMENT OF INCOME			BALANCE SHEET AS OF JANUARY 31	
Direct Material	$10,000	Sales (8,000 units × $5.00)		$40,000	ASSETS	
Direct Labor	10,000	Cost of Goods Sold:			Current Assets:	
Manufacturing Overhead:		Cost of Production (10,000 × $3.00)	$30,000			
Variable	6,000	Less: Inventory, January 31 (2,000 × 3.00)	6,000		Inventory	$6,000
Fixed	4,000	Cost of Goods Sold (8,000 × 3.00)		24,000		
Cost of Production ..	$30,000	Gross Margin on Sales		$16,000		
Unit Cost of Production:		Less: Operating Expenses:				
$30,000 ÷ 10,000 units = $3.00		Marketing Expenses	$ 4,000			
		Administrative Expenses	1,000	5,000		
		Net Operating Income		$11,000		
		Rate of Gross Margin: $16,000 ÷ $40,000 = 40%				

EXHIBIT 13–2 (*Continued*)

MONTH OF FEBRUARY

COST OF PRODUCTION

Direct Material	$ 5,000
Direct Labor	5,000
Manufacturing Overhead:	
Variable	3,000
Fixed	2,000
Cost of Production ..	$15,000

Unit Cost of Production:
$15,000 ÷ 5,000 units = $3.00

STATEMENT OF INCOME

Sales (4,000 units × $5.00)			$20,000
Cost of Goods Sold:			
Inventory, Feb. 1	(2,000 × $3.00)	$ 6,000	
Cost of Production	(5,000 × 3.00)	15,000	
Cost of Goods Available for Sale	(7,000 × 3.00)	$21,000	
Inventory, Feb. 28	(3,000 × 3.00)	9,000	
Cost of Goods Sold	(4,000 × 3.00)		12,000
Gross Margin on Sales			$ 8,000
Underapplied Fixed Manufacturing Overhead			2,000
Gross Margin on Sales (adjusted) ...			$ 6,000
Less: Operating Expenses:			
Marketing Expenses		$ 4,000	
Administrative Expenses		1,000	5,000
Net Operating Income			$ 1,000

Rate of Gross Margin:
$8,000 ÷ $20,000 = 40%

Rate of Gross Margin (adjusted):
$6,000 ÷ $20,000 = 30%

BALANCE SHEET AS OF FEBRUARY 28

ASSETS	
Current Assets:	
Inventory	$9,000

10,000 = $4,000) is identical to the actual amount of fixed manufacturing overhead charged to production in Exhibit 13–1.

In February, however, the two exhibits show different financial "results." Exhibit 13–1 shows fixed manufacturing overhead of $4,000 and a unit cost of $3.40, while Exhibit 13–2 shows fixed manufacturing overhead of only $2,000 and a unit cost of $3.00. Exhibit 13–2 has the same unit cost of production in each month, because a normal fixed manufacturing overhead rate per unit is employed. The statements of income in Exhibit 13–2 show the same rate of gross margin for both months; while the amount of February's gross margin is exactly one-half of January's, when twice as many units were produced and sold. Furthermore, none of the fixed manufacturing overhead costs in excess of $.40 per unit are placed into February's ending inventory amount as they were in Exhibit 13–1 when a normal manufacturing overhead rate was not employed. Thus, the use of a normal fixed manufacturing overhead rate eliminates the unit cost deviations which are caused by a change in volume when actual fixed manufacturing overhead costs are used,[3] and the rate of gross margin and the unit cost for inventory are the same in each period regardless of the level of activity.

Although the use of a normal fixed manufacturing overhead rate resolves unit cost difficulties which result from fluctuating activity, it creates another complexity when the actual and estimated volume of production are not identical. For example, in Exhibit 13–2, the fixed manufacturing overhead rate of $.40 is predicated on a production volume of 10,000 units. Since 10,000 units are produced in January, the fixed manufacturing overhead applied to production is equal to the actual fixed manufacturing overhead. But, when 5,000 units are produced in February, only $2,000 (5,000 units × $.40) of fixed manufacturing overhead is applied to production. This means $2,000 of the actual fixed manufacturing overhead of $4,000 has not been absorbed as a production cost. Obviously, this condition would exist any time that actual and estimated activity differ. If actual exceeds estimated activity, then normal manufacturing overhead costs are overapplied; if estimated exceeds actual activity, then normal manufacturing overhead costs are underapplied. In Exhibit 13–2, the underapplied fixed manufacturing overhead repre-

---

[3] In Exhibit 13–2 a normal rate is used for fixed manufacturing overhead costs, while the actual amount is used for variable manufacturing overhead costs. Variable costs are not normalized, because they tend to vary in proportion to activity. They could, however, be comparatively normalized by the use of an overall normal manufacturing overhead rate. For example, if normal variable manufacturing overhead costs are $6,000, then $.60 per unit could be used as a normal rate for variable manufacturing overhead costs as $.40 is used for fixed costs. Moreover, the separate variable and fixed manufacturing overhead rates could be combined into one overall normal rate which would also avoid unit cost deviations caused by a change in operating activity.

sents a monetary measure of the extent to which estimated capacity was not used (e.g., the $2,000 of underapplied fixed manufacturing overhead divided by the $.40 normal fixed manufacturing overhead unit rate provides the number of units of normal production which were not produced).

In Exhibit 13–2, the $2,000 of underapplied manufacturing overhead for February is deducted from the gross margin on sales to obtain an adjusted gross margin. (A variation of this method would provide an adjusted cost of goods sold through adding the underapplied manufacturing overhead to the initial cost of goods sold.) As a result, the net income for the month of February is reduced by the total amount of the underapplied (idle capacity) cost. An alternative treatment would be to divide it between the finished goods inventory and the cost of goods sold in the proportion of the costs which originated in the current period that each contained. Another alternative would be to eliminate it from the statement of income and to defer it on the balance sheet in expectation that it would be offset by an overapplied amount in some succeeding month of the year. This latter alternative is not a generally accepted accounting procedure for annual financial statements, but it could be used for interim internal statements. Among these possibilities, the one actually used in Exhibit 13–2 and the one which converts an initial into an adjusted cost of goods sold are the procedures having the most widespread popularity.

The second alternative method proposed on page 426 for counteracting the effect of volume changes on unit costs is a historical (actual) cost system which utilizes direct costing. Exhibit 13–3 traces the flow of manufacturing costs when the theory of direct costing is employed, and shows the effect of direct costing upon both manufacturing costs and financial statements. But, before discussing Exhibit 13–3, a brief explanation of direct costing is necessary to introduce the theory, objectives, and methodology of this costing method.

"Direct costing is a plan for providing management with information about cost-volume-profit relationships and for presenting this information in a form more readily understandable by management at all levels."[4] Under direct costing, only the direct, incremental, or out-of-pocket costs needed to produce an item comprise the manufacturing cost of production. As a result, the total cost of a manufactured item placed into inventory or transferred to cost of sales is an amount equal to the sum of the direct material, direct labor, and *variable* manufacturing overhead cost which is incurred in producing the item; it is the sum of those costs which would not have been incurred if an item had not been produced. Under direct costing, the cost of production is equal to the variable manufactur-

---

[4] N.A.C.A. Research Series No. 23, *Direct Costing* (New York, New York: National Association of Cost Accountants, 1953), p. 2.

EXHIBIT 13–3

Flow of Costs

Actual Cost System Utilizing Theory of "Direct Costing"

MONTH OF JANUARY						
COST OF PRODUCTION		STATEMENT OF INCOME			BALANCE SHEET AS OF JANUARY 31	
Direct Material	$10,000	Sales (8,000 units × $5.00)		$40,000	ASSETS	
Direct Labor	10,000	Cost of Goods Sold:			Current Assets:	
Manufacturing		Cost of Production (10,000 × $2.60)	$26,000			
Overhead:		Less: Inventory,			Inventory	$5,200
Variable	6,000	January 31 (2,000 × 2.60)	5,200			
Cost of Production . .	$26,000	Cost of Goods Sold (8,000 × 2.60)		20,800		
		Manufacturing Margin		$19,200		
		Less: Variable Operating Expenses		—		
Unit Cost of Production:		Marginal Income		$19,200		
$26,000 ÷ 10,000 units = $2.60		Less: Fixed Expenses:				
		Fixed Manufacturing Overhead . . .	$ 4,000			
		Fixed Operating Expenses	5,000	9,000		
		Net Operating Income		$10,200		

EXHIBIT 13–3 (*Continued*)

MONTH OF FEBRUARY

COST OF PRODUCTION

Direct Material	$ 5,000
Direct Labor	5,000
Manufacturing Overhead:	
Variable	3,000
Cost of Production ..	$13,000

Unit Cost of Production:
$13,000 ÷ 5,000 units = $2.60

STATEMENT OF INCOME

Sales (4,000 units × $5.00)			$20,000
Cost of Goods Sold:			
Inventory, Feb. 1	(2,000 × $2.60)	$ 5,200	
Cost of Production	(5,000 × 2.60)	13,000	
Cost of Goods Available for Sale	(7,000 × 2.60)	$18,200	
Inventory, Feb. 28	(3,000 × 2.60)	7,800	
Cost of Goods Sold	(4,000 × 2.60)		10,400
Manufacturing Margin			$ 9,600
Less: Variable Operating Expenses ..			—
Marginal Income			$ 9,600
Less: Fixed Expenses:			
Fixed Manufacturing Overhead ...		$ 4,000	
Fixed Operating Expenses		5,000	9,000
Net Operating Income			$ 600

BALANCE SHEET AS OF FEBRUARY 28

ASSETS

Current Assets:	
Inventory	$7,800

ing costs incurred; the cost of production excludes all fixed manufacturing overhead costs. Direct costing is based upon the premise that fixed manufacturing overhead costs should be given the same treatment as that given to other fixed expenses. The question of whether fixed expenses belong to administration, distribution, or manufacturing is irrelevant, since they are all a function of time, and, as such, should be charged to operations during the period in which they are incurred. Following this line of thinking, fixed manufacturing overhead costs are removed from cost of production, inventory, and cost of sales. They are deducted currently on the income statement in a manner like the deduction for the fixed administrative and marketing expenses. The diagram shown below contrasts absorption costing with direct costing by showing the composition, calculation, and flow of cost of the same unit under both costing methods.

Exhibit 13–3 shows how direct costing affects the flow of costs and related financial statements. Notice that none of the fixed manufacturing overhead costs are included in the cost of production, cost of sales, or inventory in either January or February. Instead, the $4,000 of fixed manufacturing overhead cost is deducted each month from marginal income on the statement of income. Marginal income is the difference between the revenue from sales and the variable costs of producing and selling the item sold. The relationship between marginal income and sales

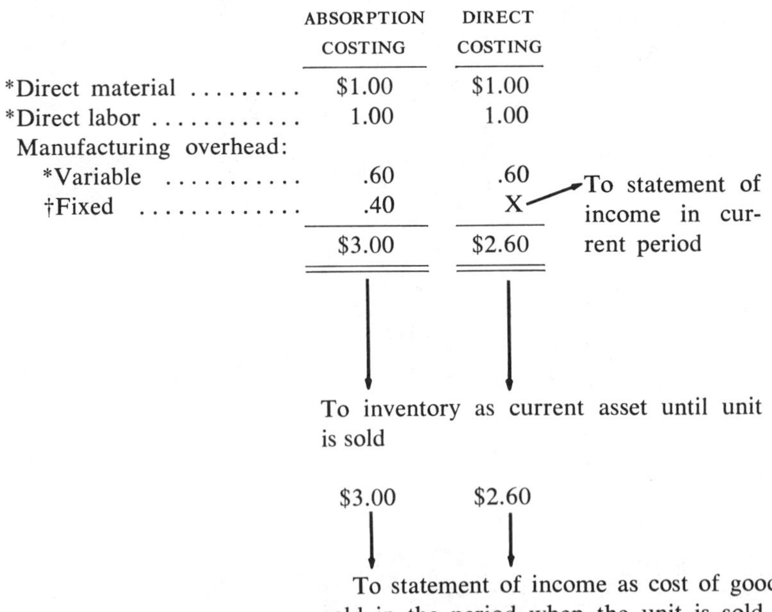

* Function of Production
† Function of time

income cannot be changed by volume; it can only be changed by different variable costs or selling prices. For example, it is 48 percent in January when 8,000 units are sold, and it is 48 percent in February when only 4,000 units are sold. Contrast this stability in the percentage of marginal income with the percentages of gross margin in Exhibit 13–1, which were vulnerable to distortion by volume fluctuations. Observe that the amount of marginal income varies in direct proportion to sales volume, while the amount of gross margin is affected by both sales volume and production volume. Notice also that unit costs remain constant regardless of the volume of activity. Consequently, no idle plant costs can be included in the inventory on the balance sheet. Clearly, the inclusion of direct costing in a cost system rectifies the confusion created by a changing volume of activity. Moreover, the marginal income information provided by direct costing is particularly useful to management in profit planning. For example, the 48 percent relationship between marginal income and sales in Exhibit 13–3 means that each dollar of sales contributes 48¢ toward covering total fixed costs. It follows that when the total fixed costs of $9,000 are divided by the 48¢ contributed by each sales dollar, a break-even point of $18,750 is readily ascertained. It should be pointed out, however, that while direct costing provides much useful information, it has certain disadvantages.

This chapter has presented an introductory coverage of manufacturing (cost) accounting. The attention of those having greater interest in this area is directed to one or more of the many books which deal exclusively with the subject of cost accounting.

QUESTIONS AND PROBLEMS

13–1. Identify the inventory of a manufacturing concern that comes closest to displaying characteristics ordinarily associated with the inventory of a trading concern. Explain.

13–2. Name and describe the three elements of manufacturing costs included in the cost of finished goods.

13–3. What are the two distinct types of manufacturing operations? How are manufacturing costs accumulated under each type of operation?

13–4. What do you consider to be the chief difference between service departments and producing departments? What is the accounting problem that is created by this difference? How may this accounting problem be solved?

13–5. Why do many manufacturing concerns employ predetermined manufacturing overhead rates? What is the major accounting problem created through the use of predetermined manufacturing overhead rates? How may this accounting problem be solved?

13–6. Identify four methods or bases used in applying or allocating manufacturing overhead expenses. What are the advantages and disadvantages of each method?
(Adapted from Uniform CPA Examination)

13–7. "Direct costing is an accounting concept, not an accounting system." Comment.

13–8. What are the basic differences between absorption costing and direct costing?

13–9. "Timing is the essential difference between absorption costing and direct costing." In what way?

13–10. The following facts were taken from the books and records of Charlie Cooper Company as of December 31, 1974:

Cash	$ 10,000
Accounts Receivable	15,000
Inventory, Raw Materials, 1/1/74	3,000
Inventory, Work in Process, 1/1/74	2,000
Inventory, Finished Goods, 1/1/74	4,000
Inventory, Raw Materials, 12/31/74	6,000
Inventory, Work in Process, 12/31/74	1,000
Inventory, Finished Goods, 12/31/74	2,000
Depreciation of Plant and Equipment	5,000
Direct Labor	25,000
Indirect Labor	3,000
Factory Supplies Used	3,000
Light, Heat and Power—Factory	4,000
Repairs to Machinery	600
Sales Salaries	9,000
Capital Stock	106,000
Retained Earnings, 1/1/74	15,800
Sales	120,000
Sales Returns and Allowances	1,700
Sales Discounts	500
Purchases, Raw Materials	60,000
Purchase Discounts	1,200
Transportation In	1,500
Retained Earnings, 12/31/74	?
Plant and Equipment	100,000
Accumulated Depreciation of Plant and Equipment	15,000
Shipping Expenses	1,200

Advertising	500
Administrative Salaries	8,000
Office Expenses	1,000
Dividends Declared	-0-

Required

Prepare the following:

a. Statement of Cost of Goods Manufactured for the year ended December 31, 1974.

b. Statement of Income for the year ended December 31, 1974. Show clearly the determination of the cost of goods sold either in the body of the statement or by an attached schedule.

c. Statement of Retained Earnings for the year ended December 31, 1974.

d. Balance Sheet as of December 31, 1974.

13–11. Ratliff Manufacturing Company manufactures and sells product "QUAD." The following facts were taken from the books and records on December 31, 1974:

Inventory of Raw Materials, 1/1/74	$ 12,000
Inventory of Work in Process, 1/1/74	14,000
Inventory of Finished Goods, 1/1/74	10,000
Plant and Equipment	450,000
Sales	440,000
Sales Returns and Allowances	4,000
Purchases of Raw Materials	242,000
Purchase Returns and Allowances	2,000
Purchase Discounts	800
Transportation In	6,000
Inventory of Raw Materials, 12/31/74	15,000
Inventory of Goods in Process, 12/31/74	8,000
Direct Labor	102,000
Indirect Labor	12,000
Light, Heat and Power—Factory	10,000
Repairs to Machinery	1,000
Factory Supplies Used	6,000
Miscellaneous Factory Expenses	2,000
Advertising	1,200
Transportation Out	2,000
Sales Salaries	36,000
Travel and Entertainment	1,400
Administrative Salaries	20,000
Office Expenses	4,400
Inventory of Finished Goods, 12/31/74	18,000
Depreciation of Plant and Equipment	9,000

Required

a. Statement of Cost of Goods Manufactured for the year ended December 31, 1974.

b. Statement of Income through the gross margin on sales. Show clearly the determination of the cost of goods sold.

13–12. The Roberts Manufacturing Company has three producing departments—A, B, C—and two service departments—maintenance and factory office. The company has been using a single manufacturing overhead cost rate. The management has been aware of the deficiencies of using such a rate and is now interested in developing departmental manufacturing overhead rates. Manufacturing overhead costs direct to departments for the period ending December 31, 1974 are:

		PRODUCING DEPARTMENTS			SERVICE DEPARTMENTS	
DIRECT COSTS	TOTAL	DEPT. A	DEPT. B	DEPT. C	MAINTE-NANCE	FACTORY OFFICE
Indirect labor .	$54,000	$5,000	$11,000	$10,000	$15,400	$12,600
Foremen salaries	25,000	2,700	6,000	5,000	5,500	5,800
Depreciation—equipment ..	6,000	2,000	1,000	2,000	800	200
Indirect material	3,000	1,100	900	500	200	300
Compensation insurance ...	1,000	100	200	200	300	200
Telephone	300					300

Manufacturing overhead costs that require allocation are:

Superintendent's salary	$12,000
Rent	15,000
Power	12,000
Light	1,000
Fire Insurance—equipment	2,000

The following data are available:

		PRODUCING DEPARTMENTS			SERVICE DEPARTMENTS	
FACTOR	AMOUNT	DEPT. A	DEPT. B	DEPT. C	MAINTE-NANCE	FACTORY OFFICE
Square footage .	30,000	6,000	10,000	9,000	2,000	3,000
No. of employees	120	20	50	30	10	10
Equipment cost	$ 50,000	$20,000	$ 5,000	$22,500	$1,000	$1,500
Horsepower hours	60,000	25,000	10,000	20,000	5,000	none
Maintenance hours	5,460	2,400	460	2,600		
Kilowatt hours .	5,000	2,000	500	2,000	300	200
Direct labor hours	240,000	50,000	100,000	90,000		

Most of the efforts of the Factory Office Department are devoted to records concerning employees. The Maintenance Department does not serve the Factory Office Department.

Required

a. Prepare a manufacturing overhead distribution sheet distributing, where applicable, service departments to appropriate service and/or producing departments.

b. Calculate the departmental manufacturing overhead costing rates per direct labor hour.

c. Compare the use of departmental manufacturing overhead rates with the practice of using a single manufacturing overhead rate for the Roberts Manufacturing Company.

(Adapted from Uniform CPA Examination)

13–13. Malandro Manufacturing Company manufactures and sells product "A." The following facts were taken from their books and records as of December 31, 1974:

Cash	$ 36,000
Accounts Receivable	72,000
Inventory of Raw Materials, 1/1/74	12,000
Inventory of Work in Process, 1/1/74	14,000
Inventory of Finished Goods, 1/1/74	10,000
Inventory of Raw Materials, 12/31/74	16,000
Inventory of Work in Process, 12/31/74	8,000
Inventory of Finished Goods, 12/31/74	18,000
Plant and Machinery	360,000
Accumulated Depreciation on Plant and Machinery	46,000
Accounts Payable	15,700
Accrued Taxes Payable	300
Capital Stock	400,000
Retained Earnings, 1/1/74	67,200
Sales	440,000
Sales Returns and Allowances	4,000
Purchases of Raw Materials	242,000
Transportation In	6,000
Purchase Returns and Allowances	2,000
Direct Labor	100,000
Indirect Labor	10,000
Property Taxes—Factory	2,000
Depreciation on Plant and Machinery	18,000
Light, Heat and Power	10,000
Repairs to Machinery	1,000
Payroll Taxes—Factory	6,000
Factory Supplies Used	4,000

Advertising	1,200
Transportation Out	2,000
Salesmen's Salaries	34,000
Payroll Taxes (Selling 2,000; Office 1,400)	3,400
Office Salaries	20,000
Office Expenses	4,000
Loss on Sale of Machinery	400
Gain on Sale of Equipment	800

Note: Apportion Light, Heat and Power as follows:
60% to manufacturing
20% to selling
20% to office

Required

Prepare the following:

a. Statement of Cost of Goods Manufactured for the year ended December 31, 1974.

b. Statement of Income and Retained Earnings for the year ended December 31, 1974.

c. Balance Sheet as of December 31, 1974.

13–14. Bryan Manufacturing Company manufactures and sells a small electric motor. From the company's books and other records, the following data were taken on December 31, 1974:

	JAN. 1, 1974	DEC. 31, 1974
Inventory of Raw Materials	$16,000	$ 18,500
Inventory of Goods in Process	12,500	18,500
Inventory of Finished Goods	24,000	?
Sales @ $30 each		533,250
Sales Returns		4,500
Cost of Goods Sold		370,125
Direct Labor		140,000
Factory Expenses, Miscellaneous		7,000
Indirect Labor		42,000
Purchases, Raw Materials		162,400
Purchase Returns and Allowances		1,400
Freight In, Raw Materials		1,500
Depreciation of Plant and Equipment		19,000
Heat, Light and Power—Factory		21,000
Indirect Materials		16,000

Note: The unit cost of production in 1973 was $20. On December 31, 1974, the inventory of finished goods included

200 units produced in 1973 and 12½ per cent of the units produced in 1974.

Required

a. Statement of Cost of Production (Cost of Goods Manufactured) for the year 1974.

b. Statement of Income as far as gross margin on sales. State the method of costing used for the inventory of finished goods (FIFO, LIFO, or specific identification).

13–15. Estes Company manufactures and sells a large electric toy. From the company's books and other records, the following data are taken on December 31, 1974:

Inventory of Finished Goods, January 1, 1974	$ 72,000
Royalties Paid	18,000
Sales Allowances	2,000
Sales Returns	12,000
Sales	660,000
Inventory of Finished Goods, December 31, 1974 .	?
Cost of Production	468,000

The inventory of finished goods on hand January 1, 1974, totaled 6,000 units, of which 600 still remain on hand at the end of 1974. A royalty of $.50 is paid the holder of the basic patent for every toy manufactured. The selling price of each electric toy is $20, and all sales returns are at the same price.

Required

a. Determine the cost of the inventory of finished goods as of December 31, 1974. Show all computations. (Assume specific identification method.)

b. Prepare a Statement of Income through gross profit on sales.

13–16. E. Scaries Manufacturing Company started business January 1, 1974. The financial statements, books, and other records disclosed the following information at December 31, 1974:

Cost of Goods Manufactured	$300,000
Net Income for the Year	$ 40,000
Number of finished units produced in 1974 ..	20,000 units
Number of units in the December 31, 1974, inventory of finished goods, all of which were produced in 1974	1,500 units

There was no inventory of work in process at December 31, 1974.

Upon audit of the books, you discover that $2,000 of Depreciation on Sales Equipment was included in manufacturing overhead as a cost of production. This $2,000 item appeared only in the statement of Cost of Goods Manufactured. No other errors were made by the Company.

Required

Compute the correct net income for the year 1974.

13–17. Capatch Production Corporation prepared the statement of income shown below (with the cost of production data incorporated therein instead of being shown as a separate statement) at the end of its first year in business.

The inventory of work in process at December 31 consists of $7,000 of direct materials, $10,000 of direct labor, and $8,000 of manufacturing overhead expenses. The amount of manufacturing overhead expenses applicable to the work in process inventory has been determined by the direct labor dollar method of apportionment.

CAPATCH PRODUCTION CORPORATION

Statement of Income
For the Year Ended December 31, 1974

Sales (47,000 units at $10 each)		$470,000
Less—Cost of Goods Sold:		
Cost of Production		
Direct Material	$120,000	
Direct Labor	100,000	
Manufacturing Overhead Expenses	80,000	
Charges to Production	$300,000	
Inventory, Work in Process, December 31	25,000	
Cost of Production	$275,000	
Inventory, Finished Goods, December 31	16,500	
Cost of Goods Sold		258,500
Gross Margin on Sales		$211,500
Marketing Expenses	$ 60,000	
Administrative Expenses	40,000	100,000
Net Income for the Year before Income Taxes		$111,500

Required

a. 50,000 units of finished goods were produced in 1974, of which 3,000 remain in inventory at December 31. Show how the $16,500 inventory amount was computed.

b. Show how the $8,000 amount of manufacturing overhead expenses applicable to the work in process inventory was determined.

c. As a step toward "direct costing," the corporation decides to remove the depreciation of plant and equipment ($20,000) from manufacturing overhead expenses and to charge it off in its entirety in the same manner as all marketing and administrative expenses. Prepare a revised statement of income for 1974.

d. Obviously, a portion of the $40,000 of administrative expenses is the result of administrative supervision of the manufacturing division of the business. Explain why many companies often make no attempt to prorate some allocable share of such expenses back to the manufacturing division as additional "manufacturing overhead expense."

13–18. XYZ Corporation is a small manufacturing company producing a highly flammable cleaning fluid. On May 31, 1974, the company had a fire which completely destroyed the in-process inventory.

After the fire a physical inventory was taken. The raw materials were valued at $30,000, the finished goods at $60,000, and supplies at $5,000.

The inventories on January 1, 1974, consisted of:

Raw materials	$ 15,000
Work in process	50,000
Finished goods	70,000
Supplies	2,000
	$137,000

A review of the accounts showed that the sales and gross profit for the last five years were:

	SALES	GROSS PROFIT
1969	$300,000	$ 86,200
1970	320,000	102,400
1971	330,000	108,900
1972	250,000	62,500
1973	280,000	84,000

The sales for the first five months of 1974 were $150,000. Raw material purchases were $50,000. Freight on purchases was $5,000.

Direct labor for the five months was $40,000; for the past five years manufacturing overhead was 50 percent of direct labor.

Required

Compute the value of inventory lost.
(Adapted from Uniform CPA Examination)

13–19. The Walsch Company manufactures a single product, a mechanical device known as "Klebo." The company maintains a process cost type of accounting system. The manufacturing operation is as follows:

Material K, a metal, is stamped to form a part which is assembled with one of the purchased parts "X." The unit is then machined and cleaned, after which it is assembled with two units of part "Y" to form the finished device known as a "Klebo." Spray priming and enameling is the final operation.

Time and motion studies indicate that of the total time required for the manufacture of a unit the first operation required 25 percent of the labor cost, the first assembly an additional 25 percent, machining and cleaning 12.5 percent, the second assembly 25 percent, and painting 12.5 percent. Manufacturing expense is considered to follow the same pattern by operations as does labor.

The following data are presented to you as of October 31, 1974, the end of the first month of operation:

Material K purchased—100,000 lbs.	$25,000
Part X purchased—80,000 units	16,000
Part Y purchased—150,000 units	15,000
Primer and enamel used	1,072
Direct labor—cost	45,415
Manufacturing expenses	24,905

	UNIT QUANTITY
Units finished and sent to finished goods warehouse	67,000
Units assembled but not painted	5,000
Units ready for the second assembly	3,000
Inventories at the end of the month:	
Finished units	7,500
Material K (lbs.)	5,800
Part X (units of part X)	5,000
Part Y (units of part Y)	6,000
Klebos in process (units)	8,000

Required

a. A schedule of equivalent labor production.

b. A schedule of total and unit costs incurred in production for:
   1. Each kind of material.
   2. Labor cost.
   3. Manufacturing expense.
   4. Total cost of production.

c. A schedule of detailed material, labor, and manufacturing costs assigned to the units left in process.

(Adapted from Uniform CPA Examination)

13–20. Match each of the ten (a through j) items with the *one* term listed below (1 through 18) which *most specifically* identifies the cost concept indicated parenthetically.

(*Caution:* An item of cost may be classified in several ways, depending on the purpose of the classification. For example, the commissions on sales of a proposed new product line might be classified as *direct, variable,* and *marginal,* among others. However, if such costs are being considered specifically as to the amount of *cash outlay* required in making a decision concerning adoption of the new line, the commissions are *out-of-pocket costs.* That would be the most *appropriate* answer in the context.)

On your answer sheet list the letters a through j. Indicate your choice of answer for each item by *printing* beside the item letter the *number* which identifies the term you select.

TERM	TERM	TERM
1. By-product costs	8. Imputed costs	14. Prime costs
2. Common or joint costs	9. Differential cost	15. Replacement costs
3. Controllable costs	10. Indirect costs	16. Standard costs
4. Direct costs	11. Opportunity costs	17. Sunk costs
5. Estimated costs	12. Original cost	18. Variable costs
6. Fixed costs	13. Out-of-pocket costs	
7. Historical cost		

ITEMS

a. The management of a corporation is considering replacing a machine which is operating satisfactorily with a more efficient new model. *Depreciation* on the cost of the existing machine is omitted from the data used in judging the proposal, because it has little or no significance with respect to such decision. (The omitted cost.)

b. In *public utility accounting,* regulatory bodies require that assets be carried at the cost to those owners who *first devoted the asset to public use.* (The cost described.)

c. One of the problems encountered by a bank in attempting to establish the cost of a *commercial-deposit* account is the fact that many facilities and services are shared by many revenue-producing activities. (Costs of the shared facilities and services.)

d. A company declined an offer received to rent one of its warehouses and elected to use the warehouse for storage of extra raw materials to insure uninterrupted production. Storage cost has been charged with *the monthly amount of the rental offered.* (This cost is known as ?)

e. A manufacturing company excludes all "fixed" costs from its valuation of inventories, assigning to inventory only *applicable portions of costs which vary with changes in volume of product.* (The term employed for the *variable* costs in this context by advocates of this costing procedure.)

f. The sales department urges an increase in production of a product and, as part of the data presented in support of its proposal, indicates the *total additional cost involved for the volume-level it proposes.* (The increase in total cost.)

g. A CPA takes exception to his client's inclusion in the cost of a fixed asset of an "interest" charge based on *the client's own funds* invested in the asset. The client states the charge was intended to obtain a cost comparable to that which would have been the case if funds had been borrowed to finance the acquisition. (The term which describes such *interest* charges.)

h. The "direct" production cost of a unit includes those portions of factory overhead, *labor and materials* which are obviously traceable directly to the unit. (The term used to specify the last *two* of the named components.)

i. Calling upon the special facilities of the production, planning, personnel, and other departments, a firm estimated its future unit cost of production and used this cost (analyzed by cost elements) in its accounts. (The term used to specify this scientifically predetermined estimate.)

j. A chemical manufacturing company produces three products originating in a common initial material mix. Each product gains a separate identity part way through processing and requires additional processing after the "split." Each contributes a significant share of revenue. The company plans to spread the costs up to the "split" among the three products by the use of relative market

values. (The term used to specify the costs accumulated up to the point of the *split.*)
(Adapted from Uniform CPA Examination)

13–21. Select the *one* answer which *best* states a logical conclusion based on the facts stated.

If a company uses a predetermined rate for application of manufacturing overhead, the volume variance is the:

a. Underapplied or overapplied fixed cost element of manufacturing overhead.

b. Underapplied or overapplied variable cost element of manufacturing overhead.

c. Difference in budgeted costs and actual costs of fixed manufacturing overhead items.

d. Difference in budgeted costs and actual costs of variable manufacturing overhead items.

e. None of the above.

(Adapted from Uniform CPA Examination)

13–22. Given below are the details pertaining to the Power Service Department.

SCHEDULE OF HORSEPOWER-HOURS

	PRODUCING DEPARTMENTS		SERVICE DEPARTMENTS	
	A	B	X	Y
Needed at capacity production	10,000	20,000	12,000	8,000
Used during the month of April	8,000	13,000	7,000	6,000

During the month of April the expenses of operating the Power Service Department amounted to $9,300; of this amount, $2,500 was considered to be fixed costs.

Required

a. What dollar amounts of the Power Service Department expense should be allocated to each producing and service department?

b. What are the reasons for allocating the costs of one service department to other service departments as well as to producing departments?

(Adapted from Uniform CPA Examination)

13–23. The Incredible Gadget Corp. manufactures a single product. Its operations are a continuing process carried on in two departments—the

Machining department and the Assembly and finishing department. *Materials are added to the product in each department without increasing the number of units produced.*

In the month of May 1956, the records showed that 75,000 units were put in production in the machining department. Of these units, 60,000 were completed and transferred to assembly and finishing, and 15,000 were left in process with all materials applied but with only ⅓ of the required labor and overhead.

In the assembly and finishing department 50,000 units were completed and transferred to the finished stock room during the month. Nine thousand units were in process on May 31, 1,000 units having been destroyed in production with no scrap value. All required materials had been applied to the 9,000 units and ⅔ of the labor and overhead, but only ½ of the prescribed material and labor had been applied to the 1,000 units lost in process.

There was no work-in-process in either department at the first of the month.

The cost of units lost in production should be treated as additional overhead in the assembly and finishing department.

Cost records showed the following charges during the month:

	MATERIALS	LABOR	OVERHEAD
Machining department	$120,000	$ 87,100	$39,000
Assembly and finishing department	41,650	101,700	56,810*

* Does not include the cost of spoiled units

Required

a. Prepare in good form a statement showing the unit cost for the month.

b. Prepare a schedule showing the details of the work-in-process inventory in each department.

(Adapted from Uniform CPA Examination)

13–24. On a lined sheet of paper alphabetize the first ten lines from a through j. Select the graph which matches the alphabetized factory cost or expense data and write the number identifying the graph on the appropriate alphabetized line.

The vertical axes of the graphs below represent *total* dollars of expense and the horizontal axes represent volume of production. In each case the zero point is at the intersction of the two axes. The graphs may be used more than once.

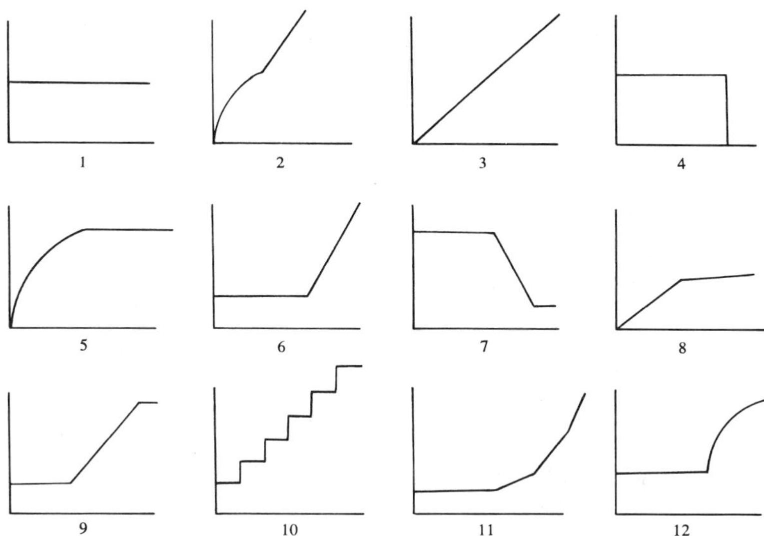

Required

a. Depreciation of equipment, where the amount of depreciation charged is computed by the machine hours method.

b. Electricity bill—a flat fixed charge, plus a variable cost after a certain number of kilowatt hours are used.

c. City water bill, which is computed as follows:

First 1,000,000 gallons or less	$1,000 flat fee
Next 10,000 gallons	.003 per gallon used
Next 10,000 gallons	.006 per gallon used
Next 10,000 gallons	.009 per gallon used
etc., etc., etc.	

d. Cost of lubricant for machines, where cost per unit decreases with each pound of lubricant used (for example, if one pound is used, the cost is $10.00; if two pounds are used, the cost is $19.98; if three pounds are used, the cost is $29.94; with a minimum cost per pound of $9.25).

e. Depreciation of equipment, where the amount is computed by the straight-line method. When the depreciation rate was established it was anticipated that the obsolescence factor would be greater than the wear and tear factor.

f. Rent on a factory building donated by the city, where the agreement calls for a fixed fee payment unless 200,000 man-hours are worked, in which case no rent need be paid.

g. Salaries of repairmen, where one repairman is needed for every 1,000 hours of machine hours or less (i.e., 0 to 1,000 hours requires one repairman, 1,001 to 2,000 hours requires two repairmen, etc.).

h. Federal unemployment compensation taxes for the year, where labor force is constant in number throughout year (average annual salary is $6,000 per worker).

i. Cost of raw material used.

j. Rent on a factory building donated by county, where agreement calls for rent of $100,000 less $1 for each direct labor hour worked in excess of 200,000 hours, but minimum rental payment of $20,000 must be paid.

(Adapted from Uniform CPA Examination)

13–25. The Baker Manufacturing Company maintains a job order cost system.

On January 1, 1972, the only work in process was job 1270 on which the following costs had been accumulated:

Direct material	$15,000
Direct labor	25,000
Manufacturing overhead	10,000
Total	$50,000

On the same date, the company's books showed a raw materials inventory of $380,000 and job 1269 which had been completed at a cost of $74,000.

During the month of January the manufacturing data are:

1.

JOB NO.	DIRECT MATERIAL	DIRECT LABOR
1270	$ 60,000	$200,000
1271	100,000	300,000
1272	110,000	220,000
	$270,000	$720,000

2. In addition $25,000 of raw materials are issued as indirect material, indirect laborers earn $75,000, and the factory superintendent earns $5,000.
3. Manufacturing overhead incurred exclusive of material issues and factory payroll costs:

Power	$30,000
Depreciation on plant and equipment	95,000
Maintenance	25,000
Insurance	15,000
Taxes	10,000
Miscellaneous	5,000

4. Manufacturing overhead is applied to jobs by use of a predetermined rate of 40% of direct labor costs. Overapplied or underapplied manufacturing overhead is closed to cost of goods sold.
5. Jobs 1270 and 1271 are completed during the month. Jobs 1269 and 1270 are shipped and billed to customers during January at 200% of the cost of production.

Required

a. Determine, in itemized form, the individual total costs of each of the jobs as of the end of January.

b. Calculate the dollar amount for each of the three inventories on January 31, 1972.

c. Prepare the Statement of Cost of Goods Manufactured for the period ending January 31, 1972.

d. Prepare the Statement of Income through the gross margin on sales for the month of January.

13–26. You have been engaged to install a cost system for Martin Company. Your investigation of the manufacturing operations of the business discloses these facts:

1. The company makes a line of lighting fixtures and lamps. The material cost of any particular item ranges from 15 percent to 60 percent of total factory cost, depending on the kind of metal and fabric used in making it.

2. The business is subject to wide cyclical fluctuations since the sales volume follows new housing construction.

3. About 60 percent of the manufacturing is normally done in the first quarter of the year.

4. For the whole plant the wage rates range from $1.25 to $3.75 an hour. However, within each of the eight individual departments, the spread between the high and low wage rate is less than 5 percent.

5. Each of the products made uses all eight of the manufacturing departments but not proportionately.

6. Within the individual manufacturing departments, manufacturing overhead ranges from 30 percent to 80 percent of conversion cost.

Required

Based on the above information, you are to prepare a statement or letter for the president of the company explaining whether in its cost system Martin Company should use:

a. A normal manufacturing overhead rate or an actual manufacturing overhead rate?

b. An overall manufacturing overhead rate or a departmental manufacturing overhead rate?

c. A method of manufacturing overhead distribution based on: direct labor hours; direct labor cost; or prime cost?

Include the *reasons* supporting *each* of your *three recommendations*. (Adapted from Uniform CPA Examination)

14

The Accounting Cycle—Recording and Accumulating Procedures

The reader should review Chapter 1 of this book where accounting is described as a process of recording, classifying, and summarizing in terms of money, transactions and events having a financial character, and interpreting the results thereof. Although this description identifies four facets of accounting, the emphasis throughout this book to this point has been on the interpretative or "how to use" aspect. The three remaining facets refer to the "how to do" aspect of accounting. They are described and illustrated in this chapter and the following one. These two chapters concentrate on the techniques and procedures which constitute the methodology for the "how to do" area of accounting.

THE ACCOUNTING EQUATION

The use of various types of economic resources is essential to the operation of a business enterprise. Some of these are publicly owned and cannot be reserved for the exclusive use of a firm. Others constitute resources whose use can be controlled because they are owned by an individual enterprise. If these latter resources can be measured in monetary terms, they comprise the financial resources of the enterprise to which they belong. For every enterprise, the sum of the financial resources owned is equal to the sum of the ownership rights associated with these resources. Every enterprise is faced with the problem of obtaining accurate information about the nature and extent of its financial resources and the ownership rights related thereto. Usually this problem is solved best by a double-entry system of record keeping which employs a methodology that provides such information readily and economically.

The financial resources or properties *owned* by a business are called *assets*. Cash, receivables, merchandise, materials, supplies, land, building, automobiles, office equipment, store equipment and fixtures, machinery, tools, patent rights, and copyrights are common examples of assets.

The rights to these assets or properties are called *equities*. These equities are of two distinct types, liabilities and ownership or capital. The equities (or rights) of the creditors constitute an interest in the assets of the enterprise; such equities represent the debts of the enterprise and are called *liabilities*. The equities of the owners are called *owners' equity* (or *capital*), and they represent the residual interest in the assets of the enterprise. The relationship between the assets and equities, as shown in Chapter 2, is expressed by the following equation:

Assets = Creditors' Equity + Owners' Equity

or

Assets = Liabilities + Capital

The preceding equation is known as the accounting equation. It shows the assets and equity relationships which exist at any point in time and is, therefore, affected by every financial transaction of an enterprise. As is discussed commencing with page 458, items of revenue earned and expenses incurred by an enterprise during a fiscal period (see also Chapter 3) affect the above equation even though their effect may not be readily apparent.

TRANSACTIONS AND THEIR EFFECT ON THE ACCOUNTING EQUATION

All transactions can be stated in terms of their effect on the elements of the accounting equation. Every transaction affects the equation in some manner, but equilibrium always exists.

When an enterprise is established, the contribution of assets, less any debts assumed by the enterprise, equals the owners' equity. Thus, the initial accounting equation is formed when an enterprise is formed. For [illegible]le, the ABC Corporation, a trucking concern, is formed on January [illegible]4, and issues 10,000 shares of $10 par value stock for cash of [illegible]0. In this transaction there is an increase in an asset, specifically [illegible]d an increase in owners' equity, specifically Capital Stock. The A[illegible]poration's initial accounting equation would appear as follows:

Assets	=	Liabilities + Owners' Equity
Cash	=	Capital Stock
[illegible]00,000	=	100,000

A ba[illegible]eet, if prepared at this point, would appear as follows:

ABC CORPORATION

Balance Sheet

January 2, 1974

[illegible]		EQUITIES	
Cash	$100,000	Capital Stock	$100,000

On January 3, [illegible]rporation purchases land and a building for $45,000 cash; $5,0[illegible] land, $40,000 for the building. As a result of this transaction, [illegible] Land and the asset Building increase and the asset Cash decre[illegible] items in the equation prior to this transaction, the transaction, [illegible] new balances after the transaction are as follows:

Assets	=	Liabilities + Owners' Equity
Cash + Land + Bu[illegible]	=	Capital Stock
100,000	=	100,000
−45,000 + 5,000 + 40,0[illegible]		
55,000 + 5,000 + 40,00[illegible]	=	100,000

A balance sheet prepared a[illegible]ime would appear as the first balance sheet shown on page 456.

On January 4, ABC Corp[illegible] purchases $20,000 of equipment; paying $15,000 cash and agre[illegible] pay the balance by a certain date in the future. The effect of this [illegible]ction is an increase of $20,000 in the asset Equipment, a decreas[illegible]15,000 in the asset Cash and an increase of $5,000 in the liabil[illegible]counts Payable. The items in the equation prior to this transactio[illegible]ransaction, and the new balances after the transaction are as follow[illegible]

Cash	+ Land	+ Building	+ Equipment	=	Accounts Payable	+ Capital Stock
55,000	+ 5,000	+ 40,000		=		100,000
−15,000			+ 20,000	=	+ 5,000	
40,000	+ 5,000	+ 40,000	+ 20,000	=	+ 5,000	+ 100,000

(Assets = Liabilities + Owners' Equity)

ABC CORPORATION

Balance Sheet

January 3, 1974

ASSETS		EQUITIES	
Cash	$ 55,000	Capital Stock	$100,000
Land	5,000		
Building	40,000		
Total Assets	$100,000	Total Equities	$100,000

A balance sheet prepared at this time would appear as follows:

ABC CORPORATION

Balance Sheet

January 4, 1974

ASSETS		EQUITIES	
Cash	$ 40,000	Liabilities:	
Land	5,000	Accounts Payable	$ 5,000
Building	40,000	Owners' Equity:	
Equipment	20,000	Capital Stock	100,000
Total Assets	$105,000	Total Equities	$105,000

Every transaction affects at least two items. For example, the issuance of capital stock for cash (the January 2 transaction) affects the asset Cash and the owners' equity item of Capital Stock. The purchase of land and building for cash (the January 3 transaction) affects the assets Land, Building and Cash. The purchase of equipment with a partial payment (the January 4 transaction) affects the assets Equipment and Cash and the liability Accounts Payable.

As illustrated above, the effect of each transaction can be shown by the use of the accounting equation, and financial statements could be revised after each transaction. Such a method, however, will not expediently record transactions as they occur; nor does management need new financial statements after *each* transaction. Instead, ledger accounts are used to record transactions properly and expediently as they occur; the nature of this system is cumulative so that periodically the *net* effect of all transactions on assets, liabilities and owners' equity (including revenue and expense items) can be determined.

ACCOUNTS

To provide for the cumulative compilation of the effect of the changes (both increases and decreases) in individual assets and equities, a separate *account* is kept for each item shown on the financial statement (see Chapters 2 and 3 for the typical items shown on financial statements). These accounts are maintained in a book or file called a ledger and thus are commonly referred to as ledger accounts.[1] The simplest form of an account is a horizontal line with the space below the line equally divided by a vertical line. Increases are recorded on one side and decreases are recorded on the other side of the vertical line. Usually each account has a separate page in a ledger.

This simplest form of an account often is called a T account because it resembles the letter T. The T account has three basic parts: (1) its name, (2) a space for recording increases, (3) a space for recording decreases. This form is illustrated below:

NAME	
Space for recording increases or decreases	Space for recording increases or decreases
DEBIT SIDE	CREDIT SIDE

The left side of the account is called the debit side; the right side of the account is called the credit side. Amounts entered on the left side of an account are called debits to the account and amounts entered on the right side of an account are called credits to the account. If the total of the debits to an account exceeds the total of the credits, the account has a *debit balance.* If the total of the credits to an account exceeds the total of the debits, the account has a *credit balance.*

[1] For a detailed discussion and illustration of specialized ledgers see Appendix B.

DEBIT AND CREDIT PROCEDURE

Every transaction affects at least two accounts. These transactions are recognized and recorded through a system known as the double-entry method which employs the following procedure:

1. *Asset Accounts*—The ledger contains a separate account for each asset. *Increases in an asset are recorded by debits, and decreases in an asset are recorded by credits.*

2. *Liability Accounts*—The ledger contains a separate account for each liability. *Increases in a liability are recorded by credits and decreases in a liability are recorded by debits.*

3. *Owners' Equity Accounts*—The ledger contains a separate account for each item constituting owners' equity. Every item of information that appears in the balance sheet, the statement of income, and the statement of retained earnings, *other than* assets and liabilities, either reveals changes in, or already is, a capital or owners' equity item. An account is maintained for each of these items. *Increases in capital or owners' equity are recorded as credits, and decreases in capital or owners' equity are recorded as debits.* Increases in capital result primarily from additional investments by owners, and profits. Decreases in capital result primarily from losses and distribution of profits (dividends). It follows from this that any decrease in profit is recorded as a debit and any increase in profit is recorded as a credit. For example, salaries (expense) are recorded as debits and sales (revenue) are recorded as credits because expenses reduce profits and revenues increase profits.

4. When a transaction is recorded, the total of the debits must equal the total of the credits.

RECORDING TRANSACTIONS IN LEDGER ACCOUNTS

To illustrate how transactions are recorded in ledger accounts by the rules of debit and credit, the transactions shown on pages 459 and 460 for ABC Corporation are recorded in the ledger accounts on page 459.

The ledger accounts on page 459 have been grouped under the major classifications of the fundamental accounting equation. Note that the revenue account which increases owners' equity and the expense accounts which decrease owners' equity appear as subdivisions of owners' equity.

Each of the given transactions should be traced carefully through the entries shown in the ledger accounts. As an aid to the tracing pro-

ASSETS = LIABILITIES + OWNERS' EQUITY

Cash

(1)	100,000	(2)	45,000
(9)	1,200	(3)	15,000
		(4)	3,000
		(5)	1,500
		(6)	50
		(8)	400
		(10)	300
		(11)	150

Accounts Payable

		(3)	5,000

Capital Stock

		(1)	100,000

Notes Payable

		(4)	8,000

Accounts Receivable

(7)	1,800	(9)	1,200

(Revenue)

Hauling Revenue

		(7)	1,800

Taxes and Licenses

(5)	1,500		

Land

(2)	5,000		

(Expenses)

Gasoline Expense

(6)	50		

Building

(2)	40,000		

Wages Expense

(8)	400		

Equipment

(3)	20,000		

Repairs Expense

(10)	300		

Trucks

(4)	11,000		

Advertising Expense

(11)	150		

1. Cash of $100,000 was received from the sale of 10,000 shares of $10 par value stock.

2. Purchased land and a building for $45,000 cash; paying $5,000 for the land and $40,000 for the building.
3. Purchased $20,000 of equipment; paying $15,000 cash and agreeing to pay the balance by a certain date in the future.
4. Purchased two trucks for $11,000; paying $3,000 cash and giving a note payable for the remainder.
5. Paid $1,500 for annual taxes and licenses.
6. Paid $50 for gasoline.
7. Billed customers $1,800 for trucking jobs completed.
8. Paid wages of truck drivers, $400 (ignore payroll taxes).
9. Received cash from a customer on account, $1,200.
10. Paid $300 for repairs to a damaged truck.
11. Paid for newspaper advertising, $150.

cedure, the entries recorded in the ledger accounts are numbered so that each debit and credit can be identified readily with the transaction. In order to obtain the maximum benefit from the illustration, the reader should confirm that the proper rule of increase or decrease for each account has been followed in each instance.

THE TRIAL BALANCE

The equality of recorded debits and credits in the ledger accounts is tested periodically, generally at the end of each month. This test of the equality of debits and credits is made in the form of a trial balance. A trial balance of account *totals* could be prepared by listing the account titles along with the total of the debits and the total of the credits for each account in the ledger. However, it is the balance of each account that is needed for the preparation of financial statements. For example, a balance sheet for the ABC Corporation prepared on January 31, 1974, from the ledger accounts shown on page 459 would show a cash *balance* of $35,800, not the total cash debits of $101,200 and the total cash credits of $65,400. Consequently, a trial balance of account balances is more useful and more widely preferred. A trial balance is a two column schedule which lists the names and balances of all the accounts in the order in which they appear in the ledger; the debit balances are listed in the left hand money column and the credit balances in the right hand money column. If the totals of the two columns agree it is proof that the ledger accounts are "in balance." A trial balance taken from the ledger of the ABC Corporation at the end of January appears on page 461.

ABC CORPORATION

Trial Balance
January 31, 1974

	Debit Balances	Credit Balances
Cash	$ 35,800	
Accounts Receivable	600	
Taxes and Licenses	1,500	
Land	5,000	
Building	40,000	
Equipment	20,000	
Trucks	11,000	
Accounts Payable		$ 5,000
Notes Payable		8,000
Capital Stock		100,000
Hauling Revenue		1,800
Gasoline Expense	50	
Wages Expense	400	
Repairs Expense	300	
Advertising Expense	150	
	$114,800	$114,800

THE JOURNAL

Normally transactions are not entered directly into the ledger accounts. Instead, a record called the *journal* is used where transactions, after being analyzed into their debit and credit components, are first recorded. The journal is sometimes referred to as the book of original entry because this is where each transaction is recorded initially. The process of recording transactions in the journal is called *journalizing*. The debits and credits recorded in the journal are subsequently transferred or *posted* to the ledger accounts.

The journal contains a chronological record of all transactions and the debit and credit components of each transaction are shown, but obviously the *balance* of any particular account is not revealed. On the other hand, ledger accounts show the debits and credits to, as well as the balance of, each asset, liability, and capital account but do not provide a chronological record of all financial transactions.

There are several different kinds of journals.[2] The type and number of journals used by a particular enterprise will depend upon the nature of its operations and the size of the enterprise. The simplest form of journal is usually referred to as a general journal. Often it has only two money columns and may be used for recording all transactions in chronological order. This form is illustrated as follows:

Journal Page

Date	Description	P. R.	Debit	Credit

To illustrate the use of the journal and to illustrate additional recording and accumulating procedures, transactions of DEF Corporation for November 1974 are recorded in the journal on pages 467–70 and posted to the ledger accounts on pages 471–74.

Each of these illustrative transactions is analyzed and discussed prior to being journalized to aid the reader in developing his ability to analyze transactions so that he may properly record them following double entry rules. Tracing each analysis to the individual journal entry will help give a clear understanding of the process of journalizing. In doing so, the following points should be noted:

1. The journal page number.
2. The columnar headings and columns which are provided for the date, description of transaction, posting reference (P.R.), debit amount and credit amount.
3. The year, month and day of the transaction are entered in the date column.
4. The title of the account debited is written to the extreme left in the description column; the account title credited is written on the following line after indenting slightly in the description column.
5. The amount of the account debited is placed in the debit (money) column opposite the account title; the amount of the account credited is placed in the credit (money) column opposite the account title.
6. Explanatory comments are placed below and indented slightly to the right of the name of the last account credited in each transaction. An explanation of each transaction should be made, unless the nature of the entry is obvious from its recording. The necessity for, and extent of, explanation is a matter of judgment.

[2] For a detailed discussion and illustration of specialized journals see Appendix B.

7. A line is skipped between recorded transactions.
8. The P.R. column is used to indicate that the amounts in the journal have been transferred to the respective ledger accounts. For example, the number 1 in the P.R. column for transaction (a) indicates that the entry has been transferred to the Cash account which is account number one in the ledger.

The November transactions of the DEF Corporation are given and analyzed below:

(a) The DEF Corporation issued 10,000 shares of $10 par value stock, at par, for cash.

This transaction results in an increase in assets and an increase in owners' equity or capital. As increases in assets are recorded as debits, the Cash account is debited because this is the specific asset that is increased. As increases in owners' equity are recorded as credits, the Capital Stock account is credited because this is the specific owners' equity item that is increased.

(b) Paid City Real Estate Company one year's rent in advance, $1,200.

In this transaction, a debit to Prepaid Rent records the increase in that asset, and a credit to Cash records the decrease in that asset.

(c) Purchased office equipment from Smith & Company for cash, $1,000.

In this transaction, a debit to Office Equipment records the increase in that asset, and a credit to Cash records the decrease in that asset.

(d) Purchase of store equipment from the Jones Company for cash, $1,500.

In this transaction, a debit to Office Equipment records the increase in that asset, and a credit to Cash records the decrease in that asset.

(e) Purchased office and store supplies from B. Runser for cash, $200.

In this transaction, a debit to Supplies records the increase in that asset, and a credit to Cash records the decrease in that asset.

(f) Purchased merchandise on account from Jay Company, $5,000. Terms, 2/10, n/30.

When a purchase of merchandise is made, the Purchases account is debited. While the Merchandise Inventory account (asset) could be debited, a separate account, Purchases (expense), is used to record the cost of merchandise purchased during an accounting period. The Merchandise Inventory account (asset) is used only to reflect the cost of merchandise on hand at the end of an accounting period. It is important to note that the Purchases account is used exclusively to record current purchases of merchandise acquired for the purpose of resale. Purchases of office supplies, equipment and other items used in the business should not be debited to Purchases, but should be debited to such accounts as Office Supplies, Equipment, etc. The credit in this transaction is to the account Accounts Payable since increases in liabilities are recorded as credits. The terms of the transaction, 2/10, n/30, mean that if the invoice is paid within 10 days, a 2 percent cash discount may be deducted from the invoice upon remittance. If the invoice is not paid within the discount period (10 days), the entire bill is due and payable in 30 days. This discount is known as a cash discount.

(g) Sale of merchandise on account to Schaeffer Company, $6,000. Terms, 2/10, n/30.

The asset Accounts Receivable is increased; therefore, a debit to the Accounts Receivable account is required. The credit to the Sales account represents an increase in owners' equity or capital because sales tend to increase profits and consequently owners' equity.

(h) Paid weekly salaries, $1,000.

A debit to Salary Expense records the increase in that expense and a credit to Cash records the decrease in that asset. Payroll taxes have been ignored in this and subsequent transactions.

(i) Purchase of merchandise on account from Hart Company, $6,000. Terms, 2/10, n/30.

A debit to Purchases records the increase in that expense and a credit to Accounts Payable records the increase in that liability.

(j) Paid weekly salaries, $1,000.

A debit to Salary Expense records the increase in that expense and a credit to Cash records the decrease in that asset.

(k) Paid Jay Company invoice dated November 3.

A debit of $5,000 to Accounts Payable records the decrease in that liability. A credit of $100 to Purchase Discounts records the decrease in the cost of the merchandise acquired because payment is being made within the discount period allowed by the vendor. A credit of $4,900 to Cash records the decrease in that asset by the amount of the check issued.

The cash discounts for prompt payment from the seller's point of view are known as *sales discounts;* the purchaser refers to them as *purchase discounts.* The seller customarily views cash discounts as reductions in sales revenue and the buyer considers them as deductions from the invoice price of the purchase. Since sales discounts are reductions in revenue and reductions in revenue are recorded as debits, the amount of the discount is recorded by the seller as a debit in an account named Sales Discounts. Thus, Sales Discounts are shown as an offset to Sales in the income statement. Also, since purchase discounts are reductions in expense and reductions in expense are recorded as credits, the amount of the discount is recorded by the buyer as a credit in an account called Purchase Discounts. Thus, Purchase Discounts are shown as an offset to Purchases in the income statement. See illustrations on the Statement of Income in Chapter 3.

(l) Paid freight charges of $200 on merchandise purchased.

A debit to Transportation In records the increase in that expense and a credit to Cash records the decrease in that asset. The costs of transportation borne by the purchaser are costs of acquiring merchandise. Sometimes this transportation charge is debited directly to the Purchases account but the use of a separate account called Transportation In facilitates subsequent verification and analysis of freight costs. Where this latter treatment is followed, Transportation In is shown as an addition to Purchases in the income statement.

(m) Received payment from Schaeffer Company for invoice of November 5.

A debit of $5,880 to Cash records the increase in that asset; a debit of $120 to Sales Discounts records the decrease in revenue (net Sales); and a credit of $6,000 to Accounts Receivable records the decrease applicable to that asset. (See analysis of transaction (k) for an explanation of Sales Discounts.)

(n) Issued debit memorandum to Hart Company for $1,000.

A debit to Accounts Payable records the decrease in that liability and a credit to Purchase Returns and Allowances records the decrease in the amount originally debited to the purchases account.

When merchandise or other items purchased on account are returned or a price adjustment is requested, the purchaser usually communicates with the seller in writing. The details may be stated on a document of the debtor (purchaser) called a debit memorandum. This document is a convenient way of informing the creditor (seller) of the amount to be debited in his account on the buyer's books and the reasons therefor. Sometimes this reduction in purchases of merchandise is credited directly to the Purchases account, but the use of a separate account called Purchase Returns and Allowances facilitates subsequent verification and analysis of returns of purchases and price allowances or adjustments. Under this latter arrangement, Purchase Returns and Allowances is shown as a deduction from Purchases in the statement of income.

(o) Sold merchandise on account to Flint Corporation, $10,000. Terms, 2/10, n/30.

A debit to Accounts Receivable records the increase in that asset and a credit to Sales records the increase in revenue.

(p) Issued Credit memorandum to Flint Corporation, $1,000.

A debit to Sales Returns and Allowances records the decrease in revenue and a credit to Accounts Receivable records the decrease in that asset. If the seller agrees to a return of merchandise or an adjustment of price, he issues a credit memorandum. The credit memorandum gives rise to a reduction in Accounts Receivable and revenue. Sometimes this reduction in revenue is debited directly to the Sales account but the use of a separate account called Sales Returns and Allowances facilitates subsequent verification and analysis of sales returns and sales price allowances or adjustments. When the latter procedure is being followed, Sales Returns and Allowances is shown as a reduction from Sales in the statement of income. See illustration on the Statement of Income in Chapter 3.

(q) Paid weekly salaries, $1,000.

A debit to Salary Expense records the increase in that expense and a credit to Cash records the decrease in that asset.

(r) Paid Hart Company invoice dated November 12.

A debit to Accounts Payable records the decrease in that liability; a credit to Purchase Discounts records the decrease in cost of merchandise purchased; a credit to Cash records the decrease in that asset. It should be noted that the discount is computed on the balance of the liability after recognizing the purchase return. (Discount is equal to 2 percent of Purchases $6,000 less Purchase Returns and Allowances $1,000, or 2 percent of $5,000.)

(s) Paid weekly salaries, $1,000.

A debit to Salary Expense records the increase in that expense and a credit to Cash records the decrease in that asset.

(t) Received check from Flint Corporation for invoice dated November 16.

A debit to Cash records the increase in that asset; a debit to Sales Discounts records the decrease in revenue; and a credit to Accounts Receivable records the decrease in that asset. (Note that the discount is computed on the balance due from Flint Corporation after recognizing the sales return, or 2 percent of $9,000.)

(u) Paid utilities, $275.

A debit to the Utilities Expense records the increase in that expense and a credit to Cash records the decrease in that asset.

(v) Sold merchandise on account to Phillips Company, $8,000. Terms, 2/10, n/30.

A debit to Accounts Receivable records the increase in that asset and a credit to Sales records the increase in revenue.

(w) Purchased merchandise on account from Tool Corporation, $7,000. Terms, 2/10, n/30.

A debit to Purchases records the increase in that expense and a credit to Accounts Payable records the increase in that liability.

POSTING TO THE ACCOUNTS

After transactions are journalized, the information in the journal is transferred to the ledger accounts through a process called *posting.* This process permits the classification and accumulation of financial data in the specific accounts identified by the journal entries.

In the process of posting, the date of the transaction, the journal page number, and the amount debited or credited are entered in the appropriate columns of the account named in the journal entry. The explanation columns of an account are used primarily for special information, such as the terms of credit as in the case of purchases or sales on account. In most cases an explanation in the account may be omitted, since detailed information is provided by the explanation given in the journal entry.

In the posting process, the journal page number from which the posting is made is entered in the posting reference (P.R.) column of the account. In addition, the ledger account number to which the entry has been posted is entered in the posting reference (P.R.) column of the journal after the posting has been made. This procedure serves several purposes. In the account, the journal page will indicate where the entire transaction has been journalized. In the journal, the ledger account numbers indicate the accounts to which postings have been made. If postings are made at irregular intervals or if the bookkeeper is interrupted while posting, the posting reference in the journal will indicate which items have been posted and which remain to be posted.

The foregoing procedures are illustrated in this chapter through the journal and the ledger accounts employed for the DEF Corporation. Tracing each entry from the journal to the accounts in the ledger will help provide a clear understanding of the posting process.

Journal Page 1

Date	Description	P.R.	Debit	Credit
	(a)			
1974				
Nov. 1	Cash	1	100,000	
	Capital Stock	30		100,000
	Issued 10,000 shares of $10 par value stock, at par			
	(b)			
1	Prepaid Rent	7	1,200	
	Cash	1		1,200
	Paid City Real Estate Company one year's rent in advance			

Journal (*Cont.*) Page 2

Date	Description	P.R.	Debit	Credit
1974	(c)			
Nov. 1	Office Equipment	10	1,000	
	Cash	1		1,000
	Purchased office equipment from Smith & Company for cash			
	(d)			
2	Store Equipment	11	1,500	
	Cash	1		1,500
	Purchased store equipment from the Jones Company for cash			
	(e)			
2	Supplies	8	200	
	Cash	1		200
	Purchased office and store supplies from B. Runser for cash			
	(f)			
3	Purchases	50	5,000	
	Accounts Payable—Jay Company	21		5,000
	Purchased merchandise from Jay Company on account, terms, 2/10, n/30			
	(g)			
5	Accounts Receivable—Schaeffer Company	4	6,000	
	Sales	40		6,000
	Sold merchandise to Schaeffer Company on account, terms, 2/10, n/30			
	(h)			
5	Salary Expense	60	1,000	
	Cash	1		1,000
	Paid weekly salaries			
	(i)			
12	Purchases	50	6,000	
	Accounts Payable—Hart Company	20		6,000
	Purchased merchandise from Hart Company on account, terms, 2/10, n/30			

Journal (*Cont.*) Page 3

Date	Description	P.R.	Debit	Credit
1974	(j)			
Nov. 12	Salary Expense	60	1,000	
	Cash	1		1,000
	Paid weekly salaries			
	(k)			
12	Accounts Payable—Jay Company	21	5,000	
	Purchase Discounts	52		100
	Cash	1		4,900
	Paid Jay Company invoice of Nov. 3, less discount			
	(l)			
15	Transportation In	51	200	
	Cash	1		200
	Paid freight on purchase of Nov. 12			
	(m)			
15	Cash	1	5,880	
	Sales Discounts	41	120	
	Accounts Receivable—Schaeffer Company	4		6,000
	Received payment for invoice of Nov. 5, less 2%			
	(n)			
15	Accounts Payable—Hart Company	20	1,000	
	Purchase Returns and Allowances	53		1,000
	Returned merchandise to Hart Company, debit memo No. 1			
	(o)			
16	Accounts Receivable—Flint Corporation	2	10,000	
	Sales	40		10,000
	Sold merchandise to Flint Corporation on account, terms, 2/10, n/30			
	(p)			
18	Sales Returns and Allowances	42	1,000	
	Accounts Receivable—Flint Corporation	2		1,000
	Issued credit memo No. 1			

Journal (*Cont.*) Page 4

Date	Description	P.R.	Debit	Credit
1974	(q)			
Nov. 19	Salary Expense	60	1,000	
	Cash	1		1,000
	Paid weekly salaries			
	(r)			
22	Accounts Payable—Hart Company	20	5,000	
	Purchase Discounts	52		100
	Cash	1		4,900
	Paid Hart Company balance due on invoice of Nov. 12, less 2%			
	(s)			
26	Salary Expense	60	1,000	
	Cash	1		1,000
	Paid weekly salaries			
	(t)			
26	Cash	1	8,820	
	Sales Discounts	41	180	
	Accounts Receivable—Flint Corporation	2		9,000
	Received from Flint Corporation balance due on invoice of Nov. 16, less 2%			
	(u)			
26	Utilities Expense	61	275	
	Cash	1		275
	Paid monthly utilities			
	(v)			
26	Accounts Receivable—Phillips Company	3	8,000	
	Sales	40		8,000
	Sold merchandise to Phillips Company on account, terms, 2/10, n/30			
	(w)			
26	Purchases	50	7,000	
	Accounts Payable—Tool Corporation	22		7,000
	Purchased merchandise from Tool Corporation on account, terms, 2/10, n/30			

LEDGER ACCOUNTS AFTER POSTING AND DETERMINATION OF BALANCES

The ledger accounts of the DEF Corporation on pages 471 to 474 are shown as they should appear after all of the November transactions have been posted. These accounts are arranged in the ledger in financial statement order; that is, assets first, followed by liabilities, owners' equity, revenue, and expense.

After the last journal entry has been posted, the balance of each account should be determined. Determination of account balances may be achieved in the following manner:

1. Add the debits in the account and insert the total in small figures just below the last entry in the debit column.
2. Add the credits in the account and insert the total in small figures just below the last entry in the credit column.
3. Compute the difference between the debit total and the credit total. If the debit total is larger than the credit total, the account has a debit balance. Enter the debit balance as a small figure to the left of the last debit amount. If the credit total is larger than the debit total in an account, the account has a credit balance. Enter the credit balance as a small figure to the left of the last credit amount.

Cash — Account 1

Date	Explanation	P.R.	Debit	Date	Explanation	P.R.	Credit
1974				1974			
Nov. 1		J1	100,000	Nov. 1		J1	1,200
15		J3	5,880	1		J2	1,000
26	96,525	J4	8,820	2		J2	1,500
			114,700	2		J2	200
				5		J2	1,000
				12		J3	1,000
				12		J3	4,900
				15		J3	200
				19		J4	1,000
				22		J4	4,900
				26		J4	1,000
				26		J4	275
							18,175

Accounts Receivable—Flint Corporation Account 2

1974			1974		
Nov. 16	J3	10,000	Nov. 18	J3	1,000
			26	J4	9,000

Accounts Receivable—Phillips Company Account 3

1974					
Nov. 26	J4	8,000			

Accounts Receivable—Schaeffer Company Account 4

1974			1974		
Nov. 5	J2	6,000	Nov. 15	J3	6,000

Prepaid Rent Account 7

1974					
Nov. 1	J1	1,200			

Supplies Account 8

1974					
Nov. 2	J2	200			

Office Equipment Account 10

1974					
Nov. 1	J2	1,000			

Store Equipment Account 11

1974					
Nov. 2	J2	1,500			

Accounts Payable—Hart Company Account 20

1974			1974		
Nov. 15	J3	1,000	Nov. 12	J2	6,000
22	J4	5,000			

Accounts Payable—Jay Company Account 21

1974			1974		
Nov. 12	J3	5,000	Nov. 3	J2	5,000

Accounts Payable—Tool Corporation Account 22

			1974		
			Nov. 26	J4	7,000

Capital Stock Account 30

			1974		
			Nov. 1	J1	100,000

Sales Account 40

			1974		
			Nov. 5	J2	6,000
			16	J3	10,000
			26	J4	8,000
					24,000

Sales Discounts Account 41

1974					
Nov. 15	J3	120			
26	J4	180			
		300			

Sales Returns and Allowances Account 42

1974					
Nov. 18	J3	1,000			

Purchases Account 50

1974					
Nov. 3	J2	5,000			
12	J2	6,000			
26	J4	7,000			
		18,000			

Transportation In Account 51

1974					
Nov. 15	J3	200			

Purchase Discounts Account 52

			1974		
			Nov. 12	J3	100
			22	J4	100
					200

Purchase Returns and Allowances Account 53

			1974		
			Nov. 15	J3	1,000

Salary Expense — Account 60

1974					
Nov. 5	J2	1,000			
12	J3	1,000			
19	J4	1,000			
26	J4	1,000			
		4,000			

Utilities Expense — Account 61

1974					
Nov. 26	J4	275			

TRIAL BALANCE

A trial balance taken from the ledger of the DEF Corporation appears below.

DEF CORPORATION
Trial Balance
November 30, 1974

Cash	$ 96,525	
Accounts Receivable	8,000	
Prepaid Rent	1,200	
Supplies	200	
Office Equipment	1,000	
Store Equipment	1,500	
Accounts Payable		$ 7,000
Capital Stock		100,000
Sales		24,000
Sales Discounts	300	
Sales Returns and Allowances	1,000	
Purchases	18,000	
Transportation In	200	
Purchase Discounts		200
Purchase Returns and Allowances		1,000
Salary Expense	4,000	
Utilities Expense	275	
	$132,200	$132,200

The trial balance of the DEF Corporation provides proof that the ledger is in balance and indicates but does not insure that (1) equal debits and credits have been recorded for all transactions; (2) the debit or credit balance of each account has been correctly computed; and (3) the addition of the account balances in the trial balance has been correctly performed.

When the sum of the debit balances disagrees with the sum of the credit balances in a trial balance, it indicates that one or more errors have been made. Typical of such errors are: (1) the recording of a debit as a credit, or vice versa; (2) arithmetical errors in computing account balances; (3) errors in copying account balances onto the trial balance; (4) listing a debit balance in the credit column of the trial balance or vice versa; and (5) errors in addition of the trial balance columns.

The preparation of a trial balance does not prove that transactions have been correctly analyzed and recorded. If the purchase of equipment was erroneously recorded by debiting the Purchases account instead of the Equipment account, the trial balance would balance. If a transaction was completely omitted from the ledger, the error would not be disclosed by the trial balance. In summary, the trial balance proves only one aspect of the ledger, and that is equality of debits and credits.

Obviously there are many mechanical methods for handling all of the procedures discussed in this chapter. At the one extreme, "pen and ink"; at the other extreme, "the computer." The actual method used by a particular company will depend upon the needs and the choice made at that enterprise.

QUESTIONS AND PROBLEMS

14–1. Total assets at all times must equal total equities. Explain.

14–2. Identify a transaction that would produce the effect desired by each of the following instructions:

a. Increase one asset and decrease another.

b. Increase an asset, decrease another asset, and increase a liability.

c. Increase an asset and increase capital.

d. Decrease an asset and decrease a liability.

e. Decrease an asset and decrease capital.

14–3. Why do expense accounts have debit balances?

14–4. Why do revenue accounts have credit balances?

14–5. What is a journal? What is a ledger? Why are both journals and ledgers used?

14–6. If the sum of the total debits is equal to the sum of the total credits on a trial balance, no errors have been committed. Comment.

14–7. Answer T (true) or F (false), whether it is possible in the same transaction to have:

a. An increase in an asset and an increase in an expense?

b. An increase in a liability and an increase in an expense?

c. An increase in an asset and a decrease in an expense?

d. A decrease in an asset and a decrease in revenue?

e. A decrease in an asset and a decrease in owners' equity?

14–8. Does an accounting entry consist of only one debit and only one credit? Explain.

14–9. What is the cross reference between the ledger and the journal?

14–10. Is the ledger a chronological record of transactions? Explain.

14–11. The December 31, 1974, balance sheet of the Morrow Corporation showed:

Assets	= Liabilities +	Owners' Equity
$100,000	= $ 40,000 +	$ 60,000

An office desk is then purchased costing $400; payment is made with $200 cash and the issuance of a $200 note. The balance sheet would then show:

Assets	= Liabilities +	Owners' Equity
$	= $	+ $

14–12. The December 31, 1974, balance sheet of the Downes Corporation showed:

Assets	= Liabilities +	Capital Stock +	Retained Earnings
$250,000	= $120,000	+ $100,000	+ $30,000

A building is then purchased costing $35,000. Cash of $10,000 and a mortgage note of $25,000 were given in payment. The balance sheet would then show:

Assets	= Liabilities +	Capital Stock +	Retained Earnings
$	= $	+ $	+ $

14–13. The December 31, 1974, balance sheet of the Spencer Corporation showed:

Assets	= Liabilities +	Stockholders' Equity
$160,000	= $110,000 +	$ 50,000

Merchandise costing $12,000 was then sold for $18,000 cash. The balance sheet would then show:

Assets = Liabilities + Stockholders' Equity
$ = $ + $

14–14. Record the debits and credits required by each of the following transactions.

TRANSACTIONS	DEBIT	CREDIT
Sold $200 of merchandise. Terms: Cash	Cash 200	Sales 200
a. Purchased $3,000 of merchandise from M. R. Jones, terms 2/10, n/30.		
b. Returned $200 of merchandise to M. R. Jones and received full credit.		
c. Sent a check to M. R. Jones for the net amount due. Check was sent within ten days.		
d. Sent a check for $3,920 to R. E. Haynes, a creditor, covering merchandise purchased less than ten days ago with terms 2/10, n/30.		
e. Sent a check to P. J. Kelly in settlement of our 60-day 6% interest-bearing note due today. Face of the note, $800. Interest $8.		
f. Sent a check for $18 to the Telephone Company for their bill received today.		
g. The store clerk took merchandise having a cost price of $40 as part of his salary.		
h. The sale of merchandise, four days ago, for $600, to Fred Wilson, was incorrectly charged to Fred Willison. Make a correcting entry.		
i. T. E. Clark returned $80 of merchandise bought yesterday for cash. His money was refunded.		
j. We returned defective merchandise to G. C. Murphy. Received credit for $120 to be applied against future purchases.		

14–15. F. Beazley opened a men's clothing store, F & B Inc. April 1, 1974 investing the following in the business:

Cash	$ 8,000
Merchandise	6,400
Showcase and other store fixtures	4,800
Store building	34,000
Land	6,000

Beazley received 5,920 shares of $10 par value stock for his investment.

Additional transactions which occurred during the month of April were as follows:

April 3 Purchased an assortment of men's furnishings, including ties, socks and handkerchiefs for cash. Total cost $240.

9 Paid $380 cash for a one-year fire insurance policy covering the building, store equipment and inventory.

16 Paid salaries for the first half of the month as follows:

Sales	$240
Office	200

18 Sold two suits on a 30-day charge to Jerry Klein. One suit was marked to sell at $90, and the other at $84.

20 Purchased a complete line of bathing supplies from the Rub-a-Dub Corporation, $376. Terms, net 30 days.

25 On April 22, returned to the Rub-a-Dub Corporation $44 of merchandise which had become soiled during shipment. A credit memorandum was received today for that amount.

26 Received a check for $60 to apply on Jerry Klein's account.

27 Issued Rub-a-Dub Corporation a 30-day non-interest bearing note for $200 to apply on account.

28 Jerry Klein returned the suit purchased on April 18 for $84. As no alterations had been made and the suit had not been worn, full credit on the return was allowed.

30 Salaries paid for the second half of the month were as follows:

Sales	$240
Office	200

Cash sales for the month amounted to $3,360.

Required

a. Record the above transactions for the month of April in the following ledger accounts: Cash; A. R.—Jerry Klein; Inventory of Merchandise; Prepaid Insurance; Land; Building; Store Equipment; A. P.—Rub-a-Dub Corp.; Notes Payable; Capital Stock; Sales; Sales Returns and Allowances; Purchases; Purchase Returns and Allowances; Sales Salaries; Office Salaries.

b. Prove the equality of the ledger account balances by preparing a trial balance as of April 30, 1974.

14–16. Record the following transactions in ledger accounts remembering to keep the debits and credits equal in every transaction. Date all entries in the ledger accounts.

May 1 J. F. Pauls began business today, the JFP Corporation, investing $4,000 cash, $6,000 of merchandise, and had the business assume the liability of a note for $2,000 which he had given to B. R. Knight. Pauls received 8,000 shares of $1 par value stock.

3 Purchased $1,200 of merchandise on account from B. Huff. Terms 2/10, n/30.

4 Sold F. Zauner $1,600 of merchandise on account. Terms 1/10, n/30.

5 Returned $200 of merchandise to B. Huff because it was received in a damaged condition. Huff allowed full credit.

6 F. Zauner returned $200 of merchandise because he had received an inferior type of goods. He was allowed full credit for the returned merchandise.

9 Sent a $400 one-month non-interest bearing note to B. Huff in partial payment of his open account balance.

10 Received a $600 one-month non-interest bearing note from F. Zauner in partial payment of his open account balance.

11 Sent check to B. Huff for balance due on open account (less discount).

12 Received check from F. Zauner for balance due on open account (less discount).

June 9 Sent check for $400 to B. Huff in payment of the note due today.

10 Received check for $600 from F. Zauner in payment of the note due today.

14–17. On December 1, 1974, Shock, Inc. started an electrical appliance business with an authorized capital stock of 15,000 shares of $50 par value stock. Transactions which occurred during the month of December were as follows:

December 2 Sold 12,000 shares of capital stock at par for cash.

4 Purchased store equipment at a cost of $7,200 from the Best Fixtures Company. Terms, cash.

December 7 Sent a $2,700 check to the United Insurance Company for the premium on a three-year insurance policy which went into effect December 1.

10 Purchased washers and dryers from the American Manufacturing Corporation for $21,600. Terms n/30 days.

12 Sold merchandise on account to W. M. Mohr. Total of invoice $25,800.

15 Paid sales salaries of $2,400 covering the two-week period ended today.

16 Received a 30-day 6% interest bearing note for $3,600 from W. M. Mohr to apply on his account.

20 Sold an additional 1,500 shares of capital stock at par for cash.

23 $1,290 of the washers which were purchased from the American Manufacturing Corporation on December 10 were found to be defective. Full credit was allowed by the vendor for the return of the defective merchandise.

29 Paid salaries of $2,400 covering the second two-week pay period of December.

31 Cash sales to date totaled $4,170.

Required

a. Record the above transactions in a general journal and post the entries to the following ledger accounts:

1. Cash
2. A. R.—W. M. Mohr
3. Notes Receivable
4. Prepaid Insurance
5. Store Equipment
6. A. P.—American Manufacturing Corp.
7. Capital Stock
8. Sales
9. Purchases
10. Purchase Returns and Allowances
11. Sales Salaries

b. Prepare a trial balance as of December 31, 1974.

14–18. On June 1, 1974, Tom Boland started a chemical supply business, the OK. Corporation, investing $16,000 cash, $8,000 merchandise, $10,000 store equipment, real estate consisting of $4,000 land and a $20,000 building. The building was mortgaged to the extent of $6,000 and the mortgage was assumed by the new concern. Boland received 5,200 shares of $10 par value stock for his net investment.

Additional transactions which occurred during the month of

June were as follows:

June 2 Purchased $1,440 of merchandise on account from the Ajax Chemical Company. Terms, 2/10, n/30.

4 Sold the Tristate Sanitation Company $1,820 of merchandise. Terms, 1/5, n/30.

5 Purchased a delivery truck from the Three Rivers Motor Company of Pittsburgh for $7,300. Terms, $1,300 cash, a 30-day 5% interest bearing note for $4,000, and the balance on open account.

6 Made a payment of $240 due on the principal of the mortgage assumed by the business.

8 Received a check from Tristate Sanitation Company for $900.90 on its purchase of June 4. Discount was allowed on the partial payment.

9 Received a bill for $52 from the Oakland Office Supply Company for stationery and other office supplies purchased today.

10 Sent a check to Ajax Chemical Company in full payment of account.

12 Sold the Comet Cleaning Company $280 of mechandise. Terms, net, 30 days.

15 Paid $90 to William Anderson, a customer, for merchandise he returned today that he had purchased yesterday for cash.

18 Filled an order from the Spotless Laundry for $340 of merchandise. Terms, 2/10, n/30. Shipping charges on the order amounted to $22 and were paid in cash by the OK. Corporation.

21 Received a check from the Comet Cleaning Co. to cover the purchase of June 12.

22 An employee gave the cashier $3.70 to cover a personal long-distance telephone call made on the office telephone.

24 The $280 check received from the Comet Cleaning Co. and deposited in the bank on June 21 was returned today marked N. S. F.

27 Some of the chemicals shipped to Spotless Laundry on the 18th were found to be sub-standard and were returned today. Credit was allowed for $40.

28 Received a check from Spotless Laundry in full settlement of account.

June 30 Paid monthly salaries amounting to $2,400.
Received the monthly telephone bill from Bell Telephone Co., $86.
Cash sales for the month amounted to $3,520.

Required

a. Record the above transactions in ledger accounts.

b. Prepare a trial balance from the ledger accounts.

14–19. On March 1, 1974, the Nuttall Supply Corporation was formed with authorized capital stock of $100,000 consisting of 2,000 shares of $50 par value stock. The following transactions were completed by the corporation during the month of March.

March 1 1200 shares of stock were issued for: cash, $20,000; land, $8,000; building, $32,000.

2 Purchased merchandise from Sisson Supply Company. Terms, 2/10, n/30. Amount, $6,000.
Purchased store equipment from Johnson Corporation, $3,600. Terms, $600 cash and a 60-day, 6% note for the balance.

3 Purchased a delivery truck costing $6,400 from Rex Motor Company. Terms, $1,600 cash and a $4,800 non-interest bearing note to be paid in equal monthly installments throughout the next 24 months.
Purchased office supplies for cash from A. C. Craft, Inc., $100.
Paid $600 premium on a 3-year insurance policy for the building.

5 Paid the Pittsburgh Press for advertising space, $500.
Purchased gas and oil from George's Service Station for the delivery truck, $14. Terms, cash.
Received electrical supplies from Bolt Brothers, $12,000. Terms, 1/10, n/30.
Paid freight charges on the shipment from Bolt Brothers, $120.

6 Sold Wilson, Inc. goods on account, $4,000. Terms, 2/10, n/30.
Paid freight charges on the goods shipped to Wilson, Inc., $40.

8 Returned defective merchandise to Sisson Supply Company receiving credit for $1,000. Sold merchandise for cash, $800.

9 $600 of merchandise sold to Wilson, Inc. on March 6 was found unsatisfactory and was returned today.
Sold R. Bryant merchandise, $5,000. Terms, 2/10, n/30.

March 10 Paid Sisson Supply Company in full.
Purchased merchandise for cash, $2,800.

12 Received a shipment of electrical supplies from King Supply Company, $7,000. Terms, n/60.

15 Received a check in full settlement of the account owed by Wilson, Inc.

17 Paid cash for a typewriter purchased from Knight and Day, $300. Received $2,450 from R. Bryant in settlement of one-half of his account. Discount was allowed on partial payment.

21 Sold merchandise for cash, $900.
Sold Oliver Company merchandise, $6,000. Terms, n/30 days.

24 Sold merchandise to Wills & Sons, $3,300. Received a 60-day, 6% note to cover the transaction.

27 Paid $6 to George's Service Station for lubricating and washing the delivery truck.

28 Issued Bolt Brothers a 30-day, 6% note to cover the purchase of March 5th.

30 Received a 60-day, 6% note from Oliver Company for their purchase on March 21st.
Paid monthly payroll divided as follows: office employees, $1,000; store employees, $1,600; delivery truck driver, $450.

Required

a. Arrange 33 ledger accounts on ledger paper and record the transactions for the month of March, 1974. Use all the following account titles to identify the ledger accounts. No additional accounts are to be employed.

1. Cash
2. A. R.—Wilson, Inc.
3. A. R.—R. Bryant
4. A. R.—Oliver Company
5. A. R.—Wills & Sons
6. Notes Receivable
7. Prepaid Insurance
8. Land
9. Building
10. Store Equipment
11. Delivery Equipment
12. Office Equipment
13. A. P.—Sisson Supply Company
14. A. P.—Johnson Corporation
15. A. P.—Bolt Brothers
16. A. P.—Rex Motor Company
17. A. P.—King Supply Company
18. Notes Payable
19. Capital Stock
20. Sales
21. Sales Returns and Allowances
22. Sales Discounts

23. Purchases
24. Purchase Returns and Allowances
25. Purchase Discounts
26. Transportation In
27. Sales Salaries
28. Advertising
29. Transportation Out
30. Delivery Salaries
31. Misc. Delivery Expenses
32. Office Salaries
33. Office Expenses

b. What entry will be made on May 29 when the note received on March 30 from Oliver Company matures with cash being received from principal and interest?

c. What entry will be made on April 27 when the note issued on March 28 to Bolt Brothers matures with cash being paid for principal and interest?

14–20. Record the following transactions completed by the Browne Supply Corporation during the month of October of the current year in appropriate ledger accounts.

October 1 The Browne Supply Corporation was formed with authorized capital stock of $160,000 consisting of 1,600 shares of $100 par value stock.

2 1,200 shares of stock were issued at par for cash.

4 Purchased a building and land for $42,000 cash. The land was valued at $5,000 and the building at $37,000.

5 Purchased Delivery Equipment for $19,000 from Shadyside Garage. Paid $5,000 in cash, gave a 20-day, 6% note for $8,400 and allowed the balance to remain on open account.

9 Purchased $5,500 of merchandise from Hughes Company on account. Terms, n/30.

11 Sold Columbia Company $5,000 of merchandise on account. Terms, 2/10, n/30.

15 Columbia Company returned $500 of the merchandise purchased on October 11. Full credit was given.

17 Sent a check for $700 to the Pitt News for advertising for the month of October.

19 Received a check for $3,000 from Columbia Company in partial payment of their account. Discount was allowed on the partial payment.

21 Paid $240 for a three-year fire insurance policy on the building.

25 Sent a check for $8,428 to Shadyside Garage for the note due them and interest of $28.

October 29 Sent a check to Hughes Company in full payment of our account.

31 Cash sales for the month, $3,500.
Paid $1,200 salaries to our employees.
The check for $3,000 received from Columbia Company was returned by the bank marked N. S. F. Protest fees of $6 were charged us by the bank.

14–21. The Foster Corporation was incorporated on January 2, 1974, and was authorized to issue 10,000 shares of $10 par value stock. The enterprise completed the following transactions during January, 1974:

January 2 Issued 4,000 shares of stock at par for cash.

4 Purchased merchandise from the Black Company for $10,000 cash.

5 Sold merchandise to Miller & Miller Co. in the amount of $16,000. Terms, 2/10, n/30; F. O. B. shipping point.

9 Purchased merchandise from the Cue Company in the amount of $12,000. Terms, cash $4,000; 60-day, 6% note payable, $4,000; and the remainder on open account.

10 Miller & Miller Co. returned defective merchandise in the amount of $4,000 to the Foster Corporation. Full credit was allowed.

12 Received a $3,000 check from the Cue Company for defective merchandise returned today.

13 Sold merchandise for cash, $20,000.

15 Paid the Cue Company account in full.

16 Received a check in the amount of $11,760 from Miller & Miller Co.

Required

a. Journalize the transactions described above.

b. Post the journal entries to ledger accounts.

c. Prepare a trial balance as of the 16th of January, 1974.

14–22. On June 1 of the current year, Ball Incorporated was formed with an authorization to issue 20,000 shares of $50 par value stock. Ball Incorporated completed the following transactions during the month of June:

June 1 Steve Rollins invested $26,800 cash, land valued at $24,000, a building valued at $160,000, and merchandise valued at $48,000. Rollins owed Tom Gorman $6,000 on open account, and the business assumed the debt. Rollins received 5,056 shares of $50 par value stock in exchange for his net investment.

June 3 Sold merchandise to G. Washington for $4,976, terms 2/10, n/30.

4 Purchased a desk for $580, office stationery for $160, and a typewriter for $600. The seller, Standard Co., extended credit for 30 days.

6 Purchased merchandise from R. B. Sims for $3,280, terms 2/10, n/30.

8 Washington returned $1,020 worth of merchandise and was allowed full credit.

9 Sold the defective merchandise received from Washington for $720 cash to A. Ashe.

10 Purchased merchandise for $12,000 from the Buy-Rite Co., terms 3/5, n/30.

12 Sent a check to Tom Gorman in full payment of account.

13 Received a check from G. Washington for the net amount due.

14 Sent a check to R. B. Sims for the amount due.

15 Paid salaries for the two-week period ending yesterday. Amount $1,400.

16 Sold merchandise to R. Sibley for $1,672, terms cash $872 and a 60-day non-interest bearing note for the balance.

17 Purchased a delivery truck for $7,800, terms $3,800 cash and a 30-day non-interest bearing note for the balance. The seller was Gem Auto Sales Co.

22 Ball Inc. presented merchandise to a charitable organization to be sold to raise funds. The merchandise cost $200 and was marked to sell at $300.

29 Paid salaries of $1,560 for the two-week period ending yesterday.

30 Cash sales for the month amounted to $10,800.

Required

a. Record the transactions for June in a two-column journal.

b. Post from the journal to appropriate ledger accounts.

c. Prepare a trial balance of the ledger accounts.

14–23. On January 1, 1974, the ledger of the Radar Corporation contained the following account balances:

Cash	$16,000	
Accounts Receivable—T. Max Davis	1,400	
Accounts Receivable—J. James	600	
Notes Receivable	4,000	
Inventory of Merchandise	15,200	
Store Equipment	10,000	
Accounts Payable—A. B. Smith		$ 800
Notes Payable		8,000
Capital Stock		36,000
Retained Earnings		2,400
	$47,200	$47,200

During the month of January, the Radar Corporation completed the following transactions:

January 2 Paid $600 to City Real Estate Company for January's rent.
Sold merchandise to I. M. King for cash, $900.
Purchased office supplies on account from the Office Supply Corporation, $90.
Purchased merchandise on account from A. B. Smith, $1,000.
Paid freight charges on mechandise purchase from Smith, $30.

5 Sent $4,000 check to M. E. Doe in payment of a non-interest bearing note which matured today.
Received from T. Max Davis a note covering the balance of his account.

6 J. James check, covering $400 of his account, arrived today.

7 Paid the balance due to Office Supply Corporation.

8 Sold merchandise to J. James, $1,600, receiving in payment $600 cash and a 60-day, 6% note for $1,000.

15 Cash sales for January 3 to 15, $1,750.

21 Purchased merchandise from the Red Wholesale Company, terms 2/10, n/30. Amount $1,400.

22 Received credit for $200 from Red Wholesale Company for the return of damaged merchandise.

29 Paid $100 to Roe Supply Company for wrapping paper, paper bags, and pasteboard cartons which were purchased today.
Purchased a store adding machine from Smith Company for cash, $550.

January 31 Paid monthly salaries divided as follows: office employees, $500; store employees $700.
Sold merchandise for cash, January 16 to 31, $2,250.
Send a check to Red Wholesale in payment of the amount due.

Required

a. Open the accounts listed and record the balances as of January 1.

b. Record in general journal form the transactions for the month.

c. Post to the general ledger.

d. Prepare a trial balance.

14–24. The Trundel-King Corporation began a wholesale sporting goods business January 2, 1974, with an authorized capital stock of 2,000 shares of $100 par value stock. Transactions which occurred during the month of January were as follows:

January 2 The corporation issued 800 shares of stock at par for cash.
Sent a check for $2,400 to the Commonwealth Real Estate Agency for six months' rent.

3 Purchased various types of sporting goods equipment from the All-American Manufacturing Company for $6,400. Terms, n/60 days.
Sold a complete line of baseball equipment to the Sportsman's Shop, billing price, $2,320. Terms, 2/10, n/30.

5 Purchased furniture for the sales display room at a cost of $1,840 from the Central Furniture Co. Terms, cash $800, a 30-day, 5% note for $800, and the balance on open account, n/60 days.

8 Purchased ten gross of tennis balls at $28.80 per gross from the Wimbeldon Netters Company for cash.

12 Received a check for $1,136.80 from the Sportsman's Shop in payment of one-half of the sale to them on January 3rd. Discount was allowed on this partial payment.

21 Purchased $240 of labels, wrapping paper, twine, and other store supplies from the Sales Supply Co. Terms n/30.

January 26 Sold 33 lettered team sweaters to the Pennapolis High School, $396. Terms, n/30 days.

31 Paid Salaries for the month, $1,400.
Cash sales for the month totaled $1,860.

Required

a. Journalize the above transactions in a two-column journal and post to ledger accounts.

b. Prepare a trial balance as of January 31, 1974.

15

The Accounting Cycle—End-of-Period Process

Certain basic steps to be followed in the accumulation of accounting data were introduced and developed in the preceding chapter. These steps in proper sequence are:

1. Analyze transactions and record appropriate journal entries.
2. Post the journal entries to the proper ledger accounts.
3. Determine the balance of each ledger account and prepare a trial balance.

The steps listed in the foregoing sequence are repeated in each accounting period to accumulate financial and accounting data. But when each accounting period ends, additional steps must be taken to adjust and properly summarize the accumulated data for financial statements and interpretive purposes (see "the accounting period" at the start of Chapter 3). These additional steps are described and illustrated in this chapter.

THE ADJUSTING PROCESS

The preparation of financial statements at the end of an accounting period would be a relatively simple matter if the balances of all of the ledger accounts as shown on the trial balance could be used, without change, on the financial statements. This is not possible because the balances of many accounts do not reflect all of the changes that occur during an accounting period. Since changes caused by transactions would be, if properly treated, reflected in the ledger accounts, unrecorded changes usually are not events which concern outside parties. Instead, these changes usually result from internal operating events which are not recognized in the accounts as they occur because it is inexpedient to do so. For example, supplies are consumed, rent and insurance prepayments expire, equipment depreciates, and wages and salaries accrue. These events, however, must be recognized in order that the accounts reflect correct balances for the preparation of financial statements.

The periodic procedure by which accounts are analyzed and, if necessary, revised, is known as the *adjusting process*. Journal entries to record any revisions resulting from these analyses are called *adjusting entries*.

Adjusting entries required at the end of a fiscal period may be classified into the following groups:

1. Adjustments for accruals (or the recognition of unrecorded, but incurred expenses and earned revenues).
2. Adjustments for prepayments and collections in advance (or the recognition of recorded costs and revenues which must be apportioned to two or more periods).
3. Adjustments for asset valuations (or the recognition of unrecorded reductions in asset amounts).

ADJUSTMENTS FOR ACCRUALS

At the end of a fiscal period there are often unrecorded expenses which have been incurred but not paid, or revenues that have been earned but not collected. For example, salaries which accrue daily may not be recorded by the end of the period because the wage payment date does not arrive until the next fiscal period. When the end of an accounting period falls between wage payment dates, the salary accounts must be brought up to date before being included on the financial statements. It is, therefore, necessary to record the salary expense incurred by an enterprise up to the close of the fiscal period, and also to record the liability for salaries owed to employees at the end of the period. Also, an enterprise may hold interest bearing notes from customers, or investments in bonds on which interest is earned. Whenever an enterprise holds an interest bearing asset at the end of the accounting period, an adjustment is necessary to reflect the interest which has been earned but not yet collected.

The principles involved in recognizing adjustments for accruals are: (1) Expenses incurred, but not yet paid and not recorded on the books at the end of a fiscal period, are expenses of that period. The amount owed should be shown as a current liability on the balance sheet and included among the expenses on the statement of income at the end of the period; and (2) Revenues earned, but not yet collected and not recorded on the books at the end of the fiscal period, are revenues of that period. The amount to be collected should be shown as a current asset on the balance sheet and included among the revenues on the statement of income at the end of the period. Although many accruals exist, the examples which follow are typical of adjusting entries necessary to recognize accruals at the end of a fiscal period.

Accrual of Salary Expenses

During the year 1974, payments actually made to employees for salaries amounted to $90,000, Salary Expense being debited and Cash credited. On December 31, 1974, additional salaries amounting to $10,000 have been earned by employees. These salaries, however, are not due for payment until January 3 of the subsequent fiscal year, 1975.

To adjust the Salary Expense account so that its balance will show a salary expense of $100,000 for 1974, and to recognize the liability for salaries owed on December 31, 1974, of $10,000, the following adjusting entry is necessary.

1974			
Dec. 31	Salary Expense	10,000	
	Salaries Payable		10,000
	To record accrued salaries, Dec. 31, 1974		

After the above entry has been posted, the two accounts would appear as follows:

Salary Expense (Debit)	Salary Expense (Credit)
1974	
Dec. 31 Bal. 90,000	
31 Adj. 10,000	

Salaries Payable (Debit)	Salaries Payable (Credit)
	1974
	Dec. 31 Adj. 10,000

The Salaries Expense account, with a balance of $100,000, representing the salary expense of 1974 is now ready for inclusion as one of the operating expenses in the statement of income. The Salaries Payable account, with a balance of $10,000, representing the liability to employees for unpaid salaries at December 31, 1974, is ready for inclusion as one of the current liabilities in the balance sheet.

Accrual of Interest Expense

On December 1, 1974, a company issued a two-month, 6 percent note payable for \$4,000 in settlement of its purchase of a delivery truck for \$4,000. Interest on the note accrues or accumulates from the date of issue and will amount to \$40 when the note matures in two months. If the life of this note fell within the fiscal period of the company, it would not be necessary to recognize the interest expense of \$40 until the maturity date of the note. Since, however, the company's fiscal period ends on December 31, 1974, it is necessary to recognize that interest charges amounting to \$20 (\$4,000 $\times$ 6 percent $\times \frac{30}{360}$) have been incurred but not paid as of December 31, 1974. The adjusting entry is shown below:

1974			
Dec. 31	Interest Expense	20	
	Interest Payable		20
	To record interest accrued for one month by Dec. 31, 1974		

After this entry has been posted, the two accounts would appear as follows:

Interest Expense

Debit		Credit
1974		
Dec. 31 Adj.	20	

Interest Payable

Debit	Credit	
	1974	
	Dec. 31 Adj.	20

The Interest Expense account, with a balance of \$20, representing the interest expense for 1974 is now ready for inclusion as one of the expenses on the statement of income. The Interest Payable account, with a balance of \$20, representing the liability for accumulated interest is ready for inclusion as one of the current liabilities in the balance sheet.

Accrual of Interest Income

On December 1, 1974, a company received a two-month, 6 percent note receivable for \$3,000 in settlement of a sale of merchandise to a customer. Interest on the note accrues or accumulates from the date of issue, and will amount to \$30 when the note matures in two months. Were it not for the timing involved, no recognition of the interest income would be necessary until the note was collected. However, the company's fiscal period ends on December 31, 1974, and it is necessary to recognize that interest amounting to \$15 (\$3,000 $\times$ 6 percent $\times \frac{30}{360}$) has been earned but not collected as of December 31, 1974. The adjusting entry is as follows:

1974			
Dec. 31	Interest Receivable	15	
	Interest Income		15
	To record interest accrued for one month by Dec. 31, 1974		

After this entry has been posted, the two accounts would appear as shown below:

Interest Receivable			
1974			
Dec. 31 Adj.	15		

Interest Income			
		1974	
		Dec. 31 Adj.	15

The Interest Income account, with a balance of $15, representing the interest earned for 1974 is now ready for inclusion as one of the revenue items on the statement of income. The Interest Receivable account, with a balance of $15, representing the claim for accumulated interest is ready for inclusion as one of the current assets on the balance sheet.

ADJUSTMENTS FOR PREPAYMENTS AND COLLECTIONS IN ADVANCE

In some instances, it is known that costs incurred and revenues collected will benefit more than one period. Such costs may be debited to asset accounts at the time of acquisition and such revenues may be credited to liability accounts at the time the collection is made. Costs of this nature are referred to as prepayments and the unearned revenues are referred to as collections in advance.

Usually business enterprises do not recognize the expiration of such prepayments until the end of the fiscal period. At that time, an adjustment is necessary to remove from each asset account that portion which has been consumed or expired and to transfer to an expense account that portion which is applicable to the current fiscal period. Because the adjusting entry apportions the asset between expired and unexpired amounts, each adjusting entry involves both expense and asset accounts.

Prepayments may be short term, as in the case of insurance, rent, interest, and supplies; or long term, as in the case of buildings and equipment.

Adjustments for collections in advance require considerations similar to those described for prepayments. The amounts received are normally credited to specific liability accounts, such as Unearned Rent. At the end of the fiscal period, it is necessary to remove from each liability account and transfer to a revenue account that portion of the collection in advance which has been earned in the current period. Because the adjusting entry apportions a collection in advance between earned and unearned amounts, each adjusting entry involves both liability and revenue accounts.

The principles involved in recognizing adjustments for prepayments and collections in advance are: (1) When costs recorded as assets have been partially consumed or expired at the end of a fiscal period, the portions consumed or expired should be transferred to expenses, so that only the unexpired portions will remain as assets. (Sometimes costs which have been recorded as expenses are wholly or partially still prepaid at the end of an accounting period. Under such circumstances, the prepaid amounts should be removed from the expense accounts and included with the assets on the balance sheet.) (2) When receipts recorded as collections in advance have been partially earned at the end of the period, the portions earned should be transferred to revenue so that only the unearned portions will remain as liabilities. (Sometimes receipts recorded as revenue are still unearned at the end of an accounting period. In such instances, the unearned amounts should be removed from the revenue accounts and included with the liabilities on the balance sheet.) The examples which follow are based on a fiscal year ending December 31 and are typical of entries necessary to recognize adjustments of prepayments and collections in advance at the end of a fiscal period.

Prepaid Insurance

On July 1, 1974, a business took out a fire insurance policy on its property. The policy was for three years and the premium paid amounted to $480. The expenditure was debited to Prepaid Insurance and credited to Cash. On December 31, 1974, the unexpired portion of the insurance premium amounted to \$400 ($\frac{30}{36} \times \$480$). To adjust the Prepaid Insurance account so that it will reveal the amount of the unexpired premium at December 31, 1974, and to record the $80 expired insurance as expense applicable to the current period, the following adjusting entry is necessary:

1974			
Dec. 31	Insurance Expense	80	
	Prepaid Insurance		80
	To record insurance expense applicable to 1974		

After the entry has been posted, the two accounts would appear as follows:

Prepaid Insurance

1974		1974	
July 1	480	Dec. 31 Adj.	80

Insurance Expense

1974			
Dec. 31 Adj.	80		

The Insurance Expense account, with a balance of $80, represents the insurance expense of 1974. The account is now ready for inclusion as one of the operating expenses in the statement of income for the year. The Prepaid Insurance account, with a balance of $400, represents the amount of prepaid insurance applicable to future periods and is ready for inclusion as one of the current assets on the balance sheet.

Depreciation

An enterprise often owns assets such as buildings, machinery, and equipment. From an accounting point of view, the cost of these assets may be considered as long-term prepayments because the services furnished by these assets are consumed over a relatively long period of time. The cost of this type of asset which is allocated to each fiscal period is called *depreciation expense.* (See Chapter 6 for a more complete discussion of depreciation.)

The amount of depreciation expense applicable to a fiscal period may be determined by dividing the cost of the asset by its estimated useful life. For example, a machine costing $10,000 with no estimated salvage value and a useful life of ten years will result in depreciation expense of $1,000 per year for each of the ten years.[1]

To illustrate the depreciation adjustment, it is assumed that on January 1, 1974, a new truck with no anticipated salvage value was purchased at a cost of $4,000. The useful life of the truck was estimated to be five years. Depreciation of the truck for the year 1974 is recorded in the following adjusting entry:

1974			
Dec. 31	Depreciation Expense—Truck	800	
	Accumulated Depreciation—Truck		800
	To record annual depreciation charge		

After this entry has been posted, the two accounts would appear as follows:

Depreciation Expense—Truck

1974			
Dec. 31 Adj.	800		

Accumulated Depreciation—Truck

		1974	
		Dec. 31 Adj.	800

---

[1] See Chapters 6 and 7 for additional methods of determining periodic depreciation charges.

The Depreciation Expense—Truck account, with a balance of $800, represents that portion of the cost of the asset Truck that has been allocated to expense. The account is now ready for inclusion as one of the operating expenses on the statement of income. The account Accumulated Depreciation—Truck is referred to as a contra-asset or offset account and is deducted from the cost of the asset Truck on the balance sheet. It represents the total amount of the cost of the asset Truck which has been allocated to expense in past and current periods. The accounts Truck and Accumulated Depreciation—Truck would appear on the balance sheet prepared as of December 31, 1974, as follows:

Truck	$4,000	
Less Accumulated Depreciation	800	$3,200

See the balance sheet in Chapter 2 for additional illustrations.

Unearned or Deferred Rent Income

Assume that on October 1, 1974, a firm enters into an agreement to lease one of its buildings for two years at an annual rental of $18,000, payable in advance. A check for $18,000 is received on October 1, 1974, and recorded as a debit to Cash and a credit to Unearned Rental Income. To adjust the Unearned Rental Income account so that the balance will represent the liability for unearned rent at December 31, 1974, of $13,500, and to record the rental income earned during the period of $4,500 ($3/12$ of $18,000), the following adjusting entry is necessary:

1974			
Dec. 31	Unearned Rental Income	4,500	
	Rental Income		4,500
	To record rent earned in the last three months of 1974		

After this entry has been posted, the two accounts would appear as follows:

Rental Income

	1974
	Dec. 31 Adj. 4,500

Unearned Rental Income

1974	1974
Dec. 31 Adj. 4,500	Oct. 1 18,000

The Rental Income account with its balance of $4,500 represents the rental income earned in 1974 and is ready for inclusion as one of the revenue items on the statement of income. The Unearned Rental Income account, with a balance of $13,500, represents the amount of rent collected in advance and applicable to future periods and is ready for inclusion as one of the current liabilities on the balance sheet as of December 31, 1974.

VALUATION ADJUSTMENTS

Many enterprises have found through past experience that accounts receivable are not always fully collectible. The difference between the total amount of the accounts receivable and the estimated realizable amount represents the amount of the accounts receivable which is estimated to be uncollectible. This uncollectible amount may be estimated by several alternative methods.

Uncollectible accounts receivable are a business expense. Instead of being considered losses chargeable against the fiscal periods in which they are proved to be uncollectible, they properly constitute losses of the fiscal periods in which they were incurred as a result of sales revenue being increased through credit sales. Accordingly, they are considered an expense chargeable against the income of the fiscal period in which the uncollectible accounts receivable originate. In order to record the bad debts expense in the current period and to evaluate the accounts receivable in terms of expected collections, an adjusting entry should be made at the end of each fiscal period. If, for example, it is estimated that $2,000 of a total of $50,000 of accounts receivable will be uncollectible, the following entry, debiting an account called Bad Debts Expense and crediting an account called Allowance for Doubtful Accounts, is made:

1974			
Dec. 31	Bad Debts Expense	2,000	
	Allowance for Doubtful Accounts		2,000
	To record estimated bad debts for the year 1974		

After this entry has been posted, the two accounts would appear as shown below:

Bad Debts Expense		Allowance for Doubtful Accounts	
1974			1974
Dec. 31 Adj. 2,000			Dec. 31 Adj. 2,000

The Bad Debts Expense account with its balance of $2,000 shows the bad debt expense recognized for 1974 and is included as one of the operating expense items on the statement of income.

The credit to Allowance for Doubtful Accounts represents a reduction in the amount of the asset Accounts Receivable. The Accounts Receivable account is not credited directly because at the time the adjustment is made, it is not known which particular customers' accounts are uncollectible. Therefore, the credit is recorded to a separate valuation account (and remains in this account until specific customers' accounts have been determined to be uncollectible). In this manner, the balance of the Accounts Receivable account remains equal to the sum of the individual customer account balances. The Accounts Receivable account and the account for Allowance for Doubtful Accounts would appear on the December 31, 1974, balance sheet as follows:

Accounts Receivable	$50,000	
Less Allowance for Doubtful Accounts	2,000	$48,000

As specific customers' accounts are determined in the future to be worthless, they would be removed from the Accounts Receivable account by debiting the Allowance for Doubtful Accounts and crediting Accounts Receivable.

The estimated amount of bad debts expense may be determined by using one of several different methods. Two commonly encountered methods are explained below:

1. As a percentage, based on past experience, of net credit sales. To illustrate, if a company should estimate the bad debts expense to be 1 percent of net credit sales of $100,000, the estimated amount of bad debts expense is $1,000 (1 percent of $100,000).

2. As a percentage, based on past experience, of accounts receivable at the end of a fiscal period. For example, a company has a $40,000 debit balance in the account Accounts Receivable and a $100 credit balance left in the account Allowance for Doubtful Accounts at the end of a fiscal period. Uncollectible accounts are estimated to equal 2 percent of the balance in the Accounts Receivable account at the end of the period. The estimate of uncollectible accounts is $800 (2 percent × $40,000). Since the account Allowance for Doubtful Accounts has a $100 credit balance, the adjustment for bad debts expense is $700, the amount needed to raise the balance in the Allowance for Doubtful Accounts to $800.

WORK SHEET

Adjustments such as those just described must, whenever required, be completed in order that the financial statements may be prepared properly. But, before the required adjusting entries are recorded in the journal and posted to the ledger, a columnar sheet is ordinarily prepared. This sheet is especially designed to organize and arrange in a systematic form all the accounting data required at the end of the fiscal period and is called a *work sheet*. The work sheet may be thought of as a rough draft of the final steps in the accounting cycle where the ledger accounts are adjusted and arranged in the general form needed for the preparation of the financial statements. It also contains the data needed for journalizing the adjusting entries as well as the closing entries which are described later in this chapter. The work sheet, while very useful, is not a part of the permanent, formal accounting records of an enterprise.

As a basis for the illustration of the preparation and uses of a work sheet, the trial balance and some additional information of the Watson Corporation is presented on pages 502–3. A commonly used ten column form of work sheet is prepared for the Watson Corporation and is illustrated on pages 506–7. Note that the heading consists of three parts: (1) name of the enterprise, (2) title, and (3) period of time covered. The body of the work sheet contains a column for account titles and five pairs of money columns entitled Trial Balance, Adjustments, Adjusted Trial Balance, Statement of Income, and Balance Sheet. Each pair of columns consists of a debit column and a credit column. The steps followed in the preparation of a work sheet are:

1. The first step in the preparation of the work sheet is to copy the titles of the accounts shown on the trial balance in the account titles column and insert the account balances of the trial balance in the first pair of columns. As soon as the account balances have been listed, these two columns should be totaled to check on the accuracy of the transcription. Often the trial balance is initially prepared directly on the work sheet by listing the titles and balances of all accounts in the order in which they appear in the ledger and totaling the debit and credit balances.

2. The adjustments (adjusting entries) required at the end of the fiscal period are inserted in the adjustments column opposite the appropriate account titles. If an account to be debited or credited in an adjustment does not appear in the trial balance, the title of the account is listed immediately below the trial balance. Note, for example, the location of Rental Income in the work sheet on page 507. The debits and credits of each adjustment should be identified by a code (letters or numbers) which will aid future reference requirements and make it easy to copy them later into the journal as formal adjusting entries. Although the adjustments made in the work sheet are *not* formal journal entries, the total of the debits must equal the total of the credits.

3. After the adjustments are placed in the second pair of columns, each account balance in the first pair of columns is combined with the appropriate adjustment amount, if any, and the resultant adjusted amount is entered in the Adjusted Trial Balance columns. In the illustration, the account Accumulated Depreciation—Building has a credit balance of $10,000 in the Trial Balance columns. This $10,000 credit amount combined with the $2,500 credit amount appearing opposite it in the Adjustments credit column produces an adjusted credit amount of $12,500 in the Adjusted Trial Balance credit column. Also, the account Supplies has a debit balance of $8,000 in the Trial Balance columns.

This $8,000 debt amount combined with the $6,000 credit appearing on the same line in the Adjustments credit column produces an adjusted debit amount of $2,000 in the Adjusted Trial Balance debit column. When the Adjustment columns are blank as they are opposite Notes Receivable, the amount in the Trial Balance columns is carried over into the Adjusted Trial Balance columns. After all appropriate amounts have been entered into the Adjusted Trial Balance columns, this pair of columns is totaled to prove arithmetical accuracy.

WATSON CORPORATION
Trial Balance
December 31, 1974

Cash	$ 42,000	
Accounts Receivable	52,000	
Allowance for Doubtful Accounts		$ 1,000
Notes Receivable	6,000	
Merchandise Inventory	75,000	
Prepaid Insurance	5,000	
Supplies	8,000	
Land	40,000	
Building	50,000	
Accumulated Depreciation—Building		10,000
Furniture and Fixtures	10,000	
Accumulated Depreciation—Furniture and Fixtures		4,000
Accounts Payable		30,000
Notes Payable		10,000
Unearned Rental Income		5,000
Capital Stock		100,000
Retained Earnings		50,000
Sales		260,000
Sales Returns and Allowances	5,000	
Sales Discounts	5,000	
Purchases	125,000	
Purchase Returns and Allowances		3,000
Purchase Discounts		2,000
Transportation In	4,000	
Advertising	6,000	
Sales Salaries	24,000	
Office Salaries	13,000	
Miscellaneous General Expense	5,000	
Interest Income		1,000
Interest Expense	1,000	
	$476,000	$476,000

The following additional information is available at December 31, 1974.

Merchandise Inventory, December 31, 1974	$80,000
Depreciation Expense:	
Buildings, 5% of cost	2,500
Furniture and Fixtures, 10% of cost	1,000
Bad Debts Expense, estimated at 1% of net sales	2,500
Prepaid Insurance, December 31, 1974	3,000
Supplies on hand, December 31, 1974	2,000
Accrued Interest on Notes Payable	300
Accrued Interest on Notes Receivable	200
Accrued sales salaries not paid	400
Accrued office salaries not paid	200
Unearned Rental Income, December 31, 1974	2,500

4. Each amount in the Adjusted Trial Balance columns is extended into the Statement of Income columns or the Balance Sheet columns depending upon the particular account involved. In addition, it should be noted that the merchandise inventory at December 31, 1974, is placed directly into the Statement of Income columns as a credit. This is done because one of the functions of the Statement of Income columns is to collect and arrange correctly all of the accounts involved in determining the cost of goods sold. By entering the ending inventory in the Statement of Income credit column, it is, in effect, being deducted from the total of beginning inventory, purchases, and transportation in, all of which are extended from the Adjusted Trial Balance debit column to the Statement of Income debit column; and Purchase Returns and Allowances and Purchase Discounts which are extended from the credit Adjusted Trial Balance column to the credit Statement of Income column. The ending inventory is also entered in the Balance Sheet debit column because this amount will appear as an asset in the Balance Sheet at the end of the fiscal period.

5. The net income or net loss for the fiscal period is determined by computing the difference between the totals of the pair of Statement of Income columns. If the credit column is larger than the debit column, the difference is the net income for the period and is entered in the *debit* column as a balancing figure of the Statement of Income columns and in the credit column of the Balance Sheet columns. The caption Net Income is written in the space for account titles to identify and explain this amount. If the debit column is larger than the credit column of the Statement of Income columns, the difference is the net loss for the period and is entered in the credit column as a balancing figure of the Statement of Income columns and in the debit column of the Balance Sheet columns.

The caption Net Loss is written in the space for account titles to identify and explain this amount.

6. After all appropriate amounts have been entered into the Balance Sheet columns, these columns are totaled to prove that the equality of the debits and credits has been retained.

FINANCIAL STATEMENTS

The formal Balance Sheet, Statement of Income, and Statement of Retained Earnings *prepared from* the work sheet of Watson Corporation appear on pages 508, 505 and 504 respectively.

WATSON CORPORATION
Statement of Retained Earnings
For the Year Ended December 31, 1974

Retained Earnings, January 1, 1974	$ 50,000
Net Income for the Year	70,800
Retained Earnings, December 31, 1974	$120,800

ADJUSTING ENTRIES

Data recorded in the Adjustments columns of the work sheet provide the information needed for the preparation of the formal adjusting entries in the journal. The adjusting entries are ordinarily taken directly from the Adjustments columns and recorded in the journal and then posted to the ledger. The adjusting journal entries of the Watson Corporation appear on page 509 and are posted to the ledger accounts appearing on pages 512 to 517.

THE CLOSING PROCESS

Revenue and expense accounts are temporary accounts used to classify changes in the owners' equity during an accounting period. At the end of the period, it is necessary to transfer balances in the revenue and expense accounts to one of the owners' equity accounts (retained earnings) on the statement of financial position. This transfer is accomplished by making a series of journal entries called closing entries.

WATSON CORPORATION

Statement of Income
For the Year Ended December 31, 1974

Sales			$260,000	
Less: Sales Returns and Allowances		$ 5,000		
Sales Discounts		5,000	10,000	
Net Sales				$250,000
Cost of Goods Sold:				
Merchandise Inventory, January 1, 1974			$ 75,000	
Purchases		$125,000		
Transportation In		4,000		
Gross Cost of Merchandise Purchased		$129,000		
Less: Purchase Returns and Allowances	$3,000			
Purchase Discounts	2,000	5,000		
Net Cost of Merchandise Purchased			124,000	
Cost of Merchandise Available for Sale			$199,000	
Less: Merchandise Inventory, December 31, 1974			80,000	
Cost of Goods Sold				119,000
Gross Margin on Sales				$131,000
Less: Operating Expenses:				
Advertising			$ 6,000	
Sales Salaries			24,400	
Bad Debts Expense			2,500	
Insurance Expense			2,000	
Supplies Expense			6,000	
Office Salaries			13,200	
Depreciation—Building			2,500	
Depreciation—Furniture & Fixtures			1,000	
Miscellaneous General Expense			5,000	
Total Operating Expenses				62,600
Net Operating Income				$ 68,400
Other Revenue and Expense				
Interest Income		$ 1,200		
Rental Income		2,500	$ 3,700	
Interest Expense			1,300	
Excess of Other Revenue over Other Expense				2,400
Net Income for the Year				$ 70,800

WATSON CORPORATION

Work Sheet

For the Year Ended December 31, 1974

Account Titles	Trial Balance		Adjustments		Adjusted Trial Balance		Statement of Income		Balance Sheet	
	Dr.	Cr.	Dr.	Cr.	Dr.	Cr.	Dr.	Cr.	Dr.	Cr.
Cash	42,000				42,000				42,000	
Accounts Receivable	52,000				52,000				52,000	
Allow. for Doubtful Accts.		1,000		3) 2,500		3,500				3,500
Notes Receivable	6,000				6,000				6,000	
Merchandise Inventory, January 1, 1974	75,000				75,000		75,000			
Prepaid Insurance	5,000			4) 2,000	3,000				3,000	
Supplies	8,000			5) 6,000	2,000				2,000	
Land	40,000				40,000				40,000	
Building	50,000				50,000				50,000	
Accumulated Depreciation—Building		10,000		1) 2,500		12,500				12,500
Furniture & Fixtures	10,000				10,000				10,000	
Accumulated Depreciation—Furniture & Fixtures		4,000		2) 1,000		5,000				5,000
Accounts Payable		30,000				30,000				30,000
Notes Payable		10,000				10,000				10,000
Unearned Rental Income		5,000	9) 2,500			2,500				2,500
Capital Stock		100,000				100,000				100,000
Retained Earnings		50,000				50,000				50,000
Sales		260,000				260,000		260,000		
Sales Returns & Allowances	5,000				5,000		5,000			
Sales Discounts	5,000				5,000		5,000			

Purchases	125,000				125,000		125,000			
Purchase Returns & Allowances		3,000				3,000		3,000		
Purchase Discounts		2,000				2,000		2,000		
Transportation In	4,000				4,000		4,000			
Advertising	6,000				6,000		6,000			
Sales Salaries	24,000		8) 400		24,400		24,400			
Office Salaries	13,000		8) 200		13,200		13,200			
Miscellaneous General Expense	5,000				5,000		5,000			
Interest Income		1,000		7) 200		1,200		1,200		
Interest Expense	1,000		6) 300		1,300		1,300			
	476,000	476,000								
Merchandise Inventory, December 31, 1974								80,000	80,000	
Depreciation—Building . . .			1) 2,500		2,500		2,500			
Depreciation—Furniture & Fixtures			2) 1,000		1,000		1,000			
Bad Debts Expense			3) 2,500		2,500		2,500			
Insurance Expense			4) 2,000		2,000		2,000			
Supplies Expense			5) 6,000		6,000		6,000			
Interest Payable				6) 300		300				300
Interest Receivable			7) 200		200				200	
Salaries Payable				8) 600		600				600
Rental Income				9) 2,500		2,500		2,500		
			17,600	17,600	483,100	483,100	277,900	348,700		
							70,800			70,800
Net Income							348,700	348,700	285,200	285,200

WATSON CORPORATION

Balance Sheet
December 31, 1974

ASSETS

Current Assets:		
Cash		$ 42,000
Accounts Receivable	$52,000	
Allowance for Doubtful Accounts	3,500	48,500
Notes Receivable		6,000
Interest Receivable		200
Merchandise Inventory		80,000
Prepaid Insurance		3,000
Supplies		2,000
Total Current Assets		$181,700
Property and Equipment:		
Land		$ 40,000
Building	$50,000	
Less: Accumulated Depreciation—Building	12,500	37,500
Furniture and Fixtures	$10,000	
Less: Accumulated Depreciation—Furniture and Fixtures	5,000	5,000
Net Property and Equipment		$ 82,500
Total Assets		$264,200

LIABILITIES

Current Liabilities:		
Accounts Payable		$30,000
Notes Payable		10,000
Interest Payable		300
Salaries Payable		600
Unearned Rental Income		2,500
Total Current Liabilities		$43,400

STOCKHOLDERS' EQUITY

Stockholders' Equity:		
Capital Stock	$100,000	
Retained Earnings	120,800	
Total Stockholders' Equity		220,800
Total Liabilities and Stockholders' Equity		$264,200

JOURNAL Page 17

Date	Description	P.R.	Debit	Credit
	Adjusting Entries			
1974	(1)			
Dec. 31	Depreciation—Building	66	2,500	
	Accumulated Depreciation—Building	12		2,500
	(2)			
	Depreciation—Furniture and Fixtures	67	1,000	
	Accumulated Depreciation—Furniture and Fixtures	14		1,000
	(3)			
	Bad Debts Expense	62	2,500	
	Allowance for Doubtful Accounts	3		2,500
	(4)			
	Insurance Expense	63	2,000	
	Prepaid Insurance	7		2,000
	(5)			
	Supplies Expense	64	6,000	
	Supplies	8		6,000
	(6)			
	Interest Expense	72	300	
	Interest Payable	22		300
	(7)			
	Interest Receivable	5	200	
	Interest Income	70		200
	(8)			
	Office Salaries	65	200	
	Sales Salaries	61	400	
	Salaries Payable	23		600
	(9)			
	Unearned Rental Income	24	2,500	
	Rental Income	71		2,500

It is possible to transfer the balances of all revenue and expense accounts directly to the retained earnings account, but additional convenience and information can be attained if the balances in these accounts are first transferred to a summary account, often called Profit and Loss Summary. The balance of the Profit and Loss Summary account, in turn, is transferred to the Retained Earnings account.

Data recorded in the Statement of Income columns of the work sheet provide the information needed for the preparation of the formal closing entries.

The entries to close the temporary accounts at the end of the period are prepared as follows:

1. Each item in the credit column of the Statement of Income columns on the work sheet is debited and the Profit and Loss Summary account is credited. This entry accomplishes two purposes: (1) it closes all of the temporary accounts on the work sheet which have credit balances, and (2) it records the merchandise inventory on hand at the end of the fiscal period. Although the ending merchandise inventory has been entered on the work sheet as a credit in the Statement of Income columns and as a debit in the Balance Sheet columns, it has never been recorded in the journal nor posted to the ledger.
2. Each item in the debit column of the Statement of Income columns on the work sheet is credited and the Profit and Loss Summary account is debited.
3. The balance in the Profit and Loss Summary account is transferred to the Retained Earnings account. For example, if a credit balance exists in the Profit and Loss Summary account, this balance is transferred to the Retained Earnings account by debiting the Profit and Loss Summary account and crediting the Retained Earnings account.
4. The balance of any profit distribution account, i.e. Dividends, is transferred to the Retained Earnings account by crediting the Dividends account and debiting the Retained Earnings account.

The closing journal entries for the Watson Corporation are presented on page 511 and are posted to the ledger accounts appearing on pages 512 to 517.

RULING AND BALANCING ACCOUNTS

After the closing entries have been journalized and posted, all ledger accounts are ruled and balanced. This step makes it possible: (1) to carry forward all financial position accounts with balances and to start the next accounting period with single amounts representing the balances at the end of the last period, and (2) to carry forward all temporary owners' equity accounts (expense, revenue, and dividends) with zero balances and thereby forego the danger of mingling entries from a prior period with those of future periods. The technique of ruling and balancing is illustrated with the ledger accounts on pages 512 to 517.

POST-CLOSING TRIAL BALANCE

After all expense, revenue, and profit distribution accounts have been closed at the end of the fiscal period, a post-closing trial balance is pre-

JOURNAL Page 18

Date	Description	P.R.	Debit	Credit
	Closing Entries			
1974				
Dec. 31	Sales	40	260,000	
	Purchase Returns and Allowances	51	3,000	
	Purchase Discounts	52	2,000	
	Interest Income	70	1,200	
	Merchandise Inventory	6	80,000	
	Rental Income	71	2,500	
	Profit and Loss Summary	32		348,700
	Profit and Loss Summary	32	277,900	
	Merchandise Inventory	6		75,000
	Sales Returns and Allowances	41		5,000
	Sales Discounts	42		5,000
	Purchases	50		125,000
	Transportation In	53		4,000
	Advertising	60		6,000
	Sales Salaries	61		24,400
	Office Salaries	65		13,200
	Miscellaneous General Expense	68		5,000
	Interest Expense	72		1,300
	Depreciation—Building	66		2,500
	Depreciation—Furniture and Fixtures	67		1,000
	Bad Debts Expense	62		2,500
	Insurance Expense	63		2,000
	Supplies Expense	64		6,000
	Profit and Loss Summary	32	70,800	
	Retained Earnings	31		70,800

pared directly from ledger accounts to prove the equality of debit and credit balances of accounts which are carried forward into the next fiscal period. Since all expense, revenue, and profit distribution accounts have been closed, the post-closing trial balance contains only financial position accounts. The post-closing trial balance is prepared by listing the balance of each account that appears in the ledger after the closing process has been completed.

The post-closing trial balance of the Watson Corporation appears on page 517.

Cash — Account 1

1974 Dec. 31	Bal.	✓	42,000				

Accounts Receivable — Account 2

1974 Dec. 31	Bal.	✓	52,000				

Allowance for Doubtful Accounts — Account 3

1974 Dec. 31	Bal.	✓	3,500	1974 Dec. 31	Bal.	✓	1,000
				31	Adj.	J17	2,500
			3,500				3,500
				1975 Jan. 1	Bal.	✓	3,500

Notes Receivable — Account 4

1974 Dec. 31	Bal.	✓	6,000				

Interest Receivable — Account 5

1974 Dec. 31	Adj.	J17	200				

Merchandise Inventory — Account 6

1974 Dec. 31	Bal.	✓	75,000	1974 Dec. 31	Closing	J18	75,000
31	Closing	J18	80,000	31	Bal.	✓	80,000
			155,000				155,000
1975 Jan. 1	Bal.	✓	80,000				

Prepaid Insurance — Account 7

1974 Dec. 31	Bal.	✓	5,000	1974 Dec. 31	Adj.	J17	2,000
				31	Bal.	✓	3,000
			5,000				5,000
1975 Jan. 1	Bal.	✓	3,000				

Supplies Account 8

1974				1974			
Dec. 31	Bal.	✓	8,000	Dec. 31	Adj.	J17	6,000
				31	Bal.	✓	2,000
			8,000				8,000
1975							
Jan. 1	Bal.	✓	2,000				

Land Account 10

1974							
Dec. 31	Bal.	✓	40,000				

Building Account 11

1974							
Dec. 31	Bal.	✓	50,000				

Accumulated Depreciation—Building Account 12

1974				1974			
Dec. 31	Bal.	✓	12,500	Dec. 31	Bal.	✓	10,000
				31	Adj.	J17	2,500
			12,500				12,500
				1975			
				Jan. 1	Bal.	✓	12,500

Furniture and Fixtures Account 13

1974							
Dec. 31	Bal.	✓	10,000				

Accumulated Depreciation—Furniture and Fixtures Account 14

1974				1974			
Dec. 31	Bal.	✓	5,000	Dec. 31	Bal.	✓	4,000
				31	Adj.	J17	1,000
			5,000				5,000
				1975			
				Jan. 1	Bal.	✓	5,000

Accounts Payable Account 20

				1974			
				Dec. 31	Bal.	✓	30,000

Notes Payable — Account 21

				1974 Dec. 31	Bal.	✓	10,000

Interest Payable — Account 22

				1974 Dec. 31	Adj.	J17	300

Salaries Payable — Account 23

				1974 Dec. 31	Adj.	J17	600

Unearned Rental Income — Account 24

1974 Dec. 31	Adj.	J17	2,500	1974 Dec. 31	Bal.		5,000
31	Bal.	✓	2,500				
			5,000				5,000
				1975 Jan. 1	Bal.		2,500

Capital Stock — Account 30

				1974 Dec. 31	Bal.	✓	100,000

Retained Earnings — Account 31

1974 Dec. 31	Bal.		120,800	1974 Dec. 31	Bal.	✓	50,000
				31	Closing	J18	70,800
			120,800				120,800
				1975 Jan. 1	Bal.		120,800

Profit and Loss Summary — Account 32

1974 Dec. 31	Closing	J18	277,900	1974 Dec. 31	Closing	J18	348,700
31	Closing	J18	70,800				
			348,700				348,700

Sales — Account 40

Date	Item	Ref.	Debit	Date	Item	Ref.	Credit
1974 Dec. 31	Closing	J18	260,000	1974 Dec. 31	Bal.	✓	260,000

Sales Returns and Allowances — Account 41

Date	Item	Ref.	Debit	Date	Item	Ref.	Credit
1974 Dec. 31	Bal.	✓	5,000	1974 Dec. 31	Closing	J18	5,000

Sales Discounts — Account 42

Date	Item	Ref.	Debit	Date	Item	Ref.	Credit
1974 Dec. 31	Bal.	✓	5,000	1974 Dec. 31	Closing	J18	5,000

Purchases — Account 50

Date	Item	Ref.	Debit	Date	Item	Ref.	Credit
1974 Dec. 31	Bal.	✓	125,000	1974 Dec. 31	Closing	J18	125,000

Purchase Returns and Allowances — Account 51

Date	Item	Ref.	Debit	Date	Item	Ref.	Credit
1974 Dec. 31	Closing	J18	3,000	1974 Dec. 31	Bal.	✓	3,000

Purchase Discounts — Account 52

Date	Item	Ref.	Debit	Date	Item	Ref.	Credit
1974 Dec. 31	Closing	J18	2,000	1974 Dec. 31	Bal.	✓	2,000

Transportation In — Account 53

Date	Item	Ref.	Debit	Date	Item	Ref.	Credit
1974 Dec. 31	Bal.	✓	4,000	1974 Dec. 31	Closing	J18	4,000

Advertising — Account 60

Date	Item	Ref.	Debit	Date	Item	Ref.	Credit
1974 Dec. 31	Bal.	✓	6,000	1974 Dec. 31	Closing	J18	6,000

Sales Salaries — Account 61

Date	Item	Ref.	Debit	Date	Item	Ref.	Credit
1974 Dec. 31	Bal.	✓	24,000	1974 Dec. 31	Closing	J18	24,400
31	Adj.	J17	400				
			24,400				24,400

Bad Debts Expense Account 62

1974				1974			
Dec. 31	Adj.	J17	2,500	Dec. 31	Closing	J18	2,500

Insurance Expense Account 63

1974				1974			
Dec. 31	Adj.	J17	2,000	Dec. 31	Closing	J18	2,000

Supplies Expense Account 64

1974				1974			
Dec. 31	Adj.	J17	6,000	Dec. 31	Closing	J18	6,000

Office Salaries Account 65

1974				1974			
Dec. 31	Bal.	✓	13,000	Dec. 31	Closing	J18	13,200
31	Adj.	J17	200				
			13,200				13,200

Depreciation—Building Account 66

1974				1974			
Dec. 31	Adj.	J17	2,500	Dec. 31	Closing	J18	2,500

Depreciation—Furniture and Fixtures Account 67

1974				1974			
Dec. 31	Adj.	J17	1,000	Dec. 31	Closing	J18	1,000

Miscellaneous General Expense Account 68

1974				1974			
Dec. 31	Bal.	✓	5,000	Dec. 31	Closing	J18	5,000

Interest Income Account 70

1974				1974			
Dec. 31	Closing	J18	1,200	Dec. 31	Bal.	✓	1,000
				31	Adj.	J17	200
			1,200				1,200

Rental Income — Account 71

1974 Dec. 31	Closing	J18	2,500	1974 Dec. 31	Adj.	J17	2,500

Interest Expense — Account 72

1974 Dec. 31	Bal.	✓	1,000	1974 Dec. 31	Closing	J18	1,300
31	Adj.	J17	300				
			1,300				1,300

WATSON CORPORATION

Post-Closing Trial Balance
December 31, 1974

Cash	$ 42,000	
Accounts Receivable	52,000	
Allowance for Doubtful Accounts		$ 3,500
Notes Receivable	6,000	
Interest Receivable	200	
Merchandise Inventory	80,000	
Prepaid Insurance	3,000	
Supplies	2,000	
Land	40,000	
Building	50,000	
Accumulated Depreciation—Building		12,500
Furniture and Fixtures	10,000	
Accumulated Depreciation—Furniture and Fixures		5,000
Accounts Payable		30,000
Notes Payable		10,000
Interest Payable		300
Salaries Payable		600
Unearned Rental Income		2,500
Capital Stock		100,000
Retained Earnings		120,800
	$285,200	$285,200

SUMMARY

The sequence of accounting procedures described and illustrated in this and the preceding chapter, constitutes a complete accounting process.

This sequence is repeated in the same order in each fiscal period and is often referred to as the accounting cycle. A brief restatement of this sequence follows:

A. Throughout an accounting period:
   1. Analyze transactions and record appropriate journal entries.
   2. Post debits and credits from the journal to the proper ledger accounts.

B. At the end of an accounting period:
   3. Prepare a trial balance of the ledger account balances.
   4. Prepare the work sheet.
   5. Prepare formal financial statements from the work sheet.
   6. Using the work sheet as a guide, enter the adjusting entries and closing entries in the journal.
   7. Post the adjusting entries and the closing entries to the ledger accounts.
   8. Rule and balance or rule the ledger accounts.
   9. Prepare a post-closing trial balance directly from the ledger accounts.

QUESTIONS AND PROBLEMS

15–1. Do the revenues of a period have any necessary relationship to the cash received in that period? Explain.

15–2. Why should the amount of insurance premiums paid in advance be treated as an asset?

15–3. Why should collections in advance be considered liabilities?

15–4. Why is the adjustment for estimated bad debts made?

15–5. The work sheet is a convenient tool used by the accountant. Explain.

15–6. Why is it desirable to prepare a post-closing trial balance?

15–7. Why is it necessary to make adjustments before preparing financial statements?

15–8. The closing process must follow the adjusting process. Explain.

15–9. Closing entries are designed to accomplish certain objectives. What are closing entries and what are their objectives?

15–10. After the books have been closed, there are no accounts with balances. True or False? Why?

15–11. a. What amount appeared in the trial balance, which showed no accruals or prepayals *prior* to adjustments, for *Interest Expense,* if the following figures were found in the balance sheet and the statement of income:

BALANCE SHEET		STATEMENT OF INCOME	
Accrued Interest Payable	$210	Interest Expense	$3,000
Interest Paid in Advance	45		

b. After all adjustments had been made and all columns totaled, but before the profit or loss was determined, a work sheet showed the following totals:

INCOME STATEMENT		BALANCE SHEET	
Dr.	Cr.	Dr.	Cr.
180,000	172,500	120,000	?

Assume the work was all done correctly.
1. What was the total of the credit Balance Sheet column?
2. What was the net profit or loss for the period? (State whether profit or loss.)

c. In preparing a work sheet, Prepaid Insurance $3,000 and Interest Income $750 were both placed in the debit Income Statement column. By how much will the work sheet be out of balance?

15–12. The information shown below was taken from the records of the Maxwell Company:

	YEAR 1974	YEAR 1975
Accounts Receivable, December 31	$90,000	$______
Allowance for Doubtful Accounts on December 31 balance sheet	$______	$2,000
Estimated bad debt allowance considered reasonable—based on Accounts Receivable at December 31	3%	2%
Allowance for Doubtful Accounts, unadjusted trial balance	$ 100(dr.)	$______
Bad Debts Expense on the statement of income	$______	$______
Accounts written off as worthless	$ 900	$2,400

What was the amount of the Allowance for Doubtful Accounts on the balance sheet at December 31, 1973? $______

Required

Fill in the blank spaces on a separate sheet of paper.

15–13. You hired a salesman on December 1, with the understanding that he would receive a commission of 10 percent on his sales. You gave him an advance of $500 cash with the understanding that this amount would be deducted from his earnings before any additional payments would be made to him, and that no additional payment would be made until January.

	ACCOUNT DEBITED WHEN THE ADVANCE WAS MADE	SALESMAN'S SALES IN DECEMBER
Case 1	Salesmen's Commissions	$6,000
Case 2	Salesmen's Commissions	4,000
Case 3	Prepaid Commissions	4,000

Required

For each case, make the necessary adjusting entry in journal form as of December 31.

15–14. The information below was taken from the records of the Alexander Company:

	YEAR 1974	YEAR 1975
Accounts Receivable, December 31	$______	$60,000
Allowance for Doubtful Accounts on December 31 Balance Sheet	$1,000	$______
Estimated bad debt allowance considered reasonable—based on Accounts Receivable at December 31	2%	3%
Allowance for Doubtful Accounts, unadjusted trial balance	$ 100(cr.)	$______
Bad Debts Expense on the statement of income	$______	$______
Accounts written off as worthless	$ 700	$ 1,400

What was the amount of the Allowance for Doubtful Accounts on the balance sheet at December 31, 1973? $______

Required

Fill in the blank spaces on a separate sheet of paper.

15–15. The balance (debit) in the Allowance for Doubtful Accounts account, before adjustment, on December 31, 1973, was $240. It was estimated that the Bad Debts Expense would be equal to ¼ of 1% of net credit sales. Total sales for the period amounted to $210,000 with credit sales amounting to $200,000 more than cash sales. Total sales returns and allowances amounted to $8,400. Credit returns and allowances were the same proportion of total returns and allowances as credit sales were of total sales.

Required

a. Record the December 31, 1973, adjusting entry for Bad Debts Expense.

b. What amount would appear as the Allowance for Doubtful Accounts on the December 31, 1973, balance sheet?

c. Record the entry on July 8, 1974, when $840 of individual customer accounts was ascertained to be uncollectible.

15–16. The following accounts were taken from the ledger of A. J. Realty Corporation. You are to interpret these accounts by answering the questions listed below.

COMMISSIONS COLLECTED IN ADVANCE

Dec. 31, 1974	38,220	Dec. 31, 1973	1,240
		During 1974 (Cash advances)	38,400

ACCRUED COMMISSIONS RECEIVABLE

Dec. 31, 1973	640	Jan. 15, 1974	640
Dec. 31, 1974	780		

COMMISSIONS EARNED

Dec. 31, 1974	39,000	Dec. 31, 1974	38,220
		Dec. 31, 1974	780

Required

a. What was the amount of Commissions Earned in the unadjusted trial balance as of December 31, 1974?

b. What was the amount of Commissions Earned in the 1974 statement of income?

c. What was the amount of Commissions Collected in Advance on the December 31, 1974, balance sheet?

d. What was the amount of Accrued Commissions Receivable on the December 31, 1974, balance sheet?

e. What was the amount of cash received for commissions:
   1. in 1974 that was income for 1973?
   2. in 1974 that was income for 1974?
   3. in 1974 that was income for 1975?
   4. in 1973 that was income for 1974?

15–17. The balance (debit) in the Allowance for Doubtful Accounts account, before adjustment, on December 31, 1973, was $240. An analysis of the Accounts Receivable account indicated that an estimated $1,160 would not be collected.

Required

a. Record the December 31, 1973, adjusting entry for Bad Debts Expense.

b. Record the entry on December 1, 1974, when $620 of individual customer accounts was ascertained to be uncollectible.

c. What amount would appear for Bad Debts Expense on the statement of income for 1974 if it was estimated that $940 of the December 31, 1974, Accounts Receivable would not be collected?

d. What amount would appear as the Allowance for Doubtful Accounts on the December 31, 1974, balance sheet?

e. An account for $350 written off as worthless on December 1, 1974, was collected on January 22, 1975. How should the $350 collection be recorded on January 22, 1975?

15–18. The following accounts were taken from the ledger of Best Corporation. You are to interpret these accounts by answering the questions listed below.

ACCRUED SALARIES PAYABLE

Jan. 4, 1974	1,880	Dec. 31, 1973	1,880
		Dec. 31, 1974	1,720

SALARIES EXPENSE

During 1974 (Cash paid)	42,400	Dec. 31, 1974	44,120
Dec. 31, 1974	1,720		

Required

a. What was the amount of Salaries Expense in the unadjusted trial balance as of December 31, 1974?

b. What was the amount of Salaries Expense on the 1974 statement of income?

c. What was the amount of Accrued Salaries Payable on the December 31, 1974, balance sheet?

d. What was the amount of Cash paid or to be paid for salaries:
1. in 1974 that was an expense of 1973?

2. in 1974 that was an expense of 1974?
3. in 1975 that was an expense of 1974?

15–19. Statements of the Stanley Company are presented below:

STANLEY COMPANY

Statement of Income
For the Month of January, 1974

Income:		
Commissions Income	$12,400	
Service Income	3,600	$16,000
Expenses:		
Salaries and Wage Expense	$11,800	
Supplies Expense	1,600	
Depreciation of Service Equipment	334	
Rent Expense	300	$14,034
Net Income		$ 1,966

STANLEY COMPANY

Balance Sheet
January 31, 1974

ASSETS		
Cash		$ 2,400
Supplies		200
Service Equipment	$32,000	
Less Accumulated Depreciation	8,334	23,666
Total Assets		$26,266
LIABILITIES		
Accrued Salaries and Wages	$ 400	
Accrued Rent Payable	300	
Unearned Service Income	2,800	
Total Liabilities		$ 3,500
OWNERS' EQUITY		
Capital Stock	$20,000	
Retained Earnings	2,766	
Total Owners' Equity		$22,766

STANLEY COMPANY

Statement of Retained Earnings
For the Month of January, 1974

Retained Earnings, January 2, 1974	$1,300
Add Net Income for January	1,966
Total	3,266
Deduct Dividends Declared in January	500
Retained Earnings, January 31, 1974	$2,766

The data from which adjusting entries were made before the above statements were prepared are summarized below:

1. Supplies used during January, $1,600.
2. Depreciation of service equipment, $334.
3. Of the unearned service income, $3,600 was earned during January.
4. Salaries and wages earned by employees, but unpaid on January 31, $400.
5. Rent payable for use of building during January, $300.

Required

Reconstruct the January 31, 1974, trial balance of the ledger of the Stanley Company before adjusting entries were made.

15–20. Following is the adjusted trial balance of the Fitzhugh Corporation on December 31, 1974.

Cash	$ 28,000	
Accounts Receivable	14,000	
Allowance for Bad Debts		$ 1,200
Accrued Interest Receivable	200	
Inventory of Merchandise	44,000	
Prepaid Insurance	1,280	
Furniture and Fixtures	48,000	
Allowance for Depreciation on Furn. & Fix.		4,800
Notes Payable		12,000
Accrued Interest Payable		80
Estimated Income Taxes Payable		6,000
Interest Collected in Advance		120
Capital Stock		100,000
Retained Earnings		7,200
Sales		180,000
Sales Returns and Allowances	2,400	
Sales Discounts	1,800	

Salaries Expense	36,000	
Insurance Expense	640	
Heat, Light, Power	1,000	
Supplies Expense	720	
Interest Expense	280	
Interest Earned		200
Purchases	124,000	
Depreciation Expense, Furn. & Fix.	2,400	
Bad Debts Expense	880	
Income Tax Expense	6,000	
	$311,600	$311,600

Required

a. Journalize closing entries. (Merchandise Inventory, Dec. 31, 1974, $48,000.)

b. What amount will appear on the December 31, 1974, balance sheet for Retained Earnings?

15–21. From the following selected facts, record the closing entries in a journal.

Inventory of Mdse. 1/1/1974	$ 8,838	Transportation In	1,080
Accrued Interest Payable	40	Prepaid Interest	120
Purchases	98,000	Purchase Returns and Allowances	2,000
Heat, Light and Power	640	Store Supplies	42
Sales Returns and Allowances	1,960	Insurance Expense	620
Depreciation of Equipment	1,404	Bad Debts Expense	500
Sales	172,800	Rent Expense	6,000
Salaries Expense	29,240	Purchase Discounts	2,040
Interest Expense	648	Gain on Sales of Equipment	1,534
Store Supplies Expense	872	Allowance for Depreciation—Equipment	2,420
Capital Stock	40,000	U.S. Treasury Bonds	5,000
Retained Earnings	4,000	Interest on Treasury Bonds	60
Loss on Sale of Investments	1,000	Inventory of Mdse. 12/31/1974	8,438
Transportation Out	470		
Allowance for Bad Debts	$ 600		

15–22. The trial balance of Dexter Co. at December 31, 1974 shows:

Accounts Receivable	$ 30,000
Allowance for Bad Debts (debit)	360
Inventory of Merchandise	150,000
Delivery Equipment	24,000
Allowance for Depreciation of Delivery Equipment	7,200
Purchases	306,000
Purchase Returns and Allowances	3,000
Transportation In	6,000
Prepaid Insurance	1,080

Adjustments are necessary for the following as of December 31, 1974:

1. Delivery equipment purchased on July 1, 2½ years ago was given an estimated life of 5 years from that date.
2. An allowance for bad debts equal to 2% of accounts receivable is considered reasonable.
3. No property taxes have been paid or recorded in 1974 and accrued taxes at the end of the year total $4,950.
4. Insurance premiums unexpired at year end amount to $720.

Required

Record all necessary adjusting journal entries at December 31, 1974.

15–23. The unadjusted trial balance of the Stowe Company at December 31, 1974, shows:

Accounts Receivable	$148,400
Purchases	364,000
Advertising Expense	12,400
Sales	280,000
Purchase Returns and Allowances	4,200
Building	120,000
Freight In	3,200
Merchandise Inventory	56,000
Rent Income	6,400
Insurance Expense	2,600
Interest Expense	1,460

The data for year-end adjustments on December 31 are as follows:

Advertising paid in advance	$ 1,240
Rent collected in advance	800
Interest accrued on notes payable	30
Insurance premiums paid in advance	320

Uncollectible Accounts estimated to be equal to ¼ of 1 percent of sales.

Building purchased January 2 of the current year was estimated to have a useful life of 20 years and no salvage value.

Required

Record the adjusting entries in general journal form.

15–24.

GLOBAL CORPORATION

Trial Balance, December 31, 1974

Cash	$ 14,818	
Accounts Receivable	5,210	
Allowance for Bad Debts		$ 148
Notes Receivable	2,400	
Inventory of Merchandise	15,832	
Inventory of Store Supplies	2,304	
Furniture and Fixtures	12,400	
Allowance for Depreciation on Furn. and Fix.		1,860
Accounts Payable		3,852
Notes Payable		4,000
Capital Stock		20,000
Retained Earnings		4,200
Sales		127,088
Sales Returns and Allowances	2,352	
Sales Discounts	1,364	
Purchases	84,748	
Purchase Returns and Allowances		1,388
Purchase Discounts		2,016
Store Salaries	19,120	
Rent Expense	4,320	
Insurance Expense	540	
Interest Expense	144	
Interest Earned		60
Rent Earned		940
	$165,552	$165,552

Supplemental information provided at December 31, 1974:

Expired insurance	$240
Inventory of store supplies	564
Accrued interest on notes receivable	30

Rent collected in advance	300
Store salaries accrued for one week	364
Interest paid in advance	20
Uncollectible accounts are estimated to be ¼ of 1 percent of net sales	
The furniture and fixtures of $12,400 were purchased July 1, 2½ years ago with an estimated life of 10 years.	

Required

Record the necessary adjusting journal entries.

15–25. The following items were taken from the trial balance of Discount House Corporation at December 31, 1974.

Cash	$19,000
Accounts Receivable	16,400
Notes Receivable	2,000
Inventory of Merchandise	10,000
Inventory of Supplies	200
Prepaid Insurance	600
Furniture and Fixtures	10,000
Accounts Payable	2,000
Notes Payable	4,000
Capital Stock	30,000
Retained Earnings	9,850
Sales	80,220
Sales Returns and Allowances	1,270
Purchases	58,400
Store Expenses	1,400
Salaries	6,000
Light, Heat, and Power	580
Interest Expense	220

Additional information provided at December 31, 1974:

Inventory of merchandise, December 31, 1974	$11,000
Interest accrued on notes receivable, December 31, 1974	10
Estimated bad debts expense	328
Accrued salaries, December 31, 1974	120
Insurance expired during 1974	200
Furniture and fixtures depreciated at the rate of 10% per year. All furniture and fixtures were purchased January 2, 1974	
Interest on notes payable at December 31, 1974	20

Required

a. Prepare a ten-column work sheet.

b. Record adjusting entries in a two-column journal.

c. Record closing entries in a two-column journal.

15–26. The accounts and their balances in the ledger of the Boone Corporation on December 31, 1974, are as follows:

Cash	$ 30,000
Accounts Receivable	16,000
Allowance for Doubtful Accounts	120
Notes Receivable	7,500
Inventory of Merchandise	22,000
Prepaid Insurance	360
Land	20,000
Building	50,000
Allowance for Depreciation—Building	10,000
Delivery Equipment	8,000
Allowance for Depreciation—Deliv. Equip.	2,400
Accounts Payable	10,000
Notes Payable	8,000
Rent Collected in Advance	1,800
Capital Stock	60,000
Retained Earnings	16,650
Sales	123,600
Sales Returns and Allowances	2,000
Sales Discounts	1,600
Purchases	66,000
Purchase Returns and Allowances	4,000
Purchase Discounts	2,000
Transportation In	1,500
Salaries Expense	12,000
Supplies Expense	500
Property Taxes Expense	1,200
Interest Earned	175
Interest Expense	85

Additional information provided at December 31, 1974:

Inventory of merchandise, December 31, 1974	$19,500
Prepaid insurance as of December 31, 1974	240
The building had an estimated life of 10 years and was purchased on January 1, 1972	
Delivery equipment had an estimated life of 5 years and was purchased on July 1, 1972	

Bad debt expense is estimated to be ¼ of 1 percent of net sales	
Salaries accrued at December 31, 1974	1,000
Supplies on hand at December 31, 1974	100
Interest accrued on notes receivable as of December 31, 1974	40
Interest accrued on notes payable as of December 31, 1974	25
Rent collected in advance, December 31, 1974	300
Interest collected in advance on notes receivable	15
Property taxes accrued as of December 31, 1974	300
Estimated federal income tax for 1974	2,700

Required

a. Prepare a ten-column work sheet.

b. Record adjusting journal entries and post to the ledger accounts.

c. Record closing journal entries and post to the ledger accounts.

d. Rule and balance the ledger accounts.

e. Prepare a post-closing trial balance.

Appendices

APPENDIX A–Excerpts from Annual Reports of

PPG Industries, Inc.
Armstrong Cork Company
Indiana Telephone Corporation

APPENDIX B–Specialized Journals, Controlling Accounts, and Subsidiary Ledgers

Appendix A

PPG INDUSTRIES, INC.

Accountants' Opinion

PPG Industries, Inc.

We have examined the financial statements of PPG Industries, Inc. and its consolidated subsidiaries for the years ended December 31, 1972 and 1971. Our examination was made in accordance with generally accepted auditing standards, and accordingly included such tests of the accounting records and such other auditing procedures as we considered necessary in the circumstances. We did not examine the financial statements of three consolidated Canadian subsidiaries, which statements reflect total assets and revenues constituting approximately 7% and 8%, respectively, of the related consolidated totals for each of the years. We were furnished with reports of other auditors on their examinations of the financial statements of these companies for the years ended December 31, 1972 and 1971. Our opinion expressed below, insofar as it relates to the amounts included for these companies, is based solely upon the reports of the other auditors.

In our opinion, based upon our examination and the reports of other auditors, the accompanying consolidated balance sheet and statements of consolidated earnings, retained earnings, and source and use of funds present fairly the financial position of PPG Industries, Inc. and consolidated subsidiaries at December 31, 1972 and 1971, and the results of their operations and sources and uses of their funds for the years then ended, in conformity with generally accepted accounting principles applied on a consistent basis.

Haskins & Sells
Pittsburgh, Pennsylvania
January 31, 1973

Summary of Accounting Policies

The following accounting principles and practices of PPG Industries, Inc., and its consolidated subsidiaries are set forth to facilitate the understanding of data presented in the financial statements.

PRINCIPLES OF CONSOLIDATION

The consolidated financial statements include the accounts of the Corporation and all significant subsidiaries, domestic and foreign, in which PPG owns more than 50 per cent of the voting stock. The investments in all companies in which PPG owns 20 to 50 per cent of the voting stock are carried at equity, and PPG's share of the earnings or losses of such equity affiliates is included in the statement of consolidated earnings. Transactions between PPG, its subsidiaries, and its equity affiliates are eliminated from the consolidated financial statements.

TRANSLATION OF FOREIGN CURRENCIES

The accounts of foreign subsidiaries and equity affiliates are translated to U. S. dollars based on the official or free rates of exchange applicable in the circumstances. Current assets, current liabilities and long-term debt are translated at the rates of exchange in effect at the end of the year. All other assets and capital shares are translated at the exchange rates prevailing when the assets were acquired or the capital stocks issued. Income and expense accounts are translated at average exchange rates for each year, except that depreciation is translated at historical rates.

Gains and losses relating to the translation of long-term debt are deferred and amortized over the life of the debt. All other gains and losses resulting from normal exchange rate fluctuations are reflected in current earnings. The Corporation maintains a reserve for gains and losses arising from major currency revaluations.

INVENTORIES

Inventories are stated generally at the lower of cost or market. Cost is determined using either average or standard factory costs, which approximate actual costs, excluding certain fixed expenses such as depreciation, property taxes and rentals.

PROPERTY AND DEPRECIATION

Property includes the cost of land, buildings, equipment, and significant improvements which add to productive capacity or extend the life of the assets. When units of property are disposed of, the cost and accumulated depreciation are removed from the accounts, and any resulting gain or loss is credited or charged to earnings.

Depreciation, for financial reporting purposes, is computed by the straight-line method based on the estimated useful lives of depreciable assets.

PRE-OPERATING COSTS

During construction of major facilities, costs are incurred for acquiring and training employees, providing light, heat, and water, and maintaining new equipment in operating condition. When such pre-operating costs are significant and there is no offsetting revenue being generated, the costs are deferred and amortized over a 10-year period.

GOODWILL

When the Corporation purchases companies for prices in excess of book values of the net assets acquired, the excess cost is accounted for as goodwill and is amortized generally over a 10-year period. Acquisitions made by exchanging common stock are generally recorded on a pooling-of-interests basis and no goodwill is recognized.

INCOME TAXES

Certain charges to earnings in the financial statements differ in amount from those deducted in tax returns. For example, depreciation is computed on accelerated methods for income tax purposes and on the straight-line method for financial reporting purposes. The tax effects of these differences are provided for as future income taxes in the financial statements.

The Corporation follows the policy of treating the investment credit allowance for capital projects as a reduction of income tax expense in the year in which the projects are completed, except for amounts which it anticipates might be recaptured. Prior to 1969, the Corporation followed the policy of deferring the investment credit allowance and amortizing the credit over the estimated useful lives of the related assets.

No provision is made for income taxes on undistributed earnings of affiliates since any taxes payable would be substantially offset by tax credits or because the Corporation intends to invest such earnings permanently.

RESEARCH AND DEVELOPMENT

Research and development expenditures, including development costs of products, processes, and product applications, are expensed in the year incurred rather than deferred.

PROVISION FOR MAINTENANCE AND REPAIRS

Current operations are charged with the cost of labor and materials incurred in maintaining properties in, and restoring properties to, good operating condition. Major furnace repairs, however, are provided for in advance by charging current operations with the estimated costs.

PROVISION FOR SELF-INSURANCE

PPG maintains a reserve which, in the Company's judgment, adequately provides for the cost of casualty losses which, if sustained, would not be covered by insurance.

PROVISION FOR LOSSES ON DISCONTINUED OPERATIONS

PPG follows the practice of providing for significant losses on terminating operations or on abandoning facilities when such losses can be reasonably estimated. Such losses are recognized as a charge against earnings concurrent with management's announcement to its customers, employees, shareholders, and other interested parties of its intention to suspend operations.

PENSION COSTS

Pension costs charged to current earnings include charges for current service and amortization of prior service costs over 30 years. The extra cost of improvements in benefits to present retirees is amortized over 10 years.

Statement of Consolidated Source and Use of Funds

		Year Ended December 31 1972	1971
Source of Funds:	Earnings before extraordinary items	$ 82,675,000	$ 63,163,000
	Extraordinary items, net of income taxes	–	(16,000,000)
	Charges to earnings not requiring funds:		
	Depreciation	62,946,000	59,061,000
	Amortization of intangible assets	3,055,000	2,989,000
	Future income taxes and investment credit	6,449,000	11,649,000
	Increase in accumulated provisions	425,000	11,946,000
	Extraordinary items	–	11,719,000
	Equity in net (earnings) losses of equity affiliates	4,909,000	(787,000)
	Funds provided from operations	**160,459,000**	**143,740,000**
	Proceeds from sale and leaseback agreements	–	31,151,000
	Issuance of long-term debt	22,783,000	67,312,000
	Disposition of property and investment	8,282,000	27,108,000
	Issuance of common shares	3,518,000	5,248,000
	Other—net	2,057,000	(544,000)
	Total	**$197,099,000**	**$274,015,000**
Use of Funds:	Expenditures for property and investment	$ 92,321,000	$123,497,000
	Cash dividends paid	30,134,000	28,798,000
	Increase in deferred charges and other assets	3,781,000	7,254,000
	Reduction in long-term debt	23,498,000	43,496,000
	Increase in working capital	47,365,000	70,970,000
	Total	**$197,099,000**	**$274,015,000**
Changes in Working Capital:	Cash and securities	$ 20,818,000	$ 34,949,000
	Notes and accounts receivable	25,314,000	29,861,000
	Inventories	11,769,000	(17,772,000)
	Prepayment and other current assets	(900,000)	(713,000)
	Notes payable	6,622,000	36,229,000
	Current maturities of long-term debt	12,163,000	(4,465,000)
	Accounts payable and accrued expenses	(11,708,000)	(17,538,000)
	Domestic and foreign taxes on income	(16,713,000)	10,419,000
	Total	**$ 47,365,000**	**$ 70,970,000**

The "Summary of Accounting Policies" and the "Notes to Financial Statements" are an integral part of this statement.

Statement of Consolidated Earnings and Retained Earnings

		Year Ended December 31, 1972	1971
Earnings for the Year:	Net sales	$1,395,921,000	$1,238,472,000
	Equity in net earnings of equity affiliates	(4,909,000)	787,000
	Other earnings	16,819,000	15,609,000
	Total	**1,407,831,000**	**1,254,868,000**
	Cost of sales	914,866,000	818,511,000
	Selling, general and administrative expenses	203,032,000	181,747,000
	Depreciation expense	62,946,000	59,061,000
	Research and development	35,101,000	32,495,000
	Taxes—exclusive of taxes on income	37,204,000	34,685,000
	Interest expense	23,106,000	25,464,000
	Other charges—net	2,909,000	2,285,000
	Total	**1,279,164,000**	**1,154,248,000**
	Earnings before income taxes, minority interest, and extraordinary items	**128,667,000**	**100,620,000**
	Domestic and foreign taxes on income	43,000,000	35,200,000
	Minority interest	2,992,000	2,257,000
	Total	**45,992,000**	**37,457,000**
	Earnings before extraordinary items	**82,675,000**	**63,163,000**
	Extraordinary items, net of income taxes	–	**(16,000,000)**
	Net Earnings	**$ 82,675,000**	**$ 47,163,000**
Earnings per Common Share:	**Before Extraordinary Items**	**$ 3.99**	**$ 3.07**
	Net Earnings	**$ 3.99**	**$ 2.29**
	Average Common Shares Outstanding	**20,705,000**	**20,596,000**
Retained Earnings:	Balance at January 1	$ 501,199,000	$ 482,724,000
	Net earnings	82,675,000	47,163,000
	Retained earnings of pooled company	–	110,000
	Total	**583,874,000**	**529,997,000**
	Cash dividends (per common share: 1972, $1.455; 1971, $1.40)	30,134,000	28,798,000
	Balance at December 31	**$ 553,740,000**	**$ 501,199,000**

The "Summary of Accounting Policies" and "Notes to Financial Statements" are an integral part of this statement.

Consolidated Balance Sheet—Assets

		December 31, 1972	1971
Current Assets:	Cash, including time deposits	$ 29,454,000	$ 34,095,000
	United States Government and other marketable securities—at lower of cost or market	50,015,000	24,556,000
	(Quoted market value: 1972, $50,037,000; 1971, $24,578,000)		
	Notes and accounts receivable (less estimated losses: 1972, $4,482,000; 1971, $3,819,000)	235,911,000	210,597,000
	Inventories	215,975,000	204,206,000
	Prepayments and other current assets	17,417,000	18,317,000
	Total Current Assets	**548,772,000**	**491,771,000**
Investments:	Investments in equity affiliates	75,366,000	74,808,000
	Other—at cost or less	7,804,000	7,824,000
	Total Investments	**83,170,000**	**82,632,000**
Property—At Cost:	Land, buildings, machinery and equipment, etc.	1,440,916,000	1,377,399,000
	Less accumulated depreciation	715,156,000	667,285,000
	Property—Net	**725,760,000**	**710,114,000**
Other Assets:	Deferred charges and other assets	**36,883,000**	**36,157,000**
	Total	**$1,394,585,000**	**$1,320,674,000**

The "Summary of Accounting Policies" and "Notes to Financial Statements" are an integral part of this statement.

Consolidated Balance Sheet—Liabilities

		December 31, 1972	1971
Current Liabilities:	Notes payable	$ 10,329,000	$ 16,951,000
	Current maturities of long-term debt	6,339,000	18,502,000
	Accounts payable and accrued expenses	156,050,000	144,342,000
	Domestic and foreign taxes on income	29,978,000	13,265,000
	Total Current Liabilities	**202,696,000**	**193,060,000**
Long-Term Debt:	Long-term debt	**300,705,000**	**301,420,000**
	Total Deferred Credits and Accumulated Provisions	**141,489,000**	**134,615,000**
Deferred Credits and Accumulated Provisions:	Future income taxes	65,968,000	57,539,000
	Investment credit—unamortized balance	10,047,000	12,027,000
	Maintenance and repairs	19,074,000	17,368,000
	Insurance and unfunded and uninsured pensions	14,938,000	13,525,000
	Discontinued operations	28,599,000	30,216,000
	Other	2,863,000	3,940,000
Minority Interest:	Minority interest in consolidated subsidiaries	**18,452,000**	**16,395,000**
Shareholders' Equity:	Cumulative preferred stock—authorized but unissued 5,000,000 shares, without par value	—	—
	Common stock—authorized 50,000,000 shares, par value $2.50	213,335,000	212,153,000
	Retained earnings	553,740,000	501,199,000
	Common stock in treasury—at cost	(35,832,000)	(38,168,000)
	Shareholders' Equity	**731,243,000**	**675,184,000**
	Total	**$1,394,585,000**	**$1,320,674,000**

Notes To Financial Statements

1. Inventories—A comparison of inventories by major components at December 31, 1972 and 1971, is as follows:

	1972	1971
Finished Products	$ 124,026,000	$ 116,482,000
Work in Process	25,295,000	23,346,000
Raw Materials	45,274,000	44,326,000
Supplies	21,380,000	20,052,000
Total	**$ 215,975,000**	**$ 204,206,000**

2. Property—A summary of total property, by major category, as of December 31, 1972 and 1971, is as follows:

	1972	1971
Land	$ 19,655,000	$ 17,972,000
Buildings	278,081,000	259,769,000
Machinery and Equipment	1,075,003,000	1,000,022,000
Other	38,823,000	36,028,000
Construction in Progress	29,354,000	63,608,000
Total	**$1,440,916,000**	**$1,377,399,000**

3. Pre-Operating Costs—At December 31, 1972 and 1971, pre-operating costs, included in deferred charges and other assets, amounted to $8,454,000 and $8,659,000, respectively. Amortization of pre-operating costs charged against earnings amounted to $914,000 in 1972 and $78,000 in 1971.

4. Goodwill—At December 31, 1972 and 1971, goodwill, included in deferred charges and other assets, amounted to $2,892,000 and $3,760,000, respectively. Amortization of goodwill charged against earnings amounted to $2,120,000 in 1972 and $2,777,000 in 1971.

5. Long-Term Debt—At December 31, 1972 and 1971, long-term debt consisted of the following:

	1972	1971
9% debentures due in 1995 for which sinking fund payments of $8,000,000 will be made in each of the years 1980 to 1994	$125,000,000	$125,000,000
5⅝% debentures due in 1991 for which sinking fund payments of $6,250,000 will be made in each of the years 1973 to 1991	112,500,000	118,750,000
European borrowings at 7% to 7¾%, due 1975 to 1986	23,886,000	23,022,000
Bank note due 1980 to 1982	16,000,000	—
Various other debts, primarily debt incurred by consolidated subsidiaries	23,319,000	34,648,000
Total	**$300,705,000**	**$301,420,000**

The aggregate maturities and sinking fund requirements for the next five years on long-term debt outstanding at December 31, 1972, are as follows:

1973	$ 6,339,000
1974	9,080,000
1975	24,535,000
1976	8,547,000
1977	8,349,000

6. Commitments and Contingencies—Lease commitments as of December 31, 1972, which are for periods in excess of two years, have aggregate annual rentals of approximately $13,800,000. The Corporation is contingently liable for approximately $8,600,000 as a guarantor of lines of credit in connection with the financing of the sale of Corporation products, loans, etc.

A number of lawsuits are pending against the Corporation, including those brought by Continental Oil Company and by Commonwealth Oil Refining Company (see page 9 for a discussion of those cases). Although the results of litigation cannot be predicted, management, upon advice of the Corporation's counsel, believes that the outcome of such litigation will not have a material adverse effect on the financial position or results of operations of PPG and its consolidated subsidiaries.

7. Capital Stock—Changes in Common Stock Issued and Common Stock in Treasury for the years ended December 31, 1972 and 1971, are as follows:

	Common Stock Issued		Common Stock in Treasury	
	Shares	Amount	Shares	Amount
Balance January 1, 1971	**21,734,157**	**$213,102,000**	**1,236,077**	**$42,451,000**
Shares issued under employee stock option plans	50,230	965,000	(58,310)	(2,011,000)
Shares delivered to retired employees under incentive compensation agreements	–	–	(2,755)	(94,000)
Changes resulting from a pooling of interest	–	(1,914,000)	(63,162)	(2,178,000)
Balance December 31, 1971	**21,784,387**	**212,153,000**	**1,111,850**	**38,168,000**
Shares issued under employee stock option plans	42,546	947,000	(11,205)	(386,000)
Shares delivered to retired employees under incentive compensation agreements	–	–	(3,009)	(99,000)
Shares issued for purchase of a company	–	235,000	(53,667)	(1,851,000)
Balance December 31, 1972	**21,826,933**	**$213,335,000**	**1,043,969**	**$35,832,000**

Amounts shown on the balance sheet for "Common Stock" represent the par value of shares issued plus capital contributed for stock in excess of par.

8. Stock Option and Incentive Compensation Plans—Information regarding stock options as of December 31, 1972 and 1971, is summarized as follows:

	1972	1971
Shares reserved for issuance upon exercise of employee stock options	241,995	295,862
Shares under option*	164,995	128,362
Options granted during year	90,500	–
Options exercised during year*	53,751	108,540
Options terminated during year	116	15,619
Exercisable	53,995	84,012

*At prices ranging from $22.53 to $45.56 per share.

The Corporation has also reserved 40,958 shares and 43,967 shares of its common stock at December 31, 1972 and 1971, respectively, for future issuance under incentive compensation agreements with certain key employees.

9. Taxes On Income—Provisions for domestic and foreign income taxes in 1972 and 1971 amounted to:

	1972	1971
Current—Federal	$28,835,000	$16,145,000
Current—foreign	3,322,000	1,988,000
Current—city and state	4,737,000	2,484,000
Deferred investment credit amortized	(1,979,000)	(1,978,000)
Future income taxes	8,085,000	16,561,000
Total	**$43,000,000**	**$35,200,000**

The current provisions for income taxes for 1972 and 1971 have been reduced by $6,223,000 and $3,564,000, respectively, for investment credits taken directly into earnings in those years. The unamortized investment credit of $10,047,000 at December 31, 1972, deferred from years prior to 1969, will be added to earnings over the next six years.

10. Extraordinary Items—The extraordinary items for 1971, after net tax credits of $17,686,000, consisted of the following:

Provision for termination of certain marginal operations	$15,818,000
Loss on sale of investment in domestic subsidiary	4,000,000
(Gain) on sale of investments and other assets	(3,818,000)
Net Loss	**$16,000,000**

11. Sale and Leaseback Agreements—In 1971, the Corporation entered into sale and leaseback agreements for a chemical tanker and related terminal facilities. Funds provided from the agreements totaled $31,151,000.

12. Earnings Per Share—Earnings per share are computed on the basis of weighted average shares outstanding during each year. Shares reserved for issuance under the Company's employee stock option plans and deferred incentive compensation agreements would not materially dilute earnings per share.

13. Reference is made to the Financial and Operating Review section, beginning on page 19, for additional information regarding income taxes; amounts required to complete capital projects approved prior to December 31, 1972; details of pension plans; and announcement of potential sale of assets.

ARMSTRONG CORK COMPANY

Accountants' Letter

PEAT, MARWICK, MITCHELL & CO.
CERTIFIED PUBLIC ACCOUNTANTS
1500 WALNUT STREET
PHILADELPHIA, PA 19102

The Board of Directors and Stockholders,
Armstrong Cork Company:

We have examined the consolidated balance sheets of Armstrong Cork Company and subsidiaries as of December 31, 1972 and 1971 and the related statements of earnings and changes in financial position for the respective years then ended. Our examination was made in accordance with generally accepted auditing standards, and accordingly included such tests of the accounting records and such other auditing procedures as we considered necessary in the circumstances.

In our opinion, the above-mentioned financial statements present fairly the financial position of Armstrong Cork Company and subsidiaries at December 31, 1972 and 1971 and the results of their operations and changes in financial position for the respective years then ended, in conformity with generally accepted accounting principles applied on a consistent basis.

Peat, Marwick, Mitchell & Co.

February 15, 1973

STATEMENTS OF CONSOLIDATED EARNINGS

Armstrong Cork Company and Subsidiaries

Years ended December 31

The Financial Review, pages 22–27, is an integral part of these statements.

	1972 (000)	1971 (000)
Current Earnings		
Income:		
Net sales	**$684,470**	$563,962
Other income, net	**6,192**	6,412
	690,662	570,374
Costs and expenses:		
Cost of goods sold	**456,400**	372,424
Selling and administrative	**122,432**	104,043
Depreciation and amortization	**27,034**	23,473
Interest expense	**6,535**	6,112
	612,401	506,052
Earnings before income taxes	**78,261**	64,322
Federal and foreign income taxes	**36,500**	28,850
NET EARNINGS	**$ 41,761**	$ 35,472
NET EARNINGS PER SHARE OF COMMON STOCK	**$ 1.60**	$ 1.36
Retained Earnings		
Amount at beginning of year	**$308,769**	$294,412
Net earnings for the year	**41,761**	35,472
	350,530	329,884
Deduct dividends:		
Preferred stock—$3.75 per share	**443**	443
Voting preferred stock—$2.375 per share	**238**	238
Common stock—$.80 per share	**20,508**	20,434
	21,189	21,115
Amount at end of year	**$329,341**	$308,769

CONSOLIDATED BALANCE SHEETS

Armstrong Cork Company and Subsidiaries

As of December 31

The Financial Review, pages 22–27, is an integral part of these statements.

	1972 (000)	1971 (000)
Assets		
Current assets:		
Cash	$ 8,243	$ 13,883
Short-term securities (at cost, which approximates market)	12,382	18,935
Accounts and notes receivable (less allowance for discounts and losses: 1972—$4,866,000; 1971—$4,258,000)	89,751	82,734
Inventories	124,074	112,884
Prepaid expenses	4,652	3,745
Total current assets	239,102	232,181
Long-term receivables	37,548	33,492
Property, plant and equipment (at cost, less accumulated depreciation and amortization: 1972—$191,039,000; 1971—$172,639,000)	300,107	290,444
Sundry assets and investments, at cost or less	11,484	4,307
	$588,241	$560,424
Liabilities and Stockholders' Equity		
Current liabilities:		
Notes payable	$ 12,608	$ 9,869
Current installments on long-term debt	816	5,399
Accounts payable and accrued expenses	53,948	47,677
Federal and foreign income taxes	6,142	16,760
Total current liabilities	73,514	79,705
Long-term debt	75,174	70,952
Deferred income taxes	23,117	18,702
Minority interest in foreign subsidiary	2,312	2,257
Stockholders' equity	414,124	388,808
	$588,241	$560,424

STATEMENTS OF CONSOLIDATED CHANGES IN FINANCIAL POSITION

Armstrong Cork Company and Subsidiaries

Years ended December 31

The Financial Review, pages 22–27, is an integral part of these statements.

	1972 (000)	1971 (000)
Funds became available from:		
Operations:		
Net earnings	$ 41,761	$ 35,472
Depreciation and amortization	27,034	23,473
Other items, including deferred income taxes	1,058	2,212
Total from operations	69,853	61,157
Long-term borrowings:		
8% sinking fund debentures	—	50,000
Other, net	4,222	6,958
Prepayment of long-term note receivable	—	5,000
Sale of common stock under option plans	1,353	1,593
Other items	—	3,432
	75,428	128,140
These funds were used for:		
Capital additions to property, plant and equipment	38,512	40,645
Dividends to stockholders	21,189	21,115
Other items	2,615	—
	62,316	61,760
INCREASE IN WORKING CAPITAL	$ 13,112	$ 66,380
Changes in working capital consist of:		
Increase (decrease) in current assets:		
Cash and short-term securities	$ (12,193)	$ 18,371
Receivables	7,017	17,475
Inventories	11,190	6,569
Other items	907	(1,272)
	6,921	41,143
Increase (decrease) in current liabilities:		
Notes payable and current installments of long-term liabilities	(1,844)	(51,397)
Accounts payable and accrued liabilities	6,271	9,400
Income taxes	(10,618)	16,760
	(6,191)	(25,237)
INCREASE IN WORKING CAPITAL	$ 13,112	$ 66,380

FINANCIAL REVIEW

Armstrong Cork Company and Subsidiaries

The accounting principles followed in this annual report are similar to those used by most industrial firms in America. The company's management has consistently used these principles because they are most suitable for directing day-to-day operations and because they provide reliable and consistent data for stockholders and the public in general.

To assist in understanding this financial review, the accounting principles used are printed in blue as are supporting tables and charts.

The consolidated financial statements and the accompanying data in this report include the accounts of the parent Armstrong Cork Company and its domestic and foreign subsidiaries. All significant items relating to transactions between the parent and subsidiaries and between subsidiaries are eliminated from consolidated statements. The parent company adjusts the carrying value of its investment in subsidiaries to reflect changes in net equity of such subsidiaries.

Consolidated Foreign Subsidiaries
Significant Assets and Liabilities at December 31

	1972 (000)	1971 (000)
Current assets	**$ 50,171**	$49,005
Current liabilities	**24,845**	29,490
Net working capital	**25,326**	19,515
Plant and other assets	**45,330**	43,496
Long-term debt	**21,850**	17,564

Net Sales and Earnings for years ended December 31

	1972 (000)	1971 (000)
Net sales	**$101,767**	$84,491
Earnings before exchange adjustments and income taxes	**11,023**	9,023
Net earnings	**5,144**	5,883

The accounts of foreign subsidiaries are translated into U. S. dollars based on appropriate rates of exchange. Monetary assets and liabilities are translated at year-end exchange rates, plant and equipment (and related depreciation) at historical rates, and income and expense items other than depreciation at average rates prevailing during the year. Exchange adjustments resulted in a loss of approximately $400,000 in 1972 and a gain of $450,000 in 1971. Exchange losses and gains are included in reported net earnings.

On June 30, 1972, the company purchased the assets and assumed certain liabilities of Cryo-Therm, Inc., a manufacturer of Armalok rigid urethane foam insulation in exchange for 86,848 shares of Armstrong common stock held in the company treasury. Substantial increases in Armalok sales in future years may require the issuance of additional shares of Armstrong common stock up to a maximum of 220,000 shares. The acquisition was accounted for as a purchase. Therefore, the results of the acquired entity since acquisition have been included, but the amounts are not material.

On September 29, 1972, the company sold Knapp & Tubbs, Inc., its wholesale showroom furniture distributor subsidiary, to an affiliate of Magnavox

Company. Knapp & Tubbs' operating results for 1972 and 1971 and the gain resulting from the sale, all immaterial in amount, are included in the financial statements.

OPERATING STATEMENT ITEMS

Net sales in 1972 totaled $684.5 million, a record level, 21% higher than the 1971 total. The amounts reported as net sales are the total of sales billed during the year less the sales value of goods returned, trade discounts and customers' allowances, and freight costs incurred in delivering products to customers.

Net earnings during 1972 amounted to $41.8 million compared with $35.5 million in 1971. Earnings per common share were $1.60 in 1972 compared with $1.36 in 1971. Earnings per share are determined by dividing net earnings, after deducting preferred dividends, by the average number of common shares outstanding. Inclusion of shares contingently issuable under the terms of stock options and outstanding convertible preferred stock would affect earnings per share by less than one cent in either year.

Net Sales by Major Product Classes

	1972 (000)	1971 (000)
Floor coverings	**$364,292**	$294,528
Ceilings	**125,890**	108,095
Furniture	**113,113**	94,177
Total Interior Furnishings	**603,295**	496,800
Industrial and other products and services	**81,175**	67,162
Net sales	**$684,470**	$563,962

Lines of business—the Interior Furnishings line contributed 92% of total operating income in 1972, compared with 91% in 1971. Operating income consists of earnings before allocating interest, certain corporate administrative expenses, and federal and foreign income taxes.

Employee compensation, including benefit costs, rose to a record $225.3 million in 1972, as average employment increased from 21,354 persons in 1971 to 22,564 in 1972.

The company and certain of its subsidiaries have pension plans covering substantially all employees. Obligations of these plans are funded through trusts and insurance. Pension costs charged to operations totaled $5.9 million in 1972 and $4.6 million in 1971. These costs consist of actuarially determined current service costs and amounts necessary to amortize prior service obligations over periods ranging up to 30 years. The company funds these pension costs currently. The unfunded past service liability amounted to approximately $13.3 million as of December 31, 1972.

Employee Compensation

	1972 (000)	1971 (000)
Wages and salaries, including vacations and holiday pay	**$200,771**	$172,002
Social Security and other payroll taxes	**10,079**	8,143
Pension costs	**5,948**	4,613
Medical, hospitalization, accident, life insurance and other benefit costs	**8,489**	7,661
	$225,287	$192,419

FINANCIAL REVIEW

Maintenance and repairs, advertising, and research and development expenditures are charged to expense as incurred, rather than deferred and amortized against future earnings.

Depreciation and amortization amounted to $27.0 million in 1972 compared with $23.5 million in 1971. The company generally uses straight-line depreciation for financial reporting purposes and accelerated depreciation as permitted for tax purposes, at rates calculated to provide for the retirement of assets at the end of their useful lives. When assets are disposed of or retired, their costs and related depreciation are removed from the books, and any gains or losses that result are reflected in earnings.

1972 Taxes Compared with Net Earnings

$57.8 million (Total Taxes)

$41.8 million (Net Earnings)

Taxes

	1972 (000)	1971 (000)
Federal income	$31,013	$25,286
Foreign income	5,487	3,564
Federal and foreign income	36,500	28,850
Social Security and other payroll	10,079	8,143
Property and miscellaneous	5,316	4,656
State income	4,894	4,126
State capital stock and franchise	1,011	1,619
	$57,800	$47,394

Taxes, as detailed at the left, totaled $57.8 million in 1972 and $47.4 million in 1971. State income taxes are treated as costs applicable to operating units in their geographical locations and, as such, are included in costs and expenses in the Statements of Consolidated Earnings. Since U.S. income taxes on unremitted foreign earnings will be substantially offset by foreign tax credits, no provision is required.

Provision for federal and foreign income taxes amounted to $36.5 million in 1972. Income taxes are based on the income and costs included in the earnings statement shown on page 19. Taxes deferred to future years ($4,415,000 in 1972 and $2,212,000 in 1971) represent timing differences resulting from the use of accelerated depreciation for tax purposes and straight-line depreciation for financial reporting, and other items that are handled differently for tax and financial reporting purposes.

Investment tax credits, amounting to $859,000 in 1972 and $293,000 in 1971, have been taken directly to income, reducing the provision for income taxes.

BALANCE SHEET ITEMS

Cash and short-term securities declined from $32.8 million at the end of 1971 to $20.6 million at the end of 1972. The operating and other factors associated with this decline are detailed in the Statements of Consolidated Changes in Financial Position on page 21.

Current receivables totaled $89.8 million at December 31, 1972. The increase of $7.0 million, or 8.5% during the year, was due principally to 1972's increased sales. Management believes provisions for possible losses are adequate.

Inventories are summarized at right. The $11.2 million increase in inventories reflects the year's higher level of business activity.

Inventories are valued at cost or market, whichever is lower. Cost is generally determined on a first-in, first-out (FIFO) basis except for certain furniture inventories valued on a last-in, first-out (LIFO) basis. LIFO-valued inventories amounted to $21,602,000 at December 31, 1972, and $24,615,000 at December 31, 1971. The excess of replacement cost over the LIFO value was $5,624,000 at the end of 1972.

Classification of Inventories

	1972 (000)	1971 (000)
Finished goods	$ 71,545	$ 67,803
Goods in process	17,256	14,388
Raw materials and supplies	35,273	30,693
	$124,074	$112,884

Working capital totaled $165.6 million, a gain of $13.1 million during 1972. The Statements of Consolidated Changes in Financial Position on page 21 summarize major sources and uses of funds as well as changes in working capital.

Working Capital

	1972 (000)	1971 (000)
Current assets	$239,102	$232,181
Current liabilities	73,514	79,705
	$165,588	$152,476

Long-term receivables include a $30,000,000 subordinated note, with interest at $9\frac{1}{2}$%, of Kerr Glass Manufacturing Corporation ("Kerr") due in annual principal installments of $2,500,000 from 1976 to maturity in 1987. Failure of Kerr to meet certain earnings tests may result in deferment of the payment of interest or principal, or both, on the note. Payment of the interest for 1972 ($2,883,000) has been deferred as provided by terms of the note and is included in long-term receivables. The note provides for mandatory principal prepayments beginning March 31, 1977, dependent upon Kerr's earnings.

Property, plant and equipment values, shown in the table at right, are stated at acquisition cost, with accumulated depreciation and amortization deducted to arrive at net carrying value. Approved but unspent capital appropriations totaled approximately $40.2 million at December 31, 1972. Substantially all this amount is expected to be spent during 1973.

Property, Plant and Equipment

	1972 (000)	1971 (000)
Land	$ 18,141	$ 17,666
Buildings	155,480	133,513
Machinery and equipment	295,767	278,627
Construction in progress	21,758	33,277
	491,146	463,083
Less accumulated depreciation and amortization	191,039	172,639
	$300,107	$290,444

FINANCIAL REVIEW

Notes Payable and Long-Term Debt

	1972 (000)	1972 Range of Interest Rates	1971 (000)	1971 Range of Interest Rates
TOTAL NOTES PAYABLE	**$12,608**	**6-8½%**	$ 9,869	5½-8%
8% sinking fund debentures due 1996	**$50,000**	**8%**	$50,000	8%
Borrowings of foreign subsidiaries due 1974-1984	**21,168**	**4-8%**	20,628	4-8½%
Mortgages and capitalized lease obligations, secured by land and buildings with net book value totaling approximately $8,446,000 at December 31, 1972, due serially to 1991	**3,765**	**5½-8½%**	3,392	5½-8½%
Other	**1,057**	**6-8⅛%**	2,331	4-8⅛%
	75,990		76,351	
Less current installments	**816**		5,399	
TOTAL LONG-TERM DEBT	**$75,174**		$70,952	
TOTAL NOTES PAYABLE AND LONG-TERM DEBT INCLUDING CURRENT INSTALLMENTS	**$88,598**		$86,220	

Stockholders' Equity

	1972 (000)	1971 (000)
Preferred stock, $3.75 cumulative, no par value. Authorized 161,821 shares; issued 161,522 shares (at redemption price of $102.75 per share)	**$ 16,596**	$ 16,596
Voting preferred stock, $2.375 cumulative convertible series, no par value. Authorized 1,500,000 shares; issued 100,000 shares (at $50.00 stated value per share); convertible into an aggregate of 210,000 shares of common stock	**5,000**	5,000
Common stock, $1.00 par value per share. Authorized 60,000,000 shares; issued: 1972—25,718,594 shares; 1971—25,669,379 shares	**25,719**	25,669
Capital surplus	**42,067**	40,389
Retained earnings	**329,341**	308,769
	418,723	396,423
Less treasury stock, at cost:		
Preferred stock, $3.75 cumulative—43,373 shares	**3,986**	3,986
Common stock: 1972—17,782 shares; 1971—104,630 shares	**613**	3,629
	4,599	7,615
	$414,124	$388,808

Long-term debt.

The 8% sinking fund debentures, sold in May 1971, are redeemable at the company's option at 107.6% prior to May 15, 1973, and at declining prices thereafter. The company may not, prior to 1981, redeem these debentures from or in anticipation of money borrowed at an annual

Scheduled Amortization of Long-Term Debt

	(000)
1973	$ 816
1974	1,170
1975	3,720
1976	1,850
1977	4,344

interest cost of less than 8%. Sinking fund payments sufficient to retire $2,500,000 principal amount of the debentures are due annually beginning May 15, 1977.

Stockholders' equity.

The voting preferred stock may be called for redemption after April 2, 1973, at an initial redemption price of $52.50 a share.

Stock options—under the option plan approved by the stockholders in 1964 there were 137,745 shares reserved for future options at December 31, 1972, and 151,610 shares at December 31, 1971. Included in option shares outstanding were 7,795 shares of common stock at December 31, 1972, in connection with options granted by a pooled company prior to combination. The option prices are not less than the closing market price of the shares on the dates the options were granted. The options are exercisable on a cumulative basis and expire five years from date of grant.

Capital surplus was increased by the excess ($1,304,000 in 1972 and $1,513,000 in 1971) of proceeds over par value of previously unissued shares of common stock (49,215 shares in 1972 and 80,491 in 1971) sold to employees upon exercise of options. The excess ($374,000) of market value over cost of 86,848 treasury common shares exchanged for assets of Cryo-Therm, Inc., accounted for the remainder of the increase in 1972.

Changes in Option Shares Outstanding During 1972 and 1971

	1972	1971
Option shares outstanding at beginning of year	**120,067**	213,050
Plus options granted	**20,060**	—
	140,127	213,050
Less:		
Options exercised	**49,215**	80,491
Options cancelled	**6,195**	12,492
	55,410	92,983
Option shares outstanding at end of year	**84,717**	120,067
Average option price per share outstanding at December 31	**$35.04**	$31.76

Contingency.

Early in 1972, the United States District Court for the Eastern District of Pennsylvania rendered a decision holding Armstrong to infringe certain patents owned by Congoleum Industries, Inc., involving a portion of the rotovinyl product line. In the opinion of outside patent counsel, this decision was erroneous particularly in the Court findings that the patents' valid scope had been infringed by Armstrong. No final judgment has been entered on this case to date, and the company is pursuing all remedial procedures.

In the opinion of management, the ultimate outcome of this action will not have a materially adverse effect on the business or the financial position of the company.

INDIANA TELEPHONE CORPORATION

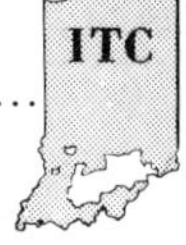

Statement of Income

	Column A Historical Cost 1972	Column A Historical Cost 1971	Column B Historical Cost Restated for Changes in Purchasing Power of Dollar 1972	Column B Historical Cost Restated for Changes in Purchasing Power of Dollar 1971
OPERATING REVENUES:				
Local service	$ 6,187,012	$ 5,744,356	$ 6,242,998	$ 5,964,020
Toll service	5,208,814	4,852,156	5,255,949	5,037,703
Miscellaneous	337,136	304,522	340,187	316,167
Total operating revenues	**11,732,962**	**10,901,034**	**11,839,134**	**11,317,890**
OPERATING EXPENSES:				
Depreciation provision, Note 1 (b)	**2,053,700**	**1,943,551**	**2,620,440**	**2,572,577**
Maintenance	1,548,758	1,486,495	1,562,773	1,550,974
Total depreciation and maintenance	**3,602,458**	**3,430,046**	**4,183,213**	**4,123,551**
Traffic	1,101,833	1,226,906	1,111,803	1,274,544
Commercial	581,311	511,661	586,571	531,227
General and administrative	1,003,875	1,055,318	1,015,121	1,100,994
State, local and miscellaneous Federal taxes	967,974	912,601	976,733	947,499
Federal income taxes, Note 1 (b)				
Currently payable	1,363,382	1,132,500	1,375,719	1,175,807
Deferred until future years	264,200	315,800	266,591	327,876
Deferred investment tax credit (net)	152,618	9,708	145,524	3,361
Total operating expenses	**9,037,651**	**8,594,540**	**9,661,275**	**9,484,859**
OPERATING INCOME	**2,695,311**	**2,306,494**	**2,177,859**	**1,833,031**
INCOME DEDUCTIONS:				
Interest on funded debt	789,579	651,195	796,724	676,097
Other deductions	41,540	36,828	53,285	41,445
Allowance for funds used during construction (credit), Note 1 (d)	(141,241)	(63,905)	(142,519)	(66,349)
Other income (credit)	(196,647)	(177,974)	(198,426)	(184,780)
Nonoperating Federal income taxes	92,500	82,000	93,337	85,136
Gain from retirement of long-term debt through operation of sinking fund (credit)	(11,985)	(15,192)	(12,093)	(15,773)
Price-level gain from retirement of long-term debt (credit), Note 1 (a)	—	—	(36,528)	(62,985)
Gain from retirement of preferred stock through operation of sinking fund (credit)	(4,709)	(5,055)	(4,752)	(5,248)
Price-level gain from retirement of preferred stock (credit), Note 1 (a)	—	—	(14,034)	(13,298)
Price-level loss from other monetary items	—	—	84,646	90,154
Total income deductions	**569,037**	**507,897**	**619,640**	**544,399**
NET INCOME, Note 1 (a)	**2,126,274**	**1,798,597**	**1,558,219**	**1,288,632**
Preferred stock dividends applicable to the period	94,890	96,209	95,749	99,888
EARNINGS APPLICABLE TO COMMON STOCK	**$ 2,031,384**	**$ 1,702,388**	**$ 1,462,470**	**$ 1,188,744**
EARNINGS PER COMMON SHARE	$ 4.16	$ 3.49	$ 3.00	$ 2.44
BOOK VALUE PER SHARE	$ 24.82	$ 21.45	$ 23.01	$ 20.81
Stations in service at end of year	**80,439**	**75,016**	**80,439**	**75,016**

The accompanying notes are an integral part of this statement.

INDIANA TELEPHONE CORPORATION

Statement of Assets—December 31, 1972

	Column A Historical Cost	Column B Historical Cost Restated for Changes in Purchasing Power of Dollar
TELEPHONE PLANT, at original cost, Note 1 (a):		
In service	$37,084,382	$47,050,796
Less—Accumulated depreciation	11,842,883	16,041,306
	25,241,499	31,009,490
Plant under construction	968,792	977,559
	26,210,291	31,987,049
WORKING CAPITAL:		
Current assets—		
Cash	795,971	795,971
Temporary cash investments accumulated for construction—at cost, which approximates market	4,482,550	4,482,550
Accounts receivable, less reserve	1,498,689	1,498,689
Materials and supplies	602,669	612,751
Prepayments	144,090	145,394
	7,523,969	7,535,355
Current liabilities—		
Sinking fund obligations, Note 2	121,000	121,000
Accounts payable	819,978	819,978
Advance billings	338,760	338,760
Dividends payable	168,904	168,904
Federal income taxes, Note 1 (b)	494,297	494,297
Other accrued taxes	677,736	677,736
Other current liabilities	986,941	986,941
	3,607,616	3,607,616
Net working capital	3,916,353	3,927,739
OTHER:		
Debt expense being amortized, Note 1 (c)	208,617	264,648
Other deferred charges	18,553	19,070
Other deferred credits	(40,818)	(41,187)
Deferred Federal income taxes, Note 1 (b)	(1,599,454)	(1,765,204)
Unamortized investment tax credit, Note 1 (e)	(544,396)	(632,744)
	(1,957,498)	(2,155,417)
TOTAL INVESTMENT IN TELEPHONE BUSINESS	$28,169,146	$33,759,371

The accompanying notes are an integral part of this statement.

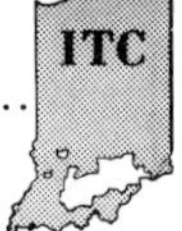

Statement of Capital—December 31, 1972

	Column A Historical Cost		Column B Historical Cost Restated for Changes in Purchasing Power of Dollar	
	Amount	Ratio	Amount	Ratio
FIRST MORTGAGE SINKING FUND BONDS:				
Series 6, 5⅜% due September 1, 1991	$ 1,820,000		$ 1,820,000	
Series 7, 4¾% due May 1, 1994	1,974,000		1,974,000	
Series 8, 4¾% due July 1, 2005	2,869,000		2,869,000	
Series 9, 6½% due October 1, 2007	2,910,000		2,910,000	
Series 10, 7¾% due June 1, 2008	4,875,000		4,875,000	
Less—Current sinking funds, Note 2	(101,000)		(101,000)	
Total first mortgage sinking fund bonds	14,347,000	51%	14,347,000	43%
PREFERRED STOCK (no maturity):				
Cumulative, sinking fund, par value $100 per share, 30,000 shares authorized of which 10,000 are unissued—				
1950 Series 4.80%	235,000		235,000	
1951 Series 4.80%	239,800		239,800	
1954 Series 5¼%	327,800		327,800	
1956 Series 5%	252,900		252,900	
1967 Series 6⅛%	679,000		679,000	
Less—Current sinking funds, Note 2	(20,000)		(20,000)	
Total preferred stock	1,714,500	6	1,714,500	5
COMMON SHAREHOLDERS' INTEREST:				
Common stock, no par value, authorized 500,000 shares, issued 492,086 shares	4,251,785		6,678,779	
Retained earnings ($3,147,223 restricted as to the payment of cash dividends on common stock, Note 4)	7,937,320		4,675,412	
	12,189,105		11,354,191	
Less—Treasury stock, 4,336 shares, at cost	(5,192)		(8,130)	
Stock discount and expense	(76,267)		(123,194)	
Total common shareholders' interest	12,107,646	43	11,222,867	33
UNREALIZED EFFECTS OF PRICE-LEVEL CHANGES, Note 1 (a)	—	—	6,475,004	19
TOTAL INVESTMENT IN TELEPHONE BUSINESS	$28,169,146	100%	$33,759,371	100%

The accompanying notes are an integral part of this statement.

INDIANA TELEPHONE CORPORATION

Statement of Changes in Financial Position

	1972	1971
FUNDS WERE PROVIDED BY:		
Operations per Column A—		
Net income	$2,126,274	$1,798,597
Items which did not require current expenditure of funds—		
Depreciation—		
Charged to income	2,053,700	1,943,551
Charged to clearing accounts	43,897	41,558
Deferred Federal income taxes	326,200	315,800
Investment tax credit (net)	152,618	9,708
Allowance for funds used during construction	(141,241)	(63,905)
Series 10 First Mortgage Sinking Fund Bonds	4,875,000	—
Net salvage on plant retirements	87,853	56,514
Miscellaneous, net	90,136	9,162
	9,614,437	4,110,985
FUNDS WERE EXPENDED FOR:		
Gross additions to telephone plant	4,586,237	3,411,941
Cash dividends declared—Common stock	365,812	182,906
—Preferred stock	118,507	72,001
Redemption of bonds and preferred stock	136,700	182,000
Refinancing First Mortgage Sinking Fund Bonds, Series 1-5	3,375,000	—
	8,582,256	3,848,848
INCREASE IN WORKING CAPITAL	$1,032,181	$ 262,137
INCREASE IN WORKING CAPITAL REPRESENTED BY CHANGES IN:		
Cash	$ 116,496	$ (22,555)
Temporary cash investments	1,408,199	960,698
Accounts receivable, less reserve	278,134	(47,043)
Materials and supplies and prepayments	143,845	43,695
Sinking fund obligations	41,000	—
Accounts payable and advance billings	(207,539)	(326,056)
Dividends payable	(145,018)	85,510
Accrued taxes	(329,450)	(87,290)
Other current liabilities	(273,486)	(344,822)
INCREASE IN WORKING CAPITAL	$1,032,181	$ 262,137

The accompanying notes are an integral part of this statement.

Statement of Retained Earnings for the Year 1972

	Column A Historical Cost	Column B Historical Cost Restated for Changes in Purchasing Power of Dollar
BALANCE, December 31, 1971	$6,295,365	$3,605,894
NET INCOME	2,126,274	1,558,219
	8,421,639	5,164,113
DEDUCT:		
Cash dividends declared—		
Common stock, annual rate—$.50 per share	365,812	369,122
Preferred stock	118,507	119,579
	484,319	488,701
BALANCE, December 31, 1972, Note 4	$7,937,320	$4,675,412

The accompanying notes are an integral part of this statement.

AUDITORS' REPORT

To the Shareholders of Indiana Telephone Corporation:

We have examined the statements of assets and capital of INDIANA TELEPHONE CORPORATION (an Indiana corporation) as of December 31, 1972, and the related statements of income, retained earnings, and changes in financial position for the year then ended. Our examination was made in accordance with generally accepted auditing standards and accordingly included such tests of the accounting records and such other auditing procedures as we considered necessary in the circumstances. We have previously examined and reported on the financial statements for the preceding year.

In our opinion, the accompanying financial statements shown under Column A present fairly the financial position of the Corporation as of December 31, 1972, and the results of its operations and the changes in its financial position for the year then ended, in conformity with generally accepted accounting principles applied on a basis consistent with that of the preceding year.

In our opinion, however, the accompanying financial statements shown under Column B more fairly present the financial position of the Corporation as of December 31, 1972, and the results of its operations for the year then ended, as recognition has been given to changes in the purchasing power of the dollar, as explained in Note 1(a).

ARTHUR ANDERSEN & CO.

Indianapolis, Indiana,
March 2, 1973.

INDIANA TELEPHONE CORPORATION

Notes to Financial Statements

1. SUMMARY OF SIGNIFICANT ACCOUNTING POLICIES

(a) EXPLANATION OF FINANCIAL STATEMENTS

In the accompanying financial statements, costs measured by the dollars disbursed at the time of the expenditure are shown in "Column A—Historical Cost." In "Column B—Historical Cost Restated For Changes in Purchasing Power of Dollar" (where the amounts in A and B differ), these dollars of cost have been restated in terms of the price level at December 31, 1972, as measured by the Gross National Product Implicit Price Deflator. Since 1954, the Corporation has presented supplemental financial information recognizing the effect of the change in the purchasing power of the dollar relating to telephone plant and depreciation expense in the annual report to shareholders.

In computing the amounts set forth in Column B of the accompanying financial statements, the Corporation has followed the methods set forth in Statement No. 3 released in June, 1969, by the Accounting Principles Board of the American Institute of Certified Public Accountants, **except that**, contrary to Statement No. 3, the effects of price-level changes on long-term debt and preferred stock have been reflected **as income in the year in which the debt and preferred stock are retired (as required by the specific instruments under which they were issued) and not refinanced.** The Accounting Principles Board has tentatively taken the position that all such amounts should be taken into income in the year of price-level change. **In the opinion of the Corporation's management and of its independent public accountants, such tentative viewpoint of the Accounting Principles Board does not result in a proper determination of income for the period.** "Unrealized Effects of Price-Level Changes" recognizes the excess of adjustments on the Statement of Assets over the adjustments of Common Shareholders' Interest.

Dollars are a means of expressing purchasing power at the time of their use. **Conversion or restatement of dollars of differing purchasing power to the purchasing power of the dollar at the date of conversion results in all the dollars being treated as mathematical likes for the purpose of significant data.** The resulting financial statements recognize the change in price levels between the periods of expenditure of funds and the periods of use of property. **Accordingly, the earnings, results of operations, assets and other data available for use by management and other readers of financial statements provide important information and comparisons not otherwise available.**

No one would attempt to add, subtract, multiply, or divide marks, dollars and pounds. The failure to change the title of the monetary unit may be partially responsible for this violation of mathematical principle. This conceals the fact that mathematical unlikes are being used and therefore unfortunate results have been produced by generally accepted accounting methods.

(b) RECOVERY OF CAPITAL AND RETURN ON CAPITAL

Under the law of Indiana, the Corporation is entitled to recover the fair value of its property used and useful in public service by accruing depreciation based on the "fair value" thereof and is entitled to earn a fair return on such "fair value." The amount shown in Column B for telephone plant approximates the fair value of the property as determined based on the principles followed by the Public Service Commission of Indiana in an order dated September 1, 1967, authorizing the Corporation to increase its subscriber rates.

In the accompanying financial statements, Column A includes depreciation expense based on historical cost and Column B includes depreciation expense, as well as other expenses, on the basis of historical cost repriced in current dollars to reflect the changes in the purchasing power of the dollar. Also, the annual reports to the Indiana Commission are in the same basic form shown herein.

It must be kept in mind that this determination of depreciation expense is a year-to-year estimate and there are involved the questions of obsolescence, foresight, and judgment giving due consideration to maintenance, but the regulatory process does not adjust even to this accurately.

In 1971 the Corporation petitioned the Indiana Commission for approval to increase its depreciation rates to a level to reflect properly these factors, but certain of these rates were not approved. If all of the requested rates were applied to the average cost of depreciable property accounts in 1972 and 1971, depreciation expense, operating income and net income (net of applicable income tax effects), as shown in the accompanying financial statements, would have been as follows:

	Column A Historical Cost	
	1972	*1971*
Depreciation provision .	$2,109,258	$1,997,871
Operating income	2,666,421	2,278,248
Net income	2,097,384	1,770,351

	Column B Historical Cost Restated for Changes in Purchasing Power of Dollar	
	1972	*1971*
Depreciation provision .	$2,690,932	$2,644,049
Operating income	2,134,276	1,788,662
Net income	1,514,636	1,244,263

If use of property, obsolescence and current denominators (in the case of monetary inflation) are used accurately by way of keeping the allowable expense of depreciation current and rates sufficient to return it along with a fair return, and the proceeds are immediately invested in property used and useful in the public service, there more likely will be a real return of capital and a fair return thereon. However, if monetary inflation continues, as it usually does, purchasing power of capital is unlikely ever to be truly returned. **It must be observed there is a substantial lag in the regulatory process. In rate making there is no guarantee of recovery of capital or of an adequate rate of return to the Corporation. This is an added risk which should be considered in estimating a fair return.**

Since the present Internal Revenue Code does not recognize the costs measured in current dollars, they are not deductible for computing Federal income tax payments, **and the Corporation in fact pays taxes on alleged earnings which do not exist in true purchasing power.** If they were deductible, as they should be, reductions in Federal income taxes as shown in Column B of $312,000 in 1972 and $274,000 in 1971 would result. By requiring the use of the Uniform System of Accounts for utility accounting and by virtue of the Internal Revenue Code, the Government has condemned and confiscated during the last 8 years over $1.3 million (in terms of the dollars of the years in which they were paid) of the assets of this Corporation through taxation of overstated earnings. This is true to a greater or lesser extent in each case where we have been able to ascertain the facts. We do not understand why this is currently concealed by management and accountants—to their detriment.

For book and financial reporting purposes, the Corporation provides for depreciation on a straight-line basis over the average service lives of the various classes of depreciable plant. In 1972, the overall rate was 6.1%. For Federal income tax purposes, beginning in 1967, an accelerated depreciation method is used and a provision is made in the Statement of Income for the taxes deferred as a result thereof.

(c) Deferred Charges

Debt expense is being amortized over the lives of the related issues. **Gains realized from reacquisition of bonds and preferred stock for sinking fund purposes are recognized in the year of retirement.**

(d) Allowance for Funds Used During Construction

The Corporation capitalizes the cost of capital employed during the period of construction on major projects. Amounts so capitalized are determined by applying a rate of 7% to the average dollar balance of these projects under construction.

(e) Unamortized Investment Tax Credit

The Corporation is deferring investment tax credits and amortizing the balance over the useful lives of the related property.

2. SINKING FUNDS

The aggregate annual sinking fund requirement on First Mortgage Sinking Fund Bonds for 1973 and 1974 is $101,000. The required annual sinking fund payment on the Series 10 Bonds begins in 1975 and is $48,750 (1%). The indenture for Series 10 Bonds also allows for an additional 1% ($48,-750) or 2% ($97,500) or a total of $146,250 in sinking fund payments, beginning in 1978, at the option of the Corporation.

As shown in the accompanying Statement of Changes in Financial Position, the level of funds provided for 1972 (which includes the $1,500,000 additional long-term funds from the issuance of the Series 10 Bonds) would have been adequate to have allowed the Corporation to make the required and optional sinking fund payments on Series 10 Bonds with sufficient remaining funds to meet construction expenditures and it would have left an increase in working capital of $885,931. The ability of the Corporation in the future to meet sinking fund payments and projected construction expenditures (to provide customer service) depends, in a large part, upon the level of earnings allowed by the Indiana Commission, with due regard to regulatory lag and monetary inflation.

At respective maturity dates, after all required sinking fund payments, the remaining balances to be paid will be as follows:

Series	*Maturity Date*	*Call Price = 100*	*Balance to be Paid at Maturity*
6	Sept. 1, 1991	1988	$1,440,000
7	May 1, 1994	1990	1,533,000
8	July 1, 2005	1985	1,909,000
9	Oct. 1, 2007	1997	1,890,000
10	June 1, 2008	2003	3,266,250

If the maximum optional sinking fund payments on Series 10 Bonds are made by the Corporation, the balance to be paid at maturity on this issue will be $341,250.

To the annual bond sinking funds aggregating $101,000 should be added the annual sinking fund requirement on preferred stock of $20,000. For the years 1973 and 1974, the total annual sinking fund requirement on both preferred stock and bonds is $121,000.

INDIANA TELEPHONE CORPORATION

3. RETIREMENT PLAN

The Corporation would prefer to pay the employees all that they earn in any year and to have no pension plan. However, the employees can have a greater amount after taxes if a qualified retirement plan is used and, accordingly, the plan exists.

Since 1966, the Corporation has maintained a money-purchase retirement plan. The plan covers all full-time employees with more than three years of service. All contributions to the plan are made by the Corporation.

In a money-purchase plan, an amount equal to a fixed percentage of the employee's earnings is paid into the plan each year, and there it is managed to produce as large a payment as possible for the employee during retirement. This is in contrast to the "fixed-benefit" plan where retirement benefits are determined by a formula. Any accumulated payments in a fixed-benefit plan not needed for benefits are returned to the employer by decreasing his payments, and any deficit in accumulated payments must be made up by the employer or his employees.

Before 1966 the Corporation had a fixed-benefit plan which required both the employer and employee to make contributions sufficient to support a pension based upon the last five years' compensation before retirement. In a fixed-benefit plan, the Internal Revenue Service does not permit an assumption of continuing monetary inflation. As a result, the amounts required to be paid in under such a plan are based upon the then existing compensation levels without recognition of the monetary inflation which will occur before retirement. As monetary inflation does occur, the actuaries require and the Internal Revenue Service permits pension contributions to make up for the failure in the past to anticipate monetary inflation. In a period of rapid monetary inflation, the contributors to the plan cannot be expected to pay the pension requirements which will be increased by the rate of monetary inflation compounded.

To avoid a pension contract which neither the employees nor the Corporation could expect to fulfill, the Corporation adopted a five percent, money-purchase plan. The annual contribution is related to the payroll of the employee and is not based upon an estimate of unknown mortality, unknown future investment return, unknown future retention of personnel, and most of all, does not depend on estimates of future salaries without adjustment for monetary inflation.

The pension payment made to the retired employee is completely divorced from social security or any other governmental program. It is hoped that the government will allow corporate management to continue to use its own best judgment in setting up private pension plans such as ours which it is believed have a more hopeful chance of surviving a period of monetary inflation.

In order to help the employees realize as much as possible from the plan—and particularly to attempt to protect the pension plan against monetary inflation, the Corporation made an extensive search for competent investment people, and finally caused the United States Trust Company of New York to be employed as the trustee to operate the fund. It is hoped that their investment skills will protect the pension fund against the continuing monetary inflation. To further help the employee in his contest with monetary inflation, the retiring employee is given **as much time to leave his funds in the care of the United States Trust Company as the Internal Revenue Service will permit.** The government has said that this is limited to the employee's life expectancy at retirement—about fifteen years. After that time, or sooner, if the employee elects a retirement annuity or obtains a lump sum, the employee himself will have to defend his property against both taxation and monetary inflation.

Historically, monetary inflation has accelerated from creeping to galloping. The end result sought is that these funds will be invested in a store of value of which some portion of value will exist after monetary inflation has run its course. That date is, of course, unknown and it is a difficult task to have both current purchasing power and a maximum remainder of stored value.

Unlike many other retirement plans, the money-purchase plan of Indiana Telephone Corporation has no unfunded liability. The Corporation considers this an important factor in its ability to survive in a society dominated by governmental regulation and monetary inflation.

The Corporation's contributions under the plan, which is fully funded each year, and other data relating to the trust fund are summarized as follows:

	1972	*1971*
Corporation contributions . . .	$103,000	$ 87,000
Cost of assets in fund at December 31	627,244	450,624
Market value of fund at December 31	836,990	572,205

4. DIVIDEND RESTRICTION

The supplemental indenture of the Series 10 First Mortgage Sinking Fund Bonds provides that cash dividends on common stock and purchases of common stock are limited to net earnings, as defined, after December 31, 1971, plus $600,000.

5. CONSTRUCTION COMMITMENTS

Construction expenditures for the year 1973 are estimated at $7,379,000. Substantial commitments have been made in connection therewith.

Appendix B

SPECIALIZED JOURNALS, CONTROLLING ACCOUNTS, AND SUBSIDIARY LEDGERS

Specialized Journals

The two-column journal illustrated in Chapter 14 is designed to record chronologically all of the financial transactions of an enterprise. It fits the needs of a relatively small business with only a few customers and creditors and a minimum of cash transactions. As the size of a business increases so will the number of resultant financial transactions. The tendency for a single two-column journal to become increasingly inadequate under such circumstances can be temporarily relieved by adding special columns for accounts frequently debited or credited. For example, a multi-column journal with special columns for "Cash-Debit" and "Cash-Credit" would eliminate writing in Cash each time a transaction required that a debit or credit be made to that account. Moreover, individual postings to the Cash account in the ledger could be avoided by posting the columnar totals of the special cash columns at the end of each period. Additional work and time could be saved through adding other special columns, such as "Accounts Receivable—Debit" and "Sales-Credit."

A multi-column journal is often adequate for an expanding business which employs only one person to keep the records; but, as the volume of business expands to hundreds or even thousands of daily transactions, it soon becomes physically impossible for one person to keep up with the daily book work. This problem could be solved readily by adding additional employees were it not for the fact that two or more people cannot work on the same journal or ledger simultaneously. Obviously, the better solution is the employment of additional people to handle the daily work load with a subdivision of labor accompanied by specialization in their duties.

To record a large volume of transactions rapidly, it is advantageous to divide the transactions into like-types and provide a specialized journal for each of those types which are repetitive in substantial volume. Since each specialized journal can be used by a different person to record a like-type of transaction, the use of special journals will permit a division of labor and will also greatly reduce the amount of detailed recording work.

The number of special journals needed by a business depends upon the variety of its like transactions which recur frequently. For example, a business that sells merchandise on credit needs a special sales journal for recording charge sales; whereas, a business which sells only for cash would not have any need for such a journal.

Just as different businesses need different types of special journals, the design of each special journal varies according to the needs of a particular business. For example, a merchandising concern offering cash discounts to customers for prompt payments of charge sales might advantageously use a special Sales Discount column in its cash receipts journal; however, a company that does not offer such discounts would find such a column in its cash receipts journal useless. It should be obvious that the design, purpose, type, and number of special journals used in business will depend upon the needs of the particular company.

Repetitive type transactions which justify the use of special journals in most enterprises are: (1) sales of merchandise on credit, (2) purchases of merchandise on credit, (3) cash receipts, and (4) cash payments. When special journals are provided for the foregoing transactions, a journal called a General Journal is still required to record other types of transactions which are non-repetitive in nature. Thus, the following journals are typically encountered:

1. Sales Journal
2. Purchases Journal
3. Cash Receipts Journal
4. Cash Payments Journal
5. General Journal

Controlling Accounts and Subsidiary Ledgers

When amounts were debited or credited to individual customer's or creditor's accounts in the illustrations in Chapter 14, they were recorded in separate accounts for each customer or creditor. Such a practice is not satisfactory when there are large numbers of customers and creditors in the regular ledger. A business having 1,000 customers and 100 creditors would require a ledger with 1,000 accounts for accounts receivable and 100 accounts for accounts payable, in addition to the accounts needed for the other assets, liabilities, owners' equity, revenue, and expense. Such a ledger would be cumbersome and unwieldy. Since only one person could work on such a ledger at a time, it would be difficult for postings to all of these accounts to be kept up to date. Furthermore, a trial balance prepared from such a ledger would be quite lengthy! If the trial balance were out of balance, the task of locating the error or errors would be extremely difficult.

An enterprise that has a large number of accounts with both customers and creditors customarily divides the ledger into three separate ledgers. All the accounts with customers are placed in a separate ledger, called the *accounts receivable ledger;* all accounts with creditors are placed in a separate ledger called the *accounts payable ledger.* Both of these ledgers are known as *subsidiary ledgers.* The ledger which retains the remaining accounts is known as the *general ledger.* In order to prevent the general ledger from being out of balance due to the removal of the individual accounts receivable and accounts payable accounts, one account receivable account and one account payable account replace the individual customer and creditor accounts in the general ledger. Each of these substitute accounts in the general ledger summarizes the many individual customer or creditor accounts located in their respective subsidiary ledger. These summarizing accounts are called *controlling accounts.*

Illustration

To illustrate the use of special journals, controlling accounts, and subsidiary ledgers, transactions of the Universal Company will be journalized and posted. The Universal Company uses the following journals (symbols to indicate posting references in the ledger accounts are indicated by letter):

1. Sales Journal (S). Every transaction recorded in this special journal is a sale of merchandise on account, and consequently every entry represents a debit to Accounts Receivable and a credit to Sales. At the end of a month, it is necessary to post to the general ledger only the monthly total of the transactions recorded in the sales journal as a debit to the Accounts Receivable control account and also as a credit to the Sales account. Evidence of such posting is indicated in the sales journal by inserting the appropriate ledger account numbers below the column total. Each debit to a customer's account is posted currently during the month from the sales journal to the individual customer's account in the Ac-

counts Receivable subsidiary ledger. The accounts in the Accounts Receivable ledger are kept in alphabetical order. When a posting is made to a customer's account, a check mark (✓) is placed in the posting reference (P.R.) column of the sales journal as evidence that the posting has been made to the subsidiary ledger. In the customer's account, symbols indicating the sales journal and page number (i.e., S3) are placed in the posting reference column as evidence of the source of the entry. The preceding posting directions must be followed correctly so that the Accounts Receivable subsidiary ledger will remain in agreement with the balance of the Accounts Receivable control account.

2. Purchases Journal (P). Every transaction recorded in this special journal (simplified as to content in this appendix) is a purchase of merchandise on account, and, consequently, every entry represents a debit to Purchases and a credit to Accounts Payable. At the end of a month, it is necessary to post to the general ledger only the monthly total of the transactions recorded in the purchases journal as a debit to the Purchases account and as a credit to the Accounts Payable control account. Evidence of such posting is indicated by inserting the appropriate ledger account numbers below the column total of the purchases journal. Each credit to a creditor's account is posted currently during the month from the purchases journal to the individual creditor's account in the Accounts Payable subsidiary ledger. The accounts in the Accounts Payable ledger are kept in alphabetical order. When a posting is made to a creditor's account, a check mark (✓) is placed in the posting reference column of the purchases journal as evidence of the posting. In the creditor's account, symbols indicating the purchases journal and page number (i.e., P4) are placed in the posting reference column as evidence of the posting. Care must be exercised in the execution of the preceding posting procedures to insure that the Accounts Payable subsidiary ledger remains in balance with the balance of the Accounts Payable control account.

3. Cash Receipts Journal (CR). Every transaction recorded in this special journal is the result of a receipt of cash. This journal typically contains five columns, entitled: Cash, Sales Discounts, Accounts Receivable, Sales, and General. The columnar arrangement of the journal provides special columns in which to record repeated debits to cash, debits to sales discounts, credits to accounts receivable, and credits to sales. Cash occasionally is received from other sources, such as from the issue of capital stock, or from the collection of notes receivable, but special columns are not justified in these cases because little or no posting effort would be saved due to their non-repetitive nature. The total of each column except the General column is posted monthly to the ledger account designated in the columnar title. Evidence of such posting is indi-

cated by inserting the appropriate ledger account number below the total of the transactions recorded under each columnar title. The total of the General column is *not posted* because it does not represent a credit to any one account. Each amount in that column must be posted individually to the proper general ledger account. Also, the individual amounts in the Accounts Receivable column must be posted currently during the month to the individual customer accounts in the Accounts Receivable subsidiary ledger. When a posting is made to a customer's account, a check mark (✓) is placed in the posting reference (P.R.) column of the cash receipts journal. It should be remembered that to keep the balance of a control account in the general ledger in agreement with the sum of the balances of the individual accounts in a subsidary ledger, every entry in a special column for customers or creditors must be posted twice—once by item to the individual's account in the subsidiary ledger, and then again as part of a column total to the control account in the general ledger.

4. Cash Payments Journal (CP). Every transaction recorded in this special journal is the result of a disbursement of cash. This journal typically contains five columns, entitled: Cash, Purchase Discounts, Accounts Payable, Purchases, and General. The columnar arrangement of the journal provides special columns in which to record repeated credits to cash, credits to purchase discounts, debits to accounts payable and debits to purchases. Cash disbursements are occasionally made for other purposes, such as a monthly utility bill or a periodic payment on a mortgage, but special columns to record such debits are not justified because little or no posting effort would be saved due to the non-repetitive nature of such transactions. The total of each column except the General column is posted monthly to the general ledger account designated in the columnar title. Such posting is evidenced by inserting the appropriate ledger account number below the total of the transactions recorded under each columnar title. The total of the General column is *not posted* because it does not represent a debit to any one account. Each amount in that column must be posted individually to the proper general ledger account. Also, the individual amounts in the Accounts Payable column must be posted currently during the month to the individual creditor accounts in the Accounts Payable subsidiary ledger to keep the subsidiary ledger in balance with the Accounts Payable control account. These postings are evidenced in the cash payments journal by the insertion of check marks in the posting reference column.

5. General Journal (J). Transactions, of a non-repetitive nature, for which special journals are not necessary are recorded in this journal. Each debit and credit amount must be posted individually. Any transaction recorded in this journal involving accounts receivable or accounts

payable must be posted twice; once to the Accounts Receivable or Accounts Payable control account in the general ledger and once to the individual account receivable or account payable account in the appropriate subsidiary ledger. Such postings must be evidenced in the general journal by inserting both the general ledger control account number and a check mark in the posting reference column.

All transactions of the Universal Company for the month of October 1974 are presented below, Analyze these transactions and study the entries in the appropriate journals; then trace the postings to the general ledger and subsidiary ledgers. This should provide a clear understanding of the use of special journals and ledgers. The various journals, general ledger, and subsidiary ledgers used in this illustration are on pages 563 to 567.

		TRANSACTIONS	JOURNAL USED
October	1	The Universal Company issued 5,000 shares of $10 par value stock, at par, for cash.	Cash Receipts
	2	Purchased merchandise on account from Ajax Company, $12,000. Invoice was dated today with terms of 2/10, n/30.	Purchases Journal
	3	Sold merchandise to Post Company, $8,000. Invoice No. 101, terms, 2/10, n/30.	Sales Journal
	5	Purchased store and office supplies from Eagle Company for cash, $400.	Cash Payments
	6	Sold merchandise for cash, $1,400.	Cash Receipts
	7	Paid two-year fire insurance policy premium, $500.	Cash Payments
	8	Purchased merchandise from Pitt Company, $11,000. Invoice dated today with terms, 1/10, n/30.	Purchases
	10	Sold merchandise to Mark Company, $6,500. Invoice No. 102, terms, 2/10, n/30.	Sales
	11	Purchased merchandise for cash, $2,500.	Cash Payments
	12	Paid Ajax Company invoice dated October 2.	Cash Payments
	13	Received payment from Post Company for invoice No. 101.	Cash Receipts
	14	Paid freight charges of $500 to C. & O.R.R. on goods purchased October 8 from Pitt Company.	Cash Payments
	15	Issued credit memo No. 1 in favor of Mark Company for return of $300 of merchandise.	General
	15	Employees were paid for first half of October, $3,500. (Ignore payroll deductions)	Cash Payments

October 18	Paid Pitt Company invoice dated October 8.	Cash Payments
19	Purchased merchandise for cash, $1,500.	Cash Payments
20	Received payment from Mark Company for invoice No. 102.	Cash Receipts
22	Sold merchandise on account to Small Company, $5,000, invoice No. 103. Terms, n/30.	Sales
23	Sold merchandise for cash, $1,700.	Cash Receipts
24	Purchased merchandise on account from Ajax Company, $1,500. Terms, 2/10, n/30.	Purchases
25	Purchased merchandise from Doubleday Company, $8,500. Invoice dated October 24 with terms of 2/10, n/60.	Purchases
26	Issued debit memo No. 1 to Doubleday Company in connection with merchandise returned today amounting to $600.	General
27	Sold merchandise on account to Arnold Company, $5,500. Invoice No. 104, terms, 2/10, n/30.	Sales
31	Paid salaries for the second half of the month, $3,500. (Ignore payroll deductions)	Cash Payments
31	Purchased store equipment from Plain Co., $8,000, paying $1,000 down and agreeing to pay the balance in 30 days.	General and Cash Payments

At the end of each accounting period, proof of the equality of debits and credits in the general ledger is established by preparation of a trial balance, as discussed and illustrated in Chapter 14. When controlling accounts and subsidiary ledgers are in use, it is *also* necessary to prove that each subsidiary ledger is in agreement with the appropriate controlling account. This proof is accomplished by preparing a schedule of accounts in each subsidiary ledger and determining that the total of each schedule agrees with the balance of the corresponding control account. The trial balance and schedules of accounts receivable and accounts payable for Universal Company at October 31, 1974, are on pages 567–68.

SALES JOURNAL — Page 1

Date	Accounts			P.R.	Amount
1974					
Oct. 3	Post Company	Invoice 101	2/10, n/30	✓	8,000
10	Mark Company	Invoice 102	2/10, n/30	✓	6,500
22	Small Company	Invoice 103	n/30	✓	5,000
27	Arnold Company	Invoice 104	2/10, n/30	✓	5,500
					25,000
					(2) (40)

PURCHASES JOURNAL Page 1

Date	Accounts		P.R.	Amount
1974				
Oct. 2	Ajax Company	2/10, n/30	✓	12,000
8	Pitt Company	1/10, n/30	✓	11,000
24	Ajax Company	2/10, n/30	✓	1,500
25	Doubleday Company	2/10, n/60	✓	8,500
				33,000
				(50) (20)

GENERAL JOURNAL Page 1

Date	Description	P.R.	Debit	Credit
1974				
Oct. 15	Sales Returns and Allowances	42	300	
	Accounts Receivable—Mark Company	2/✓		300
	Issued credit memo No. 1			
26	Accounts Payable—Doubleday Company	20/✓	600	
	Purchase Returns & Allowances	53		600
	Issued debit memo No. 1			
31	Store Equipment	10	8,000	
	Accounts Payable—Plain Company	20/✓		8,000
	Purchase of store equipment			

CASH RECEIPTS JOURNAL Page 1

			Credit			Debit	
Date	Accounts	P.R.	General	Sales	Accounts Receivable	Sales Discounts	Cash
1974							
Oct. 1	Capital Stock	30	50,000				50,000
6	Sales	—		1,400			1,400
13	Post Company	✓			8,000	160	7,840
20	Mark Company	✓			6,200	124	6,076
23	Sales	—		1,700			1,700
			50,000	3,100	14,200	284	67,016
			(✓)	(40)	(2)	(41)	(1)

CASH PAYMENTS JOURNAL Page 1

Date	Accounts	P.R.	Debit General	Debit Purchases	Debit Accounts Payable	Credit Purchase Discounts	Credit Cash
1974							
Oct. 5	Supplies	6	400				400
7	Prepaid Insurance	7	500				500
11	Purchases	—		2,500			2,500
12	Ajax Company	✓			12,000	240	11,760
14	Transportation In	51	500				500
15	Salary Expense	60	3,500				3,500
18	Pitt Company	✓			11,000	110	10,890
19	Purchases	—		1,500			1,500
31	Salary Expense	60	3,500				3,500
31	Plain Company	✓			1,000		1,000
			8,400	4,000	24,000	350	36,050
			(✓)	(50)	(20)	(52)	(1)

Cash Account 1

1974 Oct. 31	30,966	CR1	67,016	1974 Oct. 31		CP1	36,050

Accounts Receivable Account 2

1974 Oct. 31	10,500	S1	25,000	1974 Oct. 15		J1	300
				31		CR1	14,200
							14,500

Supplies Account 6

1974 Oct. 5		CP1	400				

Prepaid Insurance Account 7

1974 Oct. 7		CP1	500				

Store Equipment Account 10

1974 Oct. 31		J1	8,000				

Accounts Payable — Account 20

1974				1974			
Oct. 26		J1	600	Oct. 31		P1	33,000
31		CP1	24,000	31	16,400	J1	8,000
			24,600				41,000

Capital Stock — Account 30

				1974			
				Oct. 1		CR1	50,000

Sales — Account 40

				1974			
				Oct. 31		S1	25,000
				31	28,100	CR1	3,100

Sales Discounts — Account 41

1974							
Oct. 31		CR1	284				

Sales Returns and Allowances — Account 42

1974							
Oct. 15		J1	300				

Purchases — Account 50

1974							
Oct. 31		P1	33,000				
31	37,000	CP1	4,000				

Transportation In — Account 51

1974							
Oct. 14		CP1	500				

Purchase Discounts — Account 52

				1974			
				Oct. 15		CP1	350

Purchase Returns and Allowances — Account 53

				1974			
				Oct. 26		J1	600

Salary Expense — Account 60

1974							
Oct. 15		CP1	3,500				
31	7,000	CP1	3,500				

Accounts Receivable Ledger

Arnold Company

1974							
Oct. 27		S1	5,500				

Mark Company

1974				1974			
Oct. 10		S1	6,500	Oct. 15		J1	300
				20		CR1	6,200

Post Company

1974				1974			
Oct. 3		S1	8,000	Oct. 13		CR1	8,000

Small Company

1974							
Oct. 22		S1	5,000				

Accounts Payable Ledger

Ajax Company

1974				1974			
Oct. 12		CP1	12,000	Oct. 2		P1	12,000
				24	1,500	P1	1,500

Doubleday Company

1974				1974			
Oct. 26		J1	600	Oct. 25	7,900	P1	8,500

Pitt Company

1974				1974			
Oct. 18		CP1	11,000	Oct. 8		P1	11,000

Plain Company

1974				1974			
Oct. 31		CP1	1,000	Oct. 31	7,000	J1	8,000

UNIVERSAL COMPANY

Trial Balance
October 31, 1974

Cash	$30,966
Accounts Receivable	10,500

Supplies	400	
Prepaid Insurance	500	
Store Equipment	8,000	
Accounts Payable		$16,400
Capital Stock		50,000
Sales		28,100
Sales Discounts	284	
Sales Returns and Allowances	300	
Purchases	37,000	
Transportation In	500	
Purchase Discounts		350
Purchase Returns and Allowances		600
Salary Expense	7,000	
	$95,450	$95,450

Schedule of Accounts Receivable

October 31, 1974

Arnold Company	$ 5,500
Small Company	5,000
Total (equal to balance of controlling account)	$10,500

Schedule of Accounts Payable

October 31, 1974

Ajax Company	$ 1,500
Doubleday Company	7,900
Plain Company	7,000
Total (equal to balance of controlling account)	$16,400

HOME ASSIGNMENT PROBLEM

On January 1, 1974, the general ledger of PMT Corporation contained the following account balances:

Cash	$ 8,350
Accounts Receivable (Control)	6,200
Notes Receivable	2,000
Inventory of Merchandise	5,200

Office Furniture and Fixtures	1,500	
Accounts Payable (Control)		$ 3,500
Notes Payable		1,500
Capital Stock		15,000
Retained Earnings		3,250
	$23,250	$23,250

On January 1, 1974, the customers' and creditors' subsidiary ledgers of PMT Corporation disclosed the following account balances:

SCHEDULE A

ACCOUNTS RECEIVABLE

R. J. Allers	$2,200
E. W. Ross	3,500
B. T. Nord	500
	$6,200

SCHEDULE B

ACCOUNTS PAYABLE

Dayton Products Co.	$2,500
Rod Supply Company	1,000
	$3,500

Part I—Sales Journal, Cash Receipts Journal, and General Journal

The PMT Corporation uses special journals. In their Sales Journal, Cash Receipts Journal and General Journal, record the following transactions.

January 2 Sold merchandise to C. W. East for $800. Terms, net 30 days.

6 C. W. East returned $200 of merchandise sold to him on January 2. Full credit was allowed.

7 Sold merchandise to Jones and Company for $600. Terms, 2/10, n/30.

9 Sold merchandise with a list price of $2,000, subject to 5 percent trade discount to B. F. Smith. Terms, 1/10, n/30.

11 Received a check for $1,200 from R. J. Allers in payment of a sale made on December 14, 1973, with terms of 2/10, n/30.

13 Received a check from E. A. Ross for $1,000 and a non-interest bearing note for $2,000 in partial settlement of his January 1 account balance.

14 Sold merchandise to B. T. Nord, $2,000. Terms, cash $500, a 20-day non-interest bearing note, $1,500, and the balance on open account.

16 Received a check from Jones and Company in full of account.

18 Received a check from B. F. Smith for $990 in partial payment of the January 9 sale; applicable discount was allowed.

January 23 Sold merchandise to E. W. Ross, $600. Terms, n/30.
26 Received a check from Ray Bass for $1,000 in payment of his non-interest bearing note dated December 26, 1973.
31 Cash sales for the month of January totaled $1,500.

Part II—Purchases Journal, Cash Payments Journal, and General Journal

The PMT Corporation uses special journals. In their Purchases Journal, Cash Payments Journal and General Journal, record the following transactions:

January 2 Purchased $3,000 of merchandise from Dayton Products Co. Terms, 1/20, n/30; f.o.b. shipping point. Paid freight of $120 to Zaner Trucking Company.
5 Purchased supplies from Rod Supply Company $600. Terms, n/30.
9 Purchased merchandise from Bolt Electric Company, $2,500. Terms, cash $500, a 30-day non-interest bearing note $1,500, and the balance on open account.
10 Purchased merchandise from Marley Company, $300. Paid cash.
16 Purchased an office desk from Rug Equipment Company, $200. Terms, n/30.
19 Sent a check to Dayton Products Co., in full payment of the January 2 purchase.
23 Purchased merchandise from Dayton Products Co., $3,500. Terms, 1/20, n/30; f.o.b. shipping point. Paid freight of $150 to Zaner Trucking Company.
25 Merchandise purchased January 23 at a cost of $750 was returned to Dayton Products Co. Received full credit.
31 Cash purchases of merchandise for the month of January totaled $800.
31 Paid sales salaries for the month, $1,000. (Payroll taxes are ignored.)

Required

Part I:

a. Record the transactions listed under Part I in the appropriate journals.

b. Post all amounts that will affect the Accounts Receivable control account and the customers' subsidiary ledger.

c. Prepare a schedule of the Accounts Receivable subsidiary ledger as of January 31 and reconcile it with the balance in the Accounts Receivable control account.

Part II:

a. Record the transactions listed under Part II in the appropriate journals.

b. Post all amounts that will affect the Accounts Payable control account and the creditors' subsidiary ledger.

c. Prepare a schedule of the Accounts Payable subsidiary ledger on January 31 and reconcile it with the balance in the Accounts Payable control account.

Or, Parts I and II combined:

a. Open an account in the general ledger and subsidiary ledgers for each amount listed by the trial balance and accompanying schedules. Enter the balances in the appropriate accounts under date of January 1, 1974.

b. Record all transactions for the month of January in appropriate journals.

c. Post all journals to the appropriate ledger accounts.

d. Prepare a trial balance as of January 31, 1974.

e. Prepare schedules of the customers' and creditors' ledgers as of January 31, 1974.

f. Reconcile the balances of the Control accounts in the general ledger with the schedules prepared from the respective subsidiary ledgers.

Index